"It is impossible to understand the origins of today's fully immersive online existence without reflecting on the achievements of Richard Bartle. He conceived internet-based co-location and then willed it into existence – as an undergraduate in a small British university. Like Bede at Yarrow, from a perch distant from the intellectual centres of his time, he wrote a book read by many, one that helped define the very idea of media-in-common. It is the book you are holding in your digital hands".

Edward Castronova, *Professor of Media, Indiana University*

"The long-awaited Second Edition of *Designing Virtual Worlds* contains a lifetime of wisdom about a question central to modern game design: how and why do people play together online? Bartle entertainingly intertwines history and psychology in a way that brings insight after insight to any student of online play".

Jesse Schell, *author of* The Art of Game Design: A Book of Lenses

"The first edition of *Designing Virtual Worlds* was a major work. The second edition is in many ways quite different, but is equally as important, updating the text for the modern day and bringing fresh insight to topics ranging from legal issues to player psychology. Its relevance extends well beyond games. It is an indispensable text for understanding the what, why, and how of online worlds".

Raph Koster, *designer of* Ultima Online *and* Star Wars Galaxies

Designing Virtual Worlds

Designing Virtual Worlds, authored by a true pioneer, stands as the most comprehensive examination of virtual-world design ever written. This seminal work is a *tour de force,* remarkable for its intellectual breadth, encompassing the literary, economic, sociological, psychological, physical, technological, and ethical foundations of virtual worlds. It provides readers with a profound, well-grounded understanding of essential design principles.

This first volume of the second edition presents a rich, well-developed exploration of the foundational concepts underpinning virtual worlds. Tracing the evolution of such games from their inception, it draws upon examples ranging from the earliest MUDs to today's expansive MMORPGs. It elucidates fundamental design precepts often forgotten in the development of new games.

No other book on online games or virtual worlds matches the level of detail, historical context, and conceptual depth found in *Designing Virtual Worlds.*

Richard A. Bartle, PhD, co-wrote the first virtual world, *MUD* ("Multi-User Dungeon"), in 1978, thus being at the forefront of the online gaming industry from its very inception. He is an Emeritus Professor at the University of Essex working in both artificial intelligence and game design and is an influential writer on all aspects of virtual worlds. As an independent consultant, his thoughts have influenced almost every major online gaming company over the past 40 years. He lives with his wife, Gail, in a village just outside Colchester, England. He works in virtual worlds.

Designing Virtual Worlds: Volume I

Second Edition

Richard A. Bartle

CRC Press
Taylor & Francis Group
Boca Raton London New York

CRC Press is an imprint of the
Taylor & Francis Group, an **informa** business

Designed cover image: Jonathan Pennell

Second edition published 2026
by CRC Press
2385 NW Executive Center Drive, Suite 320, Boca Raton FL 33431

and by CRC Press
4 Park Square, Milton Park, Abingdon, Oxon, OX14 4RN

CRC Press is an imprint of Taylor & Francis Group, LLC

© 2026 Richard A. Bartle

First edition published by New Riders 2003

ISBN: 9781041174288 (hbk)
ISBN: 9781041174271 (pbk)
ISBN: 9781003689638 (ebk)

DOI: 10.1201/9781003689638

Typeset in Minion
by codeMantra

Contents

Preface to this Edition, xvi

CHAPTER 1 ▪ Definitions   1

1.1   WORLDS, SPACES AND PLACES   1
1.2   CRITERIA   3
1.3   CHARACTERS AND AVATARS   6
1.4   DESIGN   8

CHAPTER 2 ▪ History: The Text Era   13

2.1   WHY HISTORY?   13
2.2   PREHISTORY (TIME IMMEMORIAL-1978): FIRST STEPS   15
2.3   THE FIRST AGE (1978–1985): INDEPENDENT INVENTION   19
2.4   THE SECOND AGE (1985–1989): INSPIRED IMPROVEMENT   24
2.5   THE THIRD AGE (1989–1995): THE GREAT SCHISM   30
2.6   THE FOURTH AGE (1995–1997): PER-HOUR CHARGING   38

CHAPTER 3 ▪ History: The Graphics Era   42

3.1   THE FIFTH AGE (1997–2012): GRAPHICS AND SUBSCRIPTIONS 42
3.2   THE SIXTH AGE (2012–PRESENT): FREE-TO-PLAY   53
3.3   FUTURE AGES   58
3.4   LESSONS   62

CHAPTER 4 ▪ Characteristics   65

4.1   PLATFORM   65
4.2   GENRE   67
4.3   APPEARANCE   69
4.4   OPENNESS   70

4.5 REVENUE MODEL 71

4.6 INFLUENCES 73

4.7 INTERFACE 76

4.8 LUSORY ATTITUDE 78

4.9 DEVELOPER ATTENTION 80

4.10 SCALE 81

4.11 PERSISTENCE 83

4.12 CHANGEABILITY 84

4.13 PLAYER BASE 86

4.14 PHILOSOPHY 89

4.15 AGE 89

4.16 CONFIGURATION 91

CHAPTER 5 ■ Content and Meaning 92

5.1 GAMEPLAY 93

5.2 PROPERTIES OF CONTENT 94

5.3 SOURCES OF CONTENT 95

5.4 SUBSTITUTE CONTENT 96

5.5 MEANING 98

5.6 ARTISTIC STATEMENT 100

CHAPTER 6 ■ Development 103

6.1 THE STUDIO 103

6.2 PRE-PRODUCTION 106

6.3 PRODUCTION 111

6.4 ROLL-OUT 118

6.5 OPERATION 123

6.6 SUNSET 128

CHAPTER 7 ■ Architecture 130

7.1 CLIENT/SERVER 130

7.2 SERVER ARCHITECTURE 133

7.3 LOAD BALANCING 137

7.4 SECURITY 140

7.5 TELECOMMUNICATIONS 143

7.6 STREAMING 146

7.7 MOBILE PHONES 148

CHAPTER 8 ■ Interface   150

8.1   TEXT   150

8.2   GRAPHICS   152

8.3   AUGMENTED REALITY   154

8.4   VIRTUAL REALITY   154

8.5   VOICE   155

CHAPTER 9 ■ Backdrops   158

9.1   BUSINESS BACKDROP   158

       9.1.1   Intellectual Property   159

       9.1.2   Player-Operated Servers   163

9.2   LEGAL BACKDROP   164

       9.2.1   Jurisdiction   164

       9.2.2   Property   166

       9.2.3   Taxation   169

       9.2.4   Intellectual Property Revisited   169

9.3   CULTURAL BACKDROP   178

9.4   SOCIAL BACKDROP   180

9.5   POLITICAL BACKDROP   183

CHAPTER 10 ■ Demographics   185

10.1   IMPORTANT DIMENSIONS   185

10.2   DATA   190

CHAPTER 11 ■ Basic Player Types   195

11.1   WHY PLAY VIRTUAL WORLDS?   195

11.2   FUN   196

11.3   TWO DIMENSIONS   200

11.4   BEYOND THE GRAPH   204

11.5   ISSUES   206

CHAPTER 12 ■ Advanced Player Types   208

12.1   THREE DIMENSIONS   208

12.2   DEVELOPMENT TRACKS   214

12.3   DYNAMICS   221

       12.3.1   Player Type Relationships   221

       12.3.2   Details of Interactions   225

       12.3.3   Stable States   228

CHAPTER 13 ▪ Pivot: The Hero's Journey   230

13.1 AREAS OF DISAPPOINTMENT   230

13.2 SPECIFICS   232

13.3 DEPARTURE   236

    13.3.1 The Call to Adventure   236

    13.3.2 Refusal of the Call   237

    13.3.3 Supernatural Aid   238

    13.3.4 Crossing the First Threshold   239

    13.3.5 The Belly of the Whale   239

13.4 INITIATION   240

    13.4.1 The Road of Trials   240

    13.4.2 The Meeting with the Goddess   241

    13.4.3 Woman as Temptress   242

    13.4.4 Atonement with the Father   243

    13.4.5 Apotheosis   245

    13.4.6 The Ultimate Boon   246

13.5 RETURN   246

    13.5.1 Refusal of the Return   246

    13.5.2 The Magic Flight   246

    13.5.3 Rescue from Without   247

    13.5.4 Crossing the Return Threshold   247

    13.5.5 Master of the Two Worlds   247

    13.5.6 Freedom to Live   248

13.6 IN ABSTRACT   248

CHAPTER 14 ▪ Very Advanced Player Types   250

14.1 CORRESPONDENCES   250

14.2 DEPARTURE CORRESPONDENCES   252

    14.2.1 The Call to Adventure   252

    14.2.2 Refusal of the Call   253

    14.2.3 Supernatural Aid   253

    14.2.4 Crossing the First Threshold   254

    14.2.5 The Belly of the Whale   254

14.3 INITIATION CORRESPONDENCES   255

    14.3.1 The Road of Trials   255

    14.3.2 The Meeting with the Goddess   257

14.3.3 Woman as Temptress   259

14.3.4 Atonement with the Father   261

14.3.5 Apotheosis   262

14.3.6 The Ultimate Boon   263

14.4 RETURN CORRESPONDENCES   263

14.4.1 Refusal of the Return   263

14.4.2 The Magic Flight and Rescue from Without   264

14.4.3 Crossing the Return Threshold   265

14.4.4 Master of the Two Worlds   265

14.4.5 Freedom to Live   266

14.5 ANALYSIS   266

14.6 WHY PEOPLE PLAY VIRTUAL WORLDS   269

CHAPTER 15 ■ Immersion   271

15.1 TECHNICAL USES   271

15.2 DEGREES   273

15.3 PROGRESSION   275

15.4 NAMES   277

15.5 IMAGE AND SELF-IMAGE   283

15.6 IDENTITY AND IMMERSION   286

15.7 ROLE-PLAYING   288

15.8 MASQUERADING   291

CHAPTER 16 ■ Encouraging Immersion   294

16.1 PERSUADING THE MIND   295

16.2 PERSUADING THE SENSES   297

16.3 SPACE OF EXPLORATION   299

16.4 IDEAL SELVES   300

16.5 SELF-DETERMINATION   301

16.6 DEMOTING REALITY   302

16.7 INTEREST AND BOREDOM   306

16.8 FLOW   308

CHAPTER 17 ■ Applying Player Types   311

17.1 USING PLAYER TYPES   311

17.2 MISUSING PLAYER TYPES   317

17.3 OTHER APPLICATIONS   319

17.3.1 Games in General 320

17.3.2 Gamification 321

17.3.3 Teaching 322

17.3.4 There's More 325

17.4 NOT USING PLAYER TYPES 326

CHAPTER 18 ■ Other Typologies 334

18.1 MAKING IT YOUR OWN 334

18.2 USEFULNESS 341

18.3 USELESSNESS 343

18.4 PARTITIONING 346

18.4.1 Path of Ascension 346

18.4.2 Six Circles 346

18.4.3 Trojan 348

18.4.4 Desire Profiles 349

18.4.5 Funativity 349

18.4.6 4Keys2Fun 350

18.4.7 Eight Types of Fun 351

18.4.8 Self-Determination Theory 352

18.4.9 Multidimensional 353

18.4.10 Personality Metrics 356

18.4.11 BrainHex 356

18.5 SIMILARITIES 358

CHAPTER 19 ■ Community 359

19.1 OVERVIEW 359

19.2 CULTURE 363

19.3 COMMUNICATION 368

19.3.1 Communication: Shared Cultural Context 369

19.3.2 Communication: Means 370

19.3.3 Communication: Motive 375

19.3.4 Communication: Opportunity 377

19.3.5 Properties of Communication 381

19.4 GROUPS 383

19.4.1 What's a Group? 383

19.4.2 Types of Groups in MMORPGs 384

19.4.3 Parties 386

19.4.4 Guilds 386

19.4.5 Benefits of Guilds to Developers 389

19.4.6 Communication Consequences 390

19.4.7 Factions 390

19.4.8 Other Approaches 391

19.4.9 Non-Guild Play 392

19.5 LEVELS OF COMMUNITY ENGAGEMENT 392

Chapter 20 ■ Design and Community 396

20.1 COMMUNITIES AS OBJECTS 396

20.2 HOW COMMUNITIES FORM 397

20.3 COMMUNITY SIZE 400

20.4 PARTY SIZE 403

20.5 PROMOTING CONNECTIONS 404

20.6 ENCOURAGING DYADS 406

20.7 GREETERS 408

20.8 COMMUNITY MANAGEMENT 409

20.8.1 Toxicity 410

20.8.2 Toxic-Culture Prevention 412

20.8.3 Toxic-Culture Acceptance 416

20.8.4 Reputation Systems 417

20.9 COMMUNITY AND IMMERSION 420

Chapter 21 ■ Anthropology and Sociology 422

21.1 OBJECTIVE OPINION 422

21.2 ANTHROPOLOGY 423

21.2.1 Cultural Anthropology 424

21.2.2 Archaeology 426

21.3 SOCIOLOGY 428

21.3.1 Applied Sociology 429

Chapter 22 ■ Psychology's Take on Virtual Worlds 432

22.1 PSYCHOLOGISTS 435

22.2 ADDICTION 437

22.3 AGGRESSION 440

22.4 THINK OF THE CHILDREN   447

22.5 OTHER RESEARCH   449

CHAPTER 23 ■ Virtual Worlds' Take on Psychology   454

23.1 FAVOURING THE PLAYER   455

    23.1.1 Overjustification Effect   455

    23.1.2 The Uncanny Valley   456

    23.1.3 Mirror Neurons   457

    23.1.4 Theory of Mind   458

    23.1.5 Self-Perception   459

    23.1.6 Parasocial Relationships   460

23.2 NATURAL, DISFAVOURING THE PLAYER   462

    23.2.1 The Framing Effect   462

    23.2.2 Scarcity Effect   463

    23.2.3 Dunning-Kruger Effect   464

    23.2.4 Illusory Correlation   465

    23.2.5 Zeigarnik Effect   467

    23.2.6 Social Comparison Theory   467

    23.2.7 Sunk Cost Fallacy   469

    23.2.8 Loss Aversion   470

23.3 UNNATURAL, DISFAVOURING THE PLAYER   471

    23.3.1 Counterintuitiveness   472

    23.3.2 Fear of Missing Out   473

    23.3.3 Transaction Decoupling   474

    23.3.4 Operant Conditioning   476

    23.3.5 Profiling   478

23.4 RESPONSIBILITY   480

CHAPTER 24 ■ Rights   481

24.1 DESIGNER RIGHTS   482

24.2 THE COVENANT   483

24.3 PLAYER RIGHTS   485

    24.3.1 Character Rights   486

    24.3.2 Right to Liberty   489

    24.3.3 Property Rights   490

    24.3.4 Moral Rights   490

24.3.5 Right to Security of Person 490

24.3.6 Right to Privacy 491

24.4 NON-PLAYER RIGHTS 492

24.4.1 Crossfire 493

24.4.2 Consequences 493

24.4.3 Protection 494

24.4.4 *MIST* 495

CHAPTER 25 ■ Interlude 496

25.1 THIS VOLUME 496

25.2 NEXT VOLUME 498

BIBLIOGRAPHY, 503

INDEX, 539

Preface to this Edition

BACK IN THE EARLY 2000s, following the dot com boom-and-bust, I found myself with time enough on my hands to write a book: *Designing Virtual Worlds*. It sold well over many years, but time trundles along and eventually it became irredeemably dated. I asked the publishers (Pearson) to revert the rights to me, in order that I could release the text as a free download. Generously, they consented, so that's what I did.[1]

Two weeks later, it had been downloaded 100,000 times.

It occurred to me that there might be interest in a Second Edition.

0.1 THE FIRST EDITION

I wrote the First Edition because I wanted better virtual worlds.

My intention was to make its readers *think* about virtual-world design. I didn't much care whether anyone *agreed* with everything I wrote or not, so long as afterwards they advanced their own thoughts on the matter and so gained an understanding. Thinking is important: people who don't think don't gain an understanding; people who lack an understanding have to rely on either luck or the understanding of others to get by.

I therefore laid out what I had learned about the design of virtual worlds in the quarter-century that I'd been working on them. The text was aimed squarely at designers and designers-to-be, but I harboured the hope that it would also be of interest to players and academics – which indeed it was. My plan was to shovel some knowledge onto the common pile of design insights so that other designers could pick over it, with the end result that virtual worlds as a whole might improve. Rather than grimly making poorly advised incremental adjustments to the design of so-so existing worlds, designers might be allowed to avoid this fate and to let their imaginations rip.

It was an optimistic vision, and although to some extent it did inspire the spreading of creative wings, commercial virtual worlds rapidly became so expensive to make that designers were soon obliged to play it safe so as not to lose investors millions.[2]

One of the things the First Edition got right was its assertion that designing virtual worlds is an art form that is independent of other artistic endeavours. If you come at them aiming to leverage experience gained in some other creative industry – game design, literature, screenwriting, animation, … – then you'll have a useful perspective, sure, and

---

[1] It's available at https://mud.co.uk/richard/DesigningVirtualWorlds.pdf, or perhaps more permanently at https://archive.org/details/designing-virtual-worlds.

[2] I have studiously not mentioned a currency for these "millions", but if it helps then think in terms of gold pieces.

many of the capabilities you've brought with you will translate directly into virtual-world design. Many won't, though. Your problem is that at the outset, you can't be sure which will happily work and which won't. Once you *understand* virtual-world design and how to say things through it, the process becomes a lot easier. The First Edition did manage to convey this.

It also consolidated the fact that people play virtual worlds for different reasons and that these reasons are interlinked and can be used predictively. Astonishing though it may seem today, a good many people did used to design virtual worlds that they, personally, wanted to play rather than what other people wanted to play. The First Edition finally put that notion to bed, despite its not being as successful in explaining the underpinning theory as I had hoped.[3]

Although the First Edition got most of its observations right, some it got not so right. I had expected that the developers of game-oriented worlds would see sense and give them a formal end, rather than bolting an interminable succession of ever-worsening expansions onto them to trap players into a cycle of raiding for worthless gains. I had expected that the developers of non-game worlds would have recognised from the past what to expect of the present and taken steps either to mitigate or to embrace the likelihood of their world's being defined by dancing penises. I had expected that virtual worlds would have small populations of players and large populations of NPCs, not that they would be vast, soulless seas of strangers.

I still *do* expect to see these things, by the way; it was merely the timescale I got wrong. Here, have some optimism!

Now, it wouldn't have been *too* much work to update the First Edition to clarify my positions and to account for the rising cost of virtual-world development. Adding a few references to more recent virtual worlds and research papers would have given it a sheen of modernity. I could have done that.

Time moves on, though. What was new in 2003 is new no longer. Since then, we've seen newer worlds designed by newer people, some of whom have been permitted to experiment with newer ideas. We've also seen newer worlds designed by experienced people, most of whom have had a wider range of successes (but also failures) in experimenting with newer ideas. There is much goodness to assimilate. That said, we've also seen newer revenue models appear, some of which were actually old and had been so discredited prior to the First Edition that I didn't even bother mentioning them back then. Not all movement has been in a forward direction.

Bearing all this in mind, rather than patching or updating the First Edition in what programmers would immediately call a hack, I decided to write a Second Edition from scratch. Although the basic principles enshrined in the First Edition have withstood the scrutiny of time, too much else has changed in the intervening years to be ignored. The frontiers of virtual-world design have advanced afar and resolutely resist being reduced to tacked-on paragraphs or cryptic footnotes.[4]

---

[3] Behold how I effortlessly blame the book for its shortcomings, rather than its author.

[4] You read footnotes, right? Good – there are a *lot* of them in this book.

The First Edition predates *World of Warcraft* (Metzen et al., 2004), for goodness' sake! The time has come for a Second Edition.

0.2 THE SECOND EDITION

This Second Edition is, as I've said, a complete rewrite of the First Edition. There is no cutting-and-pasting from the First Edition, except for some formal definitions and the rare occasion when past-me used a turn of phrase I really like.[5]

I began my task by making a list of what I wanted to cover. It was only a series of bullet points, but it was over 30,000 words long; I realised rather too late that this was likely to convert into a full text rather lengthier than the First Edition's 266,000 words. Hence, I've split it into multiple[6] volumes.

Warning: spoilers ahead!

When I was planning the Second Edition's structure, I wanted to develop some kind of narrative thread that would take the reader naturally and logically through the content. The obvious approach (for reasons that will become apparent later) was to use the *Hero's Journey* (Campbell, 1949). Sadly, though, notwithstanding all views emanating from Hollywood to the contrary, said structure is not universally applicable to all stories; it isn't applicable to the one I wanted to tell here.

I considered using player types (Bartle, 1996) as an alternative organising methodology, but this didn't work either: too much information was spread between the types for it all to be discussed in a single-threaded, coherent manner. In the end, I went with the axes[7] that I'd used to build the player types model: players, world, acting, interacting. Following an introductory context-setting chapter and one on those practicalities of virtual-world development that designers need to know from the get-go, I would move on to describing how players impact the design of virtual worlds. This would be followed by similar chapters related to aspects of world, acting, and interacting design, ending in two meta-chapters: one on virtual-world design as art and a final one on ethics. There were to be eight chapters in total.

Had I not had as much to say as it turned out I did, all eight chapters would have fitted in one volume. That was not the case, however, and this first volume is comprised of only the first three planned chapters. Awkwardly, there seemed little point in having a book with only three chapters, especially as one of them occupied 60% of the pages, so I transformed most of what were previously sections into chapters in their own right. As a result, there are now 24 much-less-unwieldy chapters (plus an interlude, a bibliography, and this preface), better to fit in with your bedtime-reading regime.

One of the features of the First Edition that didn't stand up well for long was its discussion of research for research's sake. To be fair, there weren't many books, journals, or conference papers related to virtual worlds back then, so enumerating pretty well everything

---

[5] Laziness on my part is also a possibility.

[6] I've subtly not said exactly how many volumes, but it'll be at least two. I'm hoping for no more, but writing is a bit like programming: you never quite know how extensive the end result will be, no matter what fancy mathematics you employ to calculate it for you in advance.

[7] As in more than one axis, lumberjack fans.

of note that had been written about them wasn't onerous (just boring). As it happens, this Second Edition *does* feature a good many[8] references to academic papers, but they're not present simply because someone wrote a peer-reviewed piece that has a virtual-world connection. In general, I'll only be referencing works for one or more of the following reasons:

- They're of direct interest to designers.
- They're creative (these are mainly games or virtual worlds).
- They back up some assertions I've made that sceptics might not believe.
- I'm quoting from or paraphrasing them.
- They're examples of something I've just mentioned.
- So that you can follow up a topic without having to endure my bowdlerisation of it.
- They're cool.

A bibliography gives the impression that this is a textbook. Given that it will be sold at times under the guise of being a textbook, you might therefore be hoping to be told what you'll learn (a "what you'll learn" section in the preface or introduction being the modern fashion). Sadly, there isn't such a section. I have no idea what you'll learn because I don't know what you already know. I do know you'll learn *something* though and that whatever it is will in some way be useful to you.

Ultimately, I want virtual worlds that are better for their players. If this book can help deliver that dream then it's done its job. It won't be me who designs those worlds as I've been there, done that – but it *could* be you. I hope it *is* you. After designing a virtual world, you see the world you live in differently. More importantly, you see *yourself* differently. That's ultimately *why* you design them.

To help, I can but pass on what I've learned. Feel free to dismiss it, but only if you *know* why you're dismissing it – and know this at a non-superficial level, too. If I'm talking rubbish, you need to know *why* it's rubbish, not merely that it *is* rubbish. Then, you won't talk rubbish yourself.

I've been working with and on virtual worlds for a very long time. I'm effectively a dinosaur. I should be extinct.

Make me extinct.

---

[8] This is how we say "too many" when writing academic texts.

CHAPTER 1

Definitions

YOU WILL PERHAPS HAVE gathered from its title that this is a book about the design of virtual worlds.[1] So, what's a virtual world?

Very briefly, a *world* in this context is a space of interaction that the inhabitants of which regard as being mainly self-contained. As for *virtual*, well: *real* is that which is; *imaginary* is that which is not; *virtual* is that which is not, having the form or effect of that which is.

Virtual worlds are places where the imaginary meets the real.

Although this definition of the term *virtual world* is eminently serviceable and mercifully short, a more in-depth analysis reveals some interesting subtleties.

1.1 WORLDS, SPACES AND PLACES

In describing what I mean by a world just now, I said that its inhabitants regard it as being "mainly self-contained". That word "mainly" is there because the inhabitants may be aware of worlds beyond. For example, the ancient Romans knew of peoples and lands outside the "Roman world", but judged these to be distinct from it. Likewise, the "world of politics" is fully integrated into everyday life, but the space of interactivity it defines is largely considered to be a separate entity. Note that works of fiction usually have no world beyond, because that would break the conceit that the fiction is real: the world of *Star Trek* (Star Trek, 1966), for example, is an entire, self-contained universe.[2]

If worlds are both "spaces" and "places", it would help to know the difference between the two concepts. Very broadly, a *place* is a *space* to which meaning is attributed (Tuan, 1977). Spaces are abstract: they're moved *through*; places are material: they're moved *to*. Spaces therefore provide the interactive context for places, but places give spaces substance (Relph, 1976). Worlds, of which virtual worlds are examples, are spaces made manifest as places: you can both move through them and move to them. Thus, *World of Warcraft* is

---

[1] I intended to call it *The Design of Virtual Worlds* but was told that books with titles beginning "The" didn't sell. This must be what's been holding back *The Bible* and *The Qur'an*, then.
[2] Or multiverse, if some episodes are to be believed.

DOI: 10.1201/9781003689638-1

a virtual world and therefore a space of interaction, but it's instantiated as a place (in its case, one called Azeroth). Hence, when I say "virtual worlds are places", I'm referring to the places that they implement.[3]

As for the term *virtual*, well the definition of the term as used by philosophers, physicists and virtual world designers ultimately comes from an entry in an influential dictionary of philosophy and psychology published in 1902. I shall spare you the full quotation, but here's how it starts:

> **Virtual** [Lat. *virtus*, strength, from *vir*, a man]: Ger. *virtuell*; Fr. (1) *virtuel*; Ital. (1) *virtuale*. (1) A virtual *X* (where *X* is a common noun) is something, not an *X*, which has the efficiency (*virtus*) of an *X*.
>
> *(Peirce, 1902)*

This looks fair enough, and indeed it is, but for virtual worlds, the situation is complicated by the *world* part. Virtual worlds are places: we can go there. Doesn't this mean that to some extent they can themselves perhaps be regarded as real – just a different kind of real?

As is often the case with rhetorical questions, the answer is "yes".[4] It can plausibly be argued (Shields, 2003) that there are different kinds of real, if "real" is taken to mean "existing". The key distinction is whether something is *actual* (that is, it has a concrete existence) or *ideal* (that is, it has existence only in the mind). A physical object such as a brick would be *actually real*; a memory, dream or intention would be *ideally real*. Using this distinction, "virtual" is just another way of saying "ideally real".

For brevity, let's refer to the objective, concrete reality in which we live by the proper noun *Reality*. If we accept that Reality is actually real and virtual worlds are ideally real, what does this buy us?

Well, recall that earlier I defined the term "world" to refer to "a space of interaction that the inhabitants of which regard as being mainly self-contained". It's the "inhabitants of which" part that now kicks in. From our perspective, the virtual world is ideal but not actual, meaning it's real but not physically real. From the perspective of the non-player characters (*NPCs*) who inhabit a virtual world, though, it's actually real.[5] For them, their reality isn't virtual, it's concrete reality (just not Reality).

Adopting this argument,[6] we can legitimately interpret virtual worlds as being realities in their own right. Therefore, if "Virtual worlds are places where the imaginary meets the real" is too vague for you, try "Virtual worlds are sub-realities of Reality" instead.

---

[3] It can be argued that the space and the place are one and the same, which is convenient but beyond the scope of this book. Note that "beyond the scope of this book" is the universally accepted shorthand for "within the scope of this book but it would take me a month to write up were I to include it".

[4] Note: "no" and "it depends" are also popular answers.

[5] OK, so today's NPCs aren't anywhere smart enough to have a perspective, but tomorrow's may be. Some of the implications of this are covered in Volume II.

[6] There are other, more powerful (but more laboured) arguments, many of which I make in bleak detail in Chapter 1 of my book *How to Be a God* (Bartle, 2022). It does pick up in later chapters....

1.2 CRITERIA

Both these definitions are certain about what they exclude but non-committal about what they include. Not all sub-realities of Reality are necessarily virtual worlds (anything constructed in your imagination would qualify); not all places where the imaginary meets the real are necessarily virtual worlds (plenty of books, which are real, feature places that are imaginary). We can, however, say that objects such as shoes, which fit neither definition,[7] are not virtual worlds.

OK, so what about *Dungeons & Dragons* (Gygax & Arneson, 1974)? It's not ruled out by either definition, but that doesn't mean it's ruled in.

What we need is a definition that comes from the opposite direction: anything that matches all its criteria definitely is a virtual world; anything that does not match them all might yet be a virtual world but probably isn't. There will still be borderline cases, because unless all the criteria are somehow objectively measurable, there will be issues of judgement involved; nevertheless, the construction of such a set of criteria isn't especially difficult. A candidate system is a virtual world if it satisfies all six of the following criteria[8]:

1. The candidate system (world) operates by using an underlying, automated rule set – its *physics*.

2. Each user (henceforth *player*) is represented by an individual "in" the world – their *character*.

3. Interaction with the world takes place in *real time*.

4. The world is *shared* with other players.

5. The world doesn't end when you yourself stop playing – it's *persistent*.

6. The world is not Reality.

In lay terms, a virtual world is a system usually implemented on a computer (or network of computers) that realises an environment in software. Some of the entities in this environment act under the direct control of individual players. Because several players can be affecting the environment simultaneously, it's said to be shared (or, historically, *multi-user*). The environment continues to exist and to develop in a self-contained manner even when there are no people interacting with it.

To understand why the above criteria are necessary and pretty well sufficient, let's consider them in a little more depth.

---

[7] They only fit feet.
[8] These are my criteria, but others who have had cause to define what virtual worlds are tend to produce something similar. For example, Boellstorff et al. (2013) – a book on ethnography – present a definition that maps one-to-one onto mine, except that it omits the sixth criterion.

Criterion 1 – Physics. Virtual worlds are dynamic systems. Players perform actions that change the state of the world, thereby enabling or disabling actions that they, others or the world itself can or could potentially perform. The implementations of these actions constitute the world's physics, completely defining what can be done to the world. This implies that there's a world to have the physics, of course – a material environment that the players can change from within. For this reason, chatrooms are not virtual worlds. Also, the physics must be implemented in a consistent and automated fashion: this is why a *Dungeons & Dragons* (*D&D*) campaign is not a virtual world.

Criterion 2 – Characters. Players interact with the virtual world through the conduit of their character. This is because players only exist in Reality, not the virtual world, so they need a vehicle that does exist in the virtual world if they're to access it: this is their character. They also interact with each other through the virtual world, using its physics as a communication channel. Although a player may have several characters at their disposal (typically a *main* and one or more *alts*, all of which must be unique), they only play one of them at a time. Strategic wargames such as the *Civilization* (Meier & Shelley, 1991) or *Total War* (Simpson, 2000) series are not virtual worlds because even if one of the units may formally represent the player, the player nevertheless has direct control over multiple units. This does not mean that a player can't wield partial control over an NPC companion, an NPC party or even an NPC army in a virtual world: they can, so long as they wield that control through their character (by talking to the right NPC, say) and not independently of it. Note that there is no requirement that a character be humanoid: a character could be an aircraft, for example, if its player exercised direct executive control over it.

Criterion 3 – Real Time. When a player performs an action, the effects of that action must be executed in a timely manner. As for what a "timely manner" is, well although players are unlikely to complain if something that would take weeks in Reality takes half a second in a virtual world (learning how to ride a horse, say), they are more disposed to complain if something that should take half a second takes ten (walking through a doorway, say). Because players act through characters, actions are at the level of individuals; therefore, the processing of actions must also be at such a level. The general rule of thumb is that players should be able to perform actions at any time while they are playing, and when they do so, the virtual world needs to recognise the fact within at most four seconds.[9] This means that games with built-in turn-based components can't be virtual worlds. Also, worlds with either no push[10] or a slow automatic refresh are not virtual worlds. Although you may be able to persuade yourself (if not me) that a social media platform such as Facebook is a world with physics, it's harder to argue that it's real-time.

---

[9] This figure of four seconds comes from a study undertaken by British Telecom back in the 1980s. Unfortunately, I was not provided with a copy of the study itself, I was only told this one finding, so you'll just have to take my word (and that of the person who told me) that four seconds is the cut-off.

[10] *Push* is a general networking term used to describe a situation in which the user is presented with output without explicitly requesting it; *pull* means the user requests it.

Criterion 4 – Shared. A virtual world allows for a varying number of players to visit it at once, up to some implementation-specific maximum. The *state* of the world (that is, the current configuration of objects and their properties) is exactly the same for all these players, each of whom has meaningful abilities to change the state in ways impactful to themselves and each other. Although a virtual world that no one is playing is still a virtual world, a candidate system must be able to support at least two players simultaneously, because otherwise there'd be no possibility of sharing anything. A classic single-player role-playing[11] game such as *Skyrim* (Howard, 2011) or *The Witcher III* (Tomaszkiewicz et al., 2015) would therefore not be a virtual world, nor would a party-based game such as *Pillars of Eternity* (Sawyer, 2015) or *Baldur's Gate III* (Vincke, 2023), because the other characters are not controlled by other players.

Criterion 5 – Persistent. Virtual worlds remain playable for extended periods, their state constantly changing as a result of player action. Note that it's the operational world that needs to persist, not its state and not its players: it continues to exist and possibly to change while individuals are absent. You could leave for half an hour to have something to eat, only to find upon your return that the virtual world has noticeably altered (perhaps someone else has now slain the dragon that you were planning to slay yourself). Among other things, persistence implies a drop-in, drop-out sensibility in which different players can join and leave unpredictably. A battle royale game such as *Fortnite* (Sugg, 2020), which allows only dropping-out after the initial dropping-in, does not therefore qualify as being persistent. This, by the way, is why the definition for criterion 4 above used the word "varying": virtual worlds cannot require a fixed number of players. A two-player game is therefore not a virtual world, but, a one-or-two-player game *may* be a virtual world if it satisfies the other criteria.

Criterion 6 – Not Reality. This criterion is necessary because Reality fits all the other criteria[12] but it isn't a virtual world.[13] An escape room is not a virtual world because it uses the physics of Reality. A live-action role-playing game (*LARP*[14]) is not a virtual world because it overlays the physics of Reality, rather than implementing its own physics. Las Vegas is not a virtual world, even though that might be hard to believe at times. It's possible to argue that virtual worlds are themselves merely adjuncts of Reality (Taylor, 2008; Lehdonvirta, 2010), which implies that there's no such thing as a "virtual" world anyway; I don't hold with this view personally, largely because players actively *will* themselves not to hold it.[15] We'll see why they do this when I discuss immersion in Chapter 15.

---

[11] Note that the "role" in "role-playing" refers more to the kind found in screenplays than the kind found in job descriptions.

[12] The drop-in, drop-out feature of its persistence may rule it out if you don't believe in reincarnation.

[13] Not from our perspective, anyway. It might be from the perspective of Reality's designer(s).

[14] The verb is more often spelled *larp* these days, but after going to some effort to stop calling them LRPs, I feel I've already compromised enough.

[15] Other, more philosophical reasons, are given in Bartle (2022).

Although the above set of criteria constitutes my own definition of what a system must exhibit if it's to be called a virtual world, and is what I'll be using for the remainder of this book, I should mention that it's not the *only* such definition. Nevelsteen (2018) analysed a number of competing definitions of the term and found 23 (!) criteria in total, which he was able to condense as follows:

> [A virtual world is] a simulated environment where: many agents can virtually interact with each other, act and react to things, phenomena and the environment; agents can be zero or many human(s), each represented by many entities called a 'virtual self' (an avatar), or many software agents; all action/reaction/interaction must happen in a real-time shared spatiotemporal non-pausable virtual environment; the environment may consist of many data spaces, but the collection of data spaces should constitute a shared data space, one persistent shard.

Obviously I'm not about to disagree with this, as it's broadly in line with my own definition, but you should be aware that there *are* other definitions. I particularly like this one's use of "non-pausable".

1.3 CHARACTERS AND AVATARS

I've been calling the in-world entities that players control *characters*, but some people call them *avatars*. Neither usage is formally correct, although "character" is less incorrect. Both are members of an evolving set of related terms referring to in-world items, some of which are up-and-coming, some of which are down-and-going, and some of which are so long-established that they're entrenched where they are. Here's what you need to know:

- An *agent* (or *actor*[16]) is an entity that can act upon the virtual world from within it with some degree of autonomy. The term is mainly used by researchers in artificial intelligence (AI) to distinguish between things that act upon the world with a modicum of thinking power behind them (such as goats, swarms of bees and guided missiles) and things that act upon the world but don't (such as weather, earthquakes and traps). It's a very useful over-arching term but not one that many players would use.[17]

- A *character* is an agent that has superior thinking powers, to the extent that a player can with some effort of will believe it to be under human control.

- A *player character* is a character that is indeed under human control (or at least that the virtual world believes is under human control; if it's recognised by players to be under the control of an off-site program, it's a *bot*). When people (including me) refer to a "character", this is what they usually mean; the "player" part is only used when the context isn't clear. Player characters are sometimes called *PCs*, a hangover from tabletop role-playing games.

---

[16] *Very* formally, an actor's actions don't affect others and an agent's actions do (Gewirth, 1978).
[17] Or even many designers, although designers would recognise what it meant.

- A *non-player character* is a character that is under the control of the virtual world or some related AI-as-a-service. Although people don't usually call player characters PCs (because PCs are computers[18]), they do call non-player characters NPCs. The term is usually restricted to agents that look like player characters but aren't. Shopkeepers, pirates and robots are likely to be NPCs; dolphins, flesh-eating plants and fire elementals, not so much.

- An *avatar* is the visual appearance of a character, regardless of whether it's a player character or a non-player character. It's *not* the character itself. That said, the use of the term "avatar" to refer specifically to player characters has considerable traction, particularly among non-gamers. It's especially dominant in social worlds (which is understandable, as they're all about character appearance) and in expansions of game ideas taken in non-game directions (gamification, the Metaverse). Note that not all virtual worlds *have* characters with a visual appearance – textual worlds don't, for example – but those that do and call characters "avatars" will necessarily have another word for the visual appearance of characters, *toon* being a long-standing one.[19] See the later sidebar for an explanation of how "avatar" came to be ripped off from Hinduism to pick up its present meaning(s) in virtual worlds.

- A *companion* is an NPC that accompanies a player character, performing actions autonomously to support that character. The player may be able to give general directions to the companion, such as asking it to favour healing actions or telling it that it really needs to unleash its fireball spell right now, but on the whole, it operates self-sufficiently.

- A *drone* is a companion that has limited freedom to act of its own accord. It's essentially a functional extension of the player character. A flying eye that can scout around unexplored dungeons would be an example of a drone, as would be a remote-controlled four-rotor helicopter (*i.e.* a drone).

- A *mobile* (or *mob*) is an agent that is not a character. It's not a group of them: it's a single one (you could have a mob of mobs). Zombies, sassy raccoons and velociraptors are examples of mobiles. Note that mobiles don't actually have to be able to move: talking swords, inscrutable spaceship computers and intelligent daffodils would count.[20]

- A *monster* is an old term for an aggressive mob that really, really wants you to kill it. It's not used a lot these days, except by tabletop role-players, but it hasn't fully gone away in virtual worlds and may yet stage a recovery. If a mob has a monster mentality but doesn't look monstrous, for example a large tiger, then it may be granted the status of *creature* instead.

---

[18] They're also police constables.

[19] It sprang from the virtual world *Toontown Online* (Schell Games, 2003), which is sadly no longer with us. There is, however, a fan-based resuscitation of the game, *Toontown Rewritten* (Toontown Rewritten Team, 2014), which possibly has more players than the original game did.

[20] I can say this with some authority because I originated the term "mobile". Then again, it included NPCs at the time, so perhaps not.

- A *boss* is an abnormally powerful mob that has special, scripted behaviours at its disposal. Almost invariably, bosses are there to be defeated in combat. They are usually found at the end of a gauntlet of lesser mobs and yield much higher rewards upon defeat.

- *Trash* is what the lesser mobs before a boss are collectively called.

- A *mini-boss* is either disrespectfully applied to a boss that's easy to beat or respectfully applied to trash that gives a good account of itself. It can also refer to boss encounters made up of several powerful mobs (the mini-bosses) working together.

- An *add* is a piece of trash that is called into play during a boss encounter.

- A *critter* is something that looks to have autonomy, but it doesn't interact with anything – it's there purely for atmospheric or cosmetic reasons. Butterflies and bunnies are common examples of critters. Back in the day, "critter" was a generic term for what are now called mobs, but it was out-competed; you may find some off-the-beaten-track virtual worlds that retain this earlier usage, though.

- A *pet* is a critter that is associated with a player character. Usually, all they do is follow the character around performing scripted animations, some of which may be in response to player action. There could, however, be contexts in which they are given a degree of self-determination – *Pokémon*-style pet battles, for example. In those situations, they'd technically be companions or drones rather than pets.

Long though that list may have been, there are other terms arriving all the time, some of which will stick and some of which will go the way of *twink*.[21] Many of these terms will be elaborated upon in relevant sections later in this book, and most of them will at least be mentioned. All are going to be useful.[22]

While we're on the subject of terminology, I should mention that although I have been using the term *virtual world* as if everyone involved with them calls them that, this is not the case. There isn't, in fact, a widely accepted term that refers to what I'm calling "virtual worlds". This is for largely historical reasons, so the explanation will have to wait until I've outlined the history of virtual worlds. I'll maybe put it in a sidebar or something.[23]

1.4 DESIGN

This is a book about the design of virtual worlds. It's not a book about game design in general, although a lot of what it says is applicable beyond virtual world design. Neither is it a book about massively multiplayer online role-playing game (MMORPG) design in

---

[21] Oh, very well: the once hugely popular term *twink* was used to describe a low-level character consciously over-empowered by the generosity of a higher-level character (usually run by the same player). It's rarely used in modern game worlds because level restrictions are now added to gear specifically to prevent twinking (which was regarded as something of a scourge). The related term *mule*, to mean an alt used as a storage facility, met a similar fate.

[22] OK, so maybe not "critter".

[23] Aww, you know I will.

particular, although a lot of what it says is applicable specifically to MMORPGs (MMOs) (yes, the MMORPG acronym is so unwieldy that it has its own abbreviation[24]). This suggests that there's something particular about virtual worlds that makes them special: something they deliver that nothing else delivers, yet which isn't only delivered by a given subset of them.

Well, virtual worlds are indeed special, at least in the sense of being distinct. There is a step change between a virtual world and an environment that matches five of the defining criteria but not all six. Put formally: there are degrees of approaching being a virtual world, but no degrees of actually being a virtual world; something either *is* a virtual world or *isn't*. There's no gradual, nearly-but-not-quite continuum: only when all six criteria are present does something click, and the result – a virtual world – becomes a different experience entirely.

As an analogy, consider gunpowder: to cause an explosion, you need sulphur, charcoal, saltpetre and a flame. If you only have three, don't expect an explosion. If you have all four then it depends on the quantities of each as to how big an explosion you'll get.

When people study virtual worlds from the outside, they often don't concern themselves with this – usually for perfectly acceptable reasons. Early researchers, for example, were trying to establish ways of looking at computer play in general – as drama (Laurel, 1991), say, or literature (Murray, 1997); there was nothing to be gained from treating virtual worlds as special cases. Later researchers may be studying philosophical abstractions (Upton, 2015; Debus, 2019), or widespread psychological behaviours (Consalvo, 2007; Rigby & Ryan, 2011), or implications for society (McGonigal, 2011; Markey & Ferguson, 2017), or a host of other topics that don't rely on virtual worldliness as a central concept. This is both legitimate and justifiable, and it can easily lead to insights[25] useful in virtual world design. However, it risks overlooking something essential. Virtual worlds are not services, simulations, media or even games: they're *places*. If you bear this in mind, many design issues cease to be issues at all.

Now, cynical readers may be folding their arms at this point and asking, "so what?". I've asserted without a great deal of evidence that virtual worlds are a thing unto themselves, but even accepting this, it isn't a reason to write a book about them. The evidence and the reasons will, I hope, become apparent in the following chapters; for the moment, however, it's sufficient to note that virtual worlds *aren't* quite the same as anything else, regardless of whether or not they have unique affordances when looked at from your own favoured angle. This is because, *being* different to everything else, they need to be *designed* differently to everything else. This is a book about virtual world *design*.

---

[24] For a while, there's been a movement to apply the MMO prefix to genres of games played online that aren't virtual worlds – MMORTS, MMOFPS, MMOTBS, that kind of thing. The idea hasn't really taken off, and MMO is usually the short form of MMORPG (which is how I'll be using it here). However, bear in mind that in a different conversation, it could refer to a different kind of game.

[25] It's my observation that when an insight is referred to as being "valuable", it means the author does not, in fact, believe the insight to be valuable. This is why I have not described these insights as "valuable insights".

It's a feature of design in general that it's hard to pin down. If you could pin it down, it wouldn't be design (Redström, 2017). The definition of "design" that has perhaps found the most support is:

> courses of action aimed at changing existing situations into preferred ones
>
> *(Simon, 1969)*

My own definition is rather more prosaic: to design something is to imagine how it could be without first making it be. Also, if you express yourself through this then it's art, not design.

As I shall attempt to explain in Volume II,[26] most game design[27] is indeed art, not design, and most game designers are artists, not designers. Sadly, the term *artist* means something rather more concrete in (video-)game development, so we're stuck with *designer* whether we like it or not.

As for what it is that virtual world designers design, well the answer seems quite obvious: they design virtual worlds. Virtual worlds can be huge beasts, though, so often there will be many designers working on the same virtual world, each having different responsibilities (systems, experiences, levels, … see Chapter 6 for more), yet nevertheless all acting under the direction of a lead designer ("the" designer – see sidebar).

THE DESIGNER

The standard practice in both industry and academia is to cite games by reference to their development studio. I do not hold with this.

When we talk about creative works in other media, it's with reference to the person whose overall artistic vision shapes that of everyone else who has creative input. For example, in movies, operas and ballet, this is the director; for TV series, it's the showrunner; for rock concerts, it's the band or soloist; for classical music concerts, it's the conductor. We don't say "the film *Stagecoach* (Walter Wanger Productions, 1939)" – which refers to the production company; we don't say "the film *Stagecoach* (United Artists, 1939)" – which refers to the distributor; we say "the film *Stagecoach* (Ford, 1939)" – which refers to its director, John Ford.[28]

In games, it's usually the development studio that is cited – "the MMORPG *EverQuest* (Verant Interactive, 1999)" – or occasionally the publisher – "the MMORPG *EverQuest* (Sony Online Entertainment 1999)". We almost never see "the MMORPG *EverQuest* (Clover et al., 1999)". We're lucky even to see the name of the game honoured by italics, come to that.

---

[26] For convenience, I shall be referring to the yet-to-be-written chapters of this overall work as Volume II, but as we'll see in the interlude (at the end of this volume, Volume I), it's conceivable that there'll be more than one additional volume.

[27] Somewhat sloppily, I'll often refer to MMORPGs as "games" in this book, which is fair enough given what the G stands for in the acronym; bear in mind, however, that being a game isn't the absolute core of what they are: that's the fact that they're places (realities, in fact).

[28] Annoyingly, in the Harvard referencing system used throughout this book, films get their own special category. This renders the reference to the movie *Stagecoach* as the strangely uninformative (Stagecoach, 1939). Fortunately, I can pretend games are books to get the reference format I want — *EverQuest* (Clover et al., 1999), in the case of *EverQuest*.

The argument wheeled out for the established practice is that everyone in a studio is creative and contributed to the end product, so the studio deserves the credit rather than any individual. Accepting this as true (which it isn't[29]), it's also true of musicals, architecture and hit singles. We do have some game designers with name recognition – in the MMO space, Raph Koster, Richard Garriott and Jake Song are examples – but mostly, it's like the film industry was in the days of the studio system. People went to watch an MGM musical, not a Harry Beaumont or a Robert Z. Leonard or a W. S. Van Dyke musical. This allowed the studios to keep control of their creative talent, because (actors aside) they didn't have name recognition among the general public.

If games are to be accorded the same respect as other creative works then those whose visions are being realised must be credited. OK, so who would the equivalent of a movie director be for games, then?

In my view, it's the game designer. Given that I *am* a game designer, this probably doesn't come as a huge surprise, but there are few other contenders. Occasionally, I've met developers who argue that it's the *producer* (or *project manager*) whose vision is being realised, applying *auteur theory* to argue that this is the person most responsible for what the player experiences; this isn't a widespread view, though, even among producers.

Large games will have several designers, not just one, in which case "the" designer becomes the one in overall charge of design: the *lead designer*. Very large games – of which MMOs are prime examples – may have multiple lead designers, each in charge of a sub-system; in this case, the person with overall creative control has a different job title, such as *director*. For clarity, though, I'll stick to using the term "designer" to refer to the individual(s) most responsible for the design of a virtual world.

This, then, is why you have seen and will continue to see games and virtual worlds cited as, say, "*World of Warcraft* (Metzen et al., 2004)" rather than the "*World of Warcraft* (Blizzard Entertainment, 2004)" version you may see elsewhere. That's if the developer actually lists designers in the credits, of course. If it doesn't, OK, they win: I'll (reluctantly) cite the developer as the author.

Given that there are so many different aspects to virtual world development, the question arises: which of these should be covered in a book about virtual world design?

Well, I'll be covering all of those that are to do with the virtual world itself. I shall not, however, be casting more than a glance at the design of interfaces to virtual worlds or at the software architecture of virtual worlds. Virtual worlds can be designed for different primary input/output (I/O) methods, be they text, speech, graphics, virtual reality (VR), immersion chambers or neural implants, each of which comes with different implications

---

[29] I've met some truly uncreative people at game studios, mainly because they're needed: creative people are often easily distracted, whereas uncreative people simply get things done.

and affordances for design, play and development. Interface design[30] for these I/O methods is clearly of tremendous importance, but it's not about the design of the world itself. Similarly, the way that a virtual world's software is organised and its hardware specified is of huge significance, and designers do need to have a sense of what it allows and denies. Neither interface design nor software design is core to the design of virtual worlds themselves, though. A virtual world's design may be informed and heavily influenced by how it is to be accessed and implemented, but it's independent of it.

Therefore, as much as it's annoying for a telegraph to be smaller than the effect it's telegraphing, or for the transfer of characters between data centres to be frustratingly error-prone, I won't be looking at details such as these in this book.[31]

Likewise, although level design and encounter design are important, they can be regarded as specialist pocket areas of design separate from that of the virtual world as a whole[32]; I therefore won't be delving into those in great detail either.

I will, however, be discussing the historical context of virtual worlds, because so much of where they are today and where they're going tomorrow follows as a result of how they got here from yesterday.

I'll do that next, in fact – at rather great length, so make yourself comfy.

---

[30] Interface design goes by many names, of which UX (for User eXperience) design is perhaps the most widespread, but because virtual worlds have experiences that are disjoint from the interface, I prefer the older term. If you're interested in game design from an interface perspective, try Hodent (2017).

[31] I'll also be avoiding discussion of appalling control systems. You can breathe a sigh of relief, *Red Dead Online* (Sarwar & Sripan, 2019).

[32] Although there are plenty of good books on level design in general that can usefully be co-opted for virtual worlds (Co, 2006; Totten, 2019; Salmond, 2021), I'm still waiting for one on designing boss fights.

CHAPTER 2

History

The Text Era

Y OU WILL PERHAPS HAVE discerned that much of the terminology used for virtual worlds comes from computer games (and often *vice versa*, too). This is because that's where their origins lie. Although there are many non-game, non-entertainment virtual worlds in existence (the venerable *LinguaMOO* (Haynes & Holmevik, 1995) is used for educational purposes, for example), games still dominate and remain at the cutting edge of virtual world development. Furthermore, some have more players than all the non-game virtual worlds put together, many times over.[1] Specialists may and do use their own context-specific terms when writing about virtual worlds (an anthropologist might talk of "individuals exhibiting behaviours", for example), but even they will accept that the people who design, create or visit these worlds refer to "players playing" them, and that they'll often refer to them as "games" even when there isn't any gameplay involved.

We shall shortly examine how this state of affairs came to be, but first, let's discuss in more depth whether it's worth the effort of bothering to look.

2.1 WHY HISTORY?

Earlier, I gave two reasons why a basic knowledge of the history of virtual worlds is of use to virtual world designers: it helps them to understand how things got to be how they are; it helps them to see the trajectory of where things might be going.

The corollaries to these reasons are also important: it helps the designer understand what opportunities have been overlooked in the past and may be overlooked in the future; it helps the designer identify errors that have been made in the past that will likely be perpetuated in the future.

---

[1] It's standard practice in academic works to back up statements like this one with verifiable facts that take an age to source. It's also standard practice for these verifiable facts to date very quickly. I shall therefore not be backing up this statement, on the grounds that if it weren't true then you probably wouldn't be reading this book anyway.

An understanding of the history of virtual worlds, whether in general or through particular exemplars, enables a designer to pick up on structural and systemic commonalities beneath superficially strong differences. Earlier, when I said that I wouldn't be drilling down into the thrilling subject of interface design, that was an example of this. I will be looking at the *implications* of different interfaces, but not the ins-and-outs of the interfaces themselves. This is because when you strip away the interface, all virtual worlds still share the same essence. Interface is not part of the six-criteria definition of what makes a candidate system a virtual world.

Another reason that virtual world designers should appreciate the history of their art and profession is to counter the misguided belief that everything done in the past must be irrelevant because today's virtual worlds are "different". This is a surprisingly frequent but predictably monumental error. Brash designers coming in "to shake things up" may indeed shake things up – but not until they've repeated all the well-known-for-decades errors that they didn't think applied to their ideas because they gave virtual worlds a different label ("the Metaverse") or a different interface ("VR") or a different purpose ("education").

Historical context allows designers to discuss ideas among themselves or with knowledgeable players by referencing precedent. Rather than having to explain that a class system has inter-related skills for each class that allow a degree of customisation for particular combat roles, saying "it has talent trees like early *WoW*" will suffice. Comparisons, such as "that crafting system rips off *SWG*", are also easier if you've actually looked at the crafting system for *Star Wars Galaxies* (Koster, 2003) – which you should, by the way, even though it closed in 2011.

Yet another significant reason that virtual world designers might wish to appreciate the history of their chosen art form is that one day, they themselves will be history. If you don't respect the past, no one will respect *you* when *you're* the past. This isn't quite the act of indulgent self-preservation that it gives the impression of being: it simply follows from an examination of your own knowledge and experience. If you accept that you know things that a fresh-faced designer wouldn't, you must in turn accept that wrinkly faced designers know things that you don't. Let's put it this way: it's at least worth *asking* them, even if the result is that they wave a stick at you and tell you to get off their lawn.[2]

The final reason for acknowledging that the history of virtual worlds has importance is purely for categorical neatness. If you're not sure whether something is a virtual world or not, a good rule of thumb is to look at its heritage. If its design draws heavily from the design of a past or present virtual world, it almost certainly is one; if it doesn't, it almost certainly isn't.

History needs sources, of course. I cite plenty in this chapter, but if you want to do your own research on how virtual world design and related thinking developed, there are two absolute goldmines packed with contemporary discussions into which you can dig and delve: the MUD-DEV archives (various, 1996) and the Terra Nova blog (various, 2003). The former ran from 1996 to 2010 (petering out in about 2007) and was a moderated Usenet

---

[2] Hmm, I guess I should add that designers of the past would be foolish not to respect those of the present, too. Designers are designers: respecting one another is part of the job.

group populated by leading virtual world designers and developers; the latter operated from 2003 to 2015 (petering out in about 2013) and was a blog frequented by leading virtual world researchers from many disciplines. There are PhDs in digital history to be had in these records....

2.2 PREHISTORY (TIME IMMEMORIAL-1978): FIRST STEPS

An artist cannot endure reality; he turns away or back from it.

(Nietzsche, 1909)

We've had imaginary worlds ever since we've had imaginations.

Imaginary worlds are virtual in the sense of being ideal, but (as we shall shortly see) it wasn't until the late 1970s that they met all the criteria for being classifiable as virtual worlds. Nevertheless, worlds of the imagination did influence the genesis of virtual worlds, often in profound ways, and most of the early designers of virtual worlds either created their own imaginary worlds, were heavily informed by those of others, or (usually) both.

Although all story worlds are imaginary to some degree, the usual emphasis is on the story rather than its setting. The setting may not even be fictional – historical novels often use authenticity as a selling point, for example. When the emphasis *is* on the setting, though, and that setting *is* fictional, some world-of-the-imagination creation must have taken place. If the creator – *designer* – of that imaginary world subsequently develops the concept so that it can be used for other stories, or even simply for its own sake, then what results is called a *paracosm*.

Paracosms are not uncommon among children: around a sixth of individuals in middle childhood create them (Taylor et al., 2018), often collaboratively.[3] They are particularly favoured by children who are good at storytelling. Many well-known authors created paracosms when young, including the Brontë sisters, Robert Louis Stevenson, E. Nesbit, C. S. Lewis and the poet W. H. Auden. Some took their paracosms with them into adulthood: Austin Tappan Wright's *Islandia* (Wright, 1942) and M. A. R. Barker's role-playing world *Tékumel* (Barker, 1975) began as paracosms. Most famously, of course, Tolkien's Middle Earth (Tolkien, 1954) is a paracosm.[4]

Paracosms can also arise when a collection of works becomes sufficiently extensive that its author constructs an imaginary world about it to provide a consistent background that then takes on a life of its own; Robert E. Howard's Hyborian Age (Howard, 1936) and H. P. Lovecraft's Cthulhu Mythos (Lovecraft, 1928) came about this way. Large-scale television and film settings that have formal or informal *bibles*[5] to maintain a degree of coherence and compatibility between episodes can also become paracosms, in which context they are typically called *universes*[6]; examples include the Whoniverse of *Dr Who* (Newman et al., 1963),

---

[3] I myself created three with my brother (and several more on my own) that lasted for years.

[4] For an agreeable history of Fantasy worlds (which is now old enough to be a part of history itself), see Carter (1973).

[5] This isn't a great term, managing as it does to offend swathes of religious and non-religious people alike, but it's what they're called.

[6] Apparently, this doesn't necessarily preclude their being multiverses.

the Buffyverse of *Buffy the Vampire Slayer* (Whedon, 1997), the *Star Wars* (Lucas, 1977) universe and the Marvel Cinematic Universe (Marvel Studios, 2008). Fan fiction can seek to broaden or deepen such paracosms, but if it wantonly denies any of what is regarded as canon then other fans writing for the same setting will Not Be Pleased.

Every large-scale virtual world that has gameplay (and some that haven't) is supported fictionally by its own paracosm, the main outline of which will have been constructed in the early stages of its design. Players are exposed to this either implicitly (in the way the virtual world presents itself) or explicitly (through direct compositions that comprise its *lore*). Small-scale virtual worlds with gameplay don't need paracosms initially (or, formally, ever: it's not part of the definition of a virtual world); nevertheless, what tends to happen is that they grow their lore as they themselves grow, until they need a bible and the seeds of a paracosm are sown.

Either way, virtual world designers tend to be adept at either paracosm-enabling or paracosm-creating. If you relish the thought (if not necessarily the work) of creating your own paracosm, you're definitely MMO-designer material.[7]

Nowadays, most new designers of virtual worlds will have become familiar with the concept by playing one or more of them. Their need to design a virtual world might have derived directly from this experience, or developed as a later refinement of a more general urge to create; they may have fallen into it entirely by accident, come to that. They will usually have experimented with the basics beforehand, though, typically to explore their creativity (rather than as a planned career move). Perhaps they started out by designing and developing their own single-player role-playing games (RPGs) either from scratch or by using a tool such as RPG Maker (Gotcha Gotcha Games, 1992). Perhaps they used an online platform such as *Roblox* (Baszucki & Cassel, 2006) to create a multi-player game.[8] Perhaps, as did many of their predecessors, they built a world for a tabletop RPG such as *D&D*.

Because this section concerns the prehistory of virtual worlds, when we look for influential games that allowed early aspiring designers to cut their world-creation teeth, we find *D&D* at the forefront. It influenced many designers not only of virtual worlds but also of computer RPGs in general (King & Borland, 2003) – although not always to the same degree. There were basically two ways this tended to happen.

The first way saw the aspiring designer using *D&D* as a creative outlet. Taking the position of *Dungeon Master*[9] (DM), they created dungeons, campaigns, worlds and finally full-on paracosms. Through this, they learned the craft and the art of constructing a world that people would wish to visit, and what they could expect those people (players) to do there. They completed their transition from player to designer during this period, such that when they gained access to computers and acquired the skills to use them, they built new worlds of their imagination that bore little resemblance to *D&D*.

---

[7] If you don't relish it, you still might be; it's a sufficient criterion but not a necessary one.

[8] *Roblox* hosts some full-on virtual worlds, most notably *Adopt Me!* (Bethink, 2017).

[9] This term was trademarked by *D&D*'s publishers, Tactical Studies Rules (TSR), so other RPGs tend to go with *Game Master*, or, if they consider the "Master" part offensive, *Referee*.

The second way saw the aspiring designer assigning the position of DM to a computer before they had fully stopped being a player. By extending a game world, they learned their craft through the lens of programming until either their artistic appetite was satiated or they felt compelled to start afresh with a new, different world. For this reason, most of the games that were created along these lines shared many of *D&D*'s common tropes – the same primary attributes, similar classes and races, hit points, experience points, levels, combat, a faux-medieval, Tolkienesque milieu – some of which were carried through to the designer's second-generation games.

To some extent, this pattern can still be seen today. Some nascent designers will focus on design and then figure out the implications for implementation later, while others will focus on what the implementation allows and take it from there. Both approaches (paracosm or programming) are legitimate. With the first, you get original designs that may never reach a playable state; with the second, you get playable worlds that can seem at times to be derivative. Experienced or simply gifted designers can design worlds that are both playable and original, of course (given sufficient time).

Although other tabletop RPGs followed in *D&D*'s wake, *D&D* was the first to achieve critical mass because of its head start. Most early RPGers therefore played *D&D* rather than, say, *Tunnels & Trolls* (St Andre, 1975). This was despite the fact that some of the slightly later games, such as *RuneQuest* (Perrin et al., 1978) and *Call of Cthulhu* (Peterson, 1981), were better thought-out.

The original *D&D* rule set was descriptive, but the concept became more prescriptive with the arrival of *Advanced Dungeons & Dragons* (Gygax, 1977), which had rules for everything. This was a boon to virtual world designers coming from the direction of programming but was of less utility for designers coming from the direction of paracosms. In general terms, today's virtual worlds defer more to *Advanced Dungeons & Dragons* (*AD&D*) than they do to *D&D*.[10]

Although *D&D* in its various incarnations continued and continues to fire the imaginations of prospective virtual world designers, it's no longer as influential as it once was. In large part, this is because of the very computer RPGs that it inspired,[11] but it was already gradually losing ground as ready-made, stand-alone modules[12] gained popularity. Players no longer had to create their own dungeons, campaigns or worlds: they could simply buy a ready-made one. This meant that fewer DMs were obliged to construct their own worlds in which to play, so latent design talent went unawakened.

Although paracosms and tabletop RPGs can and do develop over time as new elements are added, they are not themselves virtual worlds: they have no physics. They can, however, become virtual worlds if endowed with such physics. Merely adding physics to a paracosm does not necessarily result in a virtual world, though, because physics is just one of the

---

[10] I shall nevertheless use *D&D* rather than *AD&D* as a shorthand for members of the set of games in the series. It's a whole keystroke shorter.

[11] For a monumental and comprehensive guide to the history of computer RPGs, with full-colour screenshots throughout, see Pepe (2022). Academics wishing to consider a career in RPG studies should also seek out Zagal & Deterding (2018) as a constructive place to start. For only the history of *D&D*, it's difficult to imagine anything more meticulous than Peterson (2024).

[12] They were called *modules* prior to the third edition of *D&D*; they're now called *adventures*.

required criteria; other kinds of game-world can result instead. As noted earlier, plenty of single-player computer RPGs implement imaginary worlds, some of which can be just as extensive and involving as those of classic, by-the-book[13] virtual worlds.

That's today, though. Back in the mists of time, when virtual worlds were on the cusp of being invented, computers were insufficiently powerful to bring life to worlds with lore as sweeping as that of contemporary paracosms. Games of that period may may have had a motivating fiction ("stop these aliens that are invading from space"), but even that wasn't obligatory ("demolish this wall" is more goal than fiction).

The immediate computer-based predecessors of virtual worlds were *adventure games*, so named because the first one (Crowther & Woods, 1976) was called *Adventure*.[14] There weren't many of these around at the time – the only other historically significant one was *Zork*[15] (Anderson et al., 1977) – but they introduced some key concepts.

Primary among these innovations was the idea that it was the *player* who was in the game world. You weren't controlling a spaceship or a lunar lander; you weren't Hammurabi, instructing people how to manage your economy; you weren't moving pieces on a board: you were your character[16], *in* the game world. Although *Adventure* didn't quite get this right to begin with ("I will be your eyes and hands"), *Zork* nailed it. This hadn't really been done before (which isn't surprising, as there wasn't much "before" in which to do it), and it opened up new avenues for computer-moderated play.

To a modern player, perhaps the most striking thing about these early games is that they employed a textual interface. Commands were input as words, and their effects were described in words. This was just how things were back then, though: most programs used a command-line interface, because it's hard to use anything else when you're communicating with a mainframe at 110 baud using what is effectively a typewriter with five reams of fanfold paper coming out of the back onto which your input and the program's output is slammed noisily in upper case through an ever-faded ribbon.[17]

That isn't to say that there weren't graphics-capable systems out there being used by people with the will to write games. In particular, the ground-breaking PLATO[18] system operated by the University of Illinois had screens with vector graphics that allowed for

---

[13] Possibly this book.

[14] It was also called *Colossal Cave, Colossal Cave Adventure* and (because the operating system it was written for only allowed six-character upper-case filenames) *ADVENT*. Crowther wrote the original version, released in 1976; Woods extended it (with Crowther's permission) in 1977, adding mythical and fantasy elements to what previously had been a straight (but humorous) representation of the Mammoth Cave system in Kentucky (Jerz, 2007).

[15] Most early players experienced this in the form of a Fortran version that was distributed on magnetic tape to institutions with DEC PDP-10 mainframes. Probably for reasons of advertising what it was, it went by the name *DUNGEN* (because of the six-letter filename limit; its introductory text called it *Dungeon*). This had later consequences for naming conventions in the virtual world genre.

[16] It's perhaps more accurate to say your character was a subset of you – the *player-subject* (Sicart, 2009).

[17] Translation for younger readers: a mainframe is a single computer with perhaps hundreds of input/output devices attached to it; 110 baud is 110 bits per second; a typewriter is like a keyboard that prints directly onto paper instead of displaying text on a screen; a ream is 500 sheets; fanfold paper consists of individual sheets connected together along perforated edges; a ribbon is an inked strip that makes a mark on paper when hit by an object (such as one with a metal letter embossed on it).

[18] This is apparently an acronym for Programmed Logic for Automatic Teaching Operations, but I suspect the acronym came first.

visual elements. As it happened, the graphics weren't all that important for virtual worlds; the fact that PLATO could handle up to a thousand users simultaneously (Woolley, 1994) was more significant. For this period of prehistory, however, the most cogent point is that PLATO's administrators were (perhaps consciously) lax at detecting inappropriate uses of resources – such as, say, the writing and playing of games by its imaginative users.

The most popular games that emerged in this environment were role-playing in nature. Some, such as *The Dungeon*[19] (Rutherford, 1975) and *The Game of Dungeons*[20] (Wood et al., 1975), were heavily inspired by *Dungeons & Dragons.*[21] Later games were written to out-do these and each other: *Orthanc Labyrinth*[22] (Resch et al., 1975), *Moria* (Duncombe & Battin, 1976) and *Oubliette* (Schwaiger et al., 1977). *Moria* was particularly revolutionary because it introduced a significant new concept: it was multi-user. Players could play in the same world at the same time in groups of up to ten (Bolingbroke, 2013) and help each other in combat (Schuller, n.d.). The opportunities for interaction were somewhat limited, though, so *Moria* doesn't really qualify as being fully shared.[23] *Oubliette* had additional interactive features,[24] but it couldn't legitimately be called real-time (combat was turn-based). Also, its persistence was questionable: characters were saved between play sessions, but the game world was fairly inert (it had random encounters in its dungeons, not autonomous NPCs). It was very close to being a virtual world, but not quite there.[25]

Adventure was not a virtual world, because it was neither shared nor persistent. *Oubliette* was shared but not persistent. Neither had NPCs that went about their business in real time. Each was an evolutionary step in the right direction, though, and it was only a matter of time before the first example of a new species, virtual worlds, would be born.

2.3 THE FIRST AGE (1978–1985): INDEPENDENT INVENTION

Virtual worlds were originally called MUDs, because *MUD* was the name of the first one to prosper.[26] Although earlier systems had been written which might today be described as being virtual worlds (depending on how charitable your definition is), they were seeds that fell on stony ground. *MUD*, by contrast, grew to produce seeds of its own.

MUD was an acronym for *Multi-User Dungeon*, but everyone called it *MUD*. It was programmed in October 1978 using MACRO-10 assembler on a DECSystem-10 mainframe at the University of Essex, England, where programming for fun was actively encouraged. Its author was a talented Computer Science undergraduate, Roy Trubshaw. Version 1 was

---

[19] Better known by its system keyword, *pedit5* – a name chosen so that administrators seeing this would think it was an editor, not a game, and so overlook it. It was still deleted roughly once a week, even so (Schuller, n.d.).

[20] Better known by its system keyword, *dnd*, this didn't suffer the same deleted-by-administrators fate as *The Dungeon* because one of its authors *was* an administrator (Schuller, n.d.).

[21] You could tell from the names, right?

[22] Usually shortened to *Orthanc*.

[23] An earlier game, *Dungeon* (Daleske, 1975), was multi-player. Its author, who also wrote the fabulously popular *Empire* (Daleske, 1973), "claims it was the first MUD on PLATO, perhaps on any computer" (Dear, 2017). Sadly, it was unresponsive and incomplete (Daleske had a cancer scare at the time); it didn't attract players.

[24] This was just as well, because it was almost impossibly difficult when playing alone.

[25] By some definitions, it may indeed qualify as a virtual world (but then so might air-traffic control systems). It depends on your definition. It doesn't by the one in this book, but I could be somewhat biased.

[26] For an extensive description, discussion and analysis of the creation of *MUD*, see Bartle (2020).

a simple test program to try out some risky coding principles[27] that he hoped to employ; two hours later, he had established that his ideas did indeed work. He immediately began work on version 2, and by mid-December had a fully functioning system that players today would be able to recognise as a virtual world.

Because version 2 was also written in assembler, it became unwieldy. In the autumn of 1979, Roy made the decision to begin work on version 3 of the game.[28] Although some assembly language was involved for the delicate parts, the vast majority of the code was in BCPL (the fore-runner of the fore-runner of C). He split the program in two: the game engine[29] and the database.[30] The way he set it up, the description of the game world and its functionality was written in a language of his own devising called MUDDL (Multi-User Dungeon Definition Language); the MUDDL code was then compiled by a program he wrote called DBASE into a form that could be loaded directly into the game engine. Running the game engine brought the virtual world to life.

Roy's purpose here was to allow for multiple virtual worlds to be written in MUDDL, which could then be run using the same, unmodified engine. He was successful in this regard, too: several games[31] were written using this approach, although none were to rival *MUD* itself.

By Easter 1980, Roy had a working shell. All the main components were present, and it did satisfy all the criteria for being a virtual world; however, it fell far short of what he had envisaged. As this was the final year of his undergraduate degree, he concluded that he didn't have time to finish it. Someone else would have to take it on.

That someone was me. From the very beginning, Roy had been very open to suggestions from his friends as to how *MUD* could be extended and improved, and had allowed a trusted few creative access to version 2. One of these, Nigel Roberts, was particularly interested in the timesharing aspects of a shared world[32]; another one, Richard Bartle,[33] was interested in the world-creation aspects. Nigel was in Roy's year, but I was a year younger and still had a year to go before I finished my BSc; Roy passed code ownership[34] of *MUD* to me.

Subsequently, I finished off the engine (Roy had done about a quarter of it, but it was the most difficult quarter) and wrote almost all the content. This version 3 of *MUD* became the paradigm for almost all subsequent virtual worlds.

Although the "D" in *MUD* stands for "Dungeon", it has only a tenuous connection with *D&D*. Roy wanted to choose a name that would give prospective players some idea of what his creation was about, and he figured that saying it was like an adventure game

---

[27] These were called *hacks* back then, before the term had been appropriated to mean something rather less positive.

[28] *MUD* was always called a game, even though versions 1 and 2 had no gameplay to speak of.

[29] This is what it would be called today; the term was not in use back in 1979.

[30] In a modern virtual world, this would equate to the *static database*, used to prime the *run-time database*.

[31] The most notable were *MIST* (Barham et al., 1984) and *ROCK* (Fox, 1983).

[32] Nigel later went on to sit on the board of the non-profit Internet Corporation for Assigned Names and Numbers (ICANN) – basically the people who stop governments from controlling the Internet. For his work in this area, he was awarded an honorary doctorate by the University of Essex in 2022.

[33] The man's a genius.

[34] As in, I had final say on what stayed in the code; it wasn't literal ownership – we shared that.

but multi-user would do the trick. Adventure games weren't called that yet, though, and because *Zork* was clearly better than *Adventure*, Roy presumed that the genre would eventually be named after the former. However, the version of *Zork* he'd played was the Fortran port called *DUNGEN*, meaning he knew the game as *Dungeon* rather than as *Zork*. Therefore, he called his own game *MUD* – it was like a multi-user *Dungeon*. The flimsy connection to *D&D* is that *Dungeon* was probably so named to attract *D&D* players. Roy had never played *D&D*, and *MUD* was never to have a dungeon.

Essex University was less than an hour's drive from what at the time was the UK's main telecommunications research centre, run by the Post Office (later, British Telecom). There were strong research links between the two establishments, and so the university was selected to pilot the Post Office's new Experimental Packet-Switching Service (EPSS). One of the possibilities this opened up was the ability to connect to the Advanced Research Project Agency (ARPA) network in the United States, which was later to evolve into the Internet. Roy invited international players to try out *MUD* in early 1979, and some did.

Other universities that also had DECsystem-10 mainframes requested copies of *MUD*, mainly in the UK and Scandinavia. For reasons explained late in Volume II, Roy and I encouraged the dissemination of *MUD* and the writing of alternatives; I duly sent the *MUD* sources to said institutions in the UK and Scandinavia.

In addition to EPSS, Essex University had some dial-in modems available for public use. News of *MUD* reached the UK's small-but-growing community of bulletin-board system (BBS) users, and they were granted permission to play when regular people were fast asleep in bed. Demand grew so much that they clubbed together and bought the university more modems.[35]

More UK universities became interested in telecoms, leading to the creation of the Joint Academic Network (JANet). EPSS ceased being experimental, and as PSS was made available to companies. As a result, many more people could and did access *MUD*. In 1984–1985, almost all the UK's specialist computer magazines ran articles about it. The idea of a virtual world was picked up by players, some of whom had design skills, and the floodgates opened.

Before I move on to discussing the virtual worlds that were inspired by *MUD*, there are two more First-Age topics to address.

The first topic concerns links to the prehistory of virtual worlds.

I began the section on virtual worlds' prehistory by describing the visualisation of imaginary worlds in the form of paracosms. I could have started it with play, or games, or self-expression through art, all of which were important factors in *MUD*'s development; none of these mark a significant step in the direction of virtual worlds in particular, however, whereas paracosms do.

Without doubt, the paracosm that has most affected the design of virtual worlds (*MUD* included) is *The Lord of the Rings*[36] (Tolkien, 1954). Many early virtual worlds drew

---

[35] This was expensive, but the people who dialled in were not short of money; if they had been, they wouldn't have been able to afford the staggeringly high cost of phone calls in the UK back then.

[36] This is another book that clearly undersold because its title began with "The".

extensively from its setting or from games such as *D&D* that took its fiction and ran with it. This isn't how it affected the design of *MUD*, though. For me, *The Lord of the Rings* presented a proof-of-concept that the worlds I had in my head could be made to feel fully real. What's more, using computers, I could allow other people to visit them as if they *were* real. I'd already designed a play-by-email campaign world that I intended to code up as a visitable reality when I gained reliable access to a computer, so when I found that Roy had already begun work on *MUD*, I swiftly dropped the idea[37] and joined him. If I hadn't read *The Lord of the Rings*, I'd probably have kept my worlds to myself.

MUD's fiction does share some of its themes and elements with Middle Earth, which perhaps suggests a deeper relationship, but it isn't true that the former drew from the latter[38]; rather, it's because they both drew from the same, older source: English folklore. I'll explain in Volume II why I chose to do this for *MUD*, but insofar as folklore is itself a communal paracosm, *MUD*'s content was influenced by that, too.

D&D owed much to *The Lord of the Rings* in its scope and fantasy setting. Although it did include some monsters from the books (such as orcs, ents and balrogs), it also featured plenty of disparate creatures from assorted mythologies (djinn, vampires, lycanthropes, pterippuses,[39] ...) and other, invented, dungeon-specific ones (gelatinous cubes, purple worms, grey oozes, ...). The foreword[40] to the original rules (Gygax & Arneson, 1974) cites the thrill of adventure found in the stories of John Carter (Burroughs, 1912), Conan (Howard, 1932) and Fafhrd and the Gray Mouser (Leiber, 1939) – all of which take place in paracosms (Barsoom, Hyboria and Newhon respectively).

Unsurprisingly, given the high intersection between people who could program and people who played tabletop RPGs,[41] *D&D* was the spark that ignited the creativity of many early computer RPG designers – so many, in fact, that it's hard to identify the cases when it wasn't. For *MUD*, the assumption that it was inspired by *D&D* is, as I've already stated, incorrect: I did take some ideas from *D&D* for version 3, notably experience points and levels, but I was looking for a solution to an anticipated problem, not seeking to emulate an existing game. I didn't even take the idea of role-playing from *D&D*, having independently come up with the idea myself circa 1972.[42]

It's a similar story with regard to the early computer games that preceded *MUD*. Roy didn't base *MUD* on *Adventure*, but he did adopt some ideas from its programming for his design for MUDDL[43] – the concept of a *travel table* being the main one. Superficially, it does look as if *MUD* might simply be an *Adventure*-style game with a multi-player component bolted on,

---

[37] A wise decision in hindsight, as it was wildly over-ambitious.

[38] *MUD* doesn't feature elves or orcs, for example, and its dwarfs aren't dwarves.

[39] These are commonly called "pegasi", or "pegasuses" if you don't use Latin pluralisation conventions for Greek words. However, mythology claims only one winged horse called Pegasus, which as a proper noun therefore needs to begin with a capital letter. It resists pluralisation, too (I guess you could ask "How many Pegasuses are there?", but it's a little contrived). None of that is going to stop players from calling winged horses "pegasi", though.

[40] It's headed "Forward...", which I hope is a deliberate pun on "Foreword" rather than a mis-spelling.

[41] I was going to add "back then", but the intersection is still high today.

[42] For a single-player game called *Dr Toddystone*. I talk a little about it in Volume II.

[43] He knew that *Dungeon/Zork* used a language called MDL, pronounced "muddle", but not what it looked like. The similarity of the names MUDDL and MDL carried serendipitous appeal, but MUDDL would have been called MUDDL regardless.

but that's not the case. Roy had written other games before encountering *Adventure*, at least one of which[44] had a command-line interface and a second-person ("You are…") descriptive format. It's easy to mis-read the past from the perspective of the present.[45]

It was years before Roy or I heard about the PLATO games (and even more years before I was able to play any of them on an emulator). They didn't affect the design of *MUD* one iota. This isn't to say they were irrelevant to the history of virtual worlds, though; as we shall shortly see, they do have a small part to play.

The final First-Age topic to be addressed is perhaps the most important: independent invention. The way I've been describing it, it's as if there was a primaeval soup of proto-virtual worlds from which *MUD* emerged as the first true example of a virtual world. Modulo different definitions of the term "virtual world", this is indeed correct. The thing is, though, that *MUD* wasn't the *only* virtual world to claw its way out of primordial chaos.

Virtual worlds were invented independently at least[46] six times. None of the creators of these worlds were aware of the existence of any others. We'll come across them all in due course (if we haven't already), but here's the full list:

- *MUD* (Trubshaw & Bartle, 1978)

- *Sceptre of Goth*[47] (Kleitz, 1978)

- *Avatar* (Maggs et al., 1979)

- *Island of Kesmai* (Flinn & Taylor, 1981)

- *Habitat* (Morningstar & Farmer, 1986)

- *Monster* (Skrenta, 1988)

It's often assumed that just because something was the first of its kind, everything else of that kind must owe something to it. This belief is especially strong when applied to the dissemination of games. For example, even though the idea of hitting a ball with a stick seems pretty obvious, and balls as playthings were invented in many cultures, there does seem to be evidence that all hit-a-ball-with-a-stick games may descend from a single game originating in ancient Persia (Tylor, 1879).[48]

This is not the case with virtual worlds, though. Multiple people had similar ideas and similar opportunities, and opted to pursue similar goals at similar times. They did so without reference to each other. *MUD* shouldn't therefore be lionised merely for being first to the punch.[49]

---

[44] A riff on *Hunt the Wumpus* (Yob, 1973) that he wrote with Nigel Roberts on Nigel's Commodore PET.

[45] This is why historians will always have a job.

[46] There may well be others yet to come to the fore. A multi-player version of *Zork* briefly existed pre-1980, for example Lebling (1980), but whether it would count as a virtual world or not isn't apparent.

[47] Also known as *Milieu*, *E*M*P*I*R*E* and *Ghost* (Alberti, 2010); *Sceptre* (or sometimes *Scepter*) *of Goth* was its commercial name.

[48] I don't hold with this view myself, on account of how *Stickball* was played by indigenous North Americans before they had any contact with indigenous Eurasians. See the sidebar on the term "Avatar".

[49] Especially as it only "beat" *Sceptre of Goth* by weeks.

These early, independently invented virtual worlds can, however, be given credit for those they inspired. They were certain to inspire them, too, because computer technology was advancing rapidly and players with design aspirations were keen to try their own hand at virtual world creation.

Although the engine for *MUD* version 3 (which was basically a MUDDL interpreter) could be used to build new, original worlds, it had its limits. It only ran on DECsystem-10 mainframes, and if more than 36 people wanted to play then a second instantiation had to be cranked up. It was inevitable that some of its players would try their hand at writing their own MUD – and we encouraged them to do so.

2.4 THE SECOND AGE (1985–1989): INSPIRED IMPROVEMENT

The first game to be written from scratch that took *MUD* as a paradigm was *PIGG*[50] (Murrell, 1980), also written at the University of Essex. It was only when players external to the university began writing their own virtual worlds that the concept of "a MUD" developed, and *MUD* itself was dubbed[51] *MUD1* to disambiguate it from the genre that now bore its name. This marked the beginning of the Second Age of virtual worlds.

The first three *MUD*-inspired MUDs to be written from scratch by its external players were *Shades* (Newell, 1985), *Gods* (Laurie, 1985) and *AMP*[52] (Blandford, 1985). *Shades* and *Gods* met with commercial success, considerably so in *Shades'* case as it was on British Telecom's Prestel system, and therefore, a local phone call away from everywhere in the UK.[53] It later found additional success in French translation on the Minitel system; *Gods* had a profitable server in Germany.

Although it remained free on Essex University, *MUD1* also went commercial. In 1986, it was launched on CompuServe (the dominant US online service of the time) as *British Legends*,[54] followed a year later by its debut on CompuNet (a UK lookalike); both services used DECsystem-10 mainframes. One of the programmers at CompuNet, Alan Lenton, took a look at *MUD1* and wrote his own virtual world, *Federation II*[55] (Lenton, 1988) – the first MUD to have a non-Fantasy setting (it was Science Fiction).

Island of Kesmai had arrived on CompuServe already. Both games suffered somewhat from the strict limitations on resource use that CompuServe imposed, which meant they had to put forced hibernations between player commands to keep below the processing budget.[56] They also endured the consequences of working with an effective monopoly (I recall one particularly fraught conversation in which the CompuServe games product manager insisted that I explain to him why CompuServe should only keep 92% of the income generated by *British Legends*).

---

[50] So-called "because it's a pig to write".

[51] Roy and I had nothing to do with this. Players call things what they want to call things, whether you like it or not.

[52] An acronym for *Adventure for Multiple Players*.

[53] Some non-local *MUD* players racked up phone bills of £2,000 to £3,000 a quarter. This was at a time when the average wage in the UK was £159.30 a week (UK Parliament, 1985).

[54] The "British" adjective was used so that I didn't have to go through all the text localising it into US English.

[55] There was no *Federation*: the name was chosen to make it look as if it was the continuation of a successful franchise.

[56] Back then, it was all about central-processing-unit usage; nowadays, it's all about frames-per-second.

Back in the UK, scores of MUDs were being written by players of the "big four": *MUD1*, *Shades*, *Gods* and *Federation II*. It was a period of great experimentation, with new ideas being tried, discarded, retried, improved – all in multiple directions. This was possible because:

- a MUD could be written by one person working alone or a small group working together;

- all games were written from scratch, so didn't have to use any systems imposed on them by game engines;

- it still took some effort to create a MUD, so the people who designed and built them were motivated to do so by the creative possibilities;

- virtual worlds, being worlds, naturally encourage experimentation.

The first virtual world engine[57] that found traction was provided by the IOWA[58] system, using a MUD definition language called Slate[59] that had its beginnings in a MUD called *MirrorWorld* (Cordrey et al., 1986). Slate allowed for a wide variety of genres but had too much built-in to present many opportunities for divergence in gameplay; most of the IOWA stable of games used Slate and were therefore different in setting but not so different to play. In the same way that the vocabulary of a language shapes what you can say in it, so game engines shape what can be written using them.

Some of the IOWA virtual worlds introduced concepts that we shall come across later, although as precursors rather than as progenitors (subsequent, independent reinventions properly established the ideas). In particular:

- *Empyrion* (Clary et al., 1990) implemented its mobs on a separate processor using a general-purpose AI programming language, Prolog. These mobs[60] were reputedly able to learn.

- *Chaos World of Wizards* (Cordrey et al., 1990) was user-extensible. Unlike *MUD* version 2, all players of *Chaos World of Wizards* had creation rights, not just those trusted to make a good job of it. The obvious game-breaking potential of this feature duly broke the game, and the chaos alluded to in its title inevitably ensued, but what if something similar were tried in a non-game context?

- *Quest* (Harling et al., 1986) claimed to be the first MUD with gambling, allowing players to bet their characters' experience points on the results of NPC gladiatorial combat. This wasn't as popular among players as had been hoped.

---

[57] Most engines of this period were implemented as interpreters for a definition language. Sometimes, the engine and the language had the same name; sometimes, they were the same but had "language", "interpreter", "system" or some such tacked onto one or both of them; sometimes they were different.

[58] Its full title was *Input/Output World of Adventure*, but (as seems to be the way with semi-contrived acronyms) everyone called it IOWA.

[59] Slate was available for license on non-IOWA systems for the sum of £3,000. Some such licenses were indeed sold.

[60] Strictly speaking, they were *bots* – see Volume II.

One IOWA game, *Avalon*[61] (Simmons et al., 1989), did have a direct influence on later virtual worlds. It was written using its own engine and language, Hourglass, which was originally coded in ARM assembler then ported to Unix. There was also a port to the PC called *Vortex*, which was used for the development of a pivotal MUD, *Achaea*[62] (Mihaly, 1996), that we shall re-encounter in due course. Many important concepts from *Avalon*, and to some extent another influential MUD, *BatMUD* (Frösen, 1990), informed the development of *Achaea*. Primary among these was the emphasis on role-playing,[63] particularly the notion of making the highest-ranking players both fictional and literal gods of the game world (an idea pioneered by, well, *Gods*); as we'll see in Volume II, this wasn't the feature with the greatest ultimate knock-on effect, however.

Avalon's commitment to innovation was such that it implemented an attractive subset of a more ambitious set of ideas that *MirrorWorld*'s lead designer, Pip Cordrey, had presented in a series of talks and articles. Cordrey's vision, called Mosaic, involved using a revolutionary grid system as a basis for structuring virtual worlds. At its core was the controversial concept of building the game world out of virtual cubic-metre blocks. Although we pressed him to implement this graphically, Cordrey was anti-graphics and refused to contemplate the idea. Thus, *Minecraft* (Persson, 2011) was not invented.

In 1985, Roy and I made the decision to rewrite *MUD* as version 4 (which came to be known as *MUD2* (Trubshaw & Bartle, 1985)). Roy wrote the front-end and account processing; I wrote the interpreter and the content (adding to the original *MUD1* land[64] plus a stand-alone zone called *VALLEY* that I'd created for periods when limits on memory usage prohibited the playing of *MUD1* in full). I discarded MUDDL and named my new language MUDDLE (Multi-User Dungeon Definition LanguagE[65]). As a full-on programming language (you could write a MUDDLE interpreter in MUDDLE), it's still used for *MUD2* to this day.

The Second Age of virtual worlds resulted in a flowering of ideas. At the Adventure '89 convention,[66] over 20 MUDs were on display, all wildly different. Non-Fantasy genres included Space Opera, Cyberpunk, ancient Britain, a generation spaceship, an underwater city, comedic and Adult.[67] Fantasy games still dominated, but even they usually had radically different features (objects and mobs that had shape, or could be decomposed, or that respawned upon destruction, or that could be created by players) and goals (focusing on combat, role-playing, economics, socialising, ….).

Parallel to this, a similar "golden age" phenomenon was occurring in single-player games (Stanton, 2015). This is what happens when a field is young: there is a window in which those who are sufficiently driven to be able to overcome the immediate obstacles

---

[61] Formally, *Avalon: the Legend Lives*. As you may by now have noticed, the full names of early virtual worlds were rarely used, a practice which today's virtual worlds are happy to perpetuate.

[62] You guessed it: it has a longer formal name that few people use – *Achaea, Dreams of Divine Lands*.

[63] You could level up in *Avalon* by having long conversations.

[64] *MUD*'s fictional world was called The Land. This may sound uninspired, but it gave the impression that the place was somehow always there, eternal – that it was real, but not of a particular place or time. See Volume II for why I wanted this.

[65] This also may sound uninspired, but that's because it was.

[66] Organised by Pip Cordrey, it was the last of the series: he abruptly left soon afterwards for a new life in Venezuela running a monkey sanctuary.

[67] I chose this word rather than "sex" because they (there were two such worlds) weren't remotely as tawdry as that makes it sound.

facing them can unleash their creativity. When the expectations of consumers increase and creation becomes more expensive to realise, the front along which experimentation and expressiveness progress narrows. Designers are obliged to go further in known directions rather than seek new pastures that may or may not be just over the next hill.

By the end of the Second Age, most of the key issues of virtual world design had been identified. It's a sad feature of virtual worlds, however, that later generations of designers sometimes aren't aware of lessons hard-learned by their metaphorical ancestors. Even though most ways of doing things are passed on from one generation to the next, the rationale does not necessarily accompany the advice. It's often "do X" rather than "do X because Y". Without knowing the Y, it's hard to ascertain whether the advice still holds or not, and therefore whether continuing to do X is a good idea or not. Sometimes, when a new technology becomes available, incoming designers will deny that X is relevant while experienced designers are shouting "no, no, because Y!" at them; sometimes, they'll take X as canon when old-timers can see that Y no longer holds. One of the aims of this book is to help connect Xs to Ys so we don't have to go through this same routine every time there's a new development affecting virtual world design.[68]

So far, this has all been *MUD, MUD, MUD*. This isn't entirely for reasons of self-aggrandizement on my part; as we'll see shortly, it's mainly because *MUD* is where today's virtual worlds overwhelmingly have their roots. It's only "overwhelmingly", though; splashes of influence from some of the other First Age virtual worlds also ripple through to the present day. That said, through sheer weight of numbers, there was much cross-pollination between MUDs, but not so much between other codebases, except when they (inevitably) encountered MUDs.

Avatar, being run as it was on a university system, was not commercially oriented. Its authors did not seek to protect its code or to discourage lookalikes (not that they needed to: *Avatar* accounted for 600,000 of the 10,000,000 hours logged by PLATO users between September 1978 and May 1985 (Woolley, 1994) – and it wasn't even released until late 1979 or early 1980 (Dear, 2017)). On the face of it, this is similar to the situation *MUD* was in – so why were so many people inspired to create their own *MUD* derivatives but not their own *Avatar* derivatives?

The answer is that *Avatar* was a bird trapped in a gilded cage. The PLATO system offered many facilities unavailable elsewhere, but that was its problem: they *weren't* available elsewhere. If you didn't have one of the special terminals, you couldn't access it; members of the general public didn't have such terminals, so couldn't access it, so didn't play *Avatar*, so weren't inspired to take the idea forward. Some individuals who did play the game went on to have major, impactful careers in the MMO industry (C. Gordon Walton[69] and David Shapiro[70] especially so), but they are few in number.

---

[68] I suspect that it's a futile aim, but I can hope.

[69] Gordon Walton is one of the best-known executive producers in the MMO industry, having worked on *Air Warrior II* (Baron, 1992), *Ultima Online* (Koster, 1997), *The Sims Online* (Trottier, 2002), *Star Wars Galaxies* (Koster, 2003), *Star Wars: the Old Republic* (Ohlen, 2011), *Crowfall* (Coleman, 2021) and many others.

[70] He's better known as Dr. Cat (or Dr Cat if you use formal British English punctuation rules and so don't put full stops (periods) after contractions, only after abbreviations). After working on a number of games in the *Ultima* (Garriott, 1981) series as a designer, programmer and both, he left to create his own virtual world, *Furcadia* (Shapiro et al., 1996), which is still going strong.

If you make a distinction between virtual worlds and their MMO subset that suggests MMOs "must be graphical" then *Avatar* can lay claim to being the first MMO.[71] *Avatar* is indeed the first virtual world to include graphics (although text dominates its screen), but the point is irrelevant: no modern virtual worlds are graphical because *Avatar* was. That said, as we'll see when we reach the Fifth Age, one of *Avatar's* precursors, *Oubliette*, can obliquely make that claim.

Although the long-term influence of *Avatar* on virtual world development is almost imperceptible, the same is not true of *Sceptre of Goth* (*Sceptre* for short). There is a still-very-visible thread of *Sceptre* in the otherwise *MUD*-woven tapestry of modern virtual worlds.

Sceptre was developed around the same time as *MUD* by Alan Klietz[72] on the Minnesota Educational Computer Consortium (MECC) mainframe using Multi-Pascal. He created it explicitly to be a multi-player *ADVENT*, using the *AD&D* rule set (Alberti, 2010). When the MECC system was closed down in 1983, he and three others[73] formed a company, GāmBit Multi Systems; Klietz rewrote the game in C to run on a modified PC. By 1985, GāmBit was grossing $70,000 a year – not far off what the top MUDs in the UK were making.[74]

GāmBit was very protective of the program code for *Sceptre*, unsurprisingly given that the company's future depended on it. It also depended on improving and maintaining *Sceptre* so that new players would be attracted and old players would remain. Unfortunately, the first programmer GāmBit hired to assist in this enterprise copied all the software[75] and, when fired for trying to sell it (through GāmBit's own chat room), promptly set up a competing system (Alberti, 2010). Furthermore, he changed the revenue model from around $2/hour to a flat $10/month.

The player base of the GāmBit server collapsed as players took the cheaper option. GāmBit responded by franchising *Sceptre*. Soon, the game was operating in 13 cities (charging each franchisee $10,000/year).

GāmBit's officers learned that they did not like running a company, so when one of their franchisees offered to buy them out, they happily accepted the offer. The franchisee collapsed shortly afterwards, in part because its president was convicted on multiple counts of tax evasion, and there *Sceptre's* own story ends.

It's not where its influence ends, however: *Sceptre* directly inspired other people to write their own virtual worlds.

Firstly, David Whatley was moved[76] to design *Gemstone][* (Whatley, 1988), which we will meet in the Fourth Age. Furthermore, to help develop it, his company, Simutronics (known as Crystal Blade at the time), snapped up five people who had toiled on *Sceptre*. Among

---

[71] At least until virtual reality interfaces become commonplace and your wilfully ignorant successors insist that MMOs "must be VR".

[72] His surname rhymes with "fleets".

[73] One of whom, Bob Alberti, is the source of most of the information about *Sceptre* provided herein; he also worked on the Gopher protocol, which was a predecessor of the Hypertext Transfer Protocol (HTTP) used by the World Wide Web.

[74] For comparison, at a time in the mid-late 1980s when the average annual UK salary had risen to around £9,000 (BBC, 2000), *Shades* was taking in around £70,000 a year.

[75] The laws protecting the ownership of programs were hazy at the time (not that they're a lot better now).

[76] He'd also heard of *Island of Kesmai*, so this wasn't all *Sceptre's* influence.

them was Scott Hartsman, who later became Sony Online Entertainment's Technical Director, working on both *EverQuest* (Clover et al., 1999) and *EverQuest II* (Waters, 2004); following this, he became CEO of Trion Worlds, the developer of *Rift* (Ffinch, 2011).

Secondly, *Sceptre* player Mark Jacobs saw such potential in virtual worlds that he taught himself to code and gave up a career as a lawyer to create *Aradath* (Jacobs, 1984). Along with Darrin Hyrup from Simutronics, he followed this up with *Dragon's Gate* (Jacobs & Hyrup, 1990), which we will also meet in the Fourth Age. He subsequently co-founded Mythic Entertainment[77] and went on to design *Dark Age of Camelot* (Jacobs et al., 2001), *Warhammer Online: Age of Reckoning* (Jacobs et al., 2008) and the long-in-development *Camelot Unchained*.

Although today's *Sceptre*-descended MMOs are still identifiable, it's in a "my grandmother was Scottish" kind of way; just because your grandmother was Scottish, it doesn't mean you are.[78] *Sceptre*'s modern descendants have married into the *MUD* family tree, and inevitably take more from that than they do from *Sceptre*.

One of the other First-Age virtual worlds, *Island of Kesmai* (*IoK*), also inspired players to develop virtual worlds of their own. *Island of Kesmai* grew out of a six-player game called *Dungeons of Kesmai* (Flinn & Taylor, 1980) completed the previous year; neither of its designers had even heard of *ADVENT* at the time.

Because the Kesmai[79] Corporation was rather better at keeping control of its code than was GāmBit, it didn't need to change course from quality to quantity and so for the most part its early games were exclusive to CompuServe. It could boast far fewer players a result, but despite this, several people[80] were inspired to design their own *IoK*-like games. The reason for this was that *IoK* was implemented as a grid-based world visualised using top-down, ASCII graphics – perfect for progressing to the kind of tile-based graphics that single-player role-playing games were pioneering at the time.

Some of *IoK*'s descendants also went on to inspire descendants of their own, but ultimately, the *IoK* family tree petered out. We'll see why when we reach the Fifth Age.

Habitat was a properly graphical virtual world, using a 2D, side-scroller perspective (without the scrolling). It was innovative in not only its use of a graphical user interface, but also its emphasis on community. It had no gameplay: it was all about interaction between players. As such, it presaged developments in the Third Age of virtual worlds.

Initially, *Habitat* was only available for players using the Commodore 64 with a modem, which limited its growth. It also ran into a number of now-familiar problems to do with social worlds (in particular, that some players are antisocial). Unusually, its main impact on later virtual world development comes not from players inspired to write their own virtual worlds, but from a classic article (Morningstar & Farmer, 1990) by the game's designers that was extremely useful for people entering the field.

---

[77] Originally, Interworld Productions; the other founders were Darrin Hyrup and Rob Denton.
[78] My grandmother was indeed Scottish, or at least both her parents were, but my other three grandparents were English. I am not, therefore, Scottish, although technically I could play for Scotland in international sporting events.
[79] I believe the name was chosen by Kelton Flinn from the output of a random-name generator he'd written.
[80] Not necessarily players – you only had to look at what *IoK* displayed to get the gist of it.

If you want to play – or, more importantly, play *with* – the original *Habitat* code, it's now been released as an open-source project, *Neohabitat* (Farmer, 2017). Have fun!

The final First-Age virtual world, *Monster,* arrived so late that it was preceded by a large number of Second Age worlds. It's not one of the better-known early worlds, but without it, one of the most significant events in the history of virtual worlds might not have happened: the Great Schism, which precipitated the Third Age of virtual worlds.

2.5 THE THIRD AGE (1989–1995): THE GREAT SCHISM

Most of the Second Age virtual worlds were written to run on (usually tricked-out) personal computers rather than mainframes. There *were* MUDs written for large, university-owned mainframe computers (and even some operated by multinational companies), but few UK institutions were as generous with their computer resources as Essex University. Even those that strove to be open-minded usually had issues with allowing random members of the general public to log in. These virtual worlds therefore tended to enjoy only local success.

The exception was *AberMUD* (Cox et al., 1987), so-called because it was a MUD[81] written at the University of Wales at Aberystwyth. It was originally written in B (the forerunner of C that BCPL was the fore-runner of) for a Honeywell L66 mainframe under GCOS3/TSS. After a year, it was ported to C, so it would run on the Unix machine at the University of Southampton. This was to be a turning point in virtual world history.

Michael Lawrie, who had been managing multiple MUDs on UK university computers (including *MIST* and for a time *MUD* at Essex University), oversaw *AberMUD* at Leeds and Southampton. He sent the code for the game to two *MIST* players in the United States where, because Unix was far more endemic than in the UK at the time, it propagated quickly among US universities. Most students had seen nothing like it before, and it became a huge success. Identical copies appeared on thousands of machines.

AberMUD was very combat-oriented in comparison to other virtual worlds of the era. It wasn't especially cutting edge in either its technology or its content, but it was a lot of fun – *if* you liked combat.

Not all players did.

In the UK, those players who didn't enjoy having their characters regularly murdered before their eyes could choose to play any of a number of more balanced virtual worlds. This was not an option in the United States, where *AberMUD* ruled. Those players who wanted a socially oriented experience had to write their own virtual worlds. This, some duly did.

The first was *TinyMUD* (Aspnes, 1989). It was a reaction to the game-like excesses of *AberMUD,* but drew its defining feature from *Monster.* Although *Monster* had not been widely played (it ran on a much-less-popular-than-Unix VAX VMS system and its server was not network-accessible), it was enough to inspire Jim Aspnes to strip it down and to focus on its core idea: object creation by players.

You may recall that *MUD* version 2 had object creation by players; some Second Age virtual worlds (particularly those on the IOWA system) also pushed the idea hard. However,

---

[81] Its lead designer and programmer, Alan Cox, was an ardent player of Essex University's *MUD.*

AberMUD did not have it, and therefore, these earlier inventions had no influence on either *Monster* or *TinyMUD*. Beware of timelines: just because someone thought of an idea first, that doesn't mean all subsequent uses of that idea necessarily owe anything to it. *Second Life* (Rosedale, 2003) ultimately had user-created content because *Monster* had it, not because *MUD* had it.

In the First and Second Ages, virtual worlds were played both by people who saw them as games and by people who saw them as societies. Although there were some differences in philosophy, in general both groups of players kept the other in check for mutual better-ment. Some virtual worlds were more game than society and some *vice versa*; some were almost entirely one-sided (such as *Habitat*). It wasn't until *TinyMUD* broke ranks, however, that the two cultures divorced. This is the Great Schism, the repercussions of which are still felt in virtual worlds today.

TinyMUD had no gameplay. People still "played" it, but the fun came from creation and socialising, not from game rules embodied in its physics. The players created a great deal, too: *MUD1* and *AberMUD* each had around 400–500 discrete locations (*rooms*, as they were known), but a popular 1990 installation of *TinyMUD* called *Islandia* (Mauldin, 1990)[82] built up over 14,000 of them in the few months of its existence – despite the fact that its administrators engaged in Wikipedia-like quality control to remove aberrant content.[83]

TinyMUDs tended to last only a few months before burning out. Even the original game, referred to as *TinyMUD Classic* (to distinguish it from other installations), ran only from 19 August 1989 to 29 April 1990 (Burka, 1992).[84] In those days, when hard disc space quotas were an issue and system administrators did not view play kindly, this was perhaps not surprising; the fact that players had to make their own fun was also a contributing factor. *TinyMUD* therefore got MUDs something of a bad name among university admin-istrators, although fortunately the quality and purpose of later virtual worlds were able to assuage this to a large extent.

TinyMUD had been written to have minimal functionality beyond object creation; it was almost proof-of-concept in its design. Many players naturally wanted more than that, so were inspired to create their own MUDs. Most notably, Stephen White created *TinyMUCK* (White, 1990), shortly followed by *MOO*[85] (White, 1990) – but not before *TinyMUCK* had moved Larry Foard to create *TinyMUSH* (Foard, 1990).

Although *TinyMUD* had allowed the creation of objects, *TinyMUCK* extended this to all aspects of the game world, including functionality. *TinyMUSH* and *MOO* incorporated their own scripting languages to make creation easier for players. Each of these derivations of *TinyMUD* – which came to be known as *codebases* – had different affordances: MUCKs

---

[82] I believe it was inspired by Austin Tappan Wright's paracosm, but could be wrong.

[83] This is still chickenfeed compared to some MUDs – *Medievia* (Smith et al., 1991) claims over four million rooms.

[84] If you want to try *TinyMUD Classic*, a version of it is cranked up once a year, on or around 19 August – Brigadoon Day (Felagund, 1999), so-called after the musical (Loewe & Lerner, 1947) in which a Scottish village only appears once every hundred years. The tradition was started by the administrator of *Islandia*.

[85] *MOO* is short for "MUD, Object-Oriented". Unlike the case with its peers, this was an actual acronym, rather than a play on the word "MUD" that was then retro-fitted as an acronym ("Multi-User Shared Hallucination", "Multi-User Created Kingdom", *etc.*).

were good for social play; MUSHes were good for role-playing[86]; MOOs were all-rounders but were especially favoured by educationalists.[87]

Aside: you may have noticed that I've been using the past tense here, but somewhat embarrassingly, my discussion of virtual world history has now reached the stage where some of the virtual worlds of the past are still very much virtual worlds of the present. There remain plenty of MOOs around, for example, so I should be saying "MOOs are" rather than "MOOs were". The reason I'll stick with the past tense, though, is that I'm framing all this in the time I'm talking about, rather than today; if I were to refer to something that happened later than this point in the historical context then it would indeed get a "MOOs are". End of Aside.

MOO spawned two significant offspring of its own: *LambdaMOO* (Curtis, 1990), which we will meet in later chapters; and *ColdMUD* (Hudson, 1993), an attempt to create a virtual world authoring system adhering to principles of software engineering.

There was a fourth codebase that came out of *TinyMUD*, but it wasn't a social world. Lars Pensjö had also played *AberMUD*, and wanted to bring user-created content to games. Thus, *LPMUD* (Pensjö, 1989) was born. *LPMUD* had a very powerful scripting language, LPC, which was based on the programming language C. LPC could be used to make very different, bespoke virtual worlds and to modify them on the fly. It flew the flag for the pre-schism balanced virtual worlds, but ultimately didn't reach its full potential: socially oriented players found LPC too hard to use, and game-oriented players didn't like the inconsistencies that invariably appear if too many creators can change a world independently.[88]

If you'd read a newspaper or magazine article about virtual worlds in the early 1990s, you might have come away with the impression that MOOs ruled. They did indeed have more players than all the TinyMUDs, MUSHes and MUCKs combined, but in truth they were niche. Most players, it turned out, were gamers.

With social players leaving in droves to play assorted social-oriented worlds, those players who liked gameplay found themselves pleasingly freed to do so. The brakes that had been there to address the needs of social players were now off. Designers could go as hard-core game as they chose. Unsurprisingly, they did.

DikuMUD (Hammer et al., 1991) was written by a group of friends studying at the Department of Computer Science, Copenhagen University (Datalogisk Institut, Københavns Universitet[89]). It was created explicitly to be a better *AberMUD*, and took *D&D* as an inspiration to achieve this goal. *LPMUD* (which the *DikuMUD* team regarded as overly buggy) and *TinyMUD* had both followed a path of allowing on-the-fly changes to their virtual worlds; *DikuMUD*'s designers headed in the opposite direction and hard-coded everything.

---

[86] It introduced event triggering and NPCs (which it called *puppets*), both of which promote role-playing.

[87] They're particularly good for natural-language learning and programming-language learning.

[88] With proper editorial control, this can be addressed. Some long-standing LPMUDs have 10,000 or more distinct locations without being the inconsistent, incoherent, incomplete messes that they might be expected to be.

[89] In case you're not entirely awake, this is where the first four letters of *DikuMUD* originate.

They hard-coded it very well, too. It was a breeze to install,[90] so people who simply wanted to set up their own installation could do so in a matter of minutes. Furthermore, non-programmers could readily add new content by modifying its data files, and because its code was well-structured, any half-decent C programmer could easily alter its physics and other systems.

Many programmers did, with the result that several major codebases were developed based on the *DikuMUD* original, the primary ones being *CircleMUD* (Elson, 1993), *SillyMUD* (Brothers et al., 1993) and *Merc* (Chastain et al., 1992).[91] *Merc*, which introduced the concept of live data editing to DikuMUDs in the form of an online creation (OLC) add-on, in turn led to *ROM*[92] (Taylor, 1993), *Envy* (Chastain et al., 1994) and a host of others.

The basic *DikuMUD* gameplay was fun and at times exhilarating. The original and its spin-offs became wildly popular. There were thousands of them available. In March 1991, before the advent of the World Wide Web, MUDs accounted for 11% of all transatlantic Internet traffic (Wakeman et al., 1991), largely because of DikuMUDs.

Other MUD codebases were brushed aside. For example, although many individual LPMUDs were good enough to hold their own, LPMUDs as a general concept weren't.[93] The best of the ideas piloted in them were subsequently implemented in DikuMUDs. Therefore, if you wanted a game world, you chose a DikuMUD. There were few good reasons to do anything else, even if your aim was to design (rather than to play or to operate) a MUD. Despite their relative inflexibility, snippets of code written for one DikuMUD codebase often worked for others with next to no adjustment. Going with a DikuMUD codebase was an easy decision to make.

So, why have I described all this?[94]

Well, there are three main reasons besides the basic historical-interest one:

Reason 1. The Third Age was the age of the codebase. No longer did designers have to make their own virtual worlds from first principles: now they could take an existing program suite and either use it off-the-shelf or adapt it to their vision. This sounds great for creativity, and indeed it is, but there are costs. In the same way that a language constrains what you can say, so a codebase constrains what you can design. If there's no word to capture the meaning you want, you have to think of your own way of expressing it – but would you even be aware that there *were* meanings beyond those that the constraints impose on you? If you think within constraints, your thinking too, is constrained. With codebases, as with modern game engines such as Unity, the built-in affordances shape their use. I've seen enough student projects to notice when people create "fresh and original" games that are basically all the same. Tools dictate what they can be used to make.

---

[90] If it had had a box, it would have run out of it.
[91] As the *Merc* team grew, they styled themselves MERC Industries.
[92] It's an acronym for "Rivers of MUD".
[93] For a late-contemporary comparison between LPMUDs and DikuMUDs, see Shah & Romine (1995).
[94] So, why am I asking a rhetorical question?

With *DikuMUD*, the pressure for designers to go in the same direction was compounded by the fact that it wasn't just an engine, it was a complete game world. It came with actual content. Although some people did throw out this content and construct their own, many others retained the basic geography and systems then expanded them – or didn't even bother, they ran the world unmodified – such that when you tried a new DikuMUD, the chances were that it would look very much like all the other DikuMUDs you'd tried. This phenomenon was called *stock MUD syndrome*. We don't see it with graphical worlds, because creating assets for textual worlds is trivially easy, whereas creating them for graphical worlds is (currently) not. However, when enormous, stylistically compatible asset packs or adequate AI assistants become available for free, do not be surprised if we then see the re-emergence of stock MMO syndrome.

Stock MUD syndrome wasn't the only problem that came from building a new virtual world on the foundations of a complete existing one. All the components of virtual worlds are present for a reason. Sometimes it's structural, like a supporting wall in a house; sometimes, it's artistic, like the form of a decorative light above an external door; sometimes, it's experimental, like the use of a new building material; sometimes, it's reflective, so the designer can come to understand why it needs to be there. Sometimes, it may even be accidental. Often, though, a component is there because the virtual world's designer is clueless. If you take an existing virtual world and augment its features without understanding why those features are there in the first place, OK, you might get lucky and it all works just fine; it's more likely, though, that you'll chip at the integrity of the virtual world. Eventually, the retaining wall will collapse, or the decoration will jar, or the experiment will be endless, or the symbol will become scenery. Accidents become fixtures. Ignorance paints over thoughtfulness.

Reason 2. The Third Age was the age of the Great Schism. The virtual worlds of the first two Ages maintained a balance between the needs of players who were there for social reasons and of players who were there for gameplay reasons. When the MUCKs, MUSHes and MOOs appeared, the new concept of a social world developed. In response to this, with DikuMUDs and their ilk, the concept of a game world developed. Virtual worlds now had two philosophically opposed branches, each catering to a particular kind of player; in other words, a schism.

This schism is still with us today, as if maintained by some collective unconscious. New social worlds define themselves by not being game worlds; new game worlds define themselves by not being social worlds. There are still some balanced worlds, but they are few and far between. Not many players – or indeed new designers – will be aware of why things are this way. It's particularly sad that few designers of social worlds seem to realise that player-created content is not a requirement. It's also frustrating that few designers of game worlds[95] seem to realise that their creations are

---

[95] Formally, this is "game-like", but I'll usually just stick with "game". Given how some players in social worlds behave, perhaps "social-like" would be a better term, too.

mutually compatible with balanced worlds and that the two can profitably be combined.[96] We'll see in Chapter 12 why these three views of virtual world – balanced, social and game – are the only stable ones (well, almost-only).

Historically, although social players did decamp to *TinyMUD*-descended virtual worlds, these were generally found to be lacking. They lacked content, because although everyone can create, not everyone can create things other people want to experience; they lacked purpose, because different people socialise in different ways to satisfy different needs; they lacked conviviality, because frustrations with resources and each other tended to give rise to acrimony; they lacked players, because a certain critical mass of people is required to enable socialising and it wasn't always regularly met. To socialise, social players want to be where other people are: the game-like worlds, to which those non-gamers who didn't give up on virtual worlds entirely reluctantly returned (only to find them even more game-like than they had been when they'd left).

Ultimately, this fate awaits all virtual worlds that offer no reason to be there aside from the presence of other people. Other people *are* compelling content, yes, but if you can't do anything together, or have nothing to talk about, not so much.[97]

Reason 3. The Third Age was the age of expansion. Tens of thousands of people, perhaps more, played virtual worlds for the first time – and the ones they played were overwhelmingly DikuMUDs or their derivatives.[98] DikuMUDs were therefore what most of the up-coming designers considered a virtual world to be. In other words, the *DikuMUD* approach was their paradigm. *DikuMUD*, it has to be said, wasn't particularly innovative – it drew heavily from *AberMUD* and *D&D* – but it identified the essential features and packaged them up into one self-consistent, accessible, well-programmed, compelling whole.

Hard though it may be for modern MMORPG players to believe that most of the gameplay of today's worlds was present in *DikuMUD*, nevertheless it's true.[99] For characters, *DikuMUD* included classes, races, pets and (in later derivatives) quests; for combat, it included aggro, cooldowns, stuns, procs, respawn timers, corpse runs and the tank/healer/DPS trinity; for grouping, it included battlefields, public quests and (to some extent) raids; for the world itself, it included banks, auction houses, housing, zones and instancing. All these concepts are still very much a part of modern MMOs, which is why I haven't explained any of them here individually – they'll be covered in later chapters. Some other features, such as procedural content-generation, were

---

[96] To find out why and how, either wait until Volume II or see Bartle (2009). Note that balanced worlds and social worlds are also mutually compatible, but there's little rationale for combining them.

[97] In (very) general, *talking* is central to adult female friendships and *doing* is central to adult male friendships (Winstead, 1986). If a virtual world provides no context for talking or doing, it has a problem.

[98] A late-1990s audit of MUDs revealed that 60% of them were DikuMUDs or derivatives (Koster, 2009). That's in terms of sites, though; my feeling is that in terms of player numbers, more than 60% played DikuMUDs (but I could be wrong so don't quote me).

[99] For an excellent overview of DikuMUDs' functionality and what modern MMOs owe to them, see Koster (2009).

fully integrated into DikuMUDs but are still somewhat fringe ideas for mainstream virtual worlds.[100]

Not everything DikuMUDs had are likely to find their way into MMOs any time soon, though. Experience-point death penalty losses and paying rent for logging off would not go down well with today's players, for example. Differences in interface (character moods aren't yet as effective in graphical worlds as they were in textual ones) and MMOs' greater scale (no administrator status for people who satisfy a "win" criterion) rule out some DikuMUD staples, too. Also, to counter the idea that modern virtual worlds are merely DikuMUDs with graphics bolted on, it's worth pointing out that today's virtual worlds do have plenty of things that DikuMUDs didn't: crafting was absent, for example. *DikuMUD* may have had a lot, but it didn't have everything.

LEXICOGRAPHY

Earlier, I gave a definition of the term *virtual world* as used in this book. Although it does enjoy a modicum of use by players, designers and academics, it isn't as popular as one (well, I) might hope.

The First-Age virtual worlds were referred to by their individual names – *MUD*, *Island of Kesmai*, *Habitat* and so on. In the Second Age, there was a sufficient number of different worlds that the need arose for a term that could be used to refer to them all collectively. The one that people settled on was "MUDs"; some effort was made to change this to "MUGs" ("Multi-User Games") and "MUAs" ("Multi-User Adventures"),[101] but to no avail.

Following the Great Schism, those who set up or played social worlds sought to distance these from the rest of the MUD family. At first, the D in MUD was said to mean "Dimension" or "Domain", but this wasn't a sufficient departure. Listing the major individual codebases was tried next: "MUCKs", "MUSHes" and "MOOs" for the social worlds and "MUDs" for the game worlds. This did gain traction. The term "MU*" was used on those occasions when there was a need to discuss all virtual worlds, * being a replace-with-whatever wildcard.

This all seems very neat, but it was completely ignored by the players and designers of game worlds, who to the frustration of their peers in social worlds referred to all virtual worlds as MUDs. It didn't help that MU* was also used by some social players to mean MUCKs, MUSHes and MOOs exclusively, on the grounds that an umbrella term implied that social and game worlds had something in common.

When graphics arrived, a distinction was made between "graphical MUDs" and "textual MUDs" (or "text MUDs", possibly because people kept writing "textural" instead of "textual"). Advocates of MU* did not extend their favoured

---

[100] The main exceptions tend to be space-travel ones such *as No Man's Sky* (Bourn, 2016) and *Elite Dangerous* (Sammarco et al., 2014).

[101] I myself pushed MUAs, because of what the D in *MUD* meant. Why yes, I was indeed wholly unsuccessful in this endeavour.

term to cover graphical worlds. This phraseology continued until external pressures required the disambiguation of graphical MUDs from other multi-player games with graphics (such as first-person shooters); this delivered the compound adjective "massively multiplayer".[102] After some dalliance with "MMPRPG" ("Massively Multiplayer Role-Playing Game") and "PW" ("Persistent World"), the consensus arrived at "MMORPG" ("Massively Multiplayer Online Role-Playing Game"). As six-letter acronyms are somewhat unwieldy, this was eventually shortened (via "MMOG" – "Massively Multiplayer Online Game") to "MMO" – but not until the prefix had been co-opted for a slew of other games with assorted claims to being massively multiplayer (such as "MMORTS" – "Massively Multiplayer Online Real-Time Strategy").

Once MMORPG became established, MUD was confined to use for textual worlds. This enabled some advocates of MMORPGs to declare that these were completely different things to MUDs, which is a little like saying paintings have nothing in common with sketches. It's the kind of attitude that grants an air of superficial superiority until the moment VR worlds use it back on its exponents.

At this point in virtual world history, the need arose for a new umbrella term to refer to social, textual and graphical worlds collectively. This is how we got "virtual worlds". Needless to say, when graphical social worlds appeared, an attempt was made to apply the term exclusively to these so as to perpetuate the effects of the Great Schism; it was even extended by some writers and academics to include social media (while still excluding MMOs), but fortunately, that didn't last.

There is a trend to use "virtual world" to mean any world implemented in 3D graphics, particularly those of computer role-playing games. I have some sympathy with this, but the thought of having to come up with yet another class name for *MUD's* descendants fills me with dread.

In this book, I therefore continue to use "virtual worlds" to refer to all examples of systems that fit the six-criterion definition I provided at the beginning. I use "social worlds" to mean virtual worlds with an emphasis on players and "game worlds" to mean virtual worlds with an emphasis on gameplay; I use "balanced worlds" to mean ones that emphasise both. I use "graphical worlds" to mean virtual worlds that have graphics and "textual worlds" or occasionally "text MUDs" to mean ones that use only text. I use "MMORPGs" and "MMOs" with reference to graphical game worlds.

What all the above shows is that terminology changes. Basically, though, regardless of your own preferences, whatever players call something, that's what it's called whether you want it to be called that or not.

---

[102] I usually hyphenate "multi-player" so as to match the case for "single-player". Proper nouns aside, I make the single exception of not doing so for "massively-multiplayer", to clarify that it's "massively-(multi-player)" rather than "(massively-multi)-player". However, as the style guide for this book doesn't allow for hyphenating adverbs, this distinction is entirely lost. The hyphens I used have therefore all been removed and despatched to hyphen heaven.

2.6 THE FOURTH AGE (1995–1997): PER-HOUR CHARGING

The Fourth Age of virtual worlds was the shortest, but for those involved the most exhilarating. It was the period during which virtual worlds finally demonstrated that they could become commercial successes.

Initially, it cost nothing to play a virtual world. However, few prospective players *could* actually play them, because they ran on university computers to which they had no access. This changed when people began creating MUDs on their own computers; now, anyone with a computer and a modem[103] could access a MUD over the public telephone network.

Most of these home-brew MUDs remained free[104] from the perspective of their developers, but players still needed to pay to connect to them. In the UK, telephone calls were charged by duration, so the longer the call, the more it cost. Also, prices varied by distance (local calls were cheaper) and time of day (peak-time morning calls were more expensive). Local off-peak calls were around £1 an hour, but a non-local mid-morning direct-dial call to *Shades* cost £19.80 an hour. People would baulk at paying that even today, after years of inflation have somewhat reduced the purchasing power of the pound, so you can imagine how difficult it was for developers to add a second charge on top of that for the game itself. In the United States, local calls were effectively free, which was a far more conducive environment for commercial virtual worlds, but it still meant you had to have a server nearby to avoid the ruinous expense of a long-distance call.

Two solutions were adopted: placing local servers directly in population centres; placing front-end computers in population centres that communicated with central servers over a private (and therefore free-to-the-user) network. *Sceptre*, *Gods* and *MUD2* tried the former, largely because they didn't have the funds to attempt the latter; they met with modest success. No virtual world tried to set up their own private networks; however, there were existing networks that were amenable to having games on them. These were known as "information providers", and I've mentioned some already: the UK's Prestel (which had *Shades*) and CompuNet (*MUD1* and *Federation II*); France's Minitel (*Shades*); and the USA's CompuServe (*Island of Kesmai* and *MUD1*).

CompuServe was one of the world's largest information providers at the time, but (thanks to the free-local-phone-calls situation) there were several others in the United States that were bigger than anything available elsewhere on the planet. Most of these – Delphi, Prodigy, The Source – shared CompuServe's attitude to games: yes, OK, they'd carry some, but not overly publicise the fact. They'd carry them, because one gamer brought in as much income as nine non-gamers; they'd tone down the publicity, because if parents believed their children could be turned into devil-worshipping school-shooters, they'd avoid the system entirely. There was a concept of *noble content*: people signed up to read the news, to manage their portfolio of stocks and to help advance their child's education, but the content they actually wanted (even if they didn't yet know it) consisted of chatrooms and games.

---

[103] "Modem" is a contraction of "modulator-demodulator". Modems converted electronic signals into and out of sounds within the audible range suitable for transmission by voice-oriented analogue telephone networks.

[104] "Free, and worth every penny", as those who charged for their virtual worlds used to say.

The most prominent exception to this prevailing view was GEnie under the visionary leadership of Bill Louden. Louden had previously been CompuServe's product manager for (among other things) games, and had become frustrated with the company's attitude to them. GEnie was owned by General Electric, which already had its own private network that sold services such as email to other companies, but it had no general information-service offering.

GEnie treated games – and their developers – with respect. It quickly signed up *GemStone][*, *Dragon's Gate* and *Federation II*, along with a host of other multi-player games, including some from Kesmai. The service was wildly popular, but couldn't expand to meet its needs, a bit like a pot-bound plant. General Electric Information Services, which was the corporate division that operated the network, regarded GEnie as something of a cash cow that existed only to give its servers something to do in the evenings and at weekends; they wouldn't add capacity to meet the needs of its growing user base.

Because modems operated at only 300 baud for most of the 1980s, all the major information providers were text-based. Prestel and Minitel did have some basic graphics capability in the form of solid blocks (colour for Prestel, monochrome for Minitel), but nothing that could really be integrated into gameplay.

In the United States, an online service called Quantum Link was launched for owners of Commodore home computers. Using a customised client, it was able to display better graphics than its competitors – but only if you had a Commodore 64 or Commodore 128. Plenty of people did, but not all of those had modems. Nevertheless, because the Commodore 64 was regarded as a games machine, Quantum Link was games-friendly – it was the home of *Habitat* (which it relaunched in 1988 as *Club Caribe*[105]).

After struggling to attract the users and content hoped for, and a so-so joint endeavour with Apple, Quantum Link released a PC client and was renamed America Online (later rebranded AOL). Games were no longer considered essential content, although 1991 saw the launch of an innovative graphical virtual world, *Neverwinter Nights* (Daglow, 1991). Based on *D&D*, *NWN* was a collaboration between TSR (Tactical Studies Rules – *D&D*'s publisher), AOL and SSI (Strategic Simulations Inc. – a respected publisher of single-player RPGs).

This was, however, still the era of information providers. Although the Internet was growing in popularity, there were restrictions on its commercial use; the biggest services, CompuServe and Prodigy, still believed they held all the cards because they, not the Internet, had the users and the content. AOL recognised that there nevertheless *was* content on the Internet, though, so added Usenet and a browser to its services. A well-conceived advertising campaign then drew people to AOL *to* access the Internet.

AOL content managers noticed a sudden spurt in *Neverwinter Nights* usage that accompanied this. They quickly concluded that people were looking not only for something to *read* online, but something to *do* online. That would be playing games, then.

---

[105] The plan was for *Habitat* to have 20,000 players – a phenomenal amount for the mid-1980s. Unfortunately, the 1986–1988 beta test, which was limited to 500 players, showed that people played for far longer than had been expected. Those 500 players took up 1% of Quantum Link's entire network capacity (Donovan, 2010). *Club Caribe* was therefore a somewhat downscaled version of the original *Habitat* vision, but even in this form, it was able to attract some 15,000 players by 1990 (King & Borland, 2003).

With GEnie hamstrung, AOL was able to tempt over some of its best games by the cunning expedient of offering a very fair royalty. *GemStone III* (Whatley, 1990), *Dragon's Gate* and *Federation II* all accepted the proposal.

A 1993 price war had ended with the result that the big information services were no longer as expensive as they had been, but they were still charged per-hour.

Hordes of game-hungry users, per-hour charging, high-quality virtual worlds and reasonable royalty arrangements were the mix that kicked off the Fourth Age of virtual worlds. People who wanted to try out this new Internet thing flocked to the big information providers (especially AOL) and played their games. The vast, vast majority didn't try the university-hosted worlds or the stand-alone ones unless they happened to hear of them through word of mouth. If you couldn't get your virtual world on one of the big systems, you were in trouble. If you *could*, money rained on you from the sky.[106]

Of all the historical ages of virtual worlds, the Fourth Age was the shortest, lasting but a year and a half. Small companies began to set themselves up as Internet service providers, but charged a flat monthly rate rather than per-hour[107]; more and more interesting content began to appear daily on the World Wide Web, and paying for every moment you looked at it began to appear untenable. In December 1996, AOL bowed to the inevitable and also went flat rate. As a consequence, it could no longer afford to pay virtual world developers per-hour royalties.[108]

Unfortunately for AOL, its contracts with external content providers assumed a per-hour charge. AOL tried to renegotiate a flat fee or much-lower per-hour rate, and some (such as *Federation II*) went along with it. Others held their ground, believing that their games were a success because of how good they were, rather than because they were benefitting from AOL's newbie hose.

A compromise "premium content" approach that charged per-hour for the hold-outs and flat-rate for everything else failed to click with players, and by mid-1997, the bonanza was over.[109]

Most of the virtual worlds that had been available via the big information providers (not just AOL) set up their own servers on the Internet-at-large. They knew that not all their players would transfer over, but they also knew that they could keep all the money their players paid, rather than just a percentage as a royalty. They only needed around 20% of their player base to make the move and they could crack open the champagne.

Sadly for them, only a hard core of 5%–10% ever did play these virtual worlds in their new, independent form. This was for three reasons:

---

[106] *Neverwinter Nights*, which was capped at 500 users, grossed $3m–$4m in 1996. *GemStone III*, *Dragon's Gate* and *Federation II* were each being played for over a million hours a month.

[107] People prefer flat-rate over per-hour, even though the latter is more equitable. The feeling that there's always a ticking clock is a big turn-off: nobody wants to be charged half a cent because they went for a quick bio break without logging off.

[108] Ironically, *Dragon's Gate*'s designer, Mark Jacobs, had written one of the very first flat-rate virtual worlds, *Aradath* (Jacobs, 1984), a dozen years earlier.

[109] Even so, in 1997, *GemStone III* grossed $10m from of the 2,500 to 3,000 simultaneous users it averaged.

- Firstly, many of their players had treated the game as part of the offering of the information provider. They objected to paying to access a game on top of paying to access the Internet (which is why AOL's premium-content approach had failed).

- Secondly, attracting new players is very, very difficult. It isn't hard when you're being sprayed with newbies the whole time, but it is when the newbies are being sprayed elsewhere.

- Thirdly, it's difficult to charge even a subscription to play a virtual world when there are thousands of *literally free* DikuMUDs, LPMUDs, MOOs, MUSHes and MUCKs out there that are just as easy to find as your game and, in some cases, of equal or even superior quality.

The somewhat ignominious end to the Fourth Age perhaps gives the impression that it doesn't merit its own, numbered period in history. It's hardly a paradigm shift, and afterwards, its virtual worlds rejoined those of the Third Age. Nevertheless, it *is* important, because what it did was demonstrate that money could be made from virtual worlds. Although the regular computer game industry had long been aware of MUDs, they'd considered them to be niche. The Fourth Age showed them that niche doesn't matter if you can make YE-GODS!-level profits. Back-of-the-envelope calculations indicated that a flat-rate subscription virtual world with 20,000 players would be in profit; double that number would be a goldmine.

CHAPTER **3**

History

The Graphics Era

THE INFORMATION PROVIDERS THAT had dominated the pre-Internet online experience were essentially text-based. This was because the speed of modems didn't allow for much else.

Modems improved, however. By the early 1980s, 110-baud acoustic couplers had already given way to 300-baud integrated modems. The 1200/75 split protocol allowed downloading at 1200 baud and uploading at 75, which was great news for MUDs because they generated text faster than users did. Although 1200 full duplex was better, it wasn't *noticeably* better; 2400 full duplex was, though, and when we reached 9600 full duplex, it became possible to start thinking about what could be done with the extra bandwidth.

3.1 THE FIFTH AGE (1997–2012): GRAPHICS AND SUBSCRIPTIONS

The virtual worlds prior to the Fifth Age were almost entirely text-based. Everyone was aware that (what at the time were called) graphical MUDs were coming, and despite the dogged belief that text was better,[1] graphics would do to MUDs what they'd done to the text adventures of the mid-1980s – sweep them aside.[2]

Most serious MUD developers also knew how to implement graphical worlds. Rather than stream as-is content to users (which is how text was typically transmitted), tokens would be sent instead that could be interpreted by client software. You don't have to send every pixel of an image: you merely have to send the instructions to display a composition of images that are already on the user's hard drive (although back then it could have had to have come off a CDROM).

What stopped most MUD developers from attempting this was the combination of a lack of artistic ability, a lack of the necessary hardware and a non-lack of a day job.

---

[1] Which it is, but only to people with an imagination.
[2] The text adventure *The Hobbit* (Megler & Mitchell, 1982), which boasted colour illustrations, sold over a million copies. Even so, its genre (nowadays referred to as *interactive fiction*) was reduced to non-mainstream status by 1990.

          DOI: 10.1201/9781003689638-3

Some, however, were allocated sufficient resources to undertake a full project (this was the case with *Habitat* and *Neverwinter Nights*); others had garnered enough commercial success with their textual worlds that they could either self-fund development or persuade a venture capitalist to chip in to create a graphical one. Kesmai's *Air Warrior* (Flinn & Taylor, 1986) and *Multiplayer BattleTech* (Flinn & Taylor, 1991), along with Simutronics' *CyberStrike* (Whatley, 1993) – all of which were on GEnie – presaged what was to come.

The data structure used to store the world in *Island of Kesmai* was a 2D grid. In an era when there was little standardisation in home computers (players could have been using any one of dozens of different machines that themselves came in multiple configurations), it made sense to use text to render the *IoK* map. Even if there had been a client for your home computer, the question of how you might actually get hold of a copy was largely unanswered.[3] A similar text-as-graphics approach was used for early tessellated-map regular games such as *Rogue* (Toy et al., 1980) and its descendants, and some quirky home-brews such as *Dwarf Fortress* (Adams & Adams, 2006).[4]

As the user bases for particular machines grew and download speeds increased, it did start to make commercial sense to create client software that addressed one or perhaps two popular home-computer platforms. Small information providers sprang up specifically to do this, with MPG-Net and ImagiNation Network (INN[5]) being two of the front-runners.

MPG-Net featured a graphical world, *Kingdom of Drakkar* (Lineberger, 1989), which came out of a MUD called *Realm* (Lineberger, 1984). The format of its graphics was heavily influenced by *IoK* and the Roguelikes *The Dungeons of Moria* (Koeneke et al., 1983) and *Hack* (Fenlason, 1984); its storyline was based on that of a long-running *AD&D* campaign. It was colourful and attractive (for the time), with a quirky, forced-perspective camera that coupled a bird's eye view of the terrain with side-on views of characters.

INN also had *The Shadow of Yserbius* (Ybarra, 1992), which took a slightly different approach. It combined static images of what the character could see (a door, a creature, a fountain, walls, …) with a tile set-up for combat. The combat was turn-based, meaning *Yserbius* wasn't strictly speaking a virtual world, but communication remained real-time. It was successful enough that it led to two sequels, *The Fates of Twinion* (Ybarra, 1993) and *The Ruins of Cawdor* (Ybarra, 1995), but then AOL bought the rights to it and closed it down (it was competing with *Neverwinter Nights*,[6] which also used a tile-based map).

Virtual worlds that use tiles and sprites are relatively inexpensive in terms of their demands on processing time and bandwidth. Design tools are quick to develop and can be used to create vast, interesting worlds – albeit not ones with many circular buildings.

---

[3] Well, except as "you won't".

[4] *Dwarf Fortress* is now available with a proper graphical interface. You can watch your dwarfs meet their inevitable ignominious ends in a manner much more easy on the eye.

[5] It was previously called the Sierra Network, but was renamed when AT&T bought a stake, apparently in the belief that the Internet would be corporate.

[6] This happens quite a lot in creative industries: you think you're signing a great deal, but it turns out your work is just going to be sat on. Many authors have sold the rights to their book in the expectation it will become a film or TV series, only to find that it won't – the rights were acquired solely to stop another company from acquiring them and competing with an in-development series.

This has been demonstrated most successfully for offline games that aren't virtual worlds, such as those using the RPG Maker (ASCII, 1992) toolset; for actual virtual worlds, the Metaplace platform (Areae, 2007) showed what could be achieved.

Although tessellated worlds are usually rendered from either a top-down or an isometric[7] perspective, this isn't always the case. It's also possible to render them from the side. *Habitat* pioneered this approach, but it wasn't the only example: *The Realm* (Nichols & Neville, 1996)[8] had each cell represent a MUD-like room, with other rooms reached by going left, right, up (*i.e.* "into" the screen) and down (*i.e.* "out of" the screen). *The Realm* also had turn-based combat, which took place in off-grid rooms[9] (uninvolved players saw the battle as an animated cloud). Side-view MMOs remained niche, however, even though some later MMOs using this perspective met with huge success: the main one to do so, *MapleStory* (Kim, 2006) – which actually did scroll – had 47 million players worldwide in February 2006 (Huhh, 2006), including 29% of the population of South Korea and 15% of the population of Taiwan.

Experiments with an isometric perspective for tessellated worlds showed promise. *DragonSpires* (Shapiro & Dee, 1994) looked beautiful by the standards of its time; it was later remade and relaunched as *Furcadia* (Shapiro et al., 1996).

With the inevitable march towards graphical MUDs, the tile-based descendants of *IoK*, and of independent reinventions such as *DragonSpires*, should have been in their element. It was expected that they would dominate the space. However, they ran either stand-alone or on smaller networks that found it hard to recruit: if they charged per hour, no one would play when they could pay a subscription; if they switched to subscription, well few people would want to have more than one or two subscriptions at once, so competition was fierce.[10] If they tried to expand their offerings, they split their player base and their games lost critical mass; if they didn't expand, they were one-trick ponies. Their graphics looked better than text but worse than what the leading offline games boasted. Only on mobile phones could they hold their own (*Tibia* (Lübke et al., 1997), in the form of its mobile edition, *TibiaME*, being the unjustly unsung flagbearer of the platform).

Nevertheless, even with the window of opportunity for isometric worlds quickly closing, there remained time enough for two genre-defining tile-based virtual worlds to appear. The Fourth Age of virtual worlds hadn't been important for its design innovations – its MUDs hadn't been ground-breaking in that respect; rather, it was the staggering amount of money they generated that changed the future of virtual worlds. Professional game designers were able to point at the success of these textual games to persuade publishers to support the development of high-quality graphical alternatives.

---

[7] Imagine an enormous chessboard with so many squares along each edge that you only see a portion of it. The board is rotated 45° instead of facing you, and the squares at the back look the same size as the ones close-up. Keep looking at it from the same angle, say 45° or 60°, and that's an isometric viewpoint. You're right: I'm not good at describing interfaces.

[8] No relation to the earlier MUD called *Realm*. Such coincidences weren't uncommon before app stores dehomogenised game names (even if they homogenised the games themselves).

[9] This is an early graphical-world example of *instancing*. I'll be looking at the general concept of instancing later.

[10] This is the fate of TV streaming channels, although their relatively lower prices mean that viewers tolerate a few more subscriptions before they reach their limit.

Jake Song's *Lineage* (Song, 1998) was developed in South Korea, based on his incredibly successful[11] earlier virtual world, *Baramue Nara* (Song, 1996), which had been launched in the West as *Nexus: the Kingdom of the Winds* (Song, 1996). Song had written *Baramue Nara* having been involved with the first MUD to use Korean-language script, *Jyulagi Gong-won*[12] (Chungryong, O, 1994), which was a modified *LPMUD*. Whereas *Baramue Nara* was rendered using a front-facing tile system, *Lineage* went properly isometric and looked much less retro. Other developers took it seriously as a result. *Baramue Nara* and *Lineage* are the virtual worlds from which most modern virtual worlds in South Korea, Japan and China descend.

In the West, the first virtual world to hit the big time was *Ultima Online* (Koster, 1997). It was the paradigm shift that brought us into the Fifth Age of virtual worlds, somewhat ironically because nothing that followed had a design anything like it. It was, and remains, a rich, vibrant world that players can and do change through their actions.

It's generally accepted that *Ultima Online* (UO) was the brainchild of Richard Garriott, who had designed and developed the much-loved *Ultima* (Garriott, 1981) series of single-player games. The idea of a multi-player (not necessarily massively multiplayer) "Multima" had been around since the mid-1980s, when one of Origin Systems' project managers, Starr Long, and one of its technical managers, Ken Demarest, started looking at the multi-player offerings then available online (MUDs included). Although some preparatory work was undertaken in 1987 and 1988, the conclusion reached was that the market wasn't yet ready for it. The idea wouldn't go away, though, and the proposal for developing a massively multiplayer Multima was pushed hard by designer/programmer David "Dr Cat" Shapiro. Although Origin Systems, the developer of the *Ultima* series, didn't have the expertise to create a virtual world in-house, the concept and the intellectual property (IP) were of great interest to GEnie, who lined up Kesmai to do the massively multiplayer part using the assets and source code of *Ultima VI* for the client. Shapiro would be in charge of the project.

Unfortunately, AOL got wind of what was going on and put in a counter-proposal. According to Shapiro (Contato, 2021), this was essentially a spoiler: AOL had no intention of developing Multima, but by spinning out the negotiations and never signing a contract, it could stop its competitor from offering the new service. Following this move, the Multima idea was put on hold again and Shapiro left to form his own company (where he developed *DragonSpires*). Origin Systems was shortly afterwards bought by Electronic Arts (EA), and the Multima idea was kept in mothballs.

DragonSpires showed that a massively multiplayer world would be more in tune with Richard Garriott's vision for *Ultima* than would a mere multi-player one. Garriott and Long pushed Electronic Arts for funding, and eventually managed to obtain $250,000 to create a demo. Unfortunately (or perhaps fortunately) for Garriott, EA wanted him to work on the up-coming *Ultima IX: Ascension* (Garriott & Mendelsohn, 1999), which meant he couldn't spend much time on what was to become *Ultima Online*. He therefore brought

---

[11] Almost half the population of South Korea had played it at some point (KH Digital 2, 2016).
[12] "Jurassic Park" in English.

in designers and developers who already had expertise in creating massively multiplayer games. These had overwhelmingly gained this expertise by designing and programming MUDs. In particular, *UO*'s lead designer, Raph Koster, had cut his teeth creating a modified *DikuMUD* called *LegendMUD* (Koster et al., 1994), which heavily informed the design of *Ultima Online* (in particular, it was classless[13]). Raph was to go on to become one of the best-known and most highly regarded of all MMO designers, by players and fellow designers alike.

UO's design was incredibly ambitious – only perhaps that of *EVE Online* (Emilsson et al., 2003) is its equal. The game's ecology and economy are of particular importance, as we shall see in Volume II, but because of its enormous scope, the demo version didn't have all the features that Koster had envisaged for it; more time was needed for its completion. Furthermore, play-testing a game that (it was wildly speculated) could attract as many as 40,000 players wasn't easy. Therefore, the decision was made to open the demo in beta and invite people to play it. To make sure they *did* actually play it, and to cover the cost of creating and sending them a CDROM (because funding was by now tight), "if you want to volunteer to be a beta tester and help us develop this game, please send us $5" (Garriott & Fisher, 2017).

Within three days, 50,000 people had done so. EA was agog, and further funding was immediately made available – along with some hitherto-absent management oversight that *UO*'s development team had been desperately lacking.

Within a year of launch, *UO* had racked up 100,000 players, each paying $9.95 a month with none of that going to retailers. The financial viability of graphical MUDs was established beyond doubt. Other developers were inspired to create their own virtual worlds, albeit with a more up-to-date approach to the graphics.

Isometric, 2D tile-based worlds are still being developed. They're still less expensive to make and they still work well on mobiles. *RuneScape* (Ogilvie, 2001),[14] which began as a browser-based game, remains one of the most popular virtual worlds in operation. *Albion Online* (Woodward, 2017), which has a Unity client, is more modern but nevertheless is basically tile-based and isometric. However, most virtual worlds launched these days present a 3D view of their virtual environments.

Even back in the Second Age, there had been attempts to write graphical MUDs with a 3D main view. None came to fruition, although *Bloodstone* (Muir, 1990) got close: issues writing a client that worked both for the Atari ST and Commodore Amiga, talking to a server that used transputers, derailed it.

During the same period that *Ultima Online* was in development, two other teams in the United States were working on graphical MUDs. These were to become *Meridian 59* (Sellers et al., 1996) and *EverQuest* (Clover et al., 1999). All three teams were aware of each other and generally on good terms (one of *Meridian 59*'s designers, Damion Schubert, was employed on the recommendation of *Ultima Online*'s lead designer, Raph Koster). Of the

---

[13] Character class is another one of those concepts I've casually introduced several chapters before I'll give a full definition of it.

[14] I assume the capital S is so that people read it as "Rune scape" rather than "Run escape".

three games, *Meridian 59* (*M59*) launched first; in so doing, it successfully claimed the title of being the earliest 3D MMORPG, although if you want to be finicky it was 2½D.[15]

Meridian 59 was inspired partly by *Sceptre of Goth* and partly by the *MUD* line. It's worth mentioning at this point that 3D first-person graphics made it to computer games in general via *Wizardry* (Woodhead & Greenberg, 1981), which had been inspired by[16] the PLATO game *Oubliette*. It could therefore be argued that *M59* ultimately came from *Oubliette* rather than *SoG* or *MUD*. If you're looking at its graphicality then yes, this is indeed the case; if you're looking at its virtual worldliness, however, it isn't. Games draw from many sources, so they have multidimensional family trees; reasoning along one dimension is legitimate, but if you use this to draw conclusions about another dimension then you have to be very careful. As an analogy, a book of fairytales ultimately comes from Gutenberg if you're looking at books and from folk stories if you're looking at fairytales; it would be hard to argue that Gutenberg was responsible for fairytales, though.

M59's early launch was precipitated by several factors, including cashflow needs, first-mover advantage and the sheer glory of it.[17] Unfortunately, it was released rather *too* early for its own good: not many people had an Internet connection at the time, and the game demanded a decent computer, too. Those who did manage to play weren't impressed by the amount of content initially available. Furthermore, its being first to launch meant it was also first to encounter whatever new difficulties graphical worlds conjured up for their operators. *Ultima Online* and *EverQuest* could learn from these and not make the same mistakes themselves. Such is the lot of pioneers.

Although *Meridian 59* was beset by many unexpected issues – misbehaving users, corrupt admins, awkward pricing structures, player-written hacks (Schubert, 2003) – it didn't encounter all of what was to come. *Ultima Online*, which launched a year later, picked up a much larger player base[18] and had to deal with the attendant problems that this brought, too. *UO* needed 20,000 players to break even and its developers were not convinced they'd get that many. When they hit 100,000, they were therefore in absolutely unknown territory. Macros became much more of a problem than they had ever been in text MUDs; griefers, who were lone wolves in text MUDs but could form gangs in *UO*, were very hard to manage and pretty well ran riot; the geography of the virtual world couldn't accommodate all the players; the economy seized up when players didn't behave as expected (and wasn't helped by bugs that allowed the creation of what were effectively money machines). Attempts to fix these issues sometimes worked and sometimes made them worse.

One of the main gripes players had about *UO* was that it had unrestricted player-*versus*-player (PvP) combat and stiff character-death penalties. Many new players were

---

[15] Imagine a chessboard with wooden blocks on it that define a scene. Throw a cloth over it. What you have looks 3D – it has independent X, Y and Z co-ordinates – but it isn't quite. You can't have caves and you can't have bridges. This is 2½D – a 2D plane with a height map. You're still right: I'm still not good at describing interfaces.

[16] This may be putting it charitably (Bolingbroke, 2013).

[17] Justifiably, as it happens: it won Gamecenter's award for 1996 RPG of the Year, beating the much-loved *Daggerfall* (Lefay et al., 1996).

[18] *M59* had 10,000 subscribers by the end of 1996 and 25,000 at its peak (Donovan, 2010).

driven away before they could reach a point where they were able to defend themselves.[19] Those who stayed complained – forcefully – which led to a souring of the atmosphere. It was in the midst of all this mess that *EverQuest* (*EQ*) finally came out. *UO*'s disgruntled players and ex-players tried it out, and many discovered that they liked it. Within six months, *EQ* had more players than *UO*; it was eventually to have twice as many.

In an attempt to stem the tide, Electronic Arts created two separate versions of *UO* (called *facets*) to address the different users' needs: Felucca kept the original gameplay; Trammel had only consensual PvP but was otherwise essentially unaltered. Some 90% of the player base went to Trammel, which had two devastating effects.

Firstly, Felucca felt deserted, so those core players who had stayed were left questioning its viability. Their disenchantment was exacerbated by the fact that all the other players on Felucca were PvPers too, meaning that fights were tougher and far more likely to end in defeat than they had been when hapless non-PvPers could be picked off (or on) at leisure.

Secondly, Trammel didn't – *couldn't* – have the Wild West atmosphere that had once made *UO* such an exhilarating experience. People went there to avoid the negative aspects of non-consensual PvP, but also found that they missed some of the secondary, more positive aspects of it.

The Felucca/Trammel split was a turning point in *UO*'s history. The game lost something of its soul and would never be the same again.[20]

EverQuest benefited greatly from *UO*'s misfortunes. That it was *EQ* and not *M59* that players switched to was down to three factors: *EQ* was new and was being publicised; *EQ* had better graphics; *M59* had problems of its own. Furthermore, when *UO* players did try out *EQ*, they found that the latter had gameplay they preferred: whereas *UO* had made significant efforts to innovate, *EQ* had stuck with the well-honed *DikuMUD* formula,[21] which was proven to work. As a consequence, most subsequent MMORPGs (as they were by then called) were also to adopt *DikuMUD*-inspired gameplay.

Another advantage that favoured the *EQ* team was that it had seen the problems faced by *M59* and *UO* and had either designed around them or put measures in place otherwise to address them. There was only one major area where they were completely blindsided: real-money trading. We'll be looking at this in some detail in Volume II, but I mention it now because, as we'll shortly see, it's ultimately what caused the Sixth Age to dawn.

Three other MMORPGs soon followed in *EQ*'s wake, each with a different take on the basic *DikuMUD* gameplay: *Asheron's Call* (Ragaini, 1999), *Anarchy Online* (Godager, 2001), and *Dark Age of Camelot* (Jacobs et al., 2001).

The first of these, *Asheron's Call* (*AC*), won a heap of awards and also managed to pick up some frustrated *UO* players, but after a while, it faded. Its launch was delayed by over a year because of the team's inexperience (not that *UO* and *EQ* met their intended launch dates

---

[19] Nowadays, sandbox MMOs with open PVP are called *gankboxes*. The term *ganking* was originally short for "gang-killing": lots of characters ganging up on another that's alone. It's now generalised to mean any tactical combat situation in which one side has such an overwhelming advantage that the other has absolutely no chance of winning.

[20] This wasn't regarded by Electronic Arts as a failure: thanks to the general expansion of Internet usage and the softening of gamer attitudes that accompanied this, player numbers went up, peaking at 270,000 in 2003.

[21] So closely, in fact, that *EQ*'s programmers were obliged to sign a sworn statement confirming that they hadn't used any of *DikuMUD*'s code.

either); had it come out immediately before *EQ*, its fate might have been different, although probably not. It was a much deeper game than *EQ*, but a much harder one, too, which was not what players were looking for at the time. It also featured an allegiance system, in which players could swear fealty to others to give benefits to both; sadly (but predictably), the idea backfired, because no one likes being a vassal.[22] *AC* did introduce two features that *EQ* lacked which are now fairly standard, though: story arcs and a seamless world. We'll come across these again in due course.

Anarchy Online (*AO*) had a Science Fiction setting, rather than yet another variety of Fantasy. Its main innovation was its dynamic, instanced[23] missions: the player could set a number of parameters, then a new, one-off area would be created into which the player was inserted and given a goal to fulfil. Sadly, the demand for a Science Fiction setting was not as high as its developer, Funcom, had hoped, and a disastrous launch didn't help, either. Nevertheless, it's one of those games that, when people like it, they *really* like it, so it's still ticking over.

Dark Age of Camelot (*DAoC*) leveraged three popular, yet public-domain, intellectual properties: Arthurian, Celtic and Norse lore. It granted each of these its own independent territory, with the central premiss that all three factions (which it called *realms*) were perpetually at war. Each player chose a faction for their character to join, thereafter to vie in perpetuity for superiority over the other two; there were attendant benefits for whichever was currently ahead. The concept had been developed in an earlier text MUD developed by Mythic Entertainment, *Darkness Falls: The Crusade* (Jacobs, 1999), which had factions of good, evil and chaos. Factional PvP combat is now a standard option in many modern MMOs.

The graphical worlds described so far were aimed at PC users, but two early entrants into the space targeted consoles. *Phantasy Star Online* (Miyoshi, 2000) was developed for the Dreamcast; *Final Fantasy XI* (Tanaka, 2002) was developed for the PlayStation 2.

Phantasy Star Online fell victim to many of the problems that had dogged the PC MMORPGs, such as bug exploitation. Cheating was worse, though, because it used a peer-to-peer architecture rather than a client/server one, which left it wide open to attack (we'll see why in Chapter 7).

Final Fantasy XI was not originally a commercial success, because although three months after launch it had 120,000 subscribers in Japan, it needed 200,000 to break even. A PC client was released to make up the shortfall, but its control system was not what players were accustomed to; also, there was some initial friction between PC users with low-level characters and console users with high-level characters. The game's culture was welcoming, though, and (because two years earlier, Sony had bought Verant Interactive, the developer of *EverQuest*) *Final Fantasy XI* avoided most of the difficulties that its predecessors had encountered.

---

[22] I often encounter this "Just imagine, being top of the tree!" idea in my consultancy work. It usually comes from people who are go-getters with expectations about their destiny. They give almost no consideration to "Just imagine, having 207,968 people above you in the tree!".

[23] Instances are like pocket universes. They're discussed in depth in Volume II.

Console games were not considered mainstream at the time, and they're still not – despite their large user bases. All the impetus is with PC games, mainly because PCs have an alphanumeric keyboard and impose far fewer constraints on developers. The fact that console platform owners want a 30% cut of any revenue stream may have something to do with it, too.

With increasing numbers of game studios keen for a piece of MMO action, the question of how to get ahead of the competition was a tricky one. A number of different tacks were tried: new genres, such as the *City of Heroes* (Emmert, 2004) and *DC Universe Online* (Andersen & Hill, 2011) Superhero offerings; new audiences, such as the youngsters targeted by *Habbo Hotel* (Karjalainen, 2001) and *Toontown Online* (Schell Games, 2003); the involvement of classy developers, such as Westwood for *Earth and Beyond* (Sperry & Castle, 2002); open source development, as with *PlaneShift* (Atomic Blue, 2002); integration with the global non-virtual economy, the selling point of *Entropia Universe* (Edman et al., 2003); co-operative play, as found in *Yohoho! Puzzle Pirates* (Three Rings Design, 2003) and *A Tale in the Desert* (Tepper, 2003); hard-core PvP, as espoused by *EVE Online* (Emilsson et al., 2003) and *Shadowbane* (Nance, 2003); and zero combat of any kind, a central tenet of *Second Life* (Rosedale, 2003).

Second Life (*SL*) caused quite a stir when it came out. It had originally been built by Linden Lab as a kind of virtual test environment for haptic hardware (Au, 2008), but once its potential became obvious, the company pivoted to concentrate on it full-time. It wasn't a game, because it had no gameplay, but neither was it a toy. It was a place where people could play if they liked, but which offered many other possibilities, too. Its focus was creativity: players could build things and sell them for in-world Linden dollars that could then be traded (with the developers' blessing) for United States dollars. As such, it became a venue for self-expression and socialising, attractive to all those people who didn't care for the win-win-win attitudes of game worlds. In this regard, it was the graphical equivalent of the text-era MUSHes, MUCKs and (especially) MOOs.

One of the lessons learned from MOOs was that when players had no game to direct their activities, they found four main ways to occupy themselves:

1. Create their own games, within the virtual world.

2. Make, trade and show off stuff for fun or as a statement.

3. Engage in politicking, usually about resource allocation so as to do 1) or 2).

4. Participate in rampant virtual sex.

SL duly followed the same pattern. Somewhat ironically, one of its early competitors, *There* (There, 2003), was more aware of these potential pitfalls and had taken precautions to avoid them (particularly the last one) – only to find that actually they were quite popular (particularly the last one); *SL* won the resulting user-acquisition battle and was to go on to become the exemplar of social worlds. Because of this, we'll see its name crop up a number of times in this book: it has influenced how Reality has viewed virtual worlds in important ways.

Despite all the different attempts that were made in the early 2000s to gain an edge for a freshly minted virtual world, the most obvious route to success was to use an existing intellectual property if possible (as *Ultima Online* and *Final Fantasy XI* had done): this would attract players who had bought into the fiction, while cutting down on expensive world-building time.[24] *The Sims Online* (Wright & Trottier, 2002) was an early example,[25] as was Raph Koster's post-*UO* project, *Star Wars Galaxies* (Koster, 2003). Sequels were another way to make use of an existing IP: *Asheron's Call 2* (Booth & Davidson, 2002), *Lineage II* (Kim, 2003) and especially *EverQuest II* (Waters, 2004) all sought to build on their earlier accomplishments.

EverQuest II (*EQ2*) was highly anticipated. *EverQuest* still dominated the MMO space by quite a margin, and a great deal of money had been spent on *EQ2* (it had 130 hours of voice acting,[26] including a role for the awesome Sir Christopher Lee). Commentators speculated that it would be the first MMORPG in the West to accumulate a million players.

It was not.

The biggest three virtual worlds by subscriber base in mid-2000 were *Ultima Online* (230,000+ on unit sales of 380,000+), *EverQuest* (300,000+ on unit sales of 600,000+) and *Asheron's Call* (90,000+ on unit sales of 200,000+[27]). Although there was definitely some crossover here – some of the 150,000 people who tried *UO* but didn't stay were in the 600,000 who tried *EQ* – it's nevertheless evident that *churn* was a big problem. From the developers' perspective, everything was rosy: their players were telling them that they loved their game, which was true – they really did. This was because the ones who didn't love it quit.[28] Half the people who bought *EQ* didn't enjoy it enough to keep playing. *EQ* was great at attracting new players but not so great at retaining them. This situation only got worse as the number of people with Internet access grew and tastes broadened.

New virtual worlds came along for people to try – *DAoC* had 200,000 subscribers six months after it launched – but it remained the case that there was a substantial rump of people who had wanted to play an MMORPG enough to buy a copy of one yet hadn't cared enough for what they'd found to keep playing. Oh, if only a more joyful, more relaxed, more *fun* virtual world were to come along, it would scoop up all those players-in-waiting who were treading water in single-player games.

On 23 November, 2004, *World of Warcraft* (Metzen et al., 2004) launched.

The designers of *World of Warcraft* (*WoW*) knew what they were doing. Rob Pardo had played *EQ* to death[29] and realised that its learning curve was a problem (Donovan, 2010). He could see that once you got into them, MMOs were hugely immersive and captivating,

---

[24] For game-based intellectual properties, it also meant that existing assets, tools and other technologies could be co-opted for the MMO.

[25] It failed because its developers were touchingly naïve about how nicely its players would behave, shrugging off the alarmed warnings of virtual world veterans who knew better.

[26] Most sources say 130 hours, but I was told pre-release that 700 hours had been recorded. I guess they weren't all used.

[27] The unit sales for *AC* are estimated, but the other figures are accurate, given to me at the time.

[28] Social media has it worse. All your friends like what you say, but only because the people who don't like what you say aren't your friends any more.

[29] Not quite literally, but he headed up a high-end *EQ* guild, Legacy of Steel (Welsh, 2014), while simultaneously being the lead designer for *Warcraft III* (Pardo, 2002) – a pairing that would certainly have killed me.

but that getting into them was not easy. In particular, all these early examples lacked direction: players didn't know what they were supposed to do, other than that it involved going up levels (which they soon found took ages).

WoW's main innovation was a quest-driven system to give players clear goals that gently led them to the places they needed to go next and indicated what they needed to do once they arrived there. There was no main storyline, just a wide selection of shorter stories[30] that pushed in the same general direction, like a fresh breeze. Players were affably introduced to content at a range of difficulty levels, enabling them to play at their own pace. Most importantly, this remained true the whole time that the player was levelling up. Everyone always had options. Unlike the situation with *EQ*, solo play in *WoW* was therefore not only feasible but also the norm.

WoW had many other things going for it, too: it co-opted Blizzard Entertainment's popular *Warcraft* franchise; the developers were allowed enough time to polish it until it gleamed; and it had a nigh-perfect launch. It went on to become the dominant virtual world for the next two decades. By 2009,[31] it had ten million subscribers, a customer support team of close to 2,400 people and over 450 developers; the 20,000 computers in its server farms played with 1.3 petabytes of data.

So successful was *WoW* that the MMO designers who immediately followed it tended to go in one of three ways:

- They flat-out copied the *WoW* paradigm.

- They set out trying not to copy the *WoW* paradigm, but couldn't see beyond it so copied it anyway.

- They tried to follow their own non-*WoW* path and broadly succeeded.

In general, if you want to pick up players then it's better to offer something that the current paradigm either doesn't have or doesn't do well, rather than merely to reproduce it wholesale. For newbies, if they like what's currently on offer then they'll already be playing it. For oldbies, "familiar but the different" works: they've tired of what they already play, but they don't want what they play instead to be *wildly* dissimilar. One big idea – or even a big intellectual property – might just be enough to sway them your way.

Post-*WoW* MMOs that were informed by it (either by trying to be it or trying not to be it) and which managed to build up a loyal following can count among their number: *Guild Wars* (Phinney, 2005), *The Lord of the Rings Online* (Kerr, 2007), *Age of Conan* (Godager & Griffin, 2008), *Star Wars: the Old Republic* (Ohlen, 2011), *Star Trek Online* (Cryptic Studios, 2010), *Rift* (Ffinch, 2011), *Warhammer Online: Age of Reckoning* (Jacobs et al., 2008) and *The Secret World* (Tørnquist & Bruusgaard, 2012). High-profile flops that, despite being innovative,[32] couldn't sustain a sufficiently large audience include: *The Matrix Online*

---

[30] These are *quest chains*. We'll take a close look at quests in Volume II.
[31] These impressive statistics that I'm about to dump on you come courtesy of Donovan (2010).
[32] Or perhaps because they were *too* innovative.

(Ragaini, 2005), *Tabula Rasa* (Garriott & Sage, 2007), *Vanguard: Saga of Heroes* (Grant et al., 2007), *WildStar* (Carbine Studios, 2014) and *Shroud of the Avatar: Forsaken Virtues* (Garriott et al., 2018).

Mentioning a batch of virtual worlds just so that I can name-check some of them later would be a flimsy reason for including two entire chapters on virtual world history. Histories have to have more of a point to them. "It's important that we know what happened in the past" is a start, but it's not enough. *Why* is it important? What lessons can we learn? What makes any of this at all relevant today?

Well, if you look back at what happened in the Fifth Age, there's a familiar ring to it. It began with some precursors (*IoK, Habitat, Kingdom of Drakkar, …*) which led to some progenitors (*M59, UO, Lineage, EQ, AC, DAoC, …*). A flowering of ideas followed, with new virtual worlds that were very different from one another (*City of Heroes, Habbo Hotel, Earth and Beyond, Yohoho! Puzzle Pirates, A Tale in the Desert, EVE Online, Shadowbane, …*). There was then a split, with non-gamers heading off into *Second Life* and gamers moving to *World of Warcraft*, which subsequently dominated the field. With a few honourable exceptions, most of what followed was a variation on the *WoW* theme.

In abstract terms, we had initial invention from scratch, followed by a period of experimentation, then a schism that led to a social branch and bigger, paradigm-driven game branch. So yes: these phases mirror what happened in the first three Ages. I could have broken the Fifth Age into three if I'd wanted[33]; I didn't, because the changes were less marked than in the text era. In particular, the schism was weaker and did not lead gamers to double down; rather, it enabled them to relax. This was because the game worlds prior to the emergence of *Second Life* had remained tight on gameplay so as to put off non-gamers; once the non-gamers had a place of their own to go to, the gamers felt less threatened and designers could ease off.

All this tells us something about what was to happen next. In the text era, the Fourth Age was a period in which virtual worlds with a critical mass of paying players met with enormous success to the detriment of most of the rest. This is what happened in the graphics era, too, but it took a change of revenue model to do it. The associated impacts on MMO design were to usher in a new Age of virtual worlds.

3.2 THE SIXTH AGE (2012–PRESENT): FREE-TO-PLAY

In 1990, GEnie charged nearly $20 an hour for daytime access to its virtual worlds. A decade later, it cost less than that a month to play one. Today, it costs nothing (at least in theory[34]).

One of the allegations levelled at games[35] with a subscription model is that the players who play significantly more often than the mean are being subsidised by everyone else. Some players felt this to be unjust, and they figured that if it was OK to gain an unfair

---

[33] The Game Archaeologist section of the Massively Overpowered website uses the following boundaries (Olivetti, 2021): graphical breakout era 1997–2000, experimental era 2001–2004, and *WoW* clone era 2004–2009.
[34] Or indeed in practice. I played *Lost Ark* for over 200 hours and *Throne and Liberty* for over 600 hours without being pushed by either game to spend a single penny (which I duly didn't).
[35] It's not much of an issue for non-game worlds.

advantage that way, it was OK to gain an unfair advantage a different way – if only to level the playing field. That different way was to buy virtual goods or currency from those other players who were willing to sell theirs for real money.

Real-money trading (RMT), as it came to be known, grew to be a huge problem. External companies industrialised the process of obtaining in-game currency, which they then sold for out-of-game currency. Some of their activities were nefarious, and even ones that were legal (if not necessarily legitimate) could deeply affect gameplay. I'll discuss all this later, but for now, all we need to know is that eventually game developers had had enough and decided "if you can't beat them, join them". They themselves would sell virtual goods to players directly, bypassing the intermediaries and all the problems that came with them.

Because most of the people making MMORPGs were also playing them, they didn't look upon RMT favourably. They were already aware of the free-to-play concept because it was in use in some text MUDs (most notably *Achaea*, which had pioneered the concept) and some MMOs in the Far East,[36] especially *MapleStory* (in which you didn't always even know what your money was buying you). In the West, all the major game worlds held firm against it, until one – *Dungeons & Dragons Online* (Eckelberry, 2006) – broke ranks in 2009. It had been struggling to attract users, perhaps in part because its IP worked against it: too many *D&D* players preferred to play *D&D* face-to-face, and even the provision of an innovative integrated voice-chat system didn't persuade them to change their minds. Furthermore, the developer, Turbine, maintained that its publisher, Atari, hadn't lived up to its obligations regarding the support that it was supposed to be getting.[37] With fewer than 100,000 players, the MMO was becoming harder to keep afloat.

The embracement of free-to-play didn't ditch subscriptions; rather, it kept them but offered a pared-back (but still eminently playable) world to non-subscribers, too. Those non-subscribers who did buy something – anything at all – had their account upgraded to an intermediate, "premium" level, which came with an additional set of closer-to-subscriber benefits.

With no real precedent to work with,[38] the revamped *Dungeons & Dragons Online* (*DDO*) introduced a whole slew of buyable options to see what worked: character slots, character classes, special content, storage space, faster movement, experience bonuses, quest step skips, login queue priority, customer service access, …. Some of these came free with a subscription; some came free with a premium account; some weren't free at all, and even subscribers had to pay[39] for them.

A rebranding changed the full name of the game from *Dungeons & Dragons Online: Stormreach* to *Dungeons & Dragons Online: Eberron Unlimited*, driving home its message. It worked.

---

[36] I've been calling territorial blocs by their usual names – "the West", "the Far East" and so on – but do recognise that this is Eurocentric. The Chinese name for China translates as "Middle Country".

[37] Turbine sued Atari over this. The dispute was settled out of court.

[38] There was *Project Entropia* (now known as *Entropia Universe*), but that had been built from the ground up around the concept of self-RMT and sold pretty well everything it could for real money.

[39] As with most games that involve micro-transactions, payment was through an intermediate currency (Turbine points, now renamed DDO points for *DDO*) that could slowly be obtained in-game through play but which were usually bought in bulk for actual money. I'll discuss such dual currencies in Volume II.

Free-to-play brought *DDO* a new revenue stream. Players from subscription MMOs, attracted by that popular concept, "free", could try the game out without committing to it – they didn't even have to buy the client software. Casual players, who felt that a subscription would cost too much given the time they spent in the game, could potter around at leisure. Those new to the concept of MMOs would perhaps try it out in preference to one that might give them a short period of free play but then sting them for a monthly ten or fifteen dollars afterwards.

Some of *DDO*'s offerings heavily affected gameplay and put people off trying it; yet, well, free is free, so a good many tried it anyway. If they felt they were being nickel-and-dimed, they left; if they didn't, they stayed – and perhaps bought something. If they then realised that they were buying things subscribers got for free, well the temptation to take out a subscription themselves presented itself. It may seem counter-intuitive that making a game free could increase subscription levels by 40% within four months, but that's exactly what happened in *DDO*'s case (Kuchera, 2009). Revenue as a whole went up 500% within six months (Alexander, 2010).

It wasn't pressure from RMT activity that caused *DDO* to adopt free-to-play (F2P): it was the recognition that, by accepting its premiss, there was money to be made. Established players of other virtual worlds did not like what they saw and expressed concern that MMOs would be ruined if the practice became the norm.[40] Most of them didn't indulge in RMT and regarded buying any kind of gameplay advantage as effectively cheating. Even those who didn't see much wrong with it were faced with increasing evidence from social media games (which had also taken up the idea) that some unsavoury practices might be involved. It wasn't a direction that the majority of players wanted to take.

There was a solution, however.

In April, 2010, *World of Warcraft* dipped a toe in the water by introducing a new mount, the "celestial steed" (commonly referred to as a "sparkle pony"). It looked different from other mounts and offered one minor functionality improvement (it could both fly and run, whereas most mounts before it could only do one or the other); apart from that, though, it was nothing special – except that there were only a limited number for sale and they cost $25 each. Nevertheless, one day of seven-hour queueing later, the result was an additional $2,000,000 or more in *WoW*'s coffers (Sellers, 2010).[41]

What *WoW* had done was to sell an item that was (almost) solely cosmetic. The "(almost)" gave enough concern to those players who hadn't bought it to raise alarm, but the principle was established. Developers could sell virtual goods and services for real money so long as those goods and services didn't affect gameplay.

The point of RMT was to sell goods (usually in-game currency) that *did* affect gameplay, though. How did the MMO developers deal with this without making themselves part of the problem?

---

[40] Looking at the current state of MMOs, they might plausibly assert that they were right, too.

[41] If you want to see some of the arguments for and against microtransactions in virtual worlds discussed in depth, read the comments accompanying this article. It's typical of the analysis often found on Terra Nova in its heyday.

Well, to some extent the problem itself grew smaller, thanks to a general downturn in RMT caused by regulatory difficulties that the big RMT companies found themselves facing (particularly in South Korea). Developers also implemented design changes to make RMT harder, such as introducing time delays in the in-game postal system. The main way they achieved it, though, was to give people little reason to buy in-world currency in the first place. In-world currency isn't itself of much intrinsic use: it's only desirable because it can be exchanged for desirable items. If those items can be purchased direct from the manufacturer, why run the risk of being ripped off by a bad actor?

Hold on, though: many of those desirable items affect gameplay. How can you sell them to players without angering people who think it's cheating? Well, you do what *DDO* did: give it to subscribers for free and sell it to non-subscribers. It won't work for big-ticket items such as powerful weapons, but it will work for the bread-and-butter staples – consumables such as potions and the like. This is ultimately the compromise that virtual world developers made: subscription with F2P characteristics.[42]

Turbine's *The Lord of the Rings Online* went F2P in September 2010, tripling its revenue in the process (Orland, 2011). *EverQuest II* experimented with a F2P server in August 2010 and as a result made all servers F2P in late 2011. The industry tipping point came in 2012: by then, all the main MMOs offered a cash shop. The trend with new games was to launch with a subscription and then switch on F2P once all the hard-core players had played it through and moved on. A game that was launched as F2P-only was seen as a bit like releasing a movie direct to video: it didn't suggest high quality.

It's now commonplace for virtual worlds to offer both subscription[43] and F2P from the get-go – although there is some creep into pay-to-win territory, which we'll be looking at in Volume II. Given that most of the new objects were cosmetic, though, how did that affect the design of MMOs? If it didn't affect it, why isn't the Sixth Age just part of the already-quite-bloated Fifth Age?

Businesses hoping to be successful attempt to maximise income while minimising expenditure. Virtual world operators are no different: they aim to maximise what each player pays them while minimising what each player costs them. How this is achieved depends on the revenue model.

With per-hour charging, as seen in the Fourth Age, you want as many people to play as possible and you want their sessions to be as frequent and as long as possible. This leads to games in which the design imperative is to make meaningful progress grindingly slow.

With subscription (per-month) charging, as seen in the Fifth Age, you want as many people to subscribe as possible but for them to play as infrequently and for as short a period as possible. This leads to games in which the players are encouraged to hang around offline either through fear of loss (say, their house would become ruined if they cancelled their subscription) or through events that can only be completed once within some time period (weekly raids, daily quests – that sort of thing).

---

[42] I am indebted to the Chinese Communist Party for the template for this ominous turn of phrase.

[43] This could be in the form of *battle passes*, which are of limited duration but offer subscription-like benefits linked to the achievement of goals.

With a F2P model, the emphasis is on cosmetic items. These can make individual play-ers feel good about their characters (so, let them have many characters) or, more impor-tantly, encourage them to look good in front of other players (so, make grouping part and parcel of the game). The same applies if your version of free-to-play includes elements of pay-to-win: players who engage in this practice are usually (although not always) doing so because of the effect on others, rather than any on themselves. As for why you'd want to group, well that depends on other aspects of the design. For example, in *Final Fantasy XIV* (Komoto & Yoshida, 2013), you group to complete (possibly mandatory) instanced content; in *Albion Online*, you group for safety.

Virtual worlds of the Sixth Age want players to play for as long and as often as possible to expose them to each other and to F2P offerings. They do still have content treadmills, loss aversion, and fear of missing out, but they're not *about* those features. They're about the social component of virtual worlds, with the game component driving it. *That's* why they get their own Age, rather than being an extension of the previous one.

If virtual worlds are driven by social relationships, this suggests that different societies with different norms will have different approaches. This is indeed the case. A culture that gives more weight to individualism will regard buying success as a bad thing (because per-sonal advancement is not based on merit); a culture that gives more weight to group member-ship will regard it as a good thing (because your own advancement helps that of your group).

We can see the effect of this latter standpoint in the virtual worlds of the Far East, particularly those of South Korea and China. The players there had little trouble with the concept of RMT, and even its gameplay-blocking aspect was often regarded as a useful service, equivalent to paying someone else to queue for you while you had fun elsewhere. This meant that the transition to free-to-pay and even pay-to-win was not resisted by play-ers, and came half a decade earlier than in the West. The result was huge revenues for the MMO developers, much of which was reinvested in creating more MMOs. The trend began in South Korea, then was picked up in China (most notably by Shanda in late 2005; its aging isometric Korean import, *Legend of Mir 2* (WeMade Entertainment, 2001), was revitalised by it and established the viability of F2P in the country).

In addition to *Lineage II* and *MapleStory*, the most notable and enduring virtual worlds to come out of South Korea and China are *Fantasy Westward Journey* (NetEase, 2001), *Silkroad Online* (Joymax, 2005) and *Black Desert Online* (Pearl Abyss, 2015); the latter, which made some effort to appeal to Western audiences, is very well-established in both regions. The commercial wisdom of attracting a Western audience has not gone unnoticed by high-end developers, with *Justice Online* (NetEase, 2018) and *Swords of Legends Online* (Wangyuan Shengtang Entertainment Technology; Aurogon Info & Tech, 2021) both hop-ing to move into the space, and *Lost Ark* (Keum, 2019) and *Throne and Liberty* (NCSoft, 2024) successfully doing so.

China also boasts a myriad of smaller virtual worlds, which tend to close down after two or three years (once their players have been migrated to another game by the same devel-oper). The Chinese-speaking population in the region is so vast that most of these products are not localised for other languages, putting them under the radar for the bulk of Western audiences (including me).

The Fifth Age of virtual worlds was dominated by *World of Warcraft*, but its design did not anticipate the change of direction that the Sixth Age took. This allowed MMOs of the Sixth Age some licence to experiment. For example, several tried action combat (make time-critical decisions from a limited choice set) because it was better for console players than was traditional MMO combat (make considered decisions from a wide choice set). Because of this flexibility, a number of smart innovations first gained traction in MMOs of the Sixth Age; we'll come across them in due course. In addition to those virtual worlds I've already mentioned, you can therefore expect in later chapters to encounter at least the following Sixth-Age worlds available to Western audiences: *Guild Wars 2* (Johanson, 2012), *Elder Scrolls Online* (Firor & Sage, 2014), *Elite Dangerous* (Sammarco et al., 2014),[44] *Trove* (Trion Worlds, 2015), *No Man's Sky* (Bourn, 2016), *Secret World: Legends* (Tørnquist & Bruusgaard, 2017), *Fallout 76* (Pagliarulo, 2018), *Crowfall* (Coleman, 2021), *New World* (Lane et al., 2021) and *Star Citizen* (Roberts, far distant future).[45]

If we look at the Fifth and Sixth Ages together and compare them to the first four Ages, something very interesting from the perspective of this book emerges.

What happens in both the text and graphics eras is as follows:

- Early examples test the boundaries of what's possible within the space of virtual world design.

- Next, designers experiment with different ideas within the boundaries established earlier.

- Following this, virtual worlds are created to exploit the knowledge acquired so as to succeed on their own terms.

- After they have succeeded, they enjoy the fruits of this success.

This same pattern – locate, discover, apply, internalise – will reappear in Chapter 12 when we look at advanced player types.

3.3 FUTURE AGES

The Sixth Age is where we are at present.[46] So, does this mean we've now reached the pinnacle of virtual world design perfection?

Guild Wars (GW) is an MMO from the Fifth Age. Its sequel, *Guild Wars 2* (GW2) is from the Sixth Age. The two are very different. In essence, GW is for people who want to play solo but like to group occasionally, whereas GW2 is for people who want to play in groups but like to solo occasionally. If GW2 didn't have "Guild Wars" in the title then (lore aside) you could be forgiven for thinking it was unrelated to GW.

---

[44] It was originally known as *Elite: Dangerous*, but dropped the : when the *Horizons* expansion came out. Otherwise, it would have been *Elite: Dangerous: Horizons*.

[45] Note that I've no way of knowing whether at the time you read this any of these will still be around. At the time of writing, *Crowfall* has closed but could yet reopen, and *Star Citizen* has been in alpha for well over a decade but could eventually be released some time before the sun runs out of hydrogen.

[46] Well, my present at the time I'm writing this: April 2025.

What will *GW3* be like? *GW4*? *GW*n? There's a lot of future out there: we've barely scratched the surface of what virtual worlds can – and will – become.

I don't know for certain what the Seventh Age of virtual worlds will bring,[47] but there do exist viable disruptors out there that are capable of forcing changes in design if things work out for them. Some are technical, some are social; some are driven by internal factors, some by external factors; some are more likely than others; some are for the near-future, some are for the far-future. All are eventually coming whether we like it or not. Pretty well any of the topics outlined in this book could lead to a new age if conditions became suddenly right. For now, though, here are the front-runners.

1. **Cloud Streaming**.

   This is a vision that has been around since at least the 1990s. You use a light, generic client to connect to a server, which sends a live video stream to your screen reflecting your play. It looks just the same as the game would do if installed on your PC or console, produced by a top-end graphics card. This means you can start playing a new game without any download. All it needs is for your Internet connection to the server to be lag- and latency-free. The shutting down of Google's Stadia system in 2022 came as no surprise to anyone whose Internet connection is not remotely lag- or latency-free. In the future, when we have bigger Internet pipes, though? I discuss cloud streaming in a little more detail in Chapter 7.

2. **Virtual Reality**.

   This is another vision that has been around for a long time. It's always five or ten years away from going mainstream. It would certainly bring about changes to virtual world design, although there is a question as to whether a VR world would satisfy criterion six of the definition of a virtual world ("The world is not Reality"). Does VR give such an impression of being Reality that this condition no longer holds? VR is given some more attention in Chapter 8.

3. **The Metaverse**.

   Definitions vary, but the Metaverse is basically the Internet with a VR/AR interface to it. As such, it has the same disruptive affordances as VR, along with some of its own. In particular, the technologies developed to bring us the Metaverse might well be useful for the creation of virtual worlds (if not necessarily the Metaverse). This could open new design possibilities for designers even if the Metaverse project itself stalls (which it did when AI came along to attract away all its investment dollars, but you never know).

4. **Blockchains**.

   There are undoubtedly some good uses for blockchain technology in virtual worlds. Whether non-fungible tokens for in-world items are among these remains to be seen, but if they're implemented *en masse* then virtual worlds would have to be designed or redesigned to accommodate them, heralding a new age.

---

[47] For a snapshot of what players of MMORPGs thought the future would be in 2007, see Achterbosch et al. (2007).

5. **Assets and Engines**.

   Back in the text era, it was the case that anyone with coding skills and a reasonable command of a natural language could create a MUD on their own. They still can, but not if they want a graphical world. However, as game engines improve and asset bundles extend, eventually development costs will drop and we'll reach a point where it won't be beyond the means of small groups of individuals to make their own full-scale graphical virtual worlds. That will certainly shake up virtual world design, even for the big developers.

6. **Artificial Intelligence**.

   There are many, many ways by which AI can have an impact on game design.[48] Volume II mentions a good few, but it's a fast-moving research field so hold on to your hats.[49] The most interesting aspects in terms of changing how we see virtual worlds concern believable NPCs, but frankly I wouldn't be surprised if we had playable, AI-designed virtual worlds within my lifetime.[50]

7. **Law-Making**.

   People in positions of political power make laws. Most of these laws are good ideas, if not always well-implemented or well-enforced. Some mean well but make matters worse. Some address political agendas that are intended to pick on certain ideologically unsound targets (such as games). Chapter 9 looks at these in more detail, but for now, ask yourself what would happen to virtual world design if, say, the EU introduced a tax on data transfers to consumers.[51]

8. **Publicity.**

   For AAA games, half the development costs go on publicity. It's no use having a brilliant game if no one knows about it. Ads can only go so far: you need people with loud voices to attract new players, along with welcoming communities to keep them. MMOs have such communities, but they still need would-be players to come through the door. Increasingly, video games are being designed to be Twitch-friendly, so that influencers can play them and show how great the experience is. MMOs are unlikely to be any different (although as we'll see in Chapter 12, having all your players think the same thing is fun doesn't make for a healthy virtual world).

9. **Revenue Models.**

   Changes in revenue model brought about the Fourth, Fifth and Sixth Ages. We have yet to exhaust all the possibilities. For example, it might be possible for a developer to make money from hosting servers operated by players (this has happened in the past with MUDs, albeit not MUDs written by the hosting companies). What difference would having 5,000 copies of an MMO with 100 players in each make, rather than having 50 copies of one with 10,000 players in each? It's also possible that

---

[48] If you can't think of any, ask an AI chat program to suggest some for you.

[49] Also, possibly, your lunch.

[50] Which is to say, within the next 150 years. I'm confident I'll live that long, or die trying.

[51] Hint: it didn't go well when it was tried in South Korea (Gahnberg et al., 2022).

old revenue models might be revisited. If the cost of a subscription dropped to $2 a month, would that work?

10. **Innovation**.

I hinted at this earlier when I said that pretty well any of the topics outlined in this book could lead to a new age if conditions became suddenly right. Designers are creative: they have ideas all the time. We could see new mechanics, new story genres; we could see worlds with different purposes or populations; we could have worlds that actually end. Why create for today's players rather than tomorrow's? Designers will always have new things to say: if they're allowed to say them, who knows what would result?

11. **Fragmentation**.

The future may not be rosy. Virtual worlds could collectively go in different directions, along linguistic, cultural, jurisdictional, designer-led, or player-led lines. We may have multiple types of virtual world operating under different environmental or creative conditions, with only limited cross-pollination. This could either strengthen or weaken virtual worlds as a whole; as for which, it would depend how long the situation lasted.

12. **Dilution**.

Virtual worlds may have no future. They could be watered-down so much as a concept that new players don't understand why they were ever popular. Aspects of them are present to various degrees in *Dungeon Fighter Online* (Neople, 2005), *Pokémon Go* (Nomura & Masuda, 2016), *Fortnite: Battle Royale* (Sugg, 2017), *World of Tanks* (Sitnikov, 2010), ….. The concept of virtual worlds is too good to disappear forever, though: it might take a reboot or reinvention, but eventually we'd get them back. That doesn't rule out the possibility of a desert age, but it does suggest it would have an end.

Whatever the future of virtual worlds may be, the past will still be relevant. There remain extant virtual worlds from all six ages. People run rogue servers for closed-down MMOs.[52] Developers operate legacy servers for earlier releases of their virtual worlds ("when it was fun"). Text MUDs are very much still a thing – see the MUD Connector (Cowan, 1995), Grapevine (Oestrich, 2018) or MudVerse (Withmore Hope, 2007) for where to find them. A few of the hundreds of MUDs listed therein have more players or are more profitable than some commercial graphical worlds. No, that's not a joke.

To round off this section, here's an old, long-term take on the future of virtual worlds.

Science Fiction author Isaac Asimov wrote a number of non-fiction essays. One of them (Asimov, 1973) discusses a seminar he went to in the late 1960s about TV cassettes (or videotapes, as they came to be known). The speaker painted a vision of the future in which

---

[52] This practice is not usually sanctioned by the developers of said closed-down MMOs, but it's often grudgingly tolerated because it's not worth the cost of bringing a court case to shut a service down until it relaunches elsewhere a month later. Rogue servers of not-closed-down MMOs can expect a slightly harder time of it.

everyone could obtain specialised TV content from cassettes, rather than having to watch the bland pap put out on broadcast TV. The TV business would therefore become more like the publishing business, and authors such as Asimov would find themselves "outmoded and replaced". Two days later, to fill in for a speaker who at short notice couldn't make it, Asimov was invited to give an off-the-cuff talk himself. Here's my adaptation of what he said, rephrased to be about virtual worlds rather than about books.

So, we started with text, but players were told they wanted realism so we got graphics. The graphics were 2D, but stereoscopic 3D became possible (even if nowhere near as popular as 3D sound). Next, it was clear that the displays we had for graphics were either bulky and immobile or portable but so small that details were too hard to pick out. The obvious step to take was to miniaturise the components, bringing them closer to the sensory organs: a VR headset, in other words. Accompanying this, we got hand-held VR controllers; next will be generally available skin-thin data gloves that can produce different pressures and feeling sensations (water, sandpaper, fur, ...), augmented by a motion base so you can run in the real world without hitting a wall. Haptic feedback wearables are already on the market, as are ball frames that you can sit in and rotate you so your inner ear's perception of your orientation matches that of your in-world self.

Projecting further, we can expect smell as an additional sensory input (we had Smell-O-Vision in the 1960s). The haptic wearable will become full-body. Why stop there, though? Give it awhile and we'll be able to immerse people in gel tanks that use precision sonar, lasers or electronics to harden or soften the gel for that full-body experience of walking through mud or being punched in the gut. Put it in a ball frame and both you and the orientation can be manipulated, too. It's going to be inconvenient, of course, and take up a lot of room: it would be so much more agreeable to cut out the senses entirely and speak directly to the brain. This is the cyberpunk trope of "jacking in": you have some kind of neural interface that connects you to the virtual world, intercepting all commands from the brain to the limbs and returning a stream of sensations appropriate to the virtual environment.

We're still not done, though! At the moment, what I've described has the virtual world talking to the brain via the senses. If I create a giant spider that's meant to scare you, well I might overdo it and make it *too* frightening, or I might get the wrong kind of spider for you (shiny *versus* hairy), or I might have the effects of its biting you feel too unpleasant – or not unpleasant enough. Really, I don't want to be talking to the brain, I want to be talking to the mind: that emergent phenomenon of the brain in which your imagination models and interprets the world. I want to be able to insert into your mind the direct, unrejectable thought that there's a spider here just frightening enough for *you*, for *your* present needs, that comes with all the sensory trimmings that *you* need to support that controlled illusion.

This sounds amazing! It's somewhat futuristic, though. When are we likely to get such a technology? As Asimov put it, "We will have it in minus five thousand years": it's text.

3.4 LESSONS

As I said at the beginning of Chapter 2, an appreciation of history helps designers to understand how things got to be how they are and to see the trajectory of where things might be going. History has this fortunate property of repeating itself at an abstract level. The rise and decline of *LambdaMOO* is mirrored by that of *Second Life*. *WoW*'s domination is no more eternal than *DikuMUD*'s. Will today's graphics be seen as dated by future generations as text is today? Certainly!

Many historical virtual worlds are still around. Sure, they're often museum pieces, and you won't get the same feel from them that the original players did any more than a visit to Pompeii will tell you what it was like to live there in ancient times. You will, however, get a sense of the conditions, of what people did, of perhaps why they did it. Seek out these old virtual worlds while you still can. Play them. See how they did what they did. Did this one take from what came before it? Did it give to what came after? What worked? What didn't? Would it work today? Don't take what I'm telling you as the inviolate truth: make up your own mind. Above all, *understand*.

Players change as people change. Yesterday's care bears are today's hard-core. Players' reasons for playing progress over time (as we shall see in later chapters), but their preferences for the *expression* of their play are generational (Pulsipher, 2012). Nevertheless, what virtual worlds offer, nothing else can replace. This is why they were invented multiple times at the beginning, and will be reinvented multiple times in the future if their time – for the moment – comes to an end. While people have imaginations and dreams, they're just too good not to exist.

The more virtual worlds there are, the better Reality will become.

THE TERM "AVATAR"

The term *avatar* originates with Hinduism, meaning the physical embodiment on Earth of a deity or other powerful spirit. From there, virtual worlds either borrowed, imported, appropriated or stole it, depending on your point of view (De Wildt et al., 2019).

There is some dispute as to which route the word took to arrive at virtual worlds. *Habitat* usually wins,[53] although the single-player game, *Ultima IV* (Garriott, 1985), also has a strong case. Somewhat earlier, of course, it had been the actual name of the PLATO virtual world, *Avatar*.[54] The distinction is between progenitor and precursor.

In my lectures, I tell my students that *Golf* was invented in China and provide evidence in the form of a Ming dynasty scroll. I also tell them it was invented in France and provide evidence in the form of a prayerbook illustration. I further tell them it was invented in Greece and Egypt, showing carvings and paintings that are also used to prove that hockey was invented there. I then mention that it was also invented in Rome, Ireland, England and the Netherlands (where it was called *Kolf*). After that,

---

[53] *Habitat* wasn't directly inspired by Hinduism to use the term; rather, it was the title of a Poul Anderson book (Anderson, 1978) Chip Morningstar was reading that made it pop into his mind (Morningstar, 2019).

[54] *Avatar* was four years in development and was originally to be called *Avathar*, taken from Tolkien's *Silmarillion* (Tolkien, 1977); it was replaced by *Avatar* because of concerns about copyright infringement (Dear, 2017). Apparently, ancient religions can't claim intellectual property rights to their terminology or concepts.

I show it was invented in Persia, coming from a version of football that people played on horseback (so like *Polo*).

The idea of hitting a ball into a hole with a stick does not require the mind of a genius. People could and did have the same idea in many places in the world at different times in history. It was reinvented independently multiple times. Nevertheless, if you track back the genealogy of the US Masters or any modern version of the game, you will end up in Scotland. Scotland's golf is the progenitor of today's *Golf*; the rest were precursors.

So it is with use of the word "avatar". People who develop games tend to have very wide knowledge, and early designers knew what an avatar was before seeing its use in a game. They attached it to what they wanted a name for: in *Ultima IV*'s case, a person leaving their real life to enter a world of fantasy as a being of power; in *Habitat*'s case, the visual representation of a character in a virtual world. The novel *Snow Crash* (Stephenson, 1992), which popularised the idea outside of virtual worlds, used it for the character itself.[55]

So, what are we to make of this?

Although the *Ultima IV* use of *avatar* perhaps does feed into the use for virtual worlds (mainly MMORPGs), as many designers had played the game,[56] it was *Habitat* that introduced the concept in a way that stuck. The first use of "avatar" in the MUD-DEV archives, from March 1997 (Lambert, 1997), uses it in the Chip-and-Randy sense. *Snow Crash* probably influenced some of the newer developers, along with players and journalists, to switch the meaning from the visual appearance of a character to that of the character itself. There was a non-fiction book called *Avatars!* (Damer, 1997) that contributed to this, too.

Golf was probably invented in China before it was invented in Scotland. We don't play Chinese golf today, though. Nevertheless, regardless of whether you think precursors trump progenitors or not, when it comes to "avatar", Hinduism wins every time.

---

[55] As I mentioned in Chapter 1, those people who used it in this sense needed another word for the visual appearance of a character and went with *toon*. This is perhaps the main contribution to virtual world history of *Toontown Online*.

[56] Not least Richard Garriott, who wrote it.

CHAPTER 4

Characteristics

V IRTUAL WORLDS ALL HAVE the same, "virtual worldliness" feel about them and have tended to follow the same developmental trends, but they are not identical. Each has its own characteristics, which as a constellation have important consequences for design. Some such characteristics change over time, some remain constant; some have a greater or lesser effect than others; some are the result of design decisions, some result in design decisions. It's by reference to these characteristics that prospective players, having decided that they want to play a virtual world, decide which virtual world to play.

These early chapters of this volume are intended to serve as an introduction to virtual worlds, establishing the foundations for later chapters. It makes sense, then, to examine the major choices that designers (or, for business-related decisions, their employers) have open to them and what these imply for the virtual worlds that exhibit them in various forms.[1] These, along with a few other characteristics, are used by players to gauge whether or not they want to try a particular virtual world.

4.1 PLATFORM

In computing, a *platform* is a framework within which software applications run. Platforms can be hardware (say, a personal computer), software (say, Unix) or distribution (say, Steam). For us, the relevant software applications are games in general and virtual worlds in particular.

Development, operations and consumer platforms can be different: a game client developed using Windows PCs under Unity might run on PlayStation, while the game's server is in the cloud; in this example, Windows, PCs, Unity and PlayStation are all platforms (as is the cloud, if you want to be liberal). Virtual worlds such as *Second Life*, which allow user-created content, can in turn be platforms themselves.

The most important platform is the hardware (and associated operating system) that the player uses. A virtual world can be offered on several of these: *Albion Online*, for example, is available for Windows, Mac, Linux, iOS and Android, all connecting

---

[1] A designer-centric, follow-on set of early decisions is considered in Volume II.

DOI: 10.1201/9781003689638-4

to the same server (if not quite engendering the same experience). Obviously, the more platforms a virtual world is available on, the more players it's likely to get; however, the less it can use the strengths of individual platforms. A PC user with a mouse will be able to navigate a screen full of icons better than will a console user with a gamepad, and a smartphone user might have real trouble even interpreting the icons. For this reason, multi-platform games are going to aim at the intersection between the affordances of each targeted platform. Sorry, PC users, but no, you won't get that screen full of icons you crave.

There's some overlap between platforms and interfaces, because of the devices that come with them. Is VR a platform, for example?[2] I'll talk about the interface-related design implications of different platform types in Chapter 8, but the general rule is that PC users have it best in terms of functionality – not least because if console users had it better then the PC users would simply buy a USB gamepad. There are things you can do with a PC that you simply can't (yet) do with other platforms, such as input lengthy freeform text at speed. There are some exceptions: it's easier for tablet and phone users to play sitting next to each other on a sofa or in impromptu settings, for example (not that many MMO designers would expect them to do this[3]). PCs and consoles (can) have headphones and microphones, so voice chat at a distance is an option; for hand-held devices, headphones (earbuds) can be assumed to be available, but social conditions dictate whether voice can: home alone in bed, yes; commuting on a train, less yes.

For PC users, the in-world camera and the character can easily be disassociated. For console and touchscreen users, it's harder. For this reason, virtual worlds designed for significant console usage will usually fix the camera on a cursor that lives in space ahead of the character and which rotates as the character rotates; they may even fix the camera angle and rotate the character, as with an isometric viewpoint (*Lost Ark* does this). Such an approach is a step down for PC users, and although it does level the playing field for *crossplay* (that is, allowing people using different platforms to play together in the same virtual world), some developers consider it to be prudent to partition servers by user platform instead.

Platforms themselves will have one of two underlying philosophies: either they're open or they're closed. An indie developer is going to choose an open platform, such as a PC or Android, where there is no gatekeeping and it's easy to make quick changes. A professional studio will be willing to jump through tiresomely strict quality assurance hoops to land on a lucrative closed platform, such as a console, and to pay whatever slice of their profits the guardians of the platform decree. A special case of a closed platform is the *walled garden*: games that run on such a platform won't run elsewhere. *Roblox* is an example of such a platform, as was PLATO in the 1970s: you have freedom to create within the parameters of the platform, but if you want your game to run anywhere else, you either have to rewrite it for the new platform or resort to some kind of emulator.

---

[2] No, it isn't.

[3] For reasons explained in Chapter 14, MMOs are more of a two-to-four hours-most-evenings kind of thing than they are a let's-have-the-gang-round one.

Ultimately, whatever platform(s) you choose will have a strong influence on the virtual world you create – not so much because of what they allow you to do, but more because of what they prohibit you from doing.

4.2 GENRE

The word "genre" has two main uses in computer games. The first refers to the type of game (real-time strategy, first-person shooter, battle royale and so on); the second refers to the type of fictional setting (post-apocalyptic, mythological, Victorian era and so on). We're not directly concerned with the former here, because this book is expressly about one such type-of genre in particular: virtual worlds. Virtual worlds have their own sub-genres, of course, and even sub-sub-genres – many of which map onto the characteristics described in this chapter. For the moment, though, it's to the virtual world's fictional setting that our attention turns.

The first thing to point out is that virtual worlds don't need a fictional setting *per se*. Social worlds in which players can create their own content rarely have them, because if players can add arbitrary content without compunction then the result will always be a chaotic mix of ideas.[4] It's therefore fair to say that almost all virtual worlds that do have a contextual genre will be game-oriented.

When players can't add out-of-context creations to a virtual world, designers will usually provide an overall setting with perhaps some sub-settings to add variety. The description of the setting is known as the virtual world's *fiction*. I'll be looking at the fiction of game worlds (and why they're a good idea) in some detail in Volume II, but for now, it's enough to note that fiction is not the same as genre. "Science Fiction" is a genre, but "the world is a generation starship on a thousand-year journey, in which passengers keep waking up from cryogenic sleep prematurely" is a fiction.

The contextual genre of a virtual world is important to players because of the tropes it comes with and the effects it has on the world's overall design. Tropes are actually important: over the years, I've had a surprising number of people independently tell me that their dislike of elves is so great that they avoid Fantasy worlds on principle.[5] For designers, the genre lays out the framework of what they wish to say and the tropes lay out what everyone expects them to say as a given within that genre.

The dominant genre in game worlds is Fantasy, followed by Science Fiction and to a minor extent Horror. In literary circles, these three genres are known as Speculative Fiction.[6]

The Fantasy genre is an ancient one, emerging from folk tales and archaic myths. It always was and yet remains a wide and varied, ever-evolving creative landscape revealing as-yet-unseen vistas and new, secret paths to undiscovered realms. Sadly for

---

[4] Albeit one likely skewed towards impropriety.

[5] OK, so the "surprising number" is probably only about six. Whether that surprises you or not may depend on whether you yourself are elfphilic, elfphobic, or elfadiaphoric.

[6] Personally, I regard this term as being a territorial move by certain Science Fiction devotees to lay claim to Fantasy and Horror, because then "everything is SF". I'm probably wrong, but being wrong has never stood in the way of a conspiracy theory before.

players, however, a lot of the Fantasy we see in virtual worlds is generic, rooted in the 1930s Sword-and-Sorcery stories of Robert E. Howard, Fritz Leiber, Fletcher Pratt and L. Sprague de Camp, with a veneer of High Fantasy inspired by J. R. R. Tolkien's works. *Alice's Adventures in Wonderland* (Carroll, 1865) is a Fantasy novel, but it's not the kind you'd see in most of today's Fantasy MMOs. Rather, you can expect a world in which some advanced ancient society has collapsed leaving magical artefacts and decaying structures everywhere you look, with populations of tired "races" battling to survive against corrupted "monsters".

From a less cynical perspective, Fantasy is the ideal genre for MMORPGs. Players experience a world that is in some ways familiar, but in other ways unfamiliar, in which they can be (or at least try to be) whoever they want to be. Wish-fulfilling dreams such as heroism, friendship and excitement flow naturally from it; jarring, unimmersive concepts such as recovery from death, physics-defying magics and binary good-or-evil natures can be explained away in context. It harks back to an ideal past that has been ruined but can yet be reclaimed. Furthermore, people actually like it – as the large number of TV series with a Fantasy theme attest. That said, if it doesn't deliver all that the players expect from a Fantasy world, it can feel incomplete; *Meridian 59*, which initially lacked many of the traditional Fantasy features that players anticipated, suffered from this problem.

Science Fiction has the same attributes as Fantasy except that not as many people like it (unless it's fantastical, as with *Star Wars* and *Dr Who*). It usually describes either an optimistic or a pessimistic future, reflecting the popular sentiments of the day. More than Fantasy, Science Fiction has strong virtual world sub-genres, including Space Opera (*EVE Online, Elite Dangerous, No Man's Sky*, …), Superhero (*City of Heroes, DC Universe Online*, …) and Post-Apocalyptic/Dystopian (*Anarchy Online, Fallout 76, Warframe* (Sinclair & McGregor, 2013), …).

Some Fantasy worlds exhibit elements of Science Fiction and *vice versa*. This is particularly notable in games with a Japanese heritage, such as *Final Fantasy XIV* (*FFXIV*) and *Phantasy Star Online*, but plenty of other examples exist; the settings for *Skyforge* (Allods Team, 2015) and *WildStar* both roam within the union of Fantasy and Science Fiction.

Horror is not a popular genre in virtual worlds, perhaps because people don't want to have the willies scared out of them for hours at a time every evening. The commercial virtual world closest to Horror in its theme is *The Secret World*, and in practice, even that only used it periodically. Elements of horror can appear in MMOs of other genres as occasional diversions, but they're not generally sustained.

Additional genres have been tried for virtual worlds, most often in the text days (when the risk of failure was less of a financial catastrophe). Some of the overall findings were:

- Anything puzzle-based (such as Detective Fiction) or surprise-based (such as Comedy) is effectively single-shot and so needs enormous amounts of content.

- Anything that discourages players from talking to one another will struggle.

- Historical authenticity can make demands uncomfortable for modern audiences.

- Romance quickly degenerates into sex.

- Lone, identikit protagonists rapidly lose their appeal; if everyone is Harry Potter, Mulan, or Morgan Le Fey then being Harry Potter, Mulan, or Morgan Le Fey isn't special.

- Genres with equaliser weapons, such as handguns in the Wild West, end up either with everyone being an incredibly bad shot or bullets that are effectively made of peas.[7]

Some genres tried in the text MUD days *were* successful, though. Recall how many were on display at the Adventure '89 convention that I mentioned earlier; sure, these might not all be popular enough to appeal to millions of players,[8] but they could perhaps carve a niche in a marketplace otherwise saturated with Fantasy. There are plenty of untapped genres out there, and always will be; it only takes a little imagination[9] to find them.

Players should not have to play the same game over and over and over again.

One of the main reasons that designers (or those who pay their wages) choose a genre is not for its design implications, but rather its ability to bring in players. It's essentially a marketing decision. Happily (because most of them are useless at it), designers don't need to understand marketing – although of course they do need to understand the prospective players to whom their game will be marketed. They also need to understand the product if they're designing for an existing intellectual property. We'll look at this in Chapter 9.

4.3 APPEARANCE

Appearance may be superficial, but it's one of the major factors that players consider when deciding to play a virtual world. It used to be that players chose between text and graphics; now, they choose between different kinds of graphics. Whether those graphics are rendered on a flat screen, in stereoscopic 3D, or in VR is important, but not as important (for appearance) as the choice of graphical style itself. A game that has a realistic look gives the player a different feel to one that has a cartoony or exaggerated look. Likewise, a game with whimsical or rotoscoped animations establishes a different atmosphere to one that has robotic-like exactness.

Players infer from the game's look what its gameplay must be like. Fortunately, most of the time, the two are indeed aligned, although occasionally they're not, deliberately or otherwise: *WildStar* was all lolloping, amusing characters in a lolloping, amusing environment who fought lolloping, amusing mobs that viciously and relentlessly slaughtered them in a merciless, uncompromising fashion.[10]

Players also make subconscious assumptions based on graphical styles, usually accurately but sometimes incorrectly and sometimes unfairly. They may, for example, assume that a game with state-of-the-art graphics is state-of-the-art in general; often it is, but sometimes the development money was directed at graphics at the expense of gameplay.

---

[7] *Red Dead Online*, which features both, was not the success its developers might have hoped it would be.

[8] OK, so Adult ones would, but appealing to millions of players isn't quite the same as acquiring and retaining millions of players.

[9] Or a glance at the chapter in Volume II where I look at genre choice from a design perspective.

[10] Well, they did if you were playing a healer. People playing other roles may have had an easier time of it than I did.

Also, players may look at a game world that has graphics that were state-of-the-art ten years earlier[11] but which now look dated, and assume that the gameplay is also dated; this could be true, but as the popularity of retro games attests, dated gameplay doesn't necessarily mean worse gameplay.

Stylistic looks date much less quickly than do attempts at photorealism. *World of Warcraft* has upgraded its graphics with more detailed textures, but its appealing visual aesthetic has remained constant – and will doubtless continue to do so. It would therefore seem to be a good commercial move to design a virtual world with a look that won't date because it's not of a time. This is indeed a reasonable suggestion – so long as the look is in tune with both the gameplay and what the designer wants to say.

To be successful, virtual worlds should have both a look that reflects their feel and a feel that reflects their gameplay. Prospective players who see the look and don't like what that implies about the feel, and thence, the gameplay can therefore be forgiven for not wanting to sign up. Appearance may be superficial, but – for virtual worlds at least – it's often an indicator of what lies in the depths.

For someone new to virtual worlds, then, appearance may be enough to win them over. To an old hand, appearance comes with associated implications for gameplay (and to some extent interface) that are ultimately more important.

4.4 OPENNESS

Openness refers to the degree of choice that a virtual world affords its players.

All games are "open" to some extent, because otherwise they're just the playing out of a series of uncontrolled events that are no more a game than is a movie.[12] In a virtual world context, though, the concept relates to how much freedom the player has to go in different gameplay directions. Its opposite isn't "closed" (which you might expect it to be), but *linear*.

A combination of factors determines how open (or linear) a game is. At the macro level, we have worlds with heavily curated experiences on one side and worlds where the player decides undirectedly what to do on the other; in virtual world terms, these are called *theme parks* and *sandboxes* respectively.[13] At the micro level, the player may be constrained (usually by terrain) to follow a certain path to reach a destination or be freer to make their own way; the former used to be known as a *gauntlet* (as in, running the gauntlet), but the term fell out of use when it became the default approach in MMOs. A typical *Final Fantasy XIV* dungeon, for example, has but one path through it, so the players never get lost and can't skip major fights.

In the text era, virtual worlds were much more open than they became in the graphical era (at least from *World of Warcraft* onwards). Even those that tended towards a theme park experience were more open than are most of today's virtual worlds. This was because much

---

[11] Especially if the game has been in development for ten years.

[12] Yes, this does mean that I don't strictly consider *Moksha Patam* (a traditional form of rule-based play from India, known to English-speakers as *Snakes and Ladders* or *Chutes and Ladders*) to be a game, because it has no decisions and therefore no gameplay. If you believe you can influence your luck (or *vice versa*) then it would be a game, though.

[13] MMOs that try to support both vertical (theme park) and horizontal (sandbox) play as separate styles, usually unsuccessfully, are *sandparks*. I guess it's better than "theme boxes".

content in those days was emergent rather than scripted, which was for two main reasons: firstly, emergent content, arising from the depth of the virtual world's physics, was less expensive to create than scripted content (and was more conducive to arousing a sense of immersion); secondly, the founding philosophical basis of virtual worlds was to give players freedom, which scripted content struggled with but emergent content delivered.

As generations of designers came in with their own ideas, the connection with freedom diminished in favour of designer-authored experiences. The result is that most virtual worlds today will focus on either *simulationism* or *stagecraft* (Koster, 2022), with more of the commercial worlds in the latter category (that is, theme parks) than the former (that is, sandboxes). Players will tend to favour one over the other, depending on their playing career to date (we'll see why in Volume II), so will take that into account when choosing a virtual world to play.

Note that although the aim of open worlds is to allow players to decide for themselves what to do, that doesn't mean they necessarily have more choice in absolute terms. A player of a theme-park world could have to choose what to do next from twenty authored quests when a player of a sandbox world might have only three realistic options resulting from ongoing emergent events. Finding the sweet spot between under- and over-constraining player choice in virtual worlds is an example of the paradox at the heart of game design: setting the boundaries of play to open up possibilities that wouldn't otherwise exist, but not making them so tight as to remove the possibility of play altogether (Salen & Zimmerman, 2003).

4.5 REVENUE MODEL

It should already be obvious that a virtual world's chosen revenue model is an important characteristic, because of the part that revenue models played in virtual world history. I'll delve into this topic in a lot more detail in Volume II, but I'm mentioning it here because for players, how they are expected to pay for a virtual world strongly influences whether they'll try it out or not in the first place. It essentially comes down to three factors: affordability, fairness and exploitativeness.

We've known from the text era that players will usually prefer a totally free virtual world of so-so quality over one they have to pay for that's of palpably higher quality. For games that players do pay to play, whether that's per-hour or subscription (*i.e.* per-month), the higher the price, the more people are turned off. This relationship is a continuum, if not necessarily linear: higher-price games become increasingly less affordable to more players, no matter how keen they are to play them.

The difference between pay and free is disjoint, though. Even slightly crossing that boundary line loses many, many potential players. These players don't regard this as an affordability issue, but one of principle: even the threat of charging a dollar a year is sufficient to dissuade them from playing.[14] Game developers do need to raise enough money to cover the cost of the pizzas that sustain them, though, so other ways of recouping

---

[14] I've asked this several times of groups of players (mainly students) over the years, and although the proportions may change, there are always a good few who seem to regard playing games for free as being some kind of human right. Perhaps it should be.

development costs must be found. Advertising doesn't work and purveying players' personal details to people who want them is mostly illegal, but selling players virtual items that can be reproduced pretty well for nothing is highly profitable. This, then, brings us to fairness.

Fairness is the idea that players can't buy an in-world advantage using external means (usually money, but if we go the same way as professional sports then we'll also occasionally see blackmail and sex as ways to influence an outcome). For virtual worlds, paying for cosmetic items is going to be acceptable to most players. Paying for anything that influences gameplay, though, is pay-to-win. Now although the definition of pay-to-win is fairly clear, there are players and commentators who have a more fuzzy attitude; for them, pay-to-win starts where their own paying-to-win ends. For example, they may persuade themselves that *quality-of-life* improvements such as extra bag space don't count, or they do accept that it's a *little* naughty but that it's negligible in comparison to the egregious advantages bought by people with fewer scruples. They may therefore decide not to play a virtual world that openly and legitimately sells outrageous advantages (and similarly not play ones that don't offer the advantages they believe are insignificant in the great scheme of things – but not so insignificant that they themselves won't pay to have them). Basically, though, anything that positively influences the gameplay or mechanics of a virtual world is "to win", and if you pay for it using real money in some fashion then it's "pay to win". You're deluding yourself if you believe otherwise.

Exploitativeness, which my word processor's dictionary insists isn't a word, is the degree to which a virtual world's revenue model is exploitative. Although this is primarily the province of F2P games, it can be a feature of other revenue models too: requiring players to kill a thousand monsters of a particular kind to gain reputation, for example, would be exploitative under a per-hour charging system. Chapter 23 discusses some cheap psychological tricks used in game design; although these can often be used for benign purposes, they can also be used malignly to wring money out of hapless players. Examples of particularly despised techniques include lockboxes,[15] non-fungible tokens and friend invitations. That's at the time of writing, though: any or all of these could eventually become acceptable, even though they're not necessarily going to be seen as positive reasons to play. Paying real money for cool-looking clothes was once unacceptable to the majority of players.

The way that a virtual world developer or operator makes enough money to develop or operate a virtual world affects that world's design, and hence influences its attractiveness to prospective players. Ideally, it wouldn't matter: designers would design virtual worlds to say something meaningful to players, and players would play virtual worlds simply because they enjoyed what was being said. This worked in the early days, when creating virtual worlds was a hobby rather than a career, but until development costs come down, some concession to the reality of making realities is inevitable.

---

[15] Also known as *lootboxes*; I use the terms interchangeably, but will try to stick with *lockboxes* in this book to be consistent (just for you).

4.6 INFLUENCES

Players will often assess a virtual world based on what influenced its design. Virtual worlds may themselves be self-contained capsules of innovation isolated from the rest of Reality, but their designs are not. Designers absorb ideas from the world (indeed worlds) around them, some of which influence their design decisions either directly or indirectly. From a player's perspective, this influence can be either positive, negative or indifferent, depending on how the player feels about its source (or about other virtual worlds drawing from that same source).

The most direct influence that players will consider is that of intellectual property (IP). Someone who is interested in *Star Wars* is more likely to give a game set in the *Star Wars* universe a try than they are one set on Telara.[16] Of course, the people who own the intellectual property may want some money for your use of it: developers therefore have to weigh up the extra income that a popular IP will bring in[17] against the amount they'll have to fork out in royalties. The MUDs of yore tended to take a more relaxed attitude to IP than laws might suggest they should, creating worlds based on pretty well any popular TV show franchise of the era; it was the game equivalent of fan fiction. Any commercial virtual world considering using a pre-existing IP would need operate under licence, though.

There are two ways to use an IP for free while remaining within the law. Firstly, you can use an IP that's solidly in the public domain, such as folklore's Robin Hood or Dumas's *The Three Musketeers* (Dumas, 1844). Secondly, you can use the genre of a novel rather than the novel itself – Cyberpunk, rather than *Neuromancer* (Gibson, 1984), say.

Direct influences on the design of virtual worlds can also come from other virtual worlds or from computer games as a whole. The history chapters of this book explained in more-detail-than-you-wanted how the design of virtual worlds developed over time, but to summarise (in case you've excised it from your mind), the key historical virtual worlds in design terms are *MUD*, *DikuMUD*, *Ultima Online* and *World of Warcraft*.[18] This is because so many other worlds either aspired to be them or aspired to be the opposite of them.

Indirect influences on virtual worlds usually come from other media. Indeed, the single work that has had the most influence on virtual worlds is a book: Tolkien's *The Lord of the Rings*. This influence is rarely overt (although clearly it is in *The Lord of the Rings Online*), and it can be felt at different levels. For me, as I mentioned earlier, it was influential as a proof-of-concept, but for others, it was its scope, or its language, or its lore, or its characters; designers tend to have enough imagination that they can (and want to) design their own worlds, so they will usually approach extant examples of designed worlds objectively and analytically rather than subjectively and immersively.

The Lord of the Rings has also had a second-order influence, via *Dungeons & Dragons* (the design of which was partially[19] inspired by Tolkien's vision) and as a result of the films

---

[16] The world of *Rift*, if you were wondering.

[17] In theory, buying in an IP can save on development time, too, because the world-building has already been done. That argument rarely impresses people who actually *want* to build worlds themselves, though, such as virtual world designers.

[18] *LambdaMoo* and *Second Life* are also key virtual worlds, but for societal reasons rather than design reasons.

[19] Not wholly, though. The magic system was based on the one described in Jack Vance's *Dying Earth* (Vance, 1950) novels, for example.

based on the books.[20] It has even had third-order effects, through virtual worlds that were themselves indirectly influenced by *D&D*. It may, therefore, be that players who don't like the kind of High Fantasy promulgated by Tolkien's fiction may still feel its effects through analogues in other fictional genres, because of its impact on underlying gameplay or thematic elements (such as the meaning of heroism).

We could go further back in time, of course. *The Lord of the Rings* and *MUD* were both influenced by folklore, and folklore itself has also been directly used as a starting point for virtual worlds – Arthurian Britain in *Dark Age of Camelot*, for example. MMOs routinely rip off mythology, in part for IP reasons but also because doing so gives players a fighting chance of understanding what they're seeing.[21] Players tend to like folklore even if they're unfamiliar with its details, because it feels authentic: it manifests the deep roots of their culture – *if* it's the folklore of their *own* culture.[22] If it's the folklore of another culture, they may regard it as simply exotic or as adding a bit of variety, or they may use it to inform their opinion of the originating culture; they're very likely to misinterpret it, whatever.

We can also go forward in time, looking at cultures yet to be.[23] More interestingly, fictional works about virtual worlds can themselves influence what virtual worlds will be like – and in turn be influenced by them. When Larry Niven and Steven Barnes wrote *Dream Park* (Niven & Barnes, 1981) and Vernor Vinge wrote *True Names* (Vinge, 1981), they had come across adventure games[24] but not MUDs; nevertheless, *Dream Park* foresaw issues to do with narrative and ownership that arose two decades later and *True Names* made points about identity masking that still haunt virtual worlds today. William Gibson's cyberpunk novel *Idoru* (Gibson, 1996) explicitly referred to virtual worlds as MUDs while making a distinction between network-as-medium and network-as-place that would still educate those numerous academics today who only see them as the former.

Perhaps the most influential futuristic book about virtual worlds is Neal Stephenson's *Snow Crash*, which not only popularised the term *avatar* but (more importantly) also introduced the concept of the *Metaverse*.[25] People who knew about virtual worlds when *Snow Crash* came out weren't especially inspired by it, as they'd already been inspired by their own visions; people who didn't know about them often were inspired, though – some sufficiently so to create their own virtual worlds (Philip Rosedale's *Second Life*, for example (Sydell, 2010)). The idea of the Metaverse later took off when advances in VR made it look as if it could become a reality,[26] leading to the rebranding of Facebook's holding company as

---

[20] I don't remember there being four endings in the book, but the film seemed to spend an age on each of them.
[21] Creative laziness is also a possibility.
[22] This is why North American players of games set in medieval times often prefer to have NPCs speak with British accents rather than American accents.
[23] This is why British players of games set in space travel times often prefer to have NPCs speak with North American accents rather than British accents.
[24] *True Names* mentions *Adventure*; *Dream Park* mentions *Zork*.
[25] I spell this with a capital letter because it's a proper noun: there's only one of it (or will be when we get it). I don't expect this to be how most people will render the word when it's a commonplace feature of life, but given that I still spell Internet with a capital letter, I'm not going to buckle to peer pressure from people yet to be born.
[26] Literally, not just figuratively.

Meta in 2021. *Snow Crash* itself described its virtual world as a dystopia into which people escaped from the even worse dystopia of Reality, so it doesn't look as if Stephenson was far wrong there. It's to be hoped that designers of the Metaverse-to-come (as opposed to those fighting to own it) may be able to leaven that situation somewhat.

There are other works that have had an influence on how virtual worlds are perceived by non-players, such as *The Matrix* (The Matrix, 1999) trilogy, the *Westworld* TV series (Westworld, 2016) and the holodeck out of *Star Trek: The Next Generation* (Star Trek: The Next Generation, 1987). Players aren't particularly affected by these archetypes in terms of deciding what to play, although such media productions may turn prospective players on to the concept of virtual worlds in general. Conversely, players may be more interested than non-players in game-aware works such as *.hack//Sign* (.hack//Sign, 2002) and *Free Guy* (Free Guy, 2021).

It's easy to list games and other creative works that will have informed and will inform designers of virtual worlds to various degrees – LARPs, murder-mystery games, escape rooms, tabletop RPGs, computer RPGs – but that isn't to say that the players will factor such influences into their decision as to whether to play a particular virtual world or not. It's also important to note that even when a designer does try to remain faithful to inspirational source material, there are always going to be departures. It's not possible for every player to be Sinbad the Sailor without stressing the virtual world's fiction to breaking point (although this can in part be mitigated by giving players some unique-sounding form of address, such as "Warrior of Light" in *FFXIV*).

Designers rarely, if ever, find the views of critics inspiring, but these views can nevertheless shape what is designed. Social media influencers can wield a great deal of power if players listen to them, and if one of them has a bee in their bonnet about some aspect of virtual world design that can be accommodated reasonably well then it may be commercially prudent to put it in. Established virtual world websites that include editorial pieces can also be influential, at least among experienced players.[27] It must be remembered, however, that even professional and semi-professional critics are not designers: their artistic skills relate to critiques of virtual worlds, not to the creation of them. Rare is the individual who is accomplished at both creation and appraisal of an art form (Archer, 1912). This is especially true of players, who generate such volumes of opinion that the result is a melange of the idiotic, the specious, the peripheral, the broad, the oddly specific, the insightful, the deep and the "whoever said that, offer them a job immediately!".

Because the design influence of players emerges through the effect of their sheer numbers on the virtual world's viability, prospective players are therefore likely to play a game populated by people just like them. If there are no players just like them, they'll need to be broad-minded. "People just like me" can never be a formal characterisation of virtual worlds, but players can often tell instinctively whether they'll fit in or not. If designers change their ongoing designs to address player complaints, suggestions or behaviours, this

---

[27] It's always a risk to list websites, because they can suddenly disappear without warning. Bearing this in mind, then, as I write this, I regularly check out *Massively Overpowered* (Overpowered Media Group, n.d.), *MMORPG.com* (MOBA Network, n.d.) and *New World Notes* (Au, n.d.).

will eventually make their world give off vibes that players-perhaps-to-be will pick up on. Whether this is good or bad will depend on how much the designer likes or resents the direction this evolution takes.

The final influence on designers of virtual worlds that it's useful to note is that of other designers of other virtual worlds. Designers do talk to one another and are happy to explain their ideas – it's not as if they could hide them anyway once a world is exposed to members of the public. Trends come and go, and whether new ideas have enough substance to them to last is almost irrelevant: if one or more MMOs can boast an attractive new concept that yours can't, it can be very tempting to implement it even if it makes little sense. It can also be sensible to wait, of course, in case the concept or its side effects turn out to be so unpopular that players won't go anywhere near anything that features it.

In the end, whether the influences on a virtual world's design are superficial, structural, historical or cultural, it's the individual player who decides whether to engage or not with it on that basis. They don't even have to notice it consciously. The simple recognition that "this is a bit like…" can be enough to make or break the deal.

Of course, in most cases, it will have no effect at all.

4.7 INTERFACE

Interface considerations are not central to this book, but they do have implications for design – not least because players will judge a game by its broad interface characteristics.

Interfaces are two-way: input and output. A player interfaces *with* a game, not *to* a game. Although a designer does have some control over the details of an interface, the general characteristics may be imposed externally.

The most obvious implications for interface derive from the choice of platform(s). A virtual world intended to be accessed using a virtual reality interface will make different demands to one intended for touchscreen use. In the first four Ages of virtual worlds, the interface of choice was text. In the Fifth Age, output was all screen and sound; input was dominated by the keyboard-and-mouse pairing. Console-style controllers gradually crept in, though, and by the Sixth Age were fairly commonplace. Touchscreens began to gain in popularity as smartphones became more powerful, which meant that smaller screens and more limited control options came with them. The design implications for these, as noted earlier, are compounded if crossplay is allowed: designers may have to pay with something that's good-for-gameplay if they're to widen their virtual world's appeal to users of different platforms or devices.[28]

Even if crossplay is required, that doesn't mean the designer is out of options. For example, *Elder Scrolls Online* uses a traditional, first-person approach that locks the camera onto a reticle fixed in space ahead of the player character; rotating the character rotates the camera with it. *Lost Ark*, on the other hand, uses a third-person approach that locks the camera on the character, presenting an almost isometric look; rotating the character doesn't rotate

---

[28] This is especially true if the virtual world is ported to a platform it wasn't designed for, as was the case with *Marvel Heroes* (Hu & Gutschera, 2013). Originally for the PC, regrettable compromises were made for ports to the PlayStation 4 and Xbox One (such as slowing down movement abilities).

the camera. *ESO*'s interface allows for immersive, one-on-one melee[29] combat; *LA*'s allows for onrushing-horde, area-of-effect combat.

In general, combat and interface design have strong implications for one another. We'll look at combat in Volume II, but for now, the main distinction to note is between action combat and traditional combat: the former has free targeting and emphasises movement, timing and reactions; the latter has locked targeting and emphasises cooldown management and reactive responses to events. Some players will definitely prefer one form over the other, so I could have listed combat as a separate characteristic of its own; it's so symbiotic with interface in this context, though, that I put them both together.

An often-overlooked effect of interface on design is convention. Players who are used to a WASD control scheme won't be pleased if you make it QWER. Even small departures from convention (such as whether E makes you turn, strafe or interact with an object) can raise a player's ire. The same applies for output: players may expect to see a mini-map in the top-right corner of the screen and be irritated if it's in the top-left; they may want their message window bottom-left and get cross if it's bottom-centre where they expect action buttons to be. All of this is easily sorted by allowing players to configure the input controls and output windows themselves, of course, but if publicity screenshots show an uncommon default then that could discourage some players.

What isn't easily fixed is whether you give them a mini-map or a chat window to begin with. Virtual worlds can have a much more eerie and intense feel to them if there isn't a mini-map, and this effect is something a designer could desire; *Fallout 76* has a compass-style direction band rather than a mini-map, for example. Flying in the face of player expectations is not always advisable, however, and although it may be acceptable not to have one in limited-area environments (where you can see everything a mini-map would show you anyway), there would be resistance doing so in a forest or city setting. Likewise, putting speech in bubbles above characters' heads could well encourage the making of new friends, rather than simply talking to old friends at a distance, but players will just use third-party tools (such as voice-over-IP solutions) to the same end.[30]

Originality suffers if everyone uses fossilised design, but for components that need to be transparent (such as those to do with interface), originality can be counter-productive. Yes, there may be better ways to do what you're doing than the stale, established ones, but when it comes to interface, it's best not to impose too many of these on the players at once.[31]

Convention can therefore work both ways. On the plus side, it informs a designer of the minimum interface features that players demand, and little tutorial training is necessary. On the negative side, it can get in the way of innovation or artistic statement.

In today's discoverability environment, streaming is becoming increasingly important. This means that a virtual world has to look good at first glance.[32] Action has to be

---

[29] Formally, this is spelled "*mêlée*", but I'll stay with *melee* in an attempt to persuade you that I'm not as pretentious as I really am.

[30] Third-party tools are how we got mini-maps, as it happens. Designers were resistant to the idea, but players took it upon themselves to create them anyway.

[31] Where "too many" means "more than one".

[32] Text doesn't, which is the principal reason it lost out to graphics.

attracting, if not necessarily attractive. Swinging a blade produces ribbon effects; spells cause huge, colourful explosions; ever-larger numbers fly from the heads of enemies hit and friends healed. As a result, it's often hard to see what's going on; the ability to switch this off (or at least to tone it down) is therefore essential.

This may all seem like common sense, because it is. It's also the subject of regulations. We'll be looking at accessibility in Volume II, but for the moment, it's sufficient to note that unless the designer has a very good reason, *not* allowing players to reduce the amount of busy visuals on screens could fall foul of the law in different jurisdictions. Whether artistic intent counts as "a very good reason" or not will depend on how well a law is formulated. It's nevertheless the case that a designer would be wise to avoid making decisions that assume players can see well, hear well, speak well, move their extremities well or think well.

4.8 LUSORY ATTITUDE

Virtual worlds aren't necessarily games, but they can share many characteristics with them. One of these is that of their *lusory attitude*.

The virtual is not real (except from the perspective of its NPCs). A player has to will themself to believe that they are in the virtual world, rather than in Reality. Although this sounds as if it's the same as the literary notion of willing suspension of disbelief (Coleridge, 1817), there is a difference: in literature, the reader wills themself to believe that the fictional world is true, even though they know it's false; in virtual worlds, the player wills themself to believe that the real world is false, even though they know it's true. Rather than will yourself to accept the fiction, you will yourself to deny the reality. It's the willing suspension of belief.

A virtual world that has no aspect of Reality-denial to it is no virtual world at all: it's merely an aspect of Reality, like a videoconference call.

This means that what some people (those playing for fun) think of as a virtual world may not be a virtual world from the perspective of other people (those not playing for fun), who consider it to be an aspect of Reality.[33] Therefore, there is a conflict between those who are *playing* the virtual world and those who are *playing in* or *with* it – or who aren't playing at all.

How players engage with a virtual world is dependent on their *lusory attitude* (Suits, 1978). It lies along two dimensions: whether they play by the rules or not; whether they play to win or not.

- *Players* play by the rules and play to win.

- *Triflers* play by the rules but don't play to win.

- *Cheaters* don't play by the rules but play to win.

- *Spoilsports* neither play by the rules nor play to win.

---

[33] Thereby failing the sixth criterion of the definition of a virtual world: "The world is not Reality".

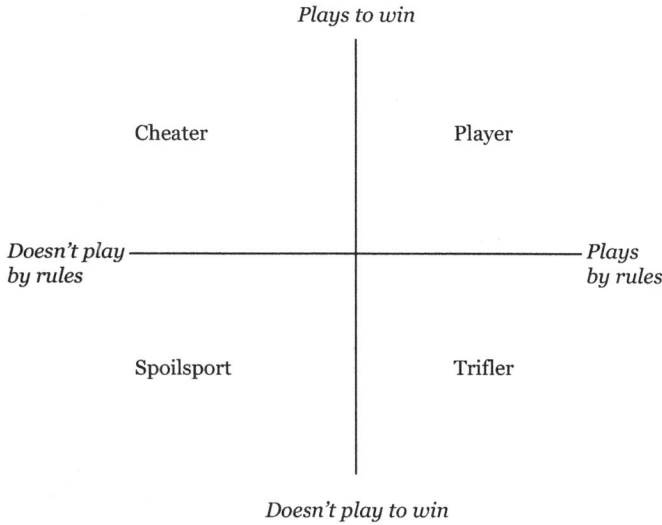

FIGURE 4.1 Lusory attitudes.

This can be summarised as the graph[34] shown in Figure 4.1.

The dominant lusory attitude of a virtual world is a factor in a player's decision as to whether to play it or not. The key dimension is that of playing by the rules or not. Those who play game worlds will want mainly players (but can tolerate triflers); those who play social worlds will want mainly triflers (but can tolerate people trying to win, even though there's no formal win condition). Cheaters and spoilsports are only acceptable to people who themselves are cheaters or spoilsports, and even then they require most other players not to be.

Interestingly, computer games and virtual worlds are different from other games when it comes to what are considered "rules". Games in general have three types of rules:

1. Physical rules (I can't hit the cue ball through other balls without also hitting those with the cue ball).

2. Written rules (if the cue ball doesn't hit another ball, it's a foul stroke).

3. Unwritten rules (take your shots in a timely manner).

In non-computer games, physical rules are coded in by the physics of the universe; written and unwritten rules are sustained by a social contract between the players.[35] Players *could* break the non-physical rules, but they choose not to in order to gain the benefits that come when all players follow the rules.

In computer games, physical and written rules are coded into the game engine directly; unwritten rules depend on the individual and are frequently ignored (on the grounds that

---

[34] Curious readers will no doubt wish to compare this to the later graphs that appear in Chapter 11.
[35] This is known as the *magic circle* (Huizinga, trans. 1949; Salen & Zimmerman, 2003).

"if the game lets me do it, I can do it"). We'll look at some of the implications of this in Volume II, but for the moment, it's enough to note that what *you* might think is an unwritten rule may not be a view shared by other players. You could well associate with those players a negative lusory attitude, and this will inform your decision as to whether or not you want to play with or alongside them.

A lusory attitude is a powerful thing. Laws in Reality are upheld by police officers and, in extreme cases, armies; rules in games are upheld entirely by consensus. At times, this gives them primacy over the laws of the land: there are things people are allowed to do in games that they are not allowed to do out of games (for example, punching each another until someone is knocked out). It would be a shame indeed if the brittle attitude to rules that players of computer games typically adopt led to a diminishment of the special protective frame enjoyed by games in general.

Whatever, lusory attitude does affect prospective players' view of a virtual world. If it's full of cheats and spoilsports, or even the merely selfish, that will affect its attractiveness either negatively or, for some people, positively.

4.9 DEVELOPER ATTENTION

Virtual worlds represent a significant time investment, so players like some degree of confidence that when they start to play one it's in good health. One way of assessing this is the amount of attention the virtual world's developers give it.

The most obvious manifestation of this is how often the virtual world software is updated. Updates typically come in four forms:

- Emergency fixes. These can happen without much warning, and are brought about to end some disastrous, show-stopping bug or exploit.[36] If the server is hanging every time a player kills a mob, for example, you'd want to implement the fix as soon as you had it.

- Weekly updates. These fix minor issues that can wait. In addition to programming bugs or irritations, they'll address art/animation bugs, text errors/ambiguities and minor gameplay balance issues. Traditionally, the patches are on Tuesdays or Thursdays.

- Content patches. These will usually coincide with a weekly update, but they add new content to the virtual world. This means they're more frequent in theme-park worlds than sandbox worlds, as the latter only need to add new functionality every once in a while. Players appreciate content patches more when they're regular, rather than unexpected or sporadic.

- Expansions. Expansions add major new content and functionality, typically involving new zones (which content patches almost never add), a slew of instanced dungeons,

---

[36] In exceptional circumstances, they can be done for external reasons. For example, if your game introduces a new "kill the king" quest and by coincidence the very next day the monarch of the UK is assassinated, you might want to roll it back. I apologise in advance if the day after this book is published, the monarch of the UK is assassinated.

some new character options (such as a new class) and a major new instalment for the main storyline. They tend to come out every two years or so, interspersed with regular content patches.[37] Unlike content patches, they often cost money to obtain.

A player looking at a virtual world that's only just come out won't be worried about the frequency of expansions. If they look at an established world and it hasn't had an expansion for several years, that could be a concern, but less so if it's still getting content patches. If content patches are few and far between, that *would* be worrying (at least for a theme-park world). If it isn't getting regular updates, that's a sign that the developers have pretty well abandoned it. If it doesn't get an emergency fix when a catastrophic problem is discovered, it definitely *has* been abandoned.

It should be noted that quantity and quality are not the same thing. A virtual world may receive lots of attention from its developer, but if this spoils the experience then it's counter-productive. *Champions Online* (Mosiondz, 2009) was pretty good at launch, but successive patches sucked out the fun and it wound up as a pale shadow of what it could have become. It's usually a good idea to announce in advance the general thrust of any up-coming major interface or gameplay changes, so if players spot problems that you don't then they can scream "Nooo!" at you before the damage is done.

Another way that developer[38] attention is perceived by players is in its public-facing activities: responses to forum or social platform queries, regularity of news items, developer blog updates – that kind of thing. An MMO may be the picture of health, but if its website is dead and its forum is dominated by rabid, unmoderated posts then the casual observer will not necessarily come away with that impression.

Players loyal to a virtual world may overlook a gradual decline in the level of attention its developer pays to it, but new players will be more objective in their assessment. If a virtual world looks to be on its deathbed, they're not going to want to make friends with it only to lose it before they've fully got to know it.

4.10 SCALE

The physical dimensions of a virtual world determine its size. The aggregation of sizes of all related, running copies of that world gives its *scale*.

There's a little more to it than this, in that it's the *perceived* or *apparent* size of the world that matters (how subjectively big it is in the players' heads) rather than its objective size in virtual square metres. This can be affected by such factors as traversal times and content density, but not in an easily measurable way. The presence of other player characters also comes into it: a world can seem physically larger if the density of player characters tails off geometrically, the further you get from busy social hubs.

---

[37] For example, *FFXIV* has expansions every two years and content patches every four months otherwise. The frequency of content addition for a virtual world is known as its *cadence*; a long period with no significant new content is called a *content drought*.

[38] Strictly speaking, this is *operator* attention, not developer attention, but as the people who run the virtual world are typically the same people who made it, the distinction is not usually significant.

Size isn't everything, though: number is also important.[39]

When two people play the same virtual world at the same time, it could be that their characters can never meet. This is because separate copies of the same game world may be running simultaneously on different servers, acting a bit like parallel universes. The programs are the same, but not the data: for example, in world X, NPC pirate96 may be alive; in world Y, NPC pirate96 may be dead. These separate worlds are known generically as either *servers* or *shards*[40]; strictly speaking, the shard is the world and the server is where the service software that implements the world runs, but in practice, the terms are interchangeable.

The concept of a shard is a little woollier than it used to be, because of newer technologies introduced to address load balancing (about which, you guessed it, more later). For example, shards can be *layered* so that one character could in theory walk across a boundary line directly behind another character and arrive in a different example of the world. They can also be collected as *megaservers*, giving players the freedom to choose at will in which copy of the world their character materialises. They may be grouped as *data centres*, with transfers between servers possible (perhaps at a cost) but with some capacity for inter-server communication and grouping for instanced content.

For the purposes of discussing scale, though, I'll take the easy approach and talk about shards in the way that players subjectively feel they exist.

Whether a virtual world with a large or small number of shards is large-scale or small-scale depends on the size of those shards. Single-shard worlds are generally of very great size and are particularly popular for virtual worlds set in the vastness of space (*EVE Online, Elite Dangerous, No Man's Sky, ...*). Most of the major commercial virtual worlds have much smaller but still quite sizeable shards (capable of accommodating perhaps 10,000 players simultaneously) and commensurately more of them. Some such shards may have different rule sets to others (usually relating to PvP and role-playing).

Being one person among 10,000 makes you a small fish in a big pond, however. It's like living in a city, rather than a village. You know the players in your guild (if you're in one), but not players in general. Most of the people you encounter, you'll never see again – or if you do, you won't remember them, they're just faces in a crowd.

Second- and third-tier virtual worlds tend to have fewer servers, with fewer players attached to each server. You may indeed find yourself bumping into the same people occasionally and remembering them. Whether you remember them for good reasons or bad[41] isn't the point: the point is that they will remember you, too.

If we look back in virtual world history, Third-Age textual worlds such as *DikuMUD* thrived (and still thrive) on having smaller communities but many more of them; furthermore, they often featured bespoke changes that offered more choice and differentiation

---

[39] I fear this line may find its way into collections of comedic, out-of-context quotations.

[40] This term originated with *Ultima Online* as a fiction to explain why there was more than one Sosaria (the game's world). An evil wizard trapped Sosaria in a crystal which was then shattered; each resulting "shard" contained a refracted copy of the world (Garriott & Fisher, 2017).

[41] I still grit my teeth when I think of a particular tank in *The Secret World* who always insisted on self-healing then would criticise my healing-specification healer for doing low damage. I'm gritting them now.

for the players. Virtual worlds on this scale aren't currently financially viable for graphical worlds, but if they were to become so then we may find more virtual worlds appear with an intimate, rather than grand-scale, atmosphere.

A final point of note regarding the number of servers a virtual world can boast is that sometimes player numbers drop off to the extent that shards begin to feel empty. At this point, a server merge may take place. This is traumatic for developers and players alike (especially if the developer didn't code for merges before release). It's usually taken as a sign that the virtual world is failing, even though it's almost guaranteed to be necessary after a virtual world has launched and the suck-it-and-see players have all left. A server merge therefore doesn't mean the virtual world *is* failing, but it could presage the receipt of less developer attention. On the plus side, the players will become more invested in the world and each other, and the community may well be stronger as a result.

Scale isn't among the most important characteristics of a virtual world, but it does have implications for other characteristics that players value. Large-scale worlds raise concerns to do with interface, player base and revenue model; small-scale worlds raise concerns about age, developer attention and appearance. Whether these implications cause or are caused by each other doesn't matter: they correlate, so that's why scale is an issue regardless of whether playing in a "big" or "popular" world is at the forefront of a prospective player's mind.

4.11 PERSISTENCE

Although persistence is one of the properties comprising the definition of a virtual world, it's not a binary value: there are different degrees of persistence. These don't usually impact on a player's decision regarding whether to play a virtual world or not – except for when they do, in which case they become critical.

The level of persistence of a virtual world is a measure of what survives a reset or reboot. We'll be looking at resets in Volume II, but for the moment, we only need to consider the concept superficially. In essence, if you have a running virtual world and switch it off then switch it back on again, its level of persistence describes how much of the state of the world before the switch-off is still there after the switch-off. At the absolute minimum, player characters must persist. The map will almost always also persist (but not if procedural map generation is a selling point), as will player inventory (but not always – it didn't in *MUD1*). Beyond that, well it depends. Will inanimate objects persist? Maybe if they're quest-critical, but otherwise possibly not. Will mobs persist? Perhaps, but they'll probably be reinitialised at their starting point instead. Will player groups persist? Will the background music that was playing continue where it left off? Will the entire state of the world persist, so that when it restarts everything will be exactly as it was before? Will extra-world functionality persist, so that new scripts that you have coded for items, NPCs or players are still operational?

These last two questions perhaps hint at when persistence becomes important. If you are in a virtual world that allows for user-created content then the user will rather expect the content they have created to persist. This is mainly of concern in non-game worlds, but even in game worlds, you might be upset if your house's contents didn't survive a server reboot.

In general, the more that persists across a reboot, the more a virtual world feels as if it's real. The world can evolve and develop a lived-in feel, which helps with immersion. A high level of persistence therefore seems on the face of it to be a good thing. Why don't virtual world designers simply make everything persist, then?

Well, there are three main reasons:

1. Saving a snapshot of the entire virtual world is a costly exercise. There's a lot of data, which takes a lot of time to dump and occupies a lot of space. Reinstating it is also expensive.[42]

2. Updates are harder to install. Developers like to make adjustments to the world to keep it fresh and to remove bugs and exploits.[43] If too much persists then reconciling the consequences of these adjustments with a saved version that may in places be incompatible with them can cause awkward problems. Even something simple such as adding a new story NPC can be tiresome if someone already happens to have a character bearing the name of that NPC.

3. It's not always desirable. If you have a detailed, responsive world that players gleefully lay waste to, you might want to reinstate it to its former glory following a reboot, rather than to leave it desolate. These days, we usually see this more for instanced sub-worlds than for the entire virtual world, though.

For a player, then, the importance of persistence depends on what the player holds dear (or holds undear). The key marker is whether the player created something or not: if they did (characters, guilds, gardens – whatever) then they'll want it to persist much more than if they didn't. This brings us neatly to a characteristic of virtual worlds that's strongly related to persistence: changeability.

4.12 CHANGEABILITY

Changeability concerns how much virtual worlds can change. The particular changes the term relates to are *tangible* (that is, physical, with respect to the virtual world) rather than *intangible* (that is, social, with respect to the players).

Virtual worlds must be able to change. If a world can't change, it has no physics, therefore it's not a virtual world. The changes don't have to be high-magnitude – simply moving around is an example of change – but there do need to be consequences for player commands. The extent of these commands is what changeability measures.

Picking a flower changes a virtual world, assuming that this action means other players can't pick the same flower (at least until it grows back[44]). Killing a mob changes the virtual world that it until-that-point inhabited. So does setting fire to a thatched roof. So does conjuring a familiar.

---

[42] Even more so if you want to save the server's internal states, so as to set up all the processes that were running exactly as they were at the precise moment the virtual world went down.

[43] These are promptly replaced by new bugs and exploits.

[44] Typically, suspiciously quickly.

How about building a house? How about creating a replica of a 1956 Vespa 150 TAP? How about introducing a system for mixing potions? How about flood-filling all object textures with the colour emerald green?

Well yes, all these actions do change a virtual world. What's more, all of them can be implemented – if you're a programmer of the virtual world in question. Some might be doable from within the virtual world; some might need a special tool; some may need to be coded using a scripting language; some may need to be hard-coded from scratch. All are possible, though, along with anything else computable. The point about changeability isn't so much *what* can be changed as *who* can do the changing. In particular, who can create things potentially outside the fictional context of the virtual world? In other words, who has *builder* privileges?

Obviously, because I've just said so, programmers can make changes (under the direction of the designer). Other trained personnel, such as artists, may be able to make wide-in-scope changes, too. Administrators will be also able to make changes, perhaps using specialist tools specifically designed for them. Furthermore, highly experienced players may on occasion be granted partial builder privileges, although that was more common in the text era than it is today (because adding textual content is far easier than adding graphical content).

Regular players tend to grow in power-to-change as they grow in experience-of-playing. For example, the spells available to someone who's been playing their mage for 1,200 hours will usually be somewhat more numerous than those available to someone who's been playing for only half a day. Do regular players get to add new material to a virtual world, though? If it's within the context of the virtual world, well certainly, but what about out-of-context items? *Do* they get builder privileges?

In a game world, they invariably don't. In a social world, they often do. In the MOOs of the Third Age of virtual worlds, even newbies could add content the moment they entered the virtual world.

The more power to change a virtual world that its players have, the higher its *player impact*[45] is said to be. Player impact is therefore strongly linked to persistence: the higher the player impact, the more of the virtual world will tend to persist. Social worlds, which emphasise building, have high player impact and high persistence; game worlds, which emphasise integrity, have low player impact and low persistence.

In a game world, the world belongs to the designers. In a social world, it belongs to the players. That's because these are the sources of the tangible content in those worlds.

Interestingly, a balanced world (such as *EVE Online*) will also belong to the designers, because players don't have builder privileges; player impact may nevertheless be considerable if players' actions can affect the landscape permanently; balanced worlds may therefore also need high persistence.

Although persistence and changeability seem relatively inconsequential when it comes to choosing what virtual world to play, together they capture something of the soul of a virtual world: whose world is it? This is an important part of what players look for when pondering which virtual world to play – so much so that it may not even cross their mind to play one with a different combination.

---

[45] The term is due to Raph Koster and Rich Vogel.

4.13 PLAYER BASE

Virtual worlds are multi-player. It should come as no surprise to learn that the nature and behaviour of the other players in a virtual world will affect who decides to play it (or not).

Virtual world designers do have an influence on who plays their worlds, although not perhaps as much as the marketing and customer service teams, or indeed as the players themselves. They can design for certain demographics and to reduce toxicity, but that doesn't mean the game will attract those demographics, nor that the players won't be toxic.

Marketing and customer service can be regarded as abstracted pressures on the virtual world's designer: the designer doesn't have to know about either of them in tremendous detail; they simply produce a steady stream of problems that must be solved. A solution may have to be designed to address these problems, but this is usually achievable on a case-by-case basis rather than requiring a wholesale redesign.[46]

When it comes to customer service, the player base you get at the start has a disproportionate effect on what you'll get later. Reputation matters more than actuality. A game with a reputation for having players who bully and harass one another will put off newbies, even if in truth it's a utopia of sweetness and light. It's therefore critical to manage expectations and to design the game from the outset to funnel in the players you want at the expense of those you don't want.

We'll be looking at designing for demographics[47] and ways to design out toxicity in Chapter 20.

Obviously, marketing will affect the kind of player your game attracts, be that at the start, or when a new expansion is released, or as an ongoing campaign. It might also have to leap into action at unexpected moments, though. There are some unfortunate positive feedback loops[48] that can kick in at any time. For example, any indication that a virtual world has a dwindling player base can swiftly become a self-fulfilling prophecy if it's not nipped in the bud; the marketing team has to do the nipping.

From the designer's perspective, marketing introduces a number of parameters that need to be accommodated. These include:

- The size of the *player base.*
- The width of the *newbie flow.*
- *Churn, retention, sink* and *drift.*

Let's take a quick look at these.

A *player base* (or *user base*) is the stable part of the current population of a virtual world. It's important because the larger it is, the more popular the virtual world is, and therefore, the better it is likely to be believed to be. Comparing the sizes of users bases is notoriously

---

[46] Wholesale redesigns sometimes happen in expansions, irrespective of whether there's a design reason that justifies them.

[47] Well, why not to design for demographics, anyway.

[48] Despite the name, these are rarely good to have.

difficult, though, because companies tend to publish the figures that make their player base (or their profits) look healthiest – that's when they publish them at all. Although established metrics do exist, they're not always informative from a player's perspective. Which is better, the number of daily active users or the number of monthly active users? Should those users be unique or aggregated? Which is more useful to know, the average session length or the average session count over some time period?

I mentioned when discussing scale that players feel the size of a virtual world subjectively; this is also the case with the magnitude of its player base. There may be a million players having a blast in China, but if you're playing on a server in France, you could still feel that the virtual world is underpopulated. The number of users playing right now at the same time you're playing will perhaps be the most relevant figure for you, but the geography of the virtual world also plays a part: a vast virtual world with 5,000 users could feel empty; a compact virtual world with 500 users could feel overcrowded. Fortunately, the physical size of a virtual world is under the direct control of its designer, so an ideal population density can be calculated then an appropriate number of different shards set up to deliver this.

A *newbie flow* is a relatively regular stream of new players that are trying out a particular virtual world. Its source can be word-of-mouth, publicity, gimmickry, search or any number of other cumulative factors. If it's under the control of an external agent who could direct it elsewhere, it becomes a *newbie hose*[49]. This is not something we see a lot of nowadays; there might be a surge while an influencer is playing, but that invariably won't last.

A virtual world expecting a large newbie flow must be designed such that the new arrivals don't interfere with each other's play as they learn the ropes; a virtual world expecting a small newbie flow must be designed such that it doesn't immediately appear to be a desolate wasteland devoid of intelligent life. Put succinctly, you want newbies coming from a large flow not to get in each other's way, but you want newbies coming from a small flow to get in each other's way.

Note that the diameter of your newbie flow is not necessarily fixed, so you could need to accommodate different volumes dynamically. When school is out, there may be an expansion; when school is in, there may be a contraction. One way of handling this is to have tutorial zones that don't feed into the main game until the players have got the hang of things; another way is to have instanced, single-player tutorials, which work well just so long as you warn the players that these *are* single-player.

Churn and retention are related concepts. *Churn* is a measure of the rate at which players leave your virtual world over a set time period. Irritatingly, in non-subscription games, it's hard to tell what "leave" truly means, as you never know whether someone has actually left or not; as a statistical measurement, though, churn remains useful. Basically, you look at how many players you have (using your favoured metric) over some set time period and then compare that to the amount you had (using the same metric) over the previous period.

---

[49] The paradigmatic example, which I mentioned earlier in passing, is when AOL directed vast numbers of newbies at the text MUDs it was hosting.

Divide the former by the latter and express it as a percentage: that gives you *retention*; subtract retention from 100% and that gives you *churn*.

Virtual worlds usually look at monthly (*day 30*) or three-monthly (*day 90*) churn, but games that don't demand such a large time investment of their players will be more interested in *day 1* and *day 7* retention. Also, because virtual worlds can sometimes acquire more players than they lose, their operators prefer to consider churn at the level of individuals rather than overall. Retention for them is not the number of people who played this month divided by the number who played last month: it's the number of people who played this month divided by the number of those *same* individuals who also played last month.[50]

For example, suppose you had 100,000 players last month. 5,000 of them left, but you got 15,000 new players. Your retention is 95% and your churn is 5%. Also, your *acquisition rate* (new players this month divided by total players last month[51]) is 15% and your *growth rate* (players gained minus players lost, divided by total players last month) is 10%. Without tracking individuals, your churn would be −10% – somewhat undermining the spirit of the concept.

So long as the number of newbies coming down in your flow at least equals the number of players lost through churn, your virtual world is viable. When players are lost faster than they are gained, that's when those who remain perceive a drop in the virtual world's popularity (and often in their own enjoyment, too). It could reach a tipping point, following which players leave in droves, or it could be a more steady exodus. Either way, if nothing is done to plug the leaks then eventually only a residue of die-hard players will be left, who won't leave except under external pressure. If that's enough to keep your virtual world operational, fine; if not, it's just a matter of time before you close it down.

Ideally, virtual worlds attract players simply because they're good. When existing players decide not to play then either the virtual world is no longer for them, or they're being attracted by one that promises to be even better, or they have a new interest or demand on their time (for example, a real-life baby). Whatever, the players in question are making a judgement about your MMO: you should accept that. The correct response is to improve your game's design. The incorrect response is to train an AI to spot patterns in player behaviour that precede an exit, then use this to tip you off about when to leap in and try to persuade the players to stay. You can ask them what's wrong, that's fine – it's not easy to obtain data concerning *why* players leave, and they may appreciate their being asked (so long as they're not a false positive). If you try to bribe them to stick around, though, we won't get better virtual worlds, just more disgruntled players.

Sink and drift are old terms little-used these days except among designers. They refer to the *reasons* that players leave. *Sink* typically happens to newbies: they try the virtual world, never fully engage with it, then sink without trace. *Drift* typically happens to oldbies: they play the virtual world for a long time but their interest gradually wanes and they drift away. Sink is about why people want to play; drift is about why they stop wanting to play.

---

[50] All these figures are invariably expressed as percentages, so assume the results of the divisions are multiplied by 100.

[51] Last month, because dividing by total players this month will usually result in a smaller figure and so look less impressive.

Contrary to what is often believed, most players don't rage quit (or if they do, they'll be back within a couple of weeks). Rather, they lose their connection with the virtual world, or failed to connect to it in the first place. The players who complain the loudest are the ones who care most passionately: they complain because they see threats to their game or their community – no way are they going to quit! External factors aside, they'll only quit if they feel they are taken for granted or they see their pessimistic predictions coming true.

We'll be considering more about the attractiveness or otherwise of the player base when we look at community in Chapter 20.

4.14 PHILOSOPHY

From a player's perspective, philosophy is a wishy-washy characteristic of virtual worlds. From a designer's perspective, it's of immense importance. Essentially, it asks: what is the virtual world about? What are you, the designer, trying to say through your design? What's the virtual world's artistic spine?

I'll be discussing this more in Volume II, but for the moment, it's enough to note that what the designer is trying to say is of less immediate influence on players than how this manifests itself. For example, a designer trying to express concepts of togetherness and friendship might do so by including content to be consumed by groups – but so might a designer saying something about party politics, or criminal gangs, or herd mentality.[52] If you like group play, you might choose to play either kind of virtual world; it's only later, when the gameplay has started to work its subtle magic, that you would start to develop a sense for what it's conveying and form a vague impression of how you feel about it. As a way to characterise virtual worlds, philosophy is therefore more for experienced players who have some notion of how to read them than it is for newbies.

I'll also add the following point, though, in case I haven't made it clear. Your virtual world belongs to *you*, the designer. It doesn't belong to the players and it certainly doesn't belong to me. Players remember the virtual worlds that are different, not the ones that are the same. Obviously I want you to read this book, but I don't want you to swallow it whole-sale: if you don't like the taste of something, spit it out; if you like the taste but it doesn't go well with what you have, spit it out; if you think something else would taste better, try it. Paradigms exist for a reason, but you should always question them.

Understand and assimilate what others think, but think for yourself. Find your voice, then use it. Don't use mine, don't use that of other designers, don't use your employer's: use *yours*.

4.15 AGE

The final notable characteristic of a virtual world that can influence a player's decision as to whether or not to play it is its age. For how long has the virtual world been running?

New virtual worlds make new promises. In general, they deliver on these, but they're easy to misread. Players want innovation, but what looks to be inventive could just be gimmicky. Superficial appeal may or may not translate into depth; obvious depth may or may

---

[52] Or indeed all three, given the amount of overlap between them.

not translate into gameplay. Designers may seek to be bold, but could instead be reckless. Almost certainly, any new virtual world is going to be unfinished; whether this is exciting or frustrating depends on the player. The same applies to the initial dearth of documentation and how-to videos available.

When a virtual world emerges in a completed state, it's usually because it's been developed and operated in another territory for some time before making it to yours. In other words, it's new to you but not *new*. It's also possible that it's a production-line world that iterates on the previous one in the series and will itself be iterated upon by its successor – like an expansion, but without the base content (and without taking player characters with it, too). Players of such worlds want a degree of familiarity and don't expect longevity; the age of the virtual world doesn't matter to them, because they know it won't live long anyway once its replacement has become established.[53]

Aging virtual worlds will have stood the test of time, so must have had something going for them at some point. If they remain vibrant and in receipt of developer attention, that's a good sign that they still do. However, the retention-by-expansion doctrine means that often they become crufty and their design loses its focus. New ideas can be picked up by later games, so that what once appeared sassy can now seem jaded. State-of-the-art graphics become past-state-of-the-art.[54] Social structures may become fossilised, so that finding friends becomes impossible; then again, fresh blood may be keenly sought-after, so new players are welcomed with genuine enthusiasm.

Fashions change, too. What was once popular may no longer be popular simply because players have, for the moment, moved on.

Most commercial virtual worlds that begin development don't make it to launch, and although some that do probably shouldn't have, the fact that they did is a point in their favour. Having launched, a virtual world can remain profitable with surprisingly few players – even AAA standard games can often get by with a player base as low as 5,000 once they've made back their development costs. There are some real gems out there if you care to look.[55]

If virtual worlds are to progress, we do need new ones; however, old ones also must remain viable, so that publishers can see that their investment will bring returns for many years. Designers of new virtual worlds must nevertheless look at old ones, so they can understand what *is* new. Likewise, designers of old virtual worlds must look at new ones, so they can see what they have to add to keep their world current.

As for players, well whether an old world is preferable to a new one or *vice versa* depends on the player. It is a characteristic they will consider, but its value is specific to the individual, not to players in general.

Aside: the First Edition of this book listed seven popular MUDs that were written 1993 or earlier and which were still running. Four of them are *still* running: *Medievia* (Smith et al., 1991), *BatMUD* (Frösen, 1990), *The Void* (Lindus, 1989) and of course *MUD1* (Trubshaw & Bartle, 1978).

---

[53] This approach is far more prevalent in China than in the West, for those Western readers wondering why they haven't come across it themselves.

[54] This is a reason why text worlds can live for extraordinarily long times: text ages much slower than graphics.

[55] I'll defend *The Secret World* to my dying breath.

4.16 CONFIGURATION

I once bought a huge bag of jelly beans boasting a range of maybe 50 or more flavours. A sheet of recipes came with them for mixing up new flavours (three apples plus one cinnamon makes apple pie, for example[56]). After trying some of these, I experimented on my own. I have to tell you, liquorice and peanut butter do not go together. The thing is, I really like liquorice and don't mind peanut butter either, but the two together created something quite staggeringly awful.

So it is with characteristics of virtual worlds. A player might look at a virtual world, go down their mental checklist of things they like and things they dislike, and find a great match. When they play the world, though, the combination of features could be a dreadful mess.[57] Similarly, they might avoid a virtual world because it checks one of their "no way!" checkboxes, but the way the rest of the world is configured renders this irrelevant.[58]

The components of virtual worlds are not orthogonal to one other. They're inter-related. The picture they paint together is dependent on all the colours used. This combination, this mix of ingredients, is what makes one virtual world distinct from all other virtual worlds.

It does people good to test their boundaries on occasion. If you don't know what challenges you, you can't learn from it.

---

[56] I loathe cinnamon, so won't eat apple pies unless I'm assured there's no cinnamon in them – and no, restaurant staff, "hardly any" is not the same as "none". In the USA, cinnamon seems to accompany so many apple products that I'm not sure apple-growers there don't cultivate cinnamon-flavour apples to save cooks the bother of adding it.

[57] Exhibit 1: *WildStar*.

[58] Exhibit 2: *LegendMUD*.

CHAPTER 5

Content and Meaning

I'VE USED THE TERM *content* multiple times[1] in this book so far but have yet to explain what I mean by it. This is often the case when designers talk about content: *they* know what they're referring to, but it's not necessarily obvious to everyone else.

In essence, if players are regarded as consumers, content is what they consume through play. It's that which the virtual world provides to hold players' interest.

This is from a designer's perspective. A lawyer might regard content entirely in terms of copyrightable material. A journalist could focus solely on fiction and story. A player may not see any content beyond the kind that interests them personally.

I'm discussing content in this early chapter not because I feel that understanding its expression is a prerequisite to understanding broad aspects of virtual world design; rather, it's because the different *modes* of expression are such prerequisites. As an analogy, if you want a 2D image of a flower then there are a number of options available to you (drawing one, painting one, photographing one, getting an AI diffusion model to create one, making a collage of one, flattening a buttercup and tracing it, …). Your choice of technique would constrain what the image *could* look like, but not determine what it *would* look like; aspects of the visual appearance of the image (composition, lighting, colour palette and so on) would need separate consideration.[2]

So it is with virtual worlds. Although in due course I will be examining the kinds of content that typically appear (or in some cases, appeared long ago) in virtual worlds, all these depend on the manner in which content is introduced into virtual worlds. It's not about what the content is, but how it gets there – the various *sources* of content. These, you do need to be aware of in advance of further discussions.

Before we look at content in detail, let's begin with an overview of something it's strongly associated with and often confused with: gameplay.

---

[1] Over 60 times, at least until members of the publisher's editing team pull out their knives.

[2] They may also cause you to revise your decision of which technique to use; this is not a unidirectional relationship.

 DOI: 10.1201/9781003689638-5

5.1 GAMEPLAY

Content is related to – but isn't the same thing as – *gameplay*.[3] All virtual worlds have content, but not all of them are games and therefore not all of them have gameplay. Gameplay is the means by which the virtual world itself introduces goals for the players to pursue. As a *very* brief overview[4]:

- Anything that's part of a game but has no impact on gameplay is *cosmetic*. The model weapons in the game *Cluedo*[5] (Pratt, 1949) are only there to add to the atmosphere; *Cluedo*'s gameplay is unchanged if they are removed.

- A game's pieces (anything that can act or be acted upon) are its *tokens*; they're sometimes called *entities* in a programming context.

- A game's *dressing* is the external context attached to its tokens, actions and cosmetic elements. Those aren't wooden cylinders, they're gangsters; that's not a stats[6] boost, it's a potion of strength.

- The statements dictating what can and cannot be done to its tokens are a game's *rules*. Any rules that are subject to rules are also tokens.[7]

- *Features*[8] emerge from tensions between rules that recommend different courses of action. Treasure is good but death is bad: do I attack the galleon? Swords are good but so is armour: which do I buy with my windfall?

- Rules and features together form the game's *mechanics*. Mechanics are the moving parts of a game, giving actions causality. Be aware that some other definitions of the term also have currency,[9] but I use the traditional one.

- *Gameplay* emerges by means of charting a course through the constraints and possibilities of the game's mechanics to achieve the player's goals.

Note that games can have different amounts of gameplay. For example, among card games, *Snap* has less gameplay than *Bridge*. Just because gameplay structures content, that doesn't mean such structuring is always of the same complexity or complicatedness.

Gameplay has a meta-relationship with content. It wields great power, and because it carries the artistic burden of games, it determines the nature of their content. It isn't

---

[3] I've only mentioned the term *gameplay* around 40 times before defining it (*pace* the editors' despair).

[4] The discussion that follows is based on the analysis in Rollings & Morris (2003).

[5] It's known as *Clue* in most countries.

[6] In RPG terms, *stats* are the basic numbers that define a character or object in terms of how it interacts with the game's mechanics. Although the word derives from *vital statistics* (as used in beauty contests back in prehistoric times), that connection is long broken, and stats are now understood to be the set of primary differentiators between related entities (characters, weapons, armour, *etc.*) in-world.

[7] This is heavily exemplified by the game *Nomic* (Suber, 1990).

[8] There are two kinds of features. The ones I'm describing here are design features; unique selling points ("realistic graphics", "unique quest system") are commercial features.

[9] Sometimes, the term *mechanics* refers to mechanisms (Hunicke et al., 2004); sometimes, it refers to tokens that can create gameplay when the player interacts with them (Rogers, 2014).

content itself, though, any more than travel is a journey or narration is a story. Gameplay is form; content is substance.[10] That doesn't mean there aren't different ways to create this substance, though.

5.2 PROPERTIES OF CONTENT

Clearly there are different kinds of content (Fantasy isn't the same as Horror, for example), but there are also different ways of bringing content into being. It's these that I shall be discussing here.

These different methods of producing content have different properties (otherwise they wouldn't be different), but some share characteristics with each other. Important defining properties include[11]:

- *Emergent* content is content created implicitly by interactions between systems, players and each other.

- *Direct* content is content created explicitly to be content.

- *Freeform* content is content that can potentially break the fiction of the virtual world at the dressing or tokens level. Depending on how free it is, it may also be able to break gameplay.

- *Contextual* content is content that does not break the fiction of the virtual world.

All four of these properties are effectively binary: each source of content either has or doesn't have the property. Furthermore, it will be one of each mutually exclusive pair (direct or emergent, freeform or contextual).

Content is also sometimes described as being *designed* if a designer designed it. This is because all contextual content is either designed, emergent or both.[12] The opposing term, *undesigned*, is rarely encountered.

Content sources can have other properties that lie more along a sliding scale. In particular, they can have different degrees of *stickiness*. Stickiness is a vague measure of how willing a player is to repeat content. There are non-vague measurements favoured by data analysts, calculated by (say) dividing the number of daily active users by the number of monthly active users, but from a designer's perspective, stickiness is more to do with how players feel about coming back to content than how often they interact with it in practice.[13]

As a non-game example, a joke isn't sticky: you don't generally want to hear it more than once. Music, however, is sticky: some people will listen to the same piece on repeat all evening, and almost everyone with hearing will periodically return to old favourites throughout their lives. As for which of bingeing or grazing better indicates the stickiness

---

[10] More prosaically, if gameplay is bones, content is flesh on those bones.

[11] "Include" is what academics put when they suspect they may have missed something obvious.

[12] See Bartle (2022) for the proof.

[13] Players may, for example, interact with something repeatedly just to be done with it, while hating every moment. This is known as *grinding*.

of content, well a data analyst might go with the former and a designer the latter; it depends on what you want from the term.

I've blithely asserted several times that there are different ways of bringing content into being. It's now time to look at these sources of content.

5.3 SOURCES OF CONTENT

There are six main[14] sources of content in virtual worlds:

- *Systems* Content
- *Procedurally Generated* Content (PGC)
- *User-Generated* Content (UGC)
- *User-Created* Content (UCC)
- *Hand-Crafted* Content (HCC)
- *Refereed* Content (also known as *Game-Mastered* Content, GMC)

Let's examine these individually.

Systems content is the default content, hence its lack of a three-letter acronym (TLA). It is designed such that it emerges from interactions between the virtual world and its players. Systems content underpins all the other forms of contents, as it implements the virtual world's physics; sandbox worlds lean heavily on it. Bugs aside, it's contextual: by definition, anything it allows is an established part of the virtual world's fiction. In a game world, it's the product of the mechanics. If its systems content isn't sticky, the virtual world is doomed.

Procedurally generated content is constructed algorithmically to programmed specifications. As such, it is emergent and contextual. It's popular among developers because it can create large amounts of token-level content with great rapidity, although it does tend to have issues with variety (a billion NPCs, all basically the same – that kind of thing), which gives it low stickiness. The increasing use of AI techniques for procedurally generating games content (Shaker et al., 2016) has mitigated this somewhat, and new diffusion models are expected to help enormously (although they're opaque, so hard to specify). Procedural content generation (PCG[15]) is especially useful for virtual worlds set in the vastness of space: *EVE Online*, *Elite Dangerous* and *No Man's Sky* are the primary examples.

User-generated content and user-created content are often mixed up, to the extent that the terms are sometimes used interchangeably. There is, however, a difference. *User-generated content* is the intangible content that emerges from interactions between users. It's free-form, but whether it's contextual or not depends on the players (on a role-playing server, it usually is; on other servers, some will be, some won't be). Designers can't force it, they can only encourage it. A good example of user-generated content is competitive PvP combat, but it can also be co-operative (as in *New World*'s elite chest runs). In general, this source

---

[14] "Main" is another word academics use when they're worried they might have overlooked something.
[15] Yes, the act of creating PGC is PCG.

of content is relatively inexpensive to implement if sometimes expensive to manage. Being largely at the gameplay level, it's very sticky for those who engage with it.

User-created content differs from user-generated content in that it's explicit: it's content created by players, for players. Those who have formal building privileges (which usually means pretty well everyone for virtual worlds with UCC) create whatever they like directly, whether it's within context or not; it's therefore generally limited to social worlds, where it doesn't matter if you create a zeppelin that looks in need of a bra. That doesn't mean that the user-created content itself has to allow user-created content, of course: *Roblox*, for example, is all about user-created content, but the sub-worlds created within it don't have to follow suit. UCC is inexpensive (for the developer) and can be fun (for the player) in a non-game world; in a game world, however, unless the player doing the creation has some design ability, even within context, the result will be content that either showers the player in rewards or is a death-trap.[16] That only holds if the game is played *within* the world and not *with* the world, though: a meta-game, in which the idea was to wreck or to enhance the creations of other players, could perhaps make sense.[17]

Hand-crafted (or *scripted*) *content* is the hallmark of theme-park worlds. It's direct, contextual and designed. It's also expensive, because it requires each piece to be constructed individually by someone who knows what they're doing; also, a large amount of it is called-for, because individually it's not sticky (although collectively it is). It's generally of a high quality and is able to convey subtleties impossible using cheaper methods. That said, such is the rate at which it's consumed that tool-wielding designers can slowly run out of ideas; if not perked up, the content will then begin to slide in the direction of boring. It's almost entirely at the level of tokens and dressing.

Refereed content is what used to be known as *game-mastered content* before people noticed that this term was gendered. It's designed (often by the referee) and although in theory it's freeform, in practice it's almost always contextual as the referee is endeavouring to produce content that's canonical. Refereed content is both the most expensive and the most high-quality source of content. It involves select groups of players engaging with content that's under the live, direct control of the referee – a bit like with tabletop RPGs such as *D&D*. It's slightly better than hand-crafted content in terms of stickiness, because the content is not entirely fixed and can change dynamically depending on what the players do. Its main disadvantage is that it is not remotely scalable and needs a lot of flexibility, so it tends to be the domain of text MUDs such as *Achaea* rather than of large-scale graphical worlds.

5.4 SUBSTITUTE CONTENT

In the same way that games can have different amounts of gameplay, virtual worlds can have different amounts of content. With non-game worlds, that's where the observation ends; with game worlds, however, the way that the content is structured (by the gameplay) will affect the player's perception of its size. A game with so many things to do that

---

[16] I outline why in Volume II.

[17] This was the premiss of the IOWA virtual world *Chaos World of Wizards*. As noted earlier, it was so successful at this that it was not a success among players.

it overwhelms the player would feel as if it had too much content – but so would one with a single, enormously long series of things-to-do from which the player couldn't stray. Too much content falls into the category of "a nice problem to have", though: the usual issue is that a game has too little content, with players feeling that they don't have anything meaningful to do.

As a general rule, the amount of content in any art form tends to correlate with the length of time it takes for an individual to work their way through it. Players will ask how many hours of gameplay a game has (by which they mean how long it takes to play it from beginning to end), usually equating more hours with a more valuable experience. If your game doesn't have much gameplay, though, you may be tempted to pad it out.

Substitute gameplay gives players choices that are effectively meaningless. It doesn't matter that there are 30 different kinds of sword, each with five different levels of proficiency, if the differences between them are effectively negligible. It doesn't matter whether you choose the dialogue option to show sympathy or coldness to the frightened NPC if some integer this increments or decrements is barely consulted. It doesn't matter if you take the long, easy route or the short, difficult route if they both lead to the same boss who drops items far more powerful than anything you'll find on the way.

Substitute gameplay aims to give players the impression that they have more agency than they actually have. Substitute content, on the other hand, aims to give them the impression that they are doing more than they are actually doing.

Substitute content can originate with any source, although it's most often hand-crafted. It *is*, formally, content – but content that's wholly unsatisfying. If you regard regular content as a hearty meal, substitute content is sawdust: sure, you can eat it, but you'd really rather not. It's there to occupy players while bringing them no benefit. In a game context, it can be even worse than this, getting in the way of other content in a manner that adds nothing to gameplay.

This doesn't sound as if it's a good idea. Why, then, would a designer include substitute content rather than meaningful or fun content?

Well, it's a lot quicker and easier to create substitute content than it is to create wider content. In the same way that false choices in a dialogue tree act as filler to give the player the impression that their actions have consequences, substitute content gives the player something to do at much less cost to the developer. Merely making tasks more time-consuming than pacing decrees is necessary will work.

The classic example of substitute content is the quest hub that's an irritatingly long walk away, which came to prominence in the Fifth Age and was refined in the Sixth. *Lost Ark* is particularly good at this: you enter the palace (it's usually a palace) and then there's 30 seconds of nothing but movement as you run to the quest-giving or quest-receiving NPC. *FFXIV* was notorious for repeatedly sending new players back and forth to a tiresome-to-get-to headquarters; it took until patch 5.3 for the designers to concede that this might be somewhat more of an annoying sink than they'd intended.

Other forms of substitute content include half-hour mazes, over-long animations for common actions, NPCs who blather on interminably about nothing, 20-move jumping puzzles that make you restart if you fail even jump 20, crafting as button-mashing,

30-minutes-too-long cut scenes, mobs with stupidly low drop rates for essential quest items, quests that break down into interminable numbers of trivial steps, … basically anything that's more about the time it takes to complete it than the fun to be had completing it.

Gameplay substitutes involve giving players inconsequential choices. Content substitutes involve giving players inconsequential tasks. Next time you're told that the world is about to end, but "before you save it, could you just put this flower on a remote shrine please?", you'll recognise the pattern.

In summary, then, content is what players consume. Virtual worlds need a lot of content – far, far more than do regular computer games. There are several ways that content can be created, not all of which are compatible with other aspects of a virtual world's design. Designers design gameplay and so shape the content (whereas level designers only design content).

Oh, speaking of designers…

5.5 MEANING

So far in this book, we've looked at:

- the definition of common terms used in virtual worlds;
- the heritage of virtual worlds;
- the characteristics that distinguish virtual worlds from one another;
- the manner in which those characteristics are embodied as substance.

There's one more concept that needs to be introduced before we can begin to dig into the practicalities, however.

What is it that virtual worlds are *about*?

It's a running theme in this book that virtual world design is an art form. As will also become apparent, there's a lot of craft involved as well, but ultimately, the designer is *saying* something through their design. Whether this is being said to the players, to other designers, to the wider world or to the designer themself is a matter of choice, but the fact is that something *is* being said. How could it not be?

One person's substance is another person's form. Working backwards: players turn their experiences into play; level designers turn content into experiences; designers turn gameplay into content; lead designers turn expression into gameplay. OK, so all designers can operate at all levels, and not all virtual worlds have gameplay anyway, but nevertheless, a chain of subjectivity and objectivity is always present and always allows for creativity in every link.

This chain is longer for games than it is for most other art forms, which means it's less immediate. For example, in poetry, the reader's here-and-now is their substance and their form is the text; for the poet, their substance is the text and their form is the shape of the poem. The art of the poet is expressed mainly in the text, which in the case of poetry includes theme, imagery, allusion and feeling, as constrained by their selection of form.

Overall, it's basically a two-link chain. In game design, however, with an interactive layer making the conversation between designer and player indirect, it's basically a three-link chain.

This can result in some confusion when games are analysed independently, because it's easy to look at the wrong link and so misinterpret substance as form. This explains why so many people who come to game reviewing from, say, a literary background or a media-studies background, focus on the content and can't quite understand why something that looks as if it should be popular isn't (or *vice versa*)[18]; someone coming from a performance background might situate the art in the play and wonder why, despite all the avenues of expression open to them, players are finding an MMO dull.

It also explains why it's often the case that designers can't easily play games for fun. What they need to be experiencing subjectively, they can't help but see objectively. Players still sense the magic, but designers know the magician's tricks. Conversely, designing an MMO requires a level of objectivity that most players don't have (and who can blame them, if the price to be paid for obtaining this objectivity is that games lose their lustre?[19]). Designing is not the same as playing: there's more to designing chocolate bars than eating chocolate bars and deciding which you most like yourself.[20]

In game design, the art must be expressed through the gameplay because that's the only thing games have that no other medium of expression has. Gameplay is determined by the (lead) designer; therefore, it reflects something the designer is trying to express. So, what is that something?

Well, that's a topic primarily for Volume II. It could be about freedom, or fighting for what's right, or companionship, or honour, or compassion, or nurture, or glory, or loss, or escape, or pretty well anything that the designer wants to say and that gameplay can encapsulate.

It can also be a directionless mess. If the design is by committee or by appropriation or by simple pick-and-mix, or if the designer has nothing specific to say other than disparate pockets of unrelated commentary and questions, the virtual world going nowhere. The craft may be excellent, but whatever art there is is at odds with itself. This syndrome is seen a lot with expansions, which can feel bitty in comparison to what went before them. When this happens, players – and indeed designers[21] – will often say that the designer is "out of ideas". The truth is, however, that the designer is out of passion. Either they've said all they wanted to say, or they can't say it in a manner consistent with the gameplay that went before it.

The designer's message pervades the virtual world. It's felt by the players at all levels, from intellectually (through the philosophy of the virtual world) to viscerally (from the

---

[18] I've read reviews that suggested gameplay is merely a form of content, which is somewhat ironic given that gameplay *is* the form of content.

[19] This loss of player-fun is common enough among designers that it has a name: *designeritis* (Koster, 2013). Designers are compensated by designer-fun, which is more cerebral but doesn't last as long. We'll look at designer-fun towards the end of Volume II.

[20] That's why there are chocolate bars with coconut filling in the party-pack mix.

[21] Myself included.

moment-to-moment core loop). It would therefore help if the designer were to be aware of what they wanted to say before they said it.

Unfortunately, that's not how it works. A designer chooses to say what they want to say *through* a virtual world; they can't say it any other way.[22] They can give multiple indications in different formats of what it is they're trying to express, but ultimately, it's going to come down to "just – just play it, just play the damned thing!".

This doesn't mean we can't look at general principles of expression, though. Although I *could* leave this until a later chapter, I'm putting it here because the earlier you understand it, the easier it will be to make sense of virtual world design as a whole.

5.6 ARTISTIC STATEMENT

Any virtual world that has a designer makes an artistic statement. If it doesn't have a designer (perhaps it's entirely procedurally generated) then it doesn't make an artistic statement – although it could *be* an artistic statement (of whoever wrote the procedural-generation software). If it has more than one designer, in the form of a ruling committee, then it may[23] make an artistic statement that's completely anodyne, or indeed several such statements. However, if one person (I've been calling them "the" designer) has overall creative authority then there's a much better chance of getting a design that actually *says* something meaningful.

I do realise that talking vapidly about nebulous concepts such as "artistic statement" and "message" doesn't really convey what these really *are*, so some examples of top-level messages might help:

- *World of Warcraft*. Be awesome.
- *EVE Online*. You are what you do.
- *Final Fantasy XIV*. Life is other people.
- *The Secret World*. You hold reality together.
- *Conan Exiles*. You have inner strength.
- *MUD*. Be and become yourself.

These may look like marketing slogans, but they're not: they're what the gameplay is saying to the player.[24]

Sorry? Did you disagree with some? You think they're about something else? Well that's great news! It means you're already attuned to reading virtual worlds. Just because *I* see it one way, that doesn't mean it's the *right* way. The rest of this chapter – the rest of this book – is going to be a lot easier for you.

---

[22] "If I could say it in words, there would be no reason to paint" – widely attributed to Edward Hopper, but I haven't managed to unearth the original source so it may just be hearsay.
[23] This is my polite, English way of saying "will".
[24] Or at least what it was saying originally, before it was scrambled by later, mishandled expansions.

If you still don't know what I'm trying to describe here, don't worry: it will come.

The artistic statement of an MMO is that which the designer is saying to the player through its gameplay and through all that follows from its gameplay. *Everything* flows from the artistic statement. It's the *soul* of the virtual world. Sure, if there are business requirements then an artistic statement should be chosen that fits them, but it shouldn't be shoehorned into them: it would feel like, and would be, a hack.

Similarly, if you compromise your artistic statement to please your intended audience, you're losing its sense of purpose. Consider what you want to say to your audience then say it, don't make concessions so it better matches what you think they want to hear. If you foresee a response that alarms you, say something different, don't say the same thing in honeyed gameplay: the players won't be fooled.

In essence: know your players and know what you want to say to them, then say it.

Whatever message your gameplay is carrying, you need to be aware of it. You don't need to know what it means in words, but you do need to know what it *means*. For example, if your gameplay compartmentalises player characters into inflexible roles, you're saying something about narrowness and conformity and security – regardless of whether you intended to or not.[25]

Sometimes, designers fret that their gameplay may be unnecessarily alienating. The key word there is "unnecessarily": it's fine for your gameplay to be alienating if that's what you want. No game can appeal to everyone. The trade-off is between a message so particular or exclusive that few people will care to hear it and a message that's so shallow and inclusive that few people will care about having heard it. There is some leeway here, in that you can often change the language of the message to make it more accessible while not substantially altering the message. For example, if you want to make a point about the beauty of nature then that's going to go down better in a medieval setting than a cyberpunk setting, simply because the players who are attracted to these genres tend to have contrasting attitudes about how marvellous trees are.

You can't tell different players different things in the same virtual world. Well, you *can*, but then then you have a hub and a set of disconnected sub-worlds. In the context of an MMO, occasional mini-games *can* carry different, self-contained messages, but ones that are common (the crafting mini-game, the combat mini-game, the farming mini-game, …) should firmly align with your overall artistic statement. It's no use creating a game that's trying to say something about how the rich exploit the poor if you have an auction house mini-game that says exactly the opposite. If your virtual world is making a heartfelt plea to take global warming seriously, don't give players the option to strip-mine it of resources to serve their own economic ends. Think about what your systems are saying; if they don't fit the artistic statement, drop them – no matter how cool or seductive you believe they are.

In summary, your artistic statement is a sense of what you want to say to your players. Use it to inform your design decisions. If there's a hard choice to be made, defer to your

---

[25] If your immediate response to this is "well players can easily change character class", you haven't understood.

artistic statement. A virtual world that doesn't reflect an artistic statement has no spine. A virtual world that has no spine is just a blob of flesh.[26]

This book may be of interest to non-designers, but principally, it talks to designers (specifically, to designers of virtual worlds). Note that having the word "designer" in your job title doesn't mean you *are* a designer; similarly, not having one doesn't mean you *aren't*. As it happens, the term "non-designers" that I used just now is actually not very helpful: *everyone* is a latent virtual world designer, because everyone is to some degree an artist; whether virtual worlds are your preferred medium of self-expression or not is the *only* thing that determines whether you're a self-realised virtual world designer. Your virtual world doesn't even have to be implemented, it only has to be designed (because that's what designers do: design).

It might help if what you design *could* actually be implemented, though.

---

[26] Or, if it's all negatives and no positives, a blob of goop inside an inflexible exoskeletal container.

CHAPTER 6

Development

I T WOULD BE WONDERFUL if designers only had to design their virtual world and then could press a button to cause it to come into being. Unfortunately, even if you close your eyes and wish *really hard*, this isn't how it currently works. Virtual worlds need to be constructed to run on hardware that has finite capabilities, by actual people[1] operating in an uncompromising social, legal and business environment within a given budget and time frame. None of these factors affect what can be *designed*, but they all affect what can be *implemented*. Therefore, if a virtual world designer wishes to see their design realised[2] then they need to account for these constraints on what, in practice, can be launched as a playable world.

Bespoke virtual worlds take a long time to make. They are large endeavours. The process of creating them is called *development*, and those individuals who develop them (including designers) are called *developers*. Often, as a synecdoche, the organisation employing developers is referred to as *the developer*, which is reasonable but can be confusing.[3]

This is not a book about development. Extrapolating from the sample of n = 1 that is me, designers regard development in general as boring; if they liked it, they'd be producers, not designers. What this means for this book is that although I'll be presenting an outline of virtual world development practicalities, I'll avoid going into minutiae. The major factors that affect and inform design will be discussed, but not the riveting, spellbinding details. If you do wish to explore these then there are excellent books that thoroughly address the topic.[4]

6.1 THE STUDIO

Virtual worlds are developed using pretty well the same set-up and processes that are used for developing regular computer games, albeit with different emphases.

---

[1] Contrary to what some TV channels might have you believe, programmers in general and game developers in particular *are*, in fact, actual people.

[2] I guess that should be *virtualised*.

[3] Compare "developers aren't paid enough" with "developers don't pay enough".

[4] The *Game Development Essentials* series (Novak, 2022) is very accessible, and I also recommend *The Game Production Handbook* (Chandler, 2013).

DOI: 10.1201/9781003689638-6

The landscape of game development is awash with categorisations that are in common use in the industry, but which aren't immediately obvious. I'll therefore clarify some terms before I describe how game (and therefore virtual world) development companies are organised.

So, games are developed by *development studios*. Companies that fund the development and distribution of computer games are called *publishers*. Companies that manufacture the platform the game runs on (a console, for example) are called *hardware manufacturers*.

A manufacturer that develops and publishes games for its own platform is a *first-party developer*. A developer contracted by a manufacture to develop games that said manufacturer will publish exclusively on their platform is a *second-party developer*. When a publisher that isn't a manufacturer publishes a game from a studio it doesn't own, that studio is a *third-party developer*. Relative to the publisher, a second-party or third-party developer is an *external developer*; a developer owned by the publisher is an *in-house* or *internal developer*. A development studio that doesn't have a recognised publisher is an *independent developer* or *indie*. An indie is effectively its own publisher.

Some publishers own in-house development studios as subsidiaries. For example, Amazon Games Orange County (the studio that developed *New World*) is part of Amazon Games (its publisher), which in turn is part of Amazon (a vast conglomerate that tries to sell me things I've already bought); it's therefore an in-house studio. The same does not apply, however, to City State Entertainment, the developer of *Camelot Unchained*; City State is self-publishing its own virtual world, so is regarded as an indie rather than an in-house publisher (although it wouldn't be an indie if it also funded third-party developers).

A studio, then, is a self-contained game-development unit with some degree of autonomy operating within a single management structure. Its relationship to its funders is relevant for situating it in an industry context, but it's within a studio (or, for some enormous in-house projects, a network of studios) that all the development action takes place.

Although a studio *can* usually work on more than one game at once, virtual worlds need so much care and attention that they tend to dominate, which makes it difficult for the studio to work on other projects. It's why in June 2023 Electronic Arts (publisher) revealed that the ongoing development and operation of *Star Wars: the Old Republic* was being moved from BioWare (internal studio) to Broadsword Online Games[5] (external developer), so that BioWare could concentrate on single-player games.

Although publishers (including hardware manufacturers) do set up their own studios from scratch occasionally, most of the studios they own started out as independents that the publisher bought. This is an important lesson for independents: your product isn't the game you're making, it's the company itself.[6] Very few people who build a start-up make a fortune from selling products; they make it from selling the start-up.

Right, let's look at how a development studio is set up.

---

[5] Broadsword had already made a success of taking over development of the ageing properties *Ultima Online* and *Dark Age of Camelot*.

[6] I'd like to claim this is my own observation, but it isn't. I got it off David Whatley, founder of the *GemStone][* developer, Simutronics.

At root, making a virtual world is a software engineering project. Everyday software houses that write code for washing machines, cranes, televisions and heart monitors are usually organised along functional lines similar to those of other engineering companies. At the top is the company executive leadership, below which are divisions that handle particular areas of activity: revenue and marketing; finance and accounting; research and development (R&D); operations and information technology (IT); administration and human resources (HR). Sometimes, these may be subdivided (sales could be separate from marketing, for example) or expanded (marketing could become marketing and public relations, perhaps), and large companies will often have their own legal department, too, but the basic architecture remains fairly constant.

In addition, there will be at least one additional, specialist division that deals with the type of product the company makes. Normally, this would be a manufacturing division of some kind, but for a software house, it means product *development* – which is traditionally part of R&D. Development is therefore separated from R&D in software houses.

A lot goes on within the development division. If the software house handles many products, they will each be assigned to a *section* (often known as a *team*) within the development division. Unless the products are very similar, these sections will have their own support and quality assurance (QA) needs, so each team will have sub-sections to address these. When there are many established product lines, each line can be treated as an independent development division; this makes them easier to spin off as a separate company if needs dictate.

Whether there is a separate section for product specification or not depends on the nature of the company. A software house developing its own products for sale will definitely need one, but if it exists primarily to service the needs of external companies (as would perhaps an app developer) or of other parts of the same corporation (the business development unit of a bank, say) then most of the specification will already have been done and the rest can be handled by the team that will be developing the product.

Game development studios generally adhere to this template, but will definitely have a section for product specification (design) and will also add sections for art and animation and perhaps audio. Larger companies, such as those making virtual worlds, will have separate sections for analytics and localisation. As before, this isn't hard-and-fast, and it depends on the kind of games the company makes. Art and animation could be two sections rather than one, for example; user experience (UX) might be taken out of design and made into a section of its own. QA is also often given section status, so it can operate independently of individual projects. All these sections typically co-operate much more than in a regular software house, by the way – it's not uncommon for artists, designers and programmers to be moved fluidly between teams in response to shifting resource requirements.

I should mention at this point that in everyday software engineering terms, *production* is that part of the development process concerning the preparation of the product for release. However, the term is often used more loosely in the computer games industry to refer to the part of the company that isn't doing hands-on development. It's a muddle, though, because it still retains its original meaning and the boundaries are fuzzy anyway.

Thus, a team doing localisation would be concerned with the production part of development, but a sales force might also off-handedly be referred to as part of production. Just go with the flow.

Virtual world studios are organised the same way that regular game studios are, but they boast a much larger design section, a larger art and animation section and an expanded operations division (including a separate, enormous, support and community management section). QA will be reabsorbed into development, because there's a lot of quality that needs to be assured as development proceeds. As we shall see, though, for a mature project, development itself could effectively become part of operations.

OK, so what does all this mean for the designers of virtual worlds?

Well, half the company is developing the virtual world and half the company is developing the company. However, in the company's upper echelons, there are more divisions concerned with the latter than with the former. This means that development may have to fight to get its voice heard, and design constraints can appear from anywhere. Worse, some of these constraints could be hard to fathom, yet the designer is obliged to accommodate them. Attempts to work around these constraints[7] are often successful, but they can result in disappointments on both sides.[8]

Fifty percent of the jobs in the games industry are in the part of the company not immediately concerned with development. All the excitement – and the reason why most people want to work for a games or virtual world studio in the first place – goes on in development. It's with their fellow developers that game designers interact the most.

6.2 PRE-PRODUCTION

The lifecycle of a virtual world goes through five stages: pre-production, production, roll-out, operation, sunset. Yes, that is another overloading of the term "production" there, and some studios call the second stage "development" or "implementation" to add to the confusion. As I said, go with the flow.

The above five stages can be summarised as follows: plan it, make it, sell it, run it, close it. A virtual world can die at any one of these stages, but only in the last one is it scheduled to do so. There is scope for overlap early on (you can start production of some parts, while others are still in pre-production), but the boundaries are nevertheless fairly distinct.

Different groups of people are involved each step of the way. The ones involved in pre-production constitute the *core team*.

The purpose of the core team is to determine what is to be made, how it is to be made and what resources will be required to make it. It usually involves around four individuals, but other senior developers may also be consulted for their opinions from time to time (particularly the QA lead).

---

[7] Or, in some cases, simply to ignore them.
[8] I wrote the following in an email this morning to a company for which I'm doing some consultancy: "You have given us a map that leads to a swamp. We want to avoid the swamp. You want us to go into the swamp. We don't know why you want us to go into the swamp. When you say OK, give me a route that doesn't go into the swamp, you complain that what we come up with doesn't go into the swamp."

The lucky four are:

1. The *producer*. This is the overall project manager. Indeed, "project manager" is sometimes their job title.

2. The *lead designer* (sometimes *design director*). The person who calls the creative shots and describes what's going to be made.

3. The *lead programmer* (sometimes *technical director*). The person in charge of turning the design into software. Some companies call programmers *engineers* so have a *lead engineer*.

4. The *lead artist* (sometimes *art director*). The person in charge of actualising the design visually.

When other people are brought in for their opinions, they are given a voice but not a say. For example, an assistant producer or combat design lead or concept artist might be asked to comment and probably will be asked to contribute, but they don't get to make the final decisions. Those are the preserve of the core-team members only.

An important point about the core team is that the members need to be able to trust one another. In pre-production, it's the lead designer who has product ownership (that is, final authority as to what goes into the game), but just as you don't want management telling you how to do your job, neither do subject experts want you telling them how to do theirs. It's OK to discuss workarounds and to suggest ways of resolving a problem, but ultimately if the producer, lead programmer or lead artist says you can't have something for reasons to do with producing, programming or artisting, take their word for it and yield.

Film screenwriters don't need to know how to act or to operate a camera, but they do need to know what can be acted and what scenes can be shot. Similarly, designers don't need to know how programmers or artists or producers do their stuff, but they do need to know what stuff can be done. If you want to push at the limits, you stand a better chance of success if you know what those limits are in the first place and why they exist.

Bearing all this in mind, then, here's how the members of the core team work together.

The producer is the project leader and the interface with the rest of the studio, who enforces the hard parameters within which the virtual world will be developed. If your budget is $50m, you don't get to design something that will take $100m to implement.[9] If it's going to be sold as a space opera, you don't get to set it in the Napoleonic era. The producer is also responsible for handling conflict management between the leads, their teams and the world in general.

The (lead) designer creates an initial *treatment* acceptable to the producer, which is then pitched to company management. If it passes muster, the designer is OKed to turn it into a full-scale design doc. Other designers with specific responsibilities will work with the lead designer on this; even so, it could take a year or more for an MMO's design to be ready.[10]

---

[9] Well, not deliberately, anyway.
[10] "Ready" rather than "completed" because game design documents are *never* completed.

Note that in many creative industries, each time a work is passed up the chain for approval, it tends to come back with suggestions for "minor revisions". Some of these may actually be good ideas that the creator happily incorporates. Others may be mediocre ones that can be inserted with partly gritted teeth. Most, however, are bad ideas that even extensive revisions couldn't save, yet if they're not accepted then the project will be cancelled. Although there is some of this unasked-for input in the virtual world industry, it's not as prevalent as it seems to be elsewhere, probably because of the more collegiate atmosphere (*everyone* in the games industry has ideas, so they're used to having them turned down). Besides, the sheer scale of the design work for a virtual world is such that even very bad ideas can often be buried where no one will find them, if indeed they are ever even implanted. I've heard more than one tale of a designer who has wilfully lied to company management in order to implement a concept that was in the designer's view essential but in the CEO's (or in one case, CCO's!) was a mere indulgence.

The pre-production phase is the most important phase in virtual world development because mistakes made here can have potentially irreparable effects on the rest of development. This is why we need designers, although the truth of the fact isn't necessarily immediately obvious. Not everyone can manage teams, not everyone can program, not everyone can do art, not everyone can compose music, not everyone can run server farms: everyone can, however, imagine a virtual world. Why, then, are designers so important?

Well, it's because when a designer messes up, the consequences can be disastrous. You therefore need people who specialise in design to do the designing; they may not be particularly good at design, but they're better than non-designers and they're *especially* better than committees of non-designers. Without a designer, there's a higher chance that seemingly minor misjudgements can lurk undiscovered until the virtual world goes live, whereupon their devastating effects become apparent. At this stage, fixing the cause may be impossible in practice, so only the symptoms can be addressed.

As an example, suppose that your game has an economy in which resources are transformed into goods that are used for obtaining more resources. Let's keep it simple and say resources are ingredients that people who like cooking turn into the food that people who like hunter-gathering need to consume to collect more ingredients. You envisage that some players will prefer the cooking and some will prefer the hunter-gathering. You realise that if insufficient food is crafted, the hunter-gatherers will become frustrated that they can't buy what they want and they'll leave; also, if too much food is crafted, the cooks will become frustrated that they can't sell what they want and they'll leave. However, when you design the game, you don't know what the proportion of cooks to hunter-gatherers you're going to get. One way to address this is to put in subtle ingredient-supply changes so that if the pendulum swings too far one way then the number of resources from which goods can be crafted increases or decreases accordingly. Perhaps if there's not enough food, the amount of ingredients obtained each collection attempt increases; if there's too much, it decreases. Using this kind of negative feedback loop to balance unknown or dynamic factors is a standard mechanic. However, let's suppose that when the game goes live, you find that when there's an under-supply of ingredients, the hunter-gatherers start cooking what they find for themselves so they're assured they'll have what they need. The cooks now have nothing to do, but they don't want to be hunter-gatherers: they're in the game for the crafting, not the combat. They leave.

In the above example, that single, seemingly innocuous idea to make cooking and hunter-gathering be different mini-games to attract different players blew up. It turned out that hunter-gatherers were grudgingly willing to do the cooking to ensure they got the food they wanted, but the cooks weren't willing to become hunter-gatherers. Now imagine it's not just food and ingredients, but every form of resource and every form of crafting and every form of end-user. How are you going to fix that?

This is why design is the most important part of virtual world creation: it has the highest cost of failure.

A common misconception is that the job of a game designer is to design games. It is not. The job of a game designer is to write game design documents. The same principle applies to virtual worlds. An idea alone is worth nothing, despite what wannabe designers may think.[11] That said, ideas expressed in design documents can be valuable. "Vision without execution is a daydream; execution without vision is a nightmare".[12]

Part of my consultancy job is to read in-progress design documents and litter them with what look to be negative comments, the bulk of which are to do with pointing out small holes in the design that need filling.[13] The comments are not negative, however, they're discussion points. They basically come to "What if...?" (or, occasionally, "You said the opposite of this elsewhere"). The more such questions are answered in pre-production, the fewer will have to be answered in production, or, even worse, operation.

Pre-production is where the lead designer and the other design leads do the bulk of their work. Much of what this book covers takes place in pre-production. In the same way that programmers regularly conduct code reviews in the production phase, designers conduct design reviews in the pre-production phase. This is as much to keep themselves on track as it is anyone else: it's very easy for designers to go off at a tangent, and the idea of design reviews is to make sure that everyone is moving in the same direction in a coherent, consistent manner without over-constraining one another.[14] A good idea should always be praised, but if it's off-topic then it's a case of "save it for the sequel" and move on.

The lead programmer may have been involved in an *ad hoc* way, while the lead designer is conceptualising the design. This is because if the lead programmer says you can't have something, you can't have it; the only way you *can* have it is if you subsequently propose a solution that the lead programmer says you can have. Designers may therefore perhaps ask for advice before boldly asserting that all NPCs will have human-level AI capabilities. The lead programmer may also help out by loaning a programmer if the lead designer wants to prototype a design idea but doesn't have the coding chops easily to do so themself.

---

[11] Even today, virtual world developers occasionally receive emails proudly announcing "I have an amazing idea for an MMO and I've chosen *you* to make it!".

[12] I am led to understand that this is a Japanese proverb. If it isn't, it deserves to be one.

[13] The rest are comments about muddled messages plus, very occasionally, ravings about how good an idea is.

[14] Unfortunately, sometimes everyone else gets on board with the tangent and a week of meaningful work is lost.

Note that the lead programmer will also be prototyping ideas of their own, and indeed that prototypes may be one of the required outputs of pre-production (to help demonstrate competence and so raise more funds for development).

The lead programmer's duties on the project really begin when the design doc is approaching completion.[15] Working together, the lead designer and the lead programmer estimate how long each software tier (client, server, back-end) will take to implement. The result will be a set of *mini-specs* for each of said tiers (for example, the back-end specs might cover account management, authentication, patching/deployment, analytics and customer support). Commercial tools exist to help with making these estimations, although experienced lead programmers will usually have a good handle on the process anyway.

The lead programmer will then prepare a *technical design document* from the mini-specs. Other programmers with particular areas of expertise will usually be involved, too. In the same way that there may be a lead combat designer (reporting to the lead designer), there may be a lead client programmer (reporting to the lead programmer).

Unlike the lead programmer, the lead artist doesn't need detailed design documentation to be able to begin preparatory work. In conversation with the lead designer, the general look and feel of the game world can be described, then fleshed out as concept art. In the past, for designers with no sketching ability, this could be a long, iterative process akin to describing to a police artist what the person who stole your handbag looked like. However, with the advent of diffusion models such as DALL-E, Stable Diffusion and Midjourney, those designers who can't draw to save their lives[16] can create sample imagery in the right kind of area that the lead artist can then use as a starting point to do properly.

Having good initial concept art is important for making sure that the designers and artists working on the virtual world have the same visual interpretation in mind, thereby ensuring (or at least encouraging) consistency. This doesn't mean that the lead artist has to *be* a concept artist (although they can be), only that they have to engage with a specialist concept artist.

While the lead designer is working on the design document, the lead artist will be working on an *art bible* (also known as a *style guide*) so that members of the art and animation team can all create works that work together. Even in a cartoon world, if one artist creates characters that seem to have come out of *The Simpsons* (Groening, 1989) and everyone else is aiming more for *Family Guy* (MacFarlane, 1999), that could be a bad look.

Lead artists rarely tell lead designers that they can't have something for artistic reasons, although they may have strong opinions as to the advisability of it. Usually, any sticking point will arise because of budgetary constraints. Yes, it would be great to use photogrammetry to capture the interior of every building from real-world examples, but that will be expensive and time-consuming; you'd need to appeal to the producer to increase the project's resources if you wanted to have it. Good luck with that. The lead artist *might* say that you can have what you want at a poorer quality level. The lead artist does not expect you to go along with this idea, so don't; it's just their way of gently letting you decide for yourself that your idea isn't as achievable as you hoped it was.

---

[15] Invariably, asymptotically.
[16] Regrettably, I have to count myself among their number.

As the game design progresses, the lead artist will work with the lead designer to estimate the range and volume of new *art assets* required. Artists don't just create characters and scenery, they create the components of these. Yes, there are indeed people whose life is spent creating textures so that bricks look like bricks from any angle and under all lighting conditions. Increasingly, artists are also given the task of turning greybox,[17] blocked-out level designs into something visually meaningful, too.

All this may sound simple, but it isn't. If you, as a designer, say you want birds in the sky, the lead artist will want to know how many kinds of birds, whether they're going to remain in the sky or maybe land at some point, whether they can be shot down, whether they can interact with one another, whether you want them individual or in flocks or both, whether they will fly in straight lines or swoop or make turns, whether people will only ever see them at a distance – basically, anything they need to know in order to create the birds that they can't derive from the established context.

The lead artist will also confer with the lead programmer to agree on a polygon budget, to get a sense of how many objects can appear on the screen at once and at what level of detail. Any tools that the artist feels may need to be created to aid the production of assets will also be discussed. The results of the lead artist's final assessment of the art load and content are compiled to give an *art specification document*.

The producer will have been actively participating in discussions between leads, in part to get a rational overview of the whole project and in part to point out when what is suggested will be too expensive in time or resources to be acceptable to higher management. There are basically two kinds of producer: ones who represent management to the development team ("You can't have more resources"); ones who represent the development team to management ("We want more resources"). The former are liked by management but resented by the development team; the latter are liked by the development team but resented by management. Such is the producer's unfortunate lot in life.

Towards the end of pre-production, the producer will take the lead designer's technical design specification and the lead programmer's art specification, and map out what needs to be made by whom and when. The result is a *production management assessment*. Product ownership is handed over from the lead designer to the producer at this point, and the production phase can begin in earnest.

6.3 PRODUCTION

The production phase is the one in which the virtual world is put together. The necessary software tools are built, the code for the product itself is written and assembled and the content is created.

Production proceeds according to the producer's production plans. The overall development methodology used is *waterfall*: the various steps are arranged in sequence such that the later steps won't be started until the deliverables of the steps they depend upon are

---

[17] *Greyboxing* (or *grayboxing*, if you don't follow the Shakespearean spelling) refers to creating and positioning placeholder objects that can easily be repositioned for level-testing before work on texturisation and other detailing begins. As it's named after the colour used for the placeholder objects, it may also be called *whiteboxing* (although some studios make a distinction between the two).

completed and tested. This allows for long-term planning (you can hire people ahead of when you'll need them, for example), but it relies on a robust set of requirements at each stage; these may not be available in the context of virtual worlds (especially MMOs).

In video-game (and thence virtual world) development, fixed sequences of processes and workflows are usually called *pipelines*. The steps in a pipeline are at the same level of abstraction as each other, but the pipelines themselves don't have to be. For example, pre-production, production, roll-out, operation and eventual sunset is the overall pipeline; concept art, modelling, texturing, rigging/animation, integration and lighting/rendering would be the overall art pipeline. Individual elements will have their own pipelines meaningful to experts.

For many components of a virtual world, an iterative methodology is preferred. This allows for some backtracking when requirements change or new requirements are introduced. The dominant methodology used is *agile*, which is popular among programmers because it prioritises working code over documentation and downplays processes and planning[18] (Beck et al., 2001). In practice, it often seems to be observed more in hope than conviction, and invariably evolves into a waterfall framework enhanced by what amounts to a muddling-through plug-in.

A third development methodology, *lean*, is a spin-off of agile. One of its key characteristics is to make decisions as late as possible, so they can be based on facts. It grants individuals autonomy and accords well with how programmers like to program, but at the organisational level, it asks for a degree of discipline that's hard to guarantee.

In summary, for a creative product such as a virtual world, the overall approach will be waterfall, with teams working in a more agile fashion and individuals tending towards lean, but with everyone following their established pipelines subject to feedback and iteration.

Now, as the production work in virtual worlds is organised around teams, let's take a brief look at said teams.

In the production phase, the core team is augmented by (in the case of commercial virtual worlds) a hundred or more other developers. Virtual worlds have a large amount of content and functionality, so they require a large number of developers to create and implement that content and functionality.[19]

The way that production is organised, the leads from the core team have their own teams to manage, which may be sufficiently large that there are specialist leads to deal with some of the sub-areas. The producer may (and usually will) work with associate producers who are (as the name suggests) associated with specific teams – design, programming, art. These may in turn have assistant producers who (as the name also suggests) assist them in their tasks. These tasks include team co-ordination, cross-team communication, reporting to stakeholders and keeping within time and budget limits. They also involve handling the production problems that arise along the way (which *will* happen, you just don't know

---

[18] OK, so it also promotes customer collaboration above contract negotiation, neither of which are particularly appealing to programmers, but requirements have got to come from somewhere.

[19] At least until AI gets its act together.

what, when or how). Because of this, producers spend much of their day in meetings. If you don't like meetings, you're not cut out to be a producer.[20]

If you're wondering why MMOs and other large-scale games need so many producers, well virtual worlds are complicated entities and there's a lot going on at once; a single producer would have to spread their efforts too thinly. Associate producers, who oversee one aspect of production, can specialise in that and reduce the load on the producer. They can also keep focus more easily and have a better understanding of their team's dynamics and how work is progressing. Assistant producers help with risk mitigation (they can take over if a more senior producer is out of action for some reason) and they can perform some of the tasks that don't require an experienced hand (such as maintaining documentation) while learning the ropes themselves.

Good producers are hard to find.[21] Theirs is a thankless job, so make sure you thank them every once in a while.[22]

It might be supposed that designers have little to do in the production phase, given the reliance on their talents in pre-production. This is not the case. The lead designer will be called upon by the producer to ensure that what the producer thinks fits the designer's vision really does fit the designer's vision, but all members of the design team will be busy. The work they do falls into three broad categories.

Category 1: Designing through Concretisation. During pre-production, designers describe what needs to be implemented. This can be at different levels of detail. For example, "There are 300 types of weapon" is not the same as "There are 300 types of weapon, with these 20 sub-types" or "There are 300 types of weapon, with these 20 sub-types, having these stat ranges" or "These are the 11,791 different weapons and their stats". Now, in specifying what needs to be made, sometimes the act of specifying takes just as long as the act of making it. If the design document calls for 14 quests in this hub at a given risk and reward setting then defining each such quest in words is going to take longer than would actually creating the quest using a tool. There's no need to delay the start of production while you decide whether the vain prince would describe his hair as flaxen or ash blonde in the flavour text. Therefore, designers can often wait until production starts before beginning such tasks: they design by making

Category 2: Concretising Abstract Designs. Describing how to make a cake is not the same as making a cake. In pre-production, designers describe what metaphorical cakes they want made; in production, everyone makes the cakes. Some of those cakes need to be made by designers, or at least by people with design skills. In regular computer games, level designers will create content within the constraints of the specification, which can involve quite some creativity. There aren't usually level designers *per se* for MMOs, but there are *experience designers*. For example, scripted boss fights are not going to be more than outlined in the design document, so someone has

---

[20] Don't despair: showing an interest in virtual world design may have already disqualified you.

[21] So are bad ones, come to that, but good ones are the harder.

[22] This has nothing to do with the fact that payroll management is often the producer's responsibility.

to design them fully during production. Another kind of design concretisation that takes place is world-building. This is traditionally the realm of designers, but these days artists are also likely undertake some – possibly almost all – of the work. Note that "world-building" here isn't at the geographic level (placing mountain ranges, making rivers flow to the sea), it's at the human level (deciding where to put windows in stables, creating patrol routes). Writers (or *narrative designers*) also do design concretisation, turning synopses into lore, story and anything else that's needed.

Category 3: Redesign. There's a difference between planning a wedding and having a wedding. Your plan did not account for what would happen if the holy oil became lumpy[23] or if the photographer took an age to pose the photos.[24] So it is with production: most of the time, everything will go to plan, but sometimes it won't.[25] There will be omissions or contradictions or inconsistencies in the design document that weren't noticed or were forgotten about; ideas that ought to have worked might not work in practice; other ideas could come out of development that are so good they need to be incorporated; content may have to be dropped because of unanticipated scheduling problems. These kinds of events, and many, many more, will require some redesign to address. Designers can therefore find themselves busy stitching up or patching over holes, or adding new flourishes, or taking things apart and putting them back together again so they're a better fit.

Those are the three main categories of work that designers will be doing during the production phase. Let's move on with a quick overview of what the other people involved are doing at the same time.

As the person responsible for the overall integrity of the software, the lead programmer's job during this period is to ensure that the members of the programming team are producing work of sufficient quality. This involves a lot of looking at other people's code, which is time-consuming. As a result, lead programmers don't get to do much programming themselves. Given that they are invariably exceptionally adept at programming, this may seem a waste of skills – which indeed it is: it would make a great deal more sense for the most accomplished programmers to be actually programming rather than looking at other programmers' outputs. Unfortunately, though, the way programmers are manufactured, they don't listen to other programmers unless they respect them. Therefore, if you want to tell a programmer what to do programming-wise, you need to be a very good programmer yourself. If only I were joking.

The technical design document will be broken down by the systems architect (who's usually the lead designer) into system specifications that can be handed to systems leads or individual programmers. The tasks will invariably be grouped together by related functionality (for example, client, server, network, data-gathering), each of which may have their

---

[23] This happened at the Hindu wedding of my niece. The officiator said, wryly, "I'm sure the gods will understand that at least we tried".

[24] This was at my own wedding. The photos weren't all that good, either, and not simply because I was in them.

[25] For example, it's one thing to make contingency plans for external events, but quite another to find your entire workforce suddenly locked down during a pandemic.

own subdivisions (user interface, AI, physics, tools, …). If there are enormous gameplay systems, such as combat, crafting, housing and the economy, then these could also have specialist sub-teams working on them.

Increasingly, the architecture of a virtual world is constrained by the engines and other prebuilt software used. Tasks that really ought to be done on the server might have to be done on the client if Unity or the Unreal Engine so decrees. This can lead to security issues if the server has to trust the client. It's less of an issue for designers as it is programmers, but because designers are increasingly having to gain programming knowledge in order to do design, it *is* still an issue.

Incidentally, I perhaps should mention that games programmers (and therefore virtual world programmers) are not the same as programmers in other industries. This is evinced by the fact that they can earn more money programming in pretty well any other industry,[26] but they stay with games. What the games industry offers that few other industries can match is the prospect of doing creative programming – self-expression through programming. This is indeed a prize. It does mean that games programmers can be tetchy if asked to program something they think is a bad idea, though, so designers need to make sure they have them on board at all levels.

In the same way that the lead programmer manages the programmers, the lead artist manages the artists. Bad art is easier to spot than bad code, so the lead artist may actually be able to spend a meaningful amount of their time arting.

The main issues to do with art are consistency and volume. There are many different kinds of artwork that need to be created for virtual worlds, and although artists are often generalists able to create art for any purpose, increasingly they're having to specialise if other skills are also required (such as world-building ones). The basic dividing line of skillsets is between static, environment art (modelling, assets, textures, …) and dynamic, character art (animation, rigging, motion capture, more modelling, ….), but there are plenty of other areas where art is required – concept art, storyboarding, user interface icons, full-motion video, visual effects – along with non-development artwork such as marketing images.[27]

Artists are often independently minded and will do things their own way even though they've been told repeatedly to do it some other way. They are particularly famed among programmers for never following naming guidelines for assets.[28] *Technical artists*, who have both artistic and programming skills, are a boon here.

Related to art is sound. Virtual worlds rely heavily on sound, but the kinds of sounds they need are very different. You wouldn't want someone whose job is to compose music also to do voice overs and to record a thousand different kinds of footsteps.[29] Each requires its own expert. They may all communicate with the same specialist sound

---

[26] Specialist programmers *can* command a large salary in the games industry, but then they can in other industries, too.

[27] Confusingly, in the same way that a day is composed of day and night, artists are sometimes referred to as being either artists or animators. They may also be referred to as being 2D artists or 3D artists, depending on whether they create flat artwork or non-flat artwork skinned with flat artwork.

[28] That said, if managing artists is like herding cats, managing programmers is like herding dead cats.

[29] 1,003 in *Half Life: Alyx* (Valve, 2020).

programmer, but other than that they're independent. Because they're so disparate, there usually won't be an audio lead; the producer or an associate producer will manage the people involved directly.[30]

Audio has a much bigger effect on player experience than players tend to suppose. From a designer's point of view, the main conversation with voice-artist wranglers, composers and (non-ambient[31]) sound designers concerns what the emotional content of the audio should be. The designer can illustrate this by referencing existing works that have a similar feel or effect, and say they want something reminiscent of that. For voice, it's possible for a designer endowed with a respectable acting ability to say key lines in the way that they want the professional to deliver them, but this isn't usually necessary as the producer will have a good enough handle on it. For music, a composer will put together some samples for approval to make sure they've got the right idea, and if so then they're free to proceed. Music that's tied to action will need to be specified at a technical level (how long each riff needs to be for combat accompaniment, for example), but the notes themselves will be the composer's responsibility.

Any, all or none of the audio components of a virtual world can be outsourced or bought in. A developer can save a lot of work by buying in a sound-effect library, for example. This is also true of some of the more expensive art requirements, such as motion capture (it's less expensive to hire a mocap studio for a couple of days than to build your own).

Programmers, artists and to some extent even designers will test their work as they go along. What they won't test, however, is how their work fits in with everyone else's, and whether it meets the specification.[32] This brings us to one of the key sections for virtual world production: quality assurance (QA).

When naïve players think about QA, they think playtesting. Who wouldn't want to spend their entire professional life playing games day in, day out?

QA is not playtesting. It's quality assurance. It's walking into every junction between every wall in the whole game environment to make sure there are no gaps, then doing the same thing while cartwheeling, teleport-jumping and being knocked back in combat. Then it's repeating all this with the smallest and largest character models.

Put another way, it's a special kind of fun for a special kind of person. Most QA technicians will burn out after 18 months of creative repetition, but those that don't are golden. Virtual world developers will do practically anything to keep them, short of paying them a decent salary. QA leads (sometimes *test managers*), who draw up the test schedules as well as doing testing themselves, are even more hard to come by; they make excellent producers, too.

Different kinds of testing take place at different stages of development. In production, a lot of it is requirements-testing (or bug-detection), but issues with the aesthetic will also be flagged up. *Compatibility testers* specialise in testing whether the virtual world runs on different hardware and software configurations[33]; this can be outsourced, but the scale

---

[30] Composers often work at home and can be so solitary that it's hard to tell if they're alive until you hear from them. Managing them is like herding Schrödinger's cat.

[31] A footstep is a footstep, but a chime telling you you've clicked the wrong icon needs to fit in.

[32] It will meet the specification in their head, but not necessarily the one in everyone else's heads.

[33] For consoles, they're called *format testers*.

of virtual worlds is such that it's going to take time. *Regression testers* check that major bug-fixes have indeed fixed the bugs and also that there aren't any new bugs that have arisen as a result of the fix.[34]

Once the code can be assembled into something playable, yes, *then* it may involve play-testing; then again, given how well the QA staff will know the game by that stage, some of it may be more informative if outsourced. Playtesting is where most of the design bugs are identified, but even if the virtual world is in dire need of new opinions from people who haven't played it before (*Kleenex testers*), there's still an important role for QA testers who have just spent the past week examining the effects of every attack animation[35] from every angle. This is because when designers design inter-related systems that involve a lot of numbers, it's often quicker to use a best-guess starting estimate than to pore over a spread-sheet for two hours before deciding that yes, +3 against short humanoids is balanced better than +2, +4 or +5. Designers can work with QA technicians to establish the actual values to be used, based on the proposed values.

Oh, I should mention that designers should always provide *some* initial value, not simply put "TBD". This is because when programmers come to code it, that's the point at which it needs to have been decided; they will therefore decide for themselves, choosing whichever of −1, 0, pi or 9,223,372,036,854,775,807 is the most likely to punish the designer for lacking specificity. Asking creative programmers to *ad lib* is a dangerous path to walk.

QA is very important for any open world and for any multi-player world; it's therefore essential for virtual worlds, especially MMOs. The QA lead has final sign-off on whether the game is in a fit state to be released or not. If the producer or someone higher up in the company overrules them, it becomes their head that will be on the block when the inevitable happens.

The final major team involved in production is customer service (CS). CS representatives (CSRs[36]) don't really come into their own until the roll-out phase, but they need to be trained on the virtual world so they will be able to anticipate and respond to the problems that players are likely throw at them (or "problems", because some players will try to game a gullible CSR for in-game advantage[37]). This will help the development of policies and protocols for dealing with such issues in the live game. CSRs will also need to familiarise themselves with the player-management tools they have been provided with, or will be provided with "soon, honest". Because they get to see across the whole spectrum of the player experience, from account set-up to account cancellation and everything in between, CSRs are often well-placed to offer a macroscopic view of the virtual world as a whole, which can complement the microscopic views that QA testers get or the tunnel-vision views that teams working in their own silos can cultivate.

---

[34] There will have been. The producer decides whether to leave them in for the next round of bug-fixing or to sort them out before then.

[35] This may sound ridiculous, but no! In *Age of Conan*, female characters had slightly longer attack animations, and because the animations were tied to hit frequency (rather than the reverse), that meant female characters did less overall damage than male characters as they hit less often.

[36] They're also called *community support representatives*, which fortunately has the same acronym. The distinction is important to those in the job, but most people just call them CSRs or CS reps.

[37] It's surprising how many *MUD2* players seemed to die in fights because their cat jumped on their keyboard just as they were about to flee.

CSRs may give the impression of being effectively call-centre workers, but there's much more to what they do than running through a checklist.[38] In particular, call-centre representatives don't have to concern themselves with disputes among the different users of the refrigerators that their employer manufactures, but CSRs do have to handle all manner of accusations that players level against one another (especially if they suspect cheating). Also, call centre workers don't have to field a relentless stream of questions in controlled social media or firefight whatever alarming misconceptions blow up in uncontrolled social media. Good CSRs, like good QA technicians, are hard to find, and experienced CSR leads, like experienced QA leads, are even harder.

This overview of what goes on in the production phase of development is all well and good, but why should designers unduly care about any of it?

Well, it helps to know during the design process how your designs will be implemented. You don't have to be *au fait* with the details, or to be able to implement any of it yourself, but it will help your colleagues tremendously if you can organise your design document in such a way that it makes it easier for them to do their jobs. Sadly, it would be dishonest of me to pretend that the outline I've just given is going to prepare you fully for the experience; each game development studio is different, and you'll need to learn its ways on the job. What I've presented here is insufficient to land you a position as a lead game designer on an MMO, but it will help you see where designers fit into the great production machine that results in the creation of a playable virtual world.

Once it is playable, of course, someone has to be persuaded to play it.

6.4 ROLL-OUT

Roll-out is the phase in which members of the public see the outcome of the studio's labours. It gets its name because the game isn't simply released to everyone on the planet at once, it's gradually opened up to more and more people.

The main reason for rolling out rather than going big bang is so that the virtual world's components, systems and content can be tested in a live environment; problems can be identified and fixed without affecting (or disaffecting) unnecessarily large numbers of players. A secondary, commercially important reason is outreach; rolling out a virtual world creates a buzz that will, if managed properly, lead to larger numbers of players in the long run.

The roll-out phase begins before production has finished and proceeds in a sequence of stages. Unfortunately, the names of these stages have been denuded over the years for publicity reasons, but I'll go with the traditional version (which is understood in the wider software industry). The stages are:

- Alpha
- Closed beta
- Open beta
- Launch

---

[38] Yes, I have indeed tried turning it off and on again.

The *alpha* stage begins when enough of the virtual world has been written that it can be put together into a rickety whole and integration-tested by the developers themselves. Once it's stable enough not to be embarrassing, small groups of trusted individuals[39] will be invited to play. It's accepted and expected that an alpha version of a virtual world will be incomplete and riddled with placeholders and bugs in not only the code but also the artwork and design.

When it begins, the alpha stage is usually called *alpha-testing* in typical software-engineering style. This is because it's the programmers who decide these things at this point. As it progresses, though, the word "testing" will gradually be dropped and developers will start saying it's "in alpha" rather than "in alpha-testing".

During alpha, the main task facing the designer is assessing whether the basic gameplay works, and if it does then whether or not it's fun. The success of large-granule concepts such as pacing (which is discussed in Volume II) can also be appraised here.

Designers may further be called upon to design around problems experienced by the other teams. If those experimental articulated vehicles that worked great on paper are a disappointment in practice then something will have to be specified to replace the space they occupied in the design.

Because the alpha stage of roll-out begins in production, there will still be plenty of subsystems being added to the virtual world as time passes. Some of the ones that were planned to be in at launch may be held back for a future patch if they look as if they'll cause problems (player housing systems are notorious for this).

Progress reports known as *developer diaries* often start to ramp up during alpha. Although they sometimes appear even in pre-production, they're much more impressive when there's an actual world to show. All leads can expect to be called upon to talk about their respective areas of expertise, usually in tandem with the producer; it's likely that someone from marketing will also be on hand to stop participants from revealing too much too soon or from making suggestions that prospective players will interpret as promises. Designers tend to be particularly in demand for developer diaries, because they can articulate all the amazing things that the players will be doing and why you really want to join them.

Although the alpha stage begins (as alpha-testing) in production, by the time it ends (as alpha), roll-out is well under way. The virtual world is in a sufficiently complete and stable state that larger numbers of players can be invited to try it out. This begins the beta stage or simply beta.[40] Most video-game developers want to go into beta as late as possible, so as not to lose momentum before launch; virtual world developers like to go into beta as soon as possible, to give ample time for bug-fixing, balancing and community-building.

There are actually two beta stages: *closed beta* and *open beta*. Closed beta comes first, usually for a limited number of players and with a requirement that they sign a non-disclosure

---

[39] These are proverbially referred to as *friends and family*, although there will typically be few of the latter. External companies specialising in playtesting may be brought in, too (*paid testers*).

[40] Most programmers will have accepted the inevitable by now and will also use this term. They know deep down that properly it's *beta-testing*, though, and may well use that invocation in the arcane ceremonies of the secret programming societies to which (for all anyone else knows) they surely belong.

agreement (NDA). This isn't simply a ruse to give the virtual world an aura of mystique and those prospective players who missed out a sense of wanting to play it even more (although, done properly, it achieves both these aims); rather, it's because there's still a lot that can go wrong and it would be unfortunate if the first uncurated glimpses of the virtual world's content were observed and reported by one and all as a series of gargantuan mishaps.

In closed beta, the pool of players with access to the virtual world is increased in size over that in alpha, but it's still limited. The control mechanism used involves the distribution of account-validation codes known as *keys*. Groups of experienced players from other virtual worlds that the developer operates may be given invites, and there may also be an application process (which could be as simple as handing a key to anyone who walks through the door at a given convention). The absolute number of keys made available is fixed, but games journalists and developers from other companies will usually have no trouble acquiring one if they ask.

One of the main advantages of having a larger number of players is simply that there *is* a larger number of players. Systems that worked fine when there were only a couple of dozen users putting them to the sword might seize up when a couple of hundred head their way. Crisp, responsive gameplay could begin to behave as if it were coated in molasses. Although some of these effects can be revealed using hordes of automated players (*bots*), these are no substitute for full-on, organised *flood tests*, in which very large numbers of players join the virtual world together and see if its banks hold. The metrics that can be gathered from having more players around are also far more useful, because the sample size is so much greater than in alpha.

CSRs are able to test some of their processes and procedures in closed beta. It's unlikely that there will be monstrous social breakdowns to sort out, but common issues are certain to emerge that affect many players. Players will also identify failings in the design and implementation that the QA team didn't get to; some of these will be obvious and the players themselves can enter them as bug reports, but others might look intentional and merit clarification from a CSR. In this respect, CSRs can provide to the development team important feedback garnered from the player base.

The main issue for MMO designers at this stage is *balance* (it's much less of a concern for social worlds). Balance is a term that's used a lot in game design, yet it's not easy to pin down. This isn't really the best place in the book to describe the concept, but that's not going to stop me. Briefly, there are three types of balance in MMOs (and in games in general):

1. **Player/Player Balance**. This is the default meaning of the term. Balance here means that the game is fair: players in competition with one another should have the same structural chance of winning.[41] If you're in a situation where you can't win then either it's your fault or you were ganged-up on (which may also be your fault).

---

[41] You can't usually "win" a virtual world, but you can win individual mini-games such as combat, and you can progress.

2. **Player/Gameplay Balance**. Balance here ensures that the game is fun, rather than too frustrating or too boring.

3. **Gameplay/Gameplay Balance**. Balance here means that all gameplay options are useful at least sometimes, and that the cost of an action is appropriate for its pay-off. Unbalanced gameplay means there's a dominant strategy (or *meta*) that players will adopt, thereby rendering all the effort put into implementing everything else redundant.

In all the above cases, near-balance is usually good enough. There is some overlap — for example, players may call a fight against an over-powered NPC "unfair" (as if it were a player rather than a component of gameplay) — but overall the distinctions are useful if only to show that there *are* different kinds of balance.

Identifying imbalance isn't easy for designers, although AI can help (Morosan, 2019). One of the problems is that balance doesn't always scale up well, and every new feature introduces new complications. The standard way to handle this is by using graduated negative feedback (that is, diminishing returns): the more power an entity or system gains, from whatever source, the less good it does them.

Identifying imbalance is easy for players, in aggregate if not individually. Imagine that your design is a bucket and that flaws in the design are holes in the bucket. In pre-production, when the design is being tested on paper and using prototypes, it's as if you fill the bucket with marbles. You're going to be able to spot the bigger holes easily that way. Come production, the QA team fills the bucket with sand. Sand is going to come out of places that marbles didn't, so you can patch those holes up, too. When it comes to roll-out, though, the players are like water. If there's a hole in your design, they're going to find it. If you're lucky (and in alpha and closed beta you almost always will be), they'll tell you about it. Later, they may keep it to themselves so they can exploit it after launch. This is another reason why you want trusted people to try out the virtual world first before you widen access.

When the closed beta is stable and the useful information (or your funding) is drying up, it's time to enter *open beta*.

Open beta is like closed beta except that many more keys are made available in tranches, perhaps in unlimited numbers overall. Open beta still retains the caveat that it's an incomplete, rough-around-the-edges product, but the NDA is lifted, and players start to act more like they will following launch. The CSR team is thus exposed to the full horror of user behaviours and can test its responses to them (and *vice versa*).

More nuanced balance tweaks are made during open beta, and the data gathered can be used for fine-tuning the virtual world's operations. Launch momentum is built by the (hopefully, good) word-of-mouth coming out from players, and late content and functionality additions are made that should have been there in the alpha, but the developers fell behind schedule.[42]

---

[42] As I'm on the developers' side here, I'd like to point out that it's just as likely the schedule ran ahead of them.

It's in open beta that we see the abuse of the perfectly good technical terms that I mentioned earlier. For example, virtual worlds may be referred to as being in alpha when actually they're in open beta, simply in order to make players feel they're getting in early and so are special.[43] Some virtual worlds seem to be in perpetual open beta,[44] which as far as I can tell is to afford a modicum of legal protection from ferocious consumer-protection regulations. There's also the concept of *paid beta*, in which players pay to be part of the beta (a bit like early access on Steam). In most creative industries, beta-testers are paid by the creator; in the virtual world industry, either they're not paid at all or it's the other way round.

At various points in both alpha and beta, the entire character database will be erased and players will have to start again from a standing start. The main difference is that in alpha, you can't always expect a warning. In closed beta, a wipe will usually accompany a substantial program update, either because the data format has changed or the designers want to see how players progress from a standing start using whatever new systems have been introduced. In open beta, it will be for *release candidate testing*[45]: the virtual world is believed to be in a good enough state that it could formally be launched, assuming no devastating bugs are discovered. When it appears as if there *are* no devastating bugs remaining,[46] there'll usually be one final character wipe and the virtual world will be launched.

There are two main kinds of launch: soft and full. In a *soft launch*, there's no marketing push; in a *full launch*, the publicity will be so great that anyone who might conceivably wish to play the virtual world will have heard of it.

A full launch is the signal to those players who have been waiting to play the virtual world for years that now is the time. They'll all pile into it at once on launch day, thereby demonstrating just how good or bad the flood testing was. The atmosphere is usually electric – launch day can be *the* best day to play a virtual world. Everything has to work, though: a botched launch – and most of them *are* botched to some extent[47] – can lose a lot of player goodwill. Botched launches are usually caused because they're premature: the developers know there are problems, but they've either run out of money (and need to launch so they can bring in income to finish the job) or they've been ordered to launch on a particular date by their parent company (because the marketing arm decided it was the best time).

Just because the players come all at once on launch day, that doesn't mean they'll still be coming all at once on launch +30 day; the server, network and CSR capacity that was necessary to deal with the influx is not going to be needed once everything has settled down. Using a +12 flamethrower of publicity is expensive, too. Because of this, many virtual worlds opt for a soft launch. It will be publicised, but not really marketed. This means that the player numbers will grow gradually, rather than start high then even out.

---

[43] This is particularly prevalent in some of the conveyor-belt MMOs developed in the Far East.

[44] At some point in the far, distant future, *Star Citizen* (Roberts, far distant future) may see its full commercial launch.

[45] Different developers use different terms here, including *gamma testing*, *going silver* and *CRC* (where the RC is short for "release candidate" and the first C is short for "code", "consumer", "customer" and probably half a dozen other variations).

[46] Note: there will be devastating bugs remaining.

[47] Even back in the early Fifth Age, it was a surprise to most of us when *Dark Age of Camelot* showed that smooth launches were possible.

The disadvantage of a soft launch is that it may be *too* soft, so hardly anyone notices. Growing from a low base is more difficult than growing from a high base, because players attract players: if you don't have a critical mass, it'll be tough going.

Two other forms of launch, which are variations of the above, are also encountered: staggered and relaunch. In a *staggered launch*, the virtual world is launched in one territory for a time (at least a year) before being made available worldwide; this is popular among Korean and Japanese developers, who like to focus their efforts on their local market first so that all the creases have been ironed out of the virtual world before everyone else gets to join in. In a *relaunch*, the virtual world receives a fresh blast of publicity, either because it only had a soft launch earlier or because some major change to its character is likely to attract new players (or old players back).[48]

The commercial launch[49] of a virtual world is formally the point at which roll-out ends and operation begins. As is the case for all these phases in a virtual world's lifecycle, there is some overlap (paid beta is effectively an unadmitted soft launch); also, ensuing expansions will have their own roll-outs. Once your players formally become paying customers, though, the focus of the developer changes from production to operation.

6.5 OPERATION

A virtual world's *operator* is the company that runs it day-to-day. If you think of a cruise ship, the operator is the company that does the advertising, pays the staff, decides the route, arranges for the embarkation and disembarkation of passengers, manages the passenger experience, tries to prevent the spread of Norovirus and generally keeps everything working. The operator of a virtual world does a metaphorically equivalent thing, but for a virtual world, not a cruise ship.

In business schools, the operation phase may be known as the *commercial exploitation phase*. We don't use that term in virtual worlds, because of the negative connotations of the word "exploitation". *Operation* is preferred because virtual worlds are vast reality machines that need to be kept up and running.

In many industries, those who manufacture particular goods don't use them: shipbuilders build ships for other companies to make use of, not for themselves to make use of. In other industries, this is not always the case: the BBC broadcasts on its own network the TV shows it makes. Which is it for virtual worlds?

Well, it's more along the latter lines. The developer of a virtual world doesn't *have* to operate it, but usually will operate it and perhaps license other operators in different territories (laws in China actually require that foreign developers have a local partner to enter the Chinese market, for example). This is because even in operation, virtual worlds are in a continual[50] state of development.

---

[48] Relaunches without some major change are rarely successful, because they smack of desperation. There are exceptions, however, most notably *Final Fantasy XIV* among modern virtual worlds.

[49] It's also known as *going gold*, from back in the day when the master CDROM from which all the ones sold in stores were copied was gold in colour.

[50] Continual from the players' perspective, continuous from the developer's.

The individuals handling the operation and development of a virtual world make up the *live team*. Paramount among them is the community support section, composed mainly of:

- CSRs on the front line within the virtual world;
- Community Support Specialists, who act as moderators for the official forum;
- Social Media Co-ordinators, who manage the wider social media channels.

If the operator operates the hardware upon which the virtual world runs (which it usually does, but times are changing as practical cloud[51]-based solutions become available) then there will be technical operations staff among the live team, too, providing network and hardware support in addition to regular company-wide IT facilities.

Ongoing development takes two forms: reaction and action. In the former, developers spend their time fixing the hailstorm of bugs and exploits uncovered by the players; in the latter, they work on new features and new content.

Bug fixes are delivered in the weekly updates, unless there's a problem so serious as to merit an emergency hot-fix. Minor content patches accompany them. Major content patches and expansions are less frequent, but propel the virtual world forward and keep it fresh (although regularity can put unpleasant time pressure on the live team[52]). Operators of a virtual world that are not also its developer have limited ability to do any kind of ongoing development, with localisation being the main exception (about which more in Chapter 9).

Alpha-testing of new code and content takes place on the developer's own internal servers. Beta-testing is done on a special *public test server*, or *public test realm* (PTR) as many players like to call them. Regular players can sign up to the PTR to see all the cool new stuff before everyone else, but because it's experimental, there will be inconveniences (character wipes, object wipes, long periods of unavailability while new changes are patched in – plus bad design ideas and the presence of sprightly new bugs that have been introduced in the process of fixing earlier bugs).

The operations leads also invest time looking at new technology and trends. If people are unflatteringly comparing your virtual world to a different virtual world because it has a flashy new feature yours doesn't then it's worth considering following in their footsteps. There is a danger that something new and shiny turns out not to remain popular for long, however, and because development takes time, you may end up implementing an idea either too late to make a difference or after it has peaked (this happened with battle royale PvP zones, for example).

It's worth mentioning at this point that the designers, programmers and artists in the live team do not have to be the same individuals that were in the development team (or

---

[51] A *cloud* is a network-accessible collection of computers and associated resources, the use of which can expand and contract dynamically and seamlessly to address users' moment-to-moment computational and storage needs. It's an example of a *distributed* system.

[52] For some reason, company leadership often seems to believe that releasing an incomplete, buggy patch or expansion on time is more important than releasing a stable, polished patch or expansion a little late.

dev team), and usually aren't. There will always be some staff turnover, of course, as people find new opportunities and move on, but that's not the same as deliberately ensuring that members of the live time are different from those of the dev team. The CSRs are always a constant, but the members of the core team and their teams[53] are often not. Several reasons are given for this phenomenon, none of which are entirely persuasive:

- The original team members are burned out, having worked on the same project for several years.

- You want your best developers working on your next product,[54] whether that's an expansion to this virtual world or it's a new virtual world entirely.

- You want fresh ideas and new thinking.

- You don't need all those expensive, experienced designers, programmers and artists now.

The counter view is that the people who have worked on a virtual world for several years are invested in it, understand it, and are more likely to be able to ensure some consistency when extending it.[55] Such may indeed also be the view of senior management – they just don't like its implications. It's easier to persuade a team that has no artistic connection to a virtual world to do things for reasons of commercial expediency than it is to persuade people who understand what the virtual world is saying to do those things. As for what "those things" are, well they're determined largely by the player base, on the grounds that it costs a lot of money to acquire new players so you want to keep the ones you've got sweet. Unfortunately, what players actually want isn't necessarily what they think they want, and what they say they want when you ask them what they want doesn't tell the whole story.

A 2021 study of what features of automobiles were highest in demand among new buyers revealed (Gorzelany, 2021) that heated seats were most popular (66%), followed by blind-spot monitoring (60%), front and rear parking sensors (55%), four-wheel drive (54%) and lane-departure warning (54%). Few drivers, it would seem, regarded brakes as particularly important. They did regard automatic emergency braking systems as *unde*-sirable, but perhaps wouldn't have mentioned even that if they hadn't specifically been asked about it. So it is with virtual worlds: players will tell you what they want, but is it what they *really* want?[56]

If you want to take the player-responsive route then one way to inform your decision is to use data mining, which is in full swing anyway during operation. The operations team will be mainly interested in: monitoring possible exploits; seeking places where inefficiency can be reduced; calculating the effects of recent design changes; and A/B testing their ideas for new ones. The rest of the company will be entirely interested in finding the best ways to

---

[53] Yes, core team members have teams of their own: sorry, I don't decide this terminology.
[54] Saying this is an easy way to insult the live team.
[55] This view, which I personally support, was pioneered by Mark Jacobs with *Dark Age of Camelot*.
[56] Thanks to the Spice Girls, we know it's not what they really, *really* want, which is "zigazig ah".

extract money from the player base while creating only minimal antagonism. Data mining is agnostic: it tells you the facts, but not the reasons behind the facts. If people are doing X a lot, that may be because they like doing X, or because it's an irritating step on the way to doing Y, or because they really want to do Z but until they can they'll reluctantly do X as the least-worst alternative. Interpreting mined data and knowing what data to mine in the first place are important skills; it's a pity more developers don't have them.

If the live team and the dev team are disjoint, it can lead to a change in the character of the virtual world – and if they have no access to the original designers, even more so.[57] Some common problems:

- The live team may perceive flaws in the design where there are none.

- The live team may adhere to a different philosophy and "correct" the design where it's at odds with this.

- The dev team's ideas may fail when exposed to actual players and require major atmosphere-changing intervention.

- There could be a difference in the creative quality of staff between the two teams.

Because the live team has control for longer, it has more time to make changes. This is fine, because virtual worlds do need to evolve if they're to develop over time, but there's a danger that it can lead to a gradual change in experience that can alienate established players while not necessarily attracting many new ones.

When virtual worlds add new content, it's almost always at the high end: that's where the majority of players are. Therefore, the later after launch a newbie enters, the more content awaits them. Now you might think that this is good news for the newbies, because there's so much more fun to be had; the thinking among developers, however, is that it's bad news because all the action is at the high end and that's where the newbies want to be. Progress at the low end is therefore accelerated, to make sure that newbies can experience as soon as possible the full pleasure of learning tiresome boss dances while being shouted at over the latest in-vogue voice-over-IP service by someone they barely know with a strangely enunciated accent. In essence, players are pushed through low-end content so they can join all the other players who were pushed through low-end content.

This dilution of content[58] takes its toll. The newbie flow reduces to a relative trickle and the size of the live team falls accordingly. Players sense that there is a downward trajectory and leave for pastures new. People change, their characters change, content becomes stale, the virtual world looks dated: eventually, what used to be a vibrant, thriving centre of fun and activity becomes a near-deserted husk, like a coastal resort in winter.

---

[57] In theory, there should be design notes that tell the live team all this. There won't be.

[58] A more detailed analysis of the causes and effects appears in Volume II. I use the word "dilution" because it thins the gameplay, but that doesn't mean the residue is objectively easy. Turning *WoW* into *Diablo* (Brevik & Schaefer, 1996) dilutes *WoW*, but that doesn't imply that the result would be easy.

The first signs are usually server merges,[59] which tend to occur when so few people are playing on a particular shard that it's in danger of losing the appearance of being multi-player. The players from one or more shards are moved to another shard, which as a result can boast a viable number of players and doesn't feel empty. Players don't like server merges at the best of times, because previously established power hierarchies fall apart during a merge. The fact that they know it's coming about because the virtual world they love is shedding players only adds to their frustration.

As it happens, not all server merges *do* occur for reasons of collapsing player numbers. *New World*, for example, opens new servers to newbies-only then after a while merges them together. This has the effect of allowing players to form relationships and groups among their peers, rather than having to find a high-power guild that's willing to accept them (and, having done so, not thereafter to ignore them) as they might in another virtual world. It's a very nice idea, but most players remain anti-merge (even though they ask for them!) and merging is still (unjustly) interpreted as a sign of failure.

Virtual worlds that don't have multiple shards are either at an advantage or a disadvantage, depending on the reason why they don't have multiple shards. Single-sharded virtual worlds, such as *EVE Online* and most social worlds, can't merge servers together because there's only the one server. If they don't keep player numbers up, they have nowhere to go. *EVE Online* has the fictional cover of "the vastness of space", but social worlds (such as those that appeared during the Metaverse boom) are not so lucky. Vacant lots and structures lie forgotten, like the relics of an ancient civilisation. All that can be done is to remove unused chunks of the world discreetly to keep everyone together, like the advancing toxic storm does in *Fortnite*.

Some other virtual worlds don't have a single server but aren't organised as shards. Rather, they're organised as *layers*. Layers are described in more detail in Volume II, but basically, they're duplicates of geographic areas of the virtual world that are created dynamically when they get full of players (player presence being the main reason response times can suffer). If the layer threshold is 50 player characters and you're following the 50th one to cross the layer boundary, you may see them disappear and find yourself in the exact same place but alone. If you don't see people disappearing, you won't necessarily even be aware that you've crossed the boundary. Virtual worlds that use a layering architecture never need server merges; all that happens is that fewer layers will come into being as player numbers decrease. If no new layers are ever created, that means there are so few players that you have other problems instead.

Falling player numbers can sometimes be arrested by taking drastic action. A simple relaunch is not going to cut it, but a relaunch after a complete top-to-bottom rewrite might (as happened with *Final Fantasy XIV* and to some extent *Elder Scrolls Online*) – if you can afford it. Similarly, you might not be able to bring in new players with a redesign, but you

---

[59] Although the terms "server" and "shard" are regarded as interchangeable by most players, this is one case in which only one is ever used. It's always a "server merge", never a "shard merge" – even though technically the latter more accurately reflects what's going on.

could staunch the outward flow of your current ones for a period (as *Star Wars Galaxies* did with its New Game Enhancements (NGE)).

All virtual worlds have a lifetime. It's a relatively long one compared to most video games, but when income becomes less than expenditure,[60] the future is bleak. That said, even modern virtual worlds need fewer players to break even than you might think. It depends on the revenue model, but a virtual world with a mere 5,000 players can still tick over if its overheads are low.[61] If no new content is added and only the most problematic bugs are fixed, a virtual world is said to have entered *maintenance mode*. If even the bugs aren't fixed, it's regarded as *abandoned*.[62] In theory, it might be given a new injection of life if external factors come into play (such as making a blockbuster movie based on its intellectual property), but players are not advised to assume it will.

6.6 SUNSET

Eventually, the loyal core of fans who have been keeping a virtual world alive will be put out of their misery and it will be closed down, or *sunsetted*, as it's known. The date and time will be announced, players will hold an impromptu party, the countdown will begin, the servers will be switched off and it's (literally, for MMOs) game over.

Ideally, a virtual world is sunsetted with three or more months of warning so that players can achieve what they want to achieve and it can close gracefully. Sometimes this is not possible for commercial or legal reasons (such as bankruptcy or unhelpful new laws), but almost never after it has been launched will a virtual world be shut down with no warning. The sun sets, it looks pretty, people leave with fond memories, and they'll only see it again if it's bought up and reignited by a different company – or if someone sets up an illegitimate *rogue server* that avoids the same fate as the original.[63]

Designers are often so insulated from the player base that they're unaware that their design improvements are costing them players. There's always another explanation. Only when rogue servers start to appear that implement the virtual world as it was in its early days is it obvious there's a problem. This happened with *World of Warcraft* and led to the creation of *World of Warcraft Classic*; from that point onwards, *WoW*[64] itself began to feel like ancient Rome in the last days of empire. You can't relive your glory days without implicitly admitting you're now in decline.

When a virtual world has been sunsetted, if possible the developers or operators should hold a post-mortem so that lessons can be learned. There will have been reviews at every phase of the virtual world's development (particularly during and at the end of production),

---

[60] Alternative: income becomes less than it would be if the resources were redeployed elsewhere.

[61] If the overheads are negligible, as is the case with most textual worlds, you don't need any players at all to keep them running.

[62] Not in the *abandonware* sense – it is still operating, just receiving neither care nor attention. Personally, I prefer the term *museum mode*, but it hasn't caught on.

[63] Rogue servers may indeed be the cause of the fate of the original. They're also known as *private servers*, in which context "private" is a euphemism for "pirate".

[64] When the context isn't clear, the latest *WoW* release is referred to as *Retail*, as opposed to *Classic*, although *Classic* itself comes in different versions: [name of expansion] *Classic* follows the original expansion path, and is an example of what's called a *progression server*; *Vanilla Classic* has no expansions; *Classic Hardcore* has permanent character death (*permadeath*); *Classic Season of* [season name] is *Vanilla* with its own new content (but a limited lifespan).

but a formal look back at its whole story is always educational and informative. Even short ones can be of use – Damion Schubert's post-mortem of *Meridian 59* (Schubert, 2003) is a classic here.[65] I won't go into detail here regarding what a game post-mortem contains or how to conduct one (which is the producer's job), but if you're interested then there are excellent post-mortems available on gamedeveloper.com (Game Developer, n.d.).[66]

It's now time to sunset this overview of the development process of virtual worlds.

No, I won't be presenting a post-mortem of it – I have too much more book to write.

---

[65] The *GDC Online Vault* contains a talk in which Damion delivers a more detailed version of this post-mortem (Schubert, 2012). Thankfully, its sound quality improves dramatically after 160 seconds....

[66] This website used to be called *Gamasutra*. All game developers knew about *Gamasutra*, and until 2021, if I'd simply said "there are excellent post-mortems available on *Gamasutra*" then I'd have been understood. Sadly, after 25 years, the name was changed for reasons to do with awkwardness when speaking to non-gamers about it and the inappropriateness of smuttiness in the corporate world.

CHAPTER 7

Architecture

To make a modern virtual world is to undertake a large software-engineering project. This won't always be the case (just as we got stock MUDs in the Third Age, we'll get stock MMORPGs in some future age), but it is for the time being.

The term *software architecture* refers to the way that the large-scale component pieces of a software system (such as a virtual world) are arranged together and talk to each other. Architecture is not the same as program code: it doesn't run and it isn't programmed. It's more of a blueprint: it describes how the parts that do run are structured and how they interact. There are specialist software architects in some organisations, but for virtual worlds, the software architect will usually also be the lead programmer.[1]

Designers don't have to be programmers (although it's useful if they are), and they certainly don't need to be software architects; it helps a lot if they nevertheless know how virtual worlds are typically put together, though, because then they can design for the architecture rather than against it.

7.1 CLIENT/SERVER

Virtual worlds are places. These places are implemented in software. Players visit them by using devices connected to the software of the virtual world.

Because virtual worlds are shared, the state of any individual shard must be maintained by a single authority. Otherwise, contradictions and inconsistencies would arise that would have to be resolved.

There are two main ways to approach this: client/server and peer-to-peer.

In a client/server model, there is a single, authoritative *host* system that maintains the truth of the virtual world: this is the *server*. Although it can be treated conceptually as a single computer, in practice for a modern graphical world it will be a cluster,[2] possibly growing and decreasing in number dynamically as part of a cloud. Each player's device runs *client*

---

[1] I'm calling them leads for simplicity's sake, but remember that there are many fancy job titles out there and the company website might say Lead Engineer, Technical Director, CTO or something entirely different.

[2] A *cluster* is a group of tightly linked, interchangeable computers that work together in such a way that they can be thought of conceptually as a single system.

 DOI: 10.1201/9781003689638-7

software that displays the virtual world as perceived by that player's character; it shows the world as it was when the last update of information from the server was sent – but it doesn't mean that the virtual world is like that *now*, because things are still happening. As an analogy, you don't know that the sun didn't explode 8 minutes ago, because it takes an average of eight minutes and 20 seconds for information from the sun to reach Earth[3]; with a virtual world, you don't know that all your client is displaying is still true because it was only true when the last message from the server arrived milliseconds ago. Mere milliseconds are rarely a problem, though, thankfully.

In a peer-to-peer system, there is no overall host; rather, the client computers themselves provide the hosting services. Each keeps a copy of the virtual world (or part of it) and informs the other peers in the network when changes are made. There is no central authority, it's a shared responsibility; this is advantageous, because it removes the single-point-of-failure problem you get using a central server. Peer-to-peer works well for multi-player games, but it has some issues for virtual worlds (which are massively multi-player, rather than merely multi-player):

- Large-scale commercial virtual worlds are often too big for a single device to handle. If you were the only player on a peer-to-peer version of *World of Warcraft*, your PC might complain.

- Peers can be hacked, so there are security issues. If you can't trust that the other peers are telling you the truth, that's the end of peer-to-peer.[4] Denial of Service attacks are also much easier in a peer-to-peer environment.

- There are limits to how many peers can be in a network before the volume of communication between them required to update the virtual world's state impacts performance.[5]

- It's difficult to provide customer service, because whatever the CSRs can do, so can the regular players (eventually, some illicit software-modification may be required).

- All the devices need to be using compatible versions of the same software. If a new patch comes out, it must emanate from an authoritative source (a central server), although distribution afterwards can be along peer-to-peer lines.

- If everyone were to quit the virtual world then to restart (perhaps following a catastrophic crash), establishing the current agreed-on world state could be problematical.

There are partial solutions to some of these difficulties. Network nodes can dynamically organise as structures to cut down on the number of messages that need to be sent between

---

[3] Obviously, if you're not on Earth when you read this then the timing may be different.
[4] Or "the end of the peer show", for Victorian-era readers.
[5] A high volume of such traffic could also hit the profits of your Internet Service Provider (ISP), leading to some degree of *throttling* – the intentional reduction of your connection speed.

peers. A blockchain can be used to distribute the storage of the world state. [6] A server can be used for patching and logging-in, with peer-to-peer handling the game itself. The security issue is pretty well insurmountable, though, so unless your MMORPG is actually only a MORPG, peer-to-peer is only going to be usable for a narrow range of activities (in particular, freeform inter-player communication works well peer-to-peer).[7]

Because a client/server architecture is reliable, maintainable, scalable and secure, most virtual worlds are implemented using some version of this approach. The basic data flow is that the server sends a stream of instruction or metadata codes (known as *tags*) to the client, which the client then interprets to update the screen; at the same time, the player issues commands via the client that are passed as requests to the server. Some of these requests cause the server to update its world model; some produce visual or auditory effects but make no changes; some are simple queries; some require an error notification. The server will also update its world model without the action of players (such as when a mob moves or the weather changes) and may provide unsolicited information (such as announcements that the server is going down shortly for maintenance). Whatever the source of the information, the server sends appropriate tags to those clients that need to know and the cycle thus continues. The process is non-blocking (neither the client nor the server waits for the other to say something before it continues). There is a further possibility, that the client receives a pre-processed video stream that it can display as-is; we'll come back to that idea soonish.

The communication of tags may use a split protocol (TCP/IP or UDP for commands; HTTP or even FTP for assets[8]). Information packets[9] sent using TCP/IP are guaranteed to get through in the order they were sent (if anything is getting through at all); UDP guarantees neither of these conditions but is much faster and usually doesn't cause issues. This is especially the case for movement: it doesn't really matter if only 46 of your 47 move-forward commands reached the server, and numbers 13 and 14 came in reverse order. Movement commands are by far the most common requests received by the server and have been since *MUD1*,[10] so UDP makes a lot of sense for those.[11]

The overall series of communications between the client and the server goes something like this:

---

[6] The massively multiplayer online real-time strategy game *Dark Forest* (Gu, 2020) promoted this idea. Blockchain updates are not exactly fast, however.

[7] *World of Warcraft* launched with a background downloader that used BitTorrent for the peer-to-peer distribution of patches, but players complained that their own bandwidth (rather than Blizzard's) was being gobbled-up to provide updates to other players. The downloader was replaced in patch 5.4.0.

[8] I'm supposed to put expansions first, then the abbreviations in parentheses, but since there are four in a row here already in parentheses: Transmission Control Protocol/Internet Protocol (TCP/IP); User Datagram Protocol (UDP); Hypertext Transfer Protocol (HTTP); File Transfer Protocol (FTP).

[9] I'll just call these *packets* henceforth. They're basically unitary blocks consisting of the data being transmitted along with associated headers that are used by the relevant protocols.

[10] I did some analysis for *MUD2* back in its heyday and found that on average some 50%–60% of commands were movement. For graphical worlds, it's more like 90% or more.

[11] Routers experiencing data collision issues will usually drop UDP packets ahead of TCP/IP packets, so if there's very heavy network congestion then using TCP/IP all the time may be the better option (although it will express itself as lag and may itself make the congestion worse).

1. The player starts up the client.

2. There's a login handshake. The client gets a unique, one-shot key from the login server using, say, Hypertext Transfer Protocol Secure (HTTPS), which it employs to establish a TCP/IP connection. This process could involve ten or more exchanges.

3. A wave of asset tags arrives to describe the appearance of the player character (if it doesn't match one saved on the client device).

4. A second wave of tags arrives, usually listing location properties. This is basically the view of the game world from the player's perspective. Again, most of the data will be saved on the client device, so it's just a case of saying what to load. The client can display the player character in their environment at this point, but it might wait until after the next step.

5. A third wave of tags arrives saying what objects are in the player character's field of view and what assets they use. The client displays these on the screen, either once they've all arrived, once groups of them have arrived (the assets for another player character, say) or as they arrive.[12]

6. Tags associated with the user interface arrive next. There aren't usually many of them; it depends on whether the player has opted to have the server save their defaults or not.

7. A stream of physics tags are sent for the client to interpret as changes to the world, while simultaneously a stream of requests are sent to the server from the client. The vast, vast bulk of the client's time will be spent here: it's wherein the player plays the virtual world. [13]

8. The client closes down. When the initial TCP/IP link is terminated, it exits.

Clearly, there's more going on here than this outline explains. There are sanity-checks at the server end for a start, to make sure that what the client is sending makes actual sense and isn't some speculative nonsense sent by a hopeful hacker. The above is sufficient for a designer to get a feel for what goes on, though, which is all that's needed at this stage. It's enough that you'll be able to follow some of what your network programmers say, anyway.

7.2 SERVER ARCHITECTURE

The way that virtual world servers are organised is not as simple as one might think. Even in the old days when a server was a single computer (or part of one, if other programs were running on it at the same time), there were different ways of doing things. For example, *MUD1* used a multi-threaded approach in which each player's process worked

---

[12] Group-at-a-time will make objects seem to pop into view. As-they-arrive will make them appear piece by piece, a process known as *resolving*, or *rezzing* for short. *Second Life* was mocked at launch for rezzing its characters feet-first.

[13] Bandwidth requirements are surprisingly low for MMOs: *World of Warcraft* uses just under 10 kb/s, whereas *Second Life* is around 100 times more (Suznjevic & Matijasevic, 2012).

independently, with a memory-locking system in place to stop two processes from trying to use the same fragment of memory at the same time[14]; *MUD2*, on the other hand, was single-threaded, with players' processes sending asynchronous requests to the game server that were then processed serially rather than in parallel.

Whether the "server" is actually one computer, a cluster of computers or a cloud-based solution,[15] the overall abstract architecture tends to be similar. There are essentially four different layers, which in closest-to-hardware order are:

- Driver
- Physics
- World definition
- Instantiation

The *driver* is effectively the virtual world's operating system, interfacing to the operating system of the server (whatever its form) upon which it runs. It implements the virtual world's input/output (I/O), packet-handling, time-outs, memory management, primitive data structures and other low-level concepts. The driver provides two fundamental concepts to the layer above: entities from which the virtual world can be constructed (*objects*) and the association of I/O channels to certain of these objects (*player characters*).

The *physics* level[16] defines the unalterable physics model that controls how objects in virtual worlds act and interact. Concepts defined will include timers, movement, communication, and (if applicable) the magic, crafting, combat and economic systems. If your virtual world has natural-world physics concepts such as volume, containment or mass/weight, they'll go here, too. Ideally, collisions between objects would also be identified and handled here, but all-too-often, they're detected and flagged up by the client (which is A Bad Idea for security reasons, but if the engine you're using is built on single-player-game foundations then that's likely what will happen).

The *world definition* defines new objects and object interactions that are consequent on the physics, but it doesn't define any new physics. That said, the boundary between what is and isn't physics is often blurry. If you implement a match that can be used to light candles, that wouldn't really count as physics; if it can be used to set fire to anything flammable, which in turn could ignite anything flammable that came close to it, well that probably would count as physics. The distinction is important, though: designers do need to decide whether something is going to be a mere effect or a physical system, because the latter has wider-ranging consequences than the former.

---

[14] This was done on a single computer under timesharing, but amounts to the same thing; besides, the Essex University's DECsystem-10 mainframe was dual-processor, so it had some formal threading to support the timesharing, too.

[15] Improbable Worlds' SpatialOS is perhaps the best-known platform-as-a-service, although it was adopted by too few developers to have the impact initially hoped for it.

[16] This used to be known as the *mudlib*, back in the day.

The world definition can be regarded as a template from which *instantiations* are created. The world definition implicitly describes all the possible states that the virtual world can be in, but an instantiation is the particular state that pertains for this shard right now.

As an analogy, consider the board game *Cluedo* (or *Clue*), which I mentioned in passing back in Chapter 5. The "operating system" it runs on is the physics of Reality: pieces are held onto the board by gravity; light reflects off the board to present to the eyes what can be interpreted as coloured images; and so on. The driver level of the game defines the tokens: the character pieces, the board and the cards. It also associates certain of these tokens with certain players: you are the red token, I'm the yellow one, our friend Alex is the green one. The physics level defines the game systems, which are the rules pertaining to movement, card types, challenges and winning. Whether specialist rules such as those concerning turn order or the movement between secret passages are at the physics level or at the world-definition level is up for debate. The names given to specific character tokens (*e.g.* Miss Scarlett), weapons (*e.g.* the candlestick) and rooms (*e.g.* the conservatory) would definitely be part of the world definition, as they're not intrinsically part of any system; house rules would be part of it, too.[17] The world definition as a whole is made up of all the rules, plus the board, pieces and dice needed to play. Given this world definition (usually in a box), it's possible for players to play a game of *Cluedo*. When they actually *are* playing it, with the pieces wherever they are on the board, particular cards in their hand and three extra ones hidden to define the crime, *that's* the game instantiation.[18]

Incidentally, if you were to write down where all the pieces were, what cards were in whose hands, which cards defined the crime and whose turn was next, that would describe the game's *state*. You'd probably need the notepads where players record what evidence they've gathered, too. Fifty years later, you could dig out the game state as written down, then given the components and the rules,[19] you and the other players could continue the instantiation where you left off. The rules are essential: we have examples of the components, board, pieces and sticks (dice-equivalents) of the ancient Egyptian game *Senet*, and even some examples of states, but we don't know the original rules so we can't play it.[20]

The state of an instantiation of a virtual world is maintained in three databases: the *run-time database* (for things that change moment-to-moment), the *static database* (for things that don't change) and the *scripting database* (likewise). The static and scripting databases are from the world definition and are the same for all shards of the same virtual world: they don't change unless a developer changes them (which may be possible without

---

[17] They'd be *plug-ins* or possibly *mods* in a virtual world context.
[18] Note that the location of the weapon tokens doesn't have to be recorded, because – as mentioned earlier – they have no part in the gameplay other than as decoration.
[19] Technically, you'd also need to know the environment. *Cluedo* wouldn't work in zero gravity as the pieces wouldn't stick to the board.
[20] We have reconstructions of the rules, but that only means is we can play *Reconstructed Senet*, which may not be what the ancient Egyptians played. For all we know, all the pieces may be decorative like *Cluedo*'s weapons, and the whole "game" is merely a way to communicate a person's horoscope.

rebooting the virtual world). The run-time database is shard-specific and updates continually, whether by player action, mob action or timer action such as day/night cycles or weather changes.

For example, the location where the NPC owner of the cheese shop is standing will change occasionally as the NPC wanders around their store: their current position would be recorded in the run-time database, so it's the same for every player on the same shard. The location and layout of the shop never change, so would be recorded in the static database. The response the NPC gives when you click on them to interact would be recorded in (and executed from) the scripting database.

I should perhaps emphasise that these are abstract descriptions of databases: how they're implemented will differ from virtual world to virtual world. Smaller virtual worlds are particularly flexible in this regard. For example, a text MUD may be able to hold the entirety of the virtual world's state in memory, so whether an element can be or won't be modified is moot – it doesn't matter. Similarly, some virtual worlds might be all script from the physics level upwards (MUSHes are like this), so everything is effectively in the script database.

The run-time database has absolute authority regarding the current state of the virtual world. If all the clients think that X is Y but the run-time database asserts that X is Z, well, X is Z. Clients synchronise with the server, not the other way round. It need not contain information only about the state of the virtual world, however: it could also store social-interaction data (friends lists, guild memberships, in-game mail messages), analytical data (for metrics or bug-solving) and infrastructure data (if applicable, what other nodes in the cluster are handling). These could alternatively be kept in their own, independent databases, of course.

There are usually a slew of other databases accompanying or perhaps comprising part of the main three. Koster (2018) lists many, including ones to help do the following:

- Govern user connections.

- Store what persists across a reboot.

- Facilitate inter-player chat.

- Authenticate users.

- Distribute patches and updates.

- Deal with real-money purchases of in-game items and services.

- Expose metadata.[21]

- Cache some of the other databases in-memory for rapid access.

- Bridge from a web client to the databases to manage them remotely.

---

[21] This could be used to allow players to look at each other's characters offline, for example.

Add others for bug-tracking,[22] project management, CSR support tickets, back-ups and the usual business activities, and you can see why the IT staff of a virtual world developer might number many people. [23]

The more that a virtual world's designer knows about the databases used, the better. However, there are diminishing returns here. Yes, you do need to know what can be stored efficiently and retrieved in milliseconds in what amounts, so you don't design with unnecessary profligacy. Yes, too, you might occasionally want to query one of the databases without bothering a programmer – but really, you're going to have better things to do than invest time in learning SQL, so sorry, programmer, you're likely to find yourself being bothered.

Although I've been careful thus far to make it clear that a virtual world "server" could be either a stand-alone computer, a cluster of computers or a cloud of computers (and associated storage), I haven't explained *why* you'd ever need more than just the one. I'll do that now.

7.3 LOAD BALANCING

The single-player game *Daggerfall* (Lefay et al., 1996) was a world at least 160,000 km² in area and contained some 15,000 dungeons and places of habitation (Blancato, 2007). Nevertheless, it fitted comfortably on an MS-DOS PC well before the turn of the century.

It's not primarily the geographical size of a virtual world that determines whether it will live happily on a single computer or not, but how much memory and processing power is required to run it. Although major drains on this could in theory come from the actions of mobs[24] or general environmental simulation effects, in practice,[25] it scales with the number of players: *activity* is the key metric, not data volume. The more players you have, the more load there is. The more load there is, the longer the virtual world will take to respond to user input.[26] Beyond some threshold, you're going to need either a bigger computer or more not-necessarily-so-big ones.

One obvious way to keep a virtual world from becoming sluggish is to cap the number of players who can access it simultaneously. This can lead to login queues, especially when a virtual world is launched or a new expansion has come out, when many more people than usual are trying to get in at once. If it leads to login queues at other times, the provision of additional shards to take in new players (or to allow existing ones to transfer to) will help reduce the problem. Not all designers want to have multiple shards, however, and single-shard worlds aren't rare: *EVE Online*, *Second Life* and *Albion Online* are examples.

As it happens, though, when a virtual world has additional shards then it's not usually for reasons to do with server load. Rather, it's because the virtual world's content is

---

[22] You did know that virtual world developers can record and save every single keystroke and mouse movement you make, didn't you? You can almost guarantee they'll do it in alpha and beta, so that when the inevitable crash happens, they can see what you did to make it happen.

[23] More than the one bloke they had in *Jurassic Park* (Jurassic Park, 1993), for sure.

[24] Much as I would love to see a virtual city populated by 100,000 autonomous NPCs, all with detailed personal lives, I suspect that's still some way off.

[25] In practice for virtual worlds, this is. Other systems, such as weather forecasting simulations, might have different ideas.

[26] This has long been known as *server lag*, although it could be argued that *server latency* would be a better term.

specified (by you, its designer) as good for a given range of player numbers, above which the environment would feel overcrowded (and below which it would feel empty). Even spreading a million players across a hundred shards still means you have to deal with ten thousand of them on each shard, which has traditionally proven to be far too many for a single non-supercomputer to handle. Therefore, as with popular single-sharded virtual worlds, developers have to use multiple computers to share the load.

As for *how* they share the load, well this is the question of *load balancing*.

The first virtual worlds of the Fifth Age used a geographic model for load balancing. Reasoning that most of the interactions between player characters occurred when the characters were in close proximity, the virtual world was split into geographic sectors (called *zones*) with a single computer dedicated to each one. Moving from one zone to another could take up to a minute, especially if the client software needed to load a new set of textures in readiness to display a different biome upon arrival (which was the case in *EverQuest*). It was therefore often covered by a loading-screen animation (at launch, *WoW*'s ship travel showed a map with the route between the departure port and the destination port gradually being filled with a line of dots).

This approach works if player characters are fairly evenly distributed throughout the virtual world. If they're not, there could be problems. In its early days, *Second Life*'s zones (which were basically square patches of land) would start to seize up if more than about 40 players were in them at the same time. The maximum number of player characters permitted in each zone was therefore capped. When events expecting a large attendance took place, the hosting zone was moved to superior hardware to allow in more people.

This form of static zoning is easy to implement but has two major drawbacks. As we've just seen, one of them is that players tend to go where the content is, which could put more of them in a zone than it can handle. The other is that lightly occupied zones are wasted resources: the server is sitting there doing very little while the server next to it could be struggling.[27]

The solution, pioneered by *Asheron's Call*, was to use *dynamic zoning*, thereby allowing for seamless worlds. In this approach, servers can change their responsibilities on-the-fly. One underloaded server could take on the management of a zone being run by another underloaded server, which in turn could be given control of half an overloaded zone. Zones in such an architecture need to be much smaller than in the static model, so that they can easily be partitioned or combined. They're still geographically granular, though, because otherwise a player might not be able to interact with another player standing two steps away across a zone boundary.

Servers can also be balanced by making sure that players don't group up in the same locations in large numbers. *Dark Age of Camelot* did this with its system of *realms* – parts of the virtual world only accessible to a subset of the player base (three subsets, in *DAoC*'s case). Interactions between the groups take place in a smaller, contested zone. This works if the different groups have similar numbers of players in them, but if one group comes to dominate overwhelmingly then it can make matters worse. Other incentives then have to

---

[27] If you want a third drawback then the inability of mobs to cross zone boundaries would be a contender.

be given to entice players to join the unpopular factions, which will have inevitable side effects of their own.[28]

Player characters are not the only cause of processing load. Sometimes, mobs and other automated systems are. In such cases, the problem can be mitigated by slowing down how often mobs move (or indeed whether they move at all). Instead of acting every so-many seconds, they act every so-many *ticks*, where the length of a tick in seconds can be increased in times of stress; the same technique can be applied to player action cooldowns. *EVE Online* famously does this for its large-scale battles, because otherwise the automatic weapons aboard spaceships would fire continuously and drones would be moving collectively while players would all be issuing commands at the same time, grinding everything to a halt. This *time dilation* solution is not a new idea (*MUD2* did it), but it's one at which *EVE Online* excels.[29]

Another method for dealing with load balancing, which helps to give the impression that a virtual world is single-shard, is *layering*. I touched on this in Chapter 6: it's when an additional copy of a zone is started up dynamically when that zone is close to getting full. Player characters entering the zoned area will be diverted to the copy, which will remain in existence while there are such characters in it. If players enter the zone as a formal group, they will all be directed to the same area if possible.[30] In general, this works well except when there's a *flash crowd*[31] (the situation in which large numbers of players suddenly attempt to get to the same location, for example to fight a *world boss*). When that happens, it's possible that you could see people running into the zone and disappearing as they're transported to a new layer (and it's also possible that the attraction is only in one layer anyway, as it might be if, say, a very rich player was giving away money for free). *The Secret World* is a good example of layering in action.

The ultimate aim of load balancing is to ensure that no server computer is overloaded. With geography-based solutions, ultimately there's going to be a minimum atomic zone size that can't be split apart any further. It's possible to break virtual worlds apart in other ways, though, in particular by object and associated functionality. This gives a much finer-grained, modular structure, allowing for the load to be easily spread dynamically in an expandable cloud (albeit with higher overheads for inter-component communication and some trickiness in creating the structure from a design document in the first place). The widespread use of such distributed systems could nevertheless be the long-term answer to the problem of load balancing.

Until then, though, designers will need to be careful with regard to controlling the number of player characters who can be in close proximity to one another, and (to a lesser extent), the number of mobs that act autonomously but non-trivially.

---

[28] *DAoC* put in a system to boost character development in unpopular realms, which worked but turned their newbie areas into ghost towns and so gave new players a bad impression of the game's popularity.

[29] It needs to, too. On 6 October, 2020, a battle known as "Fury at FWST-8" involved 8,825 players overall, peaking at 6,557 concurrently in the same vicinity (Guinness World Records, 2020).

[30] It wouldn't be possible if there were more characters in the group than fit in a fresh layer, for example. This is why designers need to be aware of this kind of thing, so they don't allow such large groups in the first place.

[31] The term comes from the title of a Larry Niven short story (Niven, 1973).

7.4 SECURITY

If you are using a client/server architecture, your client *will* be hacked. So will the graphics card and the comms links. The aphorism "the client is in the hands of the enemy" has been (often painfully) discovered by every MMO developer who hasn't had it drummed into them beforehand.

Because of this, the server can tell the client nothing that it would be bad for the player to know. Furthermore, the client must have no ability to make decisions that it would be bad to trust.

Sadly, this isn't always what happens.

Example: *EverQuest* mini-map. When *EverQuest* launched, it didn't have a mini-map. It was possible to sneak up behind player characters without their noticing your presence, except perhaps by hearing your footsteps. A lot of players liked the excitement and thrill of wandering around a new environment, constantly having to look over their shoulder in case anything was following them. However, because the player character could turn round at any moment, the *EQ* client needed to know if there was something there so it could render it at speed. Therefore, it was told the locations of everyone and everything nearby, regardless of whether they were in the player character's line of sight. As a result, a hack was written that picked up this information and displayed it as a radar mini-map. You only had to look at the mini-map and you could see whether anyone was behind you or not, or waiting in ambush behind that tree up ahead.

Example: *Air Warrior* hit-detection. Kesmai, the developers of *Air Warrior*, had a problem with their aerial dogfighting game because of lag. Sometimes, packets of information were delayed and it looked as if aircraft weren't moving. To compensate for this, the client assumed that planes continued along their last-known trajectory, so that the lag wasn't apparent; the actual location of the plane would be updated when packets finally started to arrive again. This worked most of the time, because planes did indeed tend to continue in a straight line. Sometimes, though, the pilot *had* moved and their aircraft had either to warp (ghost out from wrong location, ghost in to right location) or to slide (course-correct to get to where it should be). This meant that what was displayed on the screen was sometimes not always a true reflection of what the server decreed. People would be blasting away with all guns at a plane that fully occupied their screen, only to be told they'd missed. This caused Kesmai a lot of customer-service problems. They therefore took the decision to make the client, rather than the server, calculate whether a bullet hit or not. They knew this was a risk, but tried to finagle it by saying they'd improved lag response times. Players were not fooled, however, and soon wrote hacks that reported any shot as being a hit on whatever aircraft happened to be nearest to the client's reticle.

There are some partial solutions to the problems outlined in these examples. The *EQ* hack could have been headed off by sending encrypted data to the client that needed a very short key to decrypt it, which could be sent as a fast UDP packet; the client would have all the information it needed, but in a form unusable until the decrypt key arrived. The *AW* hack could have been mitigated by tracking lag using pulse UDP packets, so an estimate of what the client was actually displaying could be approximated. Neither of these would have made the problem go away entirely, though.[32] Eventually, mini-maps were provided as standard and tab-targeting replaced aiming until lag and latency became less of a problem.

There are plenty of such hacks. If the client is deciding whether you walked through a wall or not, well, maybe if you hold down a particular key it decides you did. Is the client handling cooldowns? Gosh, look how much faster they are now. Does the client alert the server when you get close enough to a mob to aggro it? Not now, it doesn't. Would it be handy if camouflaged enemies had big arrows pointing at them, or if walls were transparent, or if you could move 150% as fast as you should be able to move? If the client handles it, here, you can have it.

The fact that clients can be hacked is why peer-to-peer virtual worlds such as the original *Phantasy Star Online* are a bad idea. Even if you put draconian monitoring software on a client,[33] it won't help: people only have to insert a PC between your game computer and the network to gain free access to all the incoming and outgoing packets. The content of packets can be changed, new packets can be inserted, unwanted packets can be dropped.

The ability to inject packets into the communications traffic between client and server opens up the potential for *bots*. Bots[34] are stand-alone pieces of software that take on the role of the user in a software system, which in our case means they play the virtual world. Although they could have the full force of artificial intelligence behind them, they usually tend more towards mindlessness. This is because the tasks they are typically given are ones that human beings really don't want to do because they're simple but boring, such as repeatedly killing a series of mobs on a circuit for hours and hours because these very occasionally drop something desirable.

It may seem that setting up a bot is a lot of effort to go to just so you can sell felcloth to tailors in *WoW Classic*, but it's quite easy and can be done quickly at scale. A mere three weeks after its North American launch, *Lost Ark*'s operators banned over a million bot accounts (Sabo, 2022); when they repeated the exercise ten months later, the MMO's concurrent-player numbers went down from around 300,000 to more like 100,000 (Allsop, 2023). It's possible for players to buy botting software online, with Reddit communities devoted to discussing which are the best (and worst) ones for particular games.[35]

Related to bots are other forms of automatic play, such as macros. We had these in *MUD1*: players would enter a fresh game, run a macro and five minutes later be standing somewhere safe holding all the best items with a pile of points added to their score – I had to introduce multiple start points and get-in-your-way mobs to put an end to the practice. The key point about macros is that a player can be playing as normal for most of the time, then press the macro button to get that one annoying thing done quickly and efficiently, before returning to normal. A classic example would be setting up a macro to move you forward slightly then jump: rather than having to time 20 of these short combinations in a row to complete an irritating jump puzzle, you only have to line yourself up 20 times in

---

[32] Recall that UDP packets don't have to arrive in the same order they were sent, or indeed to arrive at all.

[33] Note that said draconian monitoring software is also in the hands of the enemy.

[34] I'm obliged to point out that the term *bot* is an abbreviation of the term *robot*, but I find it hard to believe that this isn't so obvious as to be perfunctory.

[35] For example, at the time of writing, the r/RunescapeBotting community has 15,000 members (Reddit, 2024).

a row and let the macro do each of the individual jumps (or macros, if there are different jump distances that require different run-up lengths).[36]

Are bots and macros a security issue? Well they are if you don't allow them, but they're not if you do. Generally, player-run bots are not allowed, because they interfere with regular players' options and play merry hell with the economy. Macros are more of a grey area, though; indeed, some virtual worlds, such as *FFXIV*, take a dim view of bots but provide in-game tools for setting up macros (that players mainly use for crafting, because it's boring but the designers haven't taken it out).

Accessibility issues can also be a reason that players use macros. When I was playing *Black Desert Online*, I became quickly frustrated by the plethora of key combinations I had not only to learn but to execute when in combat: a few minutes setting up the macro buttons on my gaming mouse soon put an end to that. OK, so this was mainly down to laziness, but I could at least have argued that the necessary finger contortions to play "properly" could have led to repetitive strain injury and hastened the onset of rheumatoid arthritis. If I'd actually had rheumatoid arthritis, macros would have been essential.

Automated play is such a problem for virtual worlds (especially free-to-play game worlds) that designers have to account for the possible effects of it in their design. Design-based countermeasures can be put in place to lessen its impact, such as prohibiting the transfer of in-game currency between characters who haven't been in the same guild for a certain minimum period. Other countermeasures can be more implementational: merely requiring multi-factor authentication will make running bots a hassle, for example.

None of this will deter the persistent bot-creator, though, and a range of detection methods will invariably have to be deployed for any virtual world with a large enough player base to attract bot activity. Artificial intelligence is making this a lot easier than it used to be, and although it can also be used to help bots evade detection by acting "naturally", they're not so much of a problem when they thereupon act naturally. Regular players don't pay a billion gold pieces for a single health potion someone has put up for sale in the auction house,[37] so an intelligent bot hoping to evade detection wouldn't do so either.

Automatic bot-detection trawls will inevitably catch some players in their nets. Said players will invariably complain about this, and not just because they were banned: it's a little insulting to be told that your play is so automated as to appear mindless. That said, detection by humans isn't guaranteed failsafe either. One of my own characters was once killed in *Albion Online* for being a bot when all I was doing was gathering resources (admittedly, an activity that was so devoid of skill it was basically a clicker game with seconds-long cooldowns between clicks).

If you are going to remove bot accounts, then, accept that you'll remove some genuine accounts, too, and have your apologies ready.

I won't go into details with regard to how bots are spotted, because this is a book about the design of virtual worlds, not security. Also, I'm no security expert and don't think I

---

[36] Guilty as charged, even though I'm very good at jump puzzles.

[37] The deal is that the person who put up the potion or whatever for sale has paid the bot-owner with real money to buy it with in-world currency. It's not as common a technique for selling gold as it used to be, because it's easy to spot and both the player's account and the bot's account get banned.

could carry off a bluff that I am. I will note that it involves the collection of large amounts of in-game metrics, and that these same metrics can be used to detect infractions by regular players, too – gameplay exploits, for example. We'll take a look at exploits in Volume II, where there's more on bots, too.

There are other security issues that don't involve gameplay.

When a virtual world is going to be patched, it's usual to pre-download the bulk of the data needed. This downloading goes on in the background while the player is playing and is low-priority so as not to introduce noticeable latency. There's nothing wrong with this, of course: players have a shorter wait time while the patch is installed and the patch server won't have as heavy bandwidth requirements.

This does mean, though, that for some time in advance, there's a collection of data sitting on the player's computer awaiting installation. It doesn't really matter for weekly updates, but for large-scale content patches, it can do. This is because a small number of players will enjoy data-mining it to find out what the up-coming patch will contain. As a result, big reveals and other secrets can be made public before you want them to be, ruining the marketing pipeline and possibly putting players off if the wrong conclusions are drawn from limited evidence.

This can be addressed, of course, by simply encrypting the patch data and not sending the decryption key until it's ready to be installed. Unfortunately, that word "simply" is not always applicable: co-ordinating a patch is a major undertaking, and sometimes what's been downloaded has itself to be patched before installation (if a late bug is found, for example, or a design decision is reversed). Developers therefore have to balance the possibility of premature information-release against the extra hassle they'd have to go to in order to prevent it. Keeping back the *really* secret stuff until the last download is a fair compromise.

In summary, developers should (and often do) log everything. They can reduce the number of bad agents by using multi-factor authentication for login, recording MAC addresses and IP addresses,[38] and by taking credit card numbers[39] and other personal details such as name, address and date of birth.

Note, though, that if you do record any player-specific information then the security of that information itself becomes an issue. You really don't want your player data to be hacked and sold to the highest bidder on the dark web. As we'll see in Volume II, privacy is important (and not only because the law says it is).

7.5 TELECOMMUNICATIONS

The connectivity between client and server is, thankfully for designers, the province of programming and operations. Nevertheless, there are implications for design that designers would do well to understand.

---

[38] MAC (Media Access Control) addresses can be faked by a compromised client and IP (Internet Protocol) addresses can also be spoofed, but they're not reusable.

[39] Obtaining a hundred thousand working credit card numbers so you can run a hundred thousand bots is, one would hope, a non-trivial undertaking.

I've mentioned some of these points already when discussing security, but they all flow from the fact that communication is not instantaneous and the client is therefore always behind the server.

As for how far behind the server the client is, well that varies user-to-user. There are three factors to consider:

- **Latency**. It takes time to send bits down fibreoptic cables, and more time to route them at each stage (especially if the routers are doing deep packet inspection for national security reasons). Firewalls can slow things down, too, as can throttling.[40] Once a connection is established, though, latency is fairly constant; it doesn't have to be the same in both directions (client-to-server may be slower than server-to-client, for example), but it's usually close. The total time in milliseconds for a round trip is the connection's overall latency. You can add in the time it takes to process a command on an empty server if you like, but it's so negligible as to be not really worth the bother.

- **Network Lag**. Despite what some players may think, lag and latency are not the same thing. Latency is fairly constant, but lag varies. If you're planning to undertake a road journey from A to B and back in the middle of the night, the time it would take you is equivalent to latency.[41] If you did it during rush hour, you'd still have basic latency, but the extra traffic would slow you down. Because network congestion spasmodically comes and goes, the result is network lag.

- **Server Lag**. When there's only a handful of players on a server, commands will be processed quickly and efficiently. When the server is close to capacity, though, there will be times when commands are coming in faster than they can be handled, or information is being generated faster than it can be transmitted.[42] This introduces the irregular delay known as server lag.

Players refer to the current response time they are getting from a virtual world (or any online game) as their *ping*. The term derives from the name of a handy Unix utility program that sends an echo request to a server and measures the time it takes to get a response. As with much player terminology, the definition isn't uniform (it may or may not include network lag, for example), but it's basically a measure of latency. Relatively speaking: *high ping* is a bad thing, indicative of network problems that impact adversely on gameplay; *low ping* is a good thing, indicative of a free-flowing connection with barely perceptible delays.

Lag is worse than latency because it's unpredictable. TV streaming services circumvent it by buffering the stream, so unless it gets really bad, there's usually a few seconds' worth of material that can be shown while the delay is clearing. This is not an option for virtual

---

[40] Net neutrality for the win!

[41] I'm optimistically assuming in this analogy that the middle of the night isn't when major roadworks take place.

[42] Visible pets are particularly bad here. If there are 50 people fighting a world boss and your pet does something cute, 50 people have to be told about it. Spell effects are also bad, for similar reasons, but they're less avoidable.

worlds, because they're real-time: if you issue a command and it takes five seconds before you find out if it worked or not, the disparity is too great and the real-time condition fails.

Although there's not a lot that can be done to stop network lag,[43] there are ways to reduce the *appearance* of lag. I touched on these *predictive models* earlier, but essentially, the trick is that the client always displays moving objects as if they're going to keep on moving in the same direction at the same speed. Usually, any instruction from the server to change an object's direction or speed comes quickly enough that the client can display the adjustment without causing weird-looking visual effects. However, when incoming movement-update packets are significantly delayed (usually by lag), the client runs the risk that its extrapolation will turn out to be incorrect. It hopes that when the period of lag is over and a flood of update packets arrive all at once, it'll be displaying the objects where the update packets say they are. Very often, this is indeed the case, so the player doesn't notice the lag. The question arises, however, as to what to do when a prediction fails and what the client has been showing the player doesn't match the latest version of the reality maintained by the server. The error must be corrected.

There are two basic ways to do this, which I touched on briefly when discussing security:

- **Warp**. The object (which is typically a player character, because few other things move non-predictively) disappears from where it was and reappears where it should be. Strictly speaking, it's only a warp if the transformation is immediate, like a cut in a movie; most virtual worlds prefer a *fade*, whereby the object becomes gradually transparent where it was while becoming gradually opaque where it should be.

- **Slide**. The object as it's shown on the screen moves "as normal" to where it's supposed to be. In practice, it will usually go somewhat faster than normal, so it can catch up with itself.[44] For short periods of lag, this is more immersive than warping, but for longer periods, it can be jarring (especially when a character runs through a wall). For best results, you should therefore use sliding when an object isn't very far from where it should be and warping for when it is. Note that the term *strafe* is sometimes used instead of slide.[45]

It's quite amusing to watch someone run off a cliff into space until they seem to notice, whereupon they plummet to their doom in the manner of Wile E. Coyote. The reason it's amusing is that it doesn't happen very often: most of the time, the client's predictions don't fail, and an episode of lag goes unnoticed. This is good for players, but it has consequences for design. In particular, you can't put anything too timing-sensitive into a virtual world, because what the client is telling the player may not match what the server defines as being true. If you expect players to dodge the jets of fire that shoot out of holes in the walls every

[43] If a player's neighbours are all watching the output of streaming services, it's not allowed for the virtual world's operator to bang on their windows and tell them to stop.
[44] You might see another character standing still like a statue for three seconds then suddenly run at comically superhuman speed to a new location.
[45] Confusingly, I've heard *fade* used for it, too. Not all historical knowledge is useful.

two seconds, you will be disappointed. Make it at least four seconds, and save the playtesters from having to tell you what you should have known already.

Designers also can't put anything too space-sensitive into a virtual world. If something needs to be where the screen is telling the player it already is, well, it might not actually be there. This bites the most in combat. We'll discuss the options in more detail in Volume II, but what it comes down to is whether you attack a space (hitting whatever happens to be there, if anything) or whether you attack a target (hitting it wherever it is, if within range and line of sight). The former is action combat with no auto-target; the latter is traditional combat with lock-on tab-targeting. As I mentioned earlier, action combat is an option if lag and latency are low (and it should be said, they are indeed both lower than they were when we had to use dial-up modems); if one or both is an issue, only tab-targeting is going to be viable.

7.6 STREAMING

The term *streaming* has three main uses in the context of virtual worlds.

One, *live streaming*, concerns playing the virtual world while you broadcast a capture of your screen (and usually of you, too, as a picture-in-picture insert) to your millions[46] of followers. I'll touch on that in Chapter 19, but it's not the kind of streaming I'm about to discuss right now.

Neither am I going to discuss *tag streaming*, which is a technical term concerning the information sent from the server to the client. This is because I've already discussed the topic earlier in this chapter.

Rather, I'm going to write a few words about *cloud streaming*, which I mentioned in Chapter 3 as a possible future for virtual worlds.

When people give presentations from their laptops, they utilise a second screen (the big one that the audience can see), but they look at their laptop's screen (so they don't have to turn round). The second screen doesn't have to be smart, it's just a screen – it could even be a simple projector.

Now, imagine that instead of interacting with the laptop, you interacted with the big screen. You could stand next to the screen and point at it and move to the next slide and so on. This is commonplace in teaching environments. The screen needs a little more programming behind it, so that it can send your touchscreen commands to the laptop for it to process, but it doesn't have to be a powerful computer itself.

Now imagine that the laptop is somewhere else and you're connecting to it from the screen over the Internet. Because no one is looking at the laptop now, it only needs to use the one screen – the remote one with which you're interacting. Also imagine that it's not a set of boring presentation slides showing on this screen, but a virtual world. You can hook up some devices to the screen, too – mouse, keyboard, controller – so you don't have to play it by touch.

That's basically what cloud streaming is.

---

[46] Well, hopefully non-zero, anyway.

Out in the cloud are powerful, dedicated computers optimised to play particular games (or virtual worlds in our case). On your home PC or console, you connect to the cloud, choose your game, and immediately you see it on your screen as if you were running it on your PC or console. It looks indistinguishable – or perhaps better, because your PC's old graphics card can't render that many polygons that quickly. It takes no time to boot up, and if it's a new game then you don't have to install it – it's right there, ready and waiting.

This set-up is, formally, client/server, but the client is very thin: it merely has to pass your input to the server and present the audiovisual stream it receives as-is.

This may sound a new idea, but it's not. *MUD* effectively worked this way, except that the cloud equivalent was a mainframe computer and the PC equivalent was a terminal so dumb that all you could do on it was type commands and read what it printed out.[47] Remote desktops use the same technology: what your screen displays looks and behaves just like it does normally, but it's actually a stream emanating from a central server somewhere.

The advantages of cloud streaming are many. You have no downloads, no patches, no waiting. Security is a breeze, because the bulk of the client is no longer in the hands of the enemy. It's a great idea!

Well, it *would* be a great idea if it weren't for latency and lag. Cloud streaming requires a lag-free, low-latency connection between your home PC or console and the cloud. If you have such a connection – as the users of Microsoft's Xbox Cloud Gaming platform do – it's a marvel.

However, if you don't have such a connection, the idea is a non-starter (at least for playing modern virtual worlds).

Text MUDs are more forgiving of latency and lag, which is why this approach worked for them. Virtual desktops (using Microsoft's Azure platform or similar) are also not unduly worried, at least they aren't if you spend most of your time filling in spreadsheets. Games that don't need real-time responses can shrug off lag by buffering the downstream in the same way that TV streaming services do, so what you see is uninterrupted but a little behind the action.[48] In graphical virtual worlds, though – or indeed any computer game that requires spatiotemporal accuracy in a fast-changing scene – buffering merely adds more latency (or, in player language, gives you a higher ping). AI-based adaptive algorithms can help overcome bandwidth issues (GeForce NOW does this), but there's not a lot that can be done to counter high latency short of placing servers close to Where You Live.

Although the likes of Stadia and OnLive ultimately failed, that doesn't mean the concept is fundamentally a bad one. If lag-free, low-latency connections can be made generally available (either by using private networks or by a massive, widespread increase in transport capacity that doesn't introduce too much latency[49]) then cloud streaming for virtual worlds may yet have its day. That day has still to come, though, at least at the time of writing.

---

[47] I don't mean "displayed", I mean literally *printed out*, on paper.

[48] If you're watching the New Year's Eve countdown to midnight on a digital TV, you could be shouting "happy new year!" several seconds late.

[49] Sadly, it looks as if satellite connections do introduce too much latency, at least for now.

7.7 MOBILE PHONES

I'll end this chapter with a short, somewhat incongruous section on virtual worlds and mobile phones. It does eventually get around to the design implications of the platform's somewhat limited affordances, but I'll begin with what I (and probably no one else) call *auxiliaries*. These are applications that provide limited information and possibly some functionality for a virtual world from outside of it. They don't put the player *in* the virtual world, so they're not formal virtual world clients, but they do have live access to the virtual world to some degree, if only its character database.

Auxiliaries are usually mobile phone apps, but they can also be web-based (an early example, *WoW*'s Armory,[50] is an example). They're not the same as a mobile version of the virtual world: you can't play the virtual world using one. You can, however, access information and perform some offline activities. For example, *FFXIV*'s Companion app lets you show other people your character, move stuff around between inventories, send retainers out on ventures and buy things from the cash shop. Needless to say, it's that final possibility that tends to greenlight the development of a modern auxiliary program; well, that and the temptation to charge players for the other functionality the auxiliary offers, too.

Virtual worlds have always had external programs that allow developers to query and to change databases.[51] Auxiliaries are just the same thing except sanitised for player use. When it comes to *playing* an actual MMO on a mobile phone, though, the platform is somewhat stymied by its combination of small screens and sucky input methods. Although there are several fully fledged phone-based MMOs out there (*TibiaME* being the earliest that I know of), in most cases, they're mobile-*only*: this is because smartphone players would be at a significant disadvantage if they had to share a cross-platform server with the players using a PC or console client. By keeping mobile and PC players apart, the gameplay available to the former can be streamlined, with fewer immediate command options and a lot of automation. Thus, although *EVE Echoes* (NetEase, 2020) tries to capture most of the *EVE Online* player experience (at which it largely succeeds), it still has to run in its own, alternate universe. Its players' ships would be absolutely shredded if exposed to the expertise of people in possession of a large screen, programmable keyboard and multi-button mouse. Likewise, *Black Desert Mobile* follows many of *Black Desert Online*'s steps, but it's a distinct game with its own servers.

That said, if the virtual world itself has fairly simple controls then cross-platform, same-server play can be feasible. *Old School RuneScape*[52] is a good example of this: its mobile-phone client rivals the concurrent-user numbers of its PC client. *Albion Online*, too, manages to allow mobile and PC players to play alongside each other on the same server without making PvP one-sided. Also, for collaborative MMOs such as *Villagers &*

---

[50] Because this is a proper noun, I feel obliged to use American English spelling. That doesn't mean I'm happy about it, though.

[51] Roy Trubshaw called the first such program he wrote for *MUD* FRIG. This is a vulgar British slang term meaning the same thing as another four-letter F word when appended by "about". For *MUD1*, it was rewritten as POWER. The upper-case letters are because of the sixbit naming system employed by the TOPS-10 operating system, by the way: all file names were in uppercase.

[52] This is what *RuneScape 2* was renamed as immediately prior to the launch of *RuneScape 3*.

Heroes (Slye, 2011), it doesn't matter much even if PC users do have an advantage (or indeed if mobile users do): being out-gunned is no big deal if you're not going to be gunned in the first place.

It remains the case, however, that if you want to design a virtual world that players can play from a phone, the best idea is to design if *for* a phone, rather than to be cross-platform. You *can* make it cross-platform, of course, but you should design it primarily for the phone as that's the lowest common denominator. *Autoplay*[53] may seem pointless, but if PC players can tolerate a dumbed-down interface to accommodate console players, console players can tolerate an even dumber one to accommodate smartphone users. Thus, successful cross-platform MMOs such as *Dragon Raja* (Archosaur Games, 2020) are born.

Talking of interfaces…

---

[53] This is pretty well what it says it is: an AI plays your character for you in the background while you yourself are otherwise occupied.

CHAPTER 8

Interface

I EXPLAINED EARLIER THAT, ALTHOUGH interface design is incredibly important to virtual worlds, I wouldn't be investing a great deal of time discussing it. Virtual worlds can succeed or fail entirely because of their interface, but ultimately, a virtual world is what the player is interfacing *with*, not the interface itself.

This is an important point. There's no fundamental difference between a world that is rendered to you through text, graphics, AR, VR or sound. A world is a world. An interface may make demands on the world (or *vice versa*), but even a text world and a VR world are both still virtual worlds, and most of what applies to one world-wise applies to the other.

That said, there are implications that different types of interface have on the design of the virtual worlds with which they are interfacing.[1] Some things you can do with one interface but not another, or you can do it but not very well. Optimising for one interface may mean deoptimising for another.

Let's take a look at a few of the more important forms.

8.1 TEXT

As I illustrated using Asimov's argument in Chapter 3, when it comes to interfaces, text is either the start point, the end point or both.

Text is incredibly immersive if you have a good imagination. Because you do have a good imagination,[2] that's not a problem for you. It may be a problem for other people, though, either because they don't have a good imagination or they do but they lack patience. Text requires more effort to get into than does graphics,[3] so unless you're prepared to invest time in reading, you're not going to bother.

One of the reasons that text is so immersive is that both input and output use the same modality. What the player tells the virtual world is in the same format and the same place

---

[1] Being bidirectional, they can also have an effect on the player, as we'll see in Chapter 15.

[2] Let's put it this way: you won't get far as a designer if you don't.

[3] "Graphics" is one of those words, like "physics", that you want sometimes to use in plural form and sometimes in singular form, but it looks the same both ways. Thus far, I've managed to get away with using the plural form the whole time, but here I'm referring to the concept of graphics, which is singular; hence, "does", not "do".

 DOI: 10.1201/9781003689638-8

as what the virtual world tells the player. Input is in text, output is in text, and as a bonus (unlike with graphics), you don't need to move your eyeline from one part of the screen to wherever the conversation box is to find out what people are saying: it's right there in front of you.

Input in text is far more nuanced than in all the other interface forms (except perhaps voice, which we'll come to later). There are as many commands as there are verbs, and they can all be modified by adverbs. You can fill a screen with icons to click on, and you'll still have nowhere near as many basic commands as you can get in a textual world.[4]

From a design perspective, text is exceptionally flexible. It's a doddle to add completely new, well, anything – objects, locations, commands, quests, whatever. For example, *MUD2* doesn't have intelligent fungi in it, but it would take me ten minutes to add them. It would take longer to give them functionality not already present in the game, such as turning mobs they killed into intelligent fungi too – maybe an hour or two, including testing. To do this in a graphical world of any kind would be non-trivial; the functionality might not be too hard, but creating and animating a completely new mob type would take weeks.

This flexibility allows for easy experimentation – you can try out ideas on impulse if you want to – leading to wondrous expressive possibilities. More can be created with text than with graphics – you could have a ten-dimensional world if you wanted (not that I'd recommend this). Many more people can write well than can architect spaces well, even in blocks worlds such as *Minecraft*, so text is more enfranchising, too.

Also, in text, the pictures are better.

In a textual world, I can stand in my own mouth, seeing my surroundings get light and dark as I open and close it. I can be part of a painting I am carrying under my arm. I can appear as a frog to one person and a beautiful princess to another. I can have internal organs. I can photograph an opinion. I can share control of my body with another player. I can drink from a Klein bottle. I can be of no gender. I can unerupt a volcano, store the world in a box, hold a soul in the palm of my hand and dance with the colour cyan.[5]

None of this matters, though, because graphics have more immediate impact than text. Unless you can't see beyond that,[6] you're not going to play a text game. You'll play what looks good at first glance.

Obviously, there are downsides to textual worlds. They're hopeless on phones because too much of the screen is needed for input. Procedural content generation is pretty well a non-starter if you want a world with any kind of depth to it. Localisation is a chore, because there's so much to translate and different parsers are required for different grammars. Voice-to-text technology opens up some interesting possibilities, but probably won't result in a renaissance of the form.

Basically, then, text is an amazingly good interface for virtual worlds, but you're not going to play a text MUD any more than you'd watch a movie of this book.

---

[4] *MUD2* has 1,610 basic commands, excluding ones composed using adverbs.
[5] This paragraph comes from a comment I made responding to a Terra Nova blog post (Ondrejka, 2005). If you want to understand more about the difference between text and graphics, this post is an excellent place to start.
[6] Or can't see at all. Text MUDs are attractive to blind players.

8.2 GRAPHICS

Although the term *graphics* only addresses output, input devices are also implied (typically mouse and keyboard for PC and controller for console[7]).

Immediately, the heaviest design consequences of interface choice are exposed: controllers can't handle text, and it's very difficult to target arbitrary points on the screen with them without turning the character to face the target. This suggests they need a fixed reticle in the middle of the screen, looking over a shoulder of the player character. Input has to be limited to button combinations (there can't be icons to click on), and thus, the range of options available to the player is limited. It's worse than that, though, because for crossplay, the range of options available to mouse/keyboard users is also limited. When an interface has to work for multiple devices, it's effectively constrained to the intersection of those devices' capabilities.

Although older virtual worlds used different visualisations (such as *The Realm*'s side-elevation approach and *Kingdom of Drakkar*'s mix of top-down for maps and side-on for characters), modern virtual worlds are pretty well[8] all 3D in appearance, adopting either a near-*isometric* perspective or a near-*first-person* one. I say "near-" because they're not quite in line with the formal definitions, and there are differences between how each virtual world handles the details. Basically, you're usually looking at either a zoomed-out screen from a high angle centred on your character ("isometric"[9]) or you're looking ahead from just above and behind your character, who is a significant presence on the screen ("first-person"). Because *first-person* implies you're seeing the virtual world through your character's eyes, some designers (myself included) prefer *second-person* if the character themself is in view.[10]

An isometric point of view shows much more of the player character's immediate surroundings but much less of the character. It's good for when you have large-scale combat with hordes of mobs throwing themselves at you in an effort to be killed first (as in *Lost Ark*), but it's weak on immersion and for looking at things far away. A first-person point of view is better for immersion, but the field of view is limited in width. Sure, you can see distant mountains, but you can't always see the tiger coming at you from behind until it's right on top of you.

There's some leeway here if the camera can be moved in and out (and especially if its orientation can be decoupled from the direction the character is facing); you can zoom in with *Lost Ark* to get a more intimate feel and you can zoom out with *FFXIV* if you want an overview. Most of the time, though, players are going to stick with one viewpoint because that's what best fits the gameplay.

---

[7] You may also be able to use a controller with a PC if you want your head handed to you on a plate by the mouse-and-keyboard users. The pointing capabilities and usability of a mouse are just so much better than those of a controller (Young et al., 2016). That said, my attempt to play *Elite Dangerous* with a mouse and keyboard instead of a hands on throttle-and-stick was torture.

[8] I wanted to say "virtually" here, but they're virtual by definition.

[9] Formally, it's *axonometric* (Totten, 2019); it's only isometric if the viewing angle is 60°.

[10] Other designers might use *third-person*, although that can also be used for the near-isometric viewpoint.

You, as the designer, decide what that gameplay is, of course. If it differs – maybe between boss fights and levelling play – then the interface will have to be flexible enough to handle the competing needs.

The original isometric games were tessellated 2D planes rotated and angled such that they looked 3D. Objects were 2D artwork, and anything that needed animation was a sprite. Early Fifth-Age virtual worlds such as *UO* and *Lineage* were like this at launch. Modern virtual worlds with an isometric viewpoint are properly modelled in 3D, which is why it's possible to move the camera around more freely than it was in the early days.

Whatever approach the interface uses to display the virtual world, the virtual world itself is independent of this. You could write a 2D client – or even a textual one – for *World of Warcraft*, given enough time. That said, there may be aspects of a virtual world's spatial design that are incompatible with a chosen interface. For example, textual worlds freely use non-geometric spaces: you can easily represent Euclidean spaces (as used by graphical worlds) within them, but the reverse isn't true. Similarly, input that might be quick and easy using a controller could be clunky and slow using a keyboard but no mouse.

Assuming that a virtual world *is* using Euclidean geometry, that doesn't necessarily mean it's fully 3D. It could be what's called *2½D* (or *2.5D*), which is 2D plus a height map. As I mentioned in Chapter 3,[11] a height map means that you can give the impression of mountains and valleys, but not caves or bridges because those can't be implemented using height maps.[12] You *can* have them by using objects and object interiors instead of terrain, but these are a nuisance to create (which is one reason why cave systems in an MMO often seem to have uncannily similar layouts).

A 2½D world would be chosen ahead of a fully 3D one because it's easier to implement. For the most part, you're only interested in surfaces. In the majority of virtual worlds, you're not going to be digging random holes in the ground, so there's no need for anything to be down there. Fully 3D volumetric spaces as used in *Minecraft* and other voxel-based worlds do indeed have something down there, and indeed possibly up there, too, but they use a lot more memory: instead of a single plane plus a number, they have to have as many planes as there are units of height.

Most graphical worlds from *M59* onwards have used 2½D, rendered by the client as if they were fully 3D. Fully 3D worlds themselves are only necessary if the design requires it, which, as you're the designer, you get to decide. Expect wails from the lead environment programmer if you do so decide and don't go with a simple blocks world with a limited number of kinds of block.

Graphical worlds are complemented well by music, sound effects and other staples from the film industry such as voice acting and motion capture. They can work on mobile devices, too, albeit with limited input offerings. Their main strength is their immediacy: a single glance is enough to show what's going on and can convey a strong sense of the

---

[11] In a footnote. Of course, if you read footnotes then you'll know that anyway, and if you don't then you won't see this. Still, who doesn't like redundant footnotes? Or rhetorical questions?

[12] A height map is one number, so like a stack of blocks. If there's a gap above these blocks before another stack starts, a simple height map won't cut it.

overall atmosphere. You don't need to do any work to take this in, unlike with text. You don't need any preparation, either, unlike with AR and VR.

Speaking of which…

8.3 AUGMENTED REALITY

Augmented reality is Reality with bits of it covered up by virtual images such that they look as if they're "really there". It's like with old movies, where a group of actors would apparently be standing in a cityscape but in actual fact were in a studio with their images superimposed onto a matte of a cityscape.

Hmm, sometimes I wonder if my easier-to-follow analogies are harder-to-follow than what they're supposedly helping to describe. Basically, AR is what you have in *Pokémon Go* or its predecessor, *Ingress* (Niantic, 2012): computer-generated images placed in front of a real image in order to give the impression that what they depict is part of Reality. The image is *diegetic* (appearing to be within the geometry of Reality) rather than *non-diegetic* (like a subtitle for a foreign-language film).

Now, given that one of the criteria for being a virtual world is that it's not Reality, and that AR worlds overlay Reality, this would suggest that they're not virtual worlds. The suggestion is correct: they're not. However, they do share many similarities, and some authorities refer to them as MMORPGs.[13]

Because of this, I shan't be saying a great deal about AR as an interface to virtual worlds except to note that merely having an AR interface *doesn't* mean a game *isn't* a virtual world. *World of Tanks*[14] has an AR interface that shows the virtual world as if it were within the real world, which, as this is exactly what a flat, 2D screen does, isn't bringing the real into the virtual so much as it's bringing the virtual into the real. The system isn't great for actually playing *WoT*, but it's excellent for giving demonstrations and for spectators watching it as an esport.

8.4 VIRTUAL REALITY

Virtual reality works by whelming the user's main senses (vision and hearing) with data presenting a perspective on a virtual world. It gives a true first-person view, as the world is seen through the character's eyes.

This sensory immersion is very powerful. The player feels that they *are* their character in the virtual world. This sounds great, because (as we'll see in Chapter 14) becoming your character is the end goal of playing a virtual world. Unfortunately, that's not really what happens with VR. The player *does* feel that they are their character, but only because the virtual world is so real-appearing that this is the starting point. It's more like they feel their character is *them*. There was never any distance between the two. This is not conducive to the kind of identity exploration that's at the heart of why people play virtual worlds.

---

[13] MobyGames' page on *Ingress* does this (Sciere, 2015). Sadly, it doesn't list the names of the people on the development team, and tracking down who actually designed *Ingress* proved to be beyond the limits of my patience.

[14] OK, so it's debatable whether *WoT* is a virtual world anyway, as its persistence is very low, but let's ignore that for now.

VR definitely brings new affordances to the player experience. OK, so there are some off-putting side effects (motion sickness, ickiness if you wear make-up, bashing into physical objects, occasional blinding headaches, feeling unsafe), and it's not great at showing text, but these issues will all be addressed in time.[15]

Designing a VR experience is a lot different from designing a regular game, at least if you want the VR to be a major feature. However, designing a *world* for VR isn't a lot different from designing it for regular graphics. Experiences can often be very computationally expensive, because you have to maintain the world all around the player, not just what's in front of them: people can turn their heads at unexpected moments, and they don't want to be faced with wooden-acting NPCs when their eyes come to rest. Control over the player experience is therefore tricky. Virtual worlds have to do all this anyway, though, so they're not as bothered by it as single-player games are.

Of course, if you're not playing up to VR's strengths by designing an experience, why would you be using VR in the first place? What value does VR add? If people can't even be bothered to wear the 3D HDMI glasses that have been able to make virtual worlds such as *WoW* look 3D[16] since 2010, why would they go to the trouble of putting on VR goggles[17]? It can't simply be that a sensory-immersive 3D world is in and of itself sufficient to attract the masses, because Reality is also a sensory-immersive 3D world and yet people will happily leave it to play games with flat, blocky graphics. Gamers might adopt it if they thought it gave them an edge, but a mouse and keyboard gives them an edge over a controller, and we haven't seen console players rushing out to buy PCs (or PC users rushing out to buy a gamer mouse).

Content is more important than interface, and until VR can either shake off its reputation of being a gimmick (by not foregrounding the technology) or becomes so easy to use that it's harder not to use it (using VR contact lenses, say), it's unlikely to become a mainstay of non-specialist virtual worlds.

Except...

Except designers *design* content. *You're* a designer. This is an open field with treasure lying on the ground for you to pick up. Don't think about experiences, don't think about proofs of concept: think about play and (for game worlds) gameplay. Virtual worlds designed *for* VR are *about* VR and aren't about anything else: the interface is the servant of the world, whereas it should be the other way round. Free yourself from that connection and you'll get more out of VR than if you focus on it, I promise.[18]

8.5 VOICE

Sound can be used to enhance a virtual world's atmosphere, through music, sound effects and voice acting in cut scenes. It can also be used as both output from a virtual world (using text-to-speech) and input to a virtual world (using speech-to-text).

---

[15] For example, motion sickness can be reduced by playing while intoxicated with alcohol. No, really: Iskenderova et al. (2017).

[16] It's not really leap-out-of-the-screen 3D, it's more looking-into-a-box 3D.

[17] Formally, these are referred to as *HMDs* – Head-Mounted Displays.

[18] For non-legally binding definitions of the word "promise" only.

Its main use, however, is for communication between players. Any gameplay that relies on co-ordinating group behaviour is going to benefit from voice, although it does interfere with the ability of users to manage multiple tasks and conversations (Wadley, 2011). It has another, more serious disadvantage, though.

Early this century, I wrote an article (Bartle, 2003) warning about the dangers of introducing voice into virtual worlds. The thing is, voice is unimmersive – your own voice, especially. When you talk, you're you, not the one-metre high ball of fun your character is.

Designers of early virtual worlds knew of this danger, but players took it out of their hands. If you're on a console, using a controller, two-way freeform communication using text is tiresome in the extreme; consequently, a succession of voice-over-IP utilities (TeamSpeak, Ventrilo, Mumble, Discord, …) were adopted by guild members to talk to one other without going through their MMO's server. Eventually, developers had to concede and began to embed the feature within their virtual worlds. You can now wander around *New World* with your microphone on, speaking to people nearby.[19]

Reliance on voice as a form of communication is not ideal. Some people, myself included, don't mind listening (through earphones) but do mind speaking (through a microphone), because speaking annoys everyone else in the house. Other people don't like using voice because it reveals something about themselves that they'd rather keep private, such as their gender or their stammer or their strong accent. This is on top of the immersion problems: the elf you're talking to may look young and beautiful and feminine, but if it sounds like a male truck-driver from Milwaukee,[20] then the illusion is hard to maintain.

If you don't want people talking to one another in an immersion-busting way, the surest method to prevent it is not to design-in any gameplay that benefits from this. Unfortunately, this rules out anything requiring co-operation or co-ordination, so is off the agenda from the start in a massively multiplayer environment. There are technical solutions, though, particularly now that AI is on the march. Speech-to-text can become speech-to-intermediate-form; text-to-speech can become intermediate-form-to-speech; the speech going in doesn't have to use the same voice as the speech coming out. Voice fonts can make you sound unique, maintaining the tone your speech (which text isn't good at[21]) while giving you a different voice to your own that's more in keeping with your character. Automatically correcting bad grammar, or even translation into another language, wouldn't be a problem. If this is embedded within a virtual world, making it easier to use than having to connect to a separate server, it could become convenient enough to be preferred by players over external solutions.

For people like me, text-to-intermediate-form could have my character speak aloud what I typed in text. For deaf people, intermediate-form-to-text could have people's speech turned into readable words. The degree to which the intermediate form would be represented in keyboard-accessible characters to show emphasis and so on could be customisable.

---

[19] Spatial propagation of voice can help with making a virtual world more persuasive, while also avoiding channel clutter (Wadley, 2011).

[20] It's traditional that they're from Milwaukee.

[21] Compare "*I* didn't do that" with "I *didn't* do that", "I didn't *do* that" and "I didn't do *that*".

The way AI is heading, the intermediate form may not be necessary. It could be possible to convert between text and speech and *vice versa* directly through a large language model. This is likely to be very computationally expensive, so would require an always-on connection to an AI-as-a-service provider, but that doesn't mean it won't happen.

Overall, though, for reasons of immersion, I personally prefer text input and text output in a textual world to anything involving sound, graphics or other sensory-specific modalities.

I would, though, wouldn't I?

CHAPTER 9

Backdrops

V IRTUAL WORLDS ARE THEIR own, separate realities, but they are designed and developed in Reality. Unless you don't intend having anyone other than you play yours, the rest of Reality will have things to say that will influence its design. These environmental factors (in the sense of the design environment, not the save-the-planet environment or the created-world's environment) can have a strong impact on what can be designed, developed and released. To avoid confusion, in this chapter, I'll be calling these external contexts "backdrops" rather than "environments", "landscapes", "ecosystems" or other vaguely geographic terms.

It's possible to break down the overall backdrop to design into a number of dominant categories: business, legal, cultural, social and political. In the following sections, I'll be discussing how each of these influences virtual world design. In truth, there is much interaction between them: there isn't just one, independent business backdrop (say), but several such backdrops depending on the prevailing legal, cultural, social and political backdrops – which in turn are affected by the business backdrop.

You may have noticed that I mentioned "legal" there. Just to be clear, I'm not a lawyer, and therefore you can't believe anything I say related to legal matters. If I *were* a lawyer, I wouldn't need to write books about virtual world design to eke out a living.

Bearing this in mind, then….

9.1 BUSINESS BACKDROP

Most of the elements of the business backdrop that can affect design have already been covered: publishers who want content changes; cross-platform implications;[1] the regularity of the update and expansion cycle; the revenue model; …. One of them is of particular importance for design, though, and needs a deeper examination.

---

[1] Note that there can be single-platform implications, too, depending on the platform. Some of these can be quite exploitative.

DOI: 10.1201/9781003689638-9

9.1.1 Intellectual Property

The most pertinent aspect of the business backdrop for designers is that of *intellectual property* (IP). Regular property is the tangible stuff you own – land, magnets, tooth-brushes, pets, 1869 maps of Europe[2]; IP is the intangible stuff you own – stories you've written, inventions you've made, logos you've bought from a graphic designer, music you've composed.

IP falls into five broad categories (World Intellectual Property Organisation; International Trade Centre, 2010):

- *Patents* grant the exclusive right to a new, industrially useful, non-obvious invention.

- *Trademarks* are distinctive signs and symbols used to identify products and their manufacturers.

- *Industrial designs* are the aesthetic qualities of an item, such as textile patterns, jewel-lery and the cool-looking shape of an E-type Jaguar.

- *Trade secrets* are pieces of business-related information that are known only within a company and that give it a competitive edge. It's a very wide area, covering ingre-dients, manufacturing processes, market research results, client lists, development strategies and Much, Much More.

- *Copyright* grants the creator of an original work a monopoly over its use, so protect-ing them from being ripped-off. It only covers expression, not ideas or information: if the unlikely hero of your novel is a parole officer, your novel itself can be subject to copyright, but the concept of a novel with a hero who's a parole officer can't be. It does cover derivative works, though.

If IP sounds insubstantial, that's because it is. Different countries have different ideas as to what counts as IP or not, and some (such as the Republic of Maldives) don't even recog-nise the concept of IP in their laws – they use common law to deal with such issues. Other countries associate different rights with IP: in 1886, the United States did not sign up to the Berne Convention for the Protection of Literary and Artistic Works (World Intellectual Property Organisation, 1979), and when it did sign up 103 years later, it explicitly excluded the section on *moral rights* (such as the right of attribution). IP is therefore strongly con-nected to the legal and political backdrops that inhere in different jurisdictions.

Because IP laws are specific to different jurisdictions and not always policed with great thoroughness, internationally they're a mess. They're also invariably a mess within juris-dictions, particularly when it comes to patents. Some patents are granted that never should have been (because of prior art or obviousness, for example), yet the cost of breaking them is far more expensive than the initial cost of obtaining them.

---

[2] I have dozens of 1869 maps of Europe.

Furthermore, there are some fairly dubious behaviours undertaken by (fortunately, a very small minority of) patent-holders that can be exceptionally annoying and deleterious, such as employing a patent granted for one purpose to something way, way out of scope,[3] or not using or publicising a patent then springing it on someone who independently invents the same thing soon after and works on it for several years.[4] Also, because companies that patent products have to make them public, this means that other companies can take the idea, modify it, persuade an overworked patent officer that it's something non-obvious, then use this to stop the original company from going in that direction unless paid off.[5] Once one company has decided it's less expensive to pay a licence fee than to challenge a patent, that establishes a precedent; the next company in line will have an even harder and more expensive time challenging it.

Patents and copyright tend to have timers on them. For patents, the timers are often meaningful (in the UK, a patent is valid for five years initially, renewable yearly thereafter until a hard, 20-year limit (UK Government, 2024a)), but copyright lasts somewhat longer (also in the UK, for written works, it lasts for 70 years after the death of the author (UK Government, 2024b)).

So, what does any of this mean for virtual worlds?

Well the good news is that game rules can't be patented or subject to other IP, so unless there's a singularly bad interpretation of existing law or a badly constructed new law, you can happily purloin gameplay ideas from other people's games without compunction. The minefield of technical patents you will have to negotiate won't be daunting if you license an existing engine or use one in the public domain. Trademark use is fine if you recognise the trademark and get permission from the owner to use it.[6] The forms of IP that affect designers the most are copyright and (to some extent) industrial designs.

If you create a virtual world that uses characters or a setting drawn from the work of other people, you must obtain permission from those people or face a legal challenge. It doesn't matter how much you change everything else: unless you obtain permission from whoever currently holds the copyright to Tolkien's works, you can't put Aragorn in your space opera and you can't put your own characters in Middle Earth. It is unlikely that such permission would be granted for free. Copyright laws do usually have *fair use* provisions that allow some flexibility (I didn't have to ask permission to mention Aragorn or Middle Earth just now[7]), but even if you had a virtual world set in the present day and an NPC disparagingly called another NPC a hobbit, you might want to check.

---

[3] I once had to advise on a patent challenge in which a company that used a conveyor-belt system for moving game-specific CD-ROMs around in its factory tried to argue that this covered all data transport for games, including transmission over the Internet.

[4] These are called *submarine patents*.

[5] This is one reason why Microsoft hasn't patented the software for Windows – it doesn't want to have to make the source code public, which patenting it would require.

[6] One of the first soccer-management games I played displayed advertising hoardings around the pitch bearing the names of real companies, to add authenticity. The developer had to *pay* those companies to show their ads. Nowadays, it's the other way round: the companies pay the developers to show pitch-side ads to players.

[7] I hope.

When it comes to virtual world design, there are four ways you can source its IP:

- **Original IP**. You create everything from scratch yourself or build on other original IP you own. *EverQuest* did the former; *Final Fantasy XIV* did the latter. Almost all non-game worlds will use original IP.

- **Public-Domain IP**. You treat as IP something that doesn't belong to anyone,[8] such as the modern world or a world of mythology. *The Secret World* did the former[9]; *Dark Age of Camelot* did the latter. Note that some "mythologies" are legally protected as indigenous cultural and intellectual property (United Nations General Assembly, 2007), and others may fall foul of blasphemy or racism laws and the like.

- **Out-of-Copyright IP**. Eventually, copyright in a work does time out. If you want to put Porthos, Athos, Aramis and D'Artagnan in your virtual world, there's nothing that the descendants of Alexandre Dumas can do about it.[10]

- **Licensed IP**. You obtain permission (usually involving a fee and royalty payments) to use the intellectual property of someone else. *Star Wars: the Old Republic* and *The Lord of the Rings Online* took this approach.

You would use original IP if you wanted to develop it further, possibly licensing it to others (for example, film-makers). You would use public-domain IP if you wanted the flexibility to add material of your own to an existing, well-known setting. You would use out-of-copyright IP if you wanted the setting but didn't want to take it in wild directions. You would use licensed IP to make more money.

The fact that the main reason for choosing licensed IP is to make more money is why I've covered IP as part of the business backdrop for game design, rather than the legal backdrop.

Although (as I mentioned in Chapter 4) there are arguments that buying in an IP saves the design team the bother of having to develop a fully rounded original IP, these are weak. Designers actively *want* to create original IP – it's fun[11]! Licensed IP has an advantage in that would-be players know what to expect from a popular, tried-and-trusted brand – but the same can be said of public-domain IP and out-of-copyright IP. As a long-term strategy, securing a licensing deal for a prestige IP can show the world that your company is a serious force, which is not something any of the other options give you but it isn't in and of itself a reason to proceed.

---

[8] It's more like intellectual non-property, then.

[9] It overlaid this with original IP.

[10] That said, there's a slight risk if copyright terms are extended. UK copyright in the early works of Sir Arthur Conan Doyle ended on 1 January 1981, only for a 1995 change in the rules to extend this to 1 January 2001 (Deazley & Meletti, 2023). Those who had freely used the Sherlock Holmes character in the interim suddenly found that they were now in breach of copyright.

[11] Blizzard looked into obtaining a *Warhammer Fantasy* (Ansell et al., 1983) licence in 1994 (Wyatt, 2012). However, its development team wanted to have full creative control, so the company devised its own setting, *Warcraft* (Wyatt, 1994), in part inspired by *Warhammer Fantasy*. Had it not done so, we probably wouldn't have got *World of Warcraft*.

The main weapon a licensed IP brings to bear that none of the other options can is cross-media publicity. While *Star Trek* movies and TV shows are still being made and shown, *Star Trek Online* will benefit. While *Dungeons & Dragons* is still played, *Dungeons & Dragons Online* will benefit. While Conan books are still being read, *Age of Conan* will benefit.

On the downside, the IP holders know this and will not be inclined to let you use their IP without paying them a fee. You have to calculate whether the (envisioned) benefits are greater than the (known) costs. It's something of a balancing act, because the income gained from the extra players that the IP attracts may be lost to royalties.[12] Also, you could find that a popular IP suddenly loses its lustre, as happened to *Buffy the Vampire Slayer* (Whedon, 1997) after accusations of workplace harassment were levelled at its showrunner. The cross-media promotion could do more harm than good, too, as anyone developing a *Game of Thrones* (Benioff & Weiss, 2011) game would have discovered after the final TV series aired. It's also important to remember that IP holders won't usually allow developers use their IP indefinitely: Mythic Entertainment's contract with Games Workshop to use the *Warhammer Fantasy* franchise ran out after five years: *Warhammer Online: Age of Reckoning* launched on 18 September 2008, and the announcement it would be closed came on 18 September 2013 (Warhammer Team, 2013); the MMO was subsequently wound down over the three months that followed and sunsetted on 18 December 2013.

As it's a business decision, the source of the IP a commercial virtual world is to use is unlikely to be left purely in the hands of the designer. If the decision is made to go with a licensed IP, this can be both constraining and liberating.

A licensed IP is constraining, because the design has to fit the franchise. Some IP owners are more relaxed than others, but many will wish to have final approval over anything that appears (author J. K. Rowling is famously very protective of her *Harry Potter* (Rowling, 1997) line). Sometimes, even things that are part of the same fictional universe may be out of bounds: I once consulted for a virtual world that had a licence for Agatha Christie's *Death on the Nile* (Christie, 1937), but no other Hercule Poirot novels, so any information or character traits revealed about the Belgian detective elsewhere weren't covered.

A licensed IP is liberating because if a licence is guaranteeing you'll have a sure-fire hit, the designer can take risks with the gameplay. Innovation with the subject matter may be difficult, but with the game itself (assuming your virtual world is an MMO), it's easier. That said, even sure-fire hits can be torpedoed by poor design decisions, as was the case with *The Sims Online* (what gameplay it had was repetitive, and for most players, it was effectively a giant chatroom[13]).

Sometimes, IP is inserted into a virtual world as a short-term gimmick to retain players who might be thinking about moving on. Often, this has literally *nothing* to do with

---

[12] The 1960s British comedy revue *Beyond the Fringe* (Cook et al., 1960), which had successful runs in the West End and Broadway, was written by and starred Peter Cook, Alan Bennett, Jonathan Miller and Dudley Moore. Cook had an agent, who negotiated for him a 10% higher weekly fee – £110 rather than £100. When the agent took his own 10% commission, Cook was left with £99 per week and the rest still had £100 (Lenburg, 1983).

[13] The MMO consultants who advised on it despaired that so few of their warnings of how players would behave were believed. They were told "Players of *The Sims* just aren't like that". It turned out that they were.

the virtual world's fiction. I have screenshots of my character in *Lost Ark* standing next to Geralt of Rivia. I blame comic books....

Most indies are going to want to create their own IP. They enjoy designing it, expect that it will have value, and they rarely have the money to pay for a licence to an existing IP anyway. Warning: sometimes, as a condition of funding development, publishers will want ownership (full or partial[14]) over any IP that results. Play your hand well. Artificial intelligence rather muddies the waters, too. You're pretty well safe to use AI to create content if you own the data it was trained upon,[15] but don't expect right now to be able to claim this creation as your intellectual property. If the AI has been trained on data you don't own (or haven't licensed from the owner), you're on even less firm ground.

There are other concerns to do with IP, some of which are technical[16] (that I won't cover here) and some of which are legal[17] (that I'll address in the next section).

9.1.2 Player-Operated Servers

Although I've looked at revenue models already, one aspect of them that I haven't discussed in as much detail as I perhaps needed to is the particular case of player-operated servers. I did touch on this in Chapter 3 when describing possible futures for virtual worlds, but I didn't suggest that it would impact design. If guilds or individuals or even small companies want to operate their own server for your virtual world, they are likely to desire a large number of customisation options to disambiguate it from other servers. They might wish to be able to turn on or off such elements as lockboxes, microtransactions, "death means death" for player characters, PvP or anything not conducive to role-playing. Of course, they might also want to make all characters female or no characters black; whether you want to facilitate this is your decision.[18]

Whatever you decide, all such conditions, in all their combinations, have to make sense when new content is added. It could be that you even have to maintain old codebases, depending on whether the operators want to accept your new content or prefer to keep to a superseded version. In the wider world of software development, legacy systems cease to be supported after a while,[19] but if you make your money from leasing servers and a significant proportion hold out, you might think differently.

This is less of a problem for non-game worlds, because their content is largely created by their players: so long as the superstructure is backwards-compatible, so is everything else. For example, users of the open-source *OpenSimulator*[20] (Guard, 2007) can set up their

---

[14] "Partial" could just be the title, for example.

[15] Note that not all AI techniques involve training. The Machine Learning ones do, but most of the rest don't.

[16] The games industry was cautious about using voxels for years, for fear of being sued by the makers of medical image scanners who held layers of patents on this somewhat obvious concept.

[17] Players' ownership or otherwise of their in-world creations is the main one.

[18] We'll look at this kind of thing in Chapter 20.

[19] Not that this stops people from sticking with them. My optician still uses Windows 98, presumably on the grounds that the one, all-encompassing piece of software they use works just fine on it and there's never any worry that an update will do Weird Things.

[20] It's often called *OpenSim* for short, but that's actually the name of an open-source system for analysing musculoskeletal structures.

own server and be reasonably sure that (unless they themselves modify the underlying software) their content will still work come the next update.

Toes have been dipped into the server-rental market over the years. Some text MUDs attempted it,[21] and operating *Minecraft* servers is a profitable business. Funcom, developer of *Conan Exiles*, seems to find it a viable revenue model for that game. Whether we'll see more of this kind of thing in future rather depends on how much risk developers are willing to take to try it out, and how well designers are able to provide flexibility over consistency. Designing for it is a significant departure from designing for other operations models, which is why I've brought it up here. You effectively have to balance for all possible combinations of settings and don't have the luxury of discarding old ideas. Rather you than me....

9.2 LEGAL BACKDROP

If you want any kind of advice concerning what the law has to say about the things that you or other people either want to do or are currently doing, engage a law firm. There are some with specialists who work in the area of virtual worlds.[22] I won't list them, because then the ones I don't list will sue me, but they're not hard to find.

In this section, I'll be outlining the main legal-backdrop issues that affect game design. I have no training in the law, so please assume that none of this is true unless backed up by the specialist law firm you engaged after reading the previous paragraph. There are some very good books that look at the topic in some detail, albeit primarily from a North American perspective; I particularly recommend[23] Boyd et al. (2019), Duranske (2008), Festinger (2005) and Lastowka (2010).[24]

9.2.1 Jurisdiction

The first point to make about how laws affect virtual world design is that of jurisdiction: different countries have different laws, and what's legal in one country might be illegal in another. Furthermore, there are several cases where laws are exact polar opposites of each other, particularly with regard to alleged historical events: country A's laws might make it illegal to *deny* that X occurred and country B's laws might make it illegal to *assert* that X occurred. I'd give examples of X, but then I'd be breaking either the laws of country A (say, Armenia) or country B (say, Türkiye).

You're definitely going to be subject to the laws of the country in which you live, but you're also often subject to the laws of the country of which you're a citizen even if you live elsewhere.[25] Just because you're in a country where some action is legal, that doesn't

---

[21] Not successfully, because extracting money from players to pay for it proved to be next to impossible when there were thousands of free alternatives out there.

[22] These people will also tend to have solid expertise in legal matters concerning computer games in general, which is a further reason for retaining their services.

[23] In alphabetical order, to reward those who, like me, had the foresight to be born with a surname that starts with a letter close to the beginning.

[24] I should perhaps mention that if you dislike the preponderance of footnotes in this book, you are *not* going to enjoy reading academic works written by lawyers.

[25] This is called *extraterritorial jurisdiction*.

mean you won't be arrested for doing it should you return to your homeland[26]; neither, however, does it mean you'll necessarily be extradited to a country where you broke local laws if you're now in a country where what you did is not illegal. For example, in Nigeria, the age of consent is 11; in Bahrain, it's 21; other countries are in between (AgeOfConsent. net, 2024). In the UK, it's 16: should[27] an adult face prosecution in the UK for having had sex with a 20-year-old in Bahrain or a 15-year-old in Nigeria? Should they be extradited to Bahrain for the former?[28]

Thankfully, child exploitation is not something that plays a great part in the virtual world design processes. It's useful, however, as an example to show the kind of grey mists that overlapping international laws throw up. "Design to the lowest common denominator" is sound advice, but some jurisdictions have such restrictive laws that the lowest common denominator is *too* low.[29] Furthermore, there are territorial differences regarding issues such as lockboxes (Federal Public Service Justice Gaming Commission, 2018), age-related playing-time restrictions (Yang & Goh, 2021), effeminate male characters (Ye, 2021), …; the list goes on. In 2022, the European Parliament, in an effort to "ensure a safe and trustworthy online environment for video games and gamers", accepted a report (Maldonado López, 2022) and adopted a resolution to regulate, among other things: the handling of user-created content; parental-control mechanisms; lockboxes;[30] manipulative and exploitative design practices; dark design patterns; in-game purchases; pay-to-win; digital purchase refunds; playability by persons with disabilities; selling virtual goods prohibited by the End-User Licence Agreement (EULA); gold farming; addiction; data use; objectifying women; hate speech; cyberbullying; and content moderation. As is often the case with EU reports, this is a mixture of good ideas, very good ideas and cataclysmically bad ones.

The report happily "stresses that video games are both tools for playing and works of art with cultural value", so that's a plus.

If you intend to have a presence in multiple jurisdictions,[31] localisation specialists can advise in advance on what constraints apply – no blood in Germany, no skulls in China, no nipples in the United States and so on. Unless you don't care about being prosecuted, it's essential that you ensure your design breaks no local laws (or that if it does, pre-launch you can accommodate local changes to make it fall within those local laws – while not breaking any extraterritorial laws that your own country might have). Small virtual worlds operating

---

[26] It's illegal to sell Kinder Surprise eggs in the USA, but US citizens are at liberty to sell them in other countries where it's legal. US state secrets, on the other hand, are a different matter.

[27] The word "should" generally indicates matters of policy. It comes with an implied (but often not stated) context, typically a legal or ethical framework but also possibly a belief system. "Should humming in public be allowed?" is implicitly prefixed with "Given your understanding of the rights and obligations of individuals and of society at large, and your personal opinions on humming:".

[28] Also, gay sex is illegal in Nigeria (Human Dignity Trust, 2024) but not in the UK: should a UK or Nigerian citizen currently in the UK be extradited for having had such sex with a 30-year-old in Nigeria?

[29] Trivially, if a country outright banned virtual worlds, the intersection of acceptable content across all jurisdictions would be the empty set.

[30] The report calls them "loot boxes" and has a *lot* to say about them.

[31] There may be several authorities that claim jurisdiction, regardless of whether you intend for them to do so. Cloud-based servers could in theory be pretty well anywhere.

within only one jurisdiction are going to have markedly fewer problems, although their players might have more if they come from elsewhere.

Players, as inhabitants of Reality, have rights (United Nations General Assembly, 1948). I'll be looking at this topic in much more detail in Chapter 24, but for the moment, I'll confine myself to noting that player characters (as opposed to players) *don't* have rights. Players, yes; their characters, no. In your design, you can do things to characters that you couldn't legally do to players, for example kill them. Perhaps surprisingly, although this was always obvious to designers it was not immediately obvious to those pioneering legal scholars and others who had an interest in virtual worlds that did not quite extend to playing them. The issue was effectively put to bed by Raph Koster's famous *A Declaration of the Rights of Avatars* (Koster, 2000),[32] later consolidated as *Declaring of the Rights of Players* because too many people didn't read beyond the title and thought its content must be saying that avatars had rights. As we'll see in Chapter 24, there are caveats to this arising from the fact that the very aim of playing a virtual world is for the player and their character to become one and the same, but the general conclusion is that so long as the context is clear (either from the outset or through play), you should be OK to have your designer way with player characters so long as in the process you do no harm to players or to wider society (Brenner, 2008).

So, having at some length established that it's not always clear which jurisdiction's laws apply,[33] and that in most jurisdictions there's a distinction between the rights of players and the rights of their characters, we now know the shape of the legal backdrop and can begin to look at its implications.

9.2.2 Property

The legal backdrop influences virtual world design in many ways. Some aspects, such as employment law, affect designers more than they affect design and aren't covered herein. The main body of law that does affect design concerns *property*.

The first issue that we as designers, and law-makers as law-makers, need to consider is what exactly property *is* in a virtual world sense. Players will happily talk about "my axe" or "my mount" or "my house", but it's actually hard to identify what any of those things *are*. There may be a pointer in a database that can be labelled as being "your" axe, but what it points to could be a single number. Do you in some sense "own" that number? The number representing "your" axe could inherit all its properties from the general concept of what an axe is; do you own that hierarchy of inheritance too? Its only association with you is that it has a relationship that you interpret as meaning "inside" with a database record that you interpret as being "the inventory" of a record that you interpret as being "my character".

Historically, when virtual worlds finally became large enough to impinge on the consciousness of legal scholars and social scientists, muscular arguments were made that you really did own "your" virtual items. There were several grounds for this, including:

---

[32] The informative MUD-DEV thread on the draft version can be found at Koster et al. (2000).

[33] There are good arguments that virtual worlds should be their own jurisdictions (Lastowka & Hunter, 2004), although this idea has not gained traction.

- Players' claims are stronger morally and logically than those of developers (Dibbell, 2006).

- Normative judgements for property in the real world apply – sometimes more strongly – in virtual worlds (Lastowka & Hunter, 2004).

- It's a limitation that restricts freedom of commerce (Fairfield, 2005).

- It's not just the developers who give objects meaning, but the players themselves as part of a community that no one can "own" (Humphreys, 2005, 2008).

These law-based arguments were largely headed-off by clauses inserted into the EULAs that all players of commercial virtual worlds assent to when they sign up to play them, but it should be noted that a EULA itself may be held unenforceable (Meehan, 2006); this defence therefore can't entirely be relied upon as being rock-solid.

In general, designers *don't* want players to own (in a legal sense) objects in a virtual world. It's worth asking why this is so.

Well, the problem is that ownership of an object comes with all kinds of rights. Some of these alarm all operators of virtual worlds; others are only a worry for MMORPG operators. The primary ones[34] of concern are:

- Protection against theft or damage to your property. If my axe wears out, the designer is responsible because they designed the virtual world that damaged it. If my character is in a prison, the guards can't confiscate my gun because that would be theft.

- The right to dispose of the property by sale, donation or destruction. I want to set up a business selling virtual currency for real currency, regardless of how it might damage the MMO's economy. I want to destroy my ground-floor house and don't care about the NPCs who live in the apartments above.

- The right to any income generated by your property. My character is part of a virtual world that people pay to access. Where are my residuals?

- The right to alter or to improve your property. I want to make this amulet bigger and shinier. You must provide the tools that allow me to do so, or you're denying me this right.

- The right to exclude others from using or otherwise accessing your property without your permission. People are looking at my character all the time on their screens. I don't want them to be able to do that; my enjoyment of my character is at its height if only *I* can look at it.

- The right to use your property. I can't use my wand while it's on cooldown. *Your* design is preventing *me* from using *my* property.

---

[34] Reminder: I'm no lawyer, so these may or may not be applicable where you live and other ones could be important that I've missed out.

In summary, if players did have full legal property rights in the virtual objects their characters own, MMORPGs at least would be unplayable. For a game world to function, it is extremely problematical for players to own "their" virtual items. For similar reasons, it's also problematical for them to own "their" characters and even "their" accounts.[35]

Designers can't really do a lot about the situation in general, but they can decide on some particulars. They are perfectly at liberty to determine that it would be beneficial to grant their players some level of ownership in "their" virtual property while not necessarily conceding that the default is they don't.

For example, if your virtual world has no gameplay then you can get round most of these issues by having the player grant usage rights in perpetuity to the operator. This is why some virtual worlds (most notably *Second Life*) are able to recognise that players *do* own their virtual goods (if not the code that implements them (Gould, 2008)).

If your virtual world has gameplay but this lacks integrity, you may also be OK with a limited form of ownership. Some virtual worlds embrace *non-fungible tokens* (NFTs), the whole point of which is that the player full-on owns them (that is, the NFTs, if not necessarily any in-world objects associated with them). A list of MMORPGs with NFT components is maintained at ChainPlay.gg (2024).

Finally, if your virtual world has gameplay built around the very concept of ownership, you may open up its rules somewhat. *Entropia Universe* comes close to this as you can sell physical objects from Reality in it (MindArk, 2024), although in 2020, it had to limit the ways you could do that following a number of scams perpetuated by players on each other.[36]

For the vast majority of virtual worlds, it's a lot safer and a lot saner not to grant players property rights in anything to do with the virtual world (Bartle, 2006). It's nothing about power or control, it's about the freedom to design and the freedom to play (Balkin, 2004; Mayer-Schönberger, 2009).

The law may (or may not) be on the side of the designer, but that doesn't mean players won't flout it. Commodification, which is the process of turning something that wasn't a commodity into a commodity, happens in virtual worlds anyway (Ondrejka, 2004). Even small virtual worlds will have an underground economy, and for the larger ones, fortunes can be made if it reaches an industrial scale. I'll discuss the underground economy in Volume II, but I mention it here so that you won't wonder why I didn't; it's not so much about the legal backdrop as the illegal one. That said, it should be noted that in some jurisdictions, most notably that of South Korea (which is a strong force in MMORPG development), the law is such that the underground economy *isn't* underground: players do own their virtual goods, at least to the extent that they can legitimately buy and sell them from and to one another (and so be taxed on these transactions). This situation arose because the underground economy grew so large unchecked that the authorities essentially capitulated to the reality and regulated it (Yoon, 2008). As a result, virtual worlds coming out of South

---

[35] "OK, I admit it, I'm a spy from another company. You still can't close my account". There are also wider concerns to do with fraud (which is why in everyday life you can't sell "your" bank account).

[36] *EVE Online* has similar scams, but they're considered to be part of the game (at least until someone wins a lawsuit that determines they're not).

Korea are designed to assume that their players own their virtual goods; the adverse consequences for this on gameplay are indeed what designers predicted they would be.

Much as designers might like their virtual worlds to be distinct from Reality, their players nevertheless hail from there and are subject to the laws of the land. Certain of these
laws make it very difficult to create virtual worlds that run counter to them, regardless
of jurisdiction. In particular, the laws around finance tend to be *very* strict pretty well
everywhere and attract stringent policing. If you create a virtual world in which players
can set themselves up as banks, don't expect "it's just a game" to spare you from judicial
oversight. Given a formal way for players to convert in-world currency to fiat currency, the
in-world currency becomes simply a proxy for it and attracts the same regulations. Few
virtual worlds (at least in the West) offer such facilities, but those that do (such as *Second
Life* and *Entropia Universe*) require players to have banking licences before they're allowed
to do it.[37] See Volume II's discussion of weaponising virtual worlds for other suggestions
of things you perhaps might not want to attempt unless you wish to spend time in prison.

9.2.3 Taxation

Taxation is another area of law from which virtual worlds can't escape. Again, this is only
likely to bite if there's some legitimate way for players to extract real-world value from virtual world possessions, but the reach of tax officials tends to be long and this is therefore
not guaranteed. For example, if (despite the provisions of the EULA) people can easily buy
and sell in-world currency on external websites, that means there's a way to assess the value
of that in-world currency. Therefore, that currency *has* a value. You, as a player, should in
theory be paying income tax on the gold pieces your character picks up from the bodies of
defeated orcs (Camp, 2007). So should NPCs, come to that. It's only the benevolence of the
tax authorities that stops Elling Trias, famed cheese vendor of Stormwind, from having to
pay real-world taxes on all the cheese he sells to player characters.[38]

Basically, then, if you're planning on having some open way for players to extract fiat
currency from your virtual world, don't expect it to be simple (Bradley, 2007).

9.2.4 Intellectual Property Revisited

In the previous section, I invested some time in discussing issues of intellectual property
(IP) and threatened to discuss them some more in this section. I shall indeed be making
good on this threat, but it's not perhaps as bad as it sounds. The points I shall raise concern:

- Player-created objects

- Fan fiction

- Rogue servers

- AI trained on your work

---

[37] *Entropia Universe* is *itself* a registered bank.

[38] You can argue that tax only needs to be paid when in-world currency is cashed out, which is how some countries handle
winnings from casinos. That doesn't mean you couldn't avoid tax by never cashing out, though, if your local pizza company accepts *WoW* gold instead of $€¥£.

I'll take these in that order.

People own the IP inherent in works they create. In some countries, they have to register a created work to assert copyright ownership, but in others, they get it automatically. Let's assume the latter, to keep it simple. So: do you own the copyright of your character?

Well, there wasn't a level-80 necromancer with these exact same properties when I started to play. I created it through my play, therefore it's a creative act. Therefore, it's mine (Reynolds, 2003).

It probably is yours, too. However, it's like a drawing done on the developer's wall using crayons that the developer provided. The developer made sure when you entered the virtual world that you signed the EULA, which if they're smart gives them a free licence in perpetuity to use anything you created in the virtual world. To make sure they have it all covered, the developer might ask for joint copyright, or even (if they get greedy) for you to grant to them, in advance, copyright ownership of anything you create. Really, though, they just want to be able to show your creation on the screens of other players and to be able to delete it if the fancy takes them. Whether you in turn can use your creation or not is less certain, because the components of your creation belong to the developer. Yes, you might have moved the sliders in a particular way to give your character a unique look, but that unique look is still made up of textures and templates created by the developer.

From a designer's point of view, this is something for the legal team to handle – unless, that is, your gameplay *asks* for players to create something new. This is the case in *A Tale in the Desert*, wherein players can create sculptures that other players can critique. It's one thing to ask for permission to display the sculpture to people who walk past it in the virtual world, but another thing entirely to claim ownership of it and to start selling 3D reproductions made out of lucite.[39] If you are calling upon players to exercise their creativity, you are best advised to let them keep ownership of what they have created – even if the law allows you to claim ownership yourself. The reaction of players if you didn't do this would be significantly bad. There aren't many subjects that players largely agree on, but the undesirability of injustice is one.

An aspect of virtual world IP that designers can affect but can't own is that of the virtual world's culture (Taylor, 2002). A designer creates the frame within and upon which their virtual world's culture grows, and in so doing, they can shape that culture. They can't instantiate it, though, and the forces they put in place to move players in desired directions can be resisted by the players themselves. Although a virtual world's culture is a huge asset and adds value to the overall IP, it's not something that can be copy-protected.

The virtual world's setting and fiction can, however, be copy-protected in a legal sense. If you don't own the virtual world's IP then your only responsibility is not to breach the terms of the licensing agreement yourself, but if you do own it – especially if it's original IP rather than derivative of folklore or out-of-copyright material – then you must be on the lookout for breaches by others. It's not usually a *criminal* offence to breach copyright, so you have to look for infractions yourself rather than to rely on the efforts of the police. This is even

---

[39] I should rapidly point out that *ATitD* doesn't do this.

more important in jurisdictions where the failure of a copyright or trademark owner to prosecute violators can lead to the loss of said copyright or trademark.

None of this is of immediate concern to the designer: it's some other poor soul's job to discover breaches and let loose the lawyers of war. Of course, in general, you probably don't want people ripping off your work, but there is one kind of copyright infringement that you might be prepared to countenance: fan fiction.

Fan fiction is a term applied to amateur works that are derivative of IP owned by someone else. It overwhelmingly takes the form of written stories, but the basic principles extend to other works such as cartoons,[40] songs, poetry and computer games. There is some debate over whether using copyrighted characters and settings without authorisation is legally protected or not, with the consensus view being that (under United States law at least), if you use very little material, transform the use in some way,[41] don't try to profit from your work and don't negatively impact the profits of the copyright holder, you're *probably* OK. If you use substantial amounts of material, shine no new light on it, sell your work and dent the income of the copyright owner, the courts are likely to find against you. You might also want to avoid mentioning the characters of other players without their permission: defamation laws are independent of IP laws.

Fan fiction does not tend to be of high literary quality, but it isn't expected to be so; it's more weighted towards characters, themes and authorial self-understanding than it is plot, style and craft. Demographic details are hard to come by, but it seems to be written and read[42] mainly by university students, around half of whom are female and a seventh of whom are male, with the rather substantial remainder being non-binary, trans or genderless (Duggan, 2020).[43]

As we'll see in Chapter 10, the typical player base of MMOs hovers around 36% female for High-Fantasy MMOs[44] and 16% female for Science Fiction MMOs[45] (Yee, 2017), with 5% trans and non-binary (Yee, 2023) and the rest male. Given this differently skewed distribution, why would a designer wish to bother directing any attention towards fan fiction?

Well … why not? You should be worried if you *don't* see fan fiction appearing, as it suggests that you have no fans. Hey, it's free publicity! You alone get to decide what's canon, and although some fan fiction is going to be misaligned with the fiction of the virtual world (describing criminally dark subjects, for example), the vast majority of it probably won't be and can be left to thrive. Besides, a 5% gain may sound low, but if you were suddenly to lose 5% of your player base, you'd soon reappraise that opinion. These fans are among the most active players, too: their views carry weight beyond their own numbers, and you really don't want to upset them unnecessarily (Garon, 2017).

---

[40] Cartoons, drawings, paintings and the like are collectively referred to as *fan art*.

[41] Parody and criticism are examples of fair use. Also, luckily for me, academics can cite chunks of copyrighted works verbatim if they want, so long as they then make some kind of point about it.

[42] So many readers of fan fiction are also writers of fan fiction that reading and writing often coalesce almost as a unitary concept.

[43] These statistics concern *Harry Potter* fan fiction, which may or may not be representative of fan fiction as a whole.

[44] *World of Warcraft* is an outlier at 23%.

[45] *Star Wars: the Old Republic* is an outlier at 29%.

Fan fiction may not usually be objectively good in and of itself, but it *is* usually objectively good for the virtual world. Encouraging it by opening the IP for non-commercial use is well worth considering. You can go further, though: you can encourage it through design. You may find that you've done this anyway if you have memorable, trope-friendly[46] NPCs that hit the spot for writers and readers, or have something in the fiction that helps.[47] You'd perhaps *want* actively to encourage it (rather than take a more *laissez-faire* approach) because it feeds into the general ecosystem surrounding virtual worlds. In particular, readers and writers of fan fiction tend to like the same things as cosplay participants,[48] which can raise the profile of your virtual world even among non-cosplayers.

Cosplay is even better than fan fiction as something a designer might be asked to encourage. Few non-fans are going to read fan fiction, but plenty of non-cosplayers will see cosplayers either at conventions or on the local TV news. This gives it more capacity for outreach than fan fiction has (although fan fiction does tell you what's likely to be cosplayed[49]).

If you want to design for cosplay, you're basically designing characters (which is addressed in Volume II) along with their look. Their look is incredibly important, because although personality is what attracts a cosplayer to a character, its appearance is what determines whether they'll go for it or not. You'll need to discuss the details with the art lead, but it's going to help if the character is humanoid, doesn't carry hard-to-make props and has either statement make-up or a distinct outfit that they wear all the time.[50] Cosplayers who want more freedom to decide what to wear can be catered-to by having characters that sport no specific uniform but are of different species (cat people, dog people, plant people, dragon people, fae people, undead people, …). If you feel the urge, you can add increasing levels of appearance difficulty for more advanced cosplayers.

Related to both fan fiction and cosplay is merchandising. If it's your IP, you'd be advised to license the manufacture and sale of merchandise to a specialist company that knows what it's doing, but you'll still need to design something merchandisable. This could be as simple as giving a key NPC a cool hat – it doesn't sound much, but when you're looking for something to sell to fans, you'll be glad you did it. You'll probably want to have more than just a cool hat, though.

Not all fans are trying to express their creativity and investment in your game through fiction or through home-made garments. Most (and this is especially true of virtual worlds, as we shall see) are expressing themselves through play. These fans – and indeed players in general – will provide you with a stream of ideas. Most will be completely unsuitable; some

---

[46] Characters who are soulmates, characters who are full of angst, characters who are hurt and need to be comforted, … .

[47] Unfortunately, the main candidates here – time-travel, identity travel, alternative universes – are difficult to pull off in a virtual world, although we'll look at some ways to fake them in Volume II. Crossovers with other IPs, which are another fan-fiction staple, are also difficult, but for other reasons; these are also discussed in Volume II.

[48] This may be because they're the very same people, but it's hard to tell: researchers tend to focus on single aspects of creative expression in fan culture (here, fan fiction and cosplay), leading to a dearth of academic papers about their intersection. Gender and sexuality angles dominate the discussions.

[49] Weight any skimpily clad female characters higher than others, and higher than the same character dressed less revealingly.

[50] Don't try wearing the same outfit all the time yourself, unless you've won a lifetime's supply of deodorant in a lottery or competition.

will match ideas you've already had that are sitting in your files; a few will be ones that are in the process of being implemented. Only rarely will one make you think, "actually, that's pretty damned good – I'm having that!".

If you send a movie script to a Hollywood producer, it will be returned unopened. Only scripts sent by agents will be considered. This isn't because Hollywood producers think works written by people who don't have an agent must be rubbish; it's because lots of people have similar ideas and they don't want to be sued because your plot happens to bear a close resemblance to that of a screenplay they've already optioned.

Game designers have a similar problem, albeit on a much smaller scale. Suppose that a player posts in the official forum "you should add flying trees as mounts", and six months later, they appear in your virtual world.[51] Let's examine some possibilities:

1. You already had the idea and were putting it in anyway.

2. You already had the idea and were bearing it in mind, but the post raised its profile.

3. You hadn't already had the idea, but it's obvious. Perhaps all your other character species have flying-mount versions, so the next time you wanted to implement a flying mount, it was always going to be the trees.

4. You and this player had the idea at the same time, perhaps inspired by the same scene in a TV cartoon that you both watched on terrestrial TV yesterday.

5. This player alone had the idea. Other people supported it, but there wouldn't be flying-tree mounts in your virtual world if this player hadn't mentioned it.

In case 1, you should have enough of an audit trail to show that it was your idea first. In case 2, you should also have some time-stamped documentation to show that it was your idea first; you can say thanks to the player for reminding you. Case 3 is tricky, yet you can probably find plenty of other players who will back up your contention that it's obvious. Case 4 is even trickier, and you may have to explain where your idea came from if the player claims credit for it – assuming you're able to do so.[52] Case 5 is the one that's of most concern.

If you implement an idea that came from a player, what obligations do you have towards that player?

• Do they deserve a thank you? Well yes, of course.

• Do they deserve recognition? Yes, it was their idea.

• Do they deserve a mention in the game credits? Hmm, that may be going too far for some ideas, but unfortunately if you do it for one idea then you'll be under pressure to do it for all, regardless of how minor they are.

---

[51] I realise I'm stretching the counterfactual here, but bear with me.

[52] Designers get ideas the whole time, so there may not actually *be* a source of inspiration – they could have thought of it simultaneously through sheer coincidence. Players heavily outnumber designers, so it's entirely likely that eventually one of them will post an idea that happens to be similar to one the designer has just had.

- Do they deserve payment? A gift might be in order as a sign of your appreciation, but actual money? How much money?

- Do they deserve royalties? It's immaterial: they're not going to get them unless a court says otherwise – and if it does, no more players' ideas will be implemented in virtual worlds ever again.

If players were to start demanding money for their ideas, designers would be in trouble – especially if they *did* actually use the ideas. Are developers going to have to take the Hollywood approach and not read any player forum posts or emails, to protect them from such accusations? If they did, case 5 would no longer be possible, so it would succeed in that regard, but then you wouldn't pick up on all the non-suggestion sentiments that come from players regarding the virtual world. Also, because the forum is external to the virtual world, the EULA isn't going to protect you (and in some countries, it wouldn't even if it were internal).

All this was known back in the first three Ages of virtual worlds. I wasn't too worried about it personally until *MUD* went commercial, but thereafter, I made sure that if I did put something in the game as a direct result of a player's suggestion, they were thanked for it. They didn't get any money, though, because unfortunately "commercial" didn't imply "profitable".

As for modern virtual worlds, well often designers are looking so far ahead that ideas coming from the player base are already outdated and unusable. Ideas to do with the UI may be more pertinent, but by the time the designer acts on them, the original poster is but one voice among many, and it's unlikely they'd succeed if they asked for a consultancy fee.

In essence, then, if you're going to take ideas from the players, be fair, be honest and be careful.

Now, casting your mind back several pages, you'll recall that I said there were four points in the legal backdrop that I was going to discuss. I've completed "ownership of player-created objects" and "fan fiction" (a pairing that came together in a satisfying manner at the end), and will now take a brief look at "rogue servers" followed by "AI trained on your work".

Rogue servers (or private servers) are unauthorised copies of the virtual world. They arise for a number of reasons, including:

- The original virtual world has closed down.

- The original virtual world is in maintenance mode.

- The original virtual world is not available to all players.

- The original virtual world isn't as good as it was back in the day.

- The original virtual world would perhaps benefit from improvements.

- The developers of the rogue server want to make a truckload of money.

I recall a conversation I once had with Raph Koster, lead designer of *Ultima Online*, who described his having been surprised to find on a visit to China that he was an MMO celebrity there for his work on *UO* – which was never released in China. He was cheerfully informed that there had been 300 *UO* servers running in the country, so all the gamers there knew who he was.

Rogue servers are not in the main of interest to designers except in the case where they offer improvements. Some of these may actually *be* improvements, or at least experiments, so it's useful to know about them. Famously, after years of being refused a pre-expansion *World of Warcraft* server by Blizzard on the grounds that building it would be a technical nightmare, a group of players successfully developed and operated their own (unauthorised) version – which proved very popular. Blizzard finally realised that setting up its own vanilla *WoW* servers might be worth the effort and announced *World of Warcraft Classic*. It's now releasing expansions while repeating fewer mistakes than it did first time round.[53]

The most obvious design observation from this is that if you continually dilute your virtual world's content so as to appeal to a wider audience, you'll lose your core audience. Better, you can see what specific design features of your later versions are problematical. Usually, it's going to fall into one of the following categories:

- You took out content that the players liked, such as popular dungeons.

- You put in unwanted content or mechanics, such as gimmicky mini-games.

- You herded players through content they hated, such as grinding or raiding.

- You mushed together important differences, such as by allowing all classes to be played by all factions.

- You added quality-of-life elements that harmed gameplay, such as antisocial looking-for-group mechanisms.

Paying attention to these might help you to design the next expansion – or, if you're designing a different virtual world, to identify what's important to players *and why*. The "*and why*" is critical: if you can't distinguish between nostalgia, content, gameplay and synergy, you could put something in or take something out that you perhaps might later rue.

The last of the four points concerning the legal backdrop that I wanted to make concerns AI trained on your work. Whether such training without your permission is legal or not is for the courts and lawmakers to decide. I'm mentioning it here not because I believe designers can do much to defend against it (or indeed to embrace it), but because of what it says about the state of virtual world design.

Clearly, it's aggravating for artists to see AI-generated visuals mimicking the style of their work in a virtual world. They can't vary their style, because they have to work to said style to ensure consistency, so they're stuck with it unless the law steps in with some form of protection. It could be that diffusion models have their uses during development for

---

[53] Not all, just fewer.

concept art or prototyping, but the concern is less to do with internal uses of the technology and more to do with external uses. If anyone can create images that look as if they come from your virtual world, anyone will. That may not always be desirable.

Perhaps less clearly, it's also possible for AI systems to generate text and quests. Type "Create a short quest for World of Warcraft Classic." into ChatGPT and prepare to be impressed.[54] Again, this could be a boon for quest-designers, but the fact that quest designs can so easily be constructed from nothingness by large language models suggests that quest design is becoming too much of a paint-by-numbers exercise.[55]

Eventually, given enough examples, AI will be able to create entire virtual worlds. For single-player games, they'll be able to do it bespoke to the individual player, but this isn't possible in a massively multiplayer environment. Nevertheless, if designers don't wish to become superfluous to design, they should consider doing some actual innovation rather than crafting the same basic mechanics over and over again with different dressings offering poor rationales. Just saying.

Finally, any discussion of the legal backdrop for virtual worlds would not be complete without mentioning that sometimes it's not the designer, developer or operator of a virtual world who does anything wrong, but one or more of the players. Players can break all kinds of laws, criminal and civil, and the virtual world's designer, developer or operator can be in the frame when the search for someone to blame begins. In cases of "your design *made* me do this bad thing!", the truth of the assertion would have to be tested in court.[56] In cases where the virtual world is merely a conduit for some other legal infraction (blackmail, money laundering, inciting riots, *lèse-majesté* in Thailand, …), it becomes a question of policing. This is getting a tad remote from design, but I'll say a little about it anyway.

If you held a party at your own house and two people started a knife fight, you'd call the police. You can't be expected to be responsible for stopping knife fights just because they're happening in your own house.[57] If you hold a soccer match in your own stadium, however, then you may well be responsible for stopping knife fights. Perhaps it's too expensive for the taxpayer to fund, or maybe there aren't enough police officers in the district to do it, or there are but they don't know how to stop knife fights, so shift the burden to you. You'd have to employ stewards to handle any knife fights, only summoning the police when the services of a warrant-holder are required.

With virtual worlds, laws tend towards the soccer-stadium model of policing rather than the home model. The operator is required to police their virtual world, only involving the actual police force either when a crime has been committed or when not reporting something would itself be a crime. This can be particularly troublesome when laws require you to do something that's impossible, such as guaranteeing that no player of your

---

[54] OK, so when I tried it just now, it suggested that the retrieval of an item from Blackrock Depths was appropriate for a level 30 character, but *apart* from that, I was impressed.

[55] When I outline the basic quest-design process in Volume II, you'll see what I mean.

[56] Where it would likely fail, because your design didn't make everyone else do it.

[57] Reminder: none of this is legal advice. For all I know, where *you* live maybe you *are* responsible for stopping knife fights in your own house.

virtual world is below a certain age.[58] All that can be done is to decide, industry-wide, on a set of best practices and then hope that conforming to this will be protection enough. Unfortunately, laws brought out to rein in large MMOs also apply all-too-often to small, hobbyist virtual worlds such as most of the MUDs we used to have and the off-the-shelf graphical worlds we may get in future; with few resources, operators of small-population worlds can only cross their fingers that nothing terrible will happen, and that if it does then a jury would see sense where the law doesn't. Headline laws aimed directly at virtual worlds, or that indirectly catch them in their net, rarely scale down well.

It's not actually as unreasonable as you might think to ask small-time virtual world operators to undertake some policing, as they'll do it anyway. There are always certain behaviours that a small number of players can be expected to engage in that are against the rules of play. Some of these can be prevented using code (a computer version of *Chess* can stop you from moving a rook like a knight, yet a physical version can't); others, though, are unpreventable using code (such as spamming chat with non-consensual insults). The uncoded rules that players must conform to are written up as the Terms of Service (TOS),[59] which may be part of or separate from the EULA; either way, all players have to accept them if they're to use the virtual world software. Some violations of the TOS will be reported by players, but others won't and will have to be dealt with proactively by someone with CSR powers. Therefore, even small-time virtual worlds will do *some* policing, although making it a legal requirement to do so (when most of the "police" are volunteers) may be excessive.

There's more on CSR responsibilities and responses in Volume II, but from a designer's perspective, the gist is that you need to specify the tools that the CSRs are going to need for:

- Detecting incidents before they happen. These are largely to do with metrics kept by the server, over which you periodically run passes. Are characters giving each other vast amounts of money for little in return? Are characters killing monsters way out of their league with ease? Are characters repeating the same, mindless actions over and over again? Is one character being gagged by multiple players who have no connection with each other? If you see the signs in advance, you may be able to head off potential problems early.

- Dealing with incidents as they happen. These include powers for screen-sharing, command-injection, object-creation, teleportation, property-setting, quest-advancement and account queries. CSRs have to deal with players, not with characters, so account access is important.

- Piecing together evidence after incidents have happened. At the very least, you'll want logging at the input level, logging at the output level, logging by server events, plus ways to search all these logs. That's right, virtual world design isn't only about the worlds themselves.[60]

---

[58] Or indeed above a certain age; laws might insist on this to prevent adults from trying to groom children in virtual worlds targeting a young audience, for example.

[59] Sometimes, it's called the Terms of Use (TOU).

[60] A fact I shall largely ignore for most of this text.

Although there are plenty of books about online community management, there are very few that are specific to virtual worlds (as opposed to ones specific to websites, social media and whatever the online bandwagon of the day is).[61] Experience matters here, so the best person to ask about this kind of thing is the CSR lead. If you don't have one, consult an outsourcing company; the people there should be able to recommend software and practices appropriate for you, even if you don't end up hiring them to handle your forums. It's unlikely that you'll have put anything in your virtual world that your CSRs will have a die-on-this-hill issue with, but you may have accidentally omitted elements that they regard as helpful (such as installing profanity filters on all accounts, default setting: on) and you could have specified features that require them to do a lot of work (such as moderating voice communications between your players). The solutions are out there, but to adopt them, you need to realise that there are problems in the first place.

9.3 CULTURAL BACKDROP

People of different cultures have different ways of thinking and acting. They have different ideas about what's appropriate and inappropriate. They also change these ideas over time and have sub-cultures that are different again. Virtual worlds address these issues by undertaking *localisation*.

Localisation isn't just about adhering to local laws, it's about adhering to local cultural norms. There's no law of the land that says you have to take your shoes off when you enter a Japanese home, but it would be impolite not to do so. In *Second Life*, logging off or teleporting away without saying goodbye first[62] is regarded as impolite because people can't tell if you've disconnected, so will wait for you to return. Likewise, although in the United States you can give distances in kilometres and temperatures in degrees Celsius, not everyone there is going to have a handle on them. As for religion and politics, they're minefields anywhere.

Although cases where laws of the land directly contradict each other are thankfully rare, it's quite common for cultures to have mutually incompatible beliefs. In the US, black cats are unlucky because they're symbols of witchcraft; in the UK, black cats are lucky because they're symbols of witchcraft. Sometimes, a culture will find a central theme of a virtual world unacceptable, in which case there's not a lot that can be done in mitigation: *Second Life* derives much of its income from virtual real estate,[63] which is contrary to the views on land ownership held by most First Nations cultures of North America (Boellstorff et al., 2013).

Many cultures share beliefs, of course, the rationale for which could be anything: in the Far East, 4 is unlucky because it sounds like the word for "death" in Cantonese, Mandarin, Japanese and Korean; in Europe, 13 is unlucky because there were 13 people present at the

---

[61] The most useful I've found is Atherton (2023). It's not structured but it contains some gems of interviews with *bona fide* virtual world designers.

[62] Teleporting away is called *poofing* in *SL* (as in, disappearing in a poof of smoke). Functions built to accompany this with a light show are *poofers*. Satisfyingly, *MUD2* drew on the same trope: when its admins teleport away, they "disappear in a puff of smoke" ("puff", rather than "poof", because "poof" is derogatory British slang for "homosexual man").

[63] Or, put another way, virtual estate.

feast where the Norse god Baldr died, 13 people present at the Last Supper, and additionally, the Romans considered it a sign of death and destruction (Dent, 2023).

Different cultures have different preoccupations. There's a reason that the *Madden NFL* games franchise (Hawkins et al., 1988) doesn't sell well in countries where people have never heard of Madden and if asked what the F might abbreviate to may correctly guess "football", by which they mean "soccer".[64]

The biggest problem with localisation is language. If you want to make your virtual world playable in places where people don't speak what you speak, you'll need help. It's not as simple as hiring a translator, either. In Volume II, I mention the distinction between a "designer of games" and a "game designer", which sounds fine to me, but when I gave a talk in Uruguay on the subject, it transpired that the Spanish for both these phrases was the same (*diseñador de juegos*) while also being different (a female game designer is a *diseñadora de juegos*). Some words don't have a direct translation into other languages: "sensible" in English translates (perhaps unsurprisingly) as *sensible* in French, but *sensible* in French back-translates (perhaps surprisingly) as "sensitive" in English.

Word length can be a problem. One of the reasons it says STOP on Welsh road signs is that STOPIWCH doesn't fit (Clark, 2012). If your quest-description boxes only have enough room to display 500 characters, you're going to have trouble when a language uses 35% more characters than yours does (which is the case if you write in English and translate into German (Sterling et al., 2012)); it can also look pretty bad in terms of empty space if the language uses 60% fewer characters (for writing in English and translating into Japanese (Sterling et al., 2012)). The range of characters that a text occupies in different languages can be very wide: the UN's *Universal Declaration of Human Rights* article 1 uses 170 characters in English but only 47 in Mandarin and a whopping 374 in Māori. If you have voice-overs, remember that different languages take longer to say things, too, so you'll need to be aware of that should you have any actions that need to be synchronised with words.

There are other differences that mean you can't rely on cross-language standards. Some languages, such as English, read left-to-right; others, such as Hebrew, read right-to-left.[65] Some have different alphabetical orders: if you want to sort words in Swedish, the order is ABCDEFGHIJKLMNOPQRSTUVWXYZÅÄÖ.

All this contrives to make it such that some techniques that are *really handy* don't work across languages. In *MUD2*, which is English-only, sentences are composed on-the-fly the whole time. Suppose I wished to inform the player that they had picked something up: I'd want to write "You pick up the" followed by [name of the object]. That wouldn't work in a gendered language, because the word for "the" would depend on the object. I might have an object that I need to specify the colour of in the description, such as a white ball or a black ball: I'd want to write "You pick up the" followed by [colour of the object] followed by [name of the object]. That wouldn't work in languages such as French that put the adjective after the object for colours (but not necessarily for other properties, such as size).

---

[64] "Soccer" is an abbreviation for *Association Football*, a term which came out of British universities to distinguish it from *Rugby Football*, or "rugger".

[65] Except numbers, which are left-to-right.

The solution that game developers have adopted, which is also used for commercial virtual worlds, is to have fixed translations. A few placeholders can exist (for player-character names to be slotted into, for example), but everything else is rigid. This means that the translations for each language can be stored in single, language-specific files that can be switched to at the player's discretion; associated voice-overs work the same way. It limits dynamic sentence creation, but tends to be one of those situations in which practicality overrules flexibility.

Different cultures have different tastes in beauty and music. They have different ideas of masculinity and femininity. They even have different ways of approaching cultural difference: some cultures welcome visitors from other cultures, but others do the opposite; some cultures regard cultural appropriation as a good thing, but others regard it as a bad thing; some cultures are cautious interacting with other cultures because they don't want to offend, but others consider this itself to be offensive because it implies they're easily offended.

Basically, if you want your virtual world to be available to multiple cultures, contact a localisation specialist towards the end of pre-production and run what you have past them. Accommodate the changes they indicate, then throw yourself at their mercy for the localisation of any text.[66]

That said…

Localisation isn't the same as translation. Translation converts the content; localisation converts the meaning of the content. Some virtual worlds are exceptionally good at localisation because their developers understand that it's not simply translation. *Final Fantasy XIV* is Japanese in origin, but its English and French translations are reputedly superb – on a par with the French-to-English translations of classic *Asterix* (Goscinny & Uderzo, 1959) cartoons. Wordplay is converted into equivalent wordplay, pop culture references are converted into equivalent pop culture references, jokes are converted into equivalent jokes. Localisation isn't therefore simply a matter of routine: there's an art to it. The trick to high-quality localisation is therefore the same as with any work of art: choose your artist then let them perform their art.

9.4 SOCIAL BACKDROP

In the first three Ages of virtual worlds, access was a privilege granted mainly to students and people with money. The doors opened in the Fourth Age, when all you needed was a computer and a modicum of tech-savviness; in the Fifth Age, they were flung wide open.

This change in population reshaped the social backdrop. What was once the domain of a select few became the domain of the less-select many. Some of the features that virtual worlds pioneered were later co-opted by and encroached upon by other media. In the same way that social worlds took balanced worlds and removed the gameplay, so social networks took social worlds and removed the play. Social worlds remain more social than social network sites are, but people don't always want to play so the latter captured their time and attention. The reason that *Second Life* didn't live up to its promise is more to do

---

[66] I particularly like the following Korean-to-English tutorial message from the mobile phone game, *Ride Zero* (Loadcomplete, 2017): "Supports and controls support and manage the support supported by a supporter".

with its being undermined by Facebook, Instagram and Twitter than its being prematurely over-hyped.

Homogenisation with other games is doing a similar thing to game worlds. When a virtual world incorporates a battle royale or a multi-player online battle arena (MOBA), you know that either its developers or its players have forgotten what makes a virtual world special.[67]

The problem is that virtual worlds designed for the kind of play popular among hard-core gamers have over time adapted to accommodate people who have a different level of enthusiasm and different expectations. This is perfectly understandable, but it means that MMOs are now in competition with other forms of play and are seen themselves as just another kind of computer game. Worse, they're increasingly regarded as a fading genre, which when they sacrifice their differences to expand their audiences they are indeed.[68]

Virtual worlds are not games and they're not play: they're places. While members of the public perceive them to be games (even social worlds, which strive *not* to be games), their unique selling point will be lost.

The social environment in which virtual worlds find themselves today is one of a battle between perceptions and preconceptions. Players of graphical worlds will rarely go anywhere near textual ones because of their preconceptions, yet they seem to find it frustrating that players of video games won't go near virtual worlds because of *their* preconceptions. If someone says that virtual worlds are an expensive time sink, what can you do? Tell them they're neither as expensive nor as much of a time sink as streamed TV? Is that going to change their mind? If they could be persuaded to try out a virtual world, OK, they might change their mind or they might not, but at least they'd have an experiential basis for their decision. Are they ever going to try one, though?[69]

Discoverability is a problem for most games, but less so for virtual worlds as there are fewer of them. Players will probably have heard of some of the more famous MMOs, and if they haven't tried one then they may well know someone who has. The cost of acquisition (that is, how much you have to pay in advertising to buy a new player) is usually more than covered by the player's lifetime value (that is, how much money this player will bring to your virtual world). Virtual worlds that launch, even if they thereupon flop, usually make back their development costs. This could change were we suddenly to be flooded with virtual worlds, as we were in stock MUD times, but for now, commercial virtual worlds can connect to enough social groupings of players that they are able to reach sufficient people who may actually play them; setting aside plenty of cash for an advertising budget is necessary, too, of course.

Getting your virtual world noticed is one thing, but the expansion of general society into the online environment makes it increasingly harder for virtual worlds to stand out as worthy of subsequent attention. What can a designer do to address this?

---

[67] One-offs are fine – we had battles royale in *MUD1*, where they were known as "spectaculars". It's when they become integrated into the gameplay that you have to worry.

[68] We'll look at the hard core *versus* mass market dialectic in more detail in Volume II.

[69] A "don't knock it if you haven't tried it" argument rarely works. I haven't tried driving a car blindfolded, but I'm still going to knock it.

Even at the start of the Fifth Age, there were arguments as to whether it was better to have a high number of players or a less-high number of hardcore players. *Meridian 59* espoused the former, *EverQuest* the latter.[70] The question remains, though: do you design for the dedicated few or the less-than-dedicated many?

I once gave a talk in Hong Kong about the decline of MMOs (Bartle, 2013). In it, I identified the following as being among the causes of this decline:

- **Development Costs**. Marketing, an ever-rising quality bar and the difficulty of raising finance.

- **Too Many Clones**. Re-use of technical assets, fixed tools, fear of failure.

- **Player Type Imbalance**. We'll come to player types in Chapter 11, but the revenue model and elder game are the main culprits.

- **Player Expectations**. Players are trained from their experience of other virtual worlds, the focus is on the short term and audience expansion.

- **Lack of Immersion**. Depth is difficult, protecting players from each other comes at a gameplay cost, and the revenue model is a problem again.

- **Lack of Understanding of Design**. Game design is an art form, but isn't treated as such. The industry doesn't recognise designers, and there's insufficient academic study of game design, which is mainly Media Studies (except for games rather than media).

In that paper, I do put forward some solutions, but the reason I mention it here is that one of the important points concerns audience expansion. After my talk, one of the other conference attendees[71] approached me and related the following anecdote.

In the 1960s, we had sports cars. These were classy, nimble, speedy, manoeuvrable and fun to drive.[72] To grow the market, manufacturers made them increasingly easier to handle and added quality-of-life changes – power steering, power braking, softer suspension, seats with vertical backs, front-wheel drive, four seats rather than two. Some of these were safety improvements, but others detracted from what a sports car *was*. In the end, sports cars started to compete with family cars made by the same manufacturers. In so doing, they lost their core audience. They became so far removed from sports cars that non-afficionados wondered why anyone ever thought so highly of them. However, in 1989, Mazda went back to basics and unveiled the MX-5. It became the best-selling sports car in history. The core audience *was* still there; it just wasn't being served.

MMO players are *also* still there – for the right MMO.

Design what MMO players want to play, not what non-MMO players want to play.

---

[70] In the end, *EQ* ended up with more of both, although some of that was because *M59* came out first and hit the bumps in the road in time for *EQ* to avoid them.

[71] He was Australian, but I didn't catch his name. Sorry if it was you!

[72] Leastwise, the ones made by British or Italian companies were.

As for *what* they want to play, well we'll be looking at that in Chapter 11. Whatever you decide, there are several years between beginning work on your virtual world and launching it. Use this time wisely: reveal to your players what they want from a virtual world, then make your virtual world give them what you've educated them to appreciate.

9.5 POLITICAL BACKDROP

This final, short section on the developmental and operational environment of virtual worlds concerns the political backdrop. It's different from the other backdrops in that it doesn't directly concern design[73]; rather, it concerns what designers need to account for when looking at virtual worlds from elsewhere.

We've seen in this chapter that for business, cultural and social reasons, different countries have different laws and development conditions. Related to this, they can have them for different political reasons, too. The political context can affect how your virtual world is treated.

Special-interest groups often wield a lot of power. Designers can feel they're treading on eggshells. Even depicting in a virtual world something that is legal where you live, such as having a view on a contentious topic, can bring opprobrium from people who hold the opposing view. Implementing something innocuous that makes perfect sense in Reality, such as having shoes come in different sizes, risk calling down accusations of all kinds of -isms when implemented in a virtual world. Constitutional rights may protect you from prosecution, and economic considerations may stay a legislative body's hand,[74] but neither will prevent people from sending hate mail, protesting outside your offices or calling for a boycott on social media.

Most virtual worlds have too small a player base to be singled out for attention or even to be noticed, so are basically just low-level noise as far as the police are concerned.[75] However, political pressure can be brought to bear on larger ones or on games in general, which can make the environment very uncomfortable. When the pressure is at governmental level, it can be backed up by threats of law changes.[76] There are four main reasons that those who hold political power might do this:

- **Populism.** The powers-that-be believe there is political capital to be made by applying pressure. Example: if large numbers of people are worried that playing virtual worlds will make their children shoot up a school,[77] then that could lead to regulation.

- **Conviction.** The powers-that-be have a set of inter-related axioms that guide their actions. If they firmly believe that the world will be a better place without computer games, they'll push that agenda simply because it's (in their view) the right thing to do.

---

[73] That isn't to say that games can't represent political systems and that designers can't say thing to players using and about such systems: they can (Kłosiński, 2024).

[74] Even the bureaucratic organisation that is the European Parliament got around to endorsing the games industry (European Parliament, 2022), largely because it wants a big one.

[75] I never did get round to putting in one of those "accept my cookies or go away" warnings on my JavaScript games.

[76] In some countries, it can also be backed up by intimidation such as baseless raids on company premises.

[77] See Chapter 22. It won't.

- **Knee-Jerk**. The powers-that-be are taken off-guard by something significant that happens and are forced to act quickly, without forethought, in response. Anything could result.

- **Fear**. The powers-that-be suspect that virtual worlds or their players represent a threat, or calculate that by overtly attacking them the general public will fail to notice the rather more subversive persecution of a different group that represents the actual threat.

Politics is a game and its rules are made by those who play.

The upshot of this, then, is that if you're a designer and you see a virtual world coming out of another country that has nonsensical or offensive elements to it or obvious holes in its gameplay, spare a thought that this might not be the fault of the designer. Also remember that some virtual worlds are decades old and are of their time[78]: consider this before judging their design or their content by the standards of today. Your own views will be thought of as antiquated soon enough.

---

[78] *The past is a foreign country: they do things differently there* (Hartley, 1953).

CHAPTER 10

Demographics

V IRTUAL WORLDS DON'T *HAVE* to have players. There's nothing in the definition of the term that says they must; the criteria covering characters, interaction and sharing merely imply that a candidate system must possess the *capability* to have players. In the same way that an unread book is still a book, an unplayed virtual world is still a virtual world.

Nevertheless, almost all virtual worlds will have players. Furthermore, nearly every major design decision will have been taken in the service of those players. If you want to speak to someone through your design, it helps to know who they are. As a designer, it's therefore crucial to understand who is going to play your virtual world and why.

That is what this chapter – and indeed the rest of Volume I – concerns.

The human beings accessing a virtual world are its players.[1] Players are distinct from the objects within the virtual world over which they exercise executive control; those are *characters*.

The difference between players and characters is of fundamental importance to virtual worlds. Characters are channels through which players act and interact with the world itself and with other players (through their respective characters). Characters exist only within the virtual world; the capacity to enter and (as a character) to remain in that world is entirely the preserve of players. The goal of designers must therefore be to provide an experience for *players*, not for characters.

So … who are these players?

10.1 IMPORTANT DIMENSIONS

If you participate in any academic survey, you can almost guarantee you'll be asked your age and gender. Such surveys often don't actually need to know either of these facts, but they ask anyway; it can help independent researchers who analyse the survey results to get a handle on how representative the sample is. For example, you might lend less weight

---

[1] A piece of software accessing a virtual as a proxy for a human being is a *bot*. Bots are discussed in Volume II.

to a survey about home ownership if your respondents were mainly undergraduates aged 20–22. Decent numbers of survey participants are expensive to find, particularly at short notice, so there's a temptation to use *convenience sampling* – a euphemism that means you look where supplies are cheap and plentiful.[2] This implies that your findings may be useful as a guide, but not be entirely paradigmatic (see sidebar on surveys).

SURVEYS

If you want to get a true picture of what the members of a population think and do, ideally you would survey all of them.[3] This is rarely practical except in a government-run census, so researchers survey a representative sample instead. From the results of this exercise, tentative[4] conclusions can be drawn regarding the general case.

The more people you ask, the better your results are likely to be. However, *selection bias* is a potential problem: you need to be careful about whom you survey. Asking 100 random people what their favourite music is may give a better reflection of the nation's musical tastes than would asking 50 times that many people at a heavy metal concert. This is why political opinion pollsters try to survey 1,000–2,000 individuals who are somehow representative of the population that they are studying, rather than hundreds of thousands who aren't.

It's also important that surveys minimise self-selection. If, instead of approaching potential survey respondents yourself, you invite them to approach you, the ones who respond may not have the same views as the non-responding majority. Notoriously, in the run-up to the 1936 US presidential election, the *Literary Digest* sent out ten million postcards to its readers asking how they would vote: they got close to a quarter back, which showed that Alfred Landon led Franklin Roosevelt 57% to 43%; this was very different from a much smaller[5] survey conducted by the upstart pollster George Gallup (The Pittsburgh Press, 1936); his final poll put Roosevelt ahead at 56%. When it came to the election itself, Roosevelt won 60.80% to Landon's 36.54% (the rest going to minority candidates). The *Literary Digest's* reputation was shattered because of this bad prediction and it closed in 1938. Part of the problem was that the magazine's readership was itself not representative of the voting public at large (whereas Gallup's sample was), but the greater issue was that the people who disliked Roosevelt felt more motivated to register their opinion – a *participation bias*.

Other possible reasons that a large survey may give false results include: the way that questions are worded; the order that questions are asked; the medium through which questions are asked (in person, over the phone, online).

---

[2] It's an old joke in academic circles that the discipline of Psychology primarily concerns the study of Psychology students.
[3] Or you could wheedle it out of a social media company, they probably know.
[4] Or, in the case of certain media titles, cast-iron guaranteed.
[5] Albeit still very large by modern standards, at 50,000 participants.

Most of the problems we see with surveys related to games and virtual worlds are indeed affected by these issues, but not as much as they're affected by survey size. Taking a cynical view, it seems that PhD students (who do most of the actual research work in academia) tend to regard 30 participants as enough to draw whatever conclusions they want from a survey. This figure of 30 comes from a seminal book on social science research methodology (Stebbins, 2001) that says you need at least 30 items of a particular kind before a statistical analysis of them will find the major ways they group together.

As an example, if you interview 30 gamers and find that ten are female, you can legitimately argue that there are at least two groups of gamers: female and not female. You can't argue that a third of all gamers are female. Nevertheless, this is the kind of thing that sometimes appears in conference papers from students looking for their first publication – and also in newspapers wishing to promote a particular perspective. I particularly remember an article in *The Guardian* (McCabe, 2008) that stated "70 percent of [female gamers] chose to construct male characters when given the option by online games". This was based on research from Nottingham Trent University (Hussain & Griffiths, 2008), which merely said that up to 70 percent of the 32 female gamers surveyed had played as a male persona in an online role-playing game at least once. *The Guardian*'s piece went on to ask "why would women choose to change their sex in far greater numbers than men opting to play women?" (which, as we'll see later in non-sidebarland, they very much don't).

There are also problems to do with self-reporting. On occasion, it's possible to check the responses people give in surveys against hard data. One celebrated[6] paper (Williams et al., 2009) asked players of *EverQuest II* how many hours a week they played, then compared this to the actual times as recorded by the servers. It turned out that male players reported playing an average of 24.10 hours/week but in fact played an average of 25.03; female players reported playing an average of 26.03 hours/week but in fact played an average of 29.32. These disparities were as a result of poor estimation by the players, along with some rounding errors; they were not caused by attempts to deceive the researchers.

You might wonder, incidentally, why no one else had noticed the discrepancy. The answer is that very few virtual world operators are willing to hand data over to researchers (Sony Online Entertainment, *EQ2*'s developer, agreed to co-operate in this particular research only because they trusted these particular researchers). This reticence is born of experience: early developers were happy to help researchers by providing anonymised data, but after their efforts were rewarded with a string of papers arguing that playing games was addictive and psychologically damaging, they had second thoughts. This is why nowadays researchers have to ask people how long they play then live with the inaccurate information they get back. Players do have access to their own data under the data-protection laws of various countries, though, so can ask for everything that a virtual world knows about them then pass that on to

---

[6] Well, I celebrate it, anyway.

academics. This kind of *data donation* has promise, although participation bias is a potential pitfall and the more players there are in a virtual world then the harder it is for researchers to reconcile what they receive.

Also, note that even though scrupulous attention to detail and terabytes of playing records can mean that the data sets collected are accurate (everyone who says they're X is indeed X), that doesn't mean they're useful.

The upshot of all this is that accurate and useful information about the players of virtual worlds is difficult to come by, but we can often gather some general pointers despite this.

The important demographic information that researchers want to ascertain for virtual worlds tends to concern the usual suspects (age, gender) along with anything relevant to the thrust of the research itself, be that race (Rowland & Barton, 2011), sexuality (Ruberg & Ruelos, 2020), personality (Dieris-Hirche et al., 2020), money spent (Yee, 2005b), ... Surveys will follow up these demographic questions with non-demographic questions also relevant to that research – the presence of toxicity (Zhu et al., 2022), say, or of sexism (Kordyaka et al., 2022), or the effects of guild membership (Pisan, 2007). This may or may not include questions specific to a given virtual world that's under investigation – ones concerning character class, for example (DiGiuseppe & Nardi, 2007).

Sadly, what researchers want to know is not necessarily what designers want to know. This isn't to say that what researchers want to know isn't important; rather, it's that some topics preponderate over others. You'll find many more Game Studies papers concerned with LGBTQ+ issues than with straight issues, for example: this may help a straight designer hoping to accommodate LGBTQ+ players, but it won't help an LGBTQ+ designer hoping to accommodate straight players.

As mentioned in Chapter 9, cultural differences prevail in Reality, which means they also prevail in virtual worlds. This isn't just a point about localisation: people of different cultures can have notably different attitudes, and if you want to make a virtual world universally acceptable then this can be difficult. It's very easy to come across as crass or insensitive, even when you try your best not to do so. The issue is primarily a problem at the surface level of the virtual world, though, not in the gameplay – showing modern Egyptian house interiors as if they were the work of Scheherazade, that kind of thing (Saleh, 2021).

There is evidence that, deeper down, players from different cultures experience virtual worlds in much the same way (Albatati et al., 2023). Yes, it may be that, in some cultures, players want to play in groups, and in others, they prefer to play alone, but it's merely a question of emphasis: some players in the former culture would want to play alone, and some in the latter would want to play in groups.

As a general rule, you won't get far if you provide content based on the proportion of people who are likely to favour it: you have to provide enough for all. If only 10% of your player base wants to play as dog people and the rest want to play as cat people, that doesn't mean you give the dog people 10% of the content and the cat people 90%: you give them the same amount. It would be like saying motorcycles should only be allowed on 3.5% of the roads in the UK because only 3.5% of the vehicles on UK roads are motorcycles (UK Government, 2024c). Therefore, if you are aiming your design at a particular culture that has particular preferences, you should give the minority preferences equal weight unless you don't want people who have those preferences to play at all. This is one reason why virtual worlds need so much content.

As we'll see soon, demographic information isn't in practice quite as useful for designers as many non-designers seem to think it should be. It may help with broad-brush generalisations ("parents of small children have to be able to quit in an instant, so we can't have 50-minute boss fights"), but if you design for stereotypes, you shouldn't be surprised if you only get those stereotypes. It's fine to design such that you don't put desired stereotypes *off*: inclusivity does work with stereotypes – it's exclusivity that you'd be wise to avoid. The most important factor isn't whom *society* thinks the player is, it's whom *they* think they are – or will become.

That said, there are practical consequences when you're designing for a specific group of individuals who all share a given characteristic. A small virtual world catering to people who suffer from arachnophobia, for example, perhaps ought not to include a great many spiders. Similarly, a virtual world intended to support people with particular emotional issues would need to be careful not to trigger those issues.

The largest demographic that needs special attention is children, as there is a never-ending supply of them and play is their default condition.[7] If you want to design for children, you have to be *exceptionally* careful: all societies take a very protective view of the child and will come down hard on you if you step over any one of countless red lines. Happily, most designers also take a protective view of the child[8] and will design accordingly; the main problems are to do with legal requirements that they may not be aware of[9] and ensuring that the CSR team has the right tools to deal with all the issues that come up (which will include identifying potential badly intentioned non-children).

For virtual worlds intended only for adults, you have much more freedom to design. Unfortunately, some children *will* play your virtual world no matter how much you try to stop them; you just have to do your best to minimise their number while not compromising the virtual world itself. Despite what politicians may wish, it's hard to prevent children from playing an MMO if they're determined to do so, much the same as it's hard to prevent them from reading a proscribed book or from watching a pornographic video. Beyond attempting age verification (which is never reliable) and not going out of your way to make your virtual world appear unnecessarily enticing to children,[10] there isn't a lot you can do. Furthermore, there isn't a lot you *should* do, if you want to keep your artistic integrity. Design what you want to design, and inform prospective players both what to expect[11] and

---

[7] You could argue that people with disabilities are the larger group, especially if you count things such as short-sightedness as a disability. We'll be looking at the design implications of this when discussing accessibility in Volume II.

[8] Hard though it may be to believe, many designers were themselves children in their early years.

[9] Or that they are aware of but believe are counter-productive.

[10] "Those kitties are *so cute!*".

[11] This is the *covenant* that designers have with players, which is discussed in Chapter 24.

what the general legal constraints are; individuals or their carers can then decide whether they ought to play or not.

Demographic surveys can provide information useful to company executives and marketers, which is often why they collect it, but whether designers find it helpful or not rather depends on its nature. For example, company executives will want to know if your design will attract players tending towards a particular social class because that will influence how much disposable income they have and thus what revenue model will be hoisted on them; designers, however, may be more concerned with the players' sense of entitlement, which will affect what they expect from the virtual world. Likewise, producers will need to know if your design will appeal to particular cultural backgrounds because they'll need to recruit CSRs who understand those backgrounds so they can communicate with the players; you as a designer merely need to know what you can assume your players will know as part of common knowledge (such as English is a language, or that magic carpets fly).

Finally, remember that demographics are statistical snapshots, not unchanging cohorts of the same people. If, today, you were to design for the 18–25 age range, how many of the individuals currently in that bracket will still be in it by the time your virtual world is launched? Fashions change. People change. Genres, both story and game, come and go in popularity. Even within the same demographic, people have different tastes. Not every person born in the same year that you were likes the same singers or movies or TV programmes that you do, and it's the same with virtual worlds: different virtual worlds will attract different players regardless of how similar their demographic make-up may be.

So, bearing this in mind, let's have a quick look at the data.

10.2 DATA

When it comes to the demographics of virtual world players, what was true ten years ago isn't necessarily true today, and what's true today won't necessarily be true ten years hence. Nevertheless, there are some general observations that can be made. One way to do this is to compare surveys from different eras.

I'll use gender as my baseline example (on the grounds that most surveys are going to include it). Note that although most surveys are going to ask if you're male or female, there's no consistency with regard to other genders; one survey might admit none at all yet another could go with "explain in your own words". In order to make a rough comparison, I'll be using the binary male/female dichotomy for this exercise – but bear in mind that one or both of these categories may include people who don't identify as either or may identify as both.[12] Incidentally, if you want to know the main differences in playing preferences between binary and non-binary players, see Yee (2023).[13]

Looking at some of the past surveys that have a decent number of respondents, then, and only at their male/female breakdown, we see the results shown in Table 10.1.

---

[12] A 2021 survey of *VRChat* (Gaylor & Joudrey, 2017) users discovered that 65.5% were male, 17% were female and 17.5% were trans/nonbinary/other (Au, 2023).

[13] Most surveys can't boast enough non-binary participants to draw meaningful inferences, but Yee's data set contains responses from over 1.25 million respondee (across all game genres), some 14,000 or so being from non-binary players; this is exceptionally good coverage.

TABLE 10.1   Demographic Surveys

Survey	Male	Female	Sample Size	Notes
Gamespot (1996)	91%	9%	2.526	MMOs, FPSs
Rejzlik (1998)	74.8%	25.2%	103	MUDs, MOOs
Schiano & White (1998)	78%	22%	515	MOOs
Roberts & Parks (1999)	51.9%	48.1%	233	MOOs
	53%	47%	202	MOOs
Utz (2001)	80.4%	19.6%	185	MUDs
Utz (2003)	82.5%	17.5%	217	MUDs
Seay et al. (2003)	89.8%	10.2%	1,836	MMOs
Stinnett (2005)	96%	4%	1,500+	*STO* pre-release
Yee (2008)	85.4%	14.6%	2,435	MMOs
Williams et al. (2009)	82.21%	17.79%	2,440	MMOs
Au (2015)	48%	52%	60	*Second Life*
Yee (2017)	64%	36%	9,949	Fantasy MMOs
	84%	16%	9,949	SF MMOs
Ye & Shih (2022)	71%	29%	millions	Mobile MMOs

Note: By mobile MMOs, I mean games played using an app on a smartphone.

Some things to note from this table:

- Social worlds attract a higher proportion of female players (or put off a higher proportion of male players) than do game worlds.

- The same researchers can conduct two surveys in close temporal proximity and get slightly different results.

- Don't expect pre-launch surveys to reflect post-launch demographics.

- The story genre of a virtual world will affect its gender breakdown.

You can make similar observations about pretty well any other demographic characteristic. Gender is just the easiest one to illustrate.

You'll observe that there was a flurry of surveys from the Third Age of virtual worlds (when the rest of the world noticed that MOOs existed) and more from the Fifth Age, but then the big-participant ones peter out. This may well be because I haven't looked in the right places (or have, but don't trust the results[14]); however, it's more likely to be because in the early days of virtual world research, there wasn't a trusted source, so people had to obtain the statistics themselves. Nick Yee's Daedalus Project (Yee, 2002b) collected data from around 40,000 players over five years and produced results in line with (but more accurate than) what smaller surveys had found; this meant that anyone who wanted to find demographic data concerning MMO players had a go-to source, which they duly went-to.

---

[14] In particular, I avoid ones on Reddit for term papers and ones with either small numbers of respondents or large numbers but they're from Mechanical Turk (Amazon, 2023).

Said state of affairs lasted for a good decade, but then the demographics shifted. Yee and a fellow researcher, Nic Ducheneaut, set up a company, Quantic Foundry, which does ongoing research based on a questionnaire that has been answered over 1.25 million times and counting. Being ongoing, it's up-to-date so is accurate and can track trends over time (that is, it's *longitudinal*). OK, so you have to pay for access to it (which many AAA developers do), but thankfully for those of us who are either poor or stingy, blog posts and Game Developers Conference talks do reveal for free the kind of information more relevant to academics and (to some extent) designers. We'll be looking at the empirical model at the heart of Quantic Foundry's research in Chapter 18.

So, returning to gender, it used to be that around 15%–20% of game world players were female (aggregated across all story genres, but mainly Fantasy), but the number is currently much higher at around 30%. Science Fiction worlds are not as appealing to female players as Fantasy is,[15] and even less appealing than social worlds are.[16] Make of this what you will.

The other piece of demographic information that researchers and marketers almost always want to know is how old the players are. Again, this changes over time – not least because players as individuals age over time. Some current players of text MUDs have been players since the 1980s, and some *Ultima Online* and *EverQuest* players aren't far behind. Virtual worlds can be played for so long that there are generational differences between them – and between their players.

It would be great if there were publicly available statistics to show the mean age of game-world players as opposed to social-world players and to players of video games in general. It would be great if there were statistics to show the mean ages for specific virtual worlds. Such statistics certainly exist – they're just not publicly available except in small-scale studies. Anecdotally, though, players of virtual worlds have until recently tended to be older than players of video games, but so many casual games are now played on phones by members of the general population that this is probably no longer the case. If we were to ignore casual games then the assertion probably still holds, although because it's possible to play MMOs *as* casual games, the distinction may be unfair. Among MMOs themselves, gateway worlds such as *RuneScape* and *WoW* will have a lower mean player age; ones that make some effort to enrich the fiction of the virtual world and to introduce some thought into play, such as *UO* and *ESO*, will have a higher mean player age; ones that require frightening amounts of patience and time investment, such as *EVE Online*, could well have a higher mean age still. Sadly, knowing this doesn't help designers a great deal, except in predicting how subtle or otherwise any griefing is likely to be.

The reason that statistics such as these are hard to come by, by the way, is twofold. Firstly, as I mentioned earlier, virtual world developers don't want to release information unnecessarily because it's ammunition that can be used against them[17]; secondly, those independent organisations that spend time and money putting together high-quality statistics invariably hope to sell their findings.[18] Academic research *is* freely available, but the

[15] *Star Wars: the Old Republic* is an exception: 29% of its players are female compared with 11.3% for its peers (Yee, 2017).
[16] Au's article on *Second Life* demographics, cited in Table 10.1, takes its data from the Quantic Foundry survey.
[17] They do actually share it between themselves informally, so they can follow industry trends.
[18] This means they're actually easy to come by, you just need to swallow the price tag.

studies are much smaller, often outdated, and are focused on the particular bee that the researcher has in their bonnet. Government-commissioned research is also free, but there isn't much of it; furthermore, it tends to take so long to compile that it's out of date before it's published.

That said, there is some public-facing information that can be captured and assessed, such as that found in company account filings. Interestingly, the data point that used to be the one most closely guarded – player numbers[19] – now no longer has to be prised from developers' cold, dead hands. By monitoring social-media activity and the live numbers reported by platforms such as Steam, and comparing these with published usage figures emanating from official sources, websites such as MMO Stats (MMO Stats, 2024) and MMO Populations (MMO Populations, 2024) can calculate a fairly consistent measure of how many people have played any given MMO in the past 24 hours (albeit not necessarily agreeing with one another in terms of the absolute numbers involved). These services are helpful for players and statistics-starved academics, but they're not particularly useful for designers except if they want to track the broad effects of a new update in which they're interested.[20]

Demographic information is mainly of interest to marketers, but this in itself is a reason that designers need to pay attention. Its use comes in two forms:

- **Actual Demographics**. If you know who's playing your virtual world, you can market it to more people in the same category in order to increase the number of players. Here, the designers design the virtual world and the marketers have to sell it as designed.

- **Target Demographics**. If you know whom you want to play your virtual world but they're not playing it, you can change the virtual world so as to appeal to them. Here, the marketers sell the virtual world and the designers have to design it as marketed.

Needless to say, the former is better from a designer's perspective than the latter. It's worth pointing out that designing for target demographics isn't intrinsically bad, by the way; it only becomes bad if the marketing group gets the idea that "what players want" gives them a licence to tell designers how to design. This is particularly unfortunate when the designer is expected to design for a demographic stereotype:

- If you design a game for a target demographic, you may only get that demographic. A game designed for girls aged 8–10 won't have a broad player base.

- You may have to design a game for a different demographic to get the one you want. The best way to attract straight, unmarried men to your virtual world could well be to attract straight, unmarried women to it.

---

[19] The reason it was closely guarded, at least when it was falling, is that it could affect stock prices.
[20] This is for other virtual worlds. For their own, they have better information in its activity logs.

- If people realise that a virtual world is stereotyping them, this can seem patronising. It's hard to think of a worse tagline than "designed for women", although "designed for women, by women" probably just about manages it.

- To embrace stereotypes is to embrace prejudice. That's fine if you actually *are* prejudiced and want to exhibit the fact,[21] but if you don't see yourself that way then you could be in for an unpleasant surprise.

I should point out that each of the examples above will offend some groups of people, for which I apologise – it wasn't intentional, although it does serve to demonstrate that even talking about demographic stereotypes is enough to demonstrate the dangers of demographic stereotyping.

Having looked at the basic demographic make-up of the players of virtual worlds, OK, what use is it? Well if you're a marketer then it will probably help you market your product; you're unlikely to *be* a marketer, though, because few marketers are going to read this far into a book on virtual world design. What it comes down to is that if you want more players that fit some demographic, you focus advertising on people of that demographic. You should not, however, design your game around demographics. People don't play virtual worlds because they're female or old or have large discretionary spending or hail from a particular culture. They play them for other reasons entirely.

---

[21] Parodies, spoofs and other critical comments on stereotypes also work. For example, the point behind making a virtual world set in, say, a 1960s spy-novel universe could be to educate people as to how relatively backward society still was back then.

CHAPTER 11

Basic Player Types

THE CONTENTS OF THIS chapter could well be the main reason you bought or otherwise acquired this book, so don your best +2 Spectacles of Cynicism and I'll begin.

11.1 WHY PLAY VIRTUAL WORLDS?

The people who market and sell virtual worlds want to know *who* is playing. Designers want to know *why* they're playing. There are many games and entertainment products out there: why play a virtual world, rather than watch TV, listen to a symphony, enjoy a first-person shooter, go for a long walk, play a card game, hit a ball into a hole with a stick, …? People have a great many options regarding leisure pursuits: why would they choose a time sink such as a virtual world? It's not even as if virtual worlds are necessarily superior to the alternatives in most respects (see sidebar).

MMORPGS *VERSUS* TABLETOP RPGS

If you compare MMORPGs with human-moderated tabletop RPGs, there are several important areas where MMORPGs come off decidedly worse.

Subjectivity. Is a player character acting in an evil way if they pickpocket a watch from an NPC? What if the NPC had been exceptionally rude to the character when they'd innocently asked what the time was? What if the NPC had pickpocketed it from the character in the first place? What if the watch belonged to the NPC but the character bought it from a pawnbroker in good faith? Humans are good at making value judgements, but computers struggle.

The unexpected. To do more damage to the vampire, the player character coats their daggers in garlic butter. If the virtual world developer has foreseen this, all is well (except perhaps for the vampire). If not, the player's ingenuity is not rewarded. There are always things that players want to do in role-playing games that fit the fiction but haven't been foreseen. Humans have little problem with this, but computers need to be told what to do.

DOI: 10.1201/9781003689638-11

Impact. If a group in a tabletop RPG wants to burn down the headquarters of the thieves' guild as an act of revenge then they can certainly attempt it. If it works, the thieves' guild will now be missing a guild house. In an MMO, the group may not be able to attempt to raze it in the first place unless it's part of a predetermined story-line, and if they do burn it down, it's unlikely to be burned down for everyone who has yet to complete that storyline.

Player needs. In a tabletop RPG, the referee can pick up on what the players want in terms of story and action, and deliver bespoke content to address that dynamically. This form of negotiated content is a feature of *Blades in the Dark* (Harper, 2017), for example. The best that an MMO can do is to offer players a multitude of options and hope they'll pick one that suits.

Meta-interaction. Players can interact with a virtual world within the context of that virtual world, but they can't argue with it. They can argue with the referee of a tabletop RPG, who may well acquiesce if they feel the players have a point ("yes, OK, there's a chance you could have pulled off the mage's boots of speed when the eagle snatched him up and carried him off – check agility, DC 25"). Some tabletop RPGs, such as *Amber* (Wujcik, 1992), are entirely a process of negotiation between the players and the referee. Tabletop RPGs don't even have to *have* a referee, come to that – *Fiasco* (Morningstar, 2009) doesn't.

None of this is to say that tabletop RPGs are necessarily better than MMORPGs, because of course MMOs have their own victories (chiefly, convenience). Smaller-scale virtual worlds, in particular text MUDs, can even do some of the things that tabletop RPGs can do but MMOs can't; for example, *Achaea* has refereed content.

Nevertheless, this does all suggest that *as RPGs*, tabletop RPGs are perhaps to be preferred.

What's the deal, then? Why *do* people play virtual worlds?

I'm going to spend the rest of this chapter explaining just that.[1]

11.2 FUN

If you ask people why they play virtual worlds, the chances are they'll tell you "it's fun". They may be a little more specific – "it's the people", "I like the world" – or they may be non-committal – "it's something to do", "TV is rubbish these days". They may even have some deeper motive – "to be someone else", "to be myself". Most often, though, they'll say it's fun. Fun is what they play to have.

You'll get the same reply for most games, of course. You'll get it for play in general. Is the fun from virtual worlds the same *kind* of fun as from other games, though? Is the fun from virtual worlds even the same for different people?

---

[1] This chapter and the three that follow, in fact....

Unfortunately, *fun* is one of those words that everyone[2] understands but no one can quite capture in words.[3] Dictionaries make the attempt, but the best definition is to experience it. For this reason, psychologists writing about games prefer the word *engagement* (which isn't a synonym for *fun*, but that doesn't seem to bother them). Some game designers dislike the word "fun" (Rogers, 2014), because if you've been working on the same content for weeks and weeks then "fun" loses all meaning.

Players aren't a lot better. Is killing the same clutch of furbolgs repeatedly for an hour to grind reputation fun? Is running the same instance[4] 30 times in a row to gain a weapon upgrade fun? Is yomping across a mob-infested swamp seeing no other player character for an entire evening fun? Yet players do this kind of thing time after time.[5]

To find our answer to the question of what people find fun *in virtual worlds*, let us cast our minds back to 1989 for some more historical context-establishing....

Back then, people recognised that virtual worlds were fun. However, it was generally assumed that each virtual world was fun in its own way: that is, all the people who played any particular virtual world played it for the same reason. That this was not actually the case should have been made copiously clear by the events of the Great Schism, but the counter-argument prevailed: if you are playing the same virtual world as I am, well you must be playing for the same reasons I am. Otherwise, you'd quit and play a different virtual world.

I knew this monolithic view of play to be wrong because, as a young game designer, I'd already been through the painful process of learning that if I designed a game that I found fun then that didn't mean everyone else would also find it fun – or even that I'd find it fun myself tomorrow. Fun is relative to the individual and the context. I wasn't about to get into an argument about it, though, because there are more players than there are mes.

Around this time, *MUD2*'s admin-level players – *wizzes*, as they were known[6] –were increasingly becoming aware that their own views on what *MUD2* was "about" did not always coincide with those of others. The main point of difference was what was called *mystique*[7]: some wizzes liked to stay in the background, manipulating the virtual world to make it interesting for regular players (known as *mortals*[8]), whereas others liked to be visible to everyone, lording it over the mortals and generally being the focus of attention.

---

[2] Well, most English speakers, anyway. Plenty of languages don't have a word for *fun* and have to make do with something not-quite-the-same instead, such as *amusant* in French. Other languages have more nuanced words for fun used in different contexts, such as *Spaß* and *Vergnügen* in German.

[3] It's what girls just wanna have (Hazard & Lauper, 1983).

[4] I talk about the nature of instances in Volume II. Players usually call them *dungeons* or (for ones involving more characters) *raids*.

[5] So do designers, but they tend to be philosophical about it as they don't personally find much fun in playing anyway. Those examples are from my personal experience in *World of Warcraft*, *Final Fantasy XIV*, and *New World*, by the way – and they're merely representative; they're by no means the most unfun things to do out there.

[6] It was short for "witches and wizards", so despite appearances was gender-neutral (even though having all witches be female and all wizards be male perhaps wasn't).

[7] A collection of terms such as this one, used in either or both of *MUD1* and *MUD2* circa 1992, can be found in the *MUDspeke Dictionary* (Bartle, 1992).

[8] Not in the sense of "not gods", but in the sense of "killable".

The first group wanted to protect the mystique of being a wiz, whereas the second group didn't see what was wrong with being in-your-face.

These inter-wiz disagreements were compounded by the fact that, at the time, we had more top-level wizzes (known as arch-wizzes) than was traditional; several wizzes had been promoted in preparation for an impending opening-up of *MUD2* to a much wider audience on British Telecom's Prestel system.[9] One of the less-recent arch-wizzes, Henry Mueller, decided that we shouldn't be squabbling when we launched on Prestel, so endeavoured to find a way to settle the differences of opinion. On 20 November 1989, he posted a long message to the wiz email list, the crux of which was the following line:

Basically, the fundamental question is: "WHAT DO YOU EXPECT FROM MUD?"

So began an intense and heated discussion that nevertheless avoided descending into the kind of acrimony typical of online discussions even in those days. In mid-January, after all the active wizzes had had their say, I put together a summary of the arguments (Bartle, 1990a) and opened this up to further debate. Further debate duly followed, the conclusions of which I analysed in May (Bartle, 1990b). Commentary on my analysis continued into late June, before it finally petered out.

Formally, this analytical process is a form of *constructivist grounded theory* (Charmaz, 2000), by the way – not that I knew this at the time, hence its rough-and-readiness. You could also categorise it as a *focus group* approach (Eklund, 2015), if you were being generous.

My conclusion following all this was that people who were playing *MUD2* for fun[10] found said fun in one of four ways. I named the playing styles I'd identified *Achievers*, *Explorers*, *Socialisers*, and *Killers*.[11] I'll discuss what they are shortly, although it's perhaps worth noting that I'd listed these four types a year earlier in an article I'd written for the *Adventurers Club Limited Member's Dossier* (Bartle, 1989),[12] so already had the basic types in mind if not their relative structure.

Having written up my analysis, over the next few years, I observed and chatted to players in *MUD2* and one or two other MUDs, surmising as a result that the model was basically correct; I didn't really do anything with it beyond that, however. Although I thought it was cool myself because of the way it neatly fitted together, I wasn't about to assume that anyone else would like it (*MUD2*'s wizzes looked at it through the lenses of their own experience, so found plenty of different lens-specific ways to fault it). I regarded it mainly

---

[9] It never happened. Rivalry between different divisions of BT, which was in the throes of privatisation, meant that the Prestel tech people wrote the interface to our specifications then their bosses went with *Shades* instead.

[10] The "for fun" is important. Note that it's referring to the fun of playing virtual worlds, rather than the fun of playing in general.

[11] The fact I went with *Killers* and not something less eye-catching may ultimately be the reason that sufficient people paid attention to this work to give it traction.

[12] They're not *quite* the same: I called Achievers "Treasure Hunters". The editor of the *Adventurers Club Limited Member's Dossier*, by the way, was Henry Mueller – the very arch-wiz who sparked off the discussion that let to my development of the player-types model.

as a curiosity that showed what fully fledged designers already knew: people play virtual worlds for different reasons.

That said, having gone to the effort of writing it, I did consider that I maybe should try to get it published. I was no longer an academic, so decided not to go for a peer-reviewed journal (not that any would have considered it anyway); instead, I chose one of the few UK semi-professional magazines exclusively covering virtual worlds: *Comms Plus!*. My article (Bartle, 1990c) was not well-received, although to be fair, few articles ever were.[13] Suitably chastened, I didn't push the model further.

However, two years later, in November 1992,[14] I was invited to speak at the Cambridge University Computer Society to a mixed audience. Reasoning that the human aspects of *MUD2* would be of more interest than the technical aspects, I wheeled my analysis out again. This talk went well (there were knowledgeable people present, including one from *Avalon*), and the post-talk discussion allowed me to defend my points. I left persuaded that the concept was robust, but in the knowledge that it was also lacking. There was no underlying theory: it explained the different kinds of fun that players of virtual worlds typically experienced, but not why they experienced these kinds in particular. Was it just to do with personality, or was there something more to it?

When I heard of the founding of the *Journal of MUD Research*, I had hopes that it would be a success.[15] I certainly wanted it to be; the more we know about virtual worlds, the better they are likely to become. In order to try to help it take off, I decided to submit a formal academic paper for the first issue. I took my analysis and rewrote it from scratch to journal standards. The *JoMR* was peer-reviewed, so my peers fittingly reviewed what I'd submitted and made requests for changes. One of these was particularly helpful, suggesting new labels for the vertical axis of the now-famous graph that I shall be discussing in the next section. The revised article was accepted and thereafter published (Bartle, 1996). It's been cited over 4,000 times and is one of the formative papers of Game Studies.[16] I appear as the answer to questions in university examinations.

So, now you know how what I'm about to describe came about. It concerned but one MUD, *MUD2*, yet I proposed that it applied to all virtual worlds. I outlined my methodology, but included neither the emails I had studied nor the tags I'd derived from them.[17] You can decide for yourself whether or not this constitutes a good enough foundation for it to merit serious attention.

Let's now look at what that 1996 paper established.

---

[13] The editor liked to be contrary and provocative, in the hope that this would stir up interest. Sadly, it all-too-often gave the impression that he didn't know what he was talking about.

[14] It was 4 November, a date I can confirm because a Take That! concert ended at the same time that my event did. The streets were awash with groups of excited teenaged girls, who inexplicably preferred listening to a boy band over falling asleep during a presentation about *MUD2*.

[15] It wasn't. Even a name change to the *Journal of Virtual Environments* couldn't save it: it folded after six years in 2002.

[16] On the basis of this, I was invited by the Digital Game Research Association to put myself forward for an inaugural Distinguished Scholar award in 2016. I obliged, whereupon my application was summarily rejected. So it goes.

[17] Remarkably, I do still have faded printouts of the emails along with my associated hand-written tagging work. I'm sure there's an AI out there that can be trained to decipher it.

11.3 TWO DIMENSIONS

The four activities pursued by people who play virtual worlds for fun are:

- **Achievement Within the Virtual World's Context**.

    Players give themselves contextual goals and set out to achieve them. Examples: collecting loot, killing mobs, and completing collections.

- **Exploration of the Virtual World**.

    Players try to uncover as much as they can about the virtual world within its context. Example: trying unusual actions, mapping, and digging into systems.

- **Socialising with Others**.

    Players use the virtual world as a context to communicate with one another. Examples: guild chat,[18] playing musical instruments, and dressing to impress.

- **Imposition on Others**.

    Players use the virtual world's affordances to cause distress to (or occasionally to boss around) other players. Examples: non-consensual attacks, verbal abuse, and running a guild.

Labelling these four abstract playing styles by terms reflecting those who engage in them, we get[19] Achievers, Explorers, Socialisers, and Killers. In the 1996 paper, I offered the alternative labelling of *hearts* (Socialisers), *clubs* (Killers), *diamonds* (Achievers), and *spades* (Explorers), but no one ever uses those.

There is a relationship between the four types – they're not independent. Achievers and Explorers are more interested in the virtual *world* than its players, whereas Socialisers and Killers are more interested in the *players* than the virtual world. Also, Achievers and Killers like *acting* on the object of their interest, bending it to their will, whereas Explorers and Socialisers prefer to *interact* with it, reacting to the responses their activities engender (Figure 11.1).

The x-axis of this *interest graph* represents the primary object of the player's interest, from an emphasis on the virtual world's players to an emphasis on the virtual world itself. The y-axis represents the manner in which the player treats that object, from acting on it to interacting with it. The x-axis can therefore handily be regarded as the noun with the y-axis the verb that is applied to that noun.

It's possible to draw the interest graph as a grid, like a mini-spreadsheet, with rows labelled players/world and columns labelled acting/interacting. However, as we'll see anon, players are in the quadrants to various extremes and may be closer to one axis than another, so a Cartesian graph is more descriptive (even though the axes don't have units).

---

[18] Message windows are generally known as *chat boxes*, and the messages that appear in them are known as *chat*. When there are multiple chat channels, a prefix may be used to identify which kind of chat is under discussion, thus *guild chat* means chat appearing in the channel associated with your guild. Guilds are defined formally in Chapter 19.

[19] I'm going to capitalise the names of player types (and related categories) in this book, so you can tell I mean the types (and the players of those types) rather than people in general. Talking about Killers isn't the same as talking about killers.

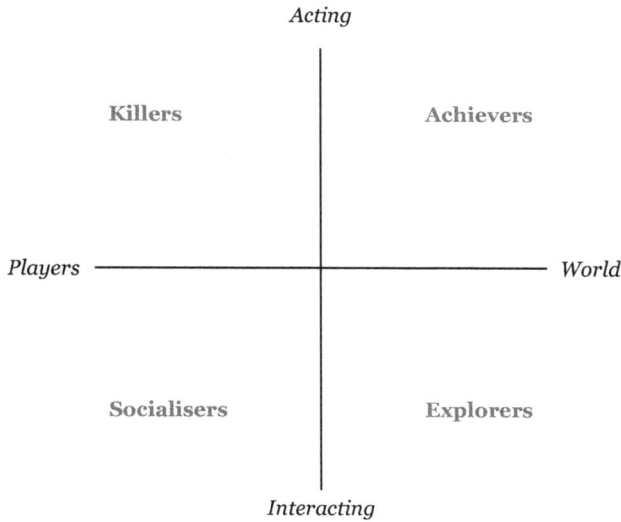

FIGURE 11.1   Interest graph.

Alert readers who didn't skip Chapter 4 will note some similarity between the graphs of Figures 4.1 and 11.1. There is indeed a relationship between them (see sidebar).

LUSORY ATTITUDE AND PLAYER INTEREST

The resemblance between the lusory attitude graph of Figure 4.1 and the player interest graph of Figure 11.1 suggests that there may be a connection between them.

It's immediately tempting to map player interests directly onto lusory attitudes:

- Achievers are players, who play by the rules to win (in the sense of "beating" whatever the virtual world throws at them).
- Explorers are triflers, who engage with the virtual world but not to win.
- Socialisers are spoilsports, who don't engage with the virtual world (just its players) and don't want to win.
- Killers are cheaters, who want to win but are prepared to break the rules to do so.

This looks OK superficially, but if we compare the axes then it doesn't really work. Are we really saying that people who are interested in the world necessarily play by the rules and those who are interested in players necessarily don't? Are we really saying that those who like to act want to win and those who like to interact don't? That's what a simple one-to-one mapping gives us.

Let's try another tack and look at player interests from the direction of lusory attitude:

- Achievers play to win, because winning is what they're interested in achieving. Explorers and Killers play to win by their own definition of winning, not the virtual world's. Socialisers don't play to win by any definition.
- Explorers play by the rules, because rules are what they're interested in exploring. Achievers and Socialisers play by their own definition of the rules, not the virtual world's. Killers don't play by any definition of the rules.

This suggests that the axes in Figure 4.1 could be relabelled with the types of players. Instead of going from *doesn't play by the rules* to *plays by the rules*, the x-axis would go from *Killers* to *Explorers*; instead of going from *plays to win* to *doesn't play to win*, the y-axis would go from *Achievers* to *Socialisers*.

Is this any use? Well it tells us: that Achievers sometimes play by the rules but are also willing to break them to win; that Explorers always play by the rules but aren't always interested in progression; that Socialisers have no interest in beating the virtual world yet will sometimes participate in the gameplay; that Killers think rules don't apply to them and will choose situationally how best to meet their goals.

This does seem to work, then.

I suppose it may be of marginal interest to a customer service representative, but it's something of an oversimplification. For executives, it might indicate where players can best be monetised during their playing career. For designers, it's merely more ingredients for the stew.

You can apply the same trick in reverse, too. This becomes a little irritating because although both graphs use the word "player", it's for different things. Also, the "spoilsport" label for the lusory attitude graph is perhaps a little harsh. Still, let's press on and see what we get:

- Players (in a lusory-attitude sense) are focused on the world. Cheaters and triflers have their own agendas. Spoilsports are focused on the player (in an interest graph sense).
- Cheaters act to cheat. Players and spoilsports are happy however their goals are met. Triflers interact to trifle.

You could therefore relabel the axes of Figure 11.1 with the classes of lusory attitude. Instead of going from *players* to *world*, the x-axis would go from *cheater* to *trifler*; instead of going from *acting* to *interacting*, the y-axis would go from *player* to *spoilsport*.

You wouldn't have to use the lusory attitude labels themselves if you didn't want (they can seem a little disparaging). You could use the axes that define Figure 4.1 quadrants instead. The x-axis of Figure 11.1 could go from *playing to win but not by the rules* to *playing by the rules but not to win*; the y-axis would go from *playing to win by the rules* to *neither playing by the rules nor to win*. The contradictions are resolved by inserting "sometimes"; for example, Achievers are playing by the rules, sometimes to win and sometimes not, whereas Killers are playing to win, sometimes by the rules and sometimes not.

So, what use, if any, is this second new graph?

Well if you're studying player interests, not a lot, really. This version looks at lusory attitudes through the lens of player interests, so tells us more about the former than the latter. It could perhaps shine a light where it hasn't been shone before, if there's a researcher out there who wants to examine lusory attitudes from a virtual world angle. The first version is perhaps of more use to designers, though.

As graphs aren't necessarily the best way to convey perspectives, here's a brief summary using examples:

- Achievers see virtual worlds as games, as in *Tennis*, *Cluedo*, and *Call of Cthulhu*.

- Explorers see virtual worlds as recreational pastimes, as in gardening, cooking, and building model railways.

- Socialisers see virtual worlds as entertainment activities, as in nightclubs, concerts, and watching spectator sports.

- Killers see virtual worlds as blood sports, as in hunting, shooting, and fishing.

Note that these player-type names are descriptive, not prescriptive. The axes are the important part: if you want to see if someone is in the bottom-left corner, you should look at whether they find fun interacting with people, not at whether some kind of count-the-number-of-interactions-with-players measure suggests that they socialise. This is because what a player finds fun is internal to that player. You can't say that simply because someone chats a lot they must be a Socialiser, or that because they run a guild they must be a benevolent Killer. Looking at behaviours will only get you so far; only the player really knows what they find fun – and even then, they may not have conceptualised it, or they may have but not have reflected on changes over time. As we'll see in Chapter 14, many elder-game players still think of themselves as Achievers while actually being Socialisers. Furthermore, Killers are particularly adept at disguising their behaviour so they don't appear to be a Killer, as it makes the result that much more exquisite when they finally show their true colours. It's also possible that players might read content differently: if you give Killers an increasingly bad reputation for offing newbies, there *will* be Achievers who'll aim to max out this bad reputation for themselves because in their eyes it's an achievement.

My aim in publishing the 1996 paper was not to say that for people who play MUDs for fun, "these are the four types of player"; it was to say "there is more than just one type of player". This may seem shiningly obvious now, but it wasn't always the case. I wasn't expecting my work to be bullet-proof: I thought a better hypothesis would materialise six months later and sweep it aside. That this hasn't happened is something of a surprise, and to some extent a frustration (because a better hypothesis means we'd get better virtual worlds). It appears that I inadvertently managed to hit on a classification that's of actual, practical value. The particular four player types I identified resonated with both professional and amateur designers, who had seen these people in their own virtual worlds,[20] and the paper's utility rapidly spread by word-of-mouth. As a result, player types have been used in the design of pretty well every commercial virtual world from the start of the Fifth Age onwards.

11.4 BEYOND THE GRAPH

So far, we don't have a theoretical basis for why players play virtual worlds; all we can say is that people who play virtual worlds for fun[21] will fall into one of four categories. There may be other, better categories using different parameters, but within their own terms, the player types are exhaustive. That doesn't mean the model is useful: after all, we can classify the entire human race by people who are aged below 64 and those who are aged 64 or over, which is exhaustive (it captures everyone) but not necessarily informative.

Not having a theoretical basis doesn't mean we can't test the integrity of our approach so far, though.

Let's suppose that we were to double down on one of the axes of the interest graph shown in Figure 11.1, at the expense of the others.

- **Players**. If we made the virtual world increasingly about the players and not so much the world, eventually the world would cease to provide a context. The result might as well be a chatroom. It would no longer qualify as a virtual world because whatever physics it had would be redundant.

- **World**. If we made the virtual world increasingly about the world and not so much the players, eventually it would be so capacious or intricate that encountering other players would be a rarity. It might as well be single-player. It would no longer qualify as a virtual world because its sharedness would be almost imperceptible.

- **Acting**. If we made the virtual world increasingly about action and not so much about interaction, eventually it would lead to rote repetition and grinding. The content would become so similar that it might as well be a first-person shooter or a farming game. It would no longer qualify as a virtual world because any sense of persistence it might have would be irrelevant.

- **Interacting**. If we made the virtual world about interaction and not so much about action, eventually players would become passive recipients of streams of events. They may as well be listening to a podcast, watching street theatre, or reading a book. It would no longer qualify as a virtual world because any real-time aspect to it would make little difference.

---

[20] Sadly, there were too few such designers on the panel that ignored my proposal to present this work at the Game Developers' Conference. What might seem obvious now wasn't always obvious – and of course, just because it does seem obvious now, that still doesn't mean it's correct.

[21] Reminder: *for fun* is important. The original data gathering didn't consider people who don't play for fun, therefore any extension in that direction is at your own risk.

From this, we can see that the model as it currently stands does connect with the definition of virtual worlds I presented in Chapter 1.[22] As for the other two points of the definition (not being Reality and being represented as a character), we'll come to those later.

This exercise presupposes that the player interest graph can be tilted to favour different ends of each axis. As luck would have it, it can indeed, although scaling up can be difficult: the necessary changes are easier to enact in a smaller, nimble virtual world than in a larger one with considerable momentum behind it. It's usually better to make your adjustments in beta (when players won't have hardened their views as much), but it's possible even post-launch.[23]

Here are some strategies (there are others) for altering a virtual world's design to favour a particular set of interests.

- **To Emphasise Acting**. introduce obstacles that are surmountable (so that players have to do things to achieve their goals); remove feedback (so that you have to act to find out whether what you did worked); allow for the creation of functional organisational hierarchies (so players can act in concert to achieve shared goals); cut down on the range of things that can happen as a result of your actions; give players clear goals.

- **To Emphasise Interacting**. limit the choice of actions available[24]; increase the range of responses to these actions; impose linear pathways (such as story arcs); make some responses vague or cryptic; add more content but lower the utility of loot; make it easy both to accept and to respond to new information; ensure that the virtual world has a consistent personality.

- **To Emphasise Players**. don't have many NPCs with their own agendas; make getting to the location of another player character easy; dilute the importance of the world by allowing out-of-context building; add many opportunities for personal expression. Typically, this latter point involves communication across multiple channels (speech, clothing, emotes, combat, …) and media (emojis, sound effects, fireworks, musical instruments, …), with friends lists to keep in touch with some people and filters to keep out of touch with others.

- **To Emphasise World**. make the world's geography large and time-consuming to traverse; make its loot extensive; make its systems deep and complex; only allow in-context building and crafting, but make it easy; reduce opportunities to communicate, either by restricting communicative actions (including combat with other player characters), inserting unnecessary steps for basic messaging (hit return, type "/say", then your message followed by another return), diluting the usefulness of social hubs

---

[22] When I constructed my definition of what a virtual world is, I hadn't yet made this connection. I was therefore quite chuffed when it turned out that there was one.

[23] Interface changes are usually the easiest way to do this. Tiny text on a mobile-phone virtual world will not endear it to Socialisers, for example.

[24] This may seem odd, but Explorers and Socialisers usually have a fairly strong idea of the direction in which they want to travel: they thrive on interpreting fresh and original responses, only occasionally interspersed with fresh and original behaviour on their part to elicit those responses.

(remote buying and selling, banking, repairs, …), encouraging transient connections with strangers you'll never meet again (random looking-for-group mechanisms), or locking players into social silos (guilds).

All this appears to be a fine cookbook for virtual world designers and operators to tune their worlds so they get more of the player types they want. Some of the changes look to affect relative numbers (adding more communication channels will attract more Socialisers and Killers without putting off Achievers or Explorers) and others look to affect absolute numbers (quality-of-life changes that make social hubs inessential will please Achievers and Explorers but could well cause Socialisers and Killers to pack their bags and play elsewhere). The atmosphere of a virtual world is contingent on where the centre of balance is between players who exhibit different playing styles, so this kind of versatility is a boon when you're trying to shape your virtual world to attract a particular player base.

Sadly, it's not as simple as it seems. Suppose you favoured players over world: it may look as if this would increase the percentage of Socialisers and Killers in the virtual world, but that isn't necessarily what would happen. This is because different types of players interact with other types of players (and their own type) in different ways. The Killers could well drive the Socialisers away. We'll be looking at the nature of these interactions in Chapter 12.

11.5 ISSUES

What I've described so far is pretty much how player types stood following the publication of my 1996 paper. Word-of-mouth brought it to the attention of designers and academics, because there was nothing like it out there at the time and it seemed reasonable. Designers could immediately compare its findings to their own virtual world and confirm that it fitted; academics could sense the beginnings of a new field of research. However, it didn't take long for either group to find issues with the idea. I was expecting they would, of course, because I'd assumed that it would be replaced by a better model in short order; nevertheless, if in the meantime I could improve what I had then I was up for that, too, as it might help others investigating this area.[25]

Academics mostly found fault in the fact that the model is not easily testable. There isn't always a good correlation between behaviour and player type (*e.g.* most players who engage in PvP aren't Killers, they're Achievers who regard winning a fight as an achievement); this is especially true in cultures where identity is in part carried by the group, not solely the individual. Also, players aren't themselves always good at judging what they find fun (recall that many elder-game players in MMOs think they're Achievers when they're actually Socialisers), or they are good at it but like to persuade themselves they're something else (*e.g.* Achievers may claim to be Explorers because they think Explorers are cooler).

This academic critique is entirely valid. Because it's very difficult – perhaps impossible – to know what a player's type *actually* is, that means the model can't be tested, which in turn means it can't be trusted. It's reflective but not normative.

---

[25] OK, so although that *was* a reason, the main one was that I didn't want to leave it unfinished. Hey, I'm a gamer – I finish my quests!

Designers took a more pragmatic view: the model matched what they saw in practice and produced results, so that was enough of an incentive to use it until something better came along. Sure, individuals might consider other factors more significant (they find the virtual world's fiction disagreeable, or they don't like the revenue model, or the servers keep crashing, …), but those are different hurdles to jump. Overall, the virtual world's design is the primary influence on play, and if there are signposts to show the designer where they can take it, well that's better than navigating by the stars.

Perhaps surprisingly, when I presented the model, there was little pushback on the topic of stereotyping (which, as I've already mentioned, is usually A Bad Thing). Most folk seemed to intuit that although the model may be stereotyping what people found fun, it wasn't stereotyping people themselves. People can change what they find fun in a virtual world, so associating groups of players with what they found fun at any particular moment wasn't condemning them to a fixed classification. That said, the model didn't address *why* players change type over time; it was merely noted that they *could* change type.

The main flaw that designers identified was that there were some types that seemed to have sub-types. The most glaring one was Killers, because there are ways to enjoy acting on people that don't involve causing them trauma; the other three types had variations, too, but these were more nuanced.

None of these objections stopped the player types model as it stood from being adopted widely by designers. It was (and still very much is) used both to drive the design of virtual worlds and to sanity-check that a preliminary design is sound.

It's irritating, though, that it's a model without a theory.

CHAPTER 12

Advanced Player Types

A s it stood, the basic player types model couldn't explain:

- Why there are two different kinds of Killer.

- How players move between types.

- Why people play virtual worlds.

Addressing these issues was going to require more than a patch: it needed an expansion.

12.1 THREE DIMENSIONS

The expansion came in the form of a third axis (the idea for which developed from the original player types study). I labelled it as being from *implicit* to *explicit*, with the former encapsulating "not thinking about" and the latter encapsulating "thinking about".[1] If the x-axis can be regarded as the noun and the y-axis the verb that is applied to that noun then the z-axis is the adverb that modifies that verb.

This immediately solves the Killers problem. The kind of Killer who likes to impose on players by griefing them doesn't tend to give much forethought to their actions, whereas the kind who imposes on players by organising them does. The first kind would be implicit Killers, the second kind explicit Killers.

Adding an extra axis to the graph makes it three-dimensional, as shown in Figure 12.1.

The squares of the 2D interest graph become cubes in the 3D version, which is illustrated in Figure 12.2. If we label the cubes, the result is the eight-type interest graph of Figure 12.3.

So, we need to look at these cube labels.

- **Politicians**. acting on players explicitly. These are those Killers from the 2D graph who openly seek to get players to do things. They're often community leaders, but can sometimes come across as being self-serving busybodies; it depends on their

---

[1] Sorry if you were hoping it might be "explicit" in the sense of "leave-nothing-to-the-imagination sexual imagery".

DOI: 10.1201/9781003689638-12

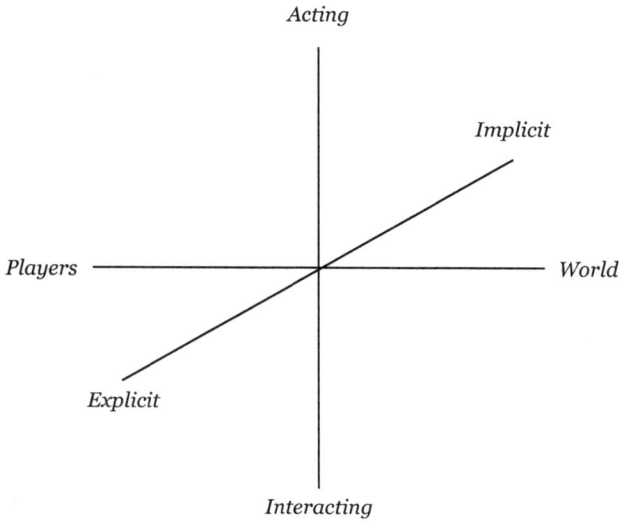

FIGURE 12.1   3D interest graph.

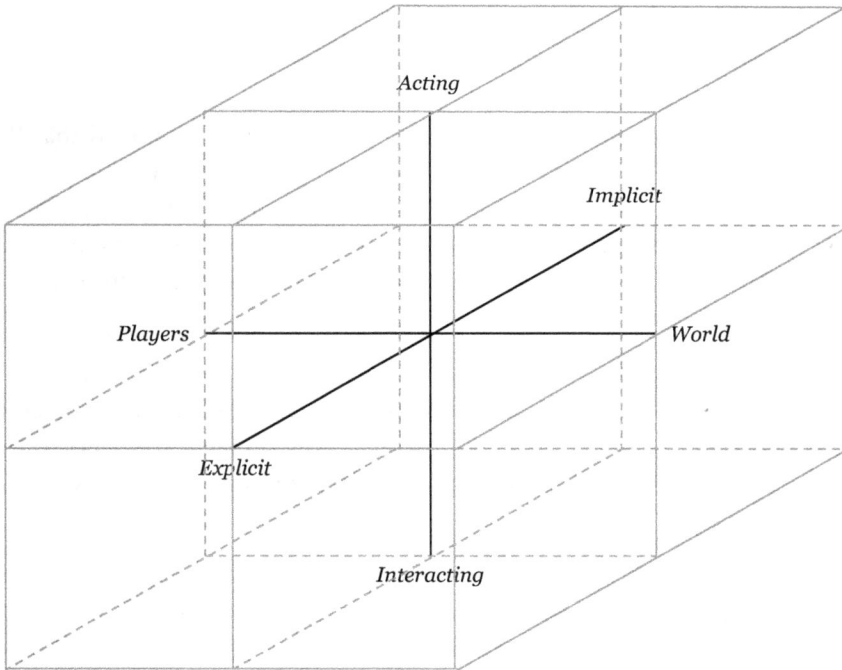

FIGURE 12.2   Interest graph cubes.

social skills. They almost always feel under-appreciated, an assessment that is rarely inaccurate.

- **Attainers**. acting on the world explicitly. These comprise the bulk of Achievers from the 2D graph, to the extent that I would have called them "Achievers" if I hadn't already

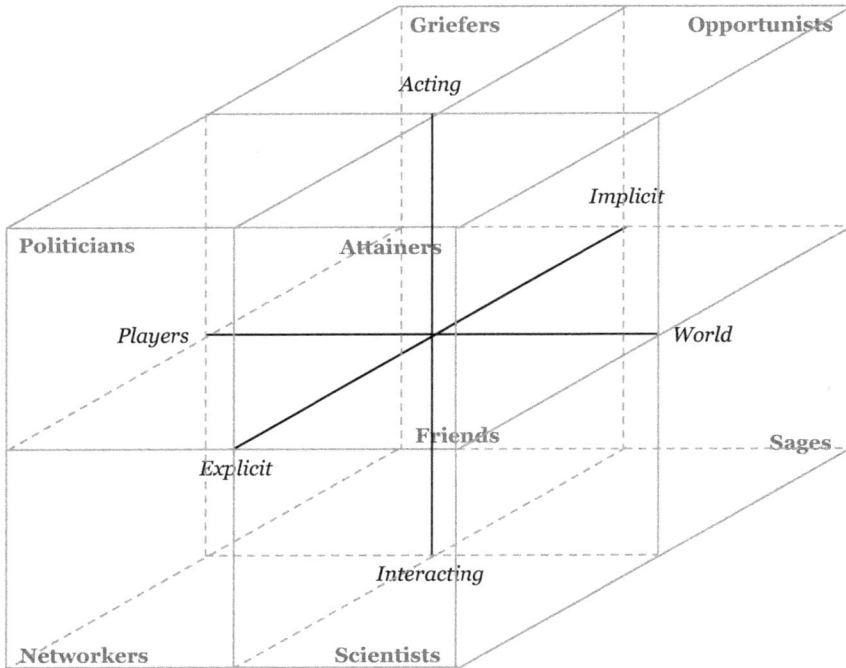

FIGURE 12.3   Eight-type interest graph.

used the word. I used to call them "Planners", but this half-implied that Politicians didn't plan, whereas they do. I chose "Attainers" as an improvement because this kind of Achiever is trying to succeed in the virtual world on its own terms. It doesn't matter that on the whole you can't formally "win" most virtual worlds, or even that some aren't even competitive: Attainers are more interested in winning battles than in winning wars.[2]

- **Networkers**. interacting with players explicitly. Networkers are Socialisers who are building a portfolio of people with whom to socialise. They enjoy the company of their acquaintances and will happily interact with complete strangers to find more. They're generally personable, if sometimes gossipy, but ruthless, social-climbing careerists do exist.

- **Scientists**. interacting with the world explicitly. Those Explorers who want to find out how the virtual world works are Scientists. They experiment to form hypotheses, then use these hypotheses predictively to test them. If they work, they treat them as theories. Scientists attempt to expand their knowledge methodically, seeking to explain phenomena.

- **Griefers**. acting on players implicitly. These are the classic kind of Killer from the 2D graph. Some may well be impulsive, insecure individuals hoping to have their existence acknowledged by others, but for the most part, Griefers are merely testing the

---

[2] Wars are simply convenient contexts for more battles.

boundaries of the virtual world's social norms. Acting in a provocative or challenging manner is their way of doing this, although not necessarily to an extreme degree. Nevertheless, to find where the boundaries are, you occasionally have to overstep them; this causes grief to those who keep within them, hence the name.

- **Opportunists**. acting on the world implicitly. Opportunists are Achievers who don't yet know enough about the virtual world to formulate long-term strategies. They therefore take their chances as they arise, looking around for things to do and trying something else if it's too hard. They flit from idea to idea like a butterfly, finding where the physical boundaries of the virtual world lie. What will it let them do and what will it not let them do? Oh look, a crocus!

- **Friends**. interacting with players implicitly. Friends play because of their friends: they're Socialisers whose friendships have been forged in the fires of the virtual world. This could happen through guild drama, near-impossible boss fights, long philosophical discussions that go on late into the night, difficult quests, …; whatever it is, the players have bonded because they've been through the mill together and have come to know each other implicitly. They don't have to *think* about how their friends would react to something, they just *know*. Conventional rules of interaction therefore need not necessarily apply.[3]

- **Sages**. interacting with the world implicitly. These are the supreme Explorers, who understand the virtual world so well that they have internalised its workings. They can tell you what will happen if you try something new, even if they've never encountered the suggestion before. Sages aspire to expand their knowledge by flights of fancy, seeking to reveal meaning. Originally, I called these "Hackers", in the original sense of the word.[4] Unfortunately, the usurped meaning[5] dominated, so I went with "Gurus". This smacked of cultural appropriation, though, so I'm now trying "Sages". It's evolution in action.

The extra dimension of implicit/explicit brings sub-types into the original model, thereby addressing one of the three charges brought against it. Naturally, having eight types instead of four somewhat complicates the inter-type dynamics, but we'll come to that later.

The extra dimension adds more depth. Whether that's useful or not depends on what you want to use the model for: virtual world designers might keep it in their armoury, but designers of regular games are less likely to find it valuable.

It's possible to add more axes, of course. Why stop at three when four might be *even better*? For example, we could use the player's level of competence to disambiguate between those who are effective at what they do and those who want to be but suck at it. Might this help identify players who need help in some way? Well, perhaps, but it looks as if it's a case of diminishing returns, in that adding new dimensions makes distinctions that are

---

[3] Put another way, they may say and do things to one another that would be totally unacceptable in other contexts.
[4] People with a mystical understanding of the workings of computers.
[5] People who want to break into computers, ruining your life.

increasingly too subtle to be informative beyond a niche application.[6] It depends what you want the model to tell you, though: it might even be that replacing an existing axis with a new, different one is more informative from your perspective. If you're interested, try some ideas yourself – you may well strike gold.

The eight-type model remains exhaustive: those people playing a virtual world for fun will be fully accommodated within it. That isn't in itself enough to validate our additional dimension, though – it may be no more relevant than "initial letter of player's name is a vowel", which also preserves exhaustiveness but is likely to be important to few designers. As it happens, though, implicit/explicit does have some merit to it.

We've already seen that the additional axis helps to explain the clear differences in attitudes with which the four-type model struggled. Another indication that it's serviceable follows from pushing its extremes beyond the graph, as we did earlier with the dimensions of player/world and acting/interacting:

- **Explicit**. If we made the virtual world increasingly about explicitness and not so much about implicitness, eventually we would disassociate ourselves with our characters. They would be objects to manipulate rather than subjective embodiments of identities. It would no longer qualify as a virtual world, because players would no longer be represented within it as characters.

- **Implicit**. If we made the virtual world increasingly about implicitness and not so much about explicitness, we wouldn't need to think about it, it would become our normality. It would no longer qualify as a virtual world because to us it would merely be part of Reality.

This addresses the two remaining elements of the definition of a Virtual World that the four-type model didn't. Again, I didn't know this when I added the new axis, so I'm rather pleased[7] about it.

As for what else the addition of the implicit/explicit axis brings us, well for that we'll need to take a look at how a player's perception of what's fun in a virtual world changes over time.

THE BARTLE TEST

After I published my 1996 paper, its findings were adapted into a test that people could take to see what player type they were (Andreasen & Downey, 1999). This was none of my doing, which perhaps explains its success; it definitely explains its name, because although my ego is inflated, it's nowhere near as inflated as it would have to be for me to name a test after myself. At the time the original version of it went offline in 2016, it was believed to be the oldest continuously running test on

---

[6] I'm sure a massively multidimensional model would please a machine-learning algorithm, but these don't buy books so I'm not directly addressing them here.
[7] You might consider the word "smug" more accurate.

the Internet. Its final home (GamerDNA, 2015), which was last archived 6 July 2016, records that 880,944 people had taken the test by then.

The original test disappeared when the company hosting it changed hands one time too many. However, it has been recreated and updated by Matthew Barr (Barr, 2016), should you wish to take it yourself. Roughly 50,000 people a year do indeed so wish, which is around the same number that the original test could boast. It consists of a series of 30 questions, each of which compares two types (from the four-type model) at a time. This means that if you're an Explorer, say, and it's asking you a question that's assessing whether you're more Killer or Socialiser, you may find it hard to answer. The results are given as percentages, adding up to 200% (because of the half-coverage for each question), and summarised as four letters (for example, EASK means you're mainly an Explorer and mainly not a Killer, with Achiever and Socialiser in between).

Because of the binary nature of its questions, the Bartle Test doesn't really meet the standards expected of Psychology surveys these days. That doesn't mean it isn't useful, though. Different virtual worlds will attract players with types in different proportions; regardless of the error bars that might accompany individual test results, they can show whether the averages are in tune with the overall trends. Of course, this only works if such information is available, which it isn't. For an example of what's possible, though, an 18 August 2000 snapshot (Andreasen, 2000) of the stats for the original Bartle Test (after 14,206 people had taken it) illustrates how it can be used to compare the player-type make-up of different virtual worlds.

Changes in trends are also identifiable: the overall breakdown of Killers, Achievers, Explorers, and Socialisers in the original test was 19%, 17%, 34%, and 27% respectively, whereas in the modern test, it's 20%, 19%, 47%, and 14%. Whether or not you believe that those figures reflect the actual proportions (personally, I don't), the values *relative* to each other are comparable. We can therefore say that the number of Explorers has increased over the years at the expense of Socialisers. As for why this might have happened, your guess is as good as mine (which is that the modern test has been taken by more players of games in general, rather than of virtual worlds in particular, so social play is less of a factor).

If you'd like a more formal and rigorous test, van den Hoven (2020) uses all eight player types.[8] Its 54 questions are formulated for a 5-point Likert scale, which avoids the issue of "I don't care either way"; furthermore, some address the axes of the graph, so that players' types can be calculated using a co-ordinate system rather than only by pairwise comparisons. It's the test you should use for the purposes of academic study or design-testing; players can use it too, although its findings are perhaps too refined to appeal to most. Should you prefer to stick with four types, Erümit et al. (2021) have an inventory of questions you can ask that use a pairwise approach across all six combinations, which looks pretty solid to me.

I perhaps ought to warn anyone conducting a survey to find out what type a respondent is that it will underestimate the number of Griefers. Hey, they're

---

[8] Using the type names as they were before I spontaneously changed them in this book.

Griefers – why would they *not* lie? This point may seem obvious, but having read many, many academic papers that survey player types I can assure you that it isn't.

Oh, and before you ask, no: I don't have a player type. I may play virtual worlds for close to a thousand hours a year, but I don't play them for fun (well, not player-fun, anyway).

12.2 DEVELOPMENT TRACKS

Not all players change type over time, but most do. This was noticed very early in virtual world development – well before player types were identified. *MUD* players would begin by trying to kill one another's characters, then once they figured out that this was a losing tactic, they moved on to exploring the world. Having gained enough knowledge to make a go of it, they transitioned to scoring points and racking up levels; in so doing, they formed friendships in adversity with people whom they could trust implicitly. Finally, they would hang out with these pals simply to have fun playing together. This exact same pattern is still apparent when I let my students loose in *MUD2* all at once in a computer lab.[9]

This change in player priorities was called *drift* – the same drift mentioned in Chapter 4 that ultimately leads players to drift away from the virtual world.

The path followed by the majority of players easily can be drawn on the 2D interest graph, although not so easily that I expect you to do it yourself. Figure 12.4 shows what it looks like.

That the connection between drift and the player interest graph was not made until after the establishment of player types is evidenced by the fact that if I'd noticed it beforehand,

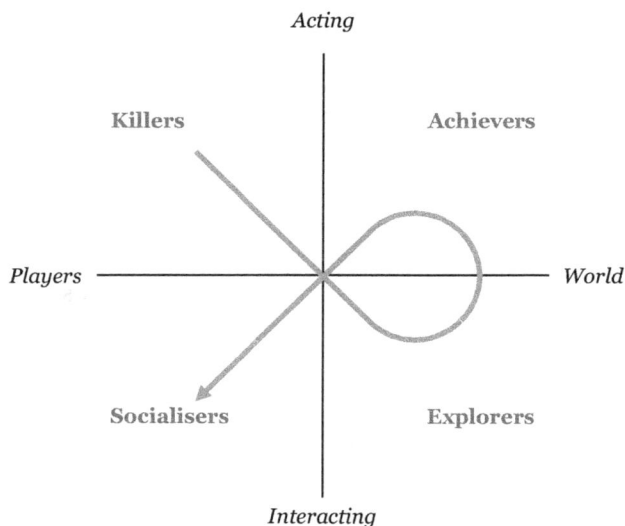

FIGURE 12.4   Main Sequence.

---

[9] Well, the first two steps are – they don't have time to get much beyond that.

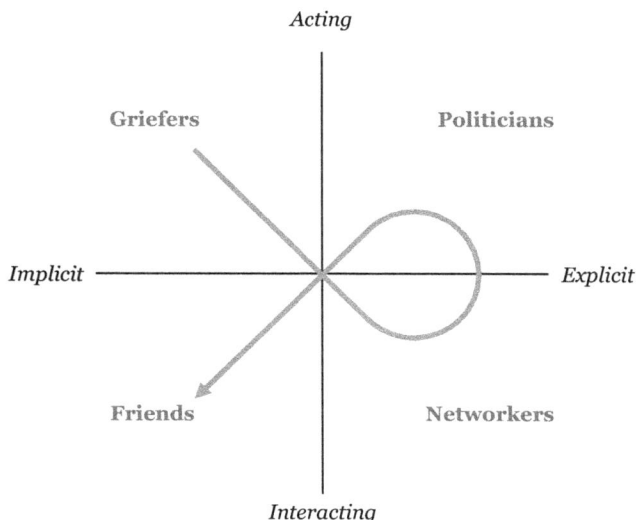

FIGURE 12.5   Main Socialiser Sequence.

I'd have changed Players/World to World/Players and got a nice alpha-shaped curve instead of a flipped version.[10]

Using eight types instead of a paltry four, this curve goes Griefer to Scientist to Attainer to Friend. It's the *Main Sequence* for player development in virtual worlds.

The Main Sequence isn't the only sequence, of course. If you observe enough players, you'll notice that some seem to go from Killer to Socialiser to Killer to Socialiser (the *Main Socialiser Sequence*); others go from Achiever to Explorer to Achiever to Explorer (the *Main Explorer Sequence*). A small minority[11] goes from Achiever to Socialiser to Achiever to Socialiser (the *Minor Sequence*). These don't make a lot of sense on the original 2D graph (without the implicit/explicit dimension), but they do on the 3D graph – or on a 2D graph with a different dimension removed (Figure 12.5).

Figures 12.5 and 12.6 show the left-hand and right-hand slices of the 3D graph as they appear looking down the player/world axis. Figure 12.6 is the Main Socialiser Sequence (which is player-oriented); Figure 12.7 is the Main Explorer Sequence (which is world-oriented).[12]

Figure 12.7 shows the Minor Sequence on the full 3D graph, hence demonstrating why I didn't draw the other three sequences this way.

In eight-type terms, then, we have four sequences that players typically follow:

---

[10] Rotating it 90 degrees clockwise makes it look like the logo of the Scottish National Party (the thistle is the national flower of Scotland).

[11] Not as small as it used to be, as players with experience in other virtual worlds increasingly follow this path when they start a new one; however, it's still smaller than before the Great Schism, when balanced worlds were the norm and it was easier to alternate between Achiever and Socialiser.

[12] I named it Main Explorer Sequence rather than Main Achiever Sequence because the end point is Explorer (in the form of Sage).

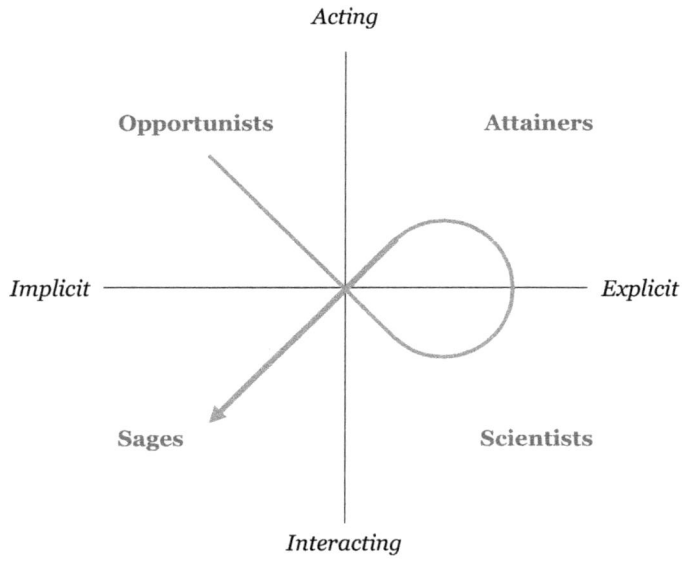

FIGURE 12.6 Main Explorer Sequence.

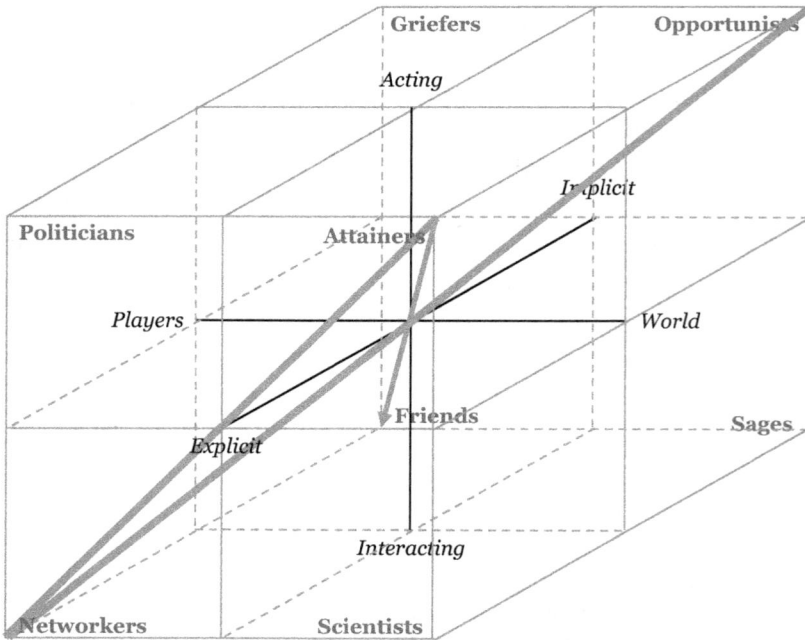

FIGURE 12.7 Minor Sequence.

- **Main Sequence**. Griefer to Scientist to Attainer to Friend
- **Main Socialiser Sequence**. Griefer to Networker to Politician to Friend.
- **Main Explorer Sequence**. Opportunist to Scientist to Attainer to Sage.
- **Minor Sequence**. Opportunist to Networker to Attainer to Friend.

It is not insignificant that three of these end in Friends.

People do occasionally switch between sequences (especially in balanced worlds, where it's easier), but this invariably happens at the intersections. For example, a player following the Main Sequence might switch after two steps and follow the Main Explorer Sequence instead, giving Griefer to Scientist to Attainer to Sage. It's my suspicion that this is usually due to external factors (such as the growing maturity of a teenaged player), but I have insufficient information to be sure; there may well be one or more better explanations.

The possible lines of travel are made more intelligible if we take the basic four sequences and combine them into *development tracks*, as illustrated in Figure 12.8.

This visualisation of the development tracks that players typically follow makes it easier to discuss the general process of movement between types.

Players of any given type will exhibit some of the characteristics of the previous and next types in the sequence they're following while they transition between them. For example, an early-stage Scientist might still find fun in behaving opportunistically on occasion, but this will reduce over time and they'll become more interested in exploring the virtual world's workings. As they continue to do so, they'll begin to find it rewarding that their understanding is correct and can be used to achieve in-world goals; these later-stage Scientists are starting to find achievement fun and are transitioning into Attainers. This supports the decision to make the interest graph of Figure 11.1 be Cartesian rather than a grid.

It's possible that during a transition a player may not like how it's going and back off. A Networker on the Main Socialiser Sequence (the upper development track in Figure 12.8) could find that becoming a Politician is too much of a time sink, for example, and switch to becoming an Attainer instead.[13] Note that this is backing off, rather than backtracking: you don't get players who have become Politicians backtracking to Networkers and then becoming Attainers, nor players who have become Friends backtracking to Attainers then becoming Sages.[14]

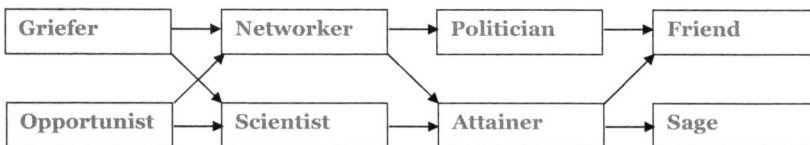

FIGURE 12.8 · Development tracks.

---

[13] Warning: becoming an Attainer is also a time sink.

[14] Contrary to what I imply in my 1996 paper, you don't get Explorers turning directly into Socialisers, either: they have to become Achievers first.

The most noticeable feature of the development tracks is the lack of a connection between Scientist and Politician and between Politician and Sage. Let's put it this way: neither transition occurs frequently enough to be noticeable.[15] I have no explanation for this anomaly. In Reality, scientists do occasionally become politicians – the 1980s Prime Minister of the UK, Margaret Thatcher, started out as a chemist – which makes the disconnect even stranger. However, just because I've chosen to *label* players who explicitly interact with the world "scientists", that doesn't mean they *are* scientists. Also, Margaret Thatcher may have been a chemist, but that doesn't imply she had fun being one (even though she worked with ice cream).

Another noticeable feature of player-drift sequences that the development tracks make easier to spot is that they all start out implicit, then go explicit, then stay explicit, then return to being implicit. This suggests that there's a general sequence: locate to discover to apply to internalise:

- **Locate**. Players begin by determining the social and physical boundaries that govern their possible actions.

- **Discover**. Next, they seek ways to string together ordered sequences of basic actions, either by asking others or by experimentation.

- **Apply**. Armed with the knowledge and expertise they need, players begin to apply it to achieve their goals.

- **Internalise**. Finally, having exercised themselves sufficiently often, players internalise their social or physical skills so they don't have to think about how to use them in future.

This mirrors quite nicely Piaget's four stages of cognitive development (Piaget, trans. 1952):

- **Sensorimotor, Ages 0–2**. Children use their body, senses, and actions to connect with the world.

- **Preoperational, Ages 2–7**. Children process the world symbolically using ideas and language.

- **Concrete Operational, Ages 7–11**. Children understand their environment and can function well in it, thinking logically and using reason.

- **Formal Operational, Ages 11–16**. Children can think reflectively and reason about hypothetical and abstract ideas.

I'm not suggesting that players of virtual worlds are basically children, but they do go through similar stages as they adapt to the new environment. [16]

---

[15] At least by me – and I have been looking. I suppose some intuitive understanding could happen within the specialised context of an elder game raid group, but whether the player concerned would find that fun is another matter.

[16] There's also an intriguing similarity to the SECI model of knowledge creation (Nonaka, 1994), but I'm not suggesting that players of virtual worlds are basically organisations, either.

EXAMINATION QUESTION

This is Question 3 from the MSc-level examination that I set for my Virtual Worlds module in 2022. Candidates had 30 minutes to answer it.

No, I won't be providing a mark scheme or a model answer – I've told you most of it already. Also, I'm mean.

Have fun!

This question concerns Player Type theory.

(a) The two-dimensional four-type model is the three-dimensional
     eight-type model with the implicit/explicit dimension removed.
        Construct a two-dimensional player type model with the
     players/world dimension removed. Draw this as a graph, giving
     each quadrant an appropriate label.
(b) Players progress through player types over time following one
     of four main paths: the *Main Sequence*, the *Main Socialiser
     Sequence*, the *Main Explorer Sequence*, and the *Minor Sequence*.
        State how each of these paths would appear on the graph you
     drew in your answer to part (a).
(c) Relate your answer to part (b) to Player Type theory's
     development tracks.
(d) More people use the four-type model than the eight-type model
     because eight types are felt to over-complicate the basic
     concept.
        Discuss whether the model you constructed in part (a) is a
     useful alternative to the usual four-type model.

This same locate/discover/apply/internalise progression appears in many situations. Recalling Chapter 2's characterisation of the development of virtual worlds, we began in the First Age by floundering around to make sense of what we'd invented, then there was a period of experimentation and learning-by-example in the Second Age; an emphasis on player-oriented and world-oriented play followed in the Third Age, culminating in the confident, successful world of the Fourth Age. The Fifth Age saw a graphical reboot, but within itself followed the first three steps of the same path.[17] Now, in the Sixth Age, we have the fourth step: old-timers treading water.

Obviously, virtual worlds don't themselves have fun because they're not people. Even though they're designed *by* people, this would only suggest that they're part of the designer's development as a designer, not that they have some industry-wide, fun-led journey of their own. Nevertheless, the repeated pattern is so prevalent that it does suggest there's something to it, by analogy if nothing else.[18]

---

[17] Avid footnote readers will remember that this is how the Fifth Age was broken down by Olivetti (2021).

[18] The progressive change in gameplay of 4X games (explore, expand, exploit, exterminate) just about fits into it, too, although labelling the location step "explore" is somewhat inconvenient.

Player types apply to all players who play virtual worlds for fun. They don't apply to players who play for other reasons. Development tracks show how players progress their ideas of what is and isn't fun. This is all neat and tidy, but there are two points worth noting that muss it up somewhat and can cause problems.

Point 1. Players sometimes get stuck. They never advance beyond a certain stage. They could be stuck forever as Griefers or as Scientists or as anything else. The reasons for this are varied, but will typically be one of the following:

- The player has no need to progress. They're quite happy where they are. People who enjoy PvP can have a ball without grinding through gameplay.

- The player has personal or personality reasons for not advancing. If they only have time to play in short bursts, they may eternally remain Opportunists.

- The virtual world prevents the player from advancing. There's no "end" to most virtual worlds, so there's no closure; players are stuck as Friends or Sages until they leave in disappointment.

Point 2. Players sometimes derail, or were never on-rail from the outset. They continue to have conventional fun while playing, but their overall motivation changes. They may become more interested in entertaining their Twitch followers than in what the virtual world is saying to them. In rare cases, something happens that outrages them so much that they turn into vengeful agents of discord and destruction. A player of type X who derails in this manner is called a *broken X*, with broken Sages the worst and broken Politicians fairly bad, too. Broken Sages are extremely knowledgeable, and if they turn that knowledge against the virtual world in a vindictive rage in response to a perceived injustice, this could have devastating, chaotic consequences, especially in smaller-scale MMOs. Regular Griefers are mere mosquitoes compared to the fire-breathing dragons that are broken Sages. As for broken Politicians, expect them either to act as pied pipers, leading their unwitting followers down a path to disaster, or to become turncoats, betraying those they lead to an enemy. Whether through gameplay or other factors, it's best to avoid distressing your players so much that they break – unless you actually want it to happen because it's part of the game.[19]

Nevertheless, development tracks do successfully address the second problematic issue that was inherent in my 1996 paper: how players move between types. The concept may lack appeal to players, and it's only going to appeal to researchers if it matches their research interests.[20] It does have some utility for designers, however, in that it can predict what kind of content players of any given type will next find fun so it can be made ready for them. Many designers pretty well know this intuitively, of course; still, it's always nice to have your intuition validated.

---

[19] To see both broken Sages and broken Politicians in action, *EVE Online* is a reliable venue.
[20] For example, if they want to prove it's wrong.

Overall, then, development tracks serve the purpose of addressing a failing of the original model, but beyond that, they're a bit "so what?". It's interesting and all to know that players instinctively adopt a structured approach to playing virtual worlds, finding fun in whatever leads them to progress along their current path, but this still doesn't tell us *why* people play virtual worlds.

Be that as is may, we'll shortly see that development tracks do unlock the answer. Before we dive in to those muddy waters, however, we need to back up a little. All that I've said so far about player types would work for single-player RPGs, and what I've been calling a "model" is actually little more than a categorisation. The player types characterisation needs an engine – something to provide pressure and give impetus to people, so they don't remain stationary forever. In short, the model needs to be *dynamic*.

12.3 DYNAMICS

All healthy virtual worlds contain some of each player type, but the ratios vary. As we've seen, each virtual world's design is largely responsible for how the player types distribute within it at a macro level, but the picture is complicated because players also act and interact at a micro level, depending on what their interests are. The implied behaviours of different types of player can encourage, discourage, or have little to no effect on the experience of other players. Killers of both kinds can have a particularly disproportionate influence on the fun experienced by others, for example.

12.3.1 Player Type Relationships

It's possible to assess the relationships between the different types. Some are quite easy to calculate: increasing or decreasing the number of Networkers will proportionally increase or decrease the number of Politicians, because Networkers are the only source of new Politicians. Of course, with some attenuation, they will thence in time become Friends, although I'll restrict this discussion to first-order effects so as to make it clearer what's going on.[21] Using this regime, a change in Politician numbers will directly influence the number of Friends, but a change in Networkers does so only indirectly so won't be discussed.

Other relationships are relatively easy to derive from their definitions. Consider the number of players in the Friends category (that is, their fun derives from their friendships with other players): it's fairly non-controversial to suppose that increasing the number of Friends will further increase the number of Friends, as there's a positive feedback loop there.

Beyond this, it starts to become a matter of observation (if not opinion). In my 1996 paper, I presented a diagram that illustrated the flow of influence between the different players types. This was only grounded in my own experience, so although it was probably not quite at the level of mere hearsay, it was nevertheless unproven. The same applies to what I shall be presenting shortly: feel free to use it as a guideline, but it would take some tiresome long-term research indeed to assess its accuracy.

Although a diagram was a reasonable way to illustrate the influence that different player types have on one another in the four-type model, it becomes a spaghetti mess to look at

---

[21] Note that "clearer" isn't the same as "clear".

when there are eight types. Rather than a mere 16 possibilities for directional inter-type interaction, there are 64. This suggests that a tabular approach may be more appropriate than one putting my limited[22] graphical-design skills under stress.

Turning tabular enables us easily to distinguish the effects of increasing and decreasing the relative numbers of a type, because we can have two tables, one for each set of effects. Having separated them out, we can then be more nuanced about both the degree of increase/decrease and the degree of effect. For example, a small increase in the number of Networkers will have a negligible impact on the number of Griefers, but a medium increase will have a small impact and a large increase will have a medium impact.[23] These impacts are over time, I should say – they're not instantaneous.[24]

It takes a special kind of grim dedication to make a pairwise comparison between all the player types, assessing the strength of influence that an increase or decrease (to one of three levels) in one will have on the other. Nevertheless, I've done it so you don't have to. The results are expressed in Tables 12.1 and 12.2.

To read these tables:

- The top-left corner says whether the effects of this table are due to increasing or decreasing the number of players of the type indicated in the column below.

- The rows show the effect of performing this increase or decrease for players of the given type on the players of each of the types in the column headers.

- Beneath each column header are three sub-columns. The first is the effect on the column-headed type of a small increase (Table 12.1) or decrease (Table 12.2) in the row-headed type; the second is for a medium change; the third is for a large change.

- The symbols in the cells are: +, ++, and +++ for small, medium, and large increases; -, --, and --- for small, medium, and large decreases; * is used instead of + and ~ is used instead of - for when the change is because of player drift to one of the next types on the development tracks.

Example: if you look at the Sage row in Table 12.2 and cross-index it with the Griefer column, you'll see a blank cell, then a + cell then a ++ cell: this means that a small decrease (Table 12.2 shows decreases) in the number of Sages won't significantly affect Griefer numbers, but a medium decrease will have a small positive effect (the number of Griefers will increase a little) and a large drop in Sage numbers will have a medium positive impact on the number of Griefers. In summary, then, this suggests that a dampening in the number of active Sages will lead to a relatively smaller amplification in the number of active Griefers.

I've been referring vaguely to "numbers" here, without really committing to detail. It doesn't matter if they're absolute or relative: increasing the absolute number of Opportunists

---

[22] OK, non-existent.

[23] Remember, these are just my observations. You can quote me on them, because I'm never one to turn down a citation, but don't take them as authoritative.

[24] If they *were* instantaneous then increasing the number of players of type X would have to be recorded as an increase in the number of players of type X, which is a tautology.

TABLE 12.1   Effect of Player Type Increase

Increase	Opportunist	Griefer	Scientist	Networker	Attainer	Politician	Sage	Friend
Opportunist	+ ++ −	+ ++ +++	* ** ***	* * **	* * **	* ** ***	+	− − −−
Griefer	− −−	−	* ** ***	* * *	−	* ** +	−	− −
Scientist		−	+	−	*** ** *	*** ** *		+
Networker	+	++ ++ +	−	+ +	* ** +	*** ** +		+ ** ***
Attainer		++ ++ +	+	−	++ ++ +	++ ++ +	** ** *	** *** ** *** * **
Politician	+	+ + −		++ ++ +	+ + −	−	+	** ** ** *** *
Sage	+	− −−		+	+ + −	+	+	+ ** **
Friend	+	++ + +++	++ +	++ + +	− +	+ +		++ +++ +++

TABLE 12.2   Effect of Player Type Decrease

Decrease	Opportunist	Griefer	Scientist	Networker	Attainer	Politician	Sage	Friend
Opportunist	− −−	− −−	? ? ? ?	? ? ?	? ? ? ?	−	−	+ ++ +++
Griefer	+ ++	+ +	? ? ?	? ? ?	+ ? ? ?	−		−
Scientist	−	+ +	−	+ −	? ? −	? ? ?		? ? ? ?
Networker		−	+	− −	−	+ −	? ?	? ? ?
Attainer		−	−	− −	−	− −	?	? ?
Politician	−	−		−	− −	+	−	−
Sage	−	+ ++				−		−
Friend	−	−		−	−	−		−

will also increase the relative number of them with respect to the other types. That said, absolute numbers do matter: doubling the number of players of each type doesn't look as if it should have much of an effect in relative terms, but it may well do because of the geometric (rather than linear) influence some types can boast. Regrettably, it's hard to quantify this, but as an analogy, if you pour half a bottle of liquid soap onto one pizza and the other half onto a second pizza that has twice the surface area of the first, the result is two ruined pizzas rather one ruined pizza and one half-ruined pizza.

Some points to note about these tables:

- Not all interactions between types have much of an impact. A small decrease in the number of any type won't affect the number of Opportunists (because Opportunists are newbies and arrive all the time).

- Some interactions are positively correlated. Increasing the number of Opportunists will increase the number of Griefers by the same relative amount; decreasing the number of Opportunists will decrease the number of Griefers by the same relative amount. This is because Griefers need someone to grief and are more likely to meet Opportunists first.

- Some interactions are negatively correlated. Increasing the number of Griefers will decrease the number of Friends by the same relative amount; decreasing the number of Griefers will increase the number of Friends by the same relative amount. All Friends will eventually drift away, but toxicity from Griefers may hasten their departure.

- Some interactions are in a feedback loop. Increasing the number of Friends will increase the number of Friends further; decreasing the number of Friends will decrease the number of Friends further. This is because Friends need Friends.

- Some interactions aren't symmetric in any way. A large increase in the number of Griefers has a small negative impact on the number of Sages (too much aggravation can put off anyone) but a large decrease in the number of Griefers has no impact on the number of Sages (people aren't encouraged to become Sages merely because there's no one bothering them).

- Some next-on-the-development-track interactions are less impactful than others. Increasing the number of Networkers has less of an effect on Attainer numbers than on Politician numbers. This is because there are fewer Politicians than Attainers in most virtual worlds, so those Networkers who become Politicians have a bigger effect on the latter's numbers.

- Some interactions are just weird. Whatever the increase in the number of Griefers, the impact on Networkers is the same (small). Two forces are at work at the same time here: the more Griefers there are, the more will convert into Networkers, but the more Networkers will quit because they don't like being griefed.

- Some interactions are too situational for the graph to capture properly. Increasing the numbers of Sages has a negative effect only on the number of Griefers, but if the virtual world's systems privileged Sages above all else then increasing the number of Sages could also have a subduing effect on Attainers.

12.3.2 Details of Interactions

I'll discuss the rationale behind some of the more opaque cell entries, so you can see why they are what they are. I've touched on some of these already, so expect a small degree of repetition (it's easier for your future-reference purposes if I do this). I'll generally ignore large-change-for-small-effect interactions, unless they're particularly odd. If you disagree with my reasoning for any of these interactions, by the way, that's fine: you're perfectly at liberty to use your own experience to fill in your own tables, I'm not trying to be a demagogue here.

Opportunist/Opportunist. Assuming a functioning newbie flow, Opportunists arrive all the time. If there are players already there – typically, other Opportunists – then they'll see the virtual world is alive and will be encouraged to stay. If there are too many, though, it can feel overcrowded so they'll stop playing and maybe come back another day (or maybe not). Small decreases in the number of Opportunists don't have any effect as the player doesn't at this stage know what the norm is anyway and is willing to give the virtual world a chance. As the number of people making the place look busy drops, though, and opportunities for spontaneous grouping diminish, players are likely to become disenchanted quicker and move on.

Opportunist/Griefer. Griefers are also newbies, and so encounter a good many Opportunists through geographic proximity during the onboarding process. The more people there are around to grief, the more likely Griefers are to stay. Opportunists don't like this, of course, but can tolerate a certain amount of it as "just part of the game". Too much pain will nevertheless put them off playing, of course.

Opportunist/Networker. The impact of Opportunists on Networkers is a progression one (some Opportunists become Networkers). More interesting is the impact of Networkers on Opportunists: they will often still be in newbie areas and so may interact with Opportunists. Making a friend[25] early on can greatly increase the chance that a player will become engaged (Rosedale & Atherton, 2023).

Opportunist/Politician. A large change in the number of Opportunists can lead to a commensurate change in the demand for Politicians, because people are more likely to become community leaders if they sense there's untapped community to lead. However, Politicians don't interact enough with Opportunists to affect their numbers (they're usually interacting with players of later types).

---

[25] Reminder: I'm capitalising player type names in the hope that everyday usages, such as "friend", are seen as such and not as a player type, such as "Friend".

Opportunist/Sage. There's a slight positive feedback loop between these two types. Sages don't seek an audience but are chuffed if they get one. Opportunists are more inclined to stay if they see wonders being performed. Sages do occasionally wander into Opportunist areas, because why wouldn't they, so the chance that they might interact with Opportunists is not as remote as it might at first appear.

Griefer/Griefer. Griefers can and do interact with other Griefers for griefing-together LOLs, but it's not sticky content for them. They're looking to find the social boundaries of the virtual world, which is essentially a solo activity. Griefers try to avoid each other (they like imposing on, not being imposed on), only affecting one another when the numbers get so high that avoidance becomes difficult and they run out of prey except each other, Malthusian-style.

Griefer/Scientist. Many Griefers progress to Scientists, although it depends on the kind of virtual world as to what the throughput is (more may progress to Networkers). Scientists can actually give Griefers a harder time than they'd like when picked on, so a large increase in Scientist numbers can depress Griefer numbers (and a large decrease can increase Griefers' enjoyment).

Griefer/Networker. Griefers often become Networkers, but they also pick on them because they're easy to wind up. As a result, increasing Griefer numbers will have a small impact on Networker activity regardless of how large the increase is. When Griefers quit (or progress to Scientists), then the number of Networkers will fall proportionately, as the griefing may have stopped but the supply of would-be Networkers has dried up. Likewise, if the number of Networkers falls, Griefers will lose some of their choicest prey and this will affect their overall enjoyment.

Griefer/Attainer. Attainers will have seen it all and be able to shrug off the effects of more Griefers unless there are so many that the feel of the virtual world changes for the worst. On the other hand, having more Attainers will encourage Griefers to grief, because they see them as senior players who are ripe for being annoyed through disruptive activities.

Griefer/Politician. If the number of Griefers becomes so large as to be a problem, other players will need to organise better to deal with them. This opens up more opportunities for Politicians. Perversely, if there are many Politicians around then this can increase griefing opportunities, because then Griefers can attack organisations rather than just individuals.

Griefer/Sage. Griefers have to be very annoying in large numbers to cause Sages to rage-quit. One-on-one, Sages will beat Griefers pretty well every single time, and although they don't seek them out to use as dishcloths, if provoked they will defend themselves extremely robustly when attacked (whatever the channel). If you have too many Griefers in a virtual world, increasing the number of Sages (and, to a lesser extent, of Scientists) is one of the few positive ways[26] to reduce their numbers.

---

[26] Negative ways, such as locking out every player, may be more effective, but the cure is worse than the disease.

Scientist/Sage. Sage numbers aren't directly affected by changes in the number of Scientists (or indeed of any other type), but a medium or large increase in the number of Sages will show Scientists that there are undiscovered glories to be found. This will encourage them to stick with it. You can think of Sages as role models for Scientists in this context.

Networker/Friend. Friends don't really need Networkers as they have friends enough already. The more Friends there are, though, the more Networkers will want to network with them and so inveigle themselves into the virtual world's social scene (or at least a part of it). Friends don't mind this, it's just not as big a deal for them as it is for Networkers.

Attainer/Attainer. This is an important relationship, as it's a positive feedback loop relating to a large group. Attainers validate themselves by the presence of other Attainers. Too few, and it looks as if playing is pointless; too many, and, well, there's no such thing – the more, the merrier! It's further justification that the player is doing something worthwhile. It shows that the virtual world is "about" achievement in its own terms.

Attainer/Politician. Politicians need someone to boss around, and for the majority of them, that's going to be Attainers. Attainers have no desire to take part in governance, they just want a benevolent dictator to help hook them up with players who have similar goals. The more Attainers there are, the more openings for Politicians there are. Reducing the number of Politicians doesn't really affect the number of Attainers, though: it just means the remaining Politicians have to do more work.

Attainer/Friend. Large numbers of Attainers become Friends, so the relationship that way round is simple. The relationship the other way round is not only more interesting but also more important. Basically, Attainers want to be "better than" other players. Networkers and (particularly) Friends don't really care about this kind of competition, so they serve as an insulating layer.[27] Friends aren't really trying to compete any more, they just want to do things together. A small increase in the number of Friends will improve all the Attainers' assessments of their relative standings, thereby giving them reason to stay and others reason to join them. A small decrease will do the opposite. A large increase in the number of Friends changes the character of the virtual world, though: it becomes "about" the social side of play, rather than about the gameplay side, which is dispiriting for Attainers and will eventually cause them to leave in disappointment. However, a large *decrease* in the number of Friends is catastrophic: the insulating layer becomes too thin, and the Attainers at the bottom no longer have enough of a sense that they're "better than" someone else. They stop playing, which means a new set of Attainers now finds itself at the bottom, and in time they stop playing too. The whole fabric frays away because there are no Friends

---

[27] Sages don't care either, but Attainers don't try to convince themselves that they're better players than them – it would be fruitless to do so, as they're not.

to act as a hem. Only a core of die-hard Attainers will remain. This is why PvP-only worlds are always going to face difficulties.

Politician/Politician. A large increase in the number of Politicians will lead to competition between them over recruits to their causes. Not all of them will be satisfied, so expect some to fall away.

12.3.3 Stable States

From this analysis, it can be seen that Griefers have disproportionate influence on other player types, which is just how they like it. Fortunately, most of them will move on to become Networkers or Scientists, but the more of them there are then the longer they'll take to do so.

What we have here is a dynamic, player-development machine with multiple interconnected components that act to promote or to demote one another and themselves. Players come in at one end, they move through their development tracks helped or hindered by players who are at other stages of their own journeys (to an extent determined by the virtual world's design) until either reaching the end or leaving before then. It's doubtless possible to model such a machine in software, but (unless you count *MUD2* as a model) I haven't done so.[28]

We can nevertheless hypothesise what would happen if such a machine were created, because we can see what happens with actual players in virtual worlds. Eventually, the virtual world reaches one of four[29] stable states:

1. **Attainers Dominate.** Networkers and Friends are preyed on by Griefers (or broken Attainers), and quit because they don't need the aggravation. Those Griefers who become Networkers and Friends suffer the same fate, leaving the virtual world with a distinct game-like feel. The situation stabilises with Griefers in equilibrium with Attainers and Politicians, their numbers capped by Sages.

2. **Friends Dominate.** Limited opportunities presented by the virtual world's design stifle Griefers, who rapidly move on to become Networkers. This allows the positive feedback loops of Networkers and Friends to come into play, snowballing their numbers. Opportunists sense that this a social-play world; those that don't become Networkers either quit or become Scientists who follow their own path in relative isolation.

3. **No Type Dominates.** Sages and Scientists are numerous enough to keep Griefers in check, but there are still enough of the latter to stop Networkers and Friends from initiating a chain reaction. Scientists and Attainers, guided by Politicians and freed from the undue attention of Griefers, are numerous enough to ensure there's a healthy supply of Sages so as to keep it that way. This is a very stable form of virtual world, but it's difficult to set up from scratch.

---

[28] I had this book to write.
[29] There may be more, but these are the principal ones.

4. **The Virtual World is Empty.** Although this is the most stable form of virtual world, there isn't much else to commend it. The main ways it comes about are:

- Griefers scare everyone off in a mess of toxicity.

- A virtual world set-up expressly for Friends has insufficient content to build a critical mass of them.

- A virtual world set-up expressly for Attainers has no protective layer and those at the bottom stop playing (as described in Attainer/Friend earlier).

- People are put off from playing for reasons nothing to do with player types. These reasons could be internal (the software is buggy, it's an old virtual world, a patch broke the gameplay, …) or external (a change to regulations, a weak advertising campaign, war, developer runs out of money, …).

- It's meant to be empty (it's under development, it's an experiment of some kind, …).

This explains why there are three relatively stable forms of non-null virtual world, as described in Chapter 3. Type 1 from the list above are game worlds; type 2 are social worlds; type 3 are balanced worlds. I used the word "relatively" there because it *is* possible for a virtual world's form to change, especially if the developer is proactive about it. Also, it's worth noting that very large, semi-partitioned virtual worlds could have different stable forms for different partitions, depending on how they're set up (social here, game there).

As an aside, this same analytical approach has something to say about newbie-hose requirements. In essence, a balanced world needs fewer newbies than a game world, which in turn needs fewer than a social world. This is because players in a balanced world stay for longer than in a game world, and players in social worlds treat each other as content so need more of the same to keep themselves satiated.

It seems reasonable to ask at this point whether there are more abstract effects at work here on top of those for individual player types. We know that the virtual world's design plays a big part, but what about general player interests? In particular, might there be a benefit to repeating this exercise so as to look at the preferences labelled on the interest graph *axes* (player/world, acting/interacting, implicit/explicit) in addition to the player types themselves?

The short answer is yes, it's a possibility, but when I tried it, I found that it didn't offer much utility beyond telling me that I really should be using player types, not axis labels.[30]

Overall, the result of this extended analysis is that players are revealed to make the virtual world a dynamic place, pushing and pulling one another along the development tracks. This tells us why we have *movement* – which is critical for any healthy virtual world – but we're still clueless as to why players *play* virtual worlds.

To obtain our answer, we're going to have to pivot.

---

[30] Have a stab at it yourself if you're keen – it's entirely possible that I missed something important.

CHAPTER 13

Pivot

The Hero's Journey

THE MERE TITLE OF this chapter will disappoint some people.

The Hero's Journey is a narrative format described by the academic Joseph Campbell in his book *The Hero with a Thousand Faces* (Campbell, 1949). Campbell was a professor of literature with an interest in mythology and religion. He noticed that myths from across the globe all seemed to follow the same basic format, in which an archetypal hero ventured into an Other World to find himself. In each myth, the names were different and the events were different, but the key elements were the same. He called this abstracted version the *Hero's Journey*, or the *Monomyth*.

I'll describe it shortly, but first I'll address those areas of disappointment (while not necessarily removing said disappointment). There are two of them.

13.1 AREAS OF DISAPPOINTMENT

The first area is that it's the *Hero's* journey, not the *Heroine's* Journey. In myth, the protagonist is invariably male. Adapting it for the modern era and allowing female protagonists would and indeed does work, but in Campbell's view, the women of the past didn't need to go on such a journey because they had another route to self-understanding (through childbirth). If this sounds sexist and patronising, well, that's the people of the past for you (or at least the people of the past whose stories reached the present). Anyway, because it's formally the Hero's Journey, I'll be referring to the protagonist (the would-be hero) using male pronouns, rather than gender-neutral ones.[1] There is a contrasting *Heroine's Journey* (Murdock, 1990),[2] which puts its protagonist through the grinder before she drags herself

---

[1] Gender-neutral pronouns are my natural dialect (East Yorkshire) when referring to uninstantiated people, so using he/him is actually harder for me than it is to go with they/them. I was in my early 20s before I discovered that the word "themself" wasn't standard English – not that this has stopped me using it in this book as if it were.

[2] Murdock wrote it in part-consultation with Campbell. There are some aspects of it that seem a little too spiritual for my liking, but the foundations are sound.

 DOI: 10.1201/9781003689638-13

out and realises that she didn't need to go on a journey in the first place; I won't be drawing on that in what follows.[3]

The second area of disappointment is that the Hero's Journey has accrued a somewhat negative reputation in recent years. It delivers compelling narratives, but because of this, it was somewhat over-used in the film industry. If every mainstream movie you watch follows the same, compelling format, after a while it ceases to be a compelling format because you know what's coming – especially if it's in-your-face about it. The results seem formulaic because they *are* formulaic. You've seen one superhero movie, you've pretty well seen them all.

It doesn't have to be this way. The less self-conscious about following the Hero's Journey a screenwriter is, the more likely it is that the resulting movie won't feel quite so formulaic. For example, viewers might not notice that the films in *The Lord of the Rings* trilogy (The Lord of the Rings: The Fellowship of the Ring, 2001; The Lord of the Rings: The Two Towers, 2002; The Lord of the Rings: The Return of the King, 2003), and the films in the *Harry Potter* series (Harry Potter and the Philosopher's Stone, 2001) … (Harry Potter and the Deathly Hallows – Part 2, 2011) follow the Hero's Journey, but they do. This could well be because they were based on books that conform to the pattern simply because that's how the story *had to be*. The same applies to some older movies that came out well before *The Hero with a Thousand Faces* was published, such as *The Wizard of Oz* (The Wizard of Oz, 1939).[4]

Part of the reason that the Hero's Journey has such a sullied reputation among today's writers is that there are multiple takes on it. Campbell's original conception has 17 steps. Seventeen is too large a number to maintain the interest of Hollywood executives, so screenwriter Christopher Vogler reduced it to 12 steps to make it easier to follow (Vogler, 1985) and distributed this revised version at Walt Disney Pictures, where he was working at the time. It was immediately used as a template for the plot of *The Lion King* (The Lion King, 1994), which became a huge hit and cemented the validity of the approach. Its present ubiquity is such that if you search for an explanation of the Hero's Journey online, you're likely to find that it refers to Vogler's characterisation ahead of Campbell's.[5]

Twelve steps is insufficiently concise for some people, too. David Adams Leeming (Leeming, 1973) had earlier used eight steps, but his work did not apparently register on Hollywood's radar until screenwriters began to look beyond Vogler; Phil Cousineau also used eight steps (Cousineau, 1990), with rather more film-industry success. It should be pointed out that Leeming, Vogler, and Cousineau are all experts in this area: they're not barging in without a clue, and all their versions are valid at different levels of abstraction.

The upshot of this, though, is that too much paint-by-numbers use of the Hero's Journey by writers who only understood it superficially has turned it into an over-used narrative trope. It also suffers from claims that it's universal (Koenitz, 2023), which it is in the sense

---

[3] After reading this chapter and the next one, the reader is invited to speculate whether the conformity of virtual worlds to the Hero's Journey rather than the Heroine's Journey might explain why male players tend to outnumber female players.

[4] This was based on a novel (Baum, 1900) that was published before Joseph Campbell was even born.

[5] ChatGPT also defaults to Vogler's version unless you tell it otherwise, much to the surprise of those among my students who get fail-level marks when they use it to write their Hero's Journey assignment for them.

that the Hero's Journey formula appears in all cultures, but isn't in the sense that all narratives follow the Hero's Journey formula.

Campbell put together the Hero's Journey after studying myths from cultures across the world, both ancient and modern, including those of Australia, Bali, Cambodia, Finland, Iceland, Ireland, Mexico, Native America, Nigeria, Persia, Peru, Phrygia, …. He looked at the epics of Arthur, Buddha, Cuchulainn, Gilgamesh, Jason, Moses, Osiris, Vishnu, ….[6] He also considered folk tales such as *The Sleeping Beauty* and *The Frog Prince*, and authored fiction such as Homer's *Odyssey*, Dante's *Inferno*, and Tolstoy's *Anna Karenina*.[7]

Campbell found that almost all of these myths, epics, folk tales, and pieces of monumental fiction conformed to the same pattern, or fragments of that pattern, which he believed was rooted in the human psyche: if everyone has a need to explain the same fundamental concepts of social, worldly, and other-worldly realities, they're all likely to come up with narratives that at some level are similar. That level is the Hero's Journey.

Discovering your place in the universe is the purpose of the Hero's Journey. The Hero's Journey is therefore a path to self-understanding.

In general,[8] the Hero's Journey is still a feature of most creative writing courses because it produces strong plots (although it can encourage laziness). Scholars of myth and folklore are ambivalent or dismissive of it, because it's too acontextual for their purposes. Psychologists question its theoretical underpinnings (which are Jungian), because these are not scientifically provable and Psychology has moved on since 1949. Anthropologists back it up, because they'd spotted it independently.

13.2 SPECIFICS

So, what are the specifics of the Hero's Journey?

Well, it's a meta-plot. You fill in the form and you get a plot. You fill in the plot's form and you get a story. You tell the story and you get a narrative.

It's important to note that the word "hero" is used in a very formal sense here, not the everyday sense. Its strict definition of a hero is someone who has completed their Hero's Journey; all other references to being a hero are using simile or metaphor. If someone dives into an icy lake and rescues a drowning dog, you might *say* that they're a hero, but what you're actually saying is that they *acted like* a hero would have done. Performing a heroic act doesn't make you a hero any more than performing a noble act makes you a noble. Only if saving the dog somehow completes your Hero's Journey would doing so qualify you to be a *bona fide* hero.

It's also important to note that it's the Hero's Journey, not the Heroes' Journey. Only one person goes on the journey: they're not accompanied by anyone else. We'll see why later. We'll also see later that not all would-be heroes complete their journey: in many stories they fail, which can still lead to an instructive tale but the would-be hero will not end it

---

[6] You will note from the preceding list that Campbell considered as myth the stories associated with figures important to some religions. It would seem that the more a story is retold orally and passed down, the more its characteristics gravitate towards the Hero's Journey.

[7] Formally, I should provide citations for these three books. The presence of this footnote attests to the fact that I haven't.

[8] This is academic code for "I'm about to say something without backing it up: I won't fight back if you disagree".

fulfilled. The would-be hero can't fail even one step: it's all or nothing. For example, I've just said that only one person goes on their Hero's Journey but [*The Lord of the Rings* spoiler alert![9]] Sam Gamgee accompanies Frodo Baggins all the way through six books (largely because Frodo is such a drip that he'd never have made it on his own); this looks as if it breaks the rules, and so it does: as a consequence, Frodo actually *fails* his Hero's Journey, refusing to destroy the One Ring at the very location he's spent hundreds of pages trying to reach. If he'd had enough character to get to the Crack of Doom on his own, he'd have had enough character to destroy the One Ring on his own. As it was, he had to rely on getting his finger bitten off by Gollum, who then helpfully lost his footing and destroyed the One Ring for him.[10]

Superficially, the Hero's Journey is merely a tried-and-tested age-old blueprint for creating plots. If you don't look beyond this, it doesn't have a lot of relevance to virtual worlds: it's just a worn-out approach to storytelling. Its usefulness comes from what's beneath the surface, though, which is something rather profound: a route map to discovering your identity. By undertaking *your* Hero's Journey, *you* can become your true self – the you that you *really* are, rather than the you that other people *tell* you you are. It's a journey of self-discovery. People have narrated stories to one another for millennia; each retelling adds some of the storyteller to the story and smooths away the excesses that previous storytellers have added. What's left, after countless retellings, is a core story that is meaningful to all who have told it, embodying all their experiences. That's what the Hero's Journey delivers.

It's common for people to take old stories, old music, old plays, and refashion them for the modern era. They explain themselves by saying this is how the medium evolves, or (somewhat more arrogantly) that this is what the original creator would have done with their work were they alive today. For something like the Hero's Journey, yes, the content of a modern rendition would be very different from one of the past; the shape of the journey would remain the same, though. It's been smoothed and polished by the seas of ten thousand retellings, and your contribution is but one more wave gently caressing the shoreline. It will remain the same regardless of how well or badly Campbell, Vogler, or anyone else interprets it, because it touches on something fundamental to all human beings: a way to get to be the person you really are.

Philosophers might argue the point here, noting that identity is a construct and there may not even be a "self", let alone a "true self". That's fine. Operationally, though, most human beings find it convenient to regard themselves and other human beings as being independent, free-thinking entities. Now, much in the same way that you can look at other people and intuitively build up a mental picture of them as individuals,[11] you automatically build up an intuitive mental picture of yourself as an individual. Most of the time, that picture will match your thoughts and emotions, but sometimes it will be discordant: there will be faults in your mental model of yourself. The model – the self that you think

---

[9] I shouldn't have to give this, because *The Lord of the Rings* ought to be on everyone's reading list ahead of the book you're currently reading.

[10] OK, so Gollum also destroyed himself, but at least he died happy.

[11] This requires having a *theory of mind*, which we'll look at in more detail in Chapter 23.

you are – will not line up with the reality – your "true self". To amend the discrepancy, you need more data – data that you may find you can't obtain in everyday life. Hence, you either have to disrupt your everyday life or to obtain it second-hand by reflecting on the deeds of others. That's where the Hero's Journey comes in.

Right, well I'm sure you've had enough of the ethereal mysticism for now. Suffice to say, people who follow the Hero's Journey know themselves more when they finish than they did when they started.

Now the thing is, in the past, it was hard to undertake a personal Hero's Journey. Rich people could do it by going on a grand tour of Europe. Scientists could do it by embarking on expeditions to remote climes. Members of the armed forces could do it by getting shot at. Almost everyone else couldn't and therefore didn't do it. The best they could manage was listening to stories of people who *had* done it, experiencing their journeys vicariously. Vicariously often isn't enough, though: *you* don't get to be a hero reading *Treasure Island* (Stevenson, 1883) – Jim Hawkins does. You can find similarities between Jim's situation and yours at various points in your life, and perhaps learn from them through introspection, but you won't become a hero that way.[12]

The central point of all this – the reason I pivoted to it – can now be stated: playing a virtual world is a way that an ordinary person can live their own Hero's Journey.

Video-game designers have known about the Hero's Journey – along with other story formats – for decades. They created role-playing games in which the main character goes on a hero's journey and returns to become a hero. Some of these games rank among my favourites – but I didn't follow a hero's journey when I played them. My *character* did, but my character wasn't me. In virtual worlds, my character *is* me – or rather, I and my character become one. As we shall shortly see, this makes all the difference.

It's about time that I started to outline the path that the Hero's Journey takes. For reasons of depth, I'll be following Campbell's original formulation, not the version you were taught in college by someone whose preference was for something simpler.[13]

So, the basic idea is as follows:

- Something is wrong with the world.

- The would-be hero needs a thing to fix it.

- The would-be hero goes to a world of excitement and adventure to get this thing.

- The would-be hero returns to the original world with the thing.

- The would-be hero fixes what's wrong with the world using the thing he specifically went to get to fix it.

- At this point, the would-be hero becomes an actual hero.

---

[12] If you prefer a more modern and overt example than *Treasure Island*, there's an entire genre of anime that uses this trope: *isekai.*

[13] Or something easier to understand. Campbell's prose is at times close to impenetrable.

What's wrong with the world could be long-standing (such as famine) or new (such as war). It sets up the context, but it isn't part of the Hero's Journey itself. Whatever it is, it needs some object – which could be known or unknown but is definitely hard-to-get – to fix it.

Some technical terms:

- The world the would-be hero starts and ends in is the *Mundane World*.

- The world of excitement and adventure is the *Other World*.[14]

- The thing the would-be hero goes to the Other World to bring back to fix the Mundane World's problem is the *Boon*.

Now, the Hero's Journey is a literal journey so involves travel.[15] It's organised as three phases:

- In the *Departure* phase, the would-be hero is in the Mundane World and sets off on his journey.

- In the *Initiation* phase, the would-be hero arrives in the Other World and obtains the Boon.

- In the *Return* phase, the would-be hero comes back to the Mundane World and uses the Boon for its intended purpose, thereby becoming a hero.

These phases aren't all the same length (and neither are the steps that comprise them). Initiation is usually the longest, with Departure some way behind and Return a poor third.

The Boon is in truth a proxy for the transformed would-be hero. What the Mundane World *really* needs is for the would-be hero himself to fix the problem. At the start, he can't because he's a nobody (or a somebody with a major attitude problem). The Boon represents the self-actualised would-be hero who *can* fix the problem. The would-be hero goes off to the Other World to get the Boon – that is, to find his true self. Fixing the Mundane World's problem is a cipher for fixing himself. The Mundane World's problem is merely fictional cover for this.

It's in the Initiation phase, which is the main one when it comes to telling the story, that the would-be hero acquires the Boon. The Boon is the gift of an unbeatable individual, the *Father*. The would-be hero can't lay a glove on the Father, who is powerful enough to destroy the would-be hero on a whim and is uncompromising enough to do just that. To obtain the Boon, the would-be hero has to approach the Father and be given it, knowing that the Father could squish him like a bug but trusting that he won't. The Father represents the would-be-hero's untransformed self; by giving the Boon to the would-be hero, the old self is saying it accepts the new self.

---

[14] It's sometimes called the *Unfamiliar World*, but I'll stick with Other World.

[15] Usually this is spatial travel, but it could be something else – time travel, say, or social-hierarchy travel, whatever. So long as the Mundane World and the Other World are in practice separate, it's fine.

OK, so that's an overview of the Hero's Journey and of what the key components mean. Even at this level, there are some common errors[16]:

- Some people solve the Mundane World's problem in the Other World, so there's no compelling reason to come back to the Mundane World.

- Some people have the Mundane World and the Other World be the same world.

- Some people have no Boon, so there's no reason to go to the Other World and, once there, the Mundane World has no reason to want the would-be hero back.

- Some people have the would-be hero go to the Other World as part of an initiation rite, thereby demonstrating that they didn't even read the names of the three phases.

From our perspective: the Mundane World is Reality, where we exist; the Other World is the virtual world, where we go to become and to be ourselves. It's not a story for our character: it's a journey for us as individuals. If your objection to the Hero's Journey is at the level of story, it doesn't apply here. Story plays no part in how we'll be using the Hero's Journey. We won't even be using the symbolism that's inherent in the story, although I'll nevertheless describe it because it helps explain what's going on.

Making an analogy between virtual worlds and Other Worlds is a fair enough insight, but as yet it's just that, an analogy. There's nothing to show that it can be substantiated as a formal, theoretically sound relationship. The whole point of this pivot is to establish such a relationship, because then we can use the Hero's Journey to explain why people play virtual worlds.

We'll do this by showing how player types map onto the Hero's Journey. Sadly, this entails looking at the steps of the Hero's Journey in detail – and as I mentioned earlier, there are 17 of them following Campbell's formulation (which I am doing). It's something of a long haul, so prepare yourself.

Are you sitting comfortably? Then I'll begin.

(Lang, 1950)

13.3 DEPARTURE

Reminder: this phase takes place in the everyday Mundane World, where the would-be hero lives.

13.3.1 The Call to Adventure

The first step exists to show that the would-be hero is not already a hero. It achieves this by presenting the protagonist with a symbol of his destiny. For example, a king-to-be might find a crown or a sceptre; a peacemaker-to-be might cross a broken bridge; a famous-actor-to-be might see a shooting star in the night sky. The would-be hero is destined to become a king

---

[16] These are drawn from the hundreds of Hero's Journeys that I've read as student assignments.

or a peacemaker or a famous actor or whatever, but he doesn't recognise the symbol so doesn't yet realise the fact.

13.3.2 Refusal of the Call

Because the would-be hero doesn't know he has a destiny, he doesn't interpret the object or event in the Call to Adventure as a symbol of it. The to-be-King Arthur pulls the sword from the stone because he wants a sword, not because he wants to be King; he Refuses the Call by giving it to his foster brother, Sir Kay.

If the would-be hero accepts the Call to Adventure (by recognising it as such) then he will fail the Refusal of the Call step. This illustrates a notable point about the Hero's Journey: if you fail a step and in so doing fail the Hero's Journey, that doesn't mean you're a "failure". The would-be hero fails this step because he *isn't* a *would-be* hero, he's already a fully qualified hero; therefore, he can't possibly be described as a failure for Refusing the Call. So it is with the other steps: failing the Hero's Journey merely means it's not right for you at this time; it doesn't mean that children will evermore be following you in the street taunting you with jibes about what a loser you are.

It's important to note that the symbol introduced in the Call to Adventure is not a key to unlock the would-be hero's destiny, but a missed sign that he has one. There's an issue here with some interpretations of the Hero's Journey, as I shall now explain.[17]

So, the Mundane World has to have some problem that the would-be hero is destined to fix, and this must set up early in the narrative. There's no step in the Hero's Journey to do it, it's just for context-setting; there couldn't be a step anyway, as the problem might be centuries old. The Hero's Journey is a general system, and each instance of its use needs its own, specific dressing. OK, so far, so good.

Now, the story as told needs: to introduce the Mundane World; to establish the would-be hero's place in it; to show that there's a problem with it that has to be fixed. All this must have been outlined by the end of step three, because (as we shall see) that's the point at which the would-be hero needs to know why he's going to the Other World. If the Mundane World doesn't start out of whack then some disruptive event must therefore occur to create the problem. Perhaps the would-be hero's village is tormented by werewolves, or a ruler demands impossibly high taxes, or there's a leak at the nearby acid factory: regardless, an event is needed so as to give the would-be hero a problem to solve.

The thing is, if you have such an event then it's *not* the Call to Adventure. The Call to Adventure is symbolic, not literal: it's a form of foreshadowing. The Mundane World must have something wrong with it that the Boon will make right, but the event that makes the Mundane World wrong is not the Call to Adventure. How could it be, when the Mundane World often starts out in bad shape and so doesn't need such an event?

For example, if you're in a museum when suddenly a group of gunmen appear and kidnap one of the visitors while spraying bullets everywhere, that isn't a Call to Adventure; therefore, you don't have to cower behind a vending machine to Refuse the Call. The Call to

---

[17] This isn't essential knowledge for mapping player types to the Hero's Journey, but if you want to use the formula for quests or narrative then it is. You can skip it if you feel the approaching embrace of boredom.

Adventure was when you looked at the tall metal basket earlier and neither realised it was a beacon nor read the description that told you it was. Your destiny is to become a shining light of hope, not to be someone who is kidnapped.

This is where the issue lies. Many interpretations of the Hero's Journey confuse the literal "the world is coming apart, please fix it" event with the symbolic "do you know your destiny?" test. Properly, the Call to Adventure is the symbol, not the set-up, and the Refusal of the Call is a failure of recognition, not a failure to act.

It's also important that the symbol remains entirely a symbol. It should not, therefore, play any further part in what subsequently happens. Coming across a watch in step one that symbolises you're going to go time-travelling is fine; pawning it in step two so you can buy food for your sick child is fine; recovering it later to go time-travelling is not fine. If the symbol does reappear, it can only do so at the very end of the Hero's Journey, when the would-be hero has become a hero and now recognises its symbolism.

It's OK to have a watch that's used for time-travel purposes, or an ancient circular tablet that opens a portal, or a wooden stick that turns into a weapon: what's not OK is for these to be the Call to Adventure's focal object. The Call to Adventure is a symbol of the would-be hero's destiny, not an active part of it. If you want such an object, give it to the would-be hero in the next step.

13.3.3 Supernatural Aid

As the would-be hero doesn't know he has a destiny (having Refused the Call), he has to be told it outright. This task is undertaken by someone with an understanding of the Other World, often called a *mentor* (but that's perhaps a little too specific).

There are two important features of Supernatural Aid: first, it has to be Supernatural; second, it has to be Aid. This may seem obvious, but if you're following a formula then it's easily missed.

The Aid the would-be hero receives has to be Supernatural so as to demonstrate the giver's qualifications. It's not something just anyone can do, there has to be a hint of Other-Worldliness about it (although not necessarily magic).

The Aid has to be Aid to show that the would-be hero can trust the person who gave it. It can take several forms, none of which are mutually exclusive. Literal Aid is acceptable (the giver rescues the would-be hero from a bad situation); contingency Aid is acceptable (the giver gives the would-be hero a charm that will be useful in the Other World); straight info-dumping is acceptable (the giver flat-out tells the would-be hero his destiny); all combinations of these, along with other forms, are acceptable.

At the end of this step, the would-be hero should know the following:

- *What the Mundane World's problem is.* It doesn't have to be detailed: "The police are corrupt!"; "My sister is dying!"; "Aliens are invading!"; ....

- *What Boon is required to remedy the problem.* Again, this doesn't have to be all that specific at this stage: "technology that can reliably detect lies"; "medicine from the future"; "the missing component of the planetary laser-cannon defence system"; ....

- *That the Boon is in an Other World of excitement and adventure.* The nature of the Other World doesn't have to be (but can be) known: "the physics research lab in the Ural Federal University campus at Ekaterinburg"; "the year 2144"; "Switzerland"; ….

- *What to do to get to the Other World.* "Join a student exchange programme"; "use this convenient time-travel machine"; "take flight BA0716 from Heathrow terminal 5 to Zurich"; ….

- *That it's his destiny to go to the Other World to obtain the Boon and to return to the Mundane World to use it to fix the Mundane World's problem.*

Having some idea of what the Boon is by this point is *exceptionally* important. The whole Return phase will make no sense if the would-be hero doesn't go into the Other World with the explicit intention of bringing back the Boon.

13.3.4 Crossing the First Threshold
The purpose of this step is for the would-be hero to commit to his journey. He does something proactively, rather than letting it happen on its own. He's no mere passenger carried along by events. Crossing a rickety rope bridge would do it, or attempting to jump over a stream, or tasting an unappetising-looking cake. Often, he'll have to defeat a *guardian*, who doesn't have to be malevolent (security screening at an airport would suffice). He *could* turn back, but he doesn't.

Sometimes, it seems as if the would-be hero Crosses the First Threshold by accident, but he doesn't: he committed himself *before* the accident. Walking in the woods and falling down a rabbit hole is not Crossing the First Threshold, but seeing a rabbit with a pocket watch and pursuing it to a rabbit hole that you then fall down by accident is.

13.3.5 The Belly of the Whale
This is the final step of the Departure phase. The would-be hero arrives in the Other World cut off from the Mundane World. His old identity is either lost or irrelevant, and no one here knows or cares who he is. The would-be hero has to start from scratch, without back-up, friends, or support. He only has himself to rely on, plus whatever charms the giver of Supernatural Aid might have handed him as a starter pack. He's being reborn with a blank slate in this Other World of excitement and adventure.

The Other World and the Mundane world are separate from one another. The Other World resembles the Mundane World after a fashion, but is different in strange ways: not everything works the same as it does back home.

The rationale for this step is that the would-be hero is in the Other World to find his true self (for which the Boon is a proxy). He can't become his true self if he's still his Mundane-World self; therefore, his original identity has to be erased in the Other World so he can begin there afresh. His formal reason for going to the Other World is to obtain the Boon, but his real reason is to find his new self through his actions and to reconcile this with his old self (represented by the Father in step nine).

The reason this step is called the Belly of the Whale, by the way, is that many myths have the would-be hero swallowed by a large creature (such as a whale) then spat out barely alive into the Other World to fend for himself. That enough stories feature this trope to lend its name to the step is no coincidence. This is because the Belly of the Whale is acting like a womb, from which the would-be hero is reborn. In practice, any dark or damp space can be used to suggest a womb, so wells, caves, and tunnels are also common.

The Other World is usually physically disjoint from the Mundane World, but really only needs to be separate from it. So long as there's no chance that anyone there will know or have access to knowledge of the would-be hero's past, it's a possibility. Being whirled into "the world of high fashion" could work, as could remaining in the Mundane World "but I'm a squirrel". In myths, the Other World is often a foreign country or some kind of spirit realm, but authored fiction has a licence to be more quirky and often is.

The would-be hero can assume or be given a different name in the Other World. If you start a new job and tell everyone your nickname is Bunny, that's what everyone will call you. If someone who knows you already works there, though, they're going to be aware that you've just made it up. This is why the Hero's Journey is a solo activity only: you can't begin your life anew with no baggage from the past if there are people there who have brought it with them for you. If the would-be hero goes into the Other World with someone else, that someone else is not going to make it very far. It's just about feasible that the giver of Supernatural Aid could nip in a short way, or that there's someone there who knows who you are but you don't know they know, but if you have to resort to such contortions then the likelihood is that you're doing something wrong.

13.4 INITIATION

Reminder: this phase takes place in the adventure-filled Other World, where the would-be hero is initially unknown.

13.4.1 The Road of Trials

This is the part of the Hero's Journey where, for explaining-virtual-worlds purposes, you need to begin paying attention.

The Road of Trials is the first step of the Initiation phase. When the would-be hero arrives in the Other World, he doesn't know how to behave. He doesn't know how it works or what its (and therefore his) limitations are. In this step, he finds out. He does this by undergoing a number of tests that allow him to establish where the physical, social, and spiritual boundaries lie. Can he fly? Can he speak to children? Can he see dead people?

The tests themselves (the Trials) often address character flaws that the would-be hero exhibited in the Departure phase. For example, perhaps he was a tad haughty: he'll have to learn to be humble when he's washed up on the shores of a remote island and needs to persuade a passing fisherman to take him to civilisation. The aim of the Road of Trials isn't specifically to iron out the would-be hero's past creases, though: it's for him to learn the ways of the Other World, and in so doing learn something about himself.

The number of Trials isn't fixed, but is usually three. The Trials are distinct and separate from one another. If the would-be hero escapes from an enemy base by swimming across a lake, stealing a motorbike, and using it to jump over a perimeter fence, that's a single escape-from-an-enemy-base Trial, not three separate Trials – even if previously he'd professed an inability to swim, exhibited a complete lack of balance and nursed traumatic memories of having been attacked by barbed wire as a small child. Individual Trials are like quest chains, not the quests that make up those chains.

Trials are obstacles that the would-be hero encounters as he works towards obtaining the Boon. They're not formal tests that someone sets and that he has to pass. If your would-be-hero needs to join a coven of witches, you can't have them give him three tests to "prove his worth" – or rather, you can but it's a push even to count all three together as one Trial.

Many tales from myths relate only to fragments of the Hero's Journey, and individual Trials from the Road of Trials are among the more popular of these as they work well stand-alone. This is because they can be cautionary: the would-be hero is allowed to fail the textual goal of a Trial so long as he learns an important lesson that helps him develop as a person. He's finding his feet in the Other World at this stage, so it makes sense that he can mess up so long as he now knows not to do it again. If he doesn't learn from his mistake then he fails the contextual goal of understanding the Other World's ways, so from that point onwards, his Hero's Journey is a lost cause.

At the end of the Road of Trials, the would-be hero should have a practical understanding of the Other World and be well on the way to obtaining the Boon. As a result, he should have an improving understanding of himself and to have made a good start towards becoming the person that he truly is.

13.4.2 The Meeting with the Goddess

At this stage, the would-be hero can be confident that he knows how to act in the Other World and of what its (and his) limitations and affordances are. However, he doesn't yet understand the full magnitude of the task ahead. In this step, he's left in no doubt. Either it'll be too much for him to cope with or he'll fully understand but carry on regardless.

The Goddess is typically a female character who represents and embodies knowledge. She is often beautiful and pure, being as she is something of a mother figure; she most certainly is not a potential girlfriend. She explains to the would-be hero what he has to do to obtain the Boon, which is the gift of the Father (whom she understands implicitly).

The Father cannot be beaten and can destroy the would-be hero with ease should he so choose. The Goddess's primary job is to make this crystal clear. Obviously, she can't help him to overcome the Father because the Father is unovercomeable; she is well able to help him get to the Father, though. Like the giver of Supernatural Aid, she can supply the would-be hero with charms or information to make the path easier.

The Goddess is useful from a narrative perspective, because she represents knowledge: she's always up for filling the hero in on anything required for this-story-specific reasons. However, she's not someone who has appeared in the would-be hero's journey before this step, and she won't appear in it after it, either; you can't have her as a recurring character drip-feeding the would-be hero with timely information.

As an example of the Meeting with the Goddess step as a stand-alone story that the would-be hero fails, see the tale of Actaeon and Artemis in the sidebar.

ACTAEON AND ARTEMIS

Several versions of this tale have made it to us from antiquity, but here's the overall gist:

> Actaeon was a famous hunter who, while out hunting on horseback with his dogs one day, spotted a magnificent stag. It ran into a wood, so Actaeon raced ahead of his pack to find it. Instead, he came across the goddess Artemis, bathing naked in a pool with some of her nymphs. He was so struck by her beauty that he stared, which displeased Artemis enough that she turned him into a stag himself, whereupon his hounds arrived and tore him to pieces.

So, Actaeon was out hunting. Artemis is the goddess of the hunt (among other things – she can multi-task). In seeing her naked, Actaeon was exposed to the full body of knowledge of hunting. What he should have done is say, "Sorry to bother you, but have you seen a magnificent stag come this way?" (in Greek). However, he was unable to comprehend what he was looking at and as a result failed the Meeting with the Goddess step of his Hero's Journey. His dogs had no such problem, and so ensured he didn't get a second chance to pass it.

13.4.3 Woman as Temptress

This is a transition step, from learning to doing. It could be regarded as a continuation of the previous step, but with a different rationale.

Having met the Goddess and understood the full extent of the task ahead, the would-be hero is confident that he can achieve it. He knows he's grown in prowess, and where previously he would have failed he will now succeed. The hard part was getting to this point; his ability to see it through is a foregone conclusion.

Does he therefore *have* to see it through?

He has nothing to prove to himself, so why waste time doing so when he could be back in the Mundane World solving its problem?

For an artist, conceptualising the work and making the sketches are the hard part; they're what make the artist improve as an artist. Doing the painting is just routine.

For a programmer, conceiving the algorithm and sketching out the data structures is what makes them grow as a programmer. Doing the coding is mechanistic and tiresome.

Why, if you've completed the difficult planning that's at the heart of what you do, must you go through with the tiresome execution? It's just a mundane activity.

Yes, I did use the word "mundane" there deliberately. The Woman as Temptress step has the would-be hero tempted to return to the Mundane World prematurely. This isn't because he thinks he's not up to it – if he did so think, he'd have failed the preceding step. Rather, it's because he feels he's done enough already and doesn't need to continue with the original plan. He could go back right now and fix the Mundane World's problem, he doesn't need some stupid Boon that's only of symbolic value anyway.

The Temptress is usually a woman, who is tempting in a physical or material sense. This is because she is acting as a stand-in for the Mundane World, reminding the would-be hero of what he's left behind and that the Mundane World needs him. He's already improved as a person, in possession of abilities, knowledge, and perhaps items that could help change the Mundane World for the better – if only he were to abandon his journey.

The would-be hero must reject the Temptress if he wants to avoid failure. Returning now, he *won't* be able to solve the Mundane World's problem: it requires the Boon. Sure, he may be able to live a life of luxury untouched by the problem, or he may be able to effect a temporary solution to give everyone some breathing space. Either way, the problem won't go away and he'll be left feeling unfulfilled. He will not have become the hero he was destined to become; he will not be the person he truly is.

The temptation here has to be genuine, so a random woman offering the would-be hero sex is unlikely to qualify. However, suppose that he encounters a young nurse who is upset because she's heard news from her family in the old country that the war is getting worse and now the "blood sickness" has broken out. The would-be hero realises that she's talking about the very war he came to the Other World to stop (by recovering an ancient document, say). Furthermore, he knows that his six-year-old son is haemophilic and wouldn't survive the "blood sickness" – yet in the would-be hero's possession right now is a panacea potion that cures all ailments. Abandoning his plan to obtain the ancient document might seem a reasonable thing to do in such a circumstance.

It doesn't have to be this convoluted, of course. If the would-be hero went to collect a magic shield but while in the Other World picked up a magic sword on the Road of Trials, he might well act on the words of a Temptress who tells him in all honesty how amazing and powerful she thinks he is, suggesting he's capable of great things. She doesn't have to have evil or selfish intent, but if that makes more sense in the context then she could indeed be a *femme fatale* opposed to the would-be hero's journey for her own reasons.

As with the Goddess, we don't encounter the Temptress outside of her own step. This implies that the Goddess and the Temptress can't be the same person, which indeed they can't be. If, in loose terms, the Goddess is like the would-be hero's mother then the Temptress is like his girlfriend. Were they the same person, it would seriously creep him out. It makes little sense anyway for someone to try to help the would-be hero to achieve his goal, only to change her mind and try to stop him immediately thereafter.

The Meeting with the Goddess and Woman as Temptress steps can be thought of as a pair. The first tests that the would-be hero is not under-confident; the second tests that he's not over-confident.

13.4.4 Atonement with the Father

Smack in the middle of the 17 steps of the Hero's Journey, Atonement with the Father is its climax. This is what everything previously has been leading up to, and what everything following will be coming down from.

The Father is the person who has been dominating the would-be hero's existence the whole time he's been in the Other World and is the only person with the ability to grant the would-be hero the Boon. So, that sounds like a boss fight, right?

Sadly (if you like boss fights), no. The Father is undefeatable by the would-be hero and can annihilate him at will, so this isn't an option. He's usually strict and inflexible, too. How, then, does the would-be hero obtain the Boon if the Father is unbeatable and not predisposed to give it? Well, the would-be hero approaches the Father knowing that the Father *could* end his existence, but trusting that he won't.

So, why wouldn't he?

Well, the would-be hero has reached a sufficient level of self-belief that he knows the Father will show him mercy. He goes to the Father not to beat him, but to be accepted by him.

In some versions of the Hero's Journey, such as Vogler's, there is no Father, just a major ordeal in which the would-be hero faces death or his greatest fear and (if successful) from which he emerges changed in some way. In this account, there could indeed be a big bad whom the would-be hero defeats. It doesn't happen in Campbell's version, though, for good reason.

Here's why. The would-be hero's efforts to get here have transformed him into a newer, different, better person – the person he truly is. To ensure that this improvement really *is* an improvement, the would-be hero needs the endorsement of his old, untransformed self. If his old self disagrees then the would-be hero has failed. The Father, as I indicated earlier, represents the would-be hero's old, Mundane-World self.[18] The would-be hero goes to the Father to be accepted. If he's not acceptable then he's failed and is obliterated. If he could defeat the Father then he wouldn't need acceptance.

That's not all, though. The transformed would-be hero's transformation is meaningless without reference to the person who went before. If you don't know who you were, you don't truly know who you are. The would-be hero's true self isn't so much the person who approaches the Father as it is the two of them together, as one individual. The would-be hero beholds the Father, sees his old self reflected in him, and in *that* moment understands who he truly is.

The etymology of the English word *atonement* is surprisingly basic. It comes from *at-one-ment* – the result of being at one with something. This was observed by Campbell himself and is an easy way to summarise what happens. The would-be hero and the Father don't literally coalesce into a single entity (which, although conceivable, messes up step 12); rather, the would-be hero reconciles his old and new selves internally. If he were to kill or otherwise defeat the Father, this wouldn't be possible: he'd be rejecting his old self. While that's perfectly fine for some journeys,[19] it isn't how the Hero's Journey is set up. You can't become one with your old self if you destroy it.

Suppose that you want to learn to drive, but only get one shot at the driving test. If you pass, you're given a licence; if you fail, you get no licence and no chance of ever taking the test again. What would you do? Well, you'd practise and practise until eventually you decided that you were ready. You'd know you could take on the test and win. It wouldn't

---

[18] You can regard "Father" here as a metaphor, if that helps: "the acorn is the father of the oak", that kind of thing. He doesn't have to be the would-be hero's literal father, and in myth hardly ever is.

[19] Trans people can expunge their mark 1 version and feel better for it.

really be winning, though: it would be the acceptance by yourself that you were fit to drive. The driving test would be recognising that you were a true driver. In this respect, it's taking on the role of the Father.

You only go to the Father when you're confident he'll accept you. If your confidence is misplaced, you'll fail. If you lack self-assurance, you'll never approach the Father *to* fail. In truth, *you* judge whether you're worthy or not, not the unchanging Father. The Father is the mechanism by which the would-be hero's assessment of his own worthiness is tested.

The sense that the Father needs to be defeated is so strong that often it's tempting to try to hack a solution. A common one[20] is to have the Father be defeated, but moments before he dies he gives the would-be hero his blessing. This doesn't work because the would-be hero has no need for his approval if he can beat him. Another common hack is to present some ineffectual figure as being the Father and have some other, more formidable character be the one the would-be hero has to defeat. This doesn't work because merely adhering a "Father" sticker to a character's forehead isn't enough to *make* them the Father. A third hack is to have the would-be hero and the Father fight under the pretext that the Father is "testing the worth" of the would-be hero, the understanding being that the Father will end the fight when it's clear the would-be hero has won ("done enough"). This doesn't work because the would-be hero should be testing his own worth in approaching the Father in the first place: the mere fact that he came asking for the Boon and trusting he'll be shown mercy is enough for the Father to be able to assess whether he's worthy or not.

If you want to have a boss to kill, the chances are this isn't the Atonement with the Father step at all, but either Crossing the First Threshold or an event in the Road of Trials.

13.4.5 Apotheosis

Apotheosis is usually a short step. Having been accepted by the Father, the would-be hero experiences a period of relaxation and congratulation. He's pleased he was accepted, relieved he wasn't despatched to oblivion, and glad that his journey from now on should be relatively plain sailing. People in the Other World are impressed that he survived his encounter and will shower him with praise and plaudits if appropriate.

Some interpretations of the Hero's Journey make Apotheosis the key step, on the grounds that it's here the would-be hero obtains spiritual self-understanding (*apotheosis* meaning "deification"). Campbell doesn't privilege the spiritual over the physical or the social, though[21]: the Hero's Journey weaves all three threads together adapting to the needs of the individual hero. For Campbell, Apotheosis is understood in its more technical sense of "glorification to the level of the divine".[22] You didn't die at the Father's hands and are heavily praised as a result.

---

[20] Common among my students, anyway.

[21] Murdock does in the *Heroine's Journey*, which is one of the aspects of it that I think needs further work.

[22] The English word *apotheosis* derives ultimately from the Greek *apo* ("from, away from; after") and *theos* ("god"). It arrived in English via Latin, where it meant "deification" in the sense of recognising that the deeds of a mortal were such that the mortal should be treated as a god. It didn't mean the mortal (typically the Roman Emperor) *was* a god, just that they had the same status as a god.

13.4.6 The Ultimate Boon

The would-be hero went to the Other World to obtain the Boon – the Holy Grail, the Golden Fleece, the Elixir of Life, whatever made sense for the fiction. Having achieved Atonement, he's now his authentic self and so is pure enough to receive it.

He can obtain it in a number of ways, including:

- **Directly**. The Father gives it to him.

- **Indirectly**. The Father allows him to collect it from its resting place.

- **Reaffirmingly**. The would-be hero obtained it moments before Atonement and offers it to the Father, who returns it after Apotheosis.

The Boon represents the would-be hero *as hero*. The would-be hero receives it now because, having attained Atonement, he's acknowledged himself to be the person he was destined to become – the hero he always was but didn't *know* he was. He has yet to show the Mundane World he is, though, hence the Boon is what the Mundane World needs to solve its problem.

13.5 RETURN

Reminder: this phase begins in the adventure-filled Other World and ends in the everyday Mundane World.

13.5.1 Refusal of the Return

This is the first step of the final, Return phase. Everyone in the Other World expects the would-be hero to return to the Mundane World now that he has the Boon, but he himself has second thoughts. In the Other World, he's just been glorified; he has status, power, and esteem. Why would he give all that up to return to the Mundane World, where everyone still thinks he's a nobody? Yes, he *intends* to return, but surely he can stay a little while longer?[23]

What's happened here is that the would-be hero has assimilated into the Other World so much that it has become his new mundane.[24] Unfortunately, the Father still controls his life in the Other World, so he doesn't have the freedom he needs to *live* his life. For that, he has to return to the Mundane World, where the Father's influence is no longer felt. Right now, though, he doesn't see it that way. He's going to have to leave the Other World under duress.

13.5.2 The Magic Flight

Because of what it represents, the Boon is worthless to the would-be hero in the Other World. He might want both to have the Boon and to stay in the Other World, but the longer he stays, the more his hold on it weakens. This is demonstrated by the presence

---

[23] In a time-disjoint Other World, there's not even time pressure for him to return. Whether he leaves for the present day in the year 2145, 2155, or 2165 makes no difference to when he arrives back.

[24] In the colonial era, this was known as *going native*. Colonisers disapproved of it, because it vaguely implied that the native culture was perhaps superior to that of the coloniser.

of powerful forces in the Other World who want the Boon for non-symbolic reasons, or who at least want him not to have it. The Father may well be unbeatable, but that doesn't necessarily bother everyone. If Zeus gave you something that Hera wanted, she'd still try to take it off you.

Thus, we get the Magic Flight step, in which the would-be hero is chased out of the Other World by people within it who have an interest in his not having the Boon. The word "Flight" here derives from "flee", by the way, not from "fly": he doesn't have to sprout wings or board a helicopter, although he can (Frodo is carried off by eagles).

13.5.3 Rescue from Without

In this context, *Without* is the Mundane World; the Other World would be *Within*.

The Mundane World still has its original problem, and it knows that the would-be hero is the one to solve it. It can't afford to lose him to his pursuers: it wants him back. People from the Mundane World therefore reach into the Other World to Rescue him from the forces of the previous step. They're not merely helping him to overcome a tiresome obstacle: it must be that if they didn't Rescue him from Without, he'd be a goner. This tells him that not only does the Mundane World need him, but he also needs the Mundane World. It's in the Mundane World where he'll become the hero he is destined to be.

13.5.4 Crossing the Return Threshold

This is such a weak step that I suspect it's only present to make sure that the Atonement with the Father step is in the middle of the sequence.

Unlike Crossing the First Threshold, in Crossing the Return Threshold, the would-be hero has no commitment to make – he's Crossing the Threshold whether he likes it or not. His challenge is to readjust to the Mundane World so that it becomes his norm again. It's like when you go on a two-week vacation[25] to a foreign country and come back having got used to where you were: the Mundane World might itself feel like an Other World to you now, until you get back into the swing of things.

13.5.5 Master of the Two Worlds

In this step, the would-be hero uses the Boon to fix the specific problem that he obtained it to fix. This makes him Master of the Mundane World, and because he became Master of the Other World upon Atonement with the Father, he's now Master of the Two Worlds. Neither of them has any mystical significance for him any more, and (if plausible within the fiction), he can travel between them without travail.

In using the Boon (which doesn't have to be destroyed in the process), the would-be hero is showing to the Mundane World that he is now the person he was destined to become. Solving its problem is indisputable evidence of this fact.

---

[25] This assumes you live in a country that has employment laws wholesome enough to make two-week vacations a regular possibility.

13.5.6 Freedom to Live

The conclusion of the Hero's Journey sees the protagonist at peace with himself and with both the Mundane and Other Worlds. He has become his true self, so has nothing left to prove. He has no fear of dying before his time, because he has accomplished all he ever needed to accomplish. Consequently, he has Freedom to Live.

The would-be hero is now a Hero.

13.6 IN ABSTRACT

So, those are the 17 steps of the Hero's Journey, as described by Campbell.[26]

It's possible to omit or to reverse steps, especially in the Return phase, but this isn't recommended – you really need to know what you're doing. If you feel that you do need to omit steps or change the order, it's very likely that you've done something wrong: the resulting narrative will feel … odd. Few ancient myths do this, because they've been retold enough times to work out the issues, but if the context demands it then it *can* still happen.

The Hero's Journey is so ingrained that people will often conform to it even when they're shoehorning plot events into the wrong steps. I regularly see students labelling the set-up the Call to Adventure, but still having a symbolic Call that's properly Refused which they don't even notice until I point it out. They'll kill a boss as Atonement with the Father, but the boss is just a guardian and the whole Initiation phase is compressed into what they call their Apotheosis and Ultimate Boon steps. It's bizarre to see, but happens every year.[27]

If people who misunderstand the Hero's Journey can write stories that nevertheless conform to it, and if established writers of the past who hadn't heard of it wrote novels that conform to it, and if myths and legends developed over hundreds or even thousands of years conform to it, there's a good chance that it has something of substance to say. This doesn't mean that people who use it for screenplays necessarily have something of substance to say, nor that it hasn't been applied over-enthusiastically to describe story forms better understood using other methods, nor that its presumed psychological underpinnings are its actual psychological underpinnings. It does, however, mean that it's something all people somehow understand intuitively at some level, with enough empirical weight behind it to count as an observable phenomenon.

What all this is saying is that in the world of everyday existence, people have scant opportunity to find out and then to be who they truly are. They're forced by circumstance and by other people into different roles with different expectations, in none of which they are truly free. They have limited sovereignty over their own lives, which restricts their personal growth and frustrates their attempts at self-understanding. By casting aside their old life, beginning with a clean slate in a new, disconnected environment, they can gain sufficient autonomy to test themselves and to discover who, at their core, they really are.

The Hero's Journey isn't the only way to self-actualise, but it's one that works when it's followed. You may not be *able* to follow it, of course: it isn't without its dangers. Many is the

---

[26] Well, by me interpreting Campbell.
[27] I tell them it happens and yet it still happens. I should probably tell them harder.

young actor who went to Hollywood to become a star and to return home with an Oscar, but who ended up as a hotel shuttle-car driver[28] instead. Success is not guaranteed.

Nevertheless, the Hero's Journey is a road map to self-understanding. You begin in your constrained reality; you go away to somewhere that allows you the freedom to experiment with your identity; you return with a better sense of who you are, which changes the constraints on you in a positive way, allowing you to live your life better.

The surface reason that people go to the Other World of college is to return with the Boon of a degree. The deeper reason is to learn more about who they *are*.

---

[28] OK, so I've only met two of these so *may* be over-generalising, but it doesn't alter the overall point that risk doesn't always result in reward.

CHAPTER 14

Very Advanced Player Types

I SPENT A LONG TIME discussing the Hero's Journey, knowing full well that some of my academic colleagues loathe the topic with a passion. The reason I nevertheless invested so many pages outlining it is that it finally allows us to explain why people play virtual worlds.[1]

The Hero's Journey involves leaving the world of the mundane, becoming reborn in a world of danger and the unknown, then returning to the world of the mundane armed with new knowledge and experience and a renewed sense of self.

Reality is the Mundane World. The virtual world is the Other World.

14.1 CORRESPONDENCES

I explained earlier that the Hero's Journey is a meta-plot: you fill in the form and you get a plot; you fill in the plot's form and you get a story. You want a story, so as to tell it as a narrative. You want a narrative, because then people who listen to it can gain insights into their own sense of who they are. They can do this because the Hero's Journey encapsulates aspects of the human psyche that resonate with everyone.

Hold on, though: isn't it a little too concrete for that? Are people *really* going to identify with someone who lives in a world so dire that they, personally, have to go someplace dangerous and come back with a tool to mend it?

Everyone has an imagination, so no, it's not too concrete for a *story* – but it *is* too concrete if you're going to live it. The Hero's Journey as *told* and the Hero's Journey as *lived* have different requirements. Campbell's 17 steps provide an outline that works for both, but the symbolic details are only necessary for creating compelling narratives; the essence of the Hero's Journey goes beyond that. Stripping away the symbolism and plot structuring, it's basically promising the following in its three phases: you recognise deep down that you're not who you truly are, but freed from everyday constraints you could discover who you are, whereupon you would be able to live your everyday life as your true self.

I'll shortly be mapping the lived Hero's Journey onto Campbell's 17 steps. I won't be using the symbolism of the narrative Hero's Journey, though, because I'm not telling a

---

[1] That's "finally". There's a way to go yet.

 DOI: 10.1201/9781003689638-14

story: through playing a virtual world, the player is living their own Hero's Journey. The resulting more-abstract characterisation still applies to the narrative form, it's just that the experience is more direct in the lived form. For example, at the end of step seven (Meeting with the Goddess), the player should know who the Father is, that the Father has the Boon, and that the Father can't be overcome; in the narrative version, this information has to be conveyed to the audience through the device of the Goddess, but in the lived version, it becomes apparent through life (or in our case, play). In either case, whether to continue or not depends on how well the player copes with obtaining full knowledge of what the task ahead involves, it's just that in the lived version you don't have to seek out someone to tell your audience what you yourself have already come to understand.

That we need this more abstract characterisation becomes immediately apparent if we try to apply the Hero's Journey as-is to the players of virtual worlds. If Reality is the Mundane World and the virtual world is the Other World, that means we need to bring a Boon back from the virtual to the real. Unfortunately, by definition, anything virtual isn't real, nor can it be made real.[2] OK, so we could perhaps attempt to sidestep the problem by creating an object in Reality and claiming it's the same thing as the object in the virtual world – a 3D-printed copy of your character, say – but this doesn't work: the two objects are *not* the same thing, and labelling them as such doesn't make them the same thing. We need a Boon that *is* the same thing in both the virtual world and Reality. That's impossible, surely?

Well, not quite. There are in fact two things that the virtual has in common with the real: time and players. We can't do much with time, because it's all-encompassing: it can't be transferred from the virtual to the real or *vice versa* as it's permanently in both (or rather, both are permanently in it). Players, though, are another matter.

A person can play a virtual world as a character. They can take that character out of the virtual world if they have *become* that character – if they're as one with it. We shall shortly see that this is exactly what happens in virtual worlds, but for the moment, we merely need to note that if we can treat the player as the Boon then we have lift-off.

Can we treat the player as the Boon, though? The would-be hero is supposed to collect the Boon, not to *be* the Boon. Well, yes, that's true in the Hero's Journey with the symbolism baked-in, but if we look at the abstract version then there isn't a problem. The Boon represents the would-be hero's transformed self: if we remove the level of indirection implied by "represents", there's little contentious in saying that the would-be hero and the Boon are one and the same. It wouldn't work in a narrative, but it works just dandy in a lived Hero's Journey.

There are consequences for this, though. The Boon is meant to fix some Mundane-World problem. If the Boon is shorn of its symbolism, so must be the problem it purports to address. This means that the set-up has to change. The would-be hero is not aiming to fix a problem with the Mundane World – that's just a fictional convenience to enable a story to be instantiated. The actual problem is with the would-be hero's self-understanding.

---

[2] An idea can be *realised* as a physical object, but the fact remains that a physical object is not an idea and an idea is not a physical object. Some philosophers may disagree, but that's fine: disagreeing is their job.

The outline of the path to be followed now looks something like this: the would-be player[3] senses a problem in their[4] self-understanding that can't easily be addressed in their everyday life (in the Mundane World); the would-be player recognises that their deeper self-understanding (Boon) can be found in a virtual world (the Other World), which has different constraints and where the necessary experience to correct faults and plug gaps in their self-understanding can be gained; the would-be player goes to the virtual world (the Other World), follows the Initiation Phase steps there, and in the process self-actualises (obtains the Boon); all that remains is to return to their everyday life (in the Mundane World) and to *be* the person that they now know they are.

That looks reasonable enough.[5] So, let's see what's now involved in mapping the (would-be) player's experience onto the steps of the Hero's Journey.

14.2 DEPARTURE CORRESPONDENCES

Reminder: this phase takes place in Reality.

14.2.1 The Call to Adventure

The Hero's Journey has a set-up to establish the fiction: something is wrong with the Mundane World that the would-be hero needs the Boon to fix. In our case, where the would-be hero is the would-be player of a virtual world, we don't need a fiction as we won't be dressing the Boon in a fictional coat: the Boon doesn't *represent* the transformed player, it *is* the transformed player. Therefore, the problem-to-be-fixed is not disguised either, and becomes the problem that the would-be player senses internally. This is individual-dependent, so could manifest in any numbers of ways. Examples might include loneliness, listlessness, frustration with society, meaninglessness, and stifled creativity – it could be pretty well any feeling of dissatisfaction with how the would-be player sees themselves.

If we did have a fictional context then the Call to Adventure would present a symbol of the would-be hero's destiny; the would-be hero's destiny is therefore defined in terms of this context. For would-be players, however, we don't have such a context; the would-be player's destiny is to correct or to expand their self-understanding in the area that's bothering them. So, what would this look like?

Well, what's basically going on here is that the would-be player is being tested to see whether they need to play a virtual world or not. If a person sees lots of other people in Reality hanging out together, this could prompt feelings of loneliness that playing a virtual world would address; similarly, perpetually hanging around with other people could prompt a yearning for solitude. If the person is happy with how things are, they won't consider it to be a problem and so wouldn't need to go on a Hero's Journey to address it. If they're not happy with it, well perhaps they do need to go on a Hero's Journey. The Call

---

[3] The use of "would-be" is not an attempt to suggest that the words "player" and "hero" are synonyms; rather, it's that until an individual starts to play a virtual world, they can't be called a player. We can call them a player far sooner than we can call a would-be hero a hero.

[4] I'm not talking about heroes now, so I am allowed to drop the masculine pronouns.

[5] True for certain optimistic definitions of "reasonable".

to Adventure captures the would-be player's awareness that their life sucks because they're having to be someone they're not.

Note that their life could suck for many other reasons that need different solutions. Playing a virtual world isn't going to cure your incurable health condition, for example (although it might help you come to terms with it).

14.2.2 Refusal of the Call

In the previous step, the Call to Adventure, the would-be player was presented with an opportunity; in the Refusal of the Call, they fail to act upon it. This could be something that they want to do but feel unable to go through with (such as being too shy to ask someone they're attracted to out on a date), or it could be something they don't want to do but feel unable to opt out of (such as attending a karaoke bar at a hen party). They know they feel bad about it, but not necessarily why. It's just how life seems to be, so they accept it.

In other words, they don't act on the opportunity to be themself, they simply carry on as before. Because there's no fiction behind it, this is likely to happen many times, rather than just the once that it needs to arise in the narrative-driven format.

14.2.3 Supernatural Aid

The would-be player must somehow be told that playing the virtual world will address their woes, or at least be given sufficient information that they feel drawn to it. This could take a traditional form, such as the recommendation of an acquaintance or a news site, or it could be less forthright, such as the use of an enticing intellectual property. Even an advertisement could do it, although plenty of those will undoubtedly have been seen (in step one) and ignored (in step two).

Let's run through the checklist and see if we're good to continue. The would-be hero should at this point know:

- *What the Mundane World's problem is.* It's that there's a misalignment between the would-be player's effective and affective selves.

- *What Boon is required to remedy the problem.* The Boon is the would-be player's true self, which has no such misalignment.

- *That the Boon is in an Other World of excitement and adventure.* The would-be player may or may not be fully aware of the Boon's nature, but they're definitely aware that something awaits them in the virtual world, and that this promises to make things right.

- *What to do to get to the Other World.* Play it!

- *That it's their destiny to go to the Other World to obtain the Boon and to return to the Mundane World to use it to fix the Mundane World's problem.* We don't have a fiction-related destiny because we don't have a fiction. The would-be player does intuitively know, however, that if they want their problem fixed then playing the virtual world will change them in a positive way that will fix it.

At the end of this step, the would-be player knows what needs to be done. All that remains is to do it.

14.2.4 Crossing the First Threshold

Sitting on my desk is a letter from my building society telling me that the annual interest on my savings account has been lowered to 0.05%. It's there to remind me that I need to change building societies. It's been doing so for exactly four years as I write this.

People often know what they need to do, but they don't actually get around to doing it. Other projects can take priority. Knowing that a virtual world offers you the freedom to become and to be yourself is one thing, but time, expense, home life, and unexpected upheavals may all intervene.

The Crossing of the First Threshold step for a virtual world is relatively simple: you connect to that world. You may have to pay money first, you may not; you may have to install client software, you may not; you may have to sign a EULA, you may not; you may have to create an account, you may not. You'll probably have to do all those things, which act as a series of guardians that must be overcome. None of them are requirements, though. What *is* a requirement is that you have an interface device (such as a personal computer or console) that you cause to connect to the virtual world.

Once you've done that, you've committed yourself to proceed.

14.2.5 The Belly of the Whale

The previous steps may have been less than persuasive because of their level of generality.[6] Fortunately, the Belly of the Whale has a more obvious and tangible connection with the Hero's Journey.

It's character creation.

When you enter a virtual world for the first time, you have to create a character. OK, so in *MUD1*, you only had to give a name and gender, but even deciding on those was no simple task. You had to envisage the person you were going to be in the virtual world. Even calling yourself some random nonsense derived from hitting the keyboard with your eyes closed tells other players *something* about you – and tells *you* something about you, too. Made-up words can come with connotations: the well-known Bouba/Kiki effect is robust across cultures and writing systems (Ćwiek et al., 2021). In modern virtual worlds, you have to go way beyond what *MUD1* did, not only choosing starting species (and possibly class) but also determining your character's appearance. Some of these systems are sufficiently detailed that it's possible to spend hours in them; *Black Desert Online*'s character-creation system is so extensive that a stand-alone character-creator was released in the West before the game itself, so would-be players could dive right in on launch day.

In character creation,[7] you are building a new identity from scratch. Other than what the law might say in certain territories, there is no stipulation that the character you create

---

[6] Having had your eyes glaze over from the New Age psychobabble may also be a factor.
[7] It's sometimes called *character customisation*, although that usually refers to changing the character's appearance after it has been played a while.

intersects at all with who you are in Reality – nor is there any requirement that it doesn't. *You're* constructing the foundation upon which *you* will build your new self.

This is *exactly* what happens in the Belly of the Whale step. Some virtual world character creation systems even default to standing the character being created in a dark (or at least dimly lit) environment.[8] The match between the Belly of the Whale and character creation is pretty well undeniable.[9]

14.3 INITIATION CORRESPONDENCES

Reminder: this phase takes place in the virtual world.

14.3.1 The Road of Trials

Thankfully, we can drop the wearisome "would-be" prefix now, because at this point, the player is actually playing.

To explain how the player's behaviour maps onto the Hero's Journey, it's going to be useful to refer to the development tracks illustrated in Figure 12.8. To save you the bother of looking back for it, I'll reproduce it here (Figure 14.1).

What I propose to do is show how the development tracks line up with the player's progress along their Hero's Journey, with the Other World being the virtual world.

In the Road of Trials, the would-be hero finds where the Other World's boundaries lie. Recapitulating what I noted earlier, it's where he learns the ways of the Other World, and in so doing learns something about himself. The player of a virtual world will have some idea of what might be possible (because the world is familiar in many respects), but not a complete idea. By pushing at the boundaries, the theatre of play can be established.

There are two boundaries in virtual worlds: social and physical.[10] If you push at the social boundaries, well they may lie well beyond the point where you'd feel uncomfortable if you crossed them, in which case they won't be a concern for you and you can focus on the physical boundaries. You might transgress them by accident, but you can take that on board and move on. If the social boundaries are closer than you would hope, you're definitely going to cross them.

If you push at the physical boundaries, again, you might be fine with what you find: you don't feel you need to be able to do everything, so you don't try to do everything. Sure,

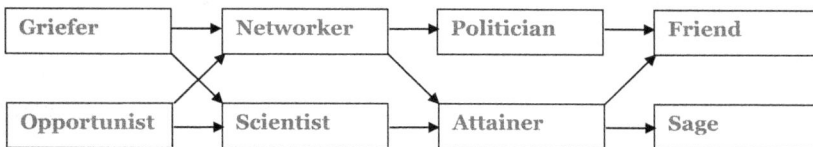

FIGURE 14.1 Development tracks.

---

[8] Examples that spring to mind include *Final Fantasy XIV, Black Desert Online, New World, Elder Scrolls Online,* … . There are doubtless many good artistic reasons underpinning each of these decisions, but it's nevertheless uncanny that so many just happen to fit the Belly of the Whale metaphor so well.

[9] I accept that this will be taken by some readers as an invitation immediately to deny it.

[10] There are three if you count the EULA as a spiritual limitation imposed by the gods, but this applies to players in Reality, not to their characters in the virtual world.

you'll attempt some things and they won't work, but you can learn from that and take it in your stride. On the other hand, if you find that the virtual world lets you do what you do, you might try something more complicated to see if it lets you do that, too. Only when it stops you do you go on to doing something else.

It's clear from this that players who emphasise social boundaries are our Griefers and players who emphasis physical boundaries are our Opportunists. For the purposes of mapping player types onto the Hero's Journey, that's all we need to show. It's somehow unsatisfactory, though, because it doesn't consider what players find fun. Player types concern what players find *fun* – they're not mere descriptions of behaviour.

OK, so if you find pushing at the social boundaries fun, why is that? Well, it suggests that you're enjoying being able to do something you can't in Reality. In other words, the aspect of self-understanding that you wish to come to grips with has a strong social element to it. How you continue once you've established the social boundaries depends on what you've learned about yourself so far. It's different for everyone, but it's not a hard sell to suggest that if you have difficulties being accepted by others then you're likely to follow the Main Sequence, whereas if you have difficulties accepting others then you're likely to follow the Main Socialiser Sequence. There are as many explanations as there are players, though.

Similarly, if you find pushing at the physical boundaries fun, well that also suggests you're enjoying being able to do something you can't in Reality. In this case, it's the lack of variety afforded you by Reality that's in question, and the aspect of self-understanding that you wish to expand upon has a strong worldly element to it. Again, how you continue once you've established the physical boundaries depends on what you've learned about yourself so far. Although this will be different for everyone, it's not unreasonable to suppose that if you have difficulties being contained by the world then you're likely to follow the Main Explorer Sequence, whereas if you have difficulties containing it then you'll follow the Minor Sequence.

Looking at what player types mean, rather than at how players might behave, has given us a much better perspective here. The connection between player types and the Hero's Journey can be seen as not simply an analogy, but something deeper.

Now, there are some caveats to this.

Some players may find pushing at *both* the social and worldly boundaries fun. They may have issues that the virtual world can't help them with, or that it can but they're unwilling to go that far. They'll either be overwhelmed and quit, or they'll stay until they can move on, or they'll stick where they are and neither move on nor quit. If they do the latter then eventually they'll have pushed the physical boundaries as far as they can, but social boundaries can be transgressed forever if there's a constant stream of newbies. Many virtual worlds have a knot of griefers like this, who may have quite extensive knowledge of gameplay but who are ultimately there to be toxic towards others. These are the ones that CSRs want to remove, rather than the ones who will become good citizens just as soon as they've established what being a good citizen means in the context of the virtual world.

Some people don't push at any of the boundaries. Perhaps they didn't need to play after all, or did need to play but the virtual world doesn't present a pathway to address their particular need. It might be that they simply don't get the very concept of virtual worlds. Whatever the cause, they won't find the virtual world fun and will likely quit either now or in the next step. It's also possible that they don't yet have enough of a handle on what they need, but if they continue to play then they might. These players will probably create a new character and start again, although they could continue to the next step and see if their experience there is more enlightening.

In addition, there will always be some people who find pushing at various boundaries fun, but for reasons nothing to do with their self-understanding: it's just an aspect of their personality. These people will continue to play, but will ultimately fail one of the steps.

Finally, you might have noticed that the Road of Trials usually has three Trials but here we have an unspecified number of them. It's quite possible that some major incidents could be strong enough to warrant being called a Trial, especially on the social side, but for most people, it's more incremental – many small Trials rather than a handful of big ones. As before, this is because actually living a Hero's Journey is not quite the same as creating a plot to form the basis of a narrative for one.

14.3.2 The Meeting with the Goddess

The next step of the Hero's Journey starts with the would-be hero equipped to function in the Other World and beginning actively to seek the Boon. To do this, he accumulates knowledge and learns new skills. At the end of the step, the full extent of what lies ahead of him is revealed through the person of the Goddess, who explains in unambiguous language exactly what the would-be hero needs to do if he's to be accepted by the Father.

If you're using the Hero's Journey to create a narrative, the Goddess is the personification of knowledge. She has to be personified so that she can convey the necessary information: who the Father is (if the would-be hero doesn't already know); that the Father has the Boon (if he doesn't already know); and that the Father cannot be overcome (regardless of whether he knows this already or not).

We don't need a personification of knowledge when living the experience of a Hero's Journey, because we don't have a narrative imperative for it. However, we do still need to make sure that the player is apprised of the necessary information. So, we have another checkpoint:

- *Does the player know who the Father is?* Yes: it's the designer of the virtual world. I'll go into more detail in step nine, but basically it's the designer who has been dominating the player's life in the virtual world so far and the designer (through their design) who gets to decide the player's fate.

- *Does the player know that the Father has the Boon?* In a game world, yes, because there's a clear end goal. If the player plays the MMO as a game and meets its definition of success, they will reap the harvest of self-understanding that is promised. It's harder for social worlds, because there's no built-in impetus: the player has to create their own goals, and it's not always obvious that succeeding at these is the designer's – or anyone else's – intention.

- *Does the player know that the Father can't be overcome?* Hacks, RMT, and vexatious lawsuits aside, yes. The designer can't be defeated within the context of the virtual world: you have to go outside of that context – back to the Mundane World – to defeat them, and you're going to fail your Hero's Journey in the process.

OK, so we can indeed check the checkpoint's points. Let's see how this step of the Hero's Journey aligns with the development tracks the player is following.

Referring back to Figure 14.1, the two player types associated with this step are Networker and Scientist. Both are in the business of gathering the knowledge and learning the skills that the player will need to continue. Players of both types know from the previous step where the boundaries lie, and both are now concerned with what they can do within those boundaries.

Networkers develop their social prowess by working to interact with other players. They will of course learn something about the virtual world's physics in the process of playing it, but aren't particularly interested in that – they can ask people on their growing list of contacts for help or information should they need it. Similarly, Scientists develop their worldly knowledge by seeking out new places and developing the skill sets that come with those new places. They will get to know more players as they do this, but that's not what's driving them.

Again, this is a good superficial match, but if I'm going to claim it reflects what the development tracks of player types are telling us, we need to look at the fun. Fortunately, a lot of this carries over from the previous step; the player is essentially continuing from where they left off.

So, Networkers are enjoying forging interactions with other people to the extent that they will go out of their way to do so. Why is this fun for them? Well, it could be because they sense that their understanding of others is increasing and that this is the direction they must follow if they are to come to understand themselves better. Then again, it could be because they sense that others' understanding of them is increasing. It could be anything, but whatever it is, it's fun because it's moving them towards their goal. Insights are coming, and more will come if they continue playing.

Scientists are enjoying experimenting with the virtual world. They can't always experiment in Reality without potentially harmful consequences, but here they're at liberty to let their imaginations run riot. That's fun. They're freed to develop analytical skills that they can bring back with them to the Mundane World when they're done – skills they would have had trouble developing if they hadn't started playing. It's not that the gap in their knowledge of the virtual world's physics is some metaphor for the gap in their self-understanding; rather, it's what knowledge-exploration tells them about their own way of thinking that's important. As for why it's important, well that depends on the individual, but if such play begins to push at previously blocked doors of creativity, or develops new ways of understanding, either of which can be applied to the self, well that would certainly do it.

The Meeting with the Goddess step fails if the would-be hero either can't cope with what he's learned or can't cope with learning it in the first place. What it boils down to is that the player will come to realise that what lies ahead is too much to contemplate despite the promised reward, so they give up. They might perceive it as too difficult, or as too time-consuming, or as too ill-formed, or as too something-else; whatever, the point is that they now know exactly what they need to do to succeed but are heartily disinclined to do it.

This has only happened to me once when playing a virtual world – and I've played dozens and dozens of them. OK, so I'm a designer, not a player, and player types therefore don't formally apply to me as I'm not playing for fun; nevertheless, I do like to reach the elder game (if it has one) before I stop, so I can wave that fact in the face of anyone who claims I'm a know-nothing ingénue when it comes to their MMO of choice. Only those former players of *WildStar* who did reach its elder game can legitimately level this charge at me. Jeez, but that was a painful grind too far....[11][12]

14.3.3 Woman as Temptress

Following the development tracks as illustrated in Figure 14.1, one might expect that this step is going to map onto the Politician/Attainer pairing – but no! It does not.

I had real trouble with this step when I was first comparing player types with the Hero's Journey, because it doesn't actually map onto any type. It would be relatively easy to finesse the issue by asserting that the Woman as Temptress step is merely the flip side of the Meeting with the Goddess, so the two can be considered as one. After all, both are about whether to continue with the Hero's Journey and both concern the player's level of confidence. I could therefore have claimed that they both matched the Networker/Scientist unit and moved swiftly onward, nothing to see here, everything's fine folks. If the ordering of the Meeting with the Goddess and Woman as Temptress steps were interchangeable then a good case for doing this could indeed be made, but sadly they're not: the Meeting with the Goddess has to come first, because until the would-be hero comprehends the full extent of what he's up against, he can't assess his ability and need to meet it in the Woman as Temptress step.

The Woman as Temptress step is therefore problematic for us,[13] because although players do go through it (that is, they do consider stopping because they feel they've already achieved enough), there isn't a player type associated with this.

Recognising the issue, I tackled it from three different directions, all of which led to the same conclusion: at this stage of their development, players pause their play while they decide whether or not to continue. Put another way, there isn't a player type here because for this step the player *isn't actually playing* (at least not for fun).

The first approach I took to try figure out what was going on was simple observation. I watched how players behaved and noted when Scientists drifted away (Networkers are harder to keep track of because they never stand still). I wasn't systematic about it, so can't provide supporting data, and I don't know whether those who have such data (virtual world operators) would back up what I noticed or tell me it's balderdash. It seemed to me,

---

[11] Players of *Elite Dangerous* also have a case, but I do still intend to return to that virtual world someday, to pick up where I left off; I'm merely waiting for its interface to be rendered usable.
[12] Oh, you can add *Albion Online*, too. It's not for solo play, and I was ganked one too many times during its "watch your character spend a minute skinning an animal" resource-gathering episodes.
[13] See how I'm subtly making it your problem now, too.

though, that people who stopped playing around this point typically did so after an absence of some kind. Mostly they would either go on vacation or switch their attention to some AAA game they wanted to play, then either return raring to go, return to find the virtual world didn't really do it for them any more, or not return at all. The ones who quit shortly after returning would offer different explanations as to why, including Mundane World obligations, loss of interest, and burn-out (although that's usually a later-step explanation), but in essence, they didn't miss the virtual world when they were offline and it no longer held the appeal it once did. Reality does intrude at other times, of course, but the intrusion here seems to be more important. Then again, it might simply have seemed that way to me because this was where I was looking.

The second way I tried to understand what was going on was to re-examine the development tracks. There are two, in parallel with cross-links. The upper track concerns the player side of the player/world axis and the lower track concerns the world side of its axis. I wondered how the other two axes played into this.

If we consider the acting/interacting axis, the player type pairs on the tracks go from acting to interacting to acting to interacting. There's a clear differentiation between each pairing, as indeed there needs to be if the player/world axis is to be split into units. Without such demarcation, the player types could be in any order.

If we consider the implicit/explicit axis, the player type pairs go from implicit to explicit to explicit to implicit. There's no differentiation in the middle. This means that the weight of the partition between the units on the track at this point is borne entirely by the acting/interacting axis. To shore up acting/interacting, we'd need to insert a break. That's what the Woman as Temptress step does here: it's creating a break, in so doing acting as a separator to make clear the explicit-to-explicit movement along the implicit/explicit axis.

What bothered me about this is that it's a programmer's explanation.[14] We could put artificial breaks between the other pairings, but we don't because they'd interrupt the flow. That said, the Woman as Temptress step does interrupt the flow of the Hero's Journey: it's a pause, a moment of reflection during which the would-be hero decides whether or not to proceed. The fact that it isn't associated with any particular player type makes it a bump in the road, but that could partially explain why there's no link from Scientist to Politician in the development tracks. Non-optimal solutions[15] have a way of doing that.

The third angle of attack I employed was to return to first principles. In the Woman as Temptress step, the Temptress represents the attractions of the Mundane World. The would-be hero is in the Other World, and the Temptress is (perhaps knowingly, perhaps not) tempting him to abandon his journey and to return to the Mundane World. For players, the Mundane World and the Other World are distinct, but travel between them is trivially easy; the player *has* to leave the Other World periodically for body-management reasons (sleeping, eating, drinking, getting rid of what you ate and drank, washing, …). The act of will involved therefore concerns not whether to *leave* the Other World; rather, it's whether to *re-enter* it having left.

---

[14] In other words, a hack.
[15] In other words, hacks.

Having reached this stage of their journey, the would-be hero reflects on what continuation would entail. During this period,[16] the would-be hero isn't actually progressing towards his goal, he's assessing whether he needs to progress any further. In a virtual world, this could involve pottering around doing side quests, or playing on an alt, or not playing at all. There's a pause while the player makes their decision.

Assembled, these three perspectives[17] allow us to understand what's going on. The player reaches a point in their play where they have a solid grounding in how the virtual world works and they're confident in their use of it. Ahead of them, they can see a long run to reach the elder game. They spend some time considering whether or not it's worth the effort to go for it, which involves a pause in their play. This pause could be imposed by Reality, or by a natural break in gameplay,[18] or simply by a feeling that it was time to ease off for a while.

There isn't a player type associated with this because the player isn't playing for fun: if they're playing at all, it's to decide whether they need to play further. Is it going to be worth their time, or is "more of the same" too much of the same?

14.3.4 Atonement with the Father

The player emerges from their period of temptation ready to rock. They're going to try to succeed on the virtual world's own terms. Once they do, they'll have found the version of themself that's all the better for this.

The Father of the virtual world is its designer. This is the person who (through the virtual world's design) has been dominating the player's existence while they were playing, and who gets to decide whether the player passes or fails. In an MMO, if you reach the level cap then you pass; if you don't, you fail. Reaching the level cap is the moment of Atonement: it's where the designer recognises that you have done all you needed to do and accepts you as you now are. You've finished the virtual world and "won" not by defeating the designer, but by attaining the designer's acceptance.

Theory-wise, the designer is acting as the player's past self – the one who at the start of the journey chose to play the virtual world. Because the player is no longer their past self (it's not the past any more), obviously they can't attain the approval of their past self directly, but they *can* meet the approval-criterion set out by their past self: finishing the virtual world.

This is all pretty well by-the-book for Attainers. They spend a great deal of time and effort making their way to the finishing line, but can nevertheless fail if they reach a point past which they can't progress; nevertheless, they're trying to do what the virtual world asks them to do, and when they've done it, they feel they've been accepted by it. They've achieved something.

Atonement is not so easy for Politicians. The problem is that the virtual world is able to record the attainment of any tangible goals that it has set, but is not able to record ones

---

[16] It doesn't have to, but can, last 40 days and 40 nights.
[17] Maybe not so much the second one.
[18] Before its first expansion, *World of Warcraft* had a drop-off at level 40. Some players stuck with it to get their mount, then called it a day. Character level distributions peaked every ten levels (Yee, 2005a).

that it has no access to because they're in the minds of the players. Sure, the designer could bring some levelling-up mechanic to reward Politicians' progress, but levelling-up is an Attainer thing, not a Politician thing: if Attainers spotted that they could reach the level cap by, say, having a thousand names on their friends list, they would organise themselves to attain just that. It's a common mistake among newbie designers (especially in gamification[19] contexts) to give to non-Attainers rewards that only Attainers value; Politicians find fun in managing players, not from levelling up. Sure, they might enjoy being given social-media-style likes, but so does everyone else – and if the virtual world uses this in a tangible way to advance progress, Attainers will mine the deuce out of it.

Politicians can't therefore rely on the virtual world to tell them they're worthy. The virtual world can't measure and therefore can't recognise their accomplishments. This means that they have to receive Atonement without being told they've succeeded. Help from the virtual world's systems can be forthcoming to guide the player in the right direction, but there's no fanfare when they get there.

Players of social worlds have an even tougher job. Politicians have no gameplay around which they can gather other players, and Attainers have no overall set goal to achieve. Neither gets any stamp of approval from the virtual world. With no gameplay, players have to decide for themselves what's meaningful and what's not. They certainly can do this, and if they do manage to receive Atonement then it can be very powerful – many are the *Second Life* players who have taken their Second Life identity back to Reality, name and all.[20] It's a long process, though, and most players don't get beyond the Meeting with the Goddess step. If the Father says "do whatever you like, it's fine by me" then that only works if they player knows what "whatever you like" means for them; if they don't, the Goddess can't tell them and they'll give up.

In game worlds, though, Atonement with the Father is a much more realistic prospect. Attainers are led along the path to enlightenment through the gameplay, and Politicians find the way themselves because they understand people and (believe it or not) are people themselves.

14.3.5 Apotheosis

Apotheosis maps onto the Friend/Sage player types at the end of the development tracks. Here, the player is relaxing having done what they came to do and is awaiting the reward (the Boon). There's no pressure on them now, so they can basically do whatever they like in the virtual world. In the case of Friends, this usually means hanging out with their pals; in the case of Sages, it usually means investigating the fabric of the virtual world.

In a narrative Hero's Journey, this step is often relatively short. As anyone who has just got engaged can testify, there are only so many times you can hear the word "congratulations" before it begins to lose its lustre. Once things have settled down, the would-be hero receives the Boon and the Return phase can begin.

---

[19] We briefly look at gamification in Chapter 17, but in essence it involves throwing out gameplay in the belief that mechanics alone make non-game activities fun.

[20] Hi, Pooky!

It's not quite like that with a lived Hero's Journey, because the Boon isn't handed over by the Father – the player has it already. If they don't realise this, they hang around for longer while they wait to be given it. Were the virtual world to make it clear what had just transpired, with some kind of "well done, you've made it, you can stop playing now" message then that would give the player permission to return to the Mundane World and they could leave with the Boon. Virtual worlds did indeed used to do something like this in the First and Second Ages and to some extent the Third. When turning a profit became more important, though, telling players they could stop playing suddenly seemed like a bad idea, and players therefore had to figure out for themselves that they didn't need to wait.

14.3.6 The Ultimate Boon

The Boon in the lived Hero's Journey is the player themself. The player doesn't have to be given it, they can leave the moment that they realise they have it – that is, when they self-actualise. As we saw for Apotheosis, though, this is easier said than done. Making that connection between finishing the levelling game and realising that you've become who you set out to become isn't obvious if not made explicit. In the narrative version, it *is* made explicit: the Father relinquishes the Boon to the would-be hero. In the lived version, where these concepts can be neither personified nor reified, it takes time for the fact they have the Boon to dawn on the player.

The Ultimate Boon step marks the end of the Initiation phase and so, for players, of the development tracks. The player no longer needs to play for fun – fun being what powered them as they progressed through the Other World to reach this very point: receipt of the Boon.

In possession of what they went to the Other World to obtain, the player can now return to the Mundane World.

14.4 RETURN CORRESPONDENCES

Reminder: this phase begins in the virtual world and ends in Reality.

14.4.1 Refusal of the Return

Now here's the thing: players who have the Boon and know they have the Boon *still* won't want to return to the Mundane World (that is, to stop playing) right away. They put a lot of effort into getting where they are. They have friends, they have obligations, they have tasks they can persuade themselves they have to do. Psychological pressures from fear of missing out, fear of loss, and the sunk cost fallacy (all of which are discussed in Chapter 23) can also work against the player.

What's happened here is that the player has spent so long regularly visiting the virtual world that it's become part of their daily routine. They need to break that routine to return to the Mundane World (and so to get on with their life). Unfortunately, players who either haven't recognised that they don't need to play, or who have reached this point prematurely, complain that the virtual world has become boring. For the former, that's as it should be: the designer is saying that you don't need to play any more. For the latter, it's not as it should be: typically, the virtual world was either too soft on the player and they're still basically following the Road of Trials, or it was too hard on the player so they used external means to progress (such as pay-to-win offerings) and therefore have already failed their Hero's Journey. Both these cases refer more to game worlds more than social worlds (in which players overcome their equivalent issues earlier).

Faced with player complaints that there's nothing to do after reaching the level cap, MMO designers introduced a second, elder game, based on what players were doing anyway to amuse themselves (in the main, raiding or PvP). Players told one another that this is where the game *really* began, so played that game instead, killing time until the next expansion. This complicates Refusal of the Return even further, because players are trapped more effectively.

This step is somewhat reminiscent of the Woman as Temptress step, except that instead of falling for the attractions of the Mundane World, the player falls for the attractions of the Other World.

The player can't stay in the Other World indefinitely, though, because there the designer's will still holds. To gain from what they've learned of themself, they have to stop playing and return to the Mundane World.

14.4.2 The Magic Flight and Rescue from Without

I'm describing these two steps together for reasons that will shortly become apparent.

In the narrative version of the Hero's Journey, the would-be hero doesn't want to leave the Other World and has to be coerced to do so. Everyone in the Other World is expecting him to return now that he has the Boon, but he doesn't; this gives other people there the opportunity to relieve him of it. They chase him in the Magic Flight, where he finds himself outmatched – but he's Rescued from Without by people from the Mundane World. This shows him that he and the Mundane World need each other.

Now in the lived version of the Hero's Journey that the player is following, this doesn't hang together. The player can stop playing at any time and isn't being hunted down anyway, so there's no need for a rescue.

Usually, the focus in the Magic Flight is on the would-be hero's desire to stay in the Other World and the incompatibility of this with his remaining there with the Boon. Let's look instead at the people who want to take the Boon from him, though. What are they after? Well, the Boon represents the would-be hero's transformed self: his pursuers want to keep this in the Other World.

This is what's happening to the player: the virtual world (in the form of its post-levelling activities and its players) is saying that it wants you to stay, but your everyday life is saying it wants you back. There's a big difference between the would-be hero's experience in the Hero's Journey narrative and the player's experience in playing a virtual world, though: in the former, the Other World wants the Boon; in the latter, it already has it so long as the player remains – it wants to draw the player back in should they attempt to leave.

We can force the player's experience to fit the Hero's Journey narrative if we wish, but it's *so* much easier (and makes a good deal more sense) if we simply reverse the usual order of the Magic Flight and Rescue from Without.

Putting Rescue from Without First. All the while the player has been playing the virtual world, the people in their mundane life have been asking "why are you playing that stupid game?". The player has not listened to them. Now, however, with the recognition that they don't need to play any more, they listen. They have been given their excuse to leave; they are being Rescued from Without.

Putting Magic Flight Second. The virtual world isn't going to give up, though. It wants the player back. It pursues the player with its nagging obligations, tempting offers of up-coming special events, perpetual social media updates from people in the virtual world whom the player knows – it's not going to let go of the player easily. The Magic Flight may succeed, yet the player could relapse. The Rescue from Without worked, but the pull back to the Other World was too strong.

Reversing the order of these two steps has achieved the same objectives in the player's lived experience as when they were in the right order in the narrative formula. The necessity for it arises from the fact that in practice the player is in the Mundane World most of the time[21] and only patches into the Other World during their free time; this is not the case in stories. That said, while reversing the order of two steps does occur in narrative versions of the Hero's Journey, it's somewhat suspect when it happens. Feel free, therefore, to keep the usual order and have an anodyne Magic Flight (the Other World doesn't need to do a great deal to keep the player) and the same Rescue from Without but with no pursuit element.

14.4.3 Crossing the Return Threshold

For a while now, the player has been spending two to four hours every evening playing the virtual world. Finally, though, they have to find other things to do with their time. This could be anything – reading, painting, basket-weaving, knitting, visiting the gym, taking up ballroom dancing, making model ships out of balsa wood, learning their children's names, watching TV, playing regular games, …. Whatever it is, adjustments will need to be made to the player's routine now that they have no need to play the virtual world any more.

14.4.4 Master of the Two Worlds

In this step, the would-be hero uses the Boon to solve the Mundane World's problem. It can be the exciting climax of a story,[22] but from the perspective of an observer is rather less exciting in the player's case: they get to *be* the person they really *are*, but that's really only meaningful to them and to those whose lives they impact.

The player can now occasionally crank up the virtual world to revisit it from time to time, but is immune to its seductive charms. That doesn't mean it can't be enjoyable, or

---

[21] One would hope….
[22] *This* is where you put your end-boss battle, folks!

that the player can't have a blast in it, it's just that it has no more mystical significance than any other place.

14.4.5 Freedom to Live

In the Hero's Journey, this is where the would-be hero becomes a hero. They have self-actualised and can live the rest of their life as their true self.

For virtual world players, the same thing happens. OK, so the virtual world probably didn't address *every* issue, and new personal circumstances can introduce fresh ones, but there are always other virtual worlds out there with things to say.

Perhaps the player may answer another Call to Adventure and begin the cycle again.

14.5 ANALYSIS

Just to make it clear, in case you saw the words "Hero's Journey" and skipped everything from the start of Chapter 13 up until now, I'm not suggesting that you should use the Hero's Journey to design narratives in virtual worlds – in fact I'd strongly advise against it for player characters. What I'm saying is that, looked upon as a whole from the player's perspective, a Hero's Journey is what you see. You don't get it from playing other games because it doesn't match other games: it only matches virtual worlds. It needs an independent world separate from Reality that an individual visits as someone they're not, simultaneously inhabited by other people, that is always there; put another way, the other world must have its own physics, not be Reality, have player characters, be real time, be shared, and be persistent. That's the definition of the term "virtual world".

As a word of caution, it should be noted that this could all be coincidence. There are plenty of examples of situations that correlate with the Hero's Journey but that have no possible theoretical connection between them. "The toast passes into the damp blackness of the mouth, where it is born anew, the teeth crunching it to adapt to the Other World of the digestive system, through which it passes only to emerge, transformed, …". I don't believe that when it comes to the players of virtual worlds it *is* a coincidence, but the sceptical reader is entitled to disagree.

There are some important differences between the would-be player's experience of a virtual world and the would-be hero's experience in a narrative. I've mentioned a few already, but in summary:

- There's no narrative framework because no narrative is being followed. The Mundane World does not need a problem to be solved beyond the fact that the would-be player doesn't feel fulfilled.

- There's no symbolic Boon, because the virtual can't return anything to the real. The Boon therefore has to be literal, rather than a proxy: the player is the Boon.

- Normally, no one who knows the would-be hero in the Mundane World can enter the Other World with them. Players may be able to do this, however, as they're protected by the frame of "it's just a game" – so long as they're only treated as their character.

- The Meeting with the Goddess step in the Hero's Journey narrative usually involves unconditional love of the Goddess by the would-be hero. We don't see that in players as the Goddess isn't personified.

- There is no player type associated with the Woman as Temptress step because the player is not playing (or is but not for fun) for its duration.

- The limited input and output to Politicians on the development tracks may or may not have something to do with the way that the inability of the virtual world to measure intangibles plays into the Woman-as-Temptress pause.

- Atonement with the Father is more difficult for Politicians than it is for Attainers, because (as in the previous point) the physics of the virtual world can't recognise the Politician's successes.

- Atonement with the Father should be acknowledged by the virtual world as the pinnacle of achievement, but usually isn't – almost entirely for commercial reasons.

- Playing a virtual world beyond Apotheosis is encouraged by a change in gameplay. Creation, raiding, and PvP combat are common elder-game activities.

- Because the player returns to the Mundane World between sessions, the Magic Flight and Rescue from Without steps make better sense if their order is reversed.

Following the Hero's Journey isn't necessary, it just helps: players can become themselves without it (especially in social worlds). Nevertheless, it explains why people play for the extended periods they do, as mentioned in Chapter 4. Not everyone can complete their Hero's Journey, nor do they necessarily need to, but most long-term players will have done. They will read this and think "well I'm not on a Hero's Journey", and they'll be right, they're not: they already completed it. Other people *are*, though, especially those who are playing their first virtual world (or at least the first one they've got into).

There are design issues that would go away were designers to understand what's going on here.

What should be happening is that players play the virtual world's levelling game, reach the end, spend some time relaxing, then they receive formal recognition of their achievement, whereupon they leave. There's no elder game, no denial of Atonement: the players leave happy and will be predisposed to play your next virtual world if it offers a different perspective. By keeping the players in the air and never letting them land, sure, that's steady money in the short term but it does more harm than good. Players can become resentful and frustrated, which breeds toxicity. The whole atmosphere changes when the virtual world is packed with people in the elder game and the levelling game is left vacuous. Guilds ossify, newcomers find it hard to fit in and so bounce off. Elder-game content is provided for players as if they were Attainers when actually they're almost all Friends and Sages, with Friends in particular wondering why things they used to think were fun no longer are. It's because the content they're being given is still telling them they're Attainers, but now that they've gone beyond that stage it doesn't do it for them.

They *think* they're Achievers because that's what the designer is telling them they are, but they're now Socialisers.

In his Daedalus Project work, Nick Yee tracked MMO players over their entire playing career and discovered that they followed a pattern (Yee, 2007b): entry, practice, mastery, burnout, and recovery. In terms of the Hero's Journey: entry is the Road of Trials; practice is the Meeting with the Goddess; mastery is Atonement with the Father; burnout is Apotheosis; and recovery is Master of the Two Worlds. That Apotheosis is described as "burnout" is problematical, because it suggests that it's a negative experience. This is supported by the data, too: players tire of raiding, grinding, and creating alts, feeling that there's nothing worthwhile left for them to do. They're supposed to be feeling at ease and relaxed – which they would, if the game had recognised that they'd won it. When the player feels that they've won but the virtual world's designer (through the virtual world's design) refuses to acknowledge the fact, the consequences are inevitable. Only when they tell the designer to stuff it, self-actualising on their own, are they free to have fun again.

Solutions to this situation do exist, but they're not always scalable or acceptable to the players[23] and would certainly ring every known alarm bell for chief finance officers.[24] Nevertheless, it's possible without being mean to the players (if not the CFOs), simply by giving the virtual world an end state.

For example, consider an "escape from a 1940s prisoner of war camp" virtual world. The whole point of it is that the player character is a prisoner who wants to escape from the camp to get back home. After acquiring equipment through immoral and imaginative means, then learning skills, watching guards, digging tunnels, and cutting wires, they eventually decide to go for it! What follows is a thrilling, challenging escape set-piece that will end in either the character's death, their recapture, or their escape. If it ends in escape, the player is elated! They took on the camp guards and won! They could have died or lost everything, but they didn't. They made it! OK, so they may want to come back as an alt to be praised by their friends, but there's nothing for them to prove any more: they ended on a high and can leave satisfied.[25]

It doesn't have to be a POW camp. It could be that you've been washed up on a desert island.[26] It could be that you've been left for dead in the wilderness.[27] Perhaps you need to raise a huge sum of credits to buy passage to beautiful Earth from the grim space station you live on (or get to the beautiful space station from grim Earth). Perhaps you stepped through a portal to Hell to retrieve your unjustly stolen soul.

Or … perhaps not. Virtual worlds cost so much to develop that it's difficult for designers to take risks with them. Most of the people who have played virtual worlds have been on their Hero's Journey already, albeit probably in a diluted form, so just want "more of the same but different". Never mind that problems such as RMT are greatly diminished if the

---

[23] See the discussion of permadeath in Volume II.

[24] "Encourage established players to leave so as to attract new players" translates as "Throw away our income stream in an attempt to recreate the exact same income stream we just threw away".

[25] Perhaps less satisfied if they messed up and the guards shot them, but hey, they were going to quit anyway. Hmm, perhaps I shouldn't have used this as an example of not being mean to players.

[26] *New World* is like this, but you can't get off said island.

[27] *Conan Exiles* is like this, and you *can* eventually leave. It's one of the few virtual worlds that tries to do it right.

virtual world has an end (it would be like buying a save file from a game of *Civilization* ten turns before your chosen civilisation is due to win it). For a high outlay, most publishers are going to prefer a low risk. As a result, low-risk worlds are what we get, and the industry is in the doldrums.

It's somewhat ironic that *MUD1* fits the Hero's Journey better than most modern virtual worlds, yet at the time I'd never heard of it.[28]

If you're interested enough to want to read an early, extended account of the Hero's Journey in a virtual world, I have two suggestions: in *My Tiny Life* (Dibbell, 1999), author Julian Dibbell completes his Hero's Journey; in *The Cybergypsies* (Sinha, 1999), author Indra Sinha fails (at the Woman as Temptress step).

14.6 WHY PEOPLE PLAY VIRTUAL WORLDS

It's been a long trek, but we're now, at last, in a position to explain why people play virtual worlds.

In an extensive review of the reasons people are enamoured of imaginary worlds, and have been for millennia, Dubourg & Baumard (2021) propose that they "co-opt our preferences for exploration, which have evolved in humans and nonhuman animals alike, to propel individuals toward new environments and new sources of reward". For virtual worlds, this is indeed the case, but the exploration is of the self, rather than of the virtual environment.

Playing virtual worlds is a hill-climbing exercise through identity space. It's a quest for identity. By being someone else in the virtual world, the player finds out who they are in Reality. Whatever they're currently doing in the virtual world to pursue that aim, they find fun.

We can show this by deriving player types then mapping those types onto an established and ancient narrative framework that has identity exploration at its core. Virtual worlds – particularly game worlds – are organised[29] to lead the player along this path, but players follow it anyway regardless until they reach the end. Even then, this might not be the end of the story: there may be other hills to climb, higher than this one. There may be a yet better you. Even if there isn't, self-affirmation arising from playing other virtual worlds is itself worthwhile.

Maslow's famous Hierarchy of Needs (Maslow, 1943) places self-actualisation at the very top of the pyramid for human beings. When all other needs are satisfied, self-actualisation is what people seek. This is why it's so compelling.[30] People want to find out who they are so they can *be* who they are. Virtual worlds aren't the only route to the successful accomplishment of this goal – it's possible through all play[31] – but they are perhaps the most accessible.

---

[28] I hadn't heard of the Hero's Journey for *MUD2*, either, even though that has a second Belly of the Whale moment – in a cave, no less.

[29] Not usually consciously, they just reflect what people seem hardwired to understand, much as the Hero's Journey does.

[30] It's therefore easily mistaken for addictiveness (and *vice versa*, although not so often).

[31] "Nevertheless the fact remains that the desire to play is fundamentally the desire to be" (Sartre, 1988).

The theory as I have described it only applies to people who play virtual worlds for fun. It's often profitably employed outside of virtual worlds, but I can't explain why it would work in such cases so make no claims that it does: the warranty doesn't apply for them.

The theory has a number of interesting properties:

- **It's Exhaustive**. There are no player types beyond the ones described (although the ones described could be subdivided further).

- **It Contains No Redundancies**. Players can be transitioning between two types, but they're never two types simultaneously.

- **It's a Dynamic (Rather than Statistical) Model**. It has moving parts.

- **It's Both Easy and Difficult to Refute**. Easy, because one counter-example to anything claiming to be exhaustive brings it down; difficult, because it relies on an understanding of what's in the player's head, which is beyond the reach of questionnaire-based or observational-based experimentation.

- **Its Axioms been Tried and Tested Multiple Times**. Player types work.[32]

Better theories almost certainly exist. It depends on what you want to use them for, of course; player types are intended for designers, but even then there will be more appropriate theories out there either waiting to be formulated, or already-formulated and waiting to be put to use. What's undeniable is that people do play virtual worlds for a reason, and that this reason is tied to identity. Players *do* behave differently in virtual worlds in comparison to Reality; they *do* maintain several characters with slightly different dispositions; they *do* learn to act in ways they couldn't in Reality, freed by the words "it's just a game"; they *do* better understand who they are as a result of all this.

Not everyone wants or needs to understand who they are, and those who try may not like what they find. For the rest, though, playing a virtual world will help them in this process regardless of whose theory is being applied to explain it.

Players say they play virtual worlds for fun, and they're not lying – they do. What they might not realise is that this hedonic surface has a eudaimonic engine to it.[33]

In Chapter 18, I'll be looking at some of the other leading ways to categorise players. Before I do so, though, and while the player types discussion still has some momentum, I need to address a potential flaw that many players (especially those who have been playing for a long time) will perhaps have detected in the player types model.

It turns out that if you ask players in surveys why they play virtual worlds, a good many of them will mention *immersion*. There isn't a player type associated with immersion.

Why is that?

---

[32] This is why I can pompously call it a theory. However, its findings haven't been rigorously tested, so if you think the explanation as to why people play virtual worlds is all stuff and nonsense, well, you could be right. That would reduce it to an hypothesis.

[33] Many do realise it, of course – at least they do for other types of game (Possler et al., 2024).

CHAPTER 15

Immersion

"IMMERSION" IS ONE OF those words that people bandy about all the time, knowing what it means intuitively, but finding it hard to define when pressed. Its primary meaning (to cover something completely in a liquid) entered late Middle English from Latin; its secondary meaning (to be thoroughly absorbed in something) derived from this in the mid-1600s. It's this secondary meaning that concerns us here.

15.1 TECHNICAL USES

Unfortunately, the word "immersion" has different technical interpretations depending on who's using it and from which direction they come. Much as some frustrated researchers would like to see the end of its use (Holter, 2007), it's not going away. With virtual worlds, it has been strongly linked to the concept of *presence*, which is itself hard to pin down.[1] It doesn't help that a feeling of presence is so subjective that it's difficult to tell when other people are experiencing it (Slater, 2003).

There are several different understandings even of presence; these were helpfully laid out by Lombard & Ditton (1997) as follows:

- Presence as *social richness*. The extent to which a medium is perceived to be intimate. The more able the user is to convey interpersonal cues, the more socially rich their experience.

- Presence as *realism*. The degree to which a medium can produce seemingly accurate representations of objects, events, and people.

- Presence as *transportation*. Either a user is transported to another place, or a place is transported to a user, or multiple users are transported to the same other space.

- Presence as *immersion*. This is perceptual immersion, whereby the senses (vision in particular) are asked to believe that the information being presented to them is true.

---

[1] In essence, it's the perceptual illusion that a mediated experience is not mediated (Lombard & Ditton, 1997).

DOI: 10.1201/9781003689638-15

- Presence as *social actor within medium*. This refers to the development of *parasocial relationships* within the medium, wherein people broadcast to the many as if they were broadcasting to the few. The classic example is believing that TV presenters are your friends.

- Presence as *medium as social actor*. Here, the medium itself is treated as if it were an actor. You get annoyed with the automated telephone voice person, even though you know they're not a person.

All of these can apply to virtual worlds to varying degrees. Textual worlds are great for social richness, which will be apparent if you took my advice a few pages back and read Dibbell (1999) or Sinha (1999). Realism is important, as we'll see in Volume II. Transportation (in the sense of "we are there") is one of the defining properties of virtual worlds[2] and was first shown to arise back in the textual era (Towell & Towell, 1997). Perceptual immersion is a given in VR worlds. Parasocial relationships can develop, as we'll see in Chapter 23. Treating the virtual world itself as social actor is more prevalent in textual worlds, where the text is addressing you in the second person and so can seem to have a personality, but it's also seen in graphical worlds through the art style.

All in all, then, virtual worlds can have different kinds of presence and therefore immersion, although two uses dominate: *spatial* immersion (following from "presence as immersion") and *emotional* immersion (following from "presence as transportation"). Of these, the second is by some distance the more immersive form (Zhang et al., 2017).

Unluckily, because of the definition of "presence as immersion", many of the academics who went on to study immersion in virtual worlds often used it in the sense of perceptual (that is, spatial) immersion. This is not how players use it. A player could be more immersed in a textual world (which has no perceptual immersion) than in a VR world with a whole head-mounted ecosystem to support it. As a result of this dichotomy in understanding, psychologists have asked players honest questions about immersion and got honest replies, while nevertheless talking at cross-purposes.

As an analogy, suppose that A asks B a series of questions about football. Did you used to play it as a child? Do you watch games regularly on TV? Is the risk of injury too great? Is it too physical? Are players paid too much? Should women be encouraged to play it? As a result of this enquiry, A can come away with useful data about football, perhaps concluding that spectators aren't as worried about some aspects of the game as lobby groups assert. Unfortunately, A is American and B is British, and they mean completely different games when they talk about "football".

So it is with "immersion". What players and designers mean by it isn't the kind of sensory immersion that researchers often mean by it.

So, let's look at what players and designers *do* mean by "immersion".

---

[2] Actually, it's two of them considered together: the world is shared, and you access it through your character.

15.2 DEGREES

The first thing to point out is that immersion is not a binary concept. There are different degrees or levels of immersion. Some players can be "more immersed" than others; some virtual worlds are "more immersive" than others. The different depths of immersion are reflected by how players refer to their player characters. Here's an overview of the stages that players go through to achieve full immersion[3]:

- **Player**. This is the human being who is sitting at the keyboard or console, interacting with the virtual world. They treat the object they are controlling as a mere construction with which they don't identify, something like a very complicated mouse pointer. They describe what they're doing using the first person, with the object they control as an unreferenced tool: "I'll pick that flower" is analogous to "I'll unscrew that screw": the object the player controls forms no more part of the user's identity than would a screwdriver.

- **Avatar**. Most users will easily come to identify with the object they control in the virtual world. They'll begin by seeing it as their representative – a superficial puppet they can manipulate, the channel through which they act. The user will refer to this object in the third person but may begin to attribute some individuality to it (designing its appearance at creation time helps here). If the object they control is named Chris, they might say something like "Chris is a bit of a daredevil", but not "I'm a bit of a daredevil".

- **Character**. These days, users have typically played enough games by the time they start with virtual worlds that they can immediately identify with the object they control at a deeper level. They don't treat it as their representative but as their representation. It's how they project facets of or extensions of themselves into the virtual world. Each such object is essentially a personality they wear when they enter the virtual world. Often, they'll have several of them (in the form of alts) that they'll try on if the one they've been wearing isn't really doing it for them at the moment. They're like friends of the user, and will be referred to either by name or in the first person as a shorthand: "I'll tank the boss" means "this individual will tank the boss". Most players who are levelling up will be immersed at this depth.

- **Persona**. There comes a point when the user and the object they control become indistinguishable. The object *is* the user, *in* the virtual world. There's no indirection, no border between user and object: the two are one and the same. This is the deepest level of immersion: identity of the user and that which they use. You feel immersed in the virtual world because *you* are *in* the virtual world. There's no distinction between who you are in and out of the virtual world. Most players who have reached the elder game will be immersed at this level.

---

[3] I'll refer to the player as the "user" here and to the player character as the "object they control", so as not to introduce any clashes in connotation.

To summarise, the player's character in the virtual world can be regarded by that player as a tool, as a puppet,[4] as a simulacrum, or as the very person of the player.

The final, persona level is what players and designers mean when they say they're immersed.[5] It can be helped or hindered by sensory immersion, but is wholly different from it. When immersed, there's no role-playing being a character, there's no assuming an identity, there's no projection of the self; there's no filtering, no shielding. What happens to your character happens to *you* – because your character *is* you, and *vice versa*.

In everyday conversation, players aren't going to be this technical. They'll use the words "player", "avatar", and "character" pretty well interchangeably. Designers are somewhat more disciplined, but aren't too fussy about it except perhaps when in conversation with other designers.

Progress through these levels will begin at the unimmersed, player level for people with no experience of role-playing games, but they'll swiftly move to avatar level. Exception: people developing the virtual world won't, because they do actually *want* a tool, not a personal representative. Experienced players will go through the avatar level during character creation, then move onto character level when they start play-proper; inexperienced players (and players of social worlds) may remain at avatar level for considerably longer. Players thereafter spend a long time at character level before becoming their character and reaching the persona level. Vastly experienced players of virtual worlds will jump straight in at this level.

Those who look on virtual worlds from the outside won't necessarily notice any difference between the character and persona levels of immersion. They might not even consider anyone to be immersed at all if they're using the word in a different technical sense. It's clear that players do entertain different levels of immersion, though, as the fact has been noted independently by several researchers[6]:

- Brown & Cairns (2004) identified the levels of immersion as *engagement, engrossment,* and *total immersion.*

- Bowman (2010) describes the stages as *genesis, development, realisation,* and *integration.*[7]

- Banks & Bowman (2013)[8] call the stages *avatar as object, avatar as other, avatar as symbiote, avatar as me.*

It's probably obvious why I've mentioned the different levels of immersion now: they relate to player types. Whether you call it "persona-level immersion", "total immersion", "integration", or "avatar as me", there's an eventual point at which the player and their

---

[4] For a period, *puppet* was used as a synonym of *avatar.* Thankfully, it didn't last.

[5] Sometimes *fully immersed* when immersion itself is the topic of discussion.

[6] Note that it is not a requirement of immersion research that the leading author's name begins with B.

[7] If you're interested in immersion in RPGs of all kinds (not just MMOs or video games) then this is the book you need to read.

[8] This is a different Bowman from the one in the previous citation: 2013 is Nicholas David Bowman; 2010 is Sarah Lynne Bowman. If you just want the Banks without the Bowman, see Banks (2015).

character become as one – a moment of at-one-ment. It's the Atonement with the Father step of the Hero's Journey.

Thus, the reason there is no player type for immersion is that immersion is a measure of how much the player identifies with their character. The further along the development tracks the player is, the more immersed they are. There's not a one-to-one correspondence, but for most players, it's going to begin with avatar-level immersion in character creation. There may be a few false starts at the Griefer/Opportunist or Networker/Scientist stages, or there may not, but by the Politician/Attainer stage, the player will be at least at the character level of immersion. If they haven't reached persona-level immersion upon entry into the Friend/Sage stage then Something Is Wrong with the virtual world's progression system.

When the player finally *becomes* their character at persona-level, that's immersion. By being someone else, they have become the person they set out to become – and always were.

Players can pick up on the fact that they are progressing, and therefore may report "immersion" as a source of fun. It's a manifestation of the player's movement through player types, though; if the player isn't progressing, they're unlikely to say that immersion is fun. It amplifies existing fun, but the fun it brings with it itself is only residual insofar as virtual worlds are concerned.

In game worlds, immersion comes naturally through the gameplay. In social worlds, it's harder because of the lack of impetus, and it may need more effort on the player's part; the work necessary to obtain immersion this way is called the *active creation of belief* (Murray, 2011).

A quick few words on alts: they're not really a part of the player's progression, but they can *play* a part. In the early stages, they're going to be different, trial versions of the player's identity and possible candidates to become the main. They may indeed *be* the player's main for a period, before being rejected (legitimately, in the Road of Trials – this isn't a failure criterion). The player won't usually want to play on an alt when they enter the Politician/Attainer stage, as that's all about the main; they may do so for secondary reasons (helping out a guild mate who needs a healer, that kind of thing), and they may play as an alt while taking the Woman as Temptress pause step, but by the Atonement with the Father step, there can only be one character (their main) so there *is* only one character. In the Friend/Sage stage, alts may reappear, as a means of relaxing and having fun with friends or of exploring esoteric aspects of the virtual world.[9]

15.3 PROGRESSION

As players progress through their journey to increased self-understanding, so their characters progress in the virtual world. The virtual world doesn't know how the player is progressing, because it has no access to the player's state of mind: as far as the code is concerned, the player's advancement is *intangible*.[10] It does, however, know how the player's character is progressing because it has access to this information: the character's advancement is *tangible*.

---

[9] Once alts start to progress collectively, as in *WoW*'s *warbands* system, this is pretty well cemented-in. It's an elder-game consequence of putting characters in class silos.

[10] Italicised to remind you that this is a technical term (albeit a rarely used one).

Basically, stats are tangible and knowledge is intangible. The designer's aim is to make the tangible progress of the character reflect the intangible progress of the player, so that the player can judge their own progress towards self-actualisation and compare it to that of others.

The character's tangible progress is defined by the designer. It's necessarily world-oriented rather than player-oriented: you can award experience points and have characters rise in levels, abilities, skills, or whatever[11]; you can't do a similar thing for how much other players like you, or how cool your character looks, or how much organisation you put in behind the scenes to co-ordinate an activity. The *existence* of intangible factors could perhaps be recognised by the virtual world, but identifying them or measuring their effect is not feasible. This is why players of social worlds (and players of game worlds following the Main Socialiser sequence) have a harder time of attaining Atonement: the virtual world can't tell where they are in their journey, so can't reflect that tangibly through their character.

In game worlds, then, the progress of a character is tangible and that of its player is effectively intangible. A relationship has to be maintained between the two, because if it's not then either the player will peak too soon (become their character but not be acknowledged for this achievement) or the character will peak too soon (be showered in congratulations that the player doesn't feel are merited). Ideally, both progressions should be in as close to lock-step as possible, so that when the player becomes one with their character, that's when the character maxes out and the celebrations can begin.

The necessity for ensuring that player and character advance in tandem is compounded by the fact that other players also see your character (and therefore you) advance. If they see someone whom they don't yet feel "deserves" to reach the level cap nevertheless do so, that will give them second thoughts about their own success. Likewise, if they see some wise, experienced player struggling to make headway, they'll feel that the virtual world has been deliberately designed to block them. Having player advancement out of tune with character advancement is therefore not only bad for the player concerned but also for other players, too.

This is why pay-to-win is such a bad thing: it's reflecting in a tangible manner pretended intangible advancement. The player has not made progress, but they're trying to give the impression through their character that they have done. Already-immersed players may defend the practice, because for them, there's no problem in having an alt zoom to the elder game – they're already there.[12] For regular players, though, there is a problem: the virtual world's measure of progress is decoupled from the player's actual progression. Worse, those players who have not availed themselves of pay-to-win facilities will feel their own progress is being undervalued.

That this difference of views is present can be seen by what happens if the developer flags up characters who have bought pay-to-win items from the official store: sales plummet. Advanced players still purchase levelling shortcuts and the like,[13] but lesser ones who

---

[11] I discuss methods for character advancement in Volume II.

[12] Designers obliged to include pay-to-win who want to keep some shred of integrity could therefore only allow it for accounts that already have a level-capped character on them.

[13] Fast-level servers are not necessarily a problem in and of themselves, but they become one if characters can then be moved to a normal server.

hope to disguise the fact that they've failed their Meeting with the Goddess won't.[14] We'll be looking at pay-to-win in more detail in Volume II.

Not all players are the same, and they'll progress at different rates. This doesn't imply that the slower ones are less bright than the faster ones – they may simply appreciate the environment or the company more. A journey doesn't have to be a race – and those who treat it as if it is are likely to break the connection between tangible and intangible progress to their own detriment. It's not as hard for designers to allow for different speeds as you might think, though, because players will self-regulate. So long as the content is there for players who aren't in a rush (via side quests, for example), they can go at their own pace.

Aged MMOs that can boast multiple expansions have a problem here, in that there's an over-abundance of legacy content. Players simply have too much that they can do. For new players, looking from the foothills at the ever-growing mountain they're expected to climb, it's going to appear daunting. More to the point, it's going to take them so long to climb it that they'll have got all they want from the virtual world well before they reach the top. For this reason, designers often speed up progress automatically – greatly increasing the rate at which the character gains experience points and so progresses. This *can* work, but it has the disadvantage that players miss a lot of content that they might have enjoyed if they hadn't been shot past it at warp speed. Also, it may need a braking mechanism if there's main-story content that must be experienced if what happens beyond it is to make any kind of sense.

Here's an exercise: take a sheet of paper in landscape orientation and draw a vertical line on the left and a horizontal line across the bottom, connecting at a right angle. Now, begin a horizontal line about half-way up the line on the left that starts to curve down then very rapidly plummets close to the bottom line; keep this line running parallel to the bottom line until you've nearly reached its right-hand edge, then have it shoot up again vertically to around the same level that it started at on the left. What you have just drawn is a graph of the approximate level distribution for pretty well every MMORPG that has levels. In practice, there'll be drop-off points along the way, but the sheer size of the suck-it-and-see early levels and the sucked-it-and-saw final level dwarf all the others.

Whatever happens,[15] players will eventually bunch up at the end. They wanted to progress, they have now progressed: all they need is permission to leave. If you don't give it to them, they're going to take it anyway – and dislike you, to boot.

15.4 NAMES

Names are identifying labels. If the player is to depart from their everyday identity – in their own eyes, too, not only in the eyes of others – then a change of name is required. Experienced players may choose a name they've used in the past, and players not playing for fun may keep their name from Reality; most players, however, will devise an appropriate new name when they create their character.

---

[14] Note that with NFTs, the fact that an item was bought rather than earned is shown whether the pay-to-winners like it or not.

[15] OK, not if permadeath happens, but like *that's* a possibility....

Although some textual worlds allow for characters comprised of multiple individuals (you're a swarm of bees, or you're Laurel and Hardy), these are mere conceits: you're still controlling only one in-world entity – your character. The virtual world and its players have to refer to that character, so it needs a name.

When I was constructing my wife's family tree, I discovered that her paternal great-grandfather was one George Martin of London. So, how many people called George Martin lived in London in the mid-1800s?

Ah. There were over 10,000 of them. Needless to say, I have not managed to track down which one was my wife's ancestor.[16]

In a textual world, names are the primary way for selecting other players (you can't simply click on their character), therefore if several people have the same name, there's a problem in deciding which character you mean. For this reason, although players in *MUD1* were allowed to give their characters the same names as one another, they weren't allowed to log in at the same time. After several awkward cases of mistaken identity, a few of jocular impersonation, and one or two of revenge-blocking, names were made unique. Only one person in the whole virtual world could have any particular name.

This is fine if the virtual world has a small player base. If it's large, you're soon going to run out of decent names. Realising that *Ultima Online* would face this problem, the decision was made to make names non-unique. The lock-out problem was avoided by allowing characters with the exact same name to be logged in at the same time. Griefers took this opportunity to impersonate as a gift and made full use of it. Later virtual worlds did not repeat this mistake.

Of course, the problem of a small name space still existed. If you have a quarter of a million players, newbies are going to have trouble finding something suitable that isn't already taken. The solution to this is to enforce uniqueness only at the server level, not across servers. When I quit *WoW* in 2012, there were 40 characters with the same name as my main (Polly), distributed across 40 different servers.

Even this has its problems, though, because sometimes you want characters from different servers to play together. For example, you may decide to cut down on wait times for instances and PvP by allowing characters from different servers to play jointly. The problem can be solved in this particular case either by making the server name a component of the character name[17] or by not putting characters with the same name together in the first place during the match-making process.

The greater issue is server merges: if servers X and Y merge and they both have a character on them called Polly, one of them is going to be disappointed to find that they've been subjected to an enforced name change so as to avoid the clash. The way around this is to give characters surnames from the outset. First names don't have to be unique and surnames don't have to be unique, but the combinations *do* have to be unique. Most of the time, players will only need to use the first name, but the surname is there if disambiguation

---

[16] I am nevertheless confident that he wasn't the Beatles' record producer.

[17] So if Reality were a virtual world, I would be Richard@Colchester or Colchester:Richard.

is required. I can continue to message Polly Smith as "Polly" even if Polly Jones shows up; only if I message "Polly Jones" directly will the default "Polly" change to her.

Whenever players are given the opportunity to type anything in freeform text, some will think it entertaining to see how far they can stress it. Names are the quintessential example. People will use names that are copyrighted, trademarked, famous, gory, profane, racist, risqué puns, unreadable, …. All of these, plus all common variations using substitute characters ("Pen15"), have to be blocked in every language known to humanity.[18] Even then, players will find creative ways around it (reversals "Sinep", palindromes "Penisinep", embeddings "Xxpenisxx", letter removal "Pnis", sound-alikes "Peenis", Spoonerisms and other anagrams "Nepis", …). The developer needs to maintain not only a list of forbidden words, but also of ways to present them, as a result of which even valid names born by real, live human beings can wind up prohibited.[19] Some headway can be made by limiting the set of characters (letters) that can be used, but if René complains that you don't permit é, Pénis will also be waiting for you to allow it.

A way of dealing with this is to turn the problem around. Instead of allowing everything and then looking for misuses, the player is given a list of permitted names from which to choose. This has the advantage of being in-context, so in a Fantasy world, there's no immersion-busting "Hans Olo" or "Winston Smith", or multi-word compound names such as "WhatTheBlazes". It has the disadvantage of making fewer names available from which to choose, and it stops players from using "the name I always use" (which is actually a good thing, as it gets them out of a rut, not that they'll necessarily see it that way). This approach was taken by *Second Life*, for which it seems to work. It could easily be used for a virtual world with a fiction in line with Reality (contemporary, historical, and possibly futuristic), because a ready supply of names is available in genealogical data. For Fantasy worlds, you'd need to have a linguist[20] on hand to design fantasy languages from which names can be derived. Those names could either be the work of the linguist or made up on the spot by the player. The way to do this is to combine syllables to which the linguist has assigned meaning: the barbarian name "Mavicron" could be "ma-vi-cron" meaning "dances-with-sword". I've seen one or two of these in text MUDs: they're quite fun to play with, but still aren't foolproof (I managed to get "Fu-qu-az-ole" out of one once). They're a good way for designers to generate NPC names, though.

Another approach to avoiding problematic names is to generate laundered ones automatically and give the player a choice of, say, ten of them. If they don't like any, they can generate more until they find one that works. *EverQuest* tried this, but the names it generated were unpopular among players so the idea was dropped. Players like their names to have meaning, either to themselves, to others, or to both. The virtual world doesn't know that the names Poppet and Icepick have different connotations, but the player does. A name you've chosen for yourself is a personal statement: if you're happy for it to be a random collection of vaguely readable letters, even that's saying something about you.

---

[18] In *WoW*'s early days, I encountered a character called Bollocks, which amused British and Irish players but meant little to those of North America.

[19] Some German surnames are *actual profanities*. "Anyone who marries someone called Scheisse must really love them".

[20] Or a designer pretending to be a linguist.

Giving players names that are devoid of meaning and asking them to bring meaning to them is a fine ideal but a hard sell.

A name is of little use if it has no permanence. Suppose that players had to rename their characters every time they played: they'd soon resort to putting numbers after an invariant beginning.[21] Virtual worlds would be full of people with names such as Legolas6718, Drizzt3307, Naruto4188, Astarion420, …. Griefers would love it, because they'd only need to come in as Legolas6719 and they could cause all manner of problems for the original Legolas.[22] Players typically want a name that doesn't identify the player but does identify the character. That way, relationships between players can develop through the medium of their characters without Reality getting in the way. Note that if players have a unique, Internet-wide identity number that other players can see, Reality *does* get in the way. Sorry, Metaverse advocates.

If someone withholds their name and doesn't consistently provide another, they're said to be *anonymous*. If someone withholds their name and does consistently provide another, they're said to be *pseudonymous*. Characters in virtual worlds are pseudonymous of their player: you may not know that it's me playing as Polly, but you do know that it's the same Polly you've been bumping into for the past three weeks while farming ironwood.

It should be mentioned that virtual worlds differ from Reality in that character names can't be hidden. If you were to stop me in the street and ask me my name, I would be under no obligation to tell you.[23] In a virtual world, you don't need to ask because my name is right there, floating above my head or embedded in my description. This doesn't have to be the case: it could be that we have to be introduced before you can use my name. This may have some benefits for immersion and for identity-reinforcement, but it's likely to become so tiresome that players will want to automate it anyway. That said, some players in pick-up groups do refer to one another by role rather than by name ("wrong stance, Tank"), so anonymity-until-pseudonymity is not perhaps as outlandish an idea as it might at first glance seem to be.

Pseudonymity shares some of anonymity's nicer features without being quite as susceptible to its nastier ones:

- Because pseudonymity is persistent, reputation counts and friendships are possible.

- Because you're not identifiable as your character, players won't prejudge you based on real-world superficialities.

- Your friends in the virtual world won't judge you by your out-of-world actions.

- Your friends in the virtual world won't judge you by your in-world actions if you use a second character they don't know is yours.

- Your friends out-of-world (that is, in Reality) won't judge you by your in-world actions.

---

[21] Like you do when you're told to change your work PC's password.

[22] Variations on the name Legolas are so common that it wouldn't surprise me if I did indeed encounter someone called Legolas6719 in a virtual world.

[23] Well, maybe if you're a law-enforcement officer I would be.

The final point (that irrevocable social consequences for the player in Reality are unlikely) allows for increased disinhibition in the virtual world; this makes identity exploration easier, because if you do screw up major big time, OK, well you can start afresh with a new character and no one will know it's you.[24] The character pushing the boundaries of their sexuality almost certainly has less to lose than the player of said character would were they to do this in Reality.

If you never encounter the same people twice, pseudonymity is pretty well the same as anonymity. This can lead either to increased or decreased levels of toxicity, depending on the virtual world's design and to some extent its culture. If it doesn't matter how mean you are to other players because you'll never see them again, some players will take this as an opportunity to be mean (because you'll never see them again) and others will take it as an opportunity not to be mean (because it doesn't matter). Virtual worlds that have a lot of forced, shared content (such as *FFXIV*) tend to have lower toxicity levels; ones that make shared content optional (such as *WoW*) tend to have higher ones. This is because in the former case, you're not guaranteeing that you're competent; in the latter case, you are.

The link of pseudonymity to the Hero's Journey is so obvious that I was in two minds as to whether to state it or not. However, for the record: in the Belly of the Whale step, you are reborn in the Other World as a different person; associating a different name with that different person enshrines the difference. If you wish to explore who you are, freed from the constraints of Reality, then being someone else is one way to do it. "Someone else" isn't you, so gets a different name.[25]

As I said, it's obvious.

One of the problems of pseudonyms is that players can become invested in them. This can make starting afresh difficult if you've gone in a wrong direction. For example, if you create a thief character and after a while realise that you don't like all the sneaking and backstabbing you have to do, you might conclude that (for you) being a thief isn't fun. Fun is what propels you, so you need to start afresh with a new character that you can take in different directions. Perhaps you feel that solo play, rather than group play, is more your style, so you choose a paladin, on the grounds that you can defend yourself, heal yourself, and kill mobs yourself (just very, very slowly[26]). You want to keep the social capital you built as your thief, though. How do you do that?

Well the modern solution is that you allow your character to have more than one class (or equivalent). *The Secret World* achieves this through skill-set selection; *FFXIV* does it by weapon specialisation. You get to start anew, but everyone still knows who you are.

This is acceptable, but not always ideal. What you regard as social capital now you may think of as baggage later. It would be better if you did start from scratch as a new character, never to return to the old one; the old one is a reminder of a past false start, but its grip is

---

[24] Notwithstanding your distinctive barking in voice chat.

[25] As an almost completely irrelevant aside, I've noticed that students who are not confident about their exams will often change their appearance shortly before taking them. That way, "it won't be me who failed, it'll be blue-hair girl". When I spot this, I try to have a word with the student to see if they need help.

[26] I once took on a naga as a paladin in *WoW*, and the fight went on unbroken for over half an hour: we both recovered health at roughly the same rate. Yes, I did win in the end (I'd have been too ashamed to mention it otherwise).

still felt in its name. Formally, what *should* happen is that you admit to yourself that you were heading in the wrong direction and dispose of that character – delete it. You've failed the Road of Trials and need to enter the Other World anew.

In the early days of virtual worlds, when permadeath was a thing, this opportunity for reinvention would naturally arise when you got killed: you'd restart either using the same name (if you were on the right track, continuing your journey) or using a different name (if you weren't, restarting it). That's not an option nowadays, because players haven't understood permadeath since the end of the 1900s; the solution designers have adopted is to allow the player to respecify their character, whereupon they'll to try to be someone else while still being regarded as who they were. The process is like trudging through toffee: you're fine once you get out of it, but it takes longer to get out of it than you might wish. That said, as this is a step on the Road of Trials, the toffee-trudging itself could teach a valuable lesson; you can fail the text of the Road of Trials and still pass the subtext. An over-rigid interpretation would force failure in both.

There's another difficulty if the problem the player has with their character is the name itself. You might have thought it a laugh to call yourself Porkstick when you started out, but now it doesn't really fit the person you feel you are. Similarly, you could have made so many enemies that you want to shed your reputation while keeping your in-world gains. In both cases, this can be solved by a name change; it would be better solved by a character change, but players don't see it that way. Sometimes, name changes are legitimate (as players who named themselves after the Egyptian goddess Isis discovered when the Islamic State of Iraq and Syria was declared in 2014), but on the whole, it means your character is a dud and you need to rewind rather than relabel.

I've been discussing all this as if players can create multiple characters with ease. They want separate identities to play with, so providing them with several character slots on their account gives them this. There is an argument, however, that each account should only have one character on it. This forces the player to focus on that character, and makes the decision to abandon it and start anew actually meaningful. *Star Wars Galaxies* did this,[27] and the result was that players were in tune with their characters much earlier than in other virtual worlds; to this day, it remains a favourite of those who played it.[28] That said, the restriction has to be absolute to work: if it's a ploy to sell players additional character slots (as in *Secret Worlds Legends*) then it won't; if it's a ploy to get players to pledge more money for a Kickstarter campaign (as in *Shroud of the Avatar: Forsaken Virtues*) then it won't.

As for what all this means for designers, well the most important lesson is that anything identity-related that's out-of-world should remain out-of-world. Yes, of course the CSR team needs access to the account details of your character, but J. Random Player doesn't. If there's any way that a regular player can uniquely identify another player in Reality without their permission, the outcry becomes very, very loud. Blizzard discovered this to its cost in 2010

---

[27] OK, so in large part it was because character data occupied so much space that a more expensive commercial database solution would have been required to store more than one character per account, but the design nevertheless leant into it.

[28] And of those who played (or play) the rogue-server version, *SWG Legends*.

when it announced, in an effort to stop trolling, that it would display alongside forum posts the poster's Real ID – basically the name of the player, not of the character. The reaction was so adverse (and not only restricted to *WoW* players) that the idea was scrapped days later.

In summary, players play virtual worlds to explore or to assert their identity. They do this through their characters, which are referenced by name. It's therefore very tempting to suggest that the name tokenises the player's identity. It doesn't, though: it tokenises the player's credentials.[29] In a virtual world, what you do is who you are. Your character's name is attached to the evidence of what you've done; it verifies that you are who you say you are – but *only* when you use that name. Other names on other characters carry other credentials with other uses. Your identity is who you are regardless of what name you use. When you and your character are the same person, you have identity – but different names.

15.5 IMAGE AND SELF-IMAGE

To play a virtual world is to hold up a mirror to the soul, and to change both reality and reflection until they become one.[30]

If the designer has got it right, players differ from their characters until they reach the elder game,[31] whereupon the player and their character are the same person. When the player starts up, the character they create is therefore unlikely to be a reflection of their true self unless they've played virtual worlds for so long that they've self-actualised already.

When the player creates their character, the practical purpose is to set out how they want it to be viewed tangibly (in terms of its stats). More importantly, though, the player decides how they want their character to be viewed intangibly (in terms of its appearance). Character creation is where the player is reborn as someone else in the Other World; it asks the question: how do you wish to present yourself to others?

Your character's look is a statement that other players will read. Every aspect of it that requires a decision on your part is saying something. Why did you choose to be a buff male half-orc fighter with green skin and a plug-ugly face? You might not actually know – but other players will still use it to inform how they react to you.

I gave a talk in *Second Life* once, several years after it had opened. My character, who had been around since the early days, had the default male skin. I think I may have made some changes to his footwear to see how customisation worked, but I reverted them after doing so. Following my talk, someone in the audience asked me why I hadn't altered my appearance. I replied that this was the wrong question. The right question was why *had* they altered *theirs*? I had no statement to make; the only decision that faced me was whether to go with the male or female default. I didn't even have to choose a name, because Linden Lab had generously set it to my own name as a one-off exception.

Why do *you* create your virtual world characters to have the appearance they do?

When the player creates their character,[32] they're setting out their stall: this is the person I am aiming to be. Indeed, because character creation is a process, creating the

---

[29] I'm grateful to David Birch for introducing me to this idea in a podcast we did together (Birch & Bartle, 2022).
[30] I first wrote this line back in 2007 (Bartle, 2007), but it's still true.
[31] This is harder in social worlds as they don't have any kind of game, let alone an elder one.
[32] The practical details of this are examined in Volume II.

character may be the very way that they home in on whom they're aiming to be. By choosing how they want others to see them, they're choosing how they want to see themself (and *vice versa*).

Of course, if you want to say something that's easy to understand, it's best to use common words. Because of this, conventions and stereotypes will play a part in a character's presentation. Likewise, if several players want to say similar things, there will be a certain amount of movement towards expressing the same sentiment. *LambdaMOO* had a disproportionate number of male characters described as "mysterious but unmistakeably powerful" (Curtis, 1992), a description that was echoed in the many other MUDs that allowed players to describe themselves in a freeform manner. There was also a widespread preponderance of female characters who were green-eyed and flame-haired, with freckled, upturned noses and heaving breasts, who moved with the catlike grace of a dancer; it would seem that the male gaze (Mulvey, 1975)[33] occurs even in a textual context. This kind of regression to archetypes also happens in graphical worlds, of course, especially those with a "choose from these possibilities" character-creation system rather than a "tune these multitudinous parameters" one. It's therefore true to say that, while everyone may be different, there may well be similarities when it comes to deciding on what clothes of identity to wear.

Much is often made of how realistic characters look. The argument runs something like this: immersion is a good thing; the more real something appears, the easier it is to accept it as real; the easier it is to accept something as real, the easier it is to become immersed; therefore, if we want immersion, we should make things appear to be real. This line of reasoning is indeed correct: the less you have to will yourself to believe is real, the easier it is to accept the virtual as real. It's using the wrong definition of immersion for our current purposes, though. Immersion is about identity, and while belief that the virtual is real does feed into that, there are limits. In particular, if the virtual is *too* real then the players treat is *as* real. If they treat it as real, they bring with it all their beliefs from Reality, in so doing limiting their ability to play with their identity.

In Hero's Journey terms, the more like the Mundane World the Other World behaves, the more like their Mundane-World self the would-be hero behaves. That being the case, you're not going to have much leeway for asserting a completely new identity if the Virtual and the Real are too close.

In his seminal work, *Understanding Comics* (McCloud, 1993), comic book author Scott McCloud explains that the more cartoony a face is, the more people it can be said to describe. If you look at a realistic drawing, you see the face of another person; if you look at a cartoon, you can see yourself. So it is with virtual worlds: if your character looks real, you see it as another person, rather than an aspirational or alternative version of you. It's hard to become your character under such circumstances – and even harder for your character to become you. With less intrusiveness from Reality, however, your options are increased. As leading games researcher Nick Yee puts it: "With *Roblox* and *Minecraft* in particular,

---

[33] I was once trying to explain what I meant by this to a friend, and only after being met with a series of confused looks did I realise she thought I was talking about "the male gays".

you see a lot more creativity when [players] aren't sociologically encouraged to be obsessed about their hair" (quoted in (Au, 2023)).

People who play virtual worlds for fun desire to discover more about themselves. In the general case, they wish to grow as a person but don't at the beginning know how. Individuals can and do have individual problems, though, and on occasion they need to address these *specific* issues if they're to increase their self-awareness. For example, the player may hold two beliefs that are both incredibly important to them but that are in opposition. Such a player will not easily address their issues by following the unassuming route laid out by the designer. What they want is a Hero's Journey that takes a less well-trodden path that they can find on their own. For that reason, they'd probably be better off playing an undirected social world than a heavily signposted game world.

When players create the character they're going to play as, there are three main strategies they can employ:

1. **Strategy One**. Choose a character who is in some major respects your opposite. The real you is somewhere in between. You do things as your character, some of which sit well with you and some of which don't. You move your character towards you as you rule out behaviours you don't like, and you move yourself towards your character when you discover behaviours you do like. Eventually, you and your character meet somewhere between their respective starting positions; at that point, you've become the person you were destined to become.

2. **Strategy Two**. Choose a character who is similar to you but not quite the same. Explore behaviours with the character, backtracking if they don't feel right and adopting them as the player if they do. As your character progresses, you follow, until eventually you catch it up; at that point, you've become the person you were destined to become.

3. **Strategy Three**. Play as yourself, taking few if any of the opportunities available to experiment with your identity.

Strategies one and two are the most popular among those playing for fun, with strategy three being the almost-exclusive preserve of people who aren't playing for fun.

Between the first two, players select the approach that they're most comfortable with; there is circumstantial evidence that more men choose the first strategy over the second, though, because (as we'll see in Volume II) proportionately more men play as female characters than women play as male characters. Both strategies involve evolving your sense of self in response to challenges, it's simply a question of choosing your preferred method of search through the space of those challenges.

I should mention at this point that when psychologists have examined the relationship between players and their characters, strategy one hardly gets a look-in. A literature review of 43 empirical studies (Sibilla & Mancini, 2018) reveals that players either use a strategy of *actualisation* (make their avatar match their own self-concept – strategy three) or of *idealisation* (make their avatar match a similar but improved version of themselves – strategy two).

This is not the experience of virtual world operators. In *Second Life*, the decision tree is as follows (Walk, 2018): players first decide if they want to try to approximate their appearance in Reality, and if so then how closely (strategy three); if they don't want to do that then they either go aspirational (tall with a large chest – strategy two), exploratory (regular human but markedly different from the player – strategy one), or extreme (drag random sliders as far as they'll go – also strategy one).

It may seem odd that not only do players change their characters but characters change their players, yet some astute players do notice this happens.[34] Furthermore, it's provable experimentally (Yee et al., 2009); it's called the *Proteus effect* (Yee & Bailensen, 2007). In the same way that we observe other people and can pick up on how they feel, we can use our characters in the virtual world as proxies to observe ourselves and change our self-perception as a result. The poet Robert Burns lamented "O wad some Pow'r the giftie gie us, *To see ourself as ithers see us!*"[35] (Burns, 1786); virtual worlds allow us to do exactly that.

It follows from the above that characters are a form of self-expression for their players: you're exercising your creativity when you construct one and continue to do so when you play it. The situation changes over time, however. Yes, characters are indeed a form of self-expression at the beginning, but by the end, they've become something else: self-affirmation. This brings us neatly to the topic of identity.

15.6 IDENTITY AND IMMERSION

I've asserted that playing a virtual world is a search for identity, which I've supported by player types, the Hero's Journey and the concept of immersion. Whether you go along with that is up to you, but it seems to me that when it comes to virtual worlds played for fun, the celebration of identity is the fundamental, critical, absolutely core point of them.

Everything the player does is ultimately in service to this. It touches all. It's why achievers achieve, explorers explore, socialisers socialise, and killers feast on human essence.

A player's development of their identity can't be measured; it can only be reflected. It can't be controlled, only frustrated. It can't be forced, only invited. It's an intrinsic property of virtual worlds, and because of this can neither be designed for nor *not* designed for: it comes with what virtual worlds *are*, and if you try to override that fact for good or ill, the changes you'd have to make would result in a design that was no longer that of a virtual world.

Now from this, it might appear that the matter is out of the designer's hands, so what's the point bothering with it?

Well, you *can't* design for identity-development in general, but you *can* design for particular expressions of identity and for ways to channel those expressions. You can put up signs that players can choose to follow (or not) and you can remove unnecessary impedances to their progress. You can position what they are likely to need where and when they are likely to need it. You can, in other words, provide focus.

---

[34] "We create our avatars, and our avatars create us": an *Uru: Ages Beyond Myst* (Miller, 2003) player, quoted (twice) in Pearce (2009).

[35] Italics and Scottish dialect original. In modern English: "Oh, would some power give us the gift *to see ourselves as other see us!*".

Through your own decisions as to the nature of your virtual world, you speak to its players; you can make them hear, but it's up to them whether or not they want to listen. You're doing this as they're finding out who they are, which gives you a certain amount of power and associated responsibility. Sadly for tyrants but happily for the rest of us, it's not the power to mould them into the people you want them to be; rather, it's the power to ensure that the people to whom you are speaking are the people to whom you wish to speak and who have a fighting chance of understanding what you're saying.

Ask a player of a virtual world why they find it fun and they'll usually respond in one of the following ways:

- Deny that they do find it fun. This could be because the virtual world no longer addresses their needs or because they're not playing it for fun anyway.[36]

- Relate their fun to the fiction or the gameplay genre. They love the *Star Wars* universe, or stealth games, or playing with their significant other. Here, they're explaining what drew them to the virtual world but not why they find it fun.

- Say they have no idea. They've invested no time in analysing the situation, because they feel no need to do so while the virtual world is delivering what they want: fun. They don't care *why* it's fun, so long as it *is* fun.

- Give an answer that fits a player type. Perhaps they like teamwork, or uncovering new information, or defeating enemies – there's some aspect of the virtual world's gameplay that's calling to them and they're aware of it.

- Answer in terms of immersion.

In the first case, if the player isn't playing for professional or meta-reasons then either they're already immersed (and are preparing to leave the virtual world) or they derailed (and the best they can do is restart from scratch). In all the other cases, the player is pursuing the goal of becoming the person they are in the virtual world. This is what immersion is, and it's why it's so highly prized by designers, developers, and players. It's the subjective feeling of how far along your personal Hero's Journey you are.

Immersion is so important that players *will* themselves to treat what they know not to be true as if it were true. By doing so, they get a chance at being the person they know they truly are but are forced by the circumstances of Reality to treat as if they weren't.

Without immersion, virtual worlds lose much of what makes them virtual worlds. This is why anything that reduces immersion is to be avoided if at all possible.

Researchers studying immersion tend not to consider its relationship with self-identity. One well-respected and well-used[37] inventory of questions to identify how immersed a player is (Jennett et al., 2008) makes no mention of identity or even of identification. Another (Lewis et al., 2008) does look at identification but not at identity. Both of these are

---

[36] Of course, they could also be lying. Hey, griefers grief.
[37] 1,200 citations and counting.

fine for most games; it's only really for virtual worlds that they fall short. Virtual worlds are places; whether they're games or not depends on how they're pitched to players.

Why do people play the same virtual world hour after hour, evening after evening, for week after week, month after month? It's not because they like the virtual world, it's because they like who it lets them *be*: themself.

15.7 ROLE-PLAYING

The acronym MMO is an abbreviation of MMORPG, which is short for "Massively Multiplayer Online Role-Playing Game". This suggests that perhaps a modicum of role-playing is involved in MMOs.

Is it?

Well, yes and no.

A *role* is a part a person plays within a given social framework. "In my role as father of the bride, I have to give a speech".[38] People usually need to change their behaviour to fit the role they're playing, but out of the role, they're under no such obligation. That said, it's long been known that undertaking a role over time can change the individual playing it (Turner, 1978), not always for the better. The Proteus effect isn't limited to people playing games.

When a professional actor plays a part, they try to get into the head of their character; in so doing, they learn something about the contents of their own head. Over the course of a stage play's run, an actor may change how they see both their character and themself, altering how they play the role. The character doesn't change, though: it's defined by the fixed words of the script. That doesn't mean the character is rigid: it allows for different interpretations, especially when played by different actors. That said, although a character's portrayal can change, nevertheless that character remains the same as it always was. Hamlet is Hamlet regardless of who's playing him.

This is what actors want, of course. Actors map themselves onto characters: if the character is written too flexibly, the actor can't figure out how it ticks; if they can't do that, they can't use it as a basis for exploring their own emotions, views, past, attitudes, or (yes) identity. I call this *hard* role-playing, because it allows for little compromise. An actor can spend six months playing a murderer, but it's not going to change the murderer into the actor.

Players of virtual worlds rarely do this kind of role-playing. Their character may be outlined ("I'm a male human warlock"), but there's plenty of room for movement – for *play* – in its definition. Players can and do change their characters as they play, in addition to changing themselves. I call this *soft* role-playing, because the character and the player are both malleable. A player can spend six months playing a barbarian and the barbarian *could* change into the player.

In hard role-playing, then, actors and character are almost always separate[39]; in soft role-playing, players and characters start off separate but eventually become one and

---

[38] It's OK, it went well. I had slides.

[39] If an actor is close to a character to begin with then they could become that character. Obviously, this is unlikely to be a problem if the actor is playing themself.

the same. This is why I said that the answer to the question as to whether role-playing is involved in virtual worlds is "yes and no": yes if you mean soft role-playing; no if you mean hard role-playing.

I'm not denigrating hard role-playing here, by the way. Players who are hard role-playing *know* they're role-playing and can be systematic about challenging themselves. Players who are soft role-playing usually don't realise they are and may not act to change their character as much as they need to, which can be frustrating for them. Their problem is that thinking about a character while playing it introduces a separation, which inhibits immersion, so although they might benefit from stepping back on occasion, the time has to be right for them to do this effectively.[40]

When players think of role-playing, they typically associate it with the hard variety, especially "art thou with me, fair lady?" cod medievalism.[41] They might use the word "role" to refer to party make-up ("the role of tank is a thankless one"), but that's in the everyday sense of the word. They rarely consider that they themselves role-play, but role-play they do.

Unfortunately, for seeing-the-whole-picture reasons, there's a temptation for designers to think in terms of roles rather than in terms of characters. As a result, a lot of the role-playing that players engage in is foisted upon them. Ever since the Third Age, when *D&D*-style character classes became standard in game worlds, players of those worlds have been steered towards playing a class rather than a character. It's far easier to design for a class than for a character, so this is understandable (regrettable, but understandable). Players *can* still play a character if they put their mind to it, of course, but classes get in the way.

A virtual world that enforces classes is said[42] to be *classbound*; with no classes, it's *classless*. *World of Warcraft* is an example of the former, *The Secret World* the latter. An MMO that allows you to change class with ease, such as *Final Fantasy XIV*, is still classbound: you can choose what class to be right now – but it's still a class.

Classbound role-playing is necessarily more restrictive than classless role-playing. Classless, you get to change yourself over time and visit untrodden ground; classbound, you don't. Put it this way: if you start off wanting to be a mage in a classbound system, you board the mage train to Mageville and the only exploration you get to do is of the train; in a classless system, you might start off as a mage but pick up a few healing spells along the way and find that you prefer to heal, then focus on that until you realise your true calling isn't healing others but stopping them from needing to be healed in the first place, so you become a paladin. In a classbound system, you could be able to take a branch line ("fire mage") but you're still stuck on the train. In a classless system, you get to explore the whole space of character options between the lines, albeit not necessarily at the same speed as the folks using public transport.

In a classbound system, if you boarded the wrong train at the outset then you pretty well have to start afresh and take a different one. It's possible to mitigate this to some extent by making players specialise late, asking them to narrow their class as they get a better

---

[40] Specifically, they're going to find relief when they reach the Woman as Temptress pause.

[41] Or furries. Furries get a look-in, too – uwu.

[42] By me, anyway. See this decades-old article I wrote on the topic for *Edge* magazine (Bartle, 2001).

understanding of what's involved.[43] This is good for newbies, because they're not rushed into choosing the wrong class. That said, they only end up in the right class from among those available, and it's still only the right class for the time being.

If you want classes in your virtual world, strive to make the class be about the character, not the character be about the class. Players shouldn't be shouting "learn your class" at people whom they feel aren't playing it right; they should be telling them how to adapt their class to match their personal playing style. That, of course, requires them to recognise that personal playing styles exist, which is harder in an MMO that's all about elder-game raiding. Still, you can try.

We'll be looking at classes more in Volume II.

Before we move on, it's worth examining how players of virtual worlds who find role-playing fun fit into the player types model. There definitely are such people (Yee, 2005d), yet there's no player type for "Role-Player". Fortunately, we don't need a player type to accommodate them:

- Some people don't play the virtual world for fun, they role-play for fun. The virtual world is simply where they choose to do it. Virtual worlds are conducive to role-playing, so are attractive in this regard. However, for the hard role-players concerned, they're largely a means to an end. Player types don't apply to these people, because (as I said in the first line) they're not playing for fun.

- Some players use role-playing as a further separation from the Mundane World. They have fun while they role-play, but role-playing isn't intrinsic to their fun; they'd also have fun if they didn't role-play. Role-playing is part of the game, but it isn't itself the game (so, a bit like faction membership). These players progress through player types as normal; for them, role-playing helps with immersion and can therefore amplify their experience, but it isn't itself the experience.

- The remainder (which is usually the majority) role-play in the service of some player type. As always with questions to do with player types, it's a good idea to look at the axes of the graph. Role-players are interested in players, so will probably be following the Main Socialiser sequence.[44] If the player is using role-playing as an aid to interaction then they'll be Networkers or Friends. If it's a form of accept-me-as-I-am acting on players, though, they'll formally be Griefers.[45] If Politicians role-play, it's to make their politicking easier.

---

[43] *EverQuest 2* was like this initially. Players started out choosing between being good and evil, then after the tutorial ended they picked what archetype to be (fighter, mage, priest, scout). At level 10, they chose a class from within the archetype; at level 20, they chose a subclass of their chosen class. This all changed in update 19, when the character's final class was decided at level 1, which made it less friendly for MMO-newbies but more friendly for alts and refugees from *WoW*.

[44] Attainers might try it competitively if there's some reward ("I'm going to be the best gosh darn role-player on the server!") and Opportunists could try it for random reasons, but the Explorer types are less likely to find it attractive.

[45] This doesn't mean they'll purposefully do any griefing (although they might); it's more that they have an "I was just role-playing" shield to hand should they push social boundaries too far.

It's worth mentioning at this point that while some people role-play in virtual worlds and not in Reality, others role-play in Reality and not in virtual worlds. For example, if you're gay but closeted, you might play a virtual world so you can be yourself in a way you can't be in your everyday life. As with role-playing, player types may or may not apply to you, depending on whether the virtual world is a means to an end for you or not. I call this *inverse role-playing*, but am probably the only person to do so.

In summary, then, a character is a mask that the player chooses to wear. By revealing less of their outer self, the player can reveal more of their inner self; they can therefore learn more about their inner self, changing both it and their character so the mask fits better. Ultimately, the two align and the player and character become a single persona.

Role-playing, then, is a paradox. The role-player is trying to become their character, but when they succeed, they're no longer role-playing.

There are actual theories that describe role-playing games, which we'll visit in Volume II. For the moment, though, let's look at a different kind of role-playing altogether.

15.8 MASQUERADING

Masquerading is the act of role-playing not a character but a player. It isn't impersonation (you're not pretending to be a known individual); rather, you make up a person in Reality – an *alter ego* – and pretend to be that person. Masqueraders don't always set out to masquerade, but tend to fall into it; the backstory and personality of the alter ego[46] are therefore often constructed on-the-fly as personal or situational needs demand.

Masquerading is not as popular as it was in the past, for two main reasons. Firstly, people are now more aware of the related form of deception known as *catfishing*, in which an individual constructs a false online identity (or, worse, steals someone else's) for a nefarious purpose.[47] Secondly, it's not as easy as it once was, what with social media and voice chat adding previously ignorable complexities.

It's also not as painful as it once was. In the innocent early days of the Internet, people who were met online were accorded the same level of trust as those met offline; it was therefore something of a shock if it turned out that they were not the person they were claiming to be. If you've formed a strong relationship with someone who's faked their identity, it can be devastating; confidence tricks, whether intended or not, are awful. For early examples, see that of Sue the Witch in *MUD1* (Bartle, 1997, 2015a) and (especially) of Karyn in *LegendMUD* (Koster, 1998; Spaight, 2003). Today's players are wise to the idea, though, and tend to twig earlier than they might have done in the past, thereby saving themselves from the emotional damage that comes from "losing" someone dear and feeling foolish in the process.

Although some masquerading is performed by schemers who plan to do it in advance, most is undertaken by guileless players who commit to it without premeditation; they don't

---

[46] Really I should be italicising this as it's from the Latin, but as it's a technical term, I'll keep it unitalicised (except when I introduced it, which, if I'd been italicising it in use, wouldn't have been italicised). Oh, the lengths I go to to appear more professional than I really am.

[47] Personally, I regard being cruel to strangers in the name of pranking as a nefarious purpose. The old, victim-blaming "can't you take a joke?" excuse no longer washes, if indeed it ever did.

mean for it to happen or for it to cause distress, they simply get in way over their heads and feel they have to continue so as to keep up the pretence. When they realise they really *have* to stop, they typically enforce a clean break from which they can't come back; this is why many such tales end in the alter ego's untimely death. The masquerader has become immersed in their alter ego, rather than in their character. That this is possible serves to demonstrate that although identity and virtual world immersion are closely related, they're not inseparable. Whether or not masquerading of this kind is likely to lead to ill effects on the masquerader is hard to say, but it's almost certain that they'll feel relieved when their deception ends.

As for the schemers, a small minority has evil intent (as always), but most will be masquerading for professional reasons. These latter are aware of the dangers and strive to avoid hurt. Examples of people who fall into this category are celebrities (we had a TV soap star[48] who played the *British Legends* incarnation of *MUD1*) and developers (especially CSRs, who want to keep an ear to the ground but don't want to be buttonholed about game issues or subjected to accusations about what they do to their own mothers). It even happens in Reality: Henry V of England used the alter ego Harry le Roy[49] to find out what his men were thinking on the eve of the Battle of Agincourt.

If you're a developer (or are famous), you're therefore one of the few people who has a vaguely legitimate reason for masquerading while playing a virtual world. It's not an enjoyable experience – you're going to be lying to people – so it may be better if you merely play *incognito*: not furnish any information about your offline existence at all. Still, if you really *must* do it, here are some tips:

- Make sure you have the time. Playing a virtual world is going to consume a great deal of it.

- Design your alter ego as a fully rounded person. Take online personality tests in-character. Read up on the design of fictional characters. [50] Know why your alter ego is playing this virtual world.

- Give your alter ego a plausible life with a plausible backstory. Include (but rarely reference) relatives and friends.

- Create an online audit trail. This means an email address, a social media presence, posts in obscure forums for people who search for you to find – whatever suggests that you're not a recent invention. Don't do everything on the same day: do it in stages.

---

[48] Sadly, I don't know his name because I don't watch any soap operas, let alone American ones, but the soap itself was something about a hospital. When he showed up at restaurant for a *BL* get-together once, he was mobbed by those non-player diners present who spent their evenings watching TV rather than playing online games. His fellow players had no idea he was famous until that point.

[49] There are probably better names he could have chosen that were less of a giveaway.

[50] I found (Card, 1988) to be pretty good, but there are probably better examples out there these days.

- Have a profile picture that makes no claims to be that of a person (a place, a pet, a doll, a cuddly toy, a comic book character – anything that doesn't imply it's of you).

- Make occasional social media posts.[51] Use other accounts to comment on these. Follow people and ask to be their friend, so you look knitted-in.

- Choose a relatively common name for your alter ego.[52] Do not use this for any of its characters in the virtual world.

- Don't claim knowledge or skills for your alter ego that you don't possess yourself. Don't use words that you can't spell.

- Have an exit strategy. Plan how your alter ego will quit. Drifting away without saying anything is perfectly acceptable.

- Don't develop any personal relationships beyond in-world norms. Be polite, participate in guild chat, but avoid giving details.

- Don't get attached to your alter ego or to the in-world character it plays. Neither will be around for the long term.

- Don't claim your alter ego has high status in Reality.

- Avoid players who really are what your alter ego is pretending to be (*e.g.* British if you're not).

- Don't introduce friends you claim to know "in real life".

- Don't take on any high-profile in-world roles.

- Don't pretend you don't have a microphone or that it's broken.

- Abandon the whole exercise the moment anyone smells a rat.

- Abandon the whole exercise the moment anyone gets emotionally invested in you. You might like to apologise, too, because it means you screwed up.

Masquerading is tawdry and exploitative. Nevertheless, it delivers knowledge and understanding that you simply can't obtain any other way. It's a bit like espionage: a dirty business, but if you can justify it on moral grounds then the rewards are often worth it.

You *do* have to justify it, though.

---

[51] You can make the first one be a complaint that this is the real you after your original account was hacked. It will need replies from your sock-puppet friends if it's to be credible, though.

[52] This is because you can sometimes get friend requests from people who think you're someone else, which can expand your follower base and look more authentic. I once created a Facebook page for a fictional character (Lizzie Lott) from a book I'd written, giving her a biography that began "I am a fictional character", yet with no effort beyond clicking on "accept", I somehow managed to rack up 700+ friends from Dar es Salaam.

CHAPTER 16

Encouraging Immersion

A PROMINENT MODEL OF INTERACTIVE digital narrative[1] (Koenitz, 2023) defines immersion as being the ability of a digital narrative to create and hold interest. Agency, which means impact through meaningful choice, builds on this, leading to transformation – changes to the artefact itself and to the person interacting with it. This in turn gives a kaleidoscopic[2] set of insights into complexity.

Such a model works well for describing a gamut of interactive experiences, but isn't quite right for virtual worlds as our definition of "immersion" is different. For us, immersion *is* transformation, and agency drives both. The timescale for virtual worlds is so much in excess of that of other sources of interactive narrative that it would actually be a surprise if the simple ability to hold players' interest was sustainable for that long. Narrative isn't the only source of immersion anyway: Reality is entirely immersive but has no narrative to it whatsoever.[3]

We can take it for granted that players have an "immersion switch" that they can flick on when they enter a virtual world and off when they leave it. They're not immersed in the virtual world while not playing it, but they are – or are becoming so – when playing it (if playing for fun). We can't, however, assume that the virtual world will have enough about it to allow the player to maintain this perspective over an extended period. Fortunately, overcoming this is something that we designers don't have to leave to chance.

Let's look at some of the ways that the design of a virtual world can encourage immersion in it.[4]

---

[1] IDNs are "Narrative expressions in the digital medium that change due to input from an audience" (Koenitz, 2023). This wide-ranging definition includes video games. Personally, I don't see the need for the medium to be digital – a *Fighting Fantasy* (Jackson & Livingstone, 1982) game is the same game whether it's in gamebook form or play-on-PC form – but then as a programmer I automatically look for minor quibbles in edge cases.

[2] This term comes from Murray (2011), upon which Koenitz's work expands.

[3] Notwithstanding some religious beliefs.

[4] This often involves not discouraging it.

DOI: 10.1201/9781003689638-16

16.1 PERSUADING THE MIND

The only thing you can be certain exists is you (Descartes, 1637). An array of senses presents your mind with a stream of inputs, which suggest the presence of an objective reality within which you exist (that is, Reality). You construct and continually update your model of Reality using what your senses and reason tell you. This is what that Reality is to you.

If you wish, it can also be what another reality is to you, such as a virtual world. This is because the world in your head doesn't *have* to mirror Reality: Reality is objective, but the world in your head is subjective. It's under the control of your imagination. You can use it predictively ("when I throw this ball, where will it go?"); you can use it reflectively ("why didn't that ball go where I thought it would?"); you can use it to create impossibilities ("I'm going to imagine a ball that only bounces off glass"). These features allow you to imagine – and to will yourself to accept as real – any world you choose.

A player who is immersed in a virtual world is immersed in themselves. The virtual world is the Other World of the Hero's Journey, in which they have reconstructed their identity. There are two key constraints on this Other World: it must be a world; it must not be Reality. If the player isn't persuaded that the virtual world is a self-sufficient, stand-alone world then they can't use it as the Other World, therefore they can't use it to become immersed. Accordingly, we need the virtual world to be *persuasive*.

We have the players on our side here, in that they *want* to become immersed and are prepared to will themselves to overlook a good many things that might tell them the virtual world is an invalid alternative to Reality, or indeed that it's simply a part of Reality itself.[5] However, the more we ask of them, the heavier the mental load the players have to bear and so the harder it becomes to maintain the conceit that the reality they are visiting is indeed real. We can therefore help with immersion by removing obstacles to this conceit. The player *knows* that it's not the reality of Reality, but the easier to accept as real we make our virtual world, then the less work the player needs to do to maintain this self-deception and the more resilient they will be to its occasional disruption.

Each player builds up an individual mental model of the virtual world. If their model largely aligns with their model of Reality, most of the time it won't need to be thought about consciously because it already makes sense to them. "When things make sense, they correspond to knowledge that we already have, so the new material can be understood, interpreted, and integrated with previously acquired material" (Norman, 2013). This allows the player to focus on the business of playing instead. Sure, there are some things we may want to have in our virtual world that Reality doesn't have, such as magic,[6] but the player will find those easier to accept if they're not also accepting a bunch of other competing (but somewhat less relevant) differences. We'll be looking at the concept of *realisticness* in Volume II, which considers this from the perspective of the virtual world's fiction; for now, though, let's see what we can do to help players accept intellectually that the virtual world is real.

---

[5] Note that researchers may choose to consider the real and the virtual together if it suits their purposes (Lehdonvirta, 2010). Doing such is unlikely to suit the purposes of designers.

[6] Notwithstanding some religious beliefs again.

We can exploit the fact that most people already have existing mental processes that help with this. The idea is that we play along with these, rather than challenge them. Suppose, for example, that in Reality, you were to visit a city in a foreign country that you've never visited before. You might not understand the language or culture, or the city's layout, or how public transport or any of the services work; you expect this, though, it's normal for visits to faraway places. You will, however, expect that gravity works like it does back home, that you'll see sights you've never seen before, and that there's a form of local government. For the first of these, it wouldn't occur to you that it might work differently, and if it did then you would be extremely alarmed. For the second, you could actively seek out points of interest or wander aimlessly and come across them by chance – or indeed do both. For the third, you'll know the general set of possibilities but not necessarily the specifics, and may be on your guard in case you accidentally violate some ordinance of which you were unaware.

People do this kind of thing automatically for new places. They've been to enough new places (even a friend's house is a new place the first time you visit it) that they have developed strategies for creating mental models. They begin with expectations: if what they encounter doesn't match up with these expectations, they have to adjust their mental model of the new place in the light of the new information; if it does match, they become more confident in their model and can flesh out its particulars further. The latter is easier than the former, but the former can be the more interesting in measured doses.

For virtual worlds, we'll be stressing the player's mental model in several areas that we know of in advance. We definitely need these; such points of dissonance with Reality may indeed be what attracted the player to the virtual world in the first place.[7] What we don't need is a cacophony of unnecessary stresses vying for attention, making it difficult for the player to concentrate on what matters most.

A lot of these unnecessary stresses can be subdued "simply" by making the virtual world have sufficient depth to it that the player doesn't notice any signs that something is amiss. This doesn't mean the virtual world has to have the same architecture, weather, and shops as Where You Live, because that isn't even the case for different places in Reality. It does mean that if you give every house split doors like a stable, rain that bounces like a rubber ball, and shops that only sell false teeth then you'd better have some in-world explanation for it. OK, so those are perhaps a little extreme, but players *will* notice repeated oddities and *will* want answers.

To help the player build up their mental model, your virtual world should be furnished with lore. Even if the players ignore it,[8] you can't ignore it yourself when you create the world because it guarantees consistency and coherence (assuming it is itself consistent and coherent). You can leave hooks for paracosm-building purposes, and add further detailing later as the virtual world develops, but even a virtual world with no history to it has to have a plausible *reason* for history's absence.

Detail makes a virtual world more persuasive than lack of detail does, because players pick up on lack of detail – especially where they're expecting detail. Therefore, holes in the

---

[7] Body dysphoria issues aside, you're not an elf in Reality, but you can be one in the right virtual world.

[8] Despite what lore-writers might wish to believe, not all players are actually interested in their creative outpourings.

virtual world's supporting lore are to be avoided except when there's a contextual promise that it will be revealed later. [9] Details are never stand-alone, though: they work together as a whole. Inconsistencies between them can therefore be jarring.

Jarringness is the enemy of immersion, because it takes the player out of the virtual world and back into Reality. Individual players have different capacities for dealing with it, so you can often get away with a little if it doesn't happen too frequently; you often can't, though. If the player trusts the designer, the jarringness will only be fleeting and the player will slip back into the virtual world with barely any effort, their expectation being that an explanation will eventually be forthcoming; if the player doesn't trust the designer, it could take a conscious decision on the player's part for them to start playing again. We'll look at this issue when we come to realisticness in Volume II, too.

The player's mental model of the virtual world concerns: the contents of the world, the relationships between these contents, and an understanding of their functionality. Such mental models are constructed routinely by people in Reality and are not restricted to virtual worlds. You have a mental model of how a car works, for example. These models don't need to be identical between individuals, or even entirely accurate: your model needs only to be serviceable for your own purposes. For virtual worlds, going one level of detail deeper than the mental model of the average player is usually sufficient to enable most people to play without being bothered by unnecessarily broken understandings. So long as they can be persuaded that this is a fully rounded world that is a valid alternative to Reality, the gateway to immersion is open.

16.2 PERSUADING THE SENSES

The ability of a virtual world to persuade the player that it's a valid alternative to Reality is crucial to its success. As with all places, the model that the player constructs is in their head, so is of primary importance. However, how the information from which to construct the model gets into the player's head in the first place is also critical. Even in Reality, people who have sensory impediments will construct different models of their surroundings in comparison to people who have none (Ricciardi et al., 2009). I, for example, am pretty well incapable of telling what direction sounds are coming from,[10] so my cognitive map of my environment is fuzzier outside my field of vision than it is for most people (although it's better within it, as I'm more attuned to my peripheral vision).

In a virtual world, the information presented to the senses provides the raw data used by the brain's interpretive apparatus to construct its world model. Both fortunately and unfortunately, the human brain has specialist hardware (the occipital lobe, at the back) that is superbly adapted for processing visual information in real time. It's fortunate, because it means sighted people can construct a model of their current environment without having to think about it; it's unfortunate, because it's evolved for Reality and we're not dealing with Reality – we're dealing with virtual worlds. If the virtual world doesn't present

[9] Or, for some story genres, the assumption that the world is so shot to pieces that it makes more sense for occasional holes never to be filled. The (non-virtual world) game *Cyberpunk 2077* (Badowski et al., 2020) has some quest chains that start but subsequently peter out, because unreliability is a feature of the Cyberpunk genre.
[10] A consequence of almost going deaf during the exact period when children develop stereophonic hearing.

visually the same way as Reality, the player will be interrupted by a call from the visual system to interpret whatever weirdness it's encountered. This will jar the player out of the virtual world come what may.

Over time, players can learn to ignore clipping errors and so on, but it would be a sorry virtual world indeed if its errors were so frequent that players became accustomed to seeing themselves standing on a floor half a metre below the actual floor, so it looked as if their legs stopped at their knees. Graphics are great when they're unnoticed for being graphics but noticed for what they display (a beautiful, panoramic view, for example). If they have odd-looking animations or eerie faces,[11] though, players will see the graphics as graphics rather than as what the graphics depict; this is bad for immersion as it tells the player the virtual world isn't real.

Note that graphical style isn't necessarily a problem, so long as it's not too abstract and is consistent throughout. Players accept that *World of Warcraft*'s graphics are cartoonish and not meant to be photorealistic. If the graphics were cubist, though, they would be less accepting; likewise, if they were as they are now but some parts looked as if they were by Disney or Hanna-Barbera, that inconsistency would interfere with immersion. Yes, it's fine if there's an explanation,[12] but if there isn't (or there is, but the players don't trust the designer enough to expect one) then immersion will suffer. Players won't believe the virtual world is real because their senses are telling them it isn't.

Textual worlds have an advantage here in that they effectively bypass the senses: words speak directly to the mind. OK, so the words have to be sensed somehow (typically visually) and they also have to adhere to standards (such as spelling, grammar, and punctuation), but the obstacles to immersion are much lower. That's if the player is good at visualisation, though: if they're not, the burden of making sense of textual descriptions of the virtual world can be unconducive to immersion.[13]

A constant stream of self-consistent elements of sensory information allows players to treat virtual worlds the same as Reality: that is, as having an objective existence. It would perhaps seem a good idea, therefore, to make the virtual as real-seeming as possible to remove more of those distractions that tell the player it isn't. This is one of the promises of VR: as we noted in Chapter 8, sensory immersion is very powerful. We also noted, however, that it can be *too* powerful: beyond a certain point, if the virtual is barely distinguishable from the real then players behave as if it were indeed the real. Yes, formally it may be an Other World, but if the players treat it as being the Mundane World then they won't be inclined to be someone else in it. One way to avoid this is to persuade the player that the virtual world *is* real, but not that it's Reality. This isn't as easy as it sounds, though. Whatever the virtual world's content, if all the sensory information the player is receiving says that they're in Reality, it's still going to be easier to regard it as if it were Reality – simply because

---

[11] We'll be looking at the *uncanny valley* in Chapter 23.

[12] The cartoon movie *Spider-Man: Across the Spider-Verse* (Spider-Man: Across the Spider-Verse, 2023) has different graphical styles for the different universes depicted.

[13] The condition of being unable to create imagery in your mind's eye is called *aphantasia*. Note that despite its visual connotations, this "imagery" doesn't have to be visual: congenitally blind people construct mental imagery based on other sensory modalities (Renzi et al., 2012), for example.

of all that hard wired processing power at the back of the brain. You may know *intellectually* that the rampaging dinosaurs aren't part of Reality, but you're still likely to close your eyes when one of them swings a claw 2 cm from your nose. Rather than willing yourself to believe that the virtual world is real, an excess of sensory immersion can require you instead to believe that what seems to be real is actually virtual. This frame-flipping makes identity immersion much harder to achieve: there's no distance between you and your character, because your character isn't distinct from you. You're player-level immersed, and there's no pressure to be anything else; there may be a desire, but it's hard to act on it.

It could be that this is only a chasm that needs to be bridged, and that if we intercept motor functions as well as hijacking the senses (by using cyberpunk-style neural implants, say) then players could be persuaded not only that their environment is Reality but that their virtual body is their own. Then, they might indeed be inclined to behave as if they were an elf or a hawk or a dolphin or whatever they rolled-up.

What would they do in this new reality, though?

Well, they'd try to escape it.

If you need no imagination to be in a virtual world, players will seek to use their imaginations to be elsewhere. Sensory immersion is not alone enough to satisfy people. After all, you're sensory-immersed in Reality, but you still read books, watch films, and play virtual worlds.

To encourage the player to become immersed, then, the designer should strive not to make the virtual world behave *unnecessarily* in ways that Reality doesn't, but not to the extent that it becomes easier for the player to accept it as real than not. Human biology and players' prior experiences will determine where the sweet spot lies, but happily it's very broad; unless you're pushing technology for technology's sake, you should be OK.

16.3 SPACE OF EXPLORATION

Exploration requires a space to explore, which in the case of virtual worlds comes primarily in the form of the player character (identity exploration) and secondarily in the form of the virtual world itself (exploring its players and its world).

The more depth the virtual world has, the less depth the character needs: the player can use their choice of what to do in the virtual world to inform the direction in which they take their character. Similarly, the more depth the character has, the less depth the world needs: the player can choose which direction to take their character in directly, with the world providing context. The former approach is favoured by sandbox MMOs, the latter by theme-park MMOs.

It's entirely possible for the virtual world to offer depth in both areas, of course, which leaves the decision with the individual player as to what's best for them. Unfortunately, it's often difficult to reconcile character depth with world depth: the two can be at odds at the systemic level. For example, if a player is exploring their character through the subtleties of the skills and rotations available to them, this would be in conflict with a world that at some point is seeking a particular solution that's not possible using those skills and rotations.

Although a virtual world's breadth and depth have implications for immersion, their greater significance is as a way for the virtual world's designer to communicate with its players. For this reason, the main discussion on this topic is in Volume II's chapter on art.

For our current purposes, we merely need to note that early on in their playing experience, players focus on breadth; only later do they move on to depth. In terms of player types, Scientists are mainly interested in the breadth of the world, and Sages are mainly interested in its depth; likewise, Networkers are primarily interested in the breadth of their relationships and Friends primarily in their depth. Therefore, as a designer, you would want to emphasise choice at the start of players' progression, gradually shifting to understanding towards the end.

Exploration begins with the general and ends with the particular (a lesson that PhD students learn the hard way).

16.4 IDEAL SELVES

Not every aspect of a player's identity necessarily needs to be explored. Players can at the outset have a partial or indistinct impression of their true self, which suggests that there are parts of their identity that won't be changing even when starting with a fresh, blank-state character. Relearning what they already know can get in the way and confuse matters, so such players often appreciate some guidance from the virtual world regarding what might be appropriate matches for the relatively fixed aspects of their sense of self. This doesn't even have to be identity-related: personality facets can also be accommodated if that keeps them out of the way of the main business in hand. For example, whether you prefer to be in the thick of things or watching from the sidelines is independent of player types.

Designers typically respond to this by suggesting target ideals, such as character classes and races (about which more in Volume II). We know that identification (the projection of the self onto some ideal) comes before identity (the projection of the self onto the self), so this is reasonable. The aim is to provide aspirational pointers, though, not tickets to ride, so it's important that the player's options are not set in stone.[14] Kits that show popular ways of organising a character are better than fixed archetypes, because they allow the player to change their mind as they develop. Say, maybe you were wrong and you *do* prefer toe-to-toe melee combat over ranged fireball-lobbing after all. Constraints can be good for gameplay (Salen & Zimmerman, 2003), but they're not necessarily conducive for immersion.

Target ideals work best when they're abstractions, because then there are fewer features that could conflict with a player's needs. It's easy to overdo this though, leading to one-dimensional archetypes; this is one reason why virtual worlds that offer dozens and dozens of character classes at the start can have problems.[15]

Although identification with their character is a stage that players need to go through, it's a bad idea to try to lock them into it. If players are made to define themselves by an ideal image, it can lead to friction between the player's developing sense of identity and that perceived of the ideal. Lucky is the player whose choice of ideal remains appropriate for their entire playing career. Player characters are mirrors in which the player can present aspects

---

[14] There may be reasons why you do want them set in stone, though, such as how they're rendered visually.

[15] Specialising later is the preferred option if you feel you *must* have fixed builds. Adding an extra dimension of "race" is a weaker approach, mainly because there are invariably gameplay-favoured combinations.

of themself, analysing what they see. For identity, they pick up on what they like and don't like about their reflection; for identification, they only pick up on how much they believe it.

To encourage immersion, then, designers need to have the target ideals fall away. They do this by giving the player opportunities to decide for themself which way to take their character. These can be guided initially, but will need to become increasingly more flexible. Whether this is achieved by giving the player new skills, gear or content depends on the virtual world, but it does need to happen. It's not simply a case of "tutorial over"; the choices must be genuine and must be staged such that players can't strive to reach an abstract ideal that will almost certainly not match their concrete ideal-self.

16.5 SELF-DETERMINATION

If players are to determine who they are for themselves, certain conditions have to be met by the virtual world's design. Fortunately, Psychology has a theory for this: *self-determination theory* (Deci & Ryan, 1985). This states that people have three essential psychological needs:

- **Autonomy**. The freedom to act, to have choice in decisions that affect you, to direct your life, and to do what you want to do. It's why players prize freedom and open-endedness.

- **Competence**. The ability to control outcomes, to be effective, and to achieve mastery in what you do. It underpins the concept of challenge in virtual worlds.

- **Relatedness**. Interacting with, connecting with, and caring for others. It makes personal expression possible and validates your progress.

Affording players these needs in the right places will help them become immersed (or, to adopt the language of the theory, help them to determine their self). Getting in the way will interfere with immersion. So:

- Anything that takes away control of the player's character is bad for autonomy and therefore for immersion. Examples include cut scenes,[16] walls to railroad where you can move, false choices, and giving characters self-awareness to protect them from player stupidity.[17] Particularly bad is forcing them to run a solo instance controlling a story character.[18] Consent has to be freely given for any of this to be acceptable.

- Anything that prevents players from being effective is bad for autonomy and therefore for immersion. Examples include: messing with the interface (to show that your character is intoxicated, say); having a one-mistake-and-start-over series of difficult

---

[16] What's good for immersing you in a story isn't necessarily good for immersing you in your character.

[17] "It's too dangerous to do that" and the like.

[18] *FFXIV* revels in this. If you can maintain a connection to your own character, though, for example by having them driving a vehicle with different abilities to their own (rather than putting them in charge of an NPC with those abilities), the ill effects can be mitigated.

jump puzzles; and asking the player to operate a vehicle without letting them (or giving them time enough to) reassign its controls.

- Anything that stops players from interacting with others is bad for relatedness and therefore for immersion. Solo instances and transient pick-up groups are classic examples, but empty wildernesses and hubs where everyone else is either a bot or conversing entirely in guild chat are also not uncommon. Perhaps worst of all is when other people's self-expression breaks the virtual world's plausibility for you.[19]

Self-determination theory isn't entirely about immersion, so I'll side-track here for a few moments. People have needs in general, therefore if a virtual world isn't delivering then they'll seek to satisfy their needs using other means. In other words, if you frustrate players' needs then they'll either stop playing or start venting their frustration on other players. You'll therefore probably want to address their needs regardless of the effect on immersion.

The general situations in which players will find their needs frustrated are given as follows (Ballou & Deterding, 2023):

- **Autonomy**: Their desired play style is constrained; their ability to play is constrained; they feel compelled to play.[20]

- **Competence**: They feel their experience is stagnant and going nowhere; they are thwarted by unfair situations; they're called upon to do things they regard as meaningless.

- **Relatedness**: They feel disconnected from other players, from communities, and from the virtual world.

Note that this works in the opposite direction, too – and powerfully so. Self-determination theory is not restricted to virtual worlds: people's needs when they're not playing can also be frustrated; what's more, they can often fulfil those needs *by playing games* (Ballou, 2023), including virtual worlds. This implies that if your virtual world openly offers players the prospect of addressing needs that are frustrated elsewhere in their lives, they will be drawn to it. When players talk about "escapism", this is often what they mean.

We'll return to self-determination theory in Chapter 18, as it can be used to categorise certain player behaviours.

16.6 DEMOTING REALITY

To persuade players that a virtual world is a valid reality, it is given behaviours and properties that resemble those of Reality. Graphics and sound effects are examples of this in action. Speech is, too – if the voice matches the character. If it doesn't, the discordance will

---

[19] If I want to believe that the virtual world is a gritty, medieval fantasy environment, that won't be easy when people are wearing outfits that say otherwise. I don't recall Tolkien having characters wearing chicken, pig, donkey, sheep, or duckling masks in *The Lord of the Rings*, but *LotRO* has them.

[20] Daily quests fall into this category. They don't affect immersion directly, but they can harm autonomy.

break immersion. You may have been looking at a gorgeous space-elf babe, but if it speaks as if it was raised in Australia and smokes 40 cigarettes a day, the illusion could be hard to maintain. Adding drops of Reality to the virtual makes the virtual less virtual-real and more Reality-real. Keep on adding drops, and eventually, it becomes too much to ignore: when this happens, the virtual is completely lost to the real.

Players can tolerate a certain amount of Reality in their virtual worlds, but that doesn't mean it's OK to have it. I can tolerate a certain amount of background noise when I'm working, but ideally wouldn't want any at all. Even people who like some background noise while they're working would draw the line at the point which, for them, it became foreground noise.[21]

As an analogy, imagine a player's model of a virtual world to be a fully inflated balloon. Reality is a knitting needle. The balloon can withstand a certain amount of pressure from the knitting needle, but if you keep pushing then eventually it's going to puncture and burst. Similarly, players can shrug off a certain amount of intrusion from Reality, but if the overall pressure is too great then at some point the whole conceit collapses. Immersion is impossible under such circumstances. Designers should therefore aim to keep Reality out of their virtual worlds as much as possible if they wish to encourage immersion.

Obviously, it's not the case that *all* aspects of Reality must be shut out. The player needs to understand the virtual world, and a great deal of that understanding derives from their understanding of Reality. I'm not suggesting that gravity should be a repelling force rather than an attracting one, for example. Rather, it's those motes of Reality that have no business being in the virtual world that I'm proposing should be avoided. It's like when you're watching a TV show and get a glimpse of a boom mike: it breaks the spell.

In *World of Warcraft*, there's a giant statue of a goblin standing on Janeiro's Point in Booty Bay, its arms outstretched.[22] It's a reference to the statue of Christ the Redeemer in Rio de Janeiro. I'm sure that whichever designer decided to put it there did so in the expectation that players would find it amusing and perhaps feel a little self-satisfied for having noticed it. It breaks immersion, though. It establishes a connection between Azeroth and Earth that has no basis to it. It tells the player that this is not a stand-alone world.

It's not just this statue. *WoW* is relentless in its references to Reality. Quest names are routinely inspired by extradiegetic turns of phrase that have little or nothing to do with the virtual world itself. Every one of them reminds the player that they're playing a game. These are so frequent that they can't even be passed off as *Easter eggs*: players don't have to seek them out, they're *right there*, unsubtly, in your face.

Pop culture references are particularly bad in this respect. They not only hurt immersion in and of themselves, but they age so poorly that players can find themselves picking up on the fact that they *are* a reference but not knowing what they're a reference *to* – they have to stop playing to look it up. It was a nice gesture when in 2019 *WoW* added a character called Stanley who says "Excelsior!", but anyone who was aged eight when they did

---

[21] I recall when my niece's husband, who is deaf, retreated from a wedding disco because the music was so loud he could feel it through the floor.
[22] Its left arm was knocked off in the *Cataclysm* expansion.

it would not necessarily get the reference upon playing the game aged 18. I'm not even going to explain it here: if you don't get it, my point is made. *Star Trek Online* contains a memorial to deceased members of the TV show's cast, which is respectful and poignant, but would be like finding a monument on Earth listing the actors who played Zeus, Hera, Ares, Athena, Poseidon, Apollo, and Artemis in ancient Greece.

WoW wasn't the first MMO to add pop culture references to virtual worlds, it merely established the practice as a norm and then went overboard with it. Examples are easy to find elsewhere. There's a character in *Dofus* (Bourgain, 2004) called Chip Endale. *Tibia* has a shopkeeper called Al Dee. There's a shout skill in *Guild Wars* named "I'll Be Back!". *Wizard101* (Coleman et al., 2008) has a Page Jimmy in Abbey Road who wants his axe, a Lesser Paul. *Blade & Soul* (Park et al., 2016) has a bear called Yo Gi. In *Lost Ark*, an NPC called Nison has a quest for you to find his daughter, Grace, [23] who has been abducted by slavers. Those are just random examples from the MMOs in question – they all have dozens, if not hundreds (or in *WoW*'s case, even thousands), of allusions to elements of Reality.

If the references give no indication that they *are* a reference and are sufficiently obscure that most people won't spot anything unusual, the damage to immersion is slight (although still present). For example, in *The Lord of the Rings Online*, there's a tavern called The Bird and Baby, which might strike players as an oddish name, but that's taverns for you; it's a nod, however, to the Cambridge pub, The Eagle and Child, where a group of academics/writers called the Inklings used to meet. One of its members was J. R. R. Tolkien, hence the allusion to it in *LotRO*. Other Inklings are also referenced in the names of NPCs there, to confirm that the connection was made deliberately. Even that isn't always necessary, though.[24]

You're pretty safe if the reference is more likely to be noticed when the player isn't actually playing. *Final Fantasy XIV* has characters called Biggs and Wedge, which aren't particularly out of place for the world – they appear in earlier games in the franchise. Most players would assume that the names were to do with the characters' respective sizes and move on. However, if you were later watching *Star Wars* and noticed that the only two X-wing pilots to survive the runs on the Death Star trenches along with Luke Skywalker were called Biggs Darklighter and Wedge Antilles, the true reason for their names would be revealed – yet in a way that wouldn't break your immersion.[25]

You're also good if you do have extradiegetic references, but the players have to seek them out consciously. For example, in *RuneScape*, there's a volcano you can use for forging certain items; if you take a gold ring there, a goblin appears that says "My Precious!!! NOOOOO!!!". The thing is, few people are going to take a gold ring there by accident – the ones that do are actively *looking* for a Mount Doom reference. *RuneScape* duly obliges,

---

[23] *Lost Ark* does endeavour to keep some of its references subtle, although it still can't resist packing them in. Here, for example, players may remember that in the film *Taken* (Taken, 2008), Liam Neeson plays a character whose daughter is abducted by human traffickers. They may not so easily recall that the kidnappee is played by Maggie Grace.

[24] London's bank in *The Secret World* is called Bartleby & Daughters. This has that slight aspect of strangeness that pervades much of *TSW*: the sense that the unusual is the usual. Whether the name of this bank is a reference to me or not (my children are both daughters) is never hinted at; I've been told informally that it is, but I am sufficiently in vain that I'm not going to ask formally in case I find out it isn't.

[25] Not in *FFXIV*, anyway. It might disrupt the attention you were paying to the movie, though.

but without breaking immersion because the player has already made that decision for themselves. This kind of traditional Easter Egg is fine so long as it's rare enough that players won't consider it to be part of the game (and yes, that does mean you can't give contextual in-world rewards for one).

Why do virtual world designers like to put in immersion-busting cultural references?

Well, many players profess to like them. They may not like the *consequences* of having them, but they don't look ahead that far. It can relieve the monotony to encounter a quest with a name that puns on that of a movie, but as a designer, you might want to ask why your virtual world is monotonous in the first place. If you're hoping that players will want to pick up the next quest to find out what jocular title it has, you're *really* in trouble.

One of the main reasons for the preponderance of pop culture references in MMOs is that some lowly level-designer was tasked with creating a minor piece of content and lacked either the time or the imagination to do it justice. You need to create a quest to kill a prehistoric wild boar. What do you call it? "Kill the prehistoric wild boar"? Oh, wait! Last night you watched a movie! Well, "Jurassic Pork" it is, then!

Pop culture references also seem to abound when a virtual world is translated from one language to another. Translators typically have little time to find new names for characters, skills, quests, or items that have no direct equivalent in the target language, so they choose ones from films, books, TV shows, sports – anything that gets it done quickly. There is some actual theory here, by the way: the idea is that by putting in pop culture references meaningful to people who speak the target language, players will feel more connected to the virtual world than if it was all from another culture. This may indeed be true, but the resulting onslaught can be exhausting.

Although occasional harmless references to the world beyond the virtual are often appreciated, having them as a matter of policy is another matter. The designer ends up scraping the bottom of the barrel for puns and other bad jokes, or getting an AI to do the scraping on their behalf. MMOs that skimp on such acontextual cultural references, such as *Elder Scrolls Online*, *The Secret World*, and *New World*, are usually perceived by players to be more immersive than the ones that don't (in particular *WoW*).

Although this may seem as if I'm criticising *WoW* and its clones here, that's only because the topic currently under discussion concerns the encouragement of immersion. If you don't want to encourage immersion, gambling that putting out a more superficial vibe will attract more players and so be more profitable in the long term, that's fine. Don't expect that you'll be able to prise players away from an extant virtual world that's taking the same approach, though.

Quality-of-life improvements are also often obstacles to immersion. The more that players get used to them, the less of a problem they become (at least in terms of immersion), but anything that basically says "we'll make the world make less sense so as to save you some bother" is undermining immersion. For example, the ability to change the appearance of your outfit so it looks as if you're wearing something else is great for character customisation, but even with the fictional cover of calling it "transmogrification" or "glamour magic", a bikini-clad tank is not really going to look the part. This is even a problem in *The Secret World*, where transmogrification isn't a thing because clothing means nothing and all the magic is in the small, discreet talismans that characters carry: have bikini, will tank.

From this, it can be seen that players are often their own worst enemies. They want to become immersed but they also want to display to other players, so may wear outlandish outfits or give themselves clever names every bit as immersion-breaking as you'd expect. They want people to treat them as if they were cool, sassy hunters, but communicate using their own voices and completely shatter this possibility (unless they actually *sound* cool, sassy, and hunterly, which I suppose some must).

The anti-immersive effects of adding voice to virtual worlds were known from the outset (Bartle, 2003), but players still wanted it. Then, when they got it, they complained that virtual worlds weren't as immersive as they used to be. Who'd have thought?

This is ultimately the conclusion reached by Nick Yee in his book, *The Proteus Paradox* (Yee, 2014). We want all the wonderful benefits that virtual worlds can offer, but we bring too much Reality into them to allow it. I'm not quite as pessimistic as Nick, because I believe that the problems virtual worlds face in this regard are cultural rather than systemic; it might take a new generation to overcome them, though.

16.7 INTEREST AND BOREDOM

Although the understanding of immersion used in Koenitz's model of interactive digital narrative doesn't apply to virtual worlds long-term, that doesn't mean it has nothing to say short-term. If a virtual world lacks the ability to create and hold interest, it's not going to lead to identity immersion. There must be something happening moment-to-moment that drives the player's personal story[26] (or at least holds the promise that it will, once it's out of the way); otherwise, the player's mind will wander and the virtual world may as well not exist. A certain amount of mind-wandering is a good thing, so long as the player's conscious thoughts snap back to the virtual world at the end of it: it means the player is confident enough in their virtual existence that they can employ their imagination without putting immersion at risk. If they're not interested in what they're doing in the virtual world, though, they'll snap back to Reality: the virtual world has then become something they are doing for reasons other than fun, and it has to be thought about from without as opposed to from within.

Interest moves towards immersion; boredom moves away from it. It's no coincidence that what Figure 11.1 depicts is called the player *interest* graph. That said, there's more to it than simply noting that (say) Achievers want to achieve, therefore they should be given a goal to achieve and some way of achieving it. Simply telling them that they have to walk from A to B gives them a goal, but if it's an uneventful journey with no obstacles to overcome then the player won't feel they've really achieved anything.

---

[26] If it's not apparent what I mean by this phrase, it will become so in Volume II. I hope.

Game worlds need *gameplay*: that which emerges by means of charting a course through the constraints and possibilities of the game's mechanics to achieve the player's goals.[27] If an MMO has gameplay and the course being charted needs correcting frequently enough that it remains in the player's thoughts then the player can engage in whatever activity they currently find fun. If, however, the regularity of the player's actions on and interactions with the virtual world and its players are infrequent, the player will direct their thoughts to other matters and lose interest. Conversely, if the frequency of events is so intense that the player spends all their time reacting rather than acting, that will also interfere with their progress. A balance is needed, but players have different ideas as to where the fulcrum should be. As is often the case in virtual world design, then, the best way to handle this is to allow the player to choose whatever level of involvement suits them best at the time. This is why people like side quests in game worlds.[28]

Social worlds don't have gameplay by design, so the situation is different for them. Their players need to have a wide range of possible activities available from which to choose what to do next. They're not charting a course through constraints and possibilities to achieve their goals: they're selecting activities that deliver their goals from a buffet of them. In practice, they'll narrow their options at a high level then drill down to find what they want – a bit like a person might do who is looking for a new novel to read or a film to watch. It's quite easy to get stuck in a rut, though, which can lead to listlessness and ennui. Ennui is also an enemy of immersion. The balance that designers of social worlds have to maintain is between discreetly presenting players with opportunities that might interest them and overwhelming them with such an abundance of options that they struggle to decide which to take.[29]

Although ennui presents problems for immersion, frustration doesn't unless it's profound enough that the player either has to stop and look up what they're doing wrong or rage-quits because this was the last straw. The main sources of frustration in virtual worlds are:

- The player is asked to do something that they aren't sufficiently competent to do.

- The player is asked to do something that they may be competent to do, but they're not sure because it's explained badly.

- The player strongly wants to do something but it's not on offer.

- The player can't get to grips with the virtual world's interface.

- The player made one tiny mistake and has to repeat a long and laborious series of actions to get back to the point where they hope they won't make it next time.

- The player can't believe how stupid the players they're playing with are.

---

[27] For your convenience and mine, I copied and- pasted this from the definition in Chapter 5.
[28] Well, alongside the loot and progress points they get from them, anyway.
[29] This is called *choice overload* (Iyengar & Lepper, 2000), or, if you prefer your terms to rhyme, *analysis paralysis*.

The designer can't do much about the last one of these, but can address the others. At the very least, strongly hinting in advance that what the player is about to attempt may be beyond them is a good idea. This is why many graphical MMOs colour-code mobs' identifiers relative to the player.[30]

In short, then, whatever the virtual world, it needs content if it's to be immersive. Too much content is much better than too little, but it has to be structured such that it's not equivalent to asking a player to choose their favourite snowflake in a snowstorm, and if players are about to shoot past something on their to-do list, they should be warned before it disappears from their radar.

16.8 FLOW

I've already discussed the concept of *presence*, which is occasionally conflated with immersion. We know that the two are not the same, because immersion stacks and presence doesn't: you can be immersed in a virtual world, go off on a daydream about the last time you were wandering through this leafy area as a greenhorn adventurer, then return to awareness and you're still in the virtual world. If you're already experiencing presence, adding further presence will either extend[31] or replace[32] it. You won't double it up. Presence enables immersion, but isn't itself immersion.

Another concept that's related to and often conflated with immersion is that of *flow* (Csikszentmihalyi, 1975). Flow is a zen-like state that people can get into when they're doing a task that's neither too hard nor too easy. They don't have to get into it, but they can.

To get into a flow state, four conditions must be met:

- There must be clear goals, so that rules and expectations are easy to grasp.

- There must be direct and immediate feedback, so that success and failure can quickly be recognised.

- The task must involve concentration and focus, so that people can delve deep into a limited field of attention.

- There must be a balance between ability and challenge, so that the task is never too easy nor too difficult.

Once an individual is in a state of flow, there are four main effects:

- They have a sense of personal control, in that what's happening is the result of their actions.

- They lose self-consciousness, in that their actions merge with their awareness.

---

[30] This way, they only frustrate those players who can't tell red from green.
[31] For example, you were controlling your character, but now your character is driving a mech so you extend your sense of presence to the mech.
[32] For example, you switch to an alt.

- They find the activity intrinsically rewarding and effortless.

- They have a distorted sense of time, which seems to pass quickly.

Most gamers will recall having experienced the last of these conditions, looking at the clock half an hour after they last looked at it and discovering that two hours have passed.

Players enjoy being in flow, and designers can encourage them to enter the state by addressing its four entry requirements:

- Make clear the options that are available.

- Ensure that when the player does something, they immediately know if it's worked or not.

- Arrange for continued play to uncover depths rather than merely increase details.

- Allow the player to find their own sweet spot between challenge and reward.

The last of these, which designers call *balance*, is the hardest to manage. In single-player games, you can do it by giving the player the opportunity to adjust the difficulty level, but that's inadvisable in virtual worlds.[33] What one player finds easy, another player may find impossible.

Through balance, flow links to fun in games. Both use the same inputs: skills and challenge. Both have a sweet spot in the middle: flow and fun. If your skills exceed the challenge, in flow terms, this leads to boredom; if the challenge exceeds your skills, it leads to frustration. You can look at games the same way: over-skilled for the challenge means the game is *no fun*; under-skilled for it means it's *unfun*. This isomorphism is illustrated in Figure 16.1.

You'll note that the axes on the graph in Figure 16.1 have no units. I'm not going to criticise it for this (after all, the player interest graph in Figure 11.1 has no units either): the point the graph is making is to do with relative values, not absolute ones, so all you need to know is which direction means "more" and which means "less".

Figure 16.1 only applies to one person at a time, though. If we compare your graph of flow with mine, and especially if we compare your idea of game balance with mine, there could well be differences. Some people enjoy games that are very difficult: for them, the angle of the fun band could be 60° compared to the median's 45. Others like games to be more relaxing, casual affairs: for them, the angle of the channel could be 30°. This difference doesn't matter for flow, but it does matter for fun. It's one reason why games that feature dynamic difficulty adjustment have issues – they don't know how stiff a test the player wishes to face moment-to-moment unless the player tells them – in which case, there's no need to adjust the difficulty dynamically, it can be set to exactly what the player wants and left at that.

---

[33] You can try it if you like, but if you do then expect pushback from those Attainers who don't leave in disgust. It works for instances where rewards can be increased for higher difficulty levels, but for open play, it's a much harder proposition.

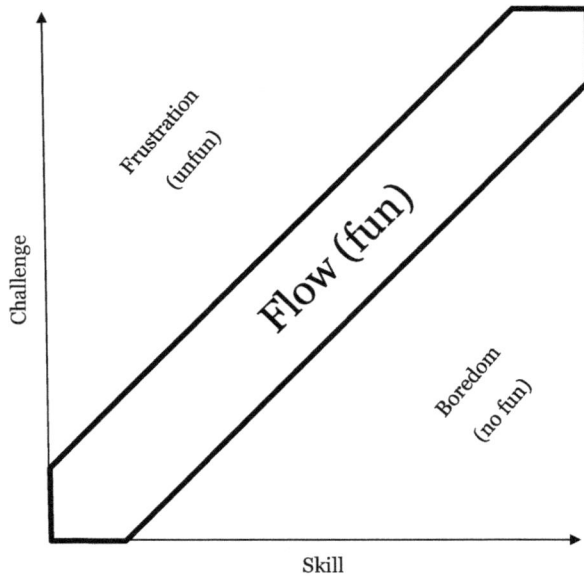

FIGURE 16.1   Flow and balance.

Flow is definitely fun, but it's not all there is to fun. In particular, you can already be having fun before you go into a flow state. Neither is flow just a fancy term that psychologists use instead of immersion: flow, like presence, doesn't stack. You can't be in a state of flow and then go into another state of flow, it's binary; however, you can be immersed in one thing and then become immersed in something else *while remaining immersed in the first thing.*

Of course, although immersion itself is fun, that doesn't mean fun is immersion, either. The kind of fun people have playing virtual worlds is reflected by how immersed they are, but fun goes way beyond virtual worlds, and even beyond games and play. Sitting on a bench on a cold winter's day watching passers-by on the other side of the road slip on the ice is fun.[34] Flow and immersion are both sufficient for fun, but neither are necessary for fun – especially in virtual worlds.

---

[34] Er, for some people. I, of course, would never amuse myself at the misfortune of others when I could easily shout a warning to help them avoid said misfortune.

CHAPTER 17

Applying Player Types

HAVING EXPLAINED AT SOME length what player types are, how they hold together, and why they're of use, the small matter of how actually to use them remains. There are more ways to misuse them than there are to use them, and they're not the only categorisations available – others may be more appropriate for your needs. You don't have to use any of them, of course: virtual worlds in the first four Ages got along just fine without such theory-based assistance.

Anyway, let's look at how to use player types in practice.

17.1 USING PLAYER TYPES

As I mentioned earlier, my primary goal when I first wrote about player types was to persuade the designers of virtual worlds that there *are* player types: such worlds are not for players who all find fun the same way. The most basic use of player types is therefore merely to acknowledge that they exist. One might have thought that this was obvious anyway but, as the vast sums squandered on the creation of wannabe-Metaverse platforms in 2021–2022 amply demonstrated, this is not the case. Some very well-funded product designers coming from outside the game-development industry[1] have no idea that there are any theories at all, let alone whether they might apply to their work or not.

You do know about player types, though, so I don't have to worry about that here.

Now, even if you're not taken by the theory behind player types (or believe that it doesn't apply in your one, particular, special, unique case), it can still serve as a sanity check in the early stages of the design process. Does a brief look at the virtual world as-envisaged suggest ways that players can have different kinds of fun? If so, you can check the checkbox and either forget about player types thereafter or take them further; if not, don't invest any of your own money in the project.

---

[1] The game-development industry is aware of player types, because the theory is widely known by developers.

Some designers like to put together a suite of imaginary-but-representative players to deploy in use cases[2] following Cooper (1999). The virtual world's target audience (as defined by the product's business requirements) is taken as a basis to identify archetypal pseudo-players; player types are then assigned to constructed examples of each important demographic group, and small, potted biographies created for imaginary individuals in said groups. These can subsequently be referred to (usually by character name) to make sure that the players they are stand-ins for will find the game fun.[3] There are plenty of examples online of use-case biography templates,[4] but see the sidebar for an example of an MMO-specific one. Note that some of its fields aren't actually *needed* for the use case (we don't care what the player's occupation is, for example), but they do help in designing the pseudo-player.[5]

USE CASE EXAMPLE

Name[6]:   Jake Blake
Player Type: Attainer
Summary: Returning ex-player
Picture:

Demographics

Age:	31
Gender:	Male (heterosexual)
Education:	BSc Computer Science, tier 2 university
Occupation:	Programmer
Family:	Married to Chloë for three years
	Daughter Olivia (six months)
Location:	Columbus OH, USA
Backstory:	Jake is a jaded contract programmer who has grown tired of constantly having to work under pressure. The recent birth of his first child has caused him to re-evaluate his life and he's currently looking for a less stressful position. He started playing MMOs because following marriage he didn't feel part of the old gang any more.

---

[2] I suspect that the ready availability of AI diffusion models to create images of imaginary people may have increased their popularity.

[3] They can also be co-opted for other purposes, such as ensuring that accessibility and identity-politics issues are addressed, but in general, it's better to keep use cases for different uses separate.

[4] These are often referred to as *personas*, an idea introduced in Cooper (1999). This is annoying for two reasons: (1) virtual world designers already have a specific meaning for the term; (2) the plural of *persona* is *personae*.

[5] They also help if you want to create a pseudo-player to masquerade as, should you so wish.

[6] I like to make my use-case character names rhyme to remind me that the individual to whom they're attached is made-up, but it's not a requirement.

Long-Term Goals:
Wants to experience the independence he lost when he married.
Immediate Goals:
Wants to relax while advancing through content with friendly people.
Wants to join a decent guild that isn't obsessed with raiding.
Quote: "Gaah! What have they done to fireballs?"

Personality

Big Five[7]:

Openness	1	2	3	[4]	5
Conscientiousness	1	2	3	4	[5]
Extraversion	1	[2]	3	4	5
Agreeableness	1	2	3	[4]	5
Neuroticism	1	2	[3]	4	5

Stats[8]:

Strength	10
Intelligence	15
Wisdom	12
Constitution	9
Dexterity	11
Charisma	15

Alignment: Neutral good.
Quirks: Doesn't like slimy creatures.
               Wilfully walks under ladders.
Beliefs: Lapsed Episcopalian.
               Votes Democrat.

In-World

Main: Florella, level 70 female human mage.
Alts: Drangie, level 66 female human priest.
               Drixie, level 54 female demonic warlock.
               Pogalog, level 38 female dwarf fighter.
               Mookx, level 25 male goblin rogue.
History: Played regularly for two years then stopped when the new baby
               came along. He's now back, but is rusty and an expansion behind

---

[7] I describe the *big five* personality types in Chapter 18 (in another sidebar).

[8] This just needs to be something that everyone easily understands. I like to use *D&D* originals, but I'm a traditionalist.

the curve. The guild he was a member of has been dissolved, and most of his friends have moved on.

Frustrations: Worried that using voice communication will wake the baby. Mage spell rotations have changed, and he doesn't like the new ones.

Preferences

Fiction: Fantasy and Science Fiction, but not both in the same world. Isn't particularly interested in the details of lore or story.

Gameplay: Action combat, casual raiding.

Challenge: Generally likes it easier than most but willing to step up if necessary.

Payment: Doesn't mind paying to play but prefers a subscription model. Loathes pay-to-win with a passion.

Media: Doesn't watch much TV except when his wife recommends a streamed show to him. Occasionally watches movies on the big screen. Occasionally reads fiction but doesn't like thick books in multi-volume series. Social media use is restricted to Facebook and Discord. Regards YouTube as a time sink.

To test your virtual world's suitability for different player types, try to imagine what examples of each one will be doing in your virtual world. Even a superficial look is better than nothing, but ideally, you'd want to go deeper than that. Important: don't imagine what players of a particular type *could* be doing, imagine what they *will* be doing. A list of possible "well they can…" opportunities has little coherence and leaves the reasoning behind the players' actions unsaid; often, these will refer to advanced set-piece activities that players stand no chance of undertaking regularly.[9] Ask what the player will *actually* be doing in your virtual world for two or more hours every evening for the next few weeks. Try not to answer using a player type ("they'll be exploring"): try to be more specific ("they'll be completing all the side quests in the northern zone because they believe there's a structure to them that could be deliberate").

In general, it's better to check what players of different types will make of planned content *before* it's implemented rather than after. More focused sanity-checking using player types is useful for instances (although not necessarily elder-game raids) and for areas as a whole, but you need to be careful that you allocate the right fun to the right type. You might, for example, think that Explorers like finding obscure items, so hide little lore nuggets around the landscape for them to come across as they potter around; this is fine, Explorers *do* like to find these, but if beyond the satisfaction of coming across one you attach *any* permanent benefit to them whatsoever (such as experience points or skill increments – or even something as innocuous as showing in the player's public profile how many of them

---

[9] Only a non-disclosure agreement has spared you from my ranting for a page about a particular game I consulted on that was exactly like this. There were several exciting things the player *could* do, but they were going to quit from directionless boredom well before they got the opportunity to do them.

they've found) then Achievers will move in. They'll want to collect them all. It's important, therefore, not only to look at content and think "yes, this will please players of type X", but also to ask yourself "what will players not of type X make of it?". What's optional for one type may be essential (but tiresome) for another.

This is enough for most designers: having given their content ideas a quick health check, they can take it from there. Player types still have more to offer, though, in particular in relation to how players move through types as they develop. It's not simply a case of having content for all player types at all points in the virtual world: that can be very wasteful, as good content is expensive to create. There's little point in providing Opportunist content in high-end regions, for example. You need content that is primed for the players who will be in the particular area you're creating. If they're mainly going to be newbies, for example, then content specific to Opportunists (and to some extent Griefers, although you'll get those come what may) would be wise, with some slight onboarding for Networkers and Scientists depending on which direction the players want to drift. Later, as players progress through regions containing areas with progressively more sophisticated content, you'd need to fade out content for earlier types, address the types you're mainly going to see, then fade in content for the types that follow.

Designers will often handle this intuitively. They know that the regions for characters in the level 10–20 range will be more focused than in the 1–10 range, so will string more content together rather than having it be mindlessly skippable.[10] They'll start adding items that players will hold onto for a couple of weeks, rather than a couple of hours, with different properties, so the player has to think about which is best – or to ask or to experiment to find out. Towards the high end, they'll be offering the player longer-term goals and better social structures, so they can drift into the next phase of their development. As I said, this is usually something a competent designer will be doing anyway, but it's always a good idea to test your work no matter how experienced you are. Because the player type model is dynamic, it allows for sanity-checking player *progression*, which gives it an advantage over static models. That said, it's easy to pace progression wrong: player types give you the ordering, but not the timing. We'll be looking at pacing in Volume II, but don't get too excited: pacing is very hard to describe, let alone to get right.

Another use of player types is to predict (and sometimes to prevent) typical progression problems. Derailment does happen, but often it's less to do with design and more to do with the behaviour of other players; this makes it a community issue rather than a player type issue (we'll look at community in Chapter 19). A more relevant problem is when players don't start on rails in the first place, either because they're not playing for fun or they are playing for fun but have situated it in the wrong place. Griefers are of particular concern, because of the disproportionate effect they have on other players. If a player starts out as an Opportunist and believes that doing what Opportunists do is what the game is about, it's not too hard to lead them to more refined content that they have to analyse or to ask about

---

[10] It's fine to skip it, but if the player is to form some sense of how they want to progress then they should at least have to think about *why* they're skipping it.

in order to progress; you can put them back on track, in other words. If a player starts out as a Griefer and believes that doing what Griefers do is what the game is about, that's much harder to counter. Players can still progress, but they take their Griefer mindset with them, leading to toxicity if it happens by default.

Such players need to be educated into the ways of the virtual world.[11] Exposure to vastly more experienced players will usually set them straight, but these two groups rarely mix naturally. They can be forced to mix (for example, by requiring that guilds have a certain percentage of low-level active members), but players don't like being forced to do anything – it strikes at their sense of autonomy. Mentoring systems can help to some degree, too, although they have problems of their own when the wrong people become mentors. *FFXIV*'s policy of putting group content on its main quest line, with rewards for high-level players who drop down to engage with it (which most of them do), does seem to work – *if* you like group content. Even interacting with alts can help convey the virtual world's culture to those Griefers who don't yet get what the game is about. Culture is passed from one generation to the next: if you don't encourage the generations to mix, don't be surprised if they come to believe different things about what your virtual world *is*.

The point I'm making here is that if you know that people might not start off on the right track, you can do something about it. If you don't know that there's even a track they should be following (but aren't) then finding a solution is much harder.

Another problem with Griefers is that they might enjoy griefing so much that they don't want to advance. It's as if they went to a restaurant and *really* liked the soup, so they ordered soup for every course. They do know what's expected of them, but boy, that soup is *so good*! To address this kind of problem, the player must experience negative consequences to sticking where they are, such as diminishing returns (basically, you add more and more salt to their soup until they don't like it any more). If griefing loses its intrinsic value to the player,[12] they'll either move on or quit; either way, you lose a Griefer, which is presumably your aim here. Players can also refuse to move on from other points in their playing career, of course, but this isn't something designers typically need to worry about; being denied the possibility of moving on when they want to is the greater problem for players (which largely affects Friends and Sages, for closure reasons explained earlier).

One of the uses first identified for player types, which I also explained earlier, was to balance a virtual world that has too many players of one type. This isn't at all practical at scale, because it takes too long. If you try to do it in one fell swoop, you'll get immediate fallout that you'll need to have prepared for in advance. Unfortunately, I can't really give any advice on how you might go about that, except to say you should begin to manage expectations well in advance. Look at *Star Wars Galaxies*' New Game Enhancements and *World of Warcraft*'s *Cataclysm* expansion and don't do what they did. Balancing or rebalancing is an

---

[11] There's an argument that players can play any game how they damned well please, so however they are playing is the "right" way by definition (Sicart, 2014). This argument may hold for single-player or small-group games, but for virtual worlds, a certain level of adherence to the magic circle is a necessity.

[12] Weirdly, as we'll see later, you could in theory achieve this by paying players to grief.

easier proposition for small-scale virtual worlds, but it still isn't easy; also, the results aren't seen immediately, so it's difficult in the short term to tell if they've worked or not.

Another use of player types that works better on a small scale than a large one is the handling of inter-player conflict. This is less of a design issue and more of an operational one. When they have thousands of players to watch over, CSRs are unable to get to know everyone; they're overstretched anyway and don't have enough time to consider all the reasons that people do what they do. CSR attention at the personal level was a lot easier to provide in MUDs that only had a few hundred players; in much larger virtual worlds, individualised player management is now generally done by the players themselves. Guild leaders in MMOs can resolve a good many conflicts before CSRs even see them, including sometimes those between guilds. They're no use for people who are guildless, though. Also, although CSRs can look at player types and figure out what's going on, guild leaders are usually Politicians still following their own path, who would have to progress to see the full picture – at which point they wouldn't want to be a guild leader. For this reason, guild leaders are more likely to rely on their people-person skills to resolve conflicts, which frankly is probably a better idea than using player types anyway.

Finally, it's worth pointing out that player types are somewhat obfuscated when players habitually play in teams. If the player attaches their identity to the group more than to their character, this can moderate their progression; essentially, the group progresses rather than the player. This behaviour is more common in cultures of the Far East, and its implications for player types are unknown.[13] It could be that some kind of group types model may be more appropriate.

Overall, then, player types are useful for setting designers off on the right track and for checking content balance at different stages of players' progression. That's pretty well about it from a practical standpoint. Their greater value is perhaps in helping designers understand their players, particularly *why they play*. The benefits of this are not felt in immediate, measurable ways, but in the long term, they produce a greater impact.

As for non-designers, player types can be used for analysing virtual worlds. This doesn't happen much in an academic context, where researchers are more interested in applying theories from other disciplines than they are in applying ones that designers actually use, but occasionally players with a sideline in game criticism will use it. J1mmy (2024)[14] is a good example of this, applying player types to *Brighter Shore* (Gower, 2024); the treatment of Killers isn't quite right, but (as we're about to see) that isn't exactly uncommon.

17.2 MISUSING PLAYER TYPES

Content in the well-received MMO *WildStar* was created specifically around the concept of player types, associating each one with what it called a *path*. The game wasn't the success it was expected to be, though. Much of this was to do with its hardcore attitude, unforgiving gameplay, over-similar classes, emphasis on gear in PvP, grouping requirements,

---

[13] Unknown by me, anyway. There may be whole bodies of work on this subject in languages I don't understand.
[14] I've no idea who J1mmy is; this is what happens when people produce videos using their YouTuber name.

reward systems, raid-attunement grind, empty feel,[15] and preponderance of bugs; however, it's worth asking why its use of player types didn't pan out.

> Bartle's breaks it down to four – you've got your killer, you've got your socialiser, you've got your explorer and your achiever. The trick there is that it applies to Paths, kind of. But Killer under Bartle's is a griefer, you get your jollies on mucking with people, ruining other people's game. We don't do that, that is not a game style that we want to cater to, we want those people in other people's games.
>
> Also, almost everybody's an Achiever to some level. So what we did was break achievement up into three different areas – collecting, combat achievement like getting better and better at fighting, and also the building style thing, the building up type of achievement.
>
> *Jeremy Gaffney, executive producer of WildStar interviewed in Meer (2011).*

So what happened was they gave players predefined paths (rails) to follow that didn't account for changes in type as the player progressed. They didn't give Griefers a path because they didn't want Griefers.[16] They split Achievers into three by content preference, causing them frustration because their preference was to do all three.

All this was fixable, but sadly the game's other problems (which were also fixable, if there hadn't been so many of them) sank it. This was a shame, because there was a lot of love for *WildStar* and what it was trying to accomplish.

At least the designers of *WildStar* understood player types; their mistake was that they didn't understand their adaptation of it. Most of the mistakes people make when they use player types come from either a misunderstanding or a complete lack of understanding of them.

Here are some of the most common misapplication errors:

- **Not Looking Beyond the Graph.** "There's a Killer player type, so that means we need PvP". No: PvP is competitive content, which is primarily for Achievers.

- **Giving One Type the Reward Desired by Another Type.** Socialisers don't want XP every time they socialise – and if they got it, Achievers would then feel they'd have to go through the motions of socialising to get it, too.[17]

- **Unknowingly Pushing the Theory Beyond Its Limits.** If you think it applies as-is to games in general, you're mistaken. More on this in the next section.

---

[15] Ironically, caused by having such good housing that no one needed to leave their houses to use most facilities.

[16] They got them anyway, they just followed other paths and leveraged those for their griefing ways.

[17] At primary school, we got a gold star if we did very well, a silver star if we did fairly well, and a star of a block colour (red, yellow, green, or blue) if we did OK. Some children didn't want gold or silver stars: they wanted stars the same colour as their friend's star. A gold star was like giving an Achiever reward to a Socialiser.

- **Knowingly Pushing the Theory Beyond Its Limits Then Forgetting You've Done So**. If you use it for regular games as an analogy ("these players act like explorers, so let's treat them as if they were"), you need to remember that an analogy is what it is. Water pipes, pumps, and valves make a great analogy for electrical circuitry until you cut a wire and all the electricity doesn't pour out of it.

- **Adapting It for a Specialist Use But Not Fully Understanding the Adaptation**. This was *WildStar*'s problem, but they weren't alone in it: pretty well the whole field of Gamification[18] did the same thing. We'll be taking a glance at gamification in the next section, too.

- **Not Looking Beyond Four Types**. Sure, you might only need the four original types, but at least check out the eight types so you can ascertain whether sticking with four is appropriate for your needs. Maybe expanding Killers into Griefers and Politicians but keeping Achievers, Explorers, and Socialisers unexpanded would work for you.

Note that player types could be close enough to what you want that it's fine to misuse them. I've misused shoes as hammers. I did *know* I was misusing them, though.

You've read this far, so I assume that you do understand player types. I've mainly included this section not because I expect you to make mistakes yourself, but because you'll see plenty of misuses out in the wild. If you're teaching people about player types, it's important that you apprise them of the most common errors, so they don't make the same mistakes themselves.

I once examined a PhD thesis, the main finding of which was that Killers were mischaracterised. They were – but by the candidate. Every player type was examined through the lens of Achiever, because the candidate was an Achiever and saw everything through an Achiever's eyes. It was an excellent thesis otherwise, so the candidate still passed, but this just goes to show that even the smartest among us can slip up when it comes to player types. Unless you're a designer, and therefore outside the framework, you need to be very careful how you apply it.

17.3 OTHER APPLICATIONS

Formally, player types as a theory only works for people who play virtual worlds for fun. As I've already mentioned, I can't explain why it would work for anything else, so make no claims to that effect. It's great[19] if it *does* work for other applications, but there's no guarantee it will.[20] In those cases, it works in practice but not in theory, which is the inverse of the

---

[18] I generally capitalise the names of fields of research (Physics is the study of physics, Psychology is the study of psychology), so have done so here. Annoyingly, it's the only time I reference the field of Gamification (er, other than in this footnote), so it looks a bit like a typographical error. It's not, though: it's merely pedantry at its best.

[19] Great for me, anyway.

[20] Some researchers question whether it can even be extended to different categories of virtual world. "It may be reasonable to say that players of fantasy-themed multi-user virtual worlds form certain player typologies (Bartle, 1996), but it would be unsatisfactory to generalize this model without a consideration (through either primary or secondary data) of players in other game genres, or even within the fantasy genre" (Boellstorff et al., 2013).

usual way that fate frustrates theorists. Pretty well every application of player types beyond virtual worlds uses the four-type model, by the way: it's easy to explain,[21] easy to understand, easy to apply, and easy to propagate. It's also harder to see why it wouldn't apply....

17.3.1 Games in General

One of the major applications of player types beyond virtual worlds is that of games in general – typically computer games rather than board games or other kinds of game, but it could be anything. Also, it will usually be for games with more than two players, so the Socialiser type makes sense; again, though, this isn't always necessary. Finally, Killers are usually equated with a certain competitive style of Achiever play, griefing being less common when social sanctions can swiftly be imposed. No players are assumed to change type, which is fair enough as they don't play long enough for that to happen.

Player types have met with some success in this domain – sufficiently so that they're taught on university modules concerned with game design in general rather than with virtual world design in particular. There is an element of self-fulfilling prophecy to this, in that if you design your game around player types then you'll find that it attracts players who match those types, therefore the exercise will seem to have worked; even so, player types are used often enough in game design that if they didn't yield *some* benefit then people would have stopped teaching them years ago. It's also the case that studies of games that didn't use player types in their design still find a good alignment with them, for example Riegelsberger at al. (2007).

Besides, just because *I* can't demonstrate that player types work for games other than virtual worlds, that doesn't mean other people can't. I was at a conference in Magdeburg, Germany, in 2009, at which a PhD student, Monica Mayer, presented her work (Mayer, 2009)[22] on applying Psi-theory (Dörner, 1999)[23] to games. Psi-theory concerns how the structure of the human mind can be implemented computationally, such that cognitive systems assume a kind of homeostatic balance when presented with a dynamically changing environment. Mayer developed an executable model based on needs satisfaction that she ran within a Psi-theory framework. She determined from the results that there were four stable types of player; these mapped *exactly* onto player types. The key point here is that Mayer *hadn't heard of player types at the time*. Because she's a psychologist, player types hadn't shown up in her initial literature search any more than her work had shown up in my research; it was only after concluding her experiment that she discovered the match. What's more, her work *wasn't concerned with virtual worlds* but with computer games in general. This suggests that there is a connection of some substance between player

---

[21] I was once doing some consulting for a *Lord of the Rings* virtual world (later canned in pre-production for corporate-politics reasons) and one of the publisher executives started explaining my own theory to me. When I told him I'd come up with it, he continued with his explanation regardless – he was so keen to ensure I understood it.

[22] It's in German but there's a .pdf version that monoglots such as I can convert into English. The title translates as *Why Live when you can Play Instead?*

[23] There doesn't appear to be an English translation of this book, the title of which means *Blueprint for a Soul*. It's therefore the only work I reference herein that I haven't read but have merely read around.

types and games in general, if not quite at the level of what that connection is. As a bonus, Mayer's work also plugs a small hole in player type theory, in that she can explain how players change type over a single session, whereas I can only explain it over the long term.

Fortunately for me, I'd proposed player types over a decade earlier than Mayer, otherwise people would be calling them Mayer types, rather than Bartle types.

There is another vector by which player types could legitimately be applied to games that aren't virtual worlds, though.

Most of the tales studied by Campbell for the Hero's Journey aren't themselves entire journeys. The story of Actaeon and Artemis, for example, is an example of a failure of the Meeting with the Goddess step: it has no reference to any of the other steps. The same could be true of individual games: you selectively change the games you play as you develop as an individual. From a design perspective, explaining games in terms of player types could therefore fit into the same theory. It wouldn't be as easy as in virtual worlds, because the player doesn't have the constant of a character to use as their proxy self, but it's still eminently possible.

I wouldn't use this argument myself to justify the application of player types to non-MMORPG games, but I wouldn't dismiss the work of those who did, either.

17.3.2 Gamification

Another major use of player types beyond virtual worlds is in *gamification*. The idea behind gamification is that techniques from games can be used to help with situations that aren't themselves games, and indeed with life in general (McGonigal, 2011). The concept itself is an old one:

> In every job that must be done, there is an element of fun. You find the fun and – snap! The job's a game.
>
> *(Mary Poppins, 1964).*

Originally, designers used the term to mean turning something that was game-like into a game[24]; it came to mean turning something not a game into something game-like (that still wasn't a game). Formally, it involves putting game design patterns to non-game use.[25]

Although gamification can have its benefits (those apps telling you how many steps you've done today use gamification, for example), it was rapidly adopted by marketers and became something of a bandwagon in the 2010s. People were given points, badges, and places on leaderboards for the most mundane of tasks and it became exploitative.[26] As with advertising, though, if everyone is doing the same thing then no one pays attention; after much over-use, basic me-too gamification stopped delivering and the marketers looked

---

[24] When I suggested to Roy Trubshaw that we embed game elements into the physics of *MUD1*, the exact words I used were "we should gamify it".

[25] Informally, it involves using fun to bribe people to do something you want them to do.

[26] Much of it fell into the category of what game designers call *cheap psychological tricks*. We'll be discussing these in Chapter 23.

elsewhere for an edge. Application-specific, bespoke gamification remains eminently viable, though, and is truer to the original concept: *find* the fun – don't force-feed the user with activities that are fun in other contexts and hope they'll work for this one.

Player types became inveigled because people new to the idea of gamification were looking for a theory to help with it. Player types, as the most visible (or at least most easily understood) theory in the gamesphere, was picked up and tried out. It wasn't the only tool in the toolbox, as there are other categorisations (as we'll see in Chapter 18); however, it struck a chord. Other categorisations look at personality or activity or world view or interests, all of which are perfectly reasonable for their intended purposes. Player types look at what people find *fun*, though – the very ore that gamification seeks to mine. As a result of this, player types became part of gamification lore, to the extent that the Gamification Summit I attended in June 2012 gave each attendee one of four different tote bags representing the four player types. See Figure 17.1 if you find that difficult to believe (they're actually quite classy).

From my perspective, using player types for gamification purposes is akin to finding a book on how to run a farm and applying it to an aquarium. A lot of it may well actually work, but there are some rather important differences. Similar views were held by many of the more thoughtful gamification practitioners, who remained working in the area after the dilettantes had left. Player types were thereafter adapted for gamification use by people who knew what they were doing, as we'll see in Chapter 18.

17.3.3 Teaching

Related to gamification are *serious games*, the vast majority of which are concerned with teaching.[27] Games did not start out as an academically respectable area of study, because of their connotations with fun; the first academics who wished to examine games for their own sake therefore had to find an acceptable way to dress them up. Serious games were that dressing. Fortunately, people more interested in education than in games have become involved since then; furthermore, games themselves have become legitimate (if not always esteemed) objects of study, so there's less pressure nowadays to use teaching as noble content.

The premise of serious games can be summarised as follows: students typically hold that games are fun but that teaching is boring, so if you combine the two, you'll get fun teaching. Sadly, all too often you get boring games. In part, this is because educators know next to nothing about game design, and game designers don't know a great deal about pedagogy either; the main problem, however, is that the kind of things educators wish to teach through games are not what games are good at teaching. Games are fantastic for developing social skills (Hoyle & Moseley, 2012) and high-order thinking skills (Rice, 2007), and they're also very good at teaching facts – so long as the game isn't *about* the facts. If you play enough games about the golden age of piracy in the Caribbean, eventually you'll know where Vera Cruz is whether you intended to memorise it or not. OK, so you may not know

---

[27] Such games were formerly promoted as *edutainment*, a term that has mercifully lost favour.

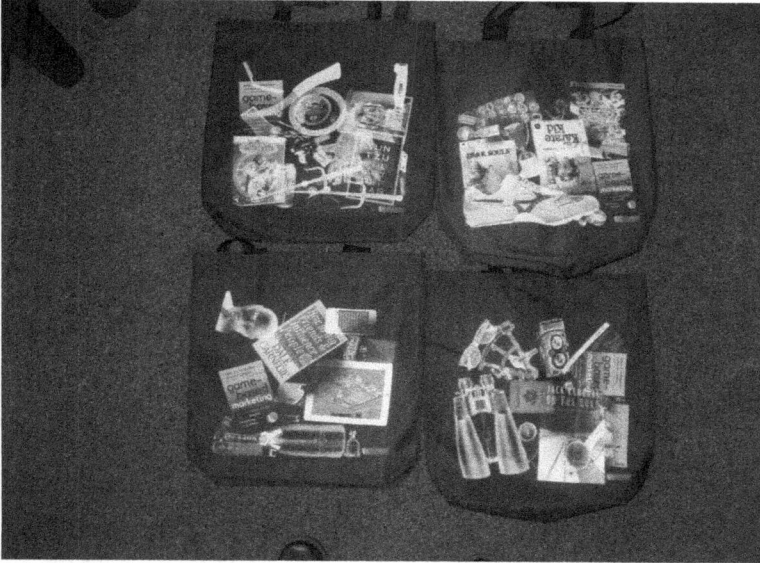

FIGURE 17.1   Gamification summit tote bags.

about the slave trade (that's usually discreetly ignored), but the geography is probably going to be relatively sound.[28]

Unfortunately, educators very often want to use games to teach intermediate skills, which is rarely a good idea: if you have the skill then you don't need to play, and if you don't have it then you're not going to get very far. It's difficult to use a game to teach people to do something as simple as line drawing, let alone to perform matrix multiplication or to predict the outcome of combining multiple industrial chemicals. You can *test* the player's skills in a game, but teaching the skills in the first place is perhaps best left to other methods. Merely being entertaining isn't enough (Elliott et al., 2002).

Player types have been used for many, many serious games, although (as a quick check on their citation counts will testify) few if any of these have made much of an impact.[29] There has been more success when it comes to systems for personalising educational games for individuals, for example using narrative game-based learning objects (Göbel et al., 2010), but on the whole, serious games researchers have largely abandoned player types and adopted gamification methods instead. These aren't having much of an impact either (Dah et al., 2024): they're too shallow; they re-use the same tropes; the overjustification effect[30] kicks in; they rely on theories that work in general but that it turns out don't work for gamification (such as self-determination theory[31]).

---

[28] Not necessarily, though. I moved a city in Spain once (Oviedo) because it was too close to an adjacent one (Gijón) for the railway-game scenario I was making. Er, that's moved it on the game map – I don't have city-moving powers in Reality.

[29] This is true of serious games in general, though, so can't entirely be laid at the door of player types.

[30] The *overjustification effect* is what happens when you give people extrinsic rewards for what they find intrinsically interesting: they lose their intrinsic interest (Lepper et al., 1973). We'll look at it in a bit more detail later in Chapter 23.

[31] As we'll see soon, sadly this theory underpins the Hexad.

Serious games are not universally liked by game designers, because it's hard to say anything through them and few of their players actually *want* to play them anyway. *Games with a purpose* (GWAPs) are slightly better, in that their aim is to leverage the skills that players already have for (usually) benign purposes, so at least their players willingly choose to play. Citizen science endeavours such as *Phrase Detectives* (Chamberlain et al., 2008) and *Foldit* (Cooper et al., 2010) are examples of GWAPs. Although player types *have* been used for GWAPs, this has primarily been via research projects with which I am peripherally associated, such as *WordClicker* (Madge et al., 2019), which don't really count.[32]

Virtual worlds began being employed for education in the Third Age, particularly via MOOs. None of these used player types as far as I know, but while we're on the topic of games and education, it's worth mentioning some of the more notable early examples all the same. The most successful one was Jeanne McWhorter's *Diversity University* (Diversity University, 1996), which was set up specifically for teaching and provided a wide range of educational tools and facilities. People held symposia, discussion classes, and lectures there; it also included some virtual representations of works of literature that could be explored interactively. Another early win was *MOOSE Crossing* (Bruckman, 1998), which leveraged the social side of virtual worlds for educational purposes: it turns out that people learn better if they're part of a community of learners who are having similar experiences to their own. Who would have guessed? Once students began to expect decent graphics in their computer games, though,[33] the popularity of educational worlds waned. This is a shame, because textual worlds such as *LinguaMOO* (Haynes & Holmevik, 1996)[34] are particularly good at teaching languages. Nowadays, it's so much hassle to organise a session in a (graphical) virtual world that those teachers who attempt it tend to do so primarily to add variety to their output, to keep their students engaged; few teach actual courses in, say, *Second Life* or *OpenSimulator*, although they're still used for research (particularly the latter).

The relationship between play and learning is so old that it predates humans[35]: *bears* play (Fagen & Fagen, 2009). It's not going away. Learning remains one of the main reasons that people play (Koster, 2013),[36] and the way that games teach in general can inform the way that we teach in particular (Gee, 2003).

When it comes to education, player types are better applied less for game design and more for understanding how players learn. One of the major ways that educators classify types of learners is using Kolb's experiential learning styles (Kolb, 1984; Kolb & Kolb, 2013), and interestingly, there's a relationship between these and player types (Hamdaoui et al., 2018). Kolb identifies the different types of learner as Divergent, Assimilative, Convergent, and Accommodative, which map onto Achiever, Killer, Explorer, and Socialiser respectively. This establishes a link between player types and learning that suggests the two

---

[32] Unhappily, this is literal: self-citations are excluded from citation counts.

[33] Academic researchers aren't typically in receipt of sufficient funding to make their graphics decent.

[34] This paper takes the form of a collection of interlinked web pages, an experimental format that was being explored at the time but didn't prove popular. It seems that many academics prefer to read an abstract and a conclusion and skip the bit in the middle. If you prefer a book, try Haynes & Holmevik (1998).

[35] Eat that, Literature!

[36] If you're a game designer who doesn't own a copy of this book, well, I have to say, you're not much of a game designer.

systems could help one another. Before you get too thrilled, however, in Kolb's approach, learners follow a cycle: concrete experience *diverges* to reflective observation, which *assimilates* to abstract conceptualisation, which *converges* to active experimentation, which then *accommodates* back to concrete experience. The transformations identify which stage of learning currently applies to the learner, from which the learner types derive their names. Unfortunately, in player types terms, this would give the ordering Achiever, Killer, Explorer, and Socialiser. We can start where we like, because Kolb's model is a cycle, but even if we begin with Killer, we get Killer to Explorer to Socialiser to Achiever. The Main Sequence for player types is Killer to Explorer to Achiever to Socialiser; it makes no sense to have Socialiser immediately before Achiever. The *types* may correspond, but the two *progressions* don't align. Although much can therefore be noted about the relationship between Kolb's learning styles and player types when static, the same cannot be said when comparing their dynamics.

For educators wishing to include commercial games in their teaching armoury, Rademacher Mena (2010) proposes a method of classifying different game genres along a number of dimensions to provide a fingerprint for each one. Genres, rather than individual games, were chosen as a proof of concept: the ultimate aim was to enable teachers to consult the fingerprints of different games to determine which best suit their needs. One of the dimensions used is player types (the other two are those of Caillois (trans. 1961) and Bloom et al (1956)).

This kind of game-profiling has quite some potential; the main problem with it is merely that someone has to profile the games. Nevertheless, this has indeed been done, albeit for use with game-recommendation systems in general. Lee & Jung (2019) gathered tag data from Steam for over 26,000 games to create fingerprints for them automatically, then combined personality-testing with their own adaptation of player types[37] to marry up profiles with fingerprints; as a result, it's possible to assess what games a player with a particular profile might like to play. The results are promising but the approach wasn't intended for educational use and would probably need to be adapted for it.

Overall, then, although player type theory has useful connections to teaching, the theory hasn't contributed much to that area. This doesn't mean it can't, only that you should proceed with caution if you want to give it a shot.

17.3.4 There's More

Player types can be used for other, more esoteric purposes such as landscape architecture (Ong, 2018), collective design (Merrick et al., 2011), and neuro-linguistic programming.[38]

Website designers were early adopters of player types (Kim, 2000).[39] The theory is only used sporadically nowadays, but the point that I set out to make – the idea that there are

[37] It's actually their own adaptation of a number of adaptations of player types. This kind of evolutionary approach to player types is not uncommon, as we'll see shortly.
[38] I don't have a reference from this, just an email requesting permission to do it. Alternatively, I did have a reference, but was neuro-linguistically programmed to forget it.
[39] She calls Killers "brats", which is a great alternative – I wish I'd thought of it! There would have been far fewer misuses of player types if I'd done so. That said, "killers" is superior for theory-marketing purposes.

different kinds of users – has become accepted as standard. In practice, the users are usu-ally instantiated as Cooper-style use cases: website designers hope to make bespoke judge-ments for bespoke sites for bespoke purposes beyond the remit of player types.[40] That said, behaviour directly related to player types can be observed in even innocuous sites such as those for baby names (Wattenberg, 2005).[41] Also, player types themselves may not always be used, but derivations of them sometimes are. Hart et al. (2013) adopt a user-typing approach based on player types to look at evaluations of user experiences with interactive websites.[42]

Overall, then, player types do seem to have applications beyond games, but it's in game design where they come into their own. While there are empirical studies that show they do work in this domain, as yet there are no theories that explain why this would be so beyond the case of virtual worlds. Given that this book is about virtual worlds, though, that isn't a problem for us here.

17.4 NOT USING PLAYER TYPES

There have been plenty of attempts in the past to try to break player types as a theory. As we've seen, some of these worked and required the theory to be repaired ("where does immersion fit in?"). Others don't apply, but are still rolled out by people whose knowledge of the theory came second-hand ("where do merchants, role-players and gold farmers fit in?"). Others are *non sequiturs* ("why doesn't it cover women?") or the results of inadequate research ("My survey of 12 students says otherwise!"). It would be great if someone *could* break the theory, because then we'd get a better theory. Would-be theory-murderers would do well to understand it before they pull the trigger, though.

Many of the criticisms of player types aren't to do with player types themselves so much as how they've been used (Hamari & Tuunanen, 2014). That said, there are definitely some situations to which player types don't apply; it would be a bad idea to pretend they do and a worse idea to apply them anyway.

The domain of player types is those people who play virtual worlds for fun. As we've seen, there is some evidence that they apply to people who play games in general, rather than only to those who play virtual worlds, but there's no persuasive explanation as to why this might pertain.

As for playing for fun, well we'll look at the ones who don't (non-player players) in Volume II, but typically the individuals involved are journalists, researchers, customer service representatives, people involved in real-money trading, or not actually people at all

---

[40] User types may be determined based on how much money the archetypal user want to spend and is able to spend, for example.

[41] If you're wondering what killers do on a baby-names site, they mock baby names. "Britney, Brittney, Britany, Brittany, Brittani, Britannie, Britni. Enough already" (Wattenberg, 2005).

[42] It turns out that the more interactive websites are superior to the less interactive ones, although I suspect there's also such a thing as too much interaction.

but bots. Designers, who can have "designer fun" playing virtual worlds, also fit into this category.[43]

Some players *are* playing for fun, but it's meta-gaming[44] fun: playing through playing. For example, two people may play a virtual world with the aim of being the first to get three complete strangers to say the word "moist" without using that word themselves: they're playing for fun (assuming that they find manipulating people without their consent fun), but the fun is in a meta-game they've overlaid on the virtual world. Similarly, they could be playing a long meta-game such as trying to be the first to reach a given level in a series of virtual worlds, with whoever wins the most such partial play-through races being the overall winner.[45]

More interesting are people who want to play for fun but don't. That's what we're going to consider now. Player types aren't much use in this situation. The argument I'll present applies to more than just virtual worlds, and possibly even to more than just games and play, but I'll restrict it to games (including MMOs) because it's easier to give examples this way. Besides, the more grandiose the claim, the thinner it becomes.

So, we have well-tested explanations for why people play games, but few for why they don't. It's often more useful to know why people aren't playing than it is to know why they are, because then you can change your game (or create another one) to widen the appeal. Given that we have player types, we can legitimately ask: are there such things as a non-player types?

Many very obvious reasons immediately come to mind as to why an individual may not play a game, including the following:

- They've never heard of it.
- They don't own the right hardware.
- They don't have the time.
- They don't have the money.
- They don't like the genre.
- They don't like the graphics.
- They can't use the interface.
- It's against their personal values.
- It's illegal.

[43] As inveterate footnote readers will recall from Chapter 5, we'll look at designer fun towards the end of Volume II.

[44] There are two principal uses of the term "meta-gaming" (or "metagaming") in games. The one I'm using here refers to playing a game for which another game is a token. The other one refers to activities related to a game that are undertaken outside the game, such as watching gameplay videos (Kahila et al., 2023).

[45] OK, so this is not common behaviour, although I have heard of guilds that sometimes do it. It's a bit like a decathlon: contestants play a number (ten) of different athletics games to try to win the decathlon game.

- They prefer to read books or stream TV shows.

- Lots more….

Let's ignore these external factors and assume that someone is already playing your game but then stops playing. Why might they stop?

Here are some suggestions:

- They finished it. OK, that's fair enough.[46]

- A better game came along. Hmm, so what makes it better (assuming a gameplay reason[47])? Well, betterness is based on why people *do* play, rather than why they *don't*, so we can explain it by referring to player types.

- **It was Too Easy**. If we look at Figure 16.1, we can see that the problem is a mismatch between the game's challenge and the player's skill. In the case of its being too easy, the game is no fun: it's asking too little of the player.

- **It was Too Hard**. Looking at Figure 16.1 again, this time the game's challenge level exceeds the player's ability (or perhaps desire) to meet it. The game is unfun: it's asking too much of the player.

- **They couldn't Engage with it**. This means they couldn't enter its magic circle: they could look at it objectively but not make the jump to do so subjectively. This isn't the same as saying it's too challenging or too complex; rather, it's that the player can't figure out what it means – it's inaccessible to them.

- **It had Too Many Flaws**. This can be for one of two main reasons: firstly, it may be buggy enough to remind the player that they're in a game, so abandoning it is perfectly reasonable; secondly, it may be bug-free, but the player keeps seeing ways to improve it. In this latter case, the player engages with it so much that they think of it objectively again, rather than subjectively.

The engagement and flaws points there concern the same thing: whether or not you understand what the game is saying to you. Either it's too heavy for you to grasp what it's saying or it's too light to meet your needs.[48] The player is asking the game for content but it responds with either too much or too little. Too much makes it inaccessible; too little makes it trivial. You won't participate unless the balance is right for *you*. As with easy/difficult, there's a sweet spot: for easy/difficult, it's where challenge balances skills; for light/heavy, it's where insight balances depth.

It's important to note that light/heavy isn't to do with intelligence. Inaccessible art merely speaks over your head: you can't get a handle on it because you don't have the requisite experience, not because you don't have the requisite brainpower. The Modern Art movement has a reputation for being like this: you have to be educated in it to make sense

---

[46] Likewise, if they dropped dead then you wouldn't really expect them to finish what they were playing.

[47] "It uses my favourite IP" is not a gameplay reason.

[48] The BoardGameGeek (Alden & Solko, 2000) rating system gives each of the games it describes a *weight* ("Community rating for how difficult a game is to understand. Lower rating (lighter weight) means easier."), against which personal preferences can be compared.

of it. This is as true of its music and sculpture as it is for its painting. Similarly, players who don't get your game aren't stupid,[49] you're just requiring that they know more than they do.

Games act as a dialogue between the designer (via the gameplay) and the player:

1. The game asks the player to do something.

2. The player answers by doing it.

3. The player's response asks the game a question.

4. The game answers by providing another piece of content, putting us back at step 1.

This usually happens at multiple levels, with the lowest one having a name: the *core loop*. The questions the game asks and the means by which they are answered can address either the player's skill or their understanding (or both) – and probably a good many other topics, too, but we'll stick with these two as they're to do with why people stop playing.

Figure 17.2 illustrates this dialogue, putting a rephrased Figure 16.1 challenge *versus* skill graph alongside a new depth *versus* insight[50] graph.

That the two concepts are orthogonal is clear, because one is active, to do with output (you can try to use your playing skill), and the other is passive, to do with input (you can't try not to use your insight). Thus, if a game is too hard then it isn't because you don't understand it, it's because it's in a language you don't fully know.

Given that the two concepts are orthogonal, we can make them axes on a handy 2D graph of the kind you (well, I) know and love – see Figure 17.3.

The dashed lines in Figure 17.3 show where the player is comfortable. Only in the central dashed square is the player definitely playing. It's possible that they could be playing outside of it if the pull towards one axis is very strong (for example, they *really* like the difficulty level but are finding it only slightly too heavy-going), but the more distant from an axis the player is, the more likely they are no longer to be playing.

Now that we have a pair of axes, it's natural to think about how to label the quadrants they define. This is a little dangerous, though, because it's game-by-game. In player types, if

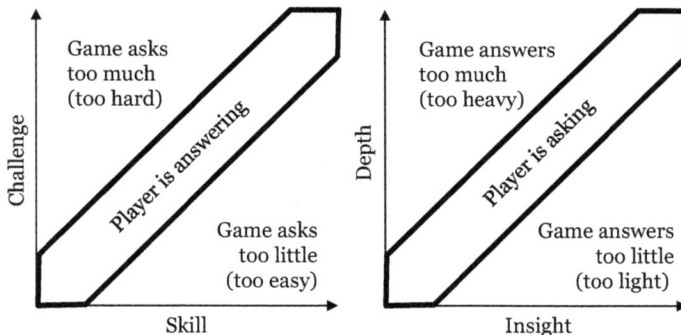

FIGURE 17.2 Challenge and depth.

---

[49] Well, some will be, but not getting your game isn't evidence of it.
[50] By "insight", I mean "capacity to understand".

you're an Achiever then you'll be one for a long time before you drift beyond; in non-player types, you may not like *this* game because it's too shallow but dislike *that* game because it's too difficult. It may be better, therefore, to think in terms of players' grievances.

For the top-right quadrant, a game that's both too hard and too shallow is one that you grasp easily, but you find it frustrating to play. For me, that would definitely include *Pong* (Alcorn, 1972)[51] and *Space Invaders* (Nishikado, 1978); for you, it would likely be different – and for future-me, too, if I practised and got better at them.[52] A game that has substance to it that you have trouble beating would be close to the x-axis, such as (in my case) *Master of Orion: Conquer the Stars* (Sena, 2016) with its brutal[53] space battles. A game with a lot of challenge but little depth would be close to the y-axis; I'd put *Tetris* (Pajitnov, 1986) and *Candy Crush Saga* (Knutsson, 2012) there.

The bottom-right quadrant contains games that are too hard and too deep. They will be full of unfathomable experiences with snail-paced progress. For me, *EVE Online* and *StarCraft* (Phinney & Metzen, 1998) are candidates for this part of the graph; it's not that I *can't* understand them, it's that I *don't* (at least as a player). A game that seems to hang together but that you're useless at would be near the x-axis – *Undertale* (Fox, 2015), *Castlevania* (Akamatsu, 1986), and *Assassin's Creed* (Désilets & Béland, 2006) for me (but of course not necessarily for you). A game you can often win but that makes little sense would be close to the y-axis; I'd put *Chess*, *Go*, and *Civilization VI* (Beach, 2016) there.

The bottom-left quadrant contains games that are easy to play but too deep to comprehend fully. *Elder Scrolls IV: Oblivion* (Rolston, 2006) fits the bill for me (mainly because of

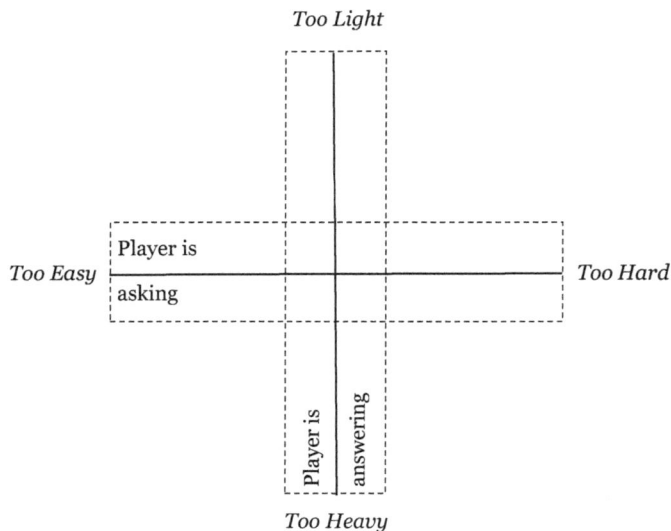

FIGURE 17.3   Disinterest graph.

---

[51] I'm hopeless at *Pong*. It's like a bullet-hell game for me.

[52] Also if I were to read more into them than is actually present and built up a whole system of interpretation about what is actually very simple, like astrologers do with the movement of the stars.

[53] This is in easy mode. Prepend the word "very" the appropriate number of times for more difficult modes.

the effects of its dynamic difficulty adjustment). Games that present context but little challenge are close to the x-axis: I'd put *Cityville* (McCormick, 2010), *Dear Esther* (Pinchbeck & Briscoe, 2012), and slot machines there. A game with achievable goals delivered by opaque systems is nearer the y-axis: *Magic: the Gathering* (Garfield, 1993) and *Football Manager <year>* (Sports Interactive, 2004) are examples in my case.

The top-left quadrant is inhabited by games with little meaning and few obstacles. They will give the impression of being both tedious and pointless. Some, such as *Cow Clicker* (Bogost, 2010), are meant to be so, of course; I'm not criticising them. Other games I'd put here myself include *Snakes and Ladders* (aka *Chutes and Ladders*) and *Noughts and Crosses* (aka *Tic-Tac-Toe*). A boring game with more depth will be near the x-axis; I'd place *SimCity* (Quigley & Librande, 2013) and *Minecraft* (Persson, 2011)[54] there. A game you fully understand but that offers major resistance would be near the y-axis: *Rogue* (Toy et al., 1980) and *Risk* (Lamorisse, 1957)[55] are my go-to examples.

Figure 17.4 shows how these games fit on the graph for me, along with some others for good measure: *Pokémon Go*, *Asteroids* (Logg & Rains, 1979), *2048* (Cirulli, 2014), *Victoria 3* (Andersson, 2022), *Dwarf Fortress* (Adams & Adams, 2006b), *Pac-Man* (Iwatani, 1980), *Gardens of Time* (Todd, 2011), *Hanabi* (Bauza, 2010), and *Poker*. Your graph will doubtless look very different. Note that I've omitted games that would fit in the central square, as this graph is about not playing, not about playing.

In summary, players will leave games that have:

- **Top-Right**. Meaningless, unnecessary obstacles (like rocks).
- **Bottom-Right**. Inarticulate, frustrating demands (like babies).
- **Bottom-Left**. Straightforward pretentions (like opera).
- **Top-Left**. Vacuous actions for vacuous reasons (like zombies).

This gives us an easy-to-remember set of labels for the quadrants: rock babes and opera zombies.

So, what can we do with this information?

Well, one option is to look at what players like before the game pushes them too far, to judge where their boundaries are. This changes the focus: rather than being about what the players don't like, we can consider the players themselves.

We know that the disinterest graph of Figure 17.3 is not an extrapolation of the interest graph in Figure 11.1 because when we extrapolate the latter the quadrants represent spaces that no longer qualify as virtual worlds. If we interpolate the disinterest graph then we should get something different.

---

[54] Yes, I do think *Minecraft* is boring. As I said, your opinions may vary.

[55] As a child, I played this game with my father and brother over 90 times and only ever won once – the last game we played together. I think they let me win.

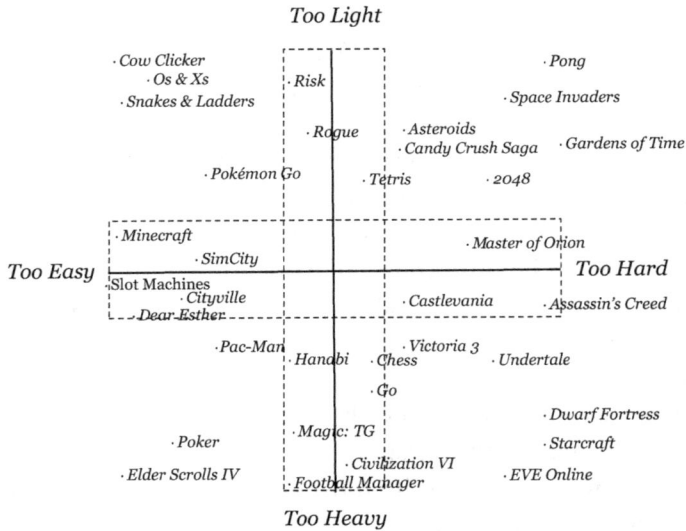

FIGURE 17.4   A personal disinterest graph.

We do indeed get something different, but not something unknown. The types of player it defines already have names in the games industry:

- Those who like lighter, challenging games are *core* gamers.
- Those who like heavier, challenging games are *hardcore* gamers.
- Those who like heavier, easier games are *care bears*.[56]
- Those who like lighter, easier games are *casual* gamers.

Figure 17.5 illustrates this.

This nicely connects previously unexpected phenomena together, but is it of any actual use? At this point, academics start using words such as "lens" and "framework" to develop methods of analysis, but although I *am* an academic, I'm first and foremost a game designer; I'll therefore do what game designers do: blunder straight in and see if and how it works.[57]

Let's take as our example, oh, the player's attitude to the free-to-play, microtransactions revenue model:

- Players won't pay to make a game harder, because they can make it harder for themselves on their own by adding their own arbitrary rules.

---

[56] This MMO-centric term is rapidly falling out of use, but its replacements are still duking it out to take over. Candidates include *chill* gamers, *story-driven* gamers, and *social* gamers. It would be inconvenient for virtual worlds if the latter won out, but unfortunately that won't be a factor in determining the result.

[57] It's not just designers – players do this all the time. If you get a new board game, say, you're going to have a trial play-through to make sure you understand the rules before you restart and play "for real". That's essentially what I'm doing here.

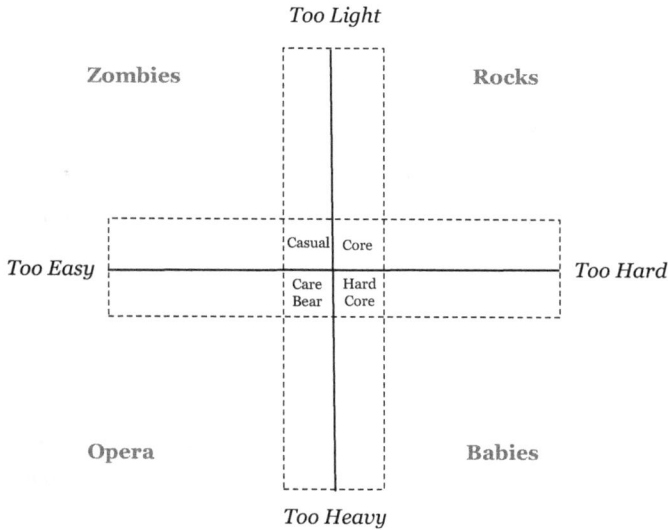

FIGURE 17.5 Gamer types.

- Players might pay to make a game less challenging if they like an easier time of things.

- Players might pay to make a game more profound in concept if they like deep games.

- Players won't pay to make a game simpler in concept as they'll feel patronised.

Applying these rules:

- Core gamers won't pay for anything.

- Hardcore gamers will pay for richer content.

- Care bear gamers will pay to remove challenges or for richer content.

- Casual gamers will pay to remove challenges.

This would suggest that free-to-play is risky for games that appeal to those players who like challenging but understood gameplay.

OK, well that seems to work! Whether it helps designers or not is another matter, but it does seem to have some utility and explanatory power.

Before I leave the topic of not using player types, I should mention that some people don't use them simply because they're not useful to them. I can't really argue with that, so won't.

We now return you to your regularly scheduled programme.

CHAPTER 18

Other Typologies

$\mathbf{P}$LAYER TYPES constitute the first and best-known player typology, but many more have appeared in their wake. Some of these are variations on or extensions of the original model. Some were inspired by player types but are otherwise original. Some are applications of existing theories from other academic disciplines. Some are independent inventions by people who had never heard of player types when they did their work.

I don't wish to give the impression that player types are the only show in town. They're not. Other typologies may well be better for your purposes, so let's take a look at some of the better-known, tried-and-tested ones.

18.1 MAKING IT YOUR OWN

Take a well-known song and have someone on a TV talent show sing it. The chances are that they will not sing the notes as written: they will sing their own interpretation of them. At times, the tune may bear such little resemblance to the original that if you didn't sing along in your head then you wouldn't recognise it. The judges will congratulate the performer for "taking that song and making it your own", regardless of whether it was significantly better when Frank Sinatra, Tina Turner, Michael Bublé, or Taylor Swift sang it. Sometimes it may well *be* better, but it's the notion of taking a song and making it your own in defiance of the songwriter's intentions that wins the applause.

Some people – researchers in particular – don't misuse player types but adapt them to their own purposes. This may be intended as a general improvement or as a specific one for a particular application. Whether it's an improvement or not is for users and would-be users to decide. If player types have slid into irrelevancy, it doesn't really matter that the theory still works, any more than it matters that the principles of galleon-construction still work: you need something that's appropriate to your present needs. Theories are only worthwhile if they have (or can lead to[1]) applications. For example, you could modify player-type theory to apply to particular mechanics rather than to virtual worlds, but to what end?[2] Just because you can, that doesn't mean you should (or indeed that you shouldn't).

---

[1] I added this comment so as not to dismiss the entire field of mathematics.
[2] Usually, the answer to this kind of question is "to get a PhD".

      DOI: 10.1201/9781003689638-18

One example of legitimately extending player types for other purposes is that proposed by Bicalho et al. (2019). In this, the four-type model is extended by adding an extra axis in the same manner that I did, but with a different domain. Rather than using implicit/explicit, they use hardcore/casual. Why? Well, they're interested in behaviour analysis concerned with the relationship between revenue and fun. For such a purpose, this extension makes good sense; experiments show that it seems serviceable, too.

One of the best-known adaptations of player types is Andrzej Marczewski's Hexad (Marczewski, 2015b), which is used in gamification. What's less well-known is that it's an adaptation of player types. It began with Andrzej's examination a number of ideas that he thought could perhaps be helpful for gamification: flow, self-determination theory, and Amy Jo Kim's player journey (Kim, 2000); the latter uses player types, which is why Andrzej got in touch with me. In our discussions, it became clear that:

1. Flow didn't work, because gamification takes place over too long a timescale.

2. Self-determination theory's autonomy and relatedness were important for gamification, with competence less important.

3. Player types in its eight-type version seemed to cover all the bases, even though formally it only applies to people who play MMOs for fun.

Andrzej thought that eight was too large a number of types (which I grudgingly accept it may well be for everyday use), but the association with self-determination theory that he'd developed gave the solution: combine into one the pair of types bound by autonomy and do the same for the pair bound by relatedness. Then, it was simply a case of giving the types appropriate names.

Here are the Hexad's six types, along with their motivations and associated player types:

- *Socialisers*, motivated by relatedness; player types' Networkers and Friends.

- *Free spirits*, motivated by autonomy and self-expression; player types' Scientists and Sages.

- *Achievers*, motivated by mastery; player types' Attainers.

- *Philanthropists*, motivated by purpose and meaning; player types' Politicians.

- *Players*, motivated by rewards; player types' Opportunists.

- *Disruptors*, motivated by change; player types' Griefers.

The Hexad itself can be extended by breaking its different types into sub-types, giving the Dodecad (Marczewski, 2015a) for those wacky people who consider eight types to be too few.

The Hexad is now standard for gamification because it's convenient and yields results. It's also being adopted for serious games, initially because Tondello et al. (2016, 2019) validated it empirically,[3] but nowadays because it has the momentum of other gamification research behind it.

GameRefinery, a company that does analytics for mobile phone games, also has a six-type model of player motivations that doubles up to 12 (Julkunen, 2020). This model intersects with that of the Hexad/Dodecad, but doesn't map onto it one-to-one. The Hexad's Disruptor and Philanthropist types are largely absent from it and its idea of what motivates Socialisers is broader than most (it includes competing against others). It adds Escapism as a motivation type and treats Expression as a type separate from social play. GameRefinery used these 12 motivations to create motivation profiles for mobile phone games – hundreds of thousands of them, automatically, from tags. Following this, they did a cluster analysis to find the most common groupings, looking for four, six, eight, and ten clusters.[4] Interestingly, they found that the best results came from eight clusters, giving the following archetypes: Treasure Hunter, Thrill Seeker, Thinker, Networker, King of the Hill, Strategist, Skill Master, and Expressionist. These correspond remarkably well to Opportunist, Griefer, Scientist, Networker, Attainer, Politician, Sage, and Friend from player types, with only the Griefer/Thrill Seeker pairing being somewhat iffy.

Another revamp of player types was constructed by Radoff (2011). This version is intended to apply to all games, not just to virtual worlds. Its x-axis goes from few players to many players and its y-axis from qualitative to quantitative. The quadrants are labelled co-operation (many/qualitative), competition (many/quantitative), achievement (few/quantitative), and immersion (few/qualitative). Although developed for new entrants when social media games were at their height, it does still see some use as a convenient way of classifying games if not necessarily their players.

The best-known advances on player types are due to Nick Yee. In Chapters 10 and 14, I mentioned his Daedalus Project, which he ran for around a decade beginning in 1999: it explored the psychology of MMO players, from which he produced a series of analyses on a wide range of topics. Any researcher new to virtual worlds who is looking at trying to figure out what makes players tick would do well to begin there.

Before we look at what the Daedalus Project has to say on the subject of why people play virtual worlds, we should start with Nick's earlier work, the Norrathian Scrolls (Yee, 2001). This was a study exclusively of *EverQuest* players. It did not ask what motivated players, so to investigate this in the Daedalus Project, Nick created a survey based on player types and what he'd learned from the Norrathian Scrolls. This time, he extended it to include players of three other MMOs (*Dark Age of Camelot*, *Asheron's Call*, and *Anarchy Online*).

---

[3] Somewhat ironically, the relationship between the Hexad and player types means that the same experiment also validates player types.

[4] This is a sound approach, because the number of clusters sought can radically affect the results. If you cluster people by DNA differences and look for five clusters, you get groups corresponding to Africans, Europeans/West Asians, East Asians, indigenous Americans, and indigenous Australians. This pleases racists, but if you look for the "sixth race of mankind" then next cluster is a tribe of 4,000 people living in northern Pakistan. This does not please racists (Rutherford, 2020).

After performing a factor analysis on the 6,665 responses he got to this, he discovered five overarching motivations that he called *facets* (Yee, 2002a). He named these as follows:

- **Relationship**. The desire to develop meaningful relationships with other people.

- **Immersion**. The desire to become immersed in a make-belief construct.

- **Grief**. The desire to objectify and use other players for ones own gains.

- **Achievement**. The desire to become powerful within the construct of a game.

- **Leadership**. The desire to play in groups; the gregariousness and assertiveness of the player often results in their being the leader of such groups.

In comparing these with player types, it's clear that: Relationship corresponds to Socialisers; Achievement corresponds to Achievers; Grief and Leadership correspond to the two types of Killer; Immersion is a thing. What about Explorers, though? Puzzled by this, Nick added some more questions that were intended to tease out explorer-related motivations in case the original questionnaire had covered the topic poorly. 500 responses later, there was still no evidence of the existence of Explorers. This was something of a blow to player types, which asserted that they did exist (but didn't have a survey of over 7,000 players to back up said assertion). Remember that Nick's work was all to do with MMOs, not with games in general, so it could not be dismissed on this basis.

So many people did seem to think that exploration was a thing that in an effort to discover what was going on, and either to validate or to refute player types empirically once and for all, Nick put together as part of the Daedalus Project a second survey with more nuanced questions to allow a finer-grained analysis. This time, he surveyed around 3,000 players from *EQ*, *DAoC*, *UO*, and *SWG*, and using a principle-component analysis unearthed ten *motivations* in three general categories (Yee, 2005a, 2005d, 2007a):

- Achievement

  - **Advancement**. Progress, power, accumulation, status.

  - **Mechanics**. Numbers, optimisation, templating, analysis.

  - **Competition**. Challenging others, provocation, domination.

- Social

  - **Socialising**. Casual chat, helping others, making friends.

  - **Relationship**. Personal, self-disclosure, find and give support.

  - **Teamwork**. Collaboration, groups, group achievements.

- Immersion

  - **Discovery**. Exploration, lore, finding hidden things.

  - **Role-Playing**. Story line, character history, roles, fantasy.

- **Customisation**. Appearances, accessories, style, colour schemes.
- **Escapism**. Relax, escape from real life, avoid real-life problems.

This analysis showed that Exploration had been absorbed by Immersion in the earlier study, so it did exist after all. Phew!

Matching these motivations with player types is straightforward in some cases but not in others. First, the clear matches:

- Advancement is a clear match with player types' Attainer.
- Mechanics is a clear match with player types' Sage.
- Socialising is a clear match with player types' Networker.
- Relationship is a clear match with player types' Friend.
- Discovery is a clear match with player types' Scientist.

Next, the partial matches:

- Competition is a match with player types' Griefer, but is muddied because some Attainers also like competition.
- Teamwork is a match with player types' Politician, but is muddied because some Friends also like teamwork.

Finally, the non-matches:

- Role-Playing, as discussed in Chapter 15, can be:
  - an invitation to choose a path to follow;
  - a manifestation of growing immersion as the player progresses through the types along the development tracks;
  - an identity worn by the player for the purposes of immersion;
  - role-playing for its own sake (hard role-playing), in which case player types don't apply.
- Customisation is a way that players acknowledge or direct their growing immersion.
- Escapism is a sign that immersion is working.

It should come as no surprise that the three immersion components don't map onto player types, because immersion isn't a player type: it's a manifestation of how close the player has come to self-actualisation. Role-playing is the player's attempt to shape the context of immersion; Customisation is how the player indicates to themself and to others how their sense of self is crystalising (or how they hope it will in the near future); Escapism is the player's recognition that the process is doing what they need it to do.

There's one player type that isn't addressed by the motivations model: Opportunists. I suspect that this is because it was caught in the same net as Scientists, but it could be that by the time anyone is presented with a questionnaire on the subject of why they play, they've already left that part of their journey (the same could perhaps be said of most Griefers, too).

These motivations describe what drives players of virtual worlds while they're playing, but not what they find fun. Of course, if players' motivations are exactly what you want to know then the motivations model is going to be of far more use to you than player types. There's no underlying theory to explain *why* players have these motivations, but there is a wealth of empirical evidence to suggest that they *do*, accompanied by comments made by players that support the findings.

The ten motivations derived in this study are a statistical model, which is static rather than dynamic: there are no moving parts. The model is silent on whether players change motivation over time, which (assuming they do change motivation over time) means that you can't tell from their current motivation what their next motivation will be. This may not matter in the elder game, though: most players there are treading water so aren't going to change type anyway. If the majority of players sampled in the motivations study were in this group (which seems likely), that would explain a lot.

The motivations approach allows for overlap, so that players can have several motivations. A player with one Social-category motivation can have other Social-category motivations, or even Achiever-category motivations. Something similar is also possible with player types, although in a constrained, fade-out, fade-in manner: it occurs as the player transitions between types. Also, it would be no surprise if motivations in the elder game were more disparate than they are in the levelling game: progress is undirected at this point, so players are obliged to seek their own goals.[5]

This research was specific to virtual worlds, but why stop there? In 2015, Nick Yee and Nic Ducheneaut, whom Nick been working with for ten years, set up Quantic Foundry (which I mentioned in Chapter 10 when I was discussing data). Beginning with a literature survey that looked at multiple existing works on motivations, they extracted around 50 items for a pilot survey. They had 600 gamers take this survey, from whose responses they could use cluster analysis to construct a motivations model. They then created an app to give other players a way of comparing themselves against the sample. They periodically re-ran the factor analysis to root out questions that were ineffective, and after 30,000 replies, they were confident that their survey was good and its results informative. They then did a media push and by 2016 had around 250,000 responses. What emerged from a cluster analysis of these were six gaming styles (so like the Hexad), each of which had two highly correlated subdivisions (so like the Dodecad). The player's degree of fit with each of the styles could be represented as a social-media-friendly spider diagram, which greatly helped the survey's uptake (Yee, 2015a).

---

[5] I see this as a flaw of modern virtual world design, not of player types. That isn't because I'm hopelessly biased towards player types, either.

The six *styles* (with handy mottos) and their subdivisions are (Quantic Foundry, 2019):

- *Action* ("Boom!"): Destruction and Excitement.

- *Social* ("Let's play together"): Competition and Community.

- *Mastery* ("Let me think"): Challenge and Strategy.

- *Achievement* ("I want more"): Completion and Power.

- *Immersion* ("Once upon a time"): Fantasy and Story.

- *Creativity* ("What if"): Design and Discovery.

Comparing these styles with the Hexad, there are several close correspondences. Social (styles) matches Socialiser (Hexad); Creativity (styles) matches Free Spirit (Hexad); Mastery (styles) matches Achiever (Hexad); Achievement (styles) matches Player (Hexad). Action (styles) and Disruptor (Hexad) are related but not the same. Immersion (style) and Philanthropist (Hexad) don't harmonise at all.

Note that Quantic Foundry's style of Achiever does not match the Hexad's Achiever type. This is what happens when people find groupings and have to assign names to them: it's not easy.[6]

With a dozen clusters, it's possible to cluster the clusters. When Quantic Foundry did this (Yee, 2015b), they discovered three such meta-clusters (all of which were present regardless of where on planet Earth the respondents lived):

- **Action-Social**. Competition, Community, Excitement, and Destruction.

- **Mastery-Achievement**. Completion, Strategy, and Challenge.

- **Immersion-Creativity**. Story, Design, and Fantasy.

The two remaining style subdivisions acted as bridges between the high-level clusters: Discovery connects Immersion-Creativity and Mastery-Achievement; Power connects Action-Social and Mastery-Achievement. This gives a hint as to how players might transition from favouring one kind of game to another over time, but unfortunately, because the model is static, it can show but not tell. Different preferences exhibited by people of different ages do suggest that movement occurs, however, if not why.

In their survey, Quantic Foundry asked respondents what their favourite games were, and from this, they were able to identify games that people with similar profiles liked; they were then able to use this as a game-recommender system. They also reversed the process, looking at the games themselves and noting what player profiles tended to like them (so, like the fingerprinting approach that we looked at in Chapter 17). They had enough data that they could follow this up to see what profiles matched what game genres or franchises.

---

[6] My own struggles with the names of what I'm calling in this book the Attainer and Sage types testify to this.

After a segment analysis of the by-then half a million people who had taken the survey, the result was nine types (Quantic Foundry, 2021):

- *Acrobat* ("Flexing my reflexes"): Challenge and Discovery.

- *Gardener* ("Quiet, relaxing task completion"): Completion.

- *Slayer* ("Cinematic mayhem with a purpose"): Fantasy, Story, and Destruction.

- *Skirmisher* ("Jumping into the fray of battle"): Destruction and Completion.

- *Gladiator* ("Dedicated, hardcore gaming"): Challenge, Completion, and Community.

- *Ninja* ("A duel of speed and skill"): Competition and Challenge.

- *Bounty Hunter* ("High-octane solo world exploration"): Destruction and Fantasy.

- *Architect* ("My empire begins with this village"): Strategy and Completion.

- *Bard* ("Playing a part in a grand story"): Design, Community, and Fantasy.

Of these, the only type that prefers MMOs over other kinds of computer game is Bard. Sure, the other types can be used in the elder game to give the players something to do while waiting for new MMO-specific content (Ninja for PvP and Gladiator for raids, for example), but if players actively *want* that kind of content then they can get it better elsewhere.

Quantic Foundry's current statistical model has travelled quite some distance from its MMO roots[7] and is backed up with astonishing amounts of data. If you want to find out what kind of people will play your game, or what kind of game your target audience will play, this is best-in-class. Its thin thread to player types is almost (but not quite) broken.

Let's now turn our attention to some other virtual world player categorisations – ones that didn't necessarily have a thread to player types to begin with. I'll begin by outlining some of the more general features that such categorisations may exhibit, before moving on to the categorisations themselves.

18.2 USEFULNESS

One way of replacing player types as a theory it to try to subsume it into another. The idea with this is that player types are just some existing, well-known model wearing different clothes. This doesn't happen very often, but it's how I heard of Piaget's work (mentioned in Chapter 12). More popular ways include using an existing theory in the first place or coming up with a new theory from scratch.

There are innumerable ways to categorise people, whether by using a statistical analysis of what they do or a psychological assessment of why they (say that they) do it. Whether any of these categorisations are useful or not depends on who wants them and

---

[7] There's even a version for board games, which has a slightly different breakdown of motivations (Quantic Foundry, 2017).

why. Categorising MMORPG players by their political ideology (Smith, 2020) might be of great interest to researchers in a range of fields, but it's not necessarily of direct use to most designers.

Knowing that there are categories doesn't in and of itself tell you what to do with them. For example, if you survey your players and discover that some like nurturing (O'Shea et al., 2022), should you provide content for them – sick animals to tend, maybe? Well you *could*, quite easily, but how many sick animals? If you provide too few, that may not satisfy them – but if you provide too many, might that not distress them? They want to help them all, but if they just keep on coming then they can't. Either way, how would they balance tending NPCs and tending other player characters?

Similarly, you might observe using in-game telemetry that some people hoard objects much more than other people do (Simpson, 1999): should you provide content for them – hoardable objects? It might seem a good idea,[8] but just because they hoard things that doesn't mean it's their favourite activity; it doesn't even mean they necessarily like it; it could be something they feel psychologically compelled to do in the same way that gambling gets a hold of some people.

Furthermore, knowing that there are categories doesn't tell you how players of one category would interact with those of another. What effect would a virtual world packed with opportunities to hoard or to nurture (or to do whatever the categories are in the theory you alight on) have on players who are interested in other things? Are you either all-in or all-out as a hoarder or nurturer, or can you have varying degrees of involvement in them? Can the same person be both a collector and a care-giver? Player types have answers to some of these questions, but if you're not a designer then you may be indifferent to them – much the same as a designer won't spend a lot of time thinking about, say, different constructs of masculinity among their players (Hellman & Majamäki, 2016), or their players' degrees of sociocultural competence (Peterson, 2012), or their players' comparative levels of creativity and innovativeness (Mikhailova, 2019), or how their players' out-of-game activities are related to their in-game activities (Kahila et al., 2023). It may be *interesting* to MMO designers (because all game designers can find pretty well anything interesting), but it isn't always of immediate relevance to design.

Because playing a virtual world involves a much longer commitment than playing most other games does (at least non-professionally), dynamic models that capture the progress of players have an advantage. A designer of a social world might take fun for granted and be more concerned with the particular behaviours of their players in terms of whether they prefer events or objects *versus* whether they prefer creating or engaging with these. This will tell the designer something they can act upon, but unless you know whether, say, object-creators transition into event-organisers over time, you won't know whether to provide the pathways for that or whether doing so would be a waste of effort.

Most of the formal categorisations of the players of virtual world are models in the statistical sense but not in the dynamic sense. The theory of player types wanders unescorted in the wilderness here.

---

[8] If the objects are stackable then it won't affect database usage: a stack of 11,000 shirts presents the same database load as a stack of one shirt – only the count has changed.

Similarly, player types are pretty well alone when it comes to looking at fun. A categorisation of motivations or engagement or behaviours isn't the same thing as fun, but they're often close enough for some alignment. Player types may be wandering by itself, but it can hear the shouts of others nearby.

18.3 USELESSNESS

Before I look at some of the independent categorisations that you might consider more useful than player types for your purposes, a few words of caution: it's easy to come up with new and different ways to categorise players, but that doesn't mean they're intrinsically useful or even informative. They may be complete (in that they cover all players) and they may be correct (in that they don't imply anything false), but that doesn't mean they're worth a jot.

To illustrate this, I'll present four ways to partition players using the basic two-axis, four-types model I used for the player interest graph of Figure 11.1, but with different axis and quadrant labels.

Partition #1, shown in Figure 18.1, is largely complete and correct. Some people might argue that there are genders that don't fit on the horizontal, or that few young people know where they are on the vertical, so you could use such a partition to stimulate debate. However, it's useless for virtual world design because it tells you nothing that you don't already know.

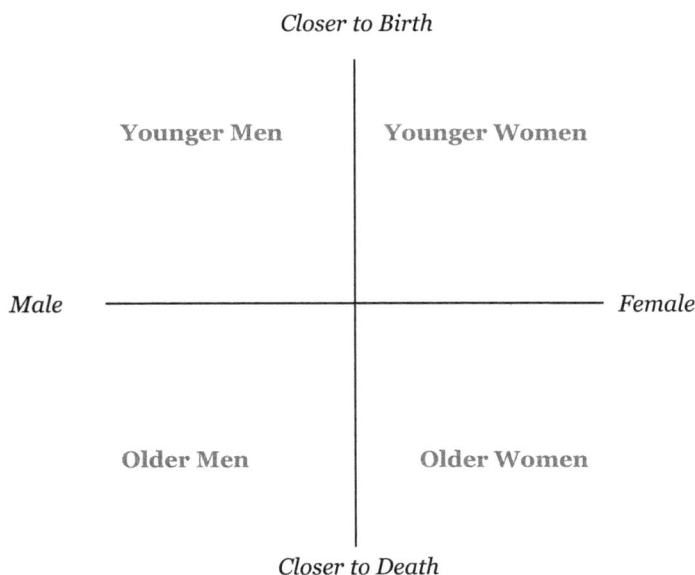

Closer to Birth

Younger Men | Younger Women

Male ——————|—————— *Female*

Older Men | Older Women

Closer to Death

FIGURE 18.1 Partition #1.

Partition #2, shown in Figure 18.2, has more interesting things to say. For example, you could use it to delineate how player interpret games, or to plot an "artist's journey" (Customer to Connoisseur to Designer to Artist).

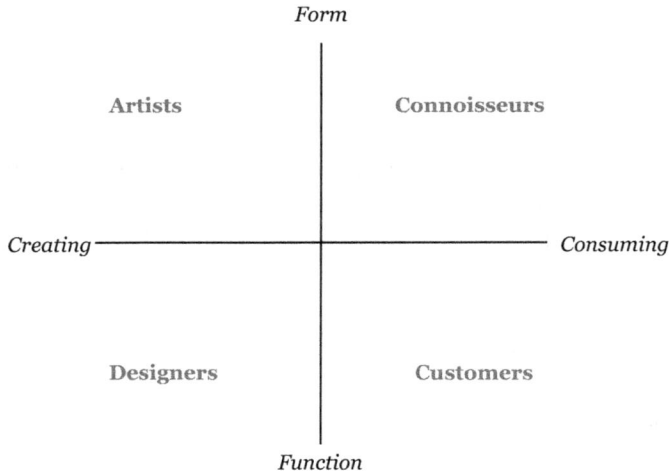

Form

Artists   Connoisseurs

Creating ———————————————— *Consuming*

Designers   Customers

Function

FIGURE 18.2   Partition #2.

Partition #3, shown in Figure 18.3, exists merely to show how by adding interesting labels to axes and quadrants you can make something superficially entertaining enough to capture the attention. You were deciding which one you were, weren't you?

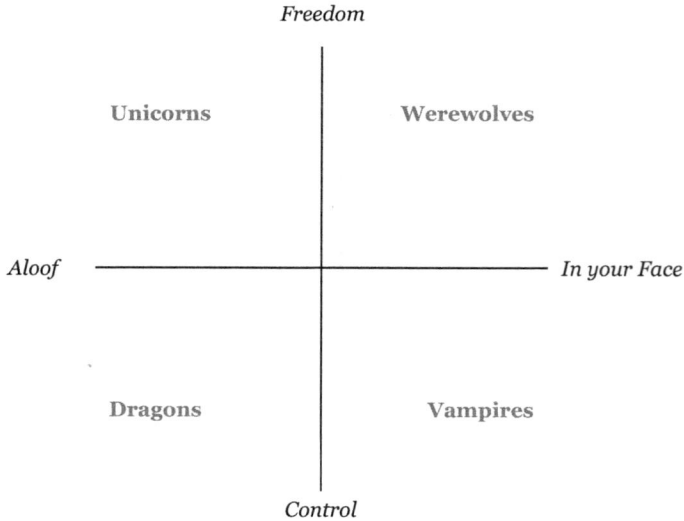

Freedom

Unicorns   Werewolves

Aloof ———————————————— *In your Face*

Dragons   Vampires

Control

FIGURE 18.3   Partition #3.

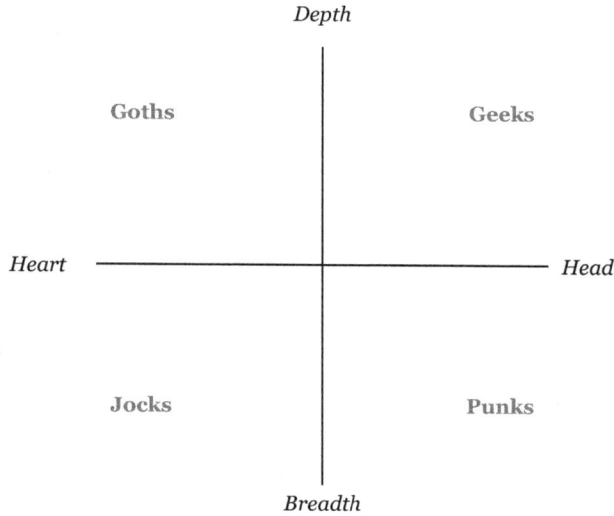

FIGURE 18.4   Partition #4.

As it happens, this one actually works for categorising virtual worlds (or at least MMOs). I created it by taking a horizontal axis of *Solo Play* on the left to *Group Play* on the right and a vertical axis taking *Sandbox* at the top to *Theme Park* at the bottom. Had I kept those labels and given the quadrants descriptive but boring labels such as Eccentric, Assertive, Detached, and Recluse, the statement would have been the same, but you wouldn't have spent even a second deciding where you fitted into it.[9]

Finally, partition #4, shown in Figure 18.4, is simply a slice of the Myers-Briggs Type Indicator (Briggs Myers, n.d.), cross-indexing Thinking/Feeling against Extraversion/Introversion. Sufficiently disguised, you can take any existing theory and pass it off as your own.[10]

Some more words of caution: it's also easy to examine other categorisations and draw parallels that may or may not be there. For example, Hu et al. (2014) looked at users of Instagram and found that they fell into five categories depending on what they posted about: activities (Achievers), a wide range (Explorers), friends (Socialisers), quotations in text (Killers/Griefers), and selfies (Killers/Politicians). I added those player type labels myself: there is nothing in the paper that suggests a link; I did it to show how easy it is to shoehorn player types (or other categorisations) into unrelated short lists and thence to claim a connection.

Then again, sometimes there may actually be more to it. You'll perhaps recall that Harry Potter follows the Hero's Journey; the houses in Hogwarts School of Witchcraft and Wizardry are Gryffindor (Achievers), Ravenclaw (Explorers), Hufflepuff (Socialisers), and Slytherin (Killers). Again, I added the player types myself, but it's a very good match. Is that because of a connection[11] (via the Hero's Journey) or is it mere coincidence?

---

[9] If you want to spend more than a second looking at a different-but-entertaining two-axis way of partitioning people, try Coates (2004).

[10] Lawyers please note that I am not attempting to pass this off as my own.

[11] Formally, this would be using the Hero's Journey as a *third variable*. I'll talk a bit more about third variables in a later sidebar.

18.4 PARTITIONING

So, bearing all this about usefulness and uselessness (for your purposes) in mind, let's examine some other ways of partitioning players of virtual worlds.

18.4.1 Path of Ascension

Randy Farmer, who along with Chip Morningstar designed the First-Age virtual world *Habitat*, describes five different kinds of people who played it (Farmer, 1988, 1992). These may be a useful starting point for people designing social worlds:

- **The *Passive*.** Half of the players fall into this category: they log in, check their messages, see if anything especially interesting is going on then join in if there is and log out if there isn't.

- **The *Active*.** The next-largest group numerically, and the ones who spend the most time in the virtual world. They speak to their friends as soon as they connect, keep up with all the goings-on, and take part in organised activities.

- **The *Motivators*.** These are the players who make the virtual world fun for others. They throw parties, open businesses, run for office, spark debates, enter competitions, and sometimes become outlaws. If you can nurture one Motivator for every 50 Passive or Active, your virtual world will be wonderful.

- **The *Caretakers*.** These are experienced Motivators. They help newbies, deal with interpersonal conflicts, record bugs, suggest worthwhile improvements, run contests, and officiate at events. They're an incredible resource. If you can manage one Caretaker for every 100 players, consider yourself lucky.

- **The *Geek Gods*.** These are the system operators, who add new content to the virtual world and fix old content. Caretakers can be elevated to this level if they've shown themselves up to the task.

The goal of the designer is to enable a progression (the *Path of Ascension*): Passive to Active to Motivator to Caretaker to Geek God. A successful, self-maintaining system will result. This path is similar to the Main Socialiser Sequence in player types, but the entry-level players aren't Griefers and the Geek Gods level refers to players who are effectively CSRs (so aren't getting their fun from playing as players).

18.4.2 Six Circles

Another approach that focuses on progression is Hedron's Six Circles (Hedron, 1998). Its author[12] created the model through the observation of players' behaviour in RPGs over the course of ten years; it's therefore grounded but has no accompanying formal study (a bit like player types, then). The focus of the model is on players' skills, knowledge, and disposition, and on the interactions between players exhibiting different stages of development

---

[12] I've no idea who Hedron is; this is what happens when people write articles using their character name.

of these. The higher the circle you occupy, the more mature you are (in terms of growth within the virtual world[13]). The Six Circles of the Adept Game Player are:

- **First Circle: *Survival*.** The main concern of newbies is acquiring enough skills and resources simply to survive. They want to be able to do things in the game without risking loss at every turn.

- **Second Circle: *Competence*.** Once a player has got themself organised, they are less concerned with avoiding defeat and more interested in developing a higher level of competence. They can overcome common challenges and the game starts to feel fun.

- **Third Circle: *Excel*.** Here, the player wants to beat the game. They get the best skills, armour, weapons, and so on, seeking out the toughest enemies to overcome.

- **Fourth Circle: *Prove Mastery*.** Having obtained the best of everything, what next? Well, these are social games, so you want to show others how good you are. You can do this either by helping them or hurting them.

- **Fifth Circle: *Seek New Challenges*.** At this stage, players have exhausted all the content programmed into the virtual world so need something else to slake their thirst. They get this from either restarting with a new, differently specified character or from interacting with the other players in one or more of the following ways: chatting with them; flaming them; PvP; engaging in inter-guild rivalries and intrigues; role-playing. If none of those appeal, they'll go play something else.

- **Sixth Circle: *Zen Game Play*.** In the final circle, everything is one. The player appreciates all the aspects the Fifth Circle has to offer and enriches the virtual world with their presence.

Looking at this, it appears as if it should be an easy mapping onto player types' development tracks, but it isn't: it intertwines the Main Explorer and Main Socialiser Sequences. The First Circle is Opportunist; the Second is Scientist; the third is Attainer; the fourth is Griefer or Politician; the Fifth is Friend; and the Sixth is Sage. What it's essentially arguing is that players who follow the Main Explorer Sequence are not fulfilled, so switch to the Main Socialiser Sequence to give that a try. When that, too, fails, they return to the Main Explorer Sequence where they continue serenely. In other words, it describes what happens when your virtual world doesn't grant players Atonement with the Father (that is, the designer doesn't concede that the player is worthy). Ideally, designers *would* concede this, but getting company management to agree to it is another matter. The Six Circles model is therefore a useful way of looking at how to structure the emergence of user-generated content in the elder game (its Fourth to Sixth Circles).

---

[13] This model actually applies to all multi-player RPGs, including face-to-face ones, but its primary sources are *Neverwinter Nights*, and *Ultima Online*.

18.4.3 Trojan

The Trojan typology (Kahn et al., 2015)[14] was developed by examining the motivations of 18,627 players of *League of Legends* (Cadwell & Feak, 2009) and 18,819 players of *Chevalier's Romance Online 3*; the former is not an MMORPG (it's a Multi-player Online Battle Arena, so has no persistence), but the latter apparently is (I can't be sure, because my attempts to track it down have come to nothing; this is also why I provide no citation for it).

The Trojan typology was developed to be cross-genre and cross-cultural (the *LoL* players were from North America; the *CRO3* players were from China). It discovered six motivations common to both constituencies:

- **Socialisers**, who wish to build and to maintain social relationships with other players.

- **Completionists**, who like to explore every element of the game to its maximum extent.

- **Competitors**, who desire to win the game and contribute to victory.

- **Escapists**, who engage in fantasy to escape from mundane Reality.

- **Story-Driven**, who are interested in the fictional context of the virtual world and its NPCs.

- **Smarty-Pants**, who play because they want to improve their brainpower and enhance their intelligence.

There's another example here of the problem of naming groups obtained by factor analysis, in that its Completionists are more to do with exploration than with the satisfaction of finishing a task (which is how Quantic Foundry uses the term). Its stand-out contribution, however, is the Smarty-Pants category,[15] which attributes to players an external motivation for playing. It strikes me that this could well be an example of survey respondents *pre-texting* (providing a plausible rationalisation to cover true intentions): spending half your free time playing games sounds more productive if you can explain it all away by saying you're brain-training rather than simply having fun, especially when you're presented with a questionnaire that explicitly asks if you do. Still, what do I know?

Because Trojan types cover two kinds of online game, it's possible to compare the differences in player motivations between them. Examining the percentage of players averaging greater than the mid-point for each of the six types (which are independent, so all range 0% to 100%), Socialisers and Completionists dominate both games, having similarly high numbers for each (around 80%). Escapists also have parity between the games, albeit with somewhat fewer players involved (low 50s%). *LoL* has many more Competitors (64%/34%) and Smarty-Pants (53%/39%) than *CRO3* does; *CRO3* has many more Story-Driven players (87%/67%) than *LoL* does. Such divergences could be due to cultural variations between

---

[14] I don't know *why* it's called the Trojan typology: it just is.

[15] This is a further example of the problem of naming groups: you might inadvertently choose something laughable that trivialises your whole study.

North America and China rather than differences between MOBAs and MMORPGs, but it seems more likely that they're not.

As for what a designer might use Trojan types for, well providing players with an excuse to justify their participation is a trick that seems to have been missed by pretty well everyone, so it might be worth a shot. Actually making your game help players develop their cognitive powers could assist with this, although (as mentioned in Chapter 17) many games are excellent at enabling players to develop social and high-order thinking skills almost by default, so this may not be necessary.

18.4.4 Desire Profiles

It's possible, although not necessarily always advisable, to apply wider research on motivation to virtual worlds. I was once consulting at a major European MMO developer and was asked what my opinion was of Reiss Desire Profiles. I told them I desired to know what they were, as I hadn't come across them before. They originated from studies of mental retardation (Reiss & Havercamp, 1998), so a lack of awareness of them is perhaps excusable on my part, but in essence, they're a set of (currently) 16 basic desires that define all human beings' goals. When I was presented with them, it was clear to me that some were probably good for virtual worlds but some were not. I was therefore somewhat alarmed when informed that the developer wanted their up-coming game to address every single element from the list.

Really? *All* of them? One of the desires was vengeance: you want to make people play your game out of revenge? Another was eating: people will play your game in order to eat?

They replied that they could put things into the game for the character to eat, but I was not persuaded: why would anyone who desired to eat be satisfied if their character ate? You don't show starving people pictures of strawberries. Immersion can only go so far.

As for revenge, I was told that it wasn't difficult to create situations such that the player would wish revenge. Well no, so much is obvious, but why would that be a good thing? I argued that players were not going to say to their friends "You *must* play this game – you get screwed over in it and will want revenge!", but I was told vengeance was a universal desire so had to be addressed. They saw no conflict between wanting revenge and not wanting to want revenge.

Treating the underlying needs of players as check-boxes to be satisfied by their characters isn't the best way to broaden the player base of virtual worlds. Still, if you want to try it, here's the full list of desires (IDS Publishing Corporation, n.d.): acceptance, beauty, curiosity, eating, family, honour, idealism, independence, order, physical activity, power, saving, social contact, status, tranquillity, and vengeance. All will work for characters' motivations in quests, if not for players' own motivations.

18.4.5 Funativity

Academics are not the only people who consider why people play: designers do, too – primarily because they *actually want to know*. They can make better games that way. Sure, their findings may lack the formal rigour required by a peer-assessed journal, but they're typically going to be of more interest to other designers because they home in on the things that actually concern designers (rather than academics).

A good example of this is Noah Falstein's Funativity (Falstein, 2004).[16] This isn't about players so much as what they find fun when they play. Approaching the topic from the direction of human evolution (as Raph Koster was later to do in his Theory of Fun), Noah considered what behaviours of prehistoric humans would have helped them to survive. For example, a hunter who comes back from a hunt and immediately goes out again risks injury from tiredness; a hunter who lounges around resting will recover from his expedition but lose sharpness and perhaps be injured next hunt as a consequence of this; a hunter who stays home but finds fun in throwing rocks at a piece of wood would both rest up and keep sharp. Evolution would therefore favour the one who played over the other two: less dead and better at hunting.

Following this through for other activities, Noah derived three different kinds of fun:

- **Physical Fun.** Hunter-gatherers with stronger muscles and co-ordination skills would survive to produce descendants who found play related to these qualities fun. Ones with good gathering skills would similarly survive, so exploring and collecting also fall into this category.

- **Social Fun.** People survive longer if they look out for each other. Bonding activities such as playing together encourage trust. Because language use enhances co-operation, storytelling also comes in here.

- **Mental Fun.** The better you are at thinking, the safer your actions will be and the quicker you can do them. Play is a way to improve your mental faculties: you can have ideas and test them out with less risk. Pattern-recognition, at which humans excel, is encouraged by this (and stops people from eating the bad mushrooms or walking where the lion tracks go).

Games don't have to focus on just one kind of fun in this model, they can (and often do) have *blended fun*. As for how you use Funativity, well the idea is that when you're considering whether a new gameplay concept will subjectively be fun (which is difficult), you should examine where it fits within Funativity to see if it will objectively be fun (which is less difficult). Even if your gameplay concept doesn't fit, the exercise could spark new ideas that will.

18.4.6 4Keys2Fun

Another approach to identifying what players find fun is to use biometrics and video evidence from people while they're actually playing them. This is what Nicole Lazzaro did to obtain her 4Keys2Fun (Lazzaro, 2004). Her model describes fun along four[17] different dimensions, expressed as balances between opposing forces:

- **Hard Fun:** mastery, balancing challenge and skill.[18]

---

[16] This is when Noah wrote up his ideas, but he'd had them brewing for some time. Randy Farmer mentions Funativity in his 1988 article on the types of *Habitat* player (Farmer, 1988).

[17] Maybe you didn't need to be told this.

[18] This captures the situation illustrated in Figure 16.1.

- **Easy Fun**: imagination, balancing the expected and the novel.

- **Serious Fun**: meaning, balancing aspiring and obtaining.

- **People Fun**: social bonding, balancing solo and group play.

The keys are further structured to show their inter-relationships, with the concept of player experience at the centre. This gives it the capacity not only to show *what* players find fun but *why* they find it fun. It's a superbly coherent and symmetric system. Any game designer who looks at the summarising diagram (XEODesign, 2010) is sure to be struck by its sheer beauty. OK, so if you're not a designer then you might not be all that impressed, but to a designer, it's an awesome piece of work.

There is some resonance with player types here: Achievers like hard fun, Explorers like easy fun, and Socialisers like people fun. Any relationship between Killers and serious fun is somewhat harder to discern, however, and enters square-peg-round-hole territory.

As for how you use 4Keys2Fun, well that's up to you. It presents a way of understanding fun, but what you do with that understanding is your own business (even if that business is gamification, where 4Keys2Fun garnered yet more fans). The model does have some overlap with player types, but it's aimed at games in general so insofar as virtual worlds are concerned has greater breadth at the expense of lesser depth.

18.4.7 Eight Types of Fun

Another designer who's had a stab at identifying different kinds of fun is Marc LeBlanc. His Eight Types of Fun (LeBlanc, 2004),[19] sometimes described as his Taxonomy of Game Pleasures, have less theoretical justification behind them than Funativity and 4Keys2Fun, but nevertheless have achieved a fair level of traction so it's reasonable to assume they're useful.[20] The Eight Types are:

- **Sensation**. Eye candy, music, physical activity, …

- **Fantasy**. Make-believe, escapism, imagination, …

- **Narrative**. Drama, plot, story, …

- **Challenge**. Obstacle course, competition, …

- **Fellowship**. Social interaction with other players.

- **Discovery**. Exploring the unknown.

- **Expression**. Self-discovery through play.

- **Submission**. Games as a pastime or hobby.

---

[19] To be honest, the article cited tells you less about the Eight Types than what I'm about to tell you here. There's a much better description in Hunicke et al. (2004).

[20] Their traction may also be due to the fact that they *are* described in Hunicke et al. (2004), which is a very well-cited paper for other reasons.

While an interesting way to categorise fun, it's not directly useful to designers. Its main purpose is to show that games have different aesthetics depending on what players consider to be fun. There is some overlap with player types, particularly with the Challenge, Fellowship, and Discovery types (and Expression, through growing immersion), but again, it's a broad typology that has to cover more than just virtual worlds, so can't treat them as anything special. It's not even intended to be exhaustive, unlike player types, Funativity, and 4Keys2Fun.

Note that Funativity, 4Keys2Fun, and LeBlanc's Eight Types are all about the fun that players experience, rather than about the players who experience said fun. This may be why player types are generally preferred (even though, formally, it's out of scope for anything other than virtual worlds).

18.4.8 Self-Determination Theory

If you're going to focus on players and why they play, it may be a good idea to examine the psychology involved. In Chapter 16, self-determination theory (SDT) was mentioned as a way to identify features that are not good for immersion. SDT can also be used to explain why people play in the first place. Ryan et al. (2006) tested exactly this idea for a number of game genres, with separate studies for each one. Study 4 concerned MMORPGs, and the results were markedly different than for the other genres examined. Their experiments looked at: player well-being following a play session; how much they enjoyed playing; their future months of play; and their weekly hours of play. The purpose of the study was to examine the psychological pull exerted by games,[21] with SDT providing the theory to explain player motivations.

Having found how much the three SDT components of competence, autonomy, and relatedness impacted each of these factors, the researchers wondered if SDT might be a better predictor of said factors than Nick Yee's motivational model (and by implication player types). When they tried this out (Przybylski et al., 2010), they discovered that this was indeed the case. Given that they'd obtained the pull results from using SDT in the first place, this is not perhaps surprising, but it does demonstrate that the model is a powerful one when applied to MMOs. It might not be of use to designers in explaining what to design, because every player is different and so prioritises different levels of competence, autonomy, and relatedness, but it's certainly useful in identifying what *not* to design.

This game-oriented work on SDT was consolidated into a system called PENS (Rigby & Ryan, 2007), an acronym for Player Experience Needs Satisfaction. It was created for use during development and playtesting, because it's easier for players to tell you how much competence, autonomy, and relationship they feel they have than it is for them to explain how much fun they're having. How the three components combine to affect more traditional measures of perceived enjoyment depends on the genre: for example, the relationship between competence and immersion is very strong in role-playing games but absent

---

[21] Unusually for research coming out of Psychology, this paper is even-handed in its approach and determines that games are actually good for players. In contrast, as we shall see in Chapter 22, most psychology research on the topic concludes that games are menaces to society (a charge that the cynical might also level at some forms of psychology research).

in strategy games, whereas with autonomy, it's very strong for both. The general finding is that the more you can address all three components the better, but that relatedness is only about half as powerful a draw as the other two are.

18.4.9 Multidimensional

Like PENS and 4Keys2Fun, veteran game designer Lew Pulsipher[22] also takes a multidimensional approach to identifying what people find fun, although he prefers the word "enjoyable" on the reasonable grounds that few *Chess*-players describe playing *Chess* as fun. His method employs a non-definitive set of sliders that range between competing imperatives (Pulsipher, 2011)[23]:

- **Role-Fulfilment *versus* Emergence**. Is the player's story dominated by a scripted, inter-connected events or by emergence from mechanics? Fiction-heavy games tend left; abstract games tend right.

- **Story *versus* Emerging Circumstances**. How directed is the player's experience? Are they led by the nose or free to roam? In MMO terms, the former are theme parks, the latter sandboxes.

- **Classical *versus* Romantic**. How much risk does the player like to take? The more Classical the player is, the more they want to know before they make their big move; the more Romantic the player is, the more they're likely to take a chance to land a knockout blow.

- **Long-Term Planning *versus* Adapting to Circumstances**. Does the player like to create grand schemes and consider alternatives before acting, or do they prefer to react to events as they arise? The more uncertainty there is in a game, the less the long-term planners will be satisfied.

- **Socialising *versus* Competition**. In player types terms, are you more of a Socialiser or more of an Achiever?

- **Entertainment *versus* Challenge**. Does the player want an easy time of it or a hard time of it? Direct competition with other players will tend towards the latter; direct co-operation with them will tend towards the former.

- **Relaxation *versus* Mastery**. How much does the player want to trade off living the dream against feeling important, powerful, and capable?

- **The Journey *versus* The Destination**. How much do players want to enjoy the game on the way to the victory in comparison to the victory itself? Older players tend to prefer the former; younger players tend to prefer the latter.

---

[22] Veteran, as in he was already an established and highly respected figure in postal gaming when I took up the hobby in 1974.

[23] This is a reposting of the original article published 4 October 2008 on GameCareerGuide.com, the link to which seems to be in a permanent state of being "temporarily down".

Overall, this approach is too nuanced to identify broad categories of players unless you focus on a small number of the eight dimensions provided. It's very informative when used for individual players, though,[24] and does have some satisfying overlaps with 4Keys2Fun.

Lew makes two other observations. Firstly, escapism pervades a lot of this: in a game, you are the central figure (which isn't the case for most of us in Reality) and can experience thrills in relative safety. Trial-and-error works, because the consequences of failure are negligible,[25] and the uncertainties of life are reduced because everything is structured.

Secondly, a lot of the differences between what a person finds enjoyable in games come down to their own personality. This nicely segues[26] into another collection of ways to categorise players, which use personality metrics as part of their analysis.

PERSONALITY ASSESSMENTS

An individual's personality tends to remain constant, although it can change over very long periods or as a result of severe trauma. Over the decades, psychologists who have studied personality have developed different metrics for describing it. There are two main approaches, *big five* and *Myers-Briggs*, each of which has a related offshoot.

The **Myers-Briggs Type Indicator**® (Briggs Myers, n.d.) was developed in the 1940s by a mother-and-daughter pair, Katharine Cook Briggs and Isabel Briggs Myers, based on work by the psychoanalyst Carl Jung. Widely used since then for psychometric tests, their system partitions personality along four dimensions:

- **Extraversion/Introversion**. Are you outgoing or private? Do you prefer to participate or to observe?
- **Sensing/Intuition**. Do you focus on the here and now or imagine possibilities? Do you prefer practice or theory?
- **Thinking/Feeling**. Are you level-headed or empathetic? Do you reason out your decisions or base them on gut instinct?
- **Judging/Perceiving**. Do you like to close options soon or keep them open? Do you respect rules and deadlines or regard them as flexible?

People typically report their personality using the letters E/I, S/N, T/F, and J/P, with each of the 16 possible combinations describing distinct personalities. The idea is that some vocations are favoured by people with one combination over those with others; for example, twice as many foreign-language interpreters are ISTJ (Introvert, Sensing, Thinking, Perceiving) than they are any other set of types (Schweda Nicholson, 2005).

Associated with Myers-Briggs are the four **Keirsey Temperaments** (Keirsey, 1998). These are based on the ancient Greek *four humours* (sanguine, choleric, melancholic, phlegmatic) updated for the modern era. Keirsey's four types are:

---

[24] They're therefore worth considering when constructing use cases.

[25] Save and reload works in games, but sadly not in Reality. If it did, I'd have gone back and changed my decision not to mine a few Bitcoins when I first heard about them.

[26] It's almost as if I plan the order in which I write about these topics.

- **Artisan**. Fun-loving, excitable, spontaneous, and bold.
- **Guardian**. Dutiful, dependable, responsible, and stable.
- **Idealist**. Spiritual, kind-hearted, romantic, and nurturing.
- **Rational**. Pragmatic, independent, strategic, and logical.

The Keirsey types are further subdivided into directive and informative *roles*, which in turn are subdivided into expressive or attentive *role variants*. This gives a set of 16 combinations that map onto the Myers-Briggs types (perhaps unsurprisingly, as Jung's work grew out of the four humours, too). The Keirsey types have an advantage over Myers-Briggs in that they're based on behaviour (which is observable) rather than thoughts and feelings (which aren't).

Unfortunately for Myers-Briggs (and thence Keirsey), there are few scientific studies to back them up (Randall et al., 2017); furthermore, their dichotomous nature is troubling and Jung's work has fallen out of favour among psychologists because of its unprovable nature.[27] As a result, Myers-Briggs and Keirsey have somewhat been rejected by the scientific community.

These earlier works have been supplanted by the **big five**[28] personality traits, which is a data-driven model. As the name might suggest, this has five components to it rather than the four of Myers-Briggs and Keirsey:

- **Openness to experience**. Inventiveness and curiosity as opposed to consistency and caution.
- **Conscientiousness**. Efficiency and organisation as opposed to extravagance and carelessness.
- **Extraversion**. Dynamism and gregariousness as opposed to solitude and reservedness.
- **Agreeableness**. Friendliness and compassionateness as opposed to criticism and judgementalism.
- **Neuroticism**. Sensitiveness and nervousness as opposed to resilience and confidence.

I have helpfully put these in order to fit the commonly used mnemonic OCEAN.[29]

Although there is some correlation with Myers-Briggs, the big five include neuroticism, about which Myers-Briggs says nothing. This is especially a problem if you want a personality assessment capable of predicting certain mental health problems related to neuroticism, such as anxiety and depression disorders.

---

[27] Note that there are few scientific studies to back up player types, either, and the Hero's Journey also has links to Jung. Player types are not made of dichotomies, though: those axes are continua, not binaries.

[28] I haven't cited an origin for it as it was developed independently by a number of research groups in the 1980s and 1990s, but if you want one then first out of the blocks were Tupes & Christal (1958) in the military, where their work languished largely unread for many years.

[29] CANOE also works. Languages other than English may have their own preferred orderings.

There's a Myers-Briggs Type Indicator® psychometric test and a Keirsey Temperament Sorter® psychometric test, so of course there's a psychometric test for the big five. This is the Minnesota Multiphasic Personality Test (Hathaway & McKinley, 1943), which was originally developed by psychiatrists for assessing patients. As it seriously predates the big five, originally there were some differences between the two models, but it has since been regularly refurbished and the two are now aligned.

18.4.10 Personality Metrics

The main personality metrics in use by industry and academia are outlined in the friendly nearby sidebar.

There are definite connections between personalities and virtual worlds. Dubourg et al. (2023) link an interest in imaginary worlds (of which virtual worlds are examples) with openness to experience. The Quantic Foundry motivations correlate moderately well with the big five assessment model, too (Yee, 2015a). Canossa et al. (2015) suggest that there's a link between personalities and in-game behaviours. However, there doesn't seem to be much of a correlation between personality types and choice of games played (Zammitto, 2010): for RPGs, only neuroticism is statistically significant – and that only barely so. Interestingly, if not entirely relevant to this book, there's a deep association between the big five personality traits and the five colours in *Magic: the Gathering* (Sabien, 2024).

Personality types are not useful to designers as categorisations, being more of a concern to CSRs (who have to deal with the outliers). Nevertheless, they can be useful for creating fictional characters. If you have a major story-significant NPC, taking a personality assessment on their behalf can be a useful exercise. Furthermore, different personality types can rub up against each other to create drama in known ways (Melissa, 2021).[30] The compatibility or otherwise of different personality permutations are usually obvious to designers, but if you're not sure then there are plenty of online dating sites happy to be surer on your behalf.

18.4.11 BrainHex

Combining personality assessments with other metrics has proven a fruitful area of games research. The Demographic Game Design (DGD1) model of Bateman & Boon (2006) uses Myers-Briggs to define four categories of players, supported by a set of case studies:

- **Conqueror**. Thinking and Judging in Myers-Briggs.

- **Manager**. Thinking and Perceiving in Myers-Briggs.

- **Wanderer**. Feeling and Perceiving in Myers-Briggs.

- **Participant**. Feeling and Judging in Myers-Briggs.

---

[30] "Melissa, MBTI Marketing Manager" doesn't appear to have a surname, but that doesn't necessarily mean she's not a real person.

It further splits the categories into hardcore and casual, which are observable in all four cases. DGD1 was mainly intended for use with regard to games in general rather than to MMOs; it noted player types, but wasn't based on them. Combining insights from DGD1 with findings in neurobiology, Nacke et al. (2011) developed a second study, DGD2, into a player-satisfaction model called BrainHex. BrainHex, which was tested on over 50,000 players, resulted in the identification of seven[31] archetypes that describe typical players' desired experiences:

- *Seekers* are curious about the game world and experience moments of awe and wonder.

- *Survivors* enjoy either fear, intense experience, or the relief of this (it's not clear which from the data).

- *Daredevils* play for thrills and risk-taking.

- *Masterminds* like solving puzzles and creating efficient strategies.

- *Conquerors* prefer to struggle against adversity yet eventually coming out on top.

- *Socialisers* find their primary source of enjoyment in other people.

- *Achievers* are like Conquerors, but instead of being oriented towards challenge, they're oriented towards goals.

BrainHex has several correspondences with Lazzaro's work, which as it's also rooted in biometric experiments is perhaps to be expected. The idea was well-received initially because of its neurobiological foundations, but subsequently lost momentum thanks to its strong connection with Mayers-Briggs, which had by then met with widespread academic disapproval.

It's often been suggested that player types and Myers-Briggs must be related, because there are four player types (in the original formulation) and four Myers-Briggs dichotomies. I don't buy this argument, not least because players change type as they play but personalities remain fairly constant.[32] However, I do like the argument made by Ethan Kennerly (Kennerly, 2004), which starts with the four playing card suits that I associated with player types, works back from those to their tarot origins, then forward from that to medieval alchemy (which is based on the four humours), thence to Jung's work and thereafter Myers-Briggs and Keirsey. I only chose playing cards as a metaphor because I needed one, and it occurred to me that I could do a nice pun on the word "suit". Let's have a round of applause for serendipity!

---

[31] With a name like BrainHex, you might have expected six, but no, it's seven.

[32] That doesn't mean I'm right, of course. Halvarsson & Winther (2009) demonstrate a relationship between personalities and player types, so there could well be something going on there that player type theory needs to address.

18.5 SIMILARITIES

Another way to riff on player types is to mix it with some other system to create a cocktail; this is what Andrzej Marczewski was initially attempting with the Hexad. In something of a *tour de force*, Stewart (2011) combines player types, Keirsey temperaments, and DGD1, along with nods to Caillois, Lazzaro, and multiple other categorisation schemes, to create a unified model that when applied to game genres nevertheless looks pretty much like player types.

Many different studies have been done to identify why players play; I could have cited many more than I have done. They come from multiple directions, but spookily seem to end up reaching similar conclusions having used different methods. Indeed, meta-analyses of a number of such player type categorisations almost[33] invariably find exactly that (Hamari & Tuunanen, 2014; Fritz & Stöckl, 2023). The key dimensions are achievement, exploration, sociability, and domination, with immersion also a possibility.

Yes, these are the four basic player types, plus or minus immersion (which is present in player types but manifests differently).

Finally, a word of caution. Almost all the qualitative research on player typologies uses questionnaires to obtain data. There's no standard approach to this, meaning that when it's cited, there is a near-complete lack of transparency as to how applicable the results are or whether their use can be justified in the given context (Hughes et al., 2023). If we're ever going to apply player typologies consistently, the sooner we can standardise the field, the better.

---

[33] I say "almost" because if you don't cluster the dimensions, you may end up with rather more than four or five. McKechnie-Martin et al. (2024) have 28.

Community

PLAYERS CAN AND OFTEN do play virtual worlds alone. *Playing* alone isn't the same as *being* alone, though. In virtual worlds, players play alone *together*. That may seem a small distinction, but it's a big one.

Having considered in more depth than you felt necessary why players play virtual worlds, let's now turn our attention to the player's place among other players in a virtual world.

19.1 OVERVIEW

Trying to pin down what is meant by the word "community" is not easy. Even back in the mid-1900s, sociologist George Hillery conducted a survey of definitions of the word "community" presented in texts by his fellow sociologists and found 94 different ones (Hillery, 1955).

The situation has, if anything, worsened in recent years with the appearance of additional nuances. In the same way that for presentation reasons construction companies now build "homes" rather than "houses", any identifiable sub-grouping of a larger grouping is often referred to as a "community" even if their members have little in common other than sharing some physical, cultural, or spiritual characteristic. Because of this, such groupings may be of different sizes, demonstrate different levels of intensity, and serve different purposes.

As a consequence of routinely calling users of a product a "community", much of the original contextual meaning of the term has been lost. Facebook may have a community standards document (Meta, n.d.), but (to paraphrase Randy Farmer) just because you use the Facebook app, that doesn't mean there's a Facebook community any more than your using a hammer means there's a hammer-using community (Morningstar et al., 2023). Facebook isn't a community unless by "community" you mean the people who use it: undeniably it *has* communities, but is it really one itself?

It's a similar thing for virtual worlds. It felt natural to speak of the *LambdaMOO* community (Curtis, 1992), but *LambdaMOO* was comparatively small. Does a *World of Warcraft* community exist? Its presumed members may not all feel they're part of such a grouping, but they have little say in the matter. Does it make sense to talk about "the community of MMO-players"? Might you just as well say "MMO-players"?

Sometimes, a larger grouping is described figuratively terms of its members, such as "the community of English-speaking nations". What became the European Union was called the European Economic Community at launch in 1957. Ultimately, though, communities are made of and by the people in them. The people of a community recognise a contextual connection with each other within a larger grouping. Such sometimes-stable, sometimes-shifting sub-groupings are what we'll be looking at in this chapter.

In 1998, I wrote an article for a magazine called *The Cursor*, which I entitled *Bad Ideas for Multi-Player Games* (Bartle, 1998). Bad idea #1 was: "If 50 simultaneous players is good and 500 is better, 5,000 must be absolutely fantastic!". Obviously, having 5,000 players is better for business than having 50 or 500, but my point was that having them all in the same shard was not the ideal solution. If people want to be nobodies, they can play Reality; if you want to make it so they can feel known to their peers then they have to be packaged up into smaller communities. A 5,000-player game becomes a 20-community game, where each community is around 250 simultaneous players. It's therefore better (although not necessarily best) to write a game for 250 players and run 20 copies of it.

Virtual worlds are cruise ships, not speedboats: you don't design them by taking a speedboat and adding more seats. Sadly, in the past, many designers nevertheless effectively did do exactly[1] that, leaving guilds to take responsibility for the community-organisation aspect of MMOs that as a consequence became somewhat pressing. Guilds *can* actually be pretty good at this, though, so long as their members follow some basic, common-sense rules (Johansson & Verhagen, 2010).

You may be wondering why I chose 250 when suggesting a community size in the paragraph-before-last. The reason is Dunbar's number (see sidebar) (note: Dunbar's number is 150, not 250; you need more than 150 in a virtual world, to allow for shifting relationships). People can only maintain a certain number of relationships, a good many of which will be with people in Reality. In a virtual world, they'll know some other players, but those other players may not all know each other. Text MUDs tended to cap out at around 250 active players before they felt too crowded and people began to lose the sense that they were a somebody; 250 gives a coherent, village-like feel, so that's why I plumped for it. Individual guilds tend to be smaller than that in terms of active player numbers,[2] but with around 250 players, the community as a whole will still feel meaningful to its members (and perhaps more importantly, they'll feel meaningful themselves, too).

---

[1] Well, metaphorically exactly.

[2] A 2006 analysis of *World of Warcraft* guild sizes (Ducheneaut et al., 2006) found that the average number of active members per guild per month was 16.8, excluding guilds with only one member (typically created as an exploit to gain access to additional storage).

DUNBAR'S NUMBER

After noticing a relationship between the size of primate groups and the size of those primates' brains, the anthropologist Robin Dunbar posited that human beings can only maintain a certain number of meaningful relationships (Dunbar, 1992). When he and other researchers checked out his hypothesis, they found that it was basically true: groups that have longevity, whether they're in businesses (Webber & Dunbar, 2020), religious organisations (Bretherton & Dunbar, 2020), the military (Dunbar, 2010), or elsewhere, all seem to be composed of structures containing no more than a relatively fixed number of people. That number, 150, is called *Dunbar's number* for reasons you can probably guess.

This isn't to say that everyone has 150 best friends. There are four different clusters of friends that make up that 150 and two more beyond it of people who are known but aren't friends (Dunbar, 1998). The smaller the cluster, the more you trust the people in it.

- **Intimate Friends**. You'll probably have around five of these; they're people you can count on in a crisis.
- **Best Friends**. Most of us have around ten of these; along with your intimate friends, you can ask them for sympathy if things aren't going well.
- **Good Friends**. These number around 35; together with intimate and best friends, they constitute most of your regular social contacts and all of your emotional and economic support.
- **Casual Friends**. The remaining 100 or so people in your 150-person friend capacity are those whom you might join without feeling embarrassed if you saw them in a social setting, yet that you don't have quite the same bonds with as you do the other layers.
- **Nodding Acquaintances**. Beyond the friend layers, there are around 350 people you might acknowledge when you see them but with whom you have little other interaction.
- **You Know Their Face**. You can also recognise another 1,500 or so people, but exceeding the overall total of 2,000, you'll start forgetting old faces when you learn a new one.

Obviously, there are differences between how this pans out for individuals, not least because of gender and how sociable you are: for intimate friends, men peak between two and five, whereas women peak between three and seven (Dunbar & Spoors, 1995). Beyond that, there are still wide variations because of the way that normal (Gaussian) distributions can extend for quite some way: some people remember names better than faces, for example (or neither very well), yet many of us might easily recognise the faces of hundreds and hundreds of actors from movies that we haven't seen for many, many years. Some people are *super-recognisers* and make a career of it: they can identify a person they've seen once before from only a glimpse in a crowd (Rice, 2016). Others are *super-connectors*, with vast numbers of friends and acquaintances; these people are central to the way that networks grow (Barabási & Albert, 1998).

On the whole, though, Dunbar's number is strongly and verifiably a thing. You don't have to *have* 150 friends, but if you want more then you're very likely to struggle to keep them all.

You can't design communities: you can only design *for* them. As for how to design for them, well that depends what kind of community you want and why. There are two imperatives: the pragmatic and the artistic. Pragmatically, it's about retention: communities are very sticky – significantly more so than perceived enjoyment (Chang et al., 2008) – so if you have communities then players are less likely to leave (unless a whole community decamps at once, which does happen). Artistically, it's for the designer's own reasons: you want communities because you wish to say something to the players by using the affordances that communities give you. As usual, there's a question as to which imperative wins when they're at odds, but often both can be achieved together. When there is an irreconcilable clash between a practical requirement and an artistic statement, one side will have to concede to the other. For example, suppose the CSR lead wants a change to be made but the lead designer objects: the CSRs have data to support their arguments whereas designers have not – they can only plead "trust me!". Neither of the parties involved are unreasonable, but trying to balance knee-jerk reaction against grandiose vision may call for there to be pre-agreed policies that can be consulted and enacted by an independent arbiter.[3]

In massively multiplayer worlds, communities are natural occurrences: if you have players, you get communities whether you want them or not. They can be encouraged by design (for example, by having hubs that people need to visit to use the services there); they can be engineered by design (for example, by having content only accessible to groups); they can be forced by design (for example, by having open PvP). All these methods (and more that we'll come to later) affect the shape of the communities that develop. Always be aware, though, that communities cannot themselves be designed.

Unfortunately, the influence of designers is perhaps only a quarter of the influence that players themselves have on the communities that form. No two guilds playing on the same shard are alike, and no two shards of the same virtual world are alike. They will have recognisable differences. Designers have only limited control over the birth and growth of communities, but they do have a say in that they can encourage or discourage particular community-related activities. It would therefore be a good idea if they had some idea of how communities work.

Happily for designers, community has been studied a great deal by academics and business people; the central ideas don't have to be rediscovered for virtual worlds unless you're one of those designers who always knows better. In essence, communities are groups of

---

[3] Typically, this will be the producer. Both sides know that producers dislike them in equal measure, so the verdict will be fair.

people of a shared cultural context who have the means, motive, and opportunity to communicate with one another. Individuals can be in more than one community at the same time and can choose the extent to which they participate in those communities. Note that all of these properties need to be true for communities to arise. If you don't understand the language, have a mouth full of marshmallows, don't have anything to say or are too far away for anyone to hear you anyway, you won't immediately be joining the pop-up community of cosplayers that's forming down the street.

There are other features of communities that aren't strictly necessary, but that can make a community stronger if they're present. These include:

- Members have a shared pool of knowledge.

- Members follow common practices.

- Members share a vision of the community's future.

- Members work together on programs to benefit the community.

- The community has a history.

This list suggests ways by which a designer can help communities develop, and we'll be discussing some of them shortly. A word of caution, though: a community that is too strong may neither need nor welcome new members. Strong communities are usually good for their members (cults perhaps excepted), but they're not always good for people who want to be members but are shut out.

Right! Let's begin by looking at a concept that affects community but that designers can influence.[4]

19.2 CULTURE

Part of the reason designers have less control over communities than they might wish is that cultural factors get in the way. Culture is anything non-biological that one generation passes on to the next. For virtual worlds, this will certainly be dependent on the demographics of the players, but it will also be carried over from the games and other virtual worlds its players have played.

That different virtual worlds have different cultures isn't difficult to demonstrate. For example, sometimes a player character in a group will jump up and down without otherwise moving. Its player is conveying something to other players through this action, but what? In some virtual worlds, jumping means "yes"; in others, it means "ready", "hurry up", or "come here", or different things in different contexts. These variations are small but visible outward expressions of cultural differences between virtual worlds.

It's undeniable that designers influence the culture of their virtual world through their designs. When architects design new housing estates, they consider what kind of community they wish to inculcate; indeed, architecture is routinely used as a vehicle for

---

[4] Be aware that it can also influence designers.

cultural regeneration (Wansborough & Mageean, 2000). It's inconceivable that an architect wouldn't know that the inhabitants of soulless tower blocks would form a different kinds of community to those in terraced houses with private gardens. The same principle applies to the designers of virtual worlds. A virtual world's culture is always shaped by its design; therefore, it's impossible to design a virtual world and *not* affect the cultural behaviour it engenders. Code *begets* community (Pargman, 2000). You can't design the culture you'll get because it's too fluid, but you *can* design the mould into which it's poured.

In the past, when most players were new to the concept of virtual worlds, they acted as foundries of culture formation (Reid, 1994). The virtual world's design played a big part in this. For example, the reason people were more open in virtual worlds than in everyday life was that they were afforded pseudonymity therein; it wasn't because they grew up in a society that prized openness. So many people have played virtual worlds nowadays, though, that the influence of design is waning. The majority of players may be new to *this* virtual world, but they're not necessarily new to virtual worlds in general; it's from their previous experiences that they bring their cultural expectations.[5] Expectations do differ between players because, although virtual world cultures are often similar, they're not homogenous, so a virtual world's formative culture derives from the mixing pot of beta-testers and early-access players, tempered by the virtual world's design. The players involved *seed* (or *preload*)[6] the culture that will develop thereafter.

Unfortunately, shortly after launch, half of these early players will go off and play the next big shiny that's in open access, while the remainder will either be hardcore fans of the genre or hardcore fans of a failed virtual world that they want this one to resemble exactly. Whatever, none of them are representative of the majority of players who will subsequently join and for whom they have defined what the culture will be.

It used to be, many years ago, that you could choose your initial player base carefully so as to increase the chance that the culture to which later players would adapt might be one conducive to civil behaviour. This is still possible for small-scale worlds, but not for ones that want 300,000 beta-testers to swarm in at once to stress test the system. Fortunately, there are ways the designer can mitigate this to manage the culture; I'll address them shortly.

If a player wants their needs in a virtual world to be satisfied, they have to play alongside other players who may have different needs. Players must therefore develop a set of mutual understandings that regulate their behaviour, so they can all have a shot at doing what they want to do and at being whom they want to be. These understandings bounce off and interact with one other until they reach a reasonably steady state, providing a context that adds meaning to players' actions (and to the players themselves). This is the *culture* of the virtual world.

Note that the culture of a virtual world is how things stand now and is shifting; its *ethos* is how things would stand ideally. Designers can set the ethos of their virtual world, but the degree to which its culture aligns with it is another matter.

---

[5] Or, if you wish they didn't bring in such expectations, cultural baggage.

[6] The Latin word *colete*, meaning "to till", is the root of the word "culture", hence for example "horticulture". This pretentious reason is why I prefer "seed" to "preload".

A virtual world's culture affects the nature of its communities, which is why we're looking at it first. It's shaped by five factors:

1. **The Limitations of Human Beings.** People can only type or speak so fast; most of
their Dunbar's number of friends will be offline or elsewhere; mind-reading isn't a
thing. We can't do much about any of these; we merely have to accept them as fact and
work with them.

2. **What Players Bring with them from Elsewhere.** This comes largely from the cultures of Reality, but it also includes the cultures of other virtual worlds and games.
Two incarnations of *MUD1* had the exact same code and exact same seed players,
but developed different cultures because one drew on US professionals and the other
drew on UK teens.

3. **The Culture of Non-Players.** This can also affect the culture of a virtual world if
its proponents are influential enough. For example, designers and players alike may
steer clear of disrespecting major religions[7] even if they really, really want to do so.

4. **The Design of the Virtual World.** We have some control over this. *EVE Online, Star
Citizen, Elite Dangerous*, and *No Man's Sky* are all space-exploration virtual worlds,
but their cultures are completely different: this is because their designs are different.

5. **The Virtual World's Existing Culture.** People who arrive and find an already-extant
culture will usually attempt to conform to it, even if it's some distance from what
they're used to (that is, they suffer *culture shock*). Yes, this is a recursive definition: a
virtual world's culture is in part shaped by that virtual world's culture.

The degree to which each of these points shapes a virtual world's culture varies between
virtual worlds: point 2 will be stronger for a virtual world that attracts people who already
share a culture or cultural interests, as is the case with *Furcadia*. The influence of the points
can also vary over time for individual virtual worlds: point 4 usually starts off strong and
gets weaker, whereas point 5 usually starts off weak and gets stronger.

Because virtual worlds themselves are cultural objects, the transfer of influence isn't unidirectional. Concepts that originated in virtual worlds have now made it to Reality, including terms such as "PK", "LOL", and "AFK".[8] I myself realised that virtual worlds had made
it to the mainstream when in the 1990s I saw a shop in Singapore called "Newbie". Other
influences are more difficult to assess, though: for example, has the fact that cross-gender
play in virtual worlds is generally accepted had any effect on wider culture? If yes, what? If
no, how come it's resisted negative cultural perceptions from both the left and right of the
political spectrum for so long? If virtual worlds *can* have a lasting impact on the cultures

---

[7] *Star Wars, Star Trek, The Lord of the Rings, …*

[8] Lest these haven't made it to your particular part of Reality: PK = "player killer", particularly popular in Far Eastern
game shows; LOL = "laugh out loud", which can be embarrassingly confused with "lots of love" AFK = "away from keyboard", meaning you're not going to pay any attention to anything that happens until you type "back" (not that you were
doing much anyway).

of Reality, that offers the faint promise of art with political effects (although these things currently cost so much to develop that art with profitable effects takes priority).

The general culture of a virtual world affects its overall tone, but there can be sub-cultures (Pearce, 2009). Large-scale virtual worlds are not monocultural; indeed, rebelling against a prevailing culture can itself be the basis for a culture to form – a *counter-culture*. Both sub-cultures and counter-cultures inherit from the general culture but seek to override parts of it.[9] Factions, guilds, and character classes can all have different cultures even if they have the same members. You may play as both Horde and Alliance characters in *WoW*, but you'll find yourself adapting to slightly different cultures when you play them. Likewise, the social norms you follow as a tank are not the same as those for a healer. It's as if there's a hierarchy of cultures, with higher-up ones abstracting lower-down ones and lower-down ones fleshing-out higher-up ones in a never-ending, evolving dialogue.

Now, as I mentioned a little earlier, designers can include mechanics for managing player culture. There are two aspects to this, both captured by that verb "to manage":

- To supervise or to control, as in "I managed a company".
- To cope with, as in "I managed the jellied moose nose but not the stinkhead".[10]

There's also the question of who's doing the managing. I'll be focusing on the designers because they're the primary audience of this book, but other groups do need to be accommodated. For example, external bodies may have something to say about how designers manage (in both senses) player culture, and players who invest their identity in a cultural group that isn't represented in a virtual world will need to manage (in the second sense) their situation.

So, following on from this, we can ask (and, because this is a rhetorical exercise, answer) some questions about designers and the management of player culture.

Why would Designers want to Cope with Player Culture? They *could* take a *laissez-faire* approach and let the dice fall how they may. Whatever emerged from the resulting inter-cultural struggles would certainly be stronger as a result. Well yes, the victorious cultural faction *would* be stronger, but the virtual world itself would in all probability go belly-up after players on the losing side quit. When it became apparent what was happening, developers would have to intervene to prevent this. Bye bye *laissez-faire*. There's a power differential between players and designers: designers have responsibility whether they want it or not. We'll be looking at this in Volume II's chapter on Ethics.

More prosaically, some people have personal problems for which the virtual world is merely the vehicle in which they happen to express them, or they have interpersonal problems with other players. Designers must anticipate such frictions and put

---

[9] Sub-culture: "The system isn't working as designed and therefore needs repairing". Counter-culture: "The system is working as designed and therefore needs replacing".

[10] These are apparently delicacies in Alaska. Let's hope they stay there.

CSR systems in place to be ready for them. Most of these solutions were known and honed in the first four Ages of virtual worlds, and modern technological tools can be bought-in both to identify potential flashpoints and to speed up dealing with them. Some cultural issues are intractable, though: you know that in large-scale worlds, commodification via RMT attacks the magic circle that previously defended virtual worlds from such activities; you know that you can't change the minds of those players who find this practice culturally acceptable; you therefore have to design the virtual world in the expectation that it will happen.

Why would Designers want to Supervise Player Culture? Obviously, fire-fighting the results of not doing so is an important reason, but designers work ahead of players and can be proactive, not merely reactive. Their main goals are essentially practical: making the virtual world socially appealing to players, especially newbies; minimising the number of direct contacts between players and CSRs. However, there's also the point that by controlling (or at least directing) the culture of a virtual world, its designer is controlling its image – which is to say the designer's own self-image.

What Aspects of Player Culture Do Designers have to Cope with? Oh, the usual: the effects of bugs, ill-judged statements by the dev team, rumours, bad patches, perceived unfairness,[11] hackers, crackers, competing virtual worlds, thick players, spammers, exploiters, griefing, journalists, generic whingeing, unrealistic expectations, use of [bad language, foreign language, scripts, hacked clients], habitual TOS violations, accidents, hordes of clueless newbies, events in Reality, inter-player rivalries, inter-player disputes, rivalries and disputes between groups of players, rivalries and disputes between CSRs, rivalries and disputes between groups of CSRs, different ideas concerning what the virtual world is about, players cheating each other, players cheating you, players cheating themselves, player betrayals, non-acceptance of your authority, actual psychopaths, the bizarre and unpredictable, …. All of these are problems anyway, but how they pan out depends on the culture of the virtual world. One player base may forgive bugs but not what they perceive as cheating by the virtual world's systems; another may be the other way round, or find both or neither to be problematical.

What Aspects of Player Culture Do Designers have to Supervise? This is rather more nebulous. Essentially, designers will want to reconfigure some or all of the players' opinions, attitudes, beliefs, values, and customs regarding how they should play the virtual world. This will usually entail a relaxation rather than a tightening up: designers seek to offer players something they can't get in Reality, which means broadening horizons and granting freedoms. The nebulosity comes from that word "something": different designers have different ideas concerning what virtual worlds in general and theirs in particular are about. The aspects of player culture that must be directed towards servicing this therefore depend on the designer's vision for the virtual world.

---

[11] It doesn't help that people can have different ideas as to what's unfair or not. Which statement do you agree with most (Johnson, 2023): "Everyone deserves to have about the same amount of financial wealth" or "People who are smarter, more creative, and more conscientious deserve more financial wealth"?

This notion of using virtual worlds to make an artistic statement is something we'll address in Volume II, but for the moment, we'll be practical about it and merely say that there's so much designers *have* to cover, so much they *need* to deal with, so much they *must* do, and so little time to do it, that the stuff they *don't* have to do – such as steering players towards an unachievable ideal – understandably takes a distant second place. Does that seem reasonable?

Well, it may *seem* reasonable, but to adopt this viewpoint is a mistake. Saying something through the design of a virtual world is not a cultural optional-extra: it's central to the notion of what virtual worlds *are*. Designers aren't designing a virtual world to address a culture or designing a culture to address a virtual world: they're designing both to reflect aspects of *themselves*. If designers are prevented from doing this, the result will be a virtual world with no soul.

As I said, we'll be looking at this in (a lot more) depth in Volume II.

19.3 COMMUNICATION

If you have communication, communities will arise inevitably and unstoppably. Even if there's nothing to do, communities will spontaneously coalesce in which people complain about having nothing to do.

In the first four Ages of virtual worlds, communication was almost entirely undertaken within the virtual world. Beginning in the Fifth Age, external communication via assorted voice-over-IP systems became more viable; it's been gradually increasing in popularity since then. Although a significant reason for this is that players who use consoles can't type into chat boxes, raids that need someone to roar instructions have also played their part, even for keyboard users.

As I also mentioned earlier, speaking with your own voice in a virtual world is not good for immersion, even though it feels more real than text does. The problem is that it feels *too* real: it's harder to situate yourself in the virtual if you bring Reality with you. Voice fonts can mitigate this, but *you* still hear your voice when you speak even if the other players hear your processed voice; they're therefore not ideal.

Bad though it may be for immersion, voice communication can be very good for communities. Often, guilds will set up private channels using their VoIP service of choice[12] and communicate using that while playing. This gives them a safe communication space, where other players and the virtual world's monitoring systems can't hear them, but it can also help with gameplay: if you're using your keyboard to move yourself out of the fire, you don't want to be typing anything in a message window at the same time.

Sadly, although private VoIP channels may be a boon for those players who are in a community, they shut out players who are not in a community. The solution that immediately presents itself is for the virtual world itself to carry voice chat, so it can broadcast to players on an open channel. However, I would only recommend this approach if you want an immediate increase in toxicity. Some efforts have been made to introduce localised voice communication; for example, *New World* allows people to speak in-game such that other

---

[12] As I write this, the service *du jour* is Discord. The services *de la veille* include Teamspeak, Ventrilo, and Mumble.

players whose characters are nearby can hear you, but it's only really of use in instances (which *New World* calls *expeditions*).

Given that communication is not only good for community but a prerequisite for it, let's take look at what designers can do to help establish and encourage communication between players.

19.3.1 Communication: Shared Cultural Context

Earlier, I asserted that in essence, communities are groups of people of a shared cultural context who have the means, motive, and opportunity to communicate with one another.

A player's *cultural context* is what they use to interpret inputs as symbols. The most obvious example is that two people who are to communicate would do well to speak the same language. It doesn't have to be a natural language – hitting someone with a club is communicating *something* – but for freeform communication, a natural language is clearly superior. We don't all speak the *same* natural languages, of course, and although automatic translation is coming along in leaps and bounds, it will often still be confused by idioms,[13] memes,[14] and other aspects of culture (when should it translate the English "you" as "tu" or "vous" in French?). It's fine for simple messaging, but not great for extended conversations or discussions.

The primary way to get a shared cultural context is therefore not design-related at all: you simply organise servers by geographic location, on the grounds that people in the same region tend to share (or at least be aware of) one another's non-virtual cultural context. You do have to be careful, though: they may share a context but that doesn't necessarily mean they generally like each other (especially if there's a recent history of wars between the nations involved). It's useful for CSR reasons to designate certain servers to be meant for speakers of a particular language (English, French, German, or whatever), but if you don't then it's often the case that players will sort themselves by cultural context anyway.

A good example of this is *WoW*, which has servers that, while not officially marked as being for Italian players, are nevertheless populated almost entirely by Italian speakers. Some virtual worlds helpfully allow players to indicate what languages they speak when they look for groups, so they don't find themselves surrounded by people they don't under-stand. It doesn't always work out, though. Once, in *FFXIV*, I joined a group of four and we successfully completed a dungeon. Two of the players left afterwards, but I and the remain-ing player wanted another run, so he signed us up for a second dungeon. It turned out that he spoke both English and German, as a result of which we were both put in a group of three German speakers plus me. I had no idea what they were saying and only the one I was already grouped with had a clue what I was saying. It was one of the more unusual groups I've been in over the years.[15]

Designers can't do much else with regard to ensuring that players share a cultural con-text. With in-world communication, it's possible to provide different channels for different

---

[13] The beast at Tanagra (Darmok, 1991).
[14] Shaka, when the walls fell (Darmok, 1991).
[15] Not as unusual as the Zul'Farrak group in *WoW* that I was invited to by four identical gnomes who only spoke Chinese and moved entirely by jumping. They were damned good players, though!

languages, but there's no guarantee that players will stick to them and it's impossible to filter their words automatically because some short sentences are the same in multiple languages. Is "halt" English or German? Is "stop" English, Croatian, Czech, Dutch, Latvian, or Romanian? Answer to both questions: yes.

One final point about shared culture: it might be affected by factors bearing little relationship to language or time zone. For example, *WoW* users who start playing *FFXIV* might wonder why so many players are uncommunicative. The reason is that *WoW* players use a PC and a good many *FFXIV* players use a console with no keyboard. The two groups of players have different cultures of interaction.

19.3.2 Communication: Means

What can designers do about means?

If players are to communicate, not only must they be able to understand one another but also they must be able to exchange messages. This is achieved by providing them with *channels*, each of which uses at least one *medium* and is either in-world or out-of-world.

Designers and developers have little control over out-of-world communication, except for that which takes place in whatever official forum there might be (which they'll then have to moderate). If people want to use VoIP or to shout across the room to their mates, well designers have no influence on these as means of communication (although they will have some indirectly on their content).

The medium could be pretty well anything, but in practice will be either text or voice or possibly both. I expect that the boundaries will become less meaningful with the increasing use of AI to convert between them (for reasons to do with immersion, convenience, and accessibility). Although this sounds as if it has no downsides, it can do. For example, you might spend quite some time parameterising your voice so that players will hear it exactly how you want it to sound, but if they're converting it all to text or sign language then they (and you) are never going to know.

In-world channels are where designers can start to influence the means by which players communicate. The usual aim is to ensure ease of use, both for sending and receiving messages (or not receiving them, if the player doesn't want them). That said, if you wish to push a particular medium at the expense of others, for example synthesised voice over raw voice, then you can do so; some players will move their messages out-of-world if they're inconvenienced too much, but others will accept your choice because it's less of a bother to do so.

Channels can be synchronous in real time (like a telephone conversation) or asynchronous (like an email conversation). You might receive them by default or have to sign up for them; they might be open to anyone or closed except to those who are invited; you might have speech-and-listening rights or only listening rights. Whatever, as a player you can usually subscribe or unsubscribe to them if your interest in their content changes.[16]

Channels can address different audiences:

---

[16] "Usually", because some messages have to get through regardless, particularly those from the operator warning of an imminent server reboot.

- **Personal**. Only one person can receive the message. If you ask someone to message you, this is what they'll assume you mean. It's sometimes called a *whisper* and sometimes a *private message*, or *PM* (a term originating with social media[17]).

- **Narrowcast**. Only the members of a group receive the message. Group chat is a good example. This is sometimes called a *direct message*, or *DM*, although there's contention over the details: some people use DM to mean PM, because that's what some more modern social media platforms (such as Discord) call it.

- **Local Broadcast**. Only those in the vicinity of the character transmitting the message receive it. This could be everyone within a certain range of the speaker (how wide a range depending on whether they say or yell their message), or in the same instance. In a text MUD, it would be all characters in the same room as you.

- **Broadcast**. Everyone receives the message. Formally, this means every player on the server wherever they are, but in use, it tends to refer to everyone within the same area or region.

Note that the above refer to the potential audience, not the actual audience. If you're the only member of your guild currently playing, saying something in guild chat would still be narrowcasting, not personal communication, even though you're effectively talking to yourself.

Channels may have multiple representations. For example, a local broadcast could be displayed both as a speech bubble and as a message in a chat window. Make sure that players can turn each on and off independently, though: some players hate speech bubbles because they're unimmersive, but others love them because they show that the place is alive (although if it's *too* alive, the bubbles will overlap and your screen will look a complete mess).

The channels you can (or must) subscribe to are usually available in a *chat window*. There's only ever one chat window, but it may have multiple *tabs* (like with a browser). Only one tab can be displayed per window, but tabs can often be detached from the main window and repositioned such that several specialised sub-windows can be seen at once. I'm just going to call them all tabs. Each tab has its own *feed*, which is the list of channels to which it subscribes. The same channel can usually appear in multiple feeds, and players can customise their feeds to meet their preferences. For example, in an instance you might want to see messages directed: to the party you're in; to the local area (in case a party member speaks by area instead of party); and to you, personally. You might not want guild messages to appear, because your guild generates a lot of them and they could out-scroll the party messages. You could arrange to have personal messages to appear in all your tabs, though, so you see them no matter which tab you have open.

From all this, it may appear that the more channels you design into your virtual world, the better. This is not, however, the case. If you provide too many channels, players can easily

---

[17] Needless to say, logging being what it is, it's not *really* private unless it's encrypted.

find it confusing. I hinted at this in the example I gave in the previous paragraph: if there are two ways to speak to everyone in the same instance (by party and by area), players may miss messages if their feed omits one of them. It's even worse if they're in the same guild.

I should perhaps mention that what I've described here is the modern approach to channels, which took hold in the Sixth Age. Some Fifth-Age virtual worlds are much less configurable when it comes to channels and feeds.[18]

Communication actions are examples of what are known as *slash commands* in today's virtual worlds. On a keyboard, slash commands are typically introduced by a / character, hence the name,[19] and are invoked whenever the bulk of the keyboard is needed for some purpose other than the default of interacting with the virtual environment. Their origin is the use of / as a switch in old mainframe software: textual worlds used them to allow players to adjust settings. For example, *MUD2* has a /VT52 slash command to tell it to send output in a format compatible with VT52 terminals. OK, so this isn't particularly useful any more because VT52 terminals were only manufactured between 1974 and 1978, but you get the idea. Other slash commands, such as /S to set the period that the game would wait with no input before timing you out, retain some utility. Later innovations, such as changing the mode of keyboard input,[20] led to what we have today.

Slash commands differ between virtual worlds, so you have to learn the ones that work for the one you're playing. Some are sufficiently obscure that most players will have no idea what they might mean. What does *New World*'s /consul command do? I had to look it up to find out.[21]

For communication purposes, an important category of slash commands is *emotes*. These cause the player character to perform an expressive action that characters nearby can witness. For example, /laugh may run a short laughter animation on your character, perhaps with an accompanying sound effect, plus a message in the general chat window stating that your character laughs. Note that emotes don't *have* to be things you can technically emote – you might be able to /volunteer, for example – but that's where their origins lie. Some emotes may accept a target: it could be that you can /point in general or at some selected character or object.

Sometimes, emotes allow for modifiers. I might be able to /laugh bitterly or /laugh sarcastically or /laugh with little enthusiasm. The problem with this idea is that the animation may not match the modifier. Likewise, some emotes come with built-in modifiers: if I /dance, I may be told that I "dance happily" – even if I'm dancing at gunpoint. This was all a lot easier in textual worlds, where animations weren't

---

[18] Virtual worlds from the textual era don't need to separate channels by tabs because they can interleave them into the scrolling text the player sees anyway when they play. Sure, they *can* separate channels into different windows if they have a fancy client, but it's not a requirement.

[19] Did I really need to say that? I think I didn't really need to say that.

[20] You don't have to /say hi in *MUD2*, you can just "hi, but if you only want to talk and not do anything else you can /". This will cause all input to be speech until toggled off by another /".

[21] To save you the trouble of doing likewise, guilds in *NW* are called *companies*. The leader is the *governor* and ranks *consul*, *officer*, and *settler* descend below. The /consul command directs messages to a private chat channel available only to the governor and consuls of your company.

a thing; it'll be easier in graphical worlds, too, once it becomes possible to modify animations on the fly (I'm looking at you here, AI: hurry up).

Because textual worlds have no problem with animation, they tend to have much more flexible emotes. They can even have freeform emotes. In *MUD2*, for example, the ; and : commands will tell nearby players that you do the text that immediately follows. For example, were I to type ;laffs then this would announce "Richard laffs" to everyone else in my room.[22] Graphical worlds can also do this, of course, albeit by foregoing any accompanying animation; it's only the fact that most of their players think slash commands have to start with a slash that prevents it – instead of ; or : they'd expect something like /act. *MUD2* even allowed emoticons as input: you could type :-) or :) and it would be the same as issuing the command smile. We had over 50 of these – they're not difficult to handle.[23]

Emotes *can* have gameplay effect, for example you may need to /kneel before a shrine to advance a quest, but in general, they don't. This makes them cosmetic, which instantly suggests that some developers may have no compunction about selling them for real money. This can be problematic: sure, Achievers don't care if you sell cosmetic emotes, but Socialisers may well be angered by it. You need to be careful which ones you put in the store.

Emotes tend to come in three categories:

- Common, such as /laugh, /wave, and /sit.

- Uncommon, such as /cough, /blush, and /plead.

- Oddly specific, such as /clutchhead, /prettyplease, and /eastern-greeting.[24]

Tempting though it may be to provide only the common emotes and sell the rest, this is not a good idea: you'd be making players pay to interact, which would discourage players from interacting – yet interaction is what you need for community. If you *must* sell emotes, sell only the oddly specific ones.

Emotes are important because they allow players to express themselves non-verbally. Non-verbal communication is still communication, and designers who want communities to develop would do well to allow as many emotes as possible (so long as players can to favourite the ones they actually use).

Freeform communication, in which players can say whatever they like to one another, is obviously the ideal. However, the Internet being the Internet, it can also lead to toxicity. There are five main ways that designers can help to mitigate this, some of which can be combined to work in concert:

---

[22] A freeform emote needs to be distinguishable from something that has actually happened. In *MUD2*, this was done by giving the player's rank for genuine actions. ;has picked up the longsword. would produce "Richard has picked up the longsword.", but the get longsword command would produce "Richard the arch-wizard has picked up the longsword.". No, ;the arch-wizard has picked up the longsword. was automatically disallowed.

[23] : and ; had identical functionality except when followed by emoticon-forming text. ;-) would be the same as using the command wink.

[24] These are from *FFXIV*.

- **Prevention**: stop all communication between strangers. This isn't *quite* as bad an idea as it might first seem, as it does prevent people from broadcasting undesirable material on open channels; unfortunately, it also stops them from broadcasting desirable material on them, too. In this approach, players have to request permission to communicate with other individual players, which many will find awkward or embarrassing. Bots don't, though, and will happily spam players with requests and then immediately deliver their message the moment you accept. This therefore isn't a great solution.

- **Canned Speech**: only allow communication using predefined phrases. *Toontown* did this with its SpeedChat functionality: a pull-down menu listed the general topics ("Emotions", "Hello", "Goodbye", "Happy" – there were about fifteen in all) and then expanded the selected one into different messages ("Hi!", "Hello!", "Hi there!", "Hey!" ...). This ensured that the environment was safe for children, and had the advantage that players could communicate with people in other languages (because the phrases could be pre-translated). For freeform communication, players needed to give the recipient a unique secret code, which couldn't be done in chat.[25] This does help a lot with child safety and toxicity reduction, but canned phrases sadly aren't popular among players because they don't always can the phrase you want to use.

- **Allowlist**[26]: only permit players to use words from a limited vocabulary. This approach defines a list of words that players can use in communication and prevents them from employing any others, at least not easily. You can see why this might be desirable in games built for children, but players can be very creative: even when forced to use a sentence constructor with a vocabulary of innocuous words, players can produce gems such as "I want to stick my long-necked Giraffe up your fluffy white bunny" (Farmer, 2007).[27]

- **Denylist**[28]: permit freeform communication but automatically filter out its worst excesses. This is a simple way to prevent people from using certain loaded words. Its main annoyance is that innocent words may also find themselves banned. I recall attempting to persuade Midjourney to draw a picture of "Al Gore standing on the Information Superhighway" and being refused because "gore" is on its banned-words list. There are two subdivisions of denylists:

  - **Profanity Filters**: these are denylists that the player can opt into or out of, at their discretion. Words on the list are usually replaced with asterisks or other punctuation marks in the text. I'll talk a little more about them shortly.

---

[25] It could, however, be given by moving objects around your house, so they formed numbers (Farmer, 2007). So much for only giving codes to people you know in Reality.

[26] These are more generally known as *whitelists*, but recently, the term has somehow acquired racist overtones.

[27] In my teens, I published a postal games zine. In one of the games I ran, players played as cavemen and I only allowed them to communicate using words from a fixed list (so their communications sounded like those of cavemen). It didn't take the players long to notice that "give", "me", and "head" were in the list, and as for what they did with "hard", "spear", "in", and "out", I'll leave that to your imagination.

[28] When matching whitelists, these are *blacklists*.

- **Dynamic Filters**: these filter out words and phrases that fit a pattern. If you don't want people advertising their gold-farming services in your MMO, you filter out anything that looks like the URL of a website that sells gold. Sure, an arms race can develop as the farmers try to find ever-more exotic ways of getting round it, but the more work the players have to do to decode it, the less they're likely to do so.

- **Player Choice**: permit full freeform communication, but allow players themselves to filter out what they don't want to see based on who said it. Even something as simple as junking messages from a given sender before they arrive (that is, *gagging* or *muting* that sender[29]) is a powerful tool. It's also just about the only tool, unless you count reporting the sender as well. Developers can track what messages prompt players to gag or to report a sender, and use these as the basis for their dynamic filters. Knowing both what and whom players gag is good for both community and company management. You can also allow plug-in writers to create their own filter systems, so players can see pre-processed versions of messages,[30] or indeed be spared from seeing them at all if they have content that offends them personally.

The means made available to players for communication should be wide and varied if you want communities to form and to flourish, but they also have to be flexible and customisable. Too many channels, and players don't know which is best to use; too few, and players have to tolerate what they don't want to see in order not to miss what they do. Sending private messages is particularly important: the ability to click on a character's name in a chat box to enter message-sending mode to that character is far safer than a `/reply` option, because in the latter case, someone might message you while you're typing it and the message goes to the wrong person when you hit return. A `/tell` option will always go to the right person, but is tiresome when people have awkward names such as `oiooioioii`.

By the way, designers, while I have your attention: for pity's sake, make it that when I enter WWWWW into a chat channel, you treat it as if I'd typed a return before it. If it's clear someone is trying to move, let them move – don't assume they have some idiosyncratic reason for actually *saying* "WWWWW". Your players will thank you.

19.3.3 Communication: Motive

What can designers do about the motive to communicate?

Well, designers can't actually do a great deal to motivate players to communicate, but then they don't need to: players will find reasons to communicate regardless.

Still, let's suppose that you do wish to motivate players to communicate more than they are doing. There are two aspects to communication: sending and receiving. People who are sending want either:

---

[29] *Final Fantasy XIV* has a gag-like *blacklist* command that not only stops the selected character's messages from reaching you, but also stops you from even seeing that character in the virtual world.

[30] I'd be interested in one that automatically translated the main language spoken in North America into English.

- to instruct ("focus on the fire elemental", "tell me what to do!");

- to provide information ("when the boss flies, get ready for a big AOE", "good game"); or

- to request information ("do you need any potions?", "what level is your healer alt?").

People who are receiving either accept what they're been told (or told to do) or they query it, in which case they become senders. In dialogue, roles will frequently alternate back and forth: receivers will become senders and senders will become receivers. Therefore, if you want to motivate players to communicate then you should either: give players reasons to order, to comment, or to ask; or give receivers reasons to become senders.

There are many ways to achieve these aims, most of which are out of your hands because they depend on the players (heated arguments, for example), but if you want to design some in then here are few suggestions:

- **Reasons to Order**: require co-ordination. The player or group needs to do something but can't unless another player acts a certain way. Examples: "talk to the guard so I can sneak into the cave"; "mage, interrupt the slime monster's second pseudopod attack or we'll all die".

- **Reasons to Comment:** surprise them. The player sees something they haven't seen before, succeeds when they were expecting to fail, or fails when they were expecting to succeed. Examples: "Whoah! How where that dragon come from?!"; "Say, there didn't used to be a river here".

- **Reasons to Ask:** be ambiguous, uninformative, or misleading. Use jargon that experienced players will know but newbies won't; be vague with directions; suggest that something might be possible at the player's level when it isn't. Examples: "What's a free company?", "Where's the Ivory Chapel?", "How do I get a mount?".

- **Reasons to Become Senders:** add uncertainty. Offer multiple methods, not all of which always work. Examples: "Wait for the patrol to pass", "Do I come at it from the north", "You need to speak to the NPC in the barn".

In general, players appreciate higher-quality communication over higher-quantity communication, but they'll take any quality if quantity is too low. Fortunately, prolific senders can service many receivers, and in some circumstances (such as raids), they're an absolute necessity. If they overdo it, though, there's a danger that the players receiving their messages will interpret them as spam, in which case the sender will be gagged and any benefits they offer to communication will be lost.[31]

---

[31] I once took a bus ride in Uxbridge and sat next to a man who promptly launched into a commentary about everything he saw – people, houses, trees, shops, shops that used to sell something else – without letting up for a moment. I have never wanted to get off a bus so badly in my life.

It's important to remember that although communication is the bedrock of communities, not all players enjoy communicating or want to communicate. You mustn't force it on them. Even some Socialisers may like being in groups but not like participating in group chat.

It's also important to remember that communication is *intrinsically* rewarding. You encourage it by giving people things to talk about, not by rewarding them for doing it. *Lost Ark* has a hidden achievement, "People Person", for signing up 50 friends. While this does cause plenty of communication when a new server opens, it's mainly from players who have no particular urge to pursue a conversation, they just want the "People Person" title and associated amethyst shards. As a result, most of the players you see with a "People Person" title are not, in fact, people people.

19.3.4 Communication: Opportunity

What can designers do about opportunity?

The opportunity to communicate is in theory always available, because the player can send a message any time they choose using any channel available to them. It's not always going to be received very well, though. If you annoy people with your messages, the messages you receive in return might not be to your liking (unless you're a Griefer). What "opportunity" means in this context, then, is an opening to communicate within the social norms of the virtual world.

The first thing to point out is that if people don't notice they've received a message then that's a missed opportunity right there. Interface options such as audio alerts and tab flagging can help, just so long as they're turn-offable. In general, the fewer people who receive a message, then the more important that message is to those who do receive it: losing a non-broadcast message in scrolling streams of guild chat and combat reports hinders communication. Unfortunately, when it comes to messages, players prize the maintenance of chronological order over making private ones hang around for longer before scrolling up, although I suppose this feature could be made an option. We're straying into interface design here, though, so I'll back off before overstepping my mark.

In most societies, there are places where people can go to socialise. They're open for hours at a time and are generally welcoming. Pubs, bars, religious buildings, gyms, coffee shops, hair stylists, street markets – they're all environments where you might get talking to someone. Collectively, these are called *third places* (Oldenburg, 1989), first places being where you live and second places being where you work. They're not the only locations where you might meet strangers and get chatting, of course, but they're ones especially suited for it.[32]

Early academic research in this area proposed that virtual worlds are also third places (Ågren, 1997; Steinkuehler & Williams, 2006). This idea was almost correct, but not quite: virtual worlds *have* third places, but aren't *themselves* third places (Ducheneaut et al., 2004).[33] In the third places of virtual worlds, players have something to do but can easily interact with

---

[32] You can make friends queueing for a bus, but few people would plan to stand in line at a bus stop with the intention of doing so.

[33] This particular paper examines *Star Wars Galaxies*, which Raph Koster specifically designed so as to have its cantinas act as third spaces (having noticed that *Ultima Online*'s taverns were almost always empty).

other people who are there for their own purposes. The designer merely needs to ensure that players have several reasons to go to and to hang around a venue. For example, if you make it that buffs from bards last longer if you listen to them in a tavern, players will go to taverns; while they're waiting for a performance to finish, they'll have a chance to talk to other people who are also hanging around there. Likewise, if you make it that armour repair isn't instant, or that goods you've bought aren't immediately delivered, players will also have reason to wait a few minutes. How they fill those minutes is up to them – leaving their computer unattended so as to make a drink or to expel what they drank earlier are definite possibilities – but at least they've been given the opportunity to communicate.

Third places within virtual worlds are generally to be applauded as important components in the establishment and continuance of communities. Sadly, under pressure from players, many designers have removed the majority of the reasons ever to go to one, by providing what are known as *quality-of-life* improvements (such as allowing hub functionality to be accessed remotely). If, while trekking in the wilderness, you can access all the facilities of the town square, why go to the town square? As a consequence, you don't feel the vibrancy[34] of the virtual world and you won't have as many serendipitous encounters with other players. It's a shame, but this is often what happens when you listen to players: they're commonly more driven by their short-term interests than by their long-term ones. Quality-of-life improvements brought in with *WoW*'s *Cataclysm* expansion had a lasting, deleterious effect on the size of the MMO's player population (Pereira, 2024).

As I mentioned earlier, an important method for giving players the opportunity to communicate is by providing optional content that requires grouping. This is only necessary for game worlds: social worlds don't have that kind of content coded-in, because players can create optional content themselves if they want it (for example, a game show might need four contestants[35]). Now, although I've used the word "optional" here (twice), there's actually some dispute over that, at least in game worlds. In favour of optionality is the fact that if you make it non-optional (for example, by denying access to later content until some non-optional group content is attempted successfully), this will put off players who really don't want to play in groups. The counter-argument is that you get better groups that way, because all the players have been through the same experience and they're more willing to cut each other some slack if they mess up. This latter approach is the one adopted by *Final Fantasy XIV*, and it does seem to have some merit to it; that said, after following this line for many years, the developers also began to provide options for running group instances alongside NPCs instead of player characters, thereby implicitly recognising that not everyone wants to race through them using standard speed-run tactics[36] while being criticised if they make mistakes by those who do so want.

---

[34] This isn't a technical term, but I use it to mean how alive and happening the virtual world feels.

[35] Playing games in a social world is somewhat ironic, but then so is socialising in a game world.

[36] Basically, the tank picks up mobs and keeps running until surrounded by vast swathes of them, whereupon the healer and tank combine to keep the tank alive, while the DPS AOE down the mob of mobs. This is boring for everyone. The problem would go away if AOEs didn't come with friendly-fire protections, but they usually do. You can also improve matters by having tanks only able to occupy a certain number of mobs before the excess start attacking other characters in the group.

Group content can be informal or formal. Examples of the former include: creating world bosses that anyone can join in fighting; creating resource-gathering or crafting collections that anyone can contribute to; creating PvP battles for control of areas in which anyone can participate. These are often very satisfying to engage in, but they don't tend to do a lot for communication except when people join as part of an organised group (in which case they already have the opportunity to communicate). Occasionally, *ad hoc* groups will form to enable healers to identify whom they should heal in a mass boss brawl, after which the players subsequently hang around together, but it's less common than one might hope.

Formal group content is the more popular approach among designers and players alike. The format is that players group up to enter instances that are honed for a particular level and a given number of players; they may also require that the players adopt set roles. Regular groups will usually be optimised for something like four to six characters (depending on the virtual world, but usually constant for that world). For example, *Final Fantasy XIV* and *Star Wars: the Old Republic* have parties of four; *World of Warcraft* and *New World* have parties of five; *EverQuest* and *Final Fantasy XI* have parties of six (six-people parties aren't as popular as they once were). Intermediate instances and raids will collect sub-parties together to form a larger group (eight-player and 24-player in *FFXIV*'s case, for example). Don't expect to be able to run such raids solo alongside NPCs instead of players, though, because the situational dynamics change too much for the AIs to be scripted; if players need to go through such content to advance in the game, well, those who don't like grouping will just have to grin and bear it (or quit).

In groups containing six players or fewer, there are great opportunities to communicate. If the players feel they're of equal status in a shared context, sending messages is much more socially easy than if they feel that others will ignore or belittle them. For groups of seven or more, players become increasingly reluctant to say anything unless they're in a leadership position.

OK, so for communication-opportunity reasons (along perhaps with some others), you'll want to create content for groups sized in the four-to-six character range. This content doesn't *have* to be instanced (and is better for immersion and vibrancy if it isn't[37]), but many players will probably expect it to be so. So, how do they form such groups?

Well, this is where it gets messy. There are going to be multiple competing methods whatever you may want, not necessarily all of which are known to the virtual world:

- **Offline**. People agree to form a group in some offline forum or other channel they use. People who follow live-streamers can form connections with one another in the chat then group up in the virtual world. The forum or channel provides and delivers the opportunity to communicate, but it's not necessarily known to or available to most players.

- **Private**. People form a group with players whom they already know, usually in the same guild or on a friends list. This gives a legitimate opportunity to communicate and to strengthen bonds, but from a limited constituency.

---

[37] *Throne and Liberty*'s open dungeons with fast-respawning mobs are like this. If you're not in a group, you can still participate – and will usually be invited into a group shortly afterwards. To stop players from spending all their time in them, for half an hour out of every two, they're PvP.

- **Notice Board**. Those who want to form or to join groups for a particular purpose go to an in-world board and peruse what's on offer. Whether its messages are freeform text or created by checking boxes (or some mix of both) depends on the virtual world.

- **Structured Chat**. Players form a group and link to it in a broadcast (or local broadcast) chat channel. People who want to join the group click on it, and if there's room then they're in. This creates *ad hoc* groups that are popular for open play, such as defeating world bosses and the like. There may be some accompanying text to indicate how full the group is ("Polly's group 2/6" means there's room for another four players[38]).

- **Unstructured Chat**. Players can try to join or to form a group by appealing through a broadcast chat channel. The typical format begins LFG ("looking for group") or LFM ("looking for more" – use *e.g.* LF2M if you want to indicate how close to being full the group is). After this opener will be some abbreviation identifying an instance or raid[39]; following that will perhaps appear some qualifiers ("got tank", "quick run", "on 3rd boss"). LFG means you want people to invite you to join a group; LFM means you have a group and want to invite more people to it. Note that if there are multiple chat channels, the bulk of requests will invariably appear in just one. This need not be the /lfg channel that you considerately created for the purpose.

- **LFG System**. This is a built-in utility that cuts out the community-building pleading in chat and replaces it with a system that automatically[40] allocates players to groups. Such groups are typically known as *PUG*s ("pick-up groups"). Character roles in short supply, such as tanks and healers, typically get into a PUG very quickly, but oversubscribed roles can often expect a long wait before their turn arrives. For unpopular instances, the wait can be long for all concerned, so virtual worlds might have to draw players from multiple shards (a *cross-server* approach, meaning that even if you do make a friend you're unlikely to meet them again). While some virtual worlds will readily allocate players to already-started instances that have lost a player (*backfilling*), some won't under any circumstances, and some will but only if the player concerned is OK with it.

Although all these methods of forming groups can be available simultaneously in a virtual world, inevitably one or other of them will dominate each use case. It's very unlikely to be the offline option, but it could be any of the rest – which may vary by context. For example, players might use chat to set up raid groups but the LFG system for regular dungeons and a noticeboard for PvP.

The LFG system approach is somewhat divisive. As a general rule:

---

[38] Before the UK decimalised its currency in 1971, 2/6 was half a crown – an eighth of £1. Frighteningly, I'm old enough to remember this.

[39] Examples from *WoW Classic*: BRD = Blackrock Depths; Strat = Stratholme; ZF = Zul'Farrak; DM = Dire Maul.

[40] In MMO PvE instances, this tends to be a fairly basic queueing system with separate queues for each character role. For group PvP, as with general games built around the concept, there's a greater need to balance player skill levels (Activision, 2024).

- Opportunists, Attainers, Scientists, and Sages like it, because they get to content quicker.

- Griefers like it because they can act without lasting consequences.

- Networkers don't like it, because the relationships are transient.

- Politicians and Friends don't like it, but they don't use it anyway.

LFG systems aren't great for community: few people in PUGs are up for forming friendships, and even when they are, it's often hard to follow up a nascent relationship afterwards. Instances may be designed to encourage sociability, but the nature of PUGs resists this (Eklund & Johansson, 2013). A way to negotiate this problem is to flag groups at formation time as being either casual or non-casual: the player gets to choose one option (but not both). There's no difference in the content (it's not that non-casual is more difficult or extreme than casual); it's to do with player attitudes. When people sign up for a more leisurely experience, they can converse, crack jokes, praise one other, and the like, without feeling under pressure to perform. The opportunities to build relationships (and thence communities) are increased immensely by this. Furthermore, if a player signs up for a casual run and then sets off apace regardless (which some will do, especially if casual runs have a shorter wait time), the others can legitimately not go along with it. Importantly, they won't lose face in doing so, which they would under normal circumstances.

Note that, as with chat channels, the player-preferred way to form groups may well be something other than what you've been telling newbies is the way to do it, in which case you may lose said newbies. This would perhaps be less likely if you were aware of the problem.[41] It's therefore worthwhile at this point to mention a general piece of advice worth heeding when operating large-scale virtual worlds: seek to recruit random newbies in order to solicit their opinions from time to time. If you want, you can – and indeed should – pay them a token amount of real money (not in-world goody bags) for their participation: the information you will obtain could save you a lot of expense in the long term, especially if, when they eventually leave the virtual world, you can elicit their reasons for doing so.

19.3.5 Properties of Communication

From the foregoing, it should be clear that designers can encourage or discourage the formation of community right from the get-go by targeting communication. Giving people the ability, reason, and occasion to communicate isn't the end of it, though: by tinkering with assorted properties of communication, designers also get to influence to some degree the nature of the community that develops.

Here are some examples:

---

[41] I say "perhaps" because it could be that whatever channel you tell newbies to use, other players will then avoid it because "it's full of newbies".

Friends Lists. I've mentioned these a few times already in this book. They're personally maintained lists of individuals with whom the player wishes to keep in touch. They can be classified using two binary dimensions: unidirectional or bidirectional; annotated or unannotated. Bidirectional ones are formed when an invite is sent from the initiator to the prospective friend; if accepted, it places each in the other's friends list. Unidirectional ones add only to the initiator's list and may not even require that the second player even knows that they've been added; they're effectively simple contact lists. For unannotated lists, the story ends there; with an annotated list, the player can add a note to a name to remind themself as to why they know this person ("friendly, did some quests together in Brimstone Sands" – that kind of thing) or indeed anything else about them ("can't spell the word 'lose'"). The designer gets to decide how to configure these two dimensions: in general, unidirectional lists are better for establishing relationships, but bidirectional ones are better for advancing them; similarly, annotated lists lead to stronger connections if the player uses them, but weaker ones if the player doesn't use them (but knows they exist).

Privacy. Some players are open to communication whatever the source, whereas others only want to hear from people they already know or with whom they themselves initiate communication. Do you want random strangers sending you private messages that are primarily spam, or are you willing to put up with that for the few that aren't? You'll probably expect that people you're grouped with are able to say things to you, but do you want that permission to persist once the group has dissolved? If you don't want unsolicited verbal communication, how about emotes such as dances or cartwheels? It's easy to add options for fine-tuning all of these: the designer's power comes in determining the defaults. Most players never change defaults, especially newbies (who won't necessarily even know what the different options mean). If you don't think this makes much of a difference, imagine a virtual world where characters' nameplates show "Unknown" until you communicate with them. As a designer, you'll immediately have an opinion as to whether that's a good idea or a bad one, along with ideas of how to improve on it regardless. It's not only speech and emotes that are important, either: are you going to allow players to examine each other to find out what level they are and how good their gear is? If so, will you notify players when they've been so examined? For some players, it can feel as if they've been violated.

Profanity Filters. Again, I touched on these earlier: they're denylists operating at the lexical level. The operator of the virtual world maintains a list of words that are considered contrary to polite conversation and replaces them with asterisks. To illustrate this, let's suppose that the English word "under" was regarded as a swearword. If I had the profanity filter switched off and someone wrote "You're a real under, you are!" then that's what I'd see. With the profanity filter switched on, I'd see "You're a real *****, you are!" (or similar – there may be a fixed number of asterisks, they may be hyphens, or they may be comic-style "@#&!" substitutions). This sounds fine: you can leave the option of having the filter on or off to the individual player; all you have to do is decide which is the default. Now although this is indeed an important decision, there are two others you need to make. Firstly, are there some words that are so beyond the pale that you don't want players to see them even if they switch the filter off? Some countries have strict blasphemy laws that you might not want to risk having the players break on your behalf, for example.[42] If so, you don't have one profanity filter, you have two – only one of which can be turned off, and the other of which can be got around anyway ("You're a real U.N.D.E.R, you are!"). The second decision you need to make is whether to censor full words or part-words. If you go with full words then a convention will rapidly develop to embed swearwords in other text ("You're a real xunderx, you are!"); if you go part-words, you're probably going to catch a lot of false positives ("Hello, Mr Sa*****s") so have to allowlist them.[43] I've no idea how text-to-speech and speech-to-text will handle any of this, by the way, but can't imagine that it'll be joyous.

19.4 GROUPS

To form a community, players need to group up.

That seems a reasonable statement, but what do we actually mean by a "group" and how do people "group up" anyway? We'll strive answer those questions in this section.

19.4.1 What's a Group?

There are three common perspectives on what makes a group a group:

- **Self-Identification**. You're in a group because you feel that you're in it. You may indeed have accepted an invitation to join the group from someone else who self-identifies as a member. You practice the social norms of the group as a consequence, and from this, will get either a sense of belonging or a case of imposter syndrome (or possibly both).

- **Categorisation**. You're in a group because someone else says you are. Other people look at your characteristics or behaviour and conclude that you're part of a group. For example, if your tribe decides you're a member then you *are* a member, like it or not. Likewise, if you act as if you're a member of a group then an observer may decide to put you in it and treat you as if you behave according to that group's norms. Stereotypes come about this way.

- **Social Cohesion**. You're in a group because you and others collectively meet objective, group-independent criteria: you have shared goals; you have roles for who does what; you have status relationships regarding decision-making powers; you have norms to govern how you do things together; you have sanctions to apply when the norms are violated.

---

[42] In the past, some virtual worlds put the names of other virtual worlds in their always-denylist. Players interpreted this as an acknowledgement of inferiority, though, so the idea lost favour.

[43] In the UK, there's a town with the name Scunthorpe. Because of letters two to five, AOL's profanity filter wouldn't let its 80,000 or so inhabitants refer to the place, so they had to use "Scanthorpe" instead. After receiving multiple complaints mocking its attitude, AOL graciously relented: the word "Scunthorpe" was added to the allowlist. Thereupon, users seized upon it as a swearword.

In virtual worlds, all three of these are important. Self-identification is the way the virtual world's implementation sees you: players are in groups because they explicitly join them. Anything beyond that is intangible, so the virtual world can't act on it. Categorisation is the basis for player types, so is useful for design purposes. Social cohesion is a quality that we want all long-term groups such as guilds to possess.

Ah, yes, guilds. I've casually mentioned several common types of group so far in this text, carrying on as if everyone knew what they were. I could have described them earlier, but because they're such a central aspect of community in virtual worlds I've held off from going into details until now. As now is indeed now, it's finally time to formalise what the various terms mean.

19.4.2 Types of Groups in MMORPGs

Group types don't really have names in social worlds, other than the generic ones prevalent in general society, but MMORPGs (well, their players, anyway) have developed their own terminology to refer to different types of group. These can be defined in terms of four basically binary parameters:

- **Exclusive or Inclusive**. When several groups exist in the same category, can a player be in more than one of them at the same time? For example, in Reality, banks are inclusive: I can hold accounts at several banks without causing any of the institutions to protest. Political parties, however, demand exclusivity: they'll kick you out if they find you're also in another one. Sometimes, the answer depends on the situation: most countries are fine with allowing dual nationality but around a quarter aren't (including China, Indonesia, and Kuwait).

- **Formal or Informal**. Formal groups are known to the virtual world's physics as tangible entities; informal groups aren't. Formal groups need programming support but informal ones don't (beyond universal systems such as chat). If there are four of us picking bubble poppies in the Waking Shores but we haven't formed a party, the virtual world can't tell whether or not we're in a group. Informal groups have no subdivisions, but formal groups come in two varieties:

  - *Hardwired* groups are coded directly into the virtual world, fixed and unchanging.

  - *Softwired* groups are created by players using coded-in group-creation software. These can often form from informal groups.

  The difference is a bit like that between hardware and software, hence the names.

- **Temporary or Persistent**. If a group disappears when all its members log off (perhaps after a short grace period), it's temporary. If it doesn't, it's persistent. In Reality, an escorted tour of a city centre involves a group that dissipates when the tour ends, making it temporary; a professional football club would still exist even if all its players resigned, making it persistent. Hardwired groups are always persistent.

- **Flat or Hierarchical**. In a flat group, every member has the same powers. In a hierarchical group, at least one member (the leader) has more powers than the rest. Minimally, a group's leader is someone who: can invite new members; can expel current members; can't be expelled by current members (at least not easily). Other common powers include being able to promote and demote players to intermediate ranks and to grant them leadership powers over ranks lower than theirs.

Using these four dimensions, it's possible to describe those configurations that appear commonly enough to have acquired names (especially in game worlds):

- A *static* is an inclusive, informal, persistent, flat association of players who meet regularly to play through content (often esoteric in nature) together.

- A *party* is an exclusive, softwired, temporary, usually flat casual adventuring band. It may also be called a *group* or (in a PvP context) a *team*; it may also have a name specific to the virtual world (such as a *fellowship* in *LotRO*).

- A *train* is an inclusive, informal, temporary, flat assortment of players charging from one piece of content to another of the same kind or in the same location, overwhelming it by sheer weight of numbers.[44] For example, in *FFXIV*, this happens with dynamic content called *FATE*s ("Full Active Time Events") and *hunts* (kill specific, named monsters); in *New World*, it happens with *chest runs* (empty the treasure chests in areas packed full of elite mobs[45]).

- A *raid group* is an exclusive, softwired, temporary, flat collection of players taking on instanced content designed for more players than the maximum regular group size. The term can refer to all the players in the raid or just to the ones in your sub-group.

- A *guild* is an exclusive,[46] softwired, persistent, hierarchical social network of disparate players. They often have a name specific to the virtual world, for example a *free company* in *FFXIV*, a *corporation* in *EVE Online*, and a *cabal* in *The Secret World*; you can still usually call them guilds, though.

- A *clan* is a cross-server (and possibly cross-world) guild, sometimes known as an[47] überguild.

- An *alliance* is an inclusive, usually informal, persistent, flat collection of guilds acting as one.

---

[44] This is the more modern use of the word "train" in MMOs. The older one is when mobs form the train, pursuing the same player character in a long line. In this sense, you can "train" the mobs on someone else by running to their location then making a quick exit. We'll touch on this later.

[45] Chest runs are more emergent – *NW*'s physics doesn't know they're taking place. FATEs and hunts are coded-in – *FFXIV*'s physics is aware of them.

[46] The ones in *Stars Reach* (Koster & Georgeson, n.d.) are inclusive, which is going to unnerve some players (probably for the better).

[47] This really should be "a" rather than "an", but few players whose native language is English pronounce that "ü" as anything other than "oo".

- A *faction* is a usually exclusive, hardwired, persistent, flat separation of characters, typically present for PvP purposes. Their existence is invariably explained by the game's lore. Because factions are hardwired, NPCs can also be members of them.

These groups are the ones that have some semblance of social cohesion to them (as described at the start of this section), rather than being based on categorisations (likewise). This is why you can speak of collections of elves, mages, males, tanks, Achievers, or crafters, but there's no matching group for any of them in the above list. Other socially coherent groups do crop up from time to time – *EVE Online*'s Council of Stellar Management is one – but none of the different types have widely used names (if indeed they have any kind of name).

Note that some of this terminology is ambiguous or has changed over time. The meaning of "clan" is particularly irritating in this regard, beginning life as just another name for a guild and then switched to a guild in the context of PvP before shoving überguild out of its way to claim ownership of the concept of cross-server guilds. It'll probably mean something else entirely by the time you read this. In a similar vein, some words have specific meanings in particular virtual worlds that aren't shared by others: for example, an "alliance" in *FFXIV* is simply an eight-person group, three of which (labelled A, B, and C) combine to make a 24-person "raid group".

The most important types of group from a community perspective are parties and guilds.

19.4.3 Parties

Parties are where most of the co-operative gameplay takes place in modern MMOs, although it can of course also happen in open play (and in elder-game content, where parties will usually give way to raid groups). Parties are superb for lubricating interactions – that is, giving players cause to interact with one another. When the number of players involved is small then all feel able to contribute both to the action and the chat. The downside is that when in a party, players are effectively cut off from the rest of the virtual world; this is especially true when the party is in an instance (the most common use case), because its members will not encounter players outside of the party. In addition, for reasons to do with the fact that there could be dozens of instances running at the same time, local broadcasts will usually be specific to the instance the party is in, rather than to the area the instance is in; players may therefore miss out on information regarding events going on in their purported vicinity. Note that for cross-server parties, this restriction helps maintain the illusion that the players share the same world, which makes the effect of such parties' existence on immersion slightly less bad.

19.4.4 Guilds

Guilds are where most of the social interaction between players takes place in modern MMOs. Again, such interaction is not exclusive to guilds – a lot of it happens in broadcast chat channels, for example – but guilds are at the heart of it. Many parties consist of members of the same guild, for example.[48] If you want to know where the communities are in large-scale virtual worlds, they're in the guilds.

Knowing what Dunbar's number implies about spending some of your relationship budget in virtual worlds, it should come as no surprise that guilds have an optimal size before they start to lose coherence: it's around 50 players (Allen, 2005). Indeed, an earlier study of *Ultima Online*'s active guilds found that their size peaked at about 60 characters then rapidly dropped off (Koster, 2003).[49]

As guilds are persistent, it's possible to associate benefits with them that can confer advantages to their members. Popular ones include a guild house where players can hang out together and a shared guild bank where they can put things they don't want but that other guild members might. A sense of common identity can be encouraged by designing a guild tabard or shield sigil that all players can display, and having the guild's name appear under the character's name in the nameplate that permanently hovers above their head.[50]

As we'll see shortly, one of the ways that communities develop is when members do things not so much for their own benefit as for that of the community. Designers have picked up on this, and many virtual worlds give guilds some equivalent of experience points so they can level up, accruing rewards for their members. For example, it might be that its members can mount rides more quickly, or get a crafting XP buff, or have access to vendors selling exclusive goods. Although this idea sounds laudable, it makes it very difficult for new guilds to succeed: they're competing with established guilds that outgun them (a *founder effect*). It also means that when a guild really ought to split, players are reluctant to leave because then they'll lose the perks of membership, which can lead to much acrimony. Furthermore, after a while, most players end up in maxed-out guilds and start to treat the bonuses as if they were the norm. I'd therefore recommend using a guild advancement system primarily for cosmetic purposes (tabard at guild level 5, size 1 guild hall available at guild level 10 – that kind of thing). Some quality-of-life improvements might also be acceptable if they benefit the guild rather than the player (say, +10 guild bank size at guild level 15).

Although parties tend to be flat (some MMOs do identify a nominal party "leader", not that players pay much attention to this), guilds are usually hierarchical in what's effectively a feudal system. There is opportunity here for the designer to shape the form that the hierarchy takes. For example, one model might be to have a guild leader, beneath whom are guild officers, beneath whom are regular guild members. Cutting out the officer layer will make guilds more autocratic and dependent on the presence of the leader in order to recruit new members; this will have the consequence of making guilds as a whole smaller

---

[48] Be cautious if you join a party in which everyone but you is in the same guild. Many are the times I've been in such a group then been voted out immediately before the final boss so that I could be replaced by another member of the same guild.

[49] If you're wondering about the discrepancy between these findings, it's because "characters" includes alts but "players" doesn't.

[50] I turn down around three-quarters of the guild invitations I receive in MMOs simply because I don't like the guild in question's name. Names *can* be great, though! I was in a guild in *WoW* that we named "Right Click for Details". People saw it and did. OK, so it *may* have broken immersion, but still....

and shorter-lasting than would be so with an officer layer. Adding a fourth layer, perhaps for new members, will have the effect of making guilds larger but perhaps less responsive.

It's also possible to allow the players themselves decide how many membership tiers there are. The most I've ever experienced personally was a guild with seven different ranks, but I know of others that had more.[51] The greater the number of ranks, however, the easier it is for players to feel affronted if they're not accorded the relative seniority (if not responsibility) that they feel they deserve. It's somewhat moot though, because as a general rule, guilds defined to have a large number of ranks tend to use only a few of them anyway.

Guilds can also often be customised by giving the leader the ability to name the guild levels, perhaps with different titles by character gender (for example, "Lord" or "Lady" – *Meridian 59* did this). Objectively, the names the players choose when given such free rein are universally bad, but subjectively they can be meaningful to members, so it's therefore fine to allow the practice.

In Reality, people tend to prefer democracies over tyrannies, but in virtual worlds, most favour benevolent dictators. That's because they're able to vote with their feet, leaving a guild if it doesn't suit them; you don't get to do that with many tyrannies on Earth. On the whole, players simply want to play, so they're happy to leave the operation of their guild to those who want to do it and are good at it (mostly Politicians, but sometimes Attainers or Friends for high-end raiding guilds). It's possible to code democracy into guilds (*M59* allowed members to vote the guild leader out of office), but most virtual worlds don't bother. If a guild collapses, that gives the opportunity for its members to start anew, whereas if it continues (even under different leadership), the result can be sterility. If players nevertheless want democracy for their guild, well, add-ons might be a possibility.

When guilds offer many benefits to their members, players can come to want those benefits for themselves. For example, if storage space is at a premium then being the only member of a guild means you can have all those extra guild-bank slots yourself. This is seen as a bad thing (particularly by those developers who hope to sell extra slots for real money), so obstacles are put in place to prevent it. Primary among these is the idea of a guild charter, which requires a number of signatories (say, ten) before the guild comes into being. To compound this, the signatories may all have to be logged in simultaneously – possibly for a certain length of time, too. This makes the creation of a new guild a commitment, thereby ensuring that players will give it a chance to prove itself before they decide whether to move on or not. However, if too many players are required for the set-up process, this can prevent small groups of players from banding together – a problem that particularly affects newbies, as they don't yet know many people.

The fact that it's difficult for newbies to set up guilds, coupled with the founder effect, is not good for virtual worlds. Newbies can feel isolated from other players, shut out of established social circles while not being able to create ones of their own. Who can blame them if they decide that this experience is not for them? Fortunately, this state of affairs can relatively easily be mitigated (once recognised):

---

[51] *Albion Online* allows up to eight tiers.

- Put new players into random cohort groups, like classes at school, and have them overlap activities. If they only encounter other people who are in their situation, they are less likely to feel disconnected and more likely to make friends.[52]

- Allow the creation of guilds with two or three members. If you're worried about the possibility of getting single-player guilds, require more signatories before the guild receives exploitable benefits.

19.4.5 Benefits of Guilds to Developers

The primary rationale behind having guilds is to increase social cohesion and thence retention. Players in guilds find it harder to quit a virtual world than do players who aren't in guilds. Not wanting to let your friends down can be a powerful incentive to keep playing long after you should perhaps have stopped. Knowing this, experienced players trying out a new-to-them virtual world may be reluctant to join a guild in the first place.

There are secondary benefits to having guilds, too. For example, most things you can sell to individual players have some equivalent that can be sold to guilds. If players can be charged a monthly fee[53] for owning a house, guilds can similarly be charged for owning a guild house. Guilds will often therefore ask their players to pay dues every now and then; indeed, such a *guild tax* may be transferred from their account automatically, using a rate set by the guild leader (*Albion Online* does this). This gives guild leaders a budget that they can use as they see fit, whether that's by paying fees, buying and upgrading gear, purchasing resources, funding projects, making welfare payments to low-level members or secretly lining their own pockets.

Many players are of the opinion that being in a guild speeds levelling-up, which if correct would suggest that the retention gains of being in a guild are, at least to some extent, offset by the fact that guild members won't be playing for as long. The evidence suggests otherwise, however: except perhaps for specialist levelling guilds, there's little material connection between guild membership and speed of character advancement (Poor, 2015). With levelling guilds, such a connection may exist, but it's paid for by a lack of social cohesion within the guilds themselves, which tend to suffer from a high turnover. This is because people of similar levels within the guild will play together and so form cliques, alienating players of higher or lower levels (Lukács et al., 2009), who then quit.

A similar thing can happen when progression is at the elder-game stage, rather than during the levelling game. A notorious example is the opening ten-player Karazhan raid introduced in *World of Warcraft*'s *Burning Crusade* expansion. It remains one of the best-loved instances in all of *WoW* – by those who were able to run it. However, those who

---

[52] *New World* seems to do something like this by opening servers for new players then merging them with other servers once they've become established. I'm not entirely persuaded that disrupting the whole social order in this manner is a good idea, but Amazon Games seems to like it.

[53] This is usually called *rent*, but given that you'll usually have to pay a lump sum up-front to "buy" the property, it's perhaps a misnomer.

couldn't get into a group of ten were stuffed. Completing the instance locked players out for the rest of the week, so if you'd run it once then you couldn't step in to help out those groups still short of numbers. Resentment, frustration, and a "haves and have nots" situation followed. Sadly, the feedback the designers were getting was telling them that the instance was superb, which indeed it was from a gameplay perspective. It wasn't so great from a social perspective, though: it was a complete guild-breaker.

19.4.6 Communication Consequences

Parties and guilds, as the bedrock of a virtual world's social organisation, will have their own intra-group communication channels. At minimum, you can speak to everyone else in your party and to everyone in the guild. You may be able to speak to an entire raid of which your party is a sub-group, and you may be able to speak to the people of the same and higher rank than you in the guild (to keep the lower-ranked ones out of the conversation), but – along with direct character-to-character communication – parties and guilds are at the heart of it. This means that on occasion, players get their wires crossed and will say something on one channel that they meant to go to another. This kind of thing has happened since the days of *MUD1* and is so common today that not only does it have its own term, *mistell*, it has its own abbreviation, *MT*. There are ways to militate against it, for example by making the number of recipients be the prompt the player gets when they issue the command to initiate message input, but they're perhaps unnecessary. Mistells help to bring players together (they've all done it themselves so they all feel your pain), and even if the occasional one does cause drama, OK, well it's only shining a light on a problem that was eventually going to emerge from the shadows anyway. At least it may be easier to clear up any misunderstandings this way (sparks being less of a problem than thunderbolts).

19.4.7 Factions

It's one thing to allow players to choose which other players to speak to and to listen to, but it's another thing entirely to prevent players from speaking to anyone at all. There are game management reasons that you might want to do this (such as stopping bot characters from coming in, advertising their RMT wares, then immediately quitting), and there are gameplay reasons, too (such as spells that take away a character's voice, not that this will have any effect on external VoIP channels). In general, though, restricting communication with those in another group is something you'd only want to do after careful thought. Players who can't communicate with those in another group will tend to objectify them, regarding them more negatively, while subjectifying those of their own group, regarding them more positively. If this is what you want, go ahead. If it isn't, be forewarned.

The best-known example of this is *WoW*, which at launch forbade inter-faction communication and grouping between Horde and Alliance characters. Players in the opposing faction knew you were saying something, but not what it was.[54] This worked fairly well in

---

[54] The concept of garbling inter-faction communication was first popularised in *Dark Age of Camelot*.

context; the idea behind it was to promote PvP. So many players started creating characters in both factions, though, that this state of affairs was eventually relaxed with the introduction of cross-factional grouping in patch 9.2.5. While in such a group, players from different factions could now communicate one-on-one or over certain channels (party, raid, instance, battleground, local broadcast, and full broadcast). I'm sure there's compelling lore to explain this.

Aside: factions are also often used to provide alternative content paths for players, with different associated storylines. For example, in *SW:TOR*, the Jedi and Sith factions each have quests not available to the other. Sadly, when it comes to factions, invariably one will be more popular than the other(s). Designers may therefore find themselves tempted to add more content for the dominant factor, on the grounds that more eyes are going to see it. This is a mistake! You have to add content in equal amounts to all playable factions. If you don't, the smaller factions are going to get even smaller, until your reason for having factions in the first place is no longer satisfied.[55]

19.4.8 Other Approaches

Social organisations in virtual worlds don't have to be organised around parties and guilds, but experiments with other arrangements have not proven successful to date. *Asheron's Call* replaced parties with what it called *fellowships*, which could have up to nine members (a leader plus one to eight followers). They were similar to parties, except that when one member of a fellowship obtained experience points, all its members got a share by default (equal if they were within five levels of one another). For example, if one member of a five-member fellowship earned 1,000 experience points, they and every other member would receive 500 points. You might regard this as unfair if you were the one who did all the work, but on another occasion, someone else could do all the work and then you yourself would benefit from having done nothing. Sadly, although dishing out 2,500 points for 1,000 points of effort sounds as if it's a good system for encouraging players to group, it doesn't encourage them to form communities (they're in it for the points). It also makes content hard to balance, but it *can* work if it's restricted to certain activities. For example, *Guild Wars 2* has something similar for its PvP *squads*, so that scouts who are away from the main action don't miss out.

Asheron's Call's other major innovation, which it used instead of guilds, was its *allegiance* system. This was another way that the game shared XP, the hope being that it would cause players to connect for extrinsic reasons that would then turn into intrinsically rewarding relationships. The way it worked, a vassal swore allegiance to a patron, who then gained a proportion of the vassal's XP; the patron's own patron would get a smaller proportion. The amount of XP gained by the vassal was unaffected, so in effect, their patron received free XP. The belief was that patrons would reward their vassals for their service with gifts, but in practice, what happened was that higher-level players swore allegiance to lower-level friends to push up their experience gains, and patrons didn't have anything their vassals wanted anyway. The system ultimately failed in its aims because there was no good reason for a new player to be a vassal.

---

[55] This is assuming your reason isn't to say something about the nature of the factions themselves. For example, a World War 2 virtual world might deliberately have more content for the Alliance than the Axis because the designer has something against fascists.

19.4.9 Non-Guild Play

One final point about groups needs forcefully to be made: not everyone likes to be in them.

> Two year olds do a great deal of what might be called playing alone together. They run together, ride tricycles together and play with buckets in the sand or water together, but these activities are also carried out each child by himself, and being together merely adds some additional satisfaction.
>
> *(McGill & Welch, 1946)*

It's to be hoped that few players of virtual worlds are two-year-olds, but nevertheless many – in fact most – still like to play alone together (Ducheneaut et al., 2006). Introverts exist. Not everyone wants to be in a community, and even if they do, not everyone wants to be in the community that they're currently in and will wish to leave it. Playing alone *has* to be viable.[56] If you set up your virtual world with an ornate and glorious system for nurturing, nourishing, and sustaining communities, but neglect those who want to play solo, you will greatly reduce your potential pool of players. Even virtual worlds that are built practically to force players into guilds, such as *Throne and Liberty*, still allow players to play alone.

The presence of others in a virtual world gives a player's own presence validity. Do not forget this. You can *ignore* it, but don't *forget* it. Even those who feel they're not alone almost always, technically, are.

> When I sit alone at the computer and gaze at a monitor I am with other people who are also alone and also gazing at a monitor. We are alone together.
>
> *(Arnold, 2002)*

19.5 LEVELS OF COMMUNITY ENGAGEMENT

In academic research, the concept of community is (perhaps unsurprisingly) owned by Sociology. There are multiple dimensions to community (Bartle, 2010),[57] and sociologists can focus on any or all of them. Each dimension can be described individually or collectively in terms of its strength; unfortunately, people being people, there is a great deal of fuzziness and overlap within any given community, with different levels of community engagement[58] coexisting at once (Smathers & Ferrari, 2018),[59] so it's hard to specify a definitive measurement of just how strong a community is. People at the centre of a community and people on the periphery will experience it differently.

---

[56] High-level guildless players are sometimes called *ronin*, a term also used to describe those seemingly listless individuals who play one virtual world for a few months then wander off to play another. That's the way of player-coined terminology.

[57] OK, I confess: out of the many I could have chosen, I selected this particular citation primarily to confuse you. Phil Bartle and I are not related.

[58] Although *levels of community engagement* is the full term, you'll often see *levels of community* when considering community as an emergent object and *levels of engagement* when considering that emergent object's members' relationship to it.

[59] OK, I confess: out of the many I could have chosen, I selected this particular citation primarily because it's a game.

That said, the journey from periphery to centre is more of a step function than a linear function: people stay at one level until they change their perspective in some way (typically through action), by which they commit to the next one. As for how many levels there are, well a quick trip to my friendly local search engine tells me there are three, four, five, seven, and eight of them,[60] so it's fair to say the jury is still out on this; it rather depends on what you want to use the concept for as to how many levels of community engagement there are.

For virtual worlds, it's most useful to consider communities at five different levels.[61] In increasing strength, they're:

- **Community of *Communication*.** People lurk in the background, hearing what's going on in the community but not actively participating beyond that.

- **Community of *Interest*.** People who have compatible goals group together to further those goals. They don't have to have them for the same reason: if I like to knit[62] and you like to sew then we might agree to set up a stall together at the village fête to sell our wares.

- **Community of *Practice*.** Members pool resources and share information about how to do things. The community is no longer merely a means to an end: it has intrinsic value. Game developers working for different companies may formally be competitors, but when they get together at an industry event, they're happy to offer solutions to one another's problems while moaning about their own.

- **Community of *Commitment*.** Members work together on projects that are important to the community, not to individuals. For example, they may engage in advocacy to get the community's collective views heard. Relationships between players at this level may spill out into Reality (Taylor, 2006; Copier, 2007), a phenomenon known as *bleed* (Montola, 2010; Bowman, 2013).

- **_Spiritual_ Community.** Individual members know and trust each other implicitly. Communication is almost intuitive, as if members' emotions are shared. You don't get this very often, but you see it in situations where individuals have proven their worth to one another time and again. A soldier doesn't charge a machine-gun nest to protect their values or way of life, or even for the sake of their family: they do it to prevent the rest of their platoon from being wiped out.

In terms of size, the general rule is that the stronger the community, then the fewer members it has, but this isn't always the case. Guilds in virtual worlds often have more members that see it as a community of practice than as a community of interest, for example (in essence, because they decide it's in their interest to engage with the community's practices).

---

[60] I'm not sure what happened to six there.
[61] I picked these up from a report I read around the turn of the century that was summarising work in the area. Unfortunately, it was one of those research documents produced by a consultancy firm that sold it for several thousand dollars, so I no longer have either a copy or the reference. You can therefore feel free to take this list with a pinch of salt.
[62] I don't. I've never tried it and have no intention of ever doing so.

With virtual worlds, communities of communication come by default. You're a member of at least one as soon as you leave the tutorial, if not before. The beginnings of the first "proper" community emerge when you start to play for real. Other people in your position will also be playing, and sometimes you can help each other. If they're killing the same pack of wolves that you are, maybe you'll double-team the critters to speed up progress. If only one of you benefits when a wolf is killed,[63] perhaps you might still help the other player, so they finish their quest sooner and you can finish yours with less competition. Maybe they'll stay after they've completed their quest to help you out with yours. Either way, after a while, you'll often notice that your activities align with those of others regularly enough that a community of interest forms. You all want to do your own thing, but it's the same "own thing" that a good many other people want to do, so you find yourself co-operating with them. It's a means to an end.

After another while, you may notice that some players are better at doing what they're doing than you seem to be, so you ask what you're doing wrong. Alternatively, you may see someone doing stupid things and feel motivated to tell them how to do it right before they drive you crazy. If you don't like chatting to players, that's fine: all the information is out there on the Internet (after you've clicked through a bunch of cookie-acceptance forms that give the relevant websites full rights to pound you with ads from all directions in perpetuity[64]). Essentially, you're drawing on the community's knowledge and perhaps contributing to it yourself. It's a community of practice.

Once you're confident, you're going to need to get organised if you're to progress. You may not want to, and indeed may decide not to, but if you can group up on a semi-permanent basis with a bunch of players who have the same outlook on the virtual world that you do and who want to play together because they like each other, that will make progression easier and perhaps more fun. OK, so you form a guild (if you weren't in one already). Perhaps, at some point, it's noticed that membership numbers are stagnant or dropping off because students are returning to college, so you offer to try to recruit replacements. In so doing, you're acknowledging that the guild is something worthwhile in and of itself: you're in a community of commitment.

Finally, after many months of playing with others, you have a small, close-knit group of friends with whom you hang out regularly. They've put their characters' lives on the line countless times to save yours, as you have done to save theirs. You know how they'll act almost implicitly. Sure, you don't know exactly what the warlock is going to say, but you do know they're going to say *something* and that it'll be witty. You're a member of a spiritual community.

Members of a community of communication need to be able to listen to one another. In a community of interest, they need to be able to speak to one another. In a community of practice, they need access to each other's pertinent data. In a community of commitment, they need to be able to act together. In a spiritual community, they need each other.

---

[63] Ah yes, "killed": often, this will be dressed up in some ecologically sound language such as "culled", or perhaps avoids mentioning death at all by merely asking for a number of wolfskins. It doesn't matter: the players are going to call it "killed" regardless.

[64] Thanks, EU General Data Protection Regulation 2016/679.

Just because I'm in a community of commitment killing mobs for a communal project, that doesn't mean I won't help you kill mobs as part of a community of interest. Communities can not only be at different levels, but they can be at different levels at the same time. Members of a community are not homogenous. The more established ones may continue to contribute to a community of commitment, but newbies will arrive who have personal motives unrelated to any overarching community goals. Formally, the larger community comprises several smaller, fluid sub-communities that constantly shift and intertwine. Whether you want to view these sub-communities separately or as integral parts of a single community is up to you; it depends on why you're looking at communities in the first place. We've had (and will have) several reasons for looking at them, but the one that I'm going to focus on right now concerns community levels as perceived by the individual.

So, the inclusion of spiritual communities is the reason I like this particular model. Sadly, the term "spiritual community" is used mainly to refer to communities of people with strong, shared religious beliefs rather than to a maximally bonded group of individuals, so it's perhaps not the best. Still, we're stuck with it.

As for *why* I like the inclusion of spiritual communities, well they're where the Friends player type can be found. Communities of commitment are where Attainers and Politicians gather. Communities of practice are the domain of Scientists and Networkers. Communities of interest are formed by Griefers and Opportunists.

In other words, a player's sense of community tracks their progression in the same way that immersion does. The difference is that immersion puts the real into the virtual, whereas community puts the virtual into the real. Immersion addresses sink (it encourages newbies to play and stay); community addresses drift (it encourages oldbies to stay and play). Immersion is the hook; community is the anchor.

Community and immersion are the great intangibles of virtual worlds: key expressions of their being, but experienced by each player subjectively and individually. Studying them is like trying to pick up water with a fork: you can do it, but you have to freeze it first and will only see one instant of the whole as a result. They're not *themselves* the fundamental concepts, though. Immersion is about freedom to *be* and community is about freedom to be *with*: identity and friendship are what players want, and therefore, what designers should foment; immersion and community are merely important and effective expressions that can be used for structuring design towards these ends.

CHAPTER **20**

Design and Community

KNOWING THAT COMMUNITY IS important, designers will usually want to design for it. This is reasonable, but it's important not to be over-enthusiastic. Community membership is voluntary: if you try to force people into communities, a good many will push back against you. As I've mentioned several times already, some people like playing virtual worlds effectively by themselves and have no desire to be part of any community beyond the basic one that comes for free with communication. It's easy to imagine a Scientist's refusal even to pursue a common interest with someone else, on the grounds that figuring things out on their own is more important to them than merely figuring things out. Indeed, you'll have noticed that earlier I didn't describe Sages as favouring any particular level of community: this is because they could be in any of them, with the weaker versions being the most likely.

20.1 COMMUNITIES AS OBJECTS

Communities can strengthen if you put them under pressure, but they can also break apart. It's fine to give the players the *option* to accept pressure, but a bad idea to put pressure on them whether they want it or not. A knowledgeable general knows that troops under fire form stronger bonds than troops not under fire, but a wise general also knows that shooting at their own troops to build a sense of camaraderie among them is to be avoided.

If you do want to give communities the opportunity to take on some stress should their members feel the need to come closer together, ensure you match it to the appropriate community strength. It would be ridiculous to plunge low-level players into a high-pressure raid, even if their characters possessed all the necessary skills to complete it, because they haven't had time to get beyond a community of interest and raids need at least a community of practice. It would be less ridiculous to present them with the chance to align their individual quests. For members of an established guild, both would make sense: although some of its players will have formed high-level sub-communities, many won't (remember, communities overlap and shift). In general, then, offer a range of opt-in stressful situations for players who have progressed further, but stick to ones that promote a community of interest or of practice for players who haven't progressed far. Offer goals to guilds that are distinct from the goals offered to individuals, but order them by community strength:

DOI: 10.1201/9781003689638-20

don't put the build-a-starship objective before the modestly-increase-storage quest or after the one-mistake-and-you-can't-try-again-for-a-month base assault.

Groups emerge from the interactions of people; communities emerge from the interactions of people in groups; societies emerge from the interactions of people in communities. Interactions are at the heart of all this. If you want to design for community development, what you're actually designing for is the set of interactions that lead to the development of communities. This isn't to say that designers can't legitimately abstract away the individuals and look at the communities as a whole, but they do need to keep it in mind that ultimately they're dealing with real people. Communities are defined by their members, not *vice versa*.

Reasons that designers might nevertheless want to consider communities as objects of design include the following:

- There are so many players that it's impractical to reach out to them at the individual level.

- Players frequently act in groups, and the adage "can't see the wood for the trees" applies.[1]

- Many of the methods available to designers for creating content for individuals also work for communities.

- If you look at communities then you can develop content for communities that isn't simply about deepening the ties between players but is worthwhile in its own right.

It's important to note that designers only have direct influence over the communities that develop in-world. There'll be external communities, too. Designers can indirectly encourage some of these (such as by making content streamer-friendly, as mentioned earlier), but not all of them (people who met playing some other virtual world may come as a ready-formed community).

20.2 HOW COMMUNITIES FORM

If you're going to design for communities in virtual worlds then you really *must* read the 2018 Project Horseshoe report on the topic: *Design Practices for Human Scale Online Games* (Youngblood et al., 2018). Written by a team of MMO designers and community managers, it tells you pretty much everything you need to know.

Assuming you don't need to know *everything*, though, here are the basics.

At their most fundamental level, communities emerge when bonds form between individuals. These start off weak, but grow stronger as friendships develop. There are four ingredients to them:

1. **Proximity**. When player characters encounter each other, chance interactions occur that present opportunities for friendships to form.

---

[1] Except in the United States, where "can't see the forest for the trees" applies instead.

2. **Similarity**. Players are more likely to become friends with people they perceive as being similar to them. There's a gender difference here: women tend to align with people who have similar values, whereas men tend to align with people who have similar interests (Winstead, 1986).

3. **Reciprocity**. Players engage in escalating back-and-forth interactions to negotiate behavioural norms (about which more shortly).

4. **Disclosure**. At higher levels of friendship, players feel safe to share information about their weaknesses.[2]

Even this short list should be sparking ideas of how to encourage players to form friendships (and thence communities). For example, it's one thing to have a hub that players regularly visit, but unless they have a reason to hang around either after or during the conduct of their business then nothing much will happen – and if they do hang around, there has to be ample opportunity for them to offer or to solicit comments or actions. If there are tempting plinths to stand on, or statues to climb, or comedy traps that freeze characters for four seconds while a spotlight shines on them, then people who are hanging around will have ways to entertain themselves and others.

Extended activities are also possible. You could design a fashion show for which three or more players constitute the audience. NPCs wearing random items of gameplay-unaffecting clothing walk past on a catwalk and the players in the audience have to vote for their favourite outfit. If they all vote for the same NPC, they each receive a random item of the clothing this NPC was modelling (therefore if they agree beforehand always to vote for NPC #1 to ensure agreement, they could miss out on something they really want that NPC #2 was wearing). They might, however, vote the way a friend wants them to vote, so their friend has a chance of acquiring the item they want.

This brings us back to reciprocity. Of the four points listed, only reciprocity is dynamic – the rest are static. Reciprocity is what builds friendships and trust (Smith, 2002). It works as a four-step series of interactions:

1. **Opening**. Player #1 performs an opening action that player #2 observes. This action has a cost to it in terms of time, skill, resources, or other players' opinions.

2. **Opportunity**. Player #2 now has the opportunity to respond. If they can't, or can but choose not to, then the interaction ends.

3. **Response**. Player #2 performs an action that acknowledges player #1. This action must also have a cost, which if too high will cause the player to abandon the response and end the interaction.[3]

---

[2] I won't be going into this one a great deal here, except when nodding in the direction of spiritual communities. If you want to learn more about trust and virtual world design, Koster (2018) is an excellent, example-laden discussion.
[3] Early Facebook games allowed you to open in step #1 by spamming all your friends with a single click of a button, but to respond, they had to register with the game and then actually play it, which was too high a reciprocation mismatch for most people.

4. **Acknowledgement**. Player #1 recognises receipt of player #2's response and the loop completes. Alternatively, player #1 ignores the response and the interaction ends.

Inappropriate responses in step 3 or step 4 can also end the interaction, but conversely new loops can be opened there that escalate the interaction, moving the relationship forward. Initially, each loop completes in a matter of seconds, but later ones take longer and are more effort.

Again, even from this short description, there are some immediate takeaways. Social relationships are reciprocal, not transactional, so if you only allow for players to do business with one another then relationships will be slow to form. Players don't even need to expect anything in return. For example, suppose there's a bell that players can whack to make a satisfying note. That may be the only reason they hit it. However, it could count as a step 1 if there's another bell within hearing range but out of immediate reach; that would present an opportunity for a passing second player to whack it in response. Maybe if the two players can whack them both at the same time, there's a nice harmony and a small reward (flowers temporarily bloom, or you get a title, or the person on the bigger bell teleports to a random bell elsewhere, or receives 100 XP[4]; it depends on which player type you want to appeal to[5]).

It's easy to construct such small, co-operative systems using this formula; so long as performing them can't be regarded as daily chores, and there aren't so many that it puts people off doing any at all, they work as little magnets to draw willing players together. They don't have to be in third places: you could put one in an instance, or at a quest hub, or in a store. You could even have mendicant NPCs approach players and ask them to introduce themselves to one another. Players don't have to participate in any of these activities and won't miss out if they don't. They can be fun breaks, though, and connect like-minded players together.

When two players have established a relationship with one another, the resulting pair is called a *dyad*.[6] All relationships are made of dyads. These don't have to be equal, and it's common for them not to be (*I* may think we're best buddies but you might regard us as merely being casual chums). It's even possible for a player to believe they're in a dyad when they're not (see the discussion on *parasocial relationships* in Chapter 23).

Relationships between three people are called *triads*,[7] which are made up of dyads. If all three members of a triad have dyadic relationships between each other, the result is a *triadic closure group*. However, if there are only two dyadic relationships (player #1 and player #2 both know player #3 but they don't know each other) then there's a *triadic gap*. It's through these friends-of-friends relationships that independent groups can connect with one another to form communities. When one of the people involved is

---

[4] You'd probably want to put a long per-player cooldown on whacking the biggest bell if you did this, although not the smaller ones.

[5] OK, so maybe the bell example *was* entirely constructed so as to make this bad pun, but it's still valid.

[6] That's not a mis-spelling of "dryad", tree-spirit fans.

[7] It's a technical term that unfortunately also applies to organised crime gangs with origins in China.

a super-connector,[8] the opportunities that different groups have to hook up with similar groups are increased dramatically.

Annoyingly, it's not easy to design to attract super-connectors. The best you can do is work to keep them once you've netted one. Most players won't need a sophisticated friends list that they can organise in a hierarchical manner with notes attached to each player and a keyword search function, but a super-connector would thank you for it – especially if it can be exported as a comma-separated value (CSV) file for easy import into a spreadsheet.

Design Practices for Human Scale Online Games has pages of very useful suggestions for how to design games (not just MMOs) that support groups. However, there are a lot of them and they're incremental; put another way, they're good but boring. Also, some of the advice is written to follow particular design philosophies that you may not necessarily adhere to yourself.[9] Nevertheless, it's a very useful piece of work, which should be read by anyone interested in this aspect of virtual worlds.

20.3 COMMUNITY SIZE

One of the ways that designers can influence the nature of the communities they get in their virtual worlds is by tinkering with their sizes. As I mentioned in Chapter 19, Dunbar's number already puts an informal limit on how large a group can be to remain coherent, but of course not all groups *have* to be coherent (evidence: any political party).

"Large" and "small" are relative, context-dependent terms, but when applied to virtual world communities, we can nevertheless make some general observations.

Larger virtual world communities are:

- **More Robust**. They can splinter off a smaller group rather than shatter.

- **Easier for Newbies to Join**. They tend to have more recruiters.

- **Few in Number**. Their mutual interests and values are therefore more abstract than specific, so are easier to design for.

- **More Powerful**. Their actions are larger-scale so can be more dramatic.

- **Inclusive**. Attainers and Politicians like them because they're large enough to have room for multiple sub-communities of commitment.

Smaller virtual world communities are:

- **More Intense**. You're a big fish in a small pond.

- **Quicker to Develop**. There's less friction from other members in negotiating norms.

---

[8] You did read the sidebar where I explained what these were, yes?

[9] No, you don't have to write down the rules: just because the United States has a written constitution, that doesn't mean everyone else has to have one too. No, decision-makers can ignore consensus: democracy works splendidly for countries, but not necessarily for other organisations such as schools, companies, and armies. I'm sure you'll find your own suggestions that you disagree with, too – but at least you'll have given the matter some thought.

- **Friendlier**. Newbies are treated as people rather than as recruits.

- **Less Fractious**. Civil wars catch fewer people in the crossfire.

- **More Bespoke**. Their special interests and values are more special.

- **Exclusive**. Griefers and opportunists like them because they have strong communities of interest: they get a response when they ask for help.

Note that tiny but long-established communities are probably going to be spiritual-level, so are a little different from other smaller communities. They are:

- **Exceptionally Friendly**. However, they avoid recruiting newbies so as not to upset the *status quo*.

- **Fun to be in**. Members of spiritual communities all know what the others want and enjoy being with them while they pursue their goals.

- **Exceptionally Exclusive**. They're pretty well Friends-only.

This all sounds wonderful, but sadly, there are negatives as well as positives.

Larger virtual world communities can and will subdivide into cliques, which might peacefully co-exist for months only to take against each other with sudden, alarming ease. Members of the cliques might also bully those who aren't in cliques, sometimes to the extent that it can become a social norm. Leaders of larger communities tend to be vision-based rather than policy-based, which is great if the vision is great but awful if the vision is awful. Larger communities are a frequent cause of community management issues, and if they're *very* large, they can pose quite a severe threat. This is because their members collectively (if not consciously) try to stop their community from disintegrating by demonising other groups. Although this is entirely to do with preventing internal conflict, the fact that the group achieves this through stoking external conflict is the cause of what can be very messy community management problems. Social worlds seem more susceptible to such rancorous behaviour than game worlds, probably because the more social a world is, the more antisocial it can become if not properly managed.

Smaller virtual world communities aren't off the hook either. Their members are constantly negotiating norms, so disagreements will inevitably arise. The resulting heated arguments can result in the cold-shouldering and bad-mouthing of the players involved (offline as well as online), which leaves an unpleasant atmosphere. In extreme cases, players will rage quit.

Tiny virtual world communities are either the rump of a failed community or the beating heart of a successful one. If the former, they're homeless. If the latter, they're a gated estate but few people have a pass key.

So, knowing the pros and cons of the different community sizes, what can you do to help shift them in the direction you prefer? We're essentially talking guilds here (although I'll say a little about parties afterwards).

The easiest way to make sure you don't have large guilds is not to implement the tools that players need to manage them. That rather punishes the players in small guilds who also need the tools, though, so is not usually a good idea.

Another easy fix is to limit the number of players (not characters, because alts) in a guild. If you put an arbitrary limit of, say, 30 on guild size, none of your guilds will exceed that. The problem here is that a guild's members aren't always online at the same time: people play on different days and at different times. There'll be overlap, obviously, but sometimes half the guild will be playing simultaneously and sometimes no members will be logged in. When you put an upper limit on guild membership numbers, you're actually putting a much lower effective upper limit on how many members will be playing at once. If that doesn't fit well with, say, your raid-group sizes, you'll have done your MMO more harm than good.

If, on the other hand, you want to ensure your guilds aren't too small, there are two easy solutions, neither of which are particularly recommended. One is to make the number of people who need to sign the guild charter be a large number; the other is to dissolve the guild if membership falls below some threshold. In the former, you do get larger guilds (at least initially), but you also get fewer guilds in the first place; in the latter, you can inadvertently prevent the formation of tiny, relatively harmless guilds of Friends. A third possibility – limiting the absolute number of guilds allowed on a server – so heavily promotes the founder effect that it's likely to cause widespread dissent; don't attempt it unless widespread dissent is what you want.

The preferred way to influence guild sizes is to partition by proximity in some dimension, although it's only truly effective when you want your guilds to be smaller. The designer places boundaries on the spaces of interaction that players inhabit, reducing the number of players near one another, so the pool of potential guild members is low. Partitioning by similarity (rather than proximity) is not effective, because the designer has no knowledge of how similar players are.

Geographic proximity is the easiest kind to control. If you start characters off in different areas and make it hard for them to leave for quite some time, you will restrict how large the guilds that initially develop will be. The nature of the barriers between starting locations can be varied indeed, but include: physical (impassable mountains); resource-based (currency or specific objects are required); mental (it will take the player hours to cross the desert); relative (your powers diminish the further you are from your home village); and quest-based (you can leave when you've done what the overlord requires). I don't endorse the idea of keeping players on low-population servers until they form guilds, then performing a sever merge with a higher-population server, because server merges always cause strife; I guess that could work in the short term, though.

Players can be partitioned along other dimensions, too, although geographic proximity will usually remain a contributing factor. If all the tanks need to go to Tanktown to learn how to tank, there's the opportunity there for guilds of tanks to form. In practice, only character experience or skill level is useful in this regard, though – it's too hard to design content for all the wilder and more varied possibilities.

One possible solution is simply to ask players if they want the chance to meet one another again. At the end of each party instance, present them with the names of the other characters and a set of radio boxes saying "yes", "no", and "reserve judgement" (the default), then next time they use the LFG system, incorporate their preferences into the algorithm. Sure, the chances that we both look for a group at the same time may be slim, but the information is still useful. *I* might not have played with character X before, but if I liked playing with characters Y and Z and they liked playing with character X, there's a chance I'll like playing with character X, too. Sadly, the prospect of having to maintain a 10,000 by 10,000 sparse array for each 10,000-character server makes this suggestion less than practical.

If you want larger guilds, you can partition by content. Suppose a certain number of people *from the same guild* are required to do content together, as with guild raids but not instanced: you're going to get communities of interest forming at the very least. You're also going to annoy solo players and close-knit groups of Friends, but if you don't care about that – or actively want to do it for design or business reasons – then go right ahead. For smaller guilds, content partitioning can be more subtle. If you limit local opportunities (for combat, resource-gathering, selling crafted products, whatever) so that players have to spread themselves out more, the players working the same patch will find it convenient to come to some arrangement; a community of practice could arise. In general, if a designer can engineer a pressure for players to play together, a chance to form a community to address that pressure will be presented. It might not be taken up, but without the pressure, it almost certainly won't be.

20.4 PARTY SIZE

I've said a lot here about promoting communities by creating needs that can be addressed by co-operating players. Many players don't have to be encouraged to band together, though: they already have a need – the need to socialise with others. Communities can form spontaneously, especially among newbies (given the chance). One way to introduce non-newbies to one another is through party-based content such as instances: pick-up groups can act as shop windows for discerning guild recruiters. Because instances are usually created for a fixed party size (they don't have to be, by the way – there's no rule that says they should), an appropriate number can be selected that encourages players to form dyads and triads and thence possibly communities.

It's not that simple, though. There are many competing considerations that have to be taken into account when deciding on what fixed party size to have. For the classic tank/healer/DPS model, you can expect that few players will want to be tanks and slightly fewer (but still few) players will want to be healers, therefore you'll need more slots for DPS so that players have a decent chance of getting into a group. How many more slots, though? How many players do you expect will want to be a damage-dealer for every player who wants to be a tank? Well, it depends on how appealing each of the roles is to any particular individual, which varies from MMO to MMO depending on the gameplay. There are stats available that show how much time people spend in each role in existing MMOs, but obviously, those figures are already shaped by the MMO itself. For example, in *WoW,* the relative amounts of time spent as a tank, healer, ranged DPS, and melee DPS are 13%, 20%,

38%, and 30% respectively[10] (Yee et al., 2011). Given that *WoW* has a default party size of five, this probably explains these particular ratios.

Another factor to think about is how many classes or skill sets you have (if two classes can tank and 22 can't, you're already discouraging tanks so will need more DPS slots). Remember, though, that the larger the number you choose for a fixed party size then the harder it will be to co-ordinate enough players to fill all the slots. Furthermore, absolute group size itself can be an issue independent of other determinants: for life in general, people find it significantly less personally satisfying to be in a group of eight or more members than they do in smaller groups (Snyder, 1975).

Nevertheless, if you're deciding on a fixed party size for community-sparking reasons, you'll want a minimum of four and a maximum of six. Here's why.

One isn't a party and two is too intimate. Three is fine if there are at least two existing dyads but is socially awkward otherwise: if two players form a dyad (or are in one already), it isolates the third. Four is the minimum satisfactory number because two isolated people can themselves form a dyad. Better, the structure of the classic tank/healer/DPS trinity (which is detailed in Volume II) affords one natural dyad between the healer and the tank and a second between the two DPS. Alternatively, there are triads-in-the-making between the healer and DPS because the tank sucks, or the tank and DPS because the healer sucks.

A party size of five or six is non-problematical, but at seven, the members start to disengage.[11] Players have to work to get their views heard among the crowd, and some will inevitably feel (legitimately so) shut out. Also, when a group gets beyond a certain size, members believe they can't express both positive and negative feelings freely without antagonising others; as for what that size is, well the sweet spot is four or five (Hackman & Vidmar, 1970), although there's more leeway for people who aren't already acquaintances (and so won't have to live with the consequences of any acrimonious fallings-out). The fact that virtual worlds have backchannels, so players can communicate privately without being observed, does mitigate this; backchannels usually mean complaints, though, so what's good for forming dyads may not be quite as good for keeping them.

This isn't to say that larger groups are a bad idea. They can function well if they have a leader (a job that normally falls to the main tank in pick-up raid groups[12]). A larger group allows for different gameplay, introducing the possibility of specific additional roles such as crowd control, buffing/debuffing, off-tanking, interrupting, and kiting. They can help strengthen the bonds between members of existing groups, too; they're just not all that great for forming new bonds.

20.5 PROMOTING CONNECTIONS

Outside of parties and raid groups, it's possible to encourage dyads through other means. For example, *FFXIV* has a *commendation system*, which allows players to be nice to strangers. Upon completing an instance, players can "commend" one of the other players in their

---

[10] The numbers are rounded to the nearest percent. I shouldn't have to tell you this, but there are people out there who will do the arithmetic and scoff at me if I don't.

[11] There's a reason that cub scouts are split into groups of six. I don't know what it *is*, but there's definitely a reason.

[12] Pick-up raid groups are not as common as pick-up dungeon groups or pre-organised raid groups, but they're not exactly uncommon either. It depends on the virtual world.

group, who when they leave will be told how many commendations they received (but not from whom). Cosmetic rewards are provided every so-many commendations, to give people an incentive to be nice,[13] with the reward for 3,000 commendations being a big, plump chick to ride as a mount.[14] OK, so all this *is* party-based, but one important consequence isn't: if you reach a given threshold of commendations and meet certain other criteria (number of instances completed, plus particular tank and healer quests), you are invited to become a mentor. This is where it gets interesting.

Mentors have access to a channel otherwise reserved for new players. Newbies can ask questions on it and get useful replies – often from fellow newbies, which is how dyads can form. Sadly, commendations are rarely awarded for having interpersonal skills, and being a commendation-attracting tank doesn't mean you necessarily have them. As a result, the *FFXIV* novice channel is often full of conversations between mentors boasting about end-game matters way over the heads of newbies. Players can feel stupid asking newbie-level questions in this context, so they don't ask any at all. The system works well when the channel isn't being dominated by people who can't stop talking, but is fitful otherwise. Restricting it entirely to newbies might be better.

Creating mutual dependencies between characters is another way to allow them to establish a rapport. Supply chains for crafting used to help a lot here, but nowadays not so much. The basic principle is that if I need objects made of wood, steel, and cloth to manufacture a sailing ship, but the virtual world limits me to two professions and two gathering skills, I have to rely on others to create some of the materials I need. The reason this doesn't help people make and maintain contacts as much as it once did is that nowadays they can buy what they need from an auction house – that's if they don't use an alt to plug the skills gap. Thus, players do get what they want, but in so doing, they don't form a connection with other players. It can still happen for very high-end components that aren't reliably available in auction houses – *BDO* has some of these – but the supply lines that arise tend to be kept in-guild, in which case the players involved will know each other anyway.[15]

The idea of mutual dependencies is to promote community, not to enforce it. In Reality, people who want to make pins don't mine the ore themselves then extract the iron, smelt it to make steel, draw it to make wire, straighten it, cut it, sharpen it, package it then sell it at auction (Smith, 1776), but in virtual worlds, some players will nevertheless wish to do exactly that. If it makes them happy, you need a good reason not to indulge them.

It's possible to provide gameplay incentives for social dependencies. Usually, designers will assume that the weak will depend on the strong; this assumption is correct, they do, but *you* get to decide who is weak and who is strong in any given context. For example, suppose that you want to encourage guilds to recruit new players. One way to do this would be to require that guild houses need regular cleaning (er, I mean regular plagues of

---

[13] In my experience, you get more commendations if you hang around longer in the instance after it's finished. People can't commend players who have already left.

[14] That's "chick" as in baby chicken; it's not some jazz-culture reference to young women.

[15] You can also put dependencies between communities. These are usually about resource management and can lead to drama. If only the elves can make bows that only the humans can hunt with, there's a dependency. If the elves make bows from wood gathered in the forests where the boars the humans hunt live, there's also a potentially interesting conflict should the number of trees starts to decline from over-felling.

ten rats that need to be killed). OK, well anyone could do that, so why wouldn't they? Well, you can give players (not characters, because then alts will do it) social levels based on how many status points they have,[16] then associate a status-point cost with performing actions below your status level. Everyone loses status points if the guild house is dirty, but whoever sweeps the floor will lose even more points if they do so when at a social level higher than some threshold. Therefore, to avoid whatever penalties come with being at lower social levels, guilds will want to sign up newbies. Newbies in turn will want to be signed up, because they get decent XP or pay for clearing out rats once or twice a week. With luck, the more experienced players will get to know the newbies, and they'll be embedded in the group by the time their own social level gets too high for "menial work". This approach inverts the usual power relationship between high-ranking and low-ranking players.

20.6 ENCOURAGING DYADS

There are ways to encourage dyad-forming beyond formal groups. Anything that encourages players to play together or to talk together can work.

Jargon, which I mentioned in Chapter 19, is a good example. If you give instances, spells, objects, or other shared content a slightly too-long name, players will abbreviate it. Other players will see the abbreviation but not necessarily know what it means. The more forward among them will ask (an opening), to which a player may provide an answer (an opportunity). If they do so (a response), the person who asked can then thank them (an acknowledgement), so closing the loop. They could, however, make a comment or ask a follow-up question, as could the person who answered, as could someone who overheard the conversation. This has all happened because "Sunken Temple" is 11 characters more to type than "ST". Players will, of course, abbreviate things you didn't name (for example, *MT* and *OT* for *Main Tank*[17] and *Off Tank*), but so long as you don't go too overboard, you can add more to the mix to help them out. Incidentally, the emergence of jargon is a good indicator that a virtual world is developing its own culture (Squire & Steinkuehler, 2006), which (if you want it to have one) is nice.

Creating interdependencies between roles is also a good way to encourage dyads (Zagalo & Gonçalves, 2014). If you need someone else's help and they need yours, this can bring you both closer together. The relationship between gatherers, crafters and combatants, is one classic example; the relationship between tanks, healers, and DPS is another. Designers have to be careful, however, because some players strongly prefer to be independent; if you force them to rely on others, they won't like it.

Informal groups can serve the same purpose as parties, but in a more *ad hoc* manner. I mentioned *trains* earlier as an example of this in action; designers merely have to provide the open events around which they can form. Events that aren't train-friendly but which do require large numbers of players to tackle them are also good catalysts for friendships to form – although not necessarily for the reasons you might suppose. For example, a world boss that can be taken down by 50 players in five minutes might be able to hold its own against 15 players who will perforce both wish and need to communicate. I've personally been invited to guilds based on my healing prowess in such fights, which is more than has

---

[16] This excellent, under-used support mechanic comes from the RPG *En Garde!* (Hany et al., 1975).

[17] Also, you'll recall, *mistell*. Players are not required to be either precise or consistent.

ever happened when I've been spamming group heals on an amorphous blob of particle effects at the boss's feet.

One of the problems of having large numbers of instances or global events is that players don't always want to do the same ones together at the same time even when they're timetabled.[18] Seasonal events are a way around this: as they're only active within a short window, more players will want to run them at the same time than is the case for generic, always-available events.

Down time is conducive to communication and can be introduced using plenty of methods independently of formal groups. These don't have to be sophisticated or rigid – simply holding events at a fixed time will do it. For example, *FFXIV* has a number of mini-games in its Manderville Gold Saucer zone that start at regular, given times: players show up a few minutes early so as not to miss them, and while they're waiting will often have little else to do but chat to their competitors or co-operators. *Throne & Liberty* has instanced boss fights at predetermined times, but the boss doesn't appear until five minutes have elapsed since the boss instance opened; players use this time to organise pick-up groups so they can benefit from group buffs and can make acquaintances this way.

Sometimes, a player will want to say something to someone but not have enough information about them. This puts off shy people (who will use any excuse not to talk to someone they don't know), but it also irritates impatient people who want to find out if a conversation is going to be worthwhile before they start it. A nice solution to this is to implement self-identity descriptors. For example, *FFXIV* has what it calls *adventurer plates*, which are basically calling cards that allow characters to display information about themselves that others can use when deciding whether or not to engage. Some of it is practical (main class and level, login times, guild membership, and so on), but it's the more expressive features that help with community building. These include a portrait that the character can pose for (which tells you a *lot* about them), plus multiple layouts and formats that also convey aspects of the character's personality. If you like what you see, you're more reassured that an interaction will go well before it starts than you would be if you went in blind.

If personal expression extends to in-world creations, this can help give players a sense of being part of the wider community. When passers-by can see how nicely you've done up your house, it doesn't matter that in practice only one person a day will actually pass by: you'll still feel that you've contributed to the virtual world and are therefore part of something bigger. This is especially important for social worlds, the players of which have been obsessed with creating personal spaces since the days of *TinyMUD*. It also scales up for group stake-holding in the form of guild houses. Housing is discussed more in Volume II.

It's clear that communal activities with nothing to do with gameplay can bring players together. Sure, there may *be* gameplay reasons for having musical instruments that characters can play, but there doesn't have to be one to encourage four of them to join up and try to play the same piece together on different instruments – they'll do that anyway. You can

---

[18] Given a range of field bosses to go after in *Lost Ark*, I seemed to have an uncanny knack for choosing whichever one too-few other people also wanted to do.

provide a venue (if not an audience) for this, which will help. It won't see much use,[19] but the players who *do* use it will greatly appreciate its existence.

20.7 GREETERS

With the Sixth-Age trend of having virtual worlds that are free to play, newbies have no incentive to stay around if they don't like what they see. For many of them, a lack of any sense of being part of a community is an issue. A new player who joins a few months after the initial launch-wave of players has subsided can feel alone and friendless, facing the prospect of playing catch-up in an impersonal world where everyone else has already found like-minded playmates. If it doesn't feel welcoming, they'll leave.

This is a problem for all virtual worlds, but it's particularly bad for social worlds: forming relationships is the very reason people play. *Second Life* gets 10,000–15,000 sign-ups every day, but only keeps a few hundred (Rosedale & Atherton, 2023). The ones that stay are typically those who managed to make a quick friend. Hiring CSRs to greet newbies is expensive,[20] and although it's something that can be done by home workers part-time, it can't be outsourced either to low-skilled labour or AI large language models without doing more harm than good. Furthermore, in the same way that few people like being approached by an over-enthusiastic sales representative in a store that they've only just entered, most newbies will be annoyed by the arrival of a perpetually sunny CSR moments after materialising in the world following character creation. In addition to being approachable and available, *greeters*[21] must have perfect timing. Nevertheless, expert after expert interviewed in Atherton (2023) says how important greeters are.

Greeters don't have to greet individuals one at a time, nor do they have to insinuate themselves into every new player's opening experience. They can simply wander around newbie areas wearing an obvious nameplate that says "here to help!" (or whatever is in keeping with the fiction); if they see someone who seems confused or to be having difficulty then they can approach them, but otherwise their presence needs only to be announced (either by the greeter themself or by the virtual world on their behalf), so they can take responses when needed.

Oh, these greeters really *should* be people, by the way, in case you were still thinking of using AIs. They can have a few variations of canned phrases to open with that they can click on to save typing, but their utility is completely undermined if the player suspects they're merely a large language model in disguise. You don't need to play a virtual world to chat to a cheerful chatbot.

Even if you don't have greeters, it's useful to examine what would be required if you *did* have them as to some extent it overlaps with what players will want to do when seeking new recruits for their guild.

---

[19] *The Secret World*'s Albion Theatre is a very pleasing rendition of a London theatre. Few players visit it, but for those who want to put on a performance of some kind it's a gift, even if only for rehearsal purposes.

[20] Even CSRs are paid to work. Well, they are now, following 1990s lawsuits in which AOL's Community Leader "volunteers" successfully argued that minimum-wage laws applied to them (Postigo, 2003).

[21] That's what they're called in the industry, hence the italics.

The first and most obvious point is that if someone speaks to you and you're a complete newbie, you need to be able to reply without having to look up how to reply. The way to do this is to have multiple methods. Click on the message, the message sender's name, the character's nameplate, or the friendly pale blue button with "reply" written on it that accompanies the message – as many alternatives as possible. Standard ways that they'll use when not a newbie (such as using /r) must also work, of course.

The second and less obvious point is that if someone says something to you, you need to be able to reply to them some time after receiving their message yet without having to figure out how to find it. If there's a physical greeter there whom you can approach in-world then that's not a problem, but if you or they have wandered off then you can't do that. One way to handle this is to have the last (or first) message from a greeter be sticky and stay in the message window until the player dismisses it or logs off. Unless you give them special privileges, this doesn't work for greeters who are players; it does for on-the-payroll greeters, though.

The third and least obvious point is that greeters probably have lives outside the virtual world and may need to log off every so often. Normally, if you try to contact a character who is no longer around then you'll be told they've logged off and that's that. With greeters, it's possible to tell the player this and *then* ask if they want the message to be forwarded to another greeter in the vicinity.[22]

To summarise this chapter (so far) and the previous chapter:

- Communities are A Good Thing.
- A virtual world's design can encourage community building.
- Not everyone wants to be in a community, nor should they be.

So, once you have communities, you're sorted, right?

20.8 COMMUNITY MANAGEMENT

This isn't a book about community management: it's a book about the design of virtual worlds. However, good design can aid with community management, so we do need to give it some consideration.[23]

Communities are about people, so you need people to form them. A lot of the community-building work therefore has to be done by people; designers must furnish them with the tools and the overall vision, but otherwise it's a case of staying out of the way and leaving it to the experts.

It's a similar situation with managing communities.

---

[22] This should also work for accounts ("should" because I haven't seen it tried). If you message me from the chat box or your friends list and I'm not logged in as that character but have enabled message-forwarding, I'll receive the message on whichever character I'm playing as instead (but be told that the message was sent to my other character – as whom I should be able to reply without switching to them).

[23] Bad design can hinder it, of course. Indeed, so can good design if hindering is what you want.

We knew about what was then called *player management* back in the 1980s. In those formative years of virtual worlds, it was a task generally undertaken by the developers, rather than by specialists.[24] This continued right up to the dawn of the Fifth Age[25]; the first professional community manager was hired for *Ultima Online*, based on what its director, Starr Long, had seen happen with *Air Warrior* (Donovan, 2010). The central issues soon became well-understood for large-scale virtual worlds, and solutions such as Koster & Vogel (2002) were freely disseminated at the Game Developers Conference.

Like policing, much community management involves helping people who need help, but some of it is to do with preventing people from causing other people problems (then identifying those who do so anyway). Sometimes, the root cause of the difficulties is the culture of the virtual world; other times, it's individual players (or organised gangs of them). Sometimes, it's a culture imported from another virtual world or from Reality that's the source of a virtual world's woes.

20.8.1 Toxicity

The word used to describe obnoxious behaviours that put other people off playing a virtual world is *toxicity*. According to Google's ngram viewer, the words "toxic behaviour" became a thing circa 2002 (Google, 2010). For virtual worlds, toxic behaviour generally includes hate speech, harassment, discrimination, bullying, trolling, … pretty much the same as what goes on elsewhere on the Internet but with the added bonus that players can attempt to defend themselves with the words "it's just a game". Toxicity is not limited to virtual worlds, though; in fact, in some ways, MMOs have it easier than non-RPGs. Competitive, team-based games such as Multi-player Online Battle Arenas (MOBAs) and first-person shooters (FPSs) have it worse, because a significant dollop of the toxicity comes from people on your own side who flame you for not being as good as they think they are themselves. You do get that in some MMO PUGs, but it's not widespread in general gameplay.

In *MUD1*, we nipped this kind of @#&! in the bud by judicious use of the FOD ("Finger of Death") command, which is highly effective in a game with permadeath but also works for ones less red-in-tooth-and-claw. This is because most toxicity oozes from a very small number of players: estimates vary, but Anti-Defamation League (2023) suggests that fewer than 3% of players produce between 30% and 60% of all toxic content and only 1% are "really awful". Preventing repeat offenders from playing to repeat their offences will do you (and your other players) a huge favour – and if you also tell other operators about them, the same individuals won't go off and ruin their virtual worlds instead.[26] Sadly, even though despatching characters and accounts to oblivion remains an option, the operators of modern virtual worlds – even the ones that don't charge players to play – seem to have a fear of it, with the result that toxicity has to be dealt with using less drastic methods.

---

[24] It's something I did myself with *MUD2*. I'm very good at it, but absolutely loathe actually doing it. So, a bit like all administration, then.

[25] Damion Schubert acted as the community service department for *Meridian 59*, despite being employed as lead designer (Schubert, 2003).

[26] This assumes you don't *want* their games to be hotbeds of toxicity, of course. I proposed keeping a communal list of banned MUD players way back in the 1980s, but it didn't fly then either.

One popular way to calm down toxicity is to use a commendation system, like the one in *FFXIV* that I described earlier. Players are encouraged to behave in a commendable way because of the supposedly cool perks that come with enough commendations. *Overwatch* (Kaplan & Metzen, 2016) has a similar system called *endorsements*: when another player endorses you, you get some (battle pass) XP and a contribution towards your endorsement rank. Players can see the endorsement ranks of one other, so can avoid those who are manifestly bad. This approach seems to work: there was a 40% drop in disruptive behaviour following the implementation of endorsements (Kidwell, 2019). *League of Legends* (Cadwell & Feak, 2009) calls its version of this tactic the *honour* system; *DOTA 2* (IceFrog, 2013) calls its *commends*.

Although commendation systems do reduce reports of toxicity, once you realise that you're not going to get a commendation then all restraints are off. Commendation systems disguise toxicity, but don't change the culture that leads to it in the first place.

Another superficial way to deal with toxicity is to use AI to check what players are saying in chat. You can even have the AI participate in chat to try to direct the conversation to another topic if you want to be sly about it (although the players *will* find out and *won't* like it[27]). This is fine if they *are* exercising their toxic tongues in chat, but won't help if they're using voice. It also generates false positives when you say something that can be interpreted as a slur but which also has a perfectly innocent use (such as "black" or "white"); people can make up their own slurs to get around it anyway.[28] *Rainbow Six: Siege* (Drapeau & Baude, 2015) tried banning players for half an hour if its AI detected the use of a slur; it wasn't a success. Again, this approach addresses the symptoms but not the disease.

Ultimately, there are two root causes of toxicity: the prevailing culture and the behaviour of individuals. Although they're interlinked, they imply different solutions. We'll start by looking at the problem players.

As with bullies in wider society, some people will behave toxically regardless of the prevailing culture. They're typically doing so because (Frommel et al., 2023): they have low in-game social capital; they have a need to satisfy relatedness; they're lonely. Therefore, the way to prevent them from acting how they do is to address these causes. If you don't, they'll do it themselves: denigrating others is their way of feeling noticed, and any response they get will count as relatedness even if it's profoundly negative.

In virtual worlds, newbies generally *do* have low social capital, which is why it comes as no surprise that many start out as Griefers (not necessarily toxically so, though; their aim is to establish the boundaries of acceptable behaviour, not to break them wilfully thereafter). Happily, most who need social capital will soon acquire it, although in an established virtual world with newbie-repelling guilds, this may not be easy. That said, being a jerk at higher levels is also something of a challenge, so on the whole, virtual worlds address the toxicity that derives from a lack of social capital reasonably well (at least in comparison to MOBAs and the like). The fact that virtual worlds are persistent is a big help here, because

---

[27] OK, well they might if it's up-front about being an AI and has an engaging personality, but that will affect immersion. If you want to try to manipulate players this way, save it for the forum and expect rage.

[28] Recall AOL's problems with Scunthorpe.

it means that social capital isn't borne entirely by player or character stats, and disruptive behaviour comes with longer-lasting consequences.

The need to satisfy relatedness is managed by the methods that are used for promoting dyads. Unfortunately, because people have different personalities, not everyone is comfortable with approaching anyone they don't know; some will use aggression as a way to push through. Victim self-defence mechanisms, such as gagging, can alleviate the situation for individuals but exacerbate it in general: toxic players who are ignored will only be frustrated further, leading to a possible escalation of their activities. A friendly CSR case worker might be able to put a nascent toxic player straight if they're spotted reasonably early, but as CSRs are both expensive and perpetually busy, this isn't an easily scalable solution.

What's needed, then, is for *other* players to approach the one who's behaving toxically. There are actual ways to encourage this, by ignoring toxicity and treating everyone as if they were regular players. For example, suppose a particular instance attractive to high-level players were to need a low-level, non-alt character to be in the party: any higher-level characters who want to run that instance will actively seek out such a character. The requirement could be justified in-fiction, such as an escort quest where the low-level character is the one being escorted, or it could simply be mandated, as in the novel *Dream Park* (Niven & Barnes, 1981). It's not hard to think up such activities; you merely have to recognise that they need to be thought-up in the first place. When higher-level players do the approaching, the lower-level players they approach get a relationship boost even if they turn down the offer. This reduces the propensity of the toxically inclined to satisfy their needs in less salubrious ways, but non-toxic players also benefit.

20.8.2 Toxic-Culture Prevention

When the source of toxicity in a virtual world is its culture, rather than its players, the problem is less tractable. Changing the culture of a virtual world is difficult, and the best option is not to develop a toxic culture in the first place. Designers can't do a lot once a toxic culture is established, but they can put measures in place to stop them from prospering beyond controllable limits.

Some of the most effective ways to prevent a toxic culture aren't actually design-based. Tips for developers and operators include:

- Outline what the virtual world is about in clear language. Strangling it in legal terms deep in the Terms of Service will leave players ignorant of the virtual world's philosophy.[29] Each player needs to know what everyone is signing up for – and to have a reasonable expectation that all the other players also know. It shouldn't be possible to misinterpret either the virtual world's fictional context or its accompanying basic standards of behaviour.

---

[29] This may come as a shock to the legal team, but here goes: even though every player says they've read the Terms of Service, *not all have done so.*

- Make sure that the virtual world is indeed about what you claim it's about. Telling players one thing and then doing the opposite or the orthogonal will only confuse and anger them. No one likes to be lied to, even by accident. Periodically check that you haven't drifted off course. If the *players* have drifted off course, either reinforce the message or follow them and hope for the best.

- Don't tolerate it if the development company's principals have no principles and behave contrary to how the players have been told to behave. There may not be much you can do about it, but if you see it happening then your virtual world is heading for A Bad Place.

- Listen to what the players are saying. This doesn't only mean in forum posts, which are dominated by the same voices: by using sentiment analysis (Liu, 2010) on log files, you can extract the views of the silent majority as well. If the players point out a problem then either fix it or (if it's working as intended) fix the perception that it *is* a problem.

- Don't deal with reports of toxicity superficially. Log them all and name names in your records. Check to see if the same people are being toxic time and time again. Everyone has bad days and needs to let off steam occasionally, and a modicum of drama can be good for a community's health, so don't be too zealous in your initial response. However, people who repeatedly cause problems need first to be identified, then dealt with by following the Terms of Service provisions to the letter. This could even include allowing the player body to decide on the punishment, as with *League of Legends'* now-defunct *tribunal* system.[30]

As for what *designers* can do, well it depends on the nature of the virtual world. If you have a game world with open PvP then the obvious first steps are:

- Don't reward toxicity. *Ultima Online* implements a joint *karma* and *fame* reputation system,[31] granting those with the lowest level of the former and the highest level of the latter the title Dread Lord or Dread Lady. That's a cool title. All you have to do is murder enough characters and you'll get it.

- Punish toxic acts through gameplay. If the player sees that the virtual world doesn't want them to do something, that tells them they perhaps ought not to do it. Example: the longer a character stands near a spawn point, the more you debuff them; "it's the stench of death".

- Discourage repeat offences. Example: the more recently you attacked another character, the more XP you lose; "the madness is taking hold". Use character time for this, not real time, so people can't just log off and wait it out.

---

[30] The fact that it's now-defunct might of course suggest that you shouldn't implement it.

[31] I'll discuss reputation systems shortly.

- Discourage players from behaving toxically in groups. Example: have people in close proximity who have negative reputations debuff one another; evil people have to watch their backs in the presence of other evil people.[32] *Realm of the Mad God* (Carobus et al., 2011) awards XP to people nearby a mob when it's defeated; there's no reason why you can't remove XP from people nearby a player who's defeated if you so want.

If you have a game world with only consensual PvP (or none at all), try the following:

- Make it easy to form and to find a guild, as discussed earlier. Running a guild is a form of community management undertaken by players, who are often far more ruthless and intolerant of misbehaviour than are CSRs. If non-toxic players can find others of their ilk and only play with those, they'll have a safe haven and a fun time even a virtual world that otherwise has box-jellyfish levels of toxicity.

- I don't actually recommend this, but others do so I'll give you the option: create toxic islands. The idea here is that players who have a reputation for toxicity are made to live with one another, for example by only allowing them to group with other players who are also flagged as toxic. The reason I don't favour this is that sure, if you lock five people in the same room who all believe they're Napoleon then only one will come out still believing they are, but that one will *really* believe they are. Toxic islands make some toxic players even more toxic.

If you have any kind of virtual world, including social worlds,[33] these ideas are also among those worth considering:

- Implement simple self-defence measures such as gagging. Note that this is a response-only solution: by the time there's cause to use it, the initial damage will already have been done. It merely helps limit further damage.

- Implement a report system so that CSRs can act on egregious behaviour. Note that if this is to have any effect, the CSRs do actually need to take action: industry-wide, only around 1% of all reports are acted upon (Machkovech, 2022). I personally must have reported RMT spam in *FFXIV* over a hundred times, but it nevertheless kept on coming, using the same words, usually from the same scratch characters. You can automate some of this, for goodness' sake! If 200 disparate players all complain about a message at once, that's surely a sign you need to Do Something Quickly.[34]

---

[32] People who do the bidding of evil people usually do so because they're afraid of what will happen if they don't; they're not necessarily evil themselves. Furthermore, those who *are* evil themselves won't find being led by someone else who's evil satisfying.

[33] Social worlds tend to present more griefing opportunities because they feature extradiegetic content. However, they're more resistant to toxicity because they're all about community, so the interpersonal bonds in them are usually more concentrated and hence stronger.

[34] Example: Shoot Now And Ask Questions Later.

- Implement aide-memoirs. Don't simply give each player a personalised "friends" list: make it a "known" list that they can annotate privately. Include a headline field that can be displayed just for you in the nameplate of individual characters on your known list, so you know why you know them and what you think of them. Allow something similar at guild level.

- Don't permit name changes. This may hurt, because charging for name changes is a money mine, but it will prevent toxic players from easily evading the consequences of their nefarious deeds. Name changes are bad for both community and immersion, so they really need to be avoided if possible. Should a player *really* need to change their character's name (perhaps it suddenly becomes a term of racist abuse, for example), they can ask for a change only if they have a certain number of hours of playing time behind them (to discourage applications aimed at wasting the operator's time).

- Use the addlist/denylist systems described earlier to intercept possibly offensive messages before they are sent. You don't have to block them (although you can if you like), because there are sure to be false positives; rather, you need merely point out to the sender that there's an issue and ask them to confirm that they're sure they want to send the message in question. Pleasingly, this is often enough for them to rethink any spur-of-the-moment words they would immediately regret, but if it isn't then pass the message to the intended recipient anyway. Friends can and do swear at each other.[35]

- If your virtual world is already perceived by players to be toxic, display an anti-toxicity warning message in red on the loading screen. The mere fact it's in red will reduce toxicity (Cummings, 2013). I'm not a fan of this approach because I don't like mind-control tricks, but if you're either OK with them or desperate then go for it.

- Don't be afraid to try novel solutions. If the EULA says you can charge an administration fee for banning an account, you can indeed do exactly that. Just make absolutely sure that you have clear and publishable evidence that the culprit did what you say they did before you ask for a payment from their credit card company.

- Recognise that some people are going to be toxic whatever you do, because it's down to their nature rather than their nurture. You can do little but deal with these on a case-by-case basis. Therefore, make sure your CSRs are trained to do so.

Remember that the bad guys can weaponise allegations of toxic behaviour, so don't automate any of this unless the effects are temporary and the number of people who would have to work together to subvert it is huge.

Diversity and inclusivity can help promote cultural change from the outside, but if pushed too heavily, they can become oppressive. If people with low self-esteem are constantly told they're privileged by someone who has been elevated to a position of palpably

---

[35] It's probably safe to allow players to state that they'll accept, unmoderated, anything another named player sends them. Although players who are controlling will enforce this setting on the people whom they're controlling, they're very likely to be communicating out-of-world anyway (they know that operators log everything).

higher privilege, you can see how that's not instantly going to make the virtual world a better place. Also, remember that games don't *have* to have a diverse or inclusive player base: if for some artistic reason you want it to be narrow or exclusive or both, you can have that. You're the designer: it's *your* game.

20.8.3 Toxic-Culture Acceptance

Now, having spent some time outlining approaches to dealing with toxicity (that can be summarised as "hire the best customer service lead you can afford"), I'll spend a little while discussing its possible benefits. Yes, there are some. This won't include ways to promote toxicity (you'll get it whether you want it or not), but will cover some of the positives you can expect if you decide to suck it up.

Responding to toxic behaviour through design rather than through social measures is not ideal. It tends to dilute what virtual worlds *are*. It's the reason that my character can walk straight through yours. It's the reason that when a grenade explodes it only hurts enemies. It's the reason that all of us can loot the same treasure chest. It would be a wild fiction in which any of these made sense, but they're now staples. Likewise: open PvP is disfavoured because of ganking; non-instanced bosses are disfavoured because of *camping*[36]; out-of-inventory object persistence is disfavoured because of RMT; and fast resource-respawning is disfavoured because of *farming*.[37] Therefore, you might wonder if it's better to be true to your design ideals and take the toxicity hit that might come with this.

This is what effectively happened with *Fallout 76*, which swiftly gained a reputation of having nuclear-wasteland levels of toxicity when played in survival mode.[38] Interestingly, this disruptive environment caused those non-toxic players who weren't dissuaded from playing to form very strong communities. In games with open PvP, players are really taking a risk when they step up to help a stranger, and the bonds that form among people under fire can lead to spiritual-level communities surprisingly quickly. The risk of death in a virtual world is what makes life there meaningful (Klastrup, 2008). Most players aren't toxic, they're friendly; for these, the acts of a few toxic players can act as a catalyst to speed up the friendship reaction. It's a similar situation in *EVE Online*.

Such worlds are not appealing to everyone, but they can offer lifelong friendships to others. Importantly, neither *Fallout 76* nor *EVE Online* insists that you join or form a guild – you can have a fun time playing alone – but they do offer many dyad-making opportunities to inveigle people into doing so. Toxicity isn't a good thing, especially when it spills into Reality, but the response to it can be. If you want to take this toxicity-agnostic approach, you could indeed make a success of it; just make sure you have plenty of white

---

[36] Waiting next to the spawn point doing nothing until the target appears, then instantly attacking it. Bots are very good at this, especially in swarms. We'll briefly re-encounter the concept in Chapter 24.
[37] Repeatedly and reliably harvesting a resource. This can be as simple as picking flowers or mining ores, or as complex as emptying an entire instance of everything worth having. Guilds will sometimes boast that they have a difficult instance "on farm".
[38] I chose this metaphor because *Fallout 76* is set in a nuclear wasteland, but it's nevertheless somehow appropriate.

hats on your playtesting team and that players are completely clear about what awaits them when they sign up.

20.8.4 Reputation Systems

Now, I mentioned reputation systems a while back there.

Formally, a *reputation system* is a set of one or more interacting *reputation models*. A reputation model describes all the *reputation statements* for a particular reputation *context*[39]; a reputation statement involves a *source* making a claim about a *target* (Farmer & Glass, 2010).[40] Reputation systems have seen a great deal of use in social media, but they're also important for virtual worlds.

Obviously, the reputation *of* a virtual world is a thing, but from a design perspective, it's more useful to consider how reputation *within* a virtual world could be a thing. Reputation can concern anything – how difficult an instance is, how useful a created object is, what the best healing build is – but we're almost always going to be most interested in the reputations of characters and players and, occasionally, guilds. This is because designers have limited abilities to interfere with content reputations built using word-of-mouth, and little need to do so anyway. Sure, monitoring such reputations can help inform the designer as to what works and what doesn't, but fashions change and reputations could be different from one month to the next.

Designers usually think about reputation in the context of characters and their players. In general, character reputation is useful for gameplay reasons and player reputation is useful for community management reasons.

Character reputation tends to be handled using a fairly simple model. Some NPC or body of NPCs maintains a view of the character that can be raised or lowered by that character's actions. Basically, there's a counter that numbers are added to or subtracted from until some threshold is reached, whereupon benefits are gained or lost. Typical ways to increase the counter include undertaking quests (particularly daily quests) and killing large numbers of perceived enemies. Often, two reputation groups are in opposition and use the same counter: gaining reputation in the eyes of one therefore reduces reputation in the eyes of the other.[41]

Gaining reputation for a character is invariably grindy, and if you're a completionist, it's even worse (because for the opposing groups, you have to grind reputation for one, then grind it away before grinding reputation for the other). Concessions are sometimes made, such as binding reputation to an account behind some kind of "all the characters are in the same family" fiction, but that merely reduces the number of times you have to grind reputation, not the fact that it takes many hours to grind it in the first place.

---

[39] Reputation models also describe the events and processes for reputation contexts, but I won't be going into those here. Incidentally, I would normally have written "delving" rather than "going" there, but I don't want you to think I'm ChatGPT.

[40] Yes, this is the same Randy Farmer who co-developed *Habitat*. The programmers among you may be pleased to know that *Habitat*'s other developer, Chip Morningstar, helped create the JSON data-interchange format. Their accomplishments are not limited to virtual worlds.

[41] The Aldor and Scryer factions in *WoW*'s *Burning Crusade* expansion were originally like this.

OK, so that's the kind of reputation system used for gameplay-if-you-can-call-it-that purposes. In the context of toxicity, designers look at a completely distinct kind of reputation: that of the individual player.

The basic idea is the same: implement reputation models by adding or subtracting numbers from a running total, then act when some threshold is met. It tends to be more sophisticated, though, because models can be combined to give more nuanced measures of reputation, resulting in a fully fledged reputation system.

The reputation statements used in these models will have sources that are from either the virtual world itself or its players (or, occasionally, its CSRs). The virtual world handles the reputation of players much as it does characters: certain actions are deemed to be reputation-relevant, and when someone performs one, a number is changed accordingly. It's a bit like the way the ancient Egyptian god Anubis weighed the heart of a dead person against the feather of the goddess Ma'at to determine if they got to ascend to the Field of Reeds (pleasant) or be eaten by the crocodile-lion-hippopotamus goddess, Ammit (unpleasant). The advantages of this approach are that it's clean, easy to implement, and is done without the need for human intervention. The disadvantage is that context makes a difference, and unless you know *why* an action was performed, you can't always tell whether to increment or to decrement a counter. This is why countries have courts. Yes, killing someone is bad, but there are plenty of situations where it can be justified; you *do* need to justify it, though.

Coded-in detection of reputational actions is therefore not ideal, but it can highlight patterns of behaviour. For example, if a player routinely quits PUGs after the first boss fight yet most other players don't then that player is definitely being disruptive; whether they either know or care that what they're doing is spoiling the virtual world for others is for a CSR to decide, but at least the problem has been identified as being in need of investigation.

The fact that virtual worlds lack knowledge of context is a problem that pervades all attempts to code in responses to player behaviour. It's very hard to tell programmatically why people do what they do and how they read whatever's done to them. Therefore, it makes sense to give them a voice so they can tell you. This is where reputation statements with players as the source make their entrance.

I've already mentioned the most popular of these – commendation systems – but others do exist. To gag another player is to make a statement pertaining to their behaviour, for example, as (to a lesser extent) is adding them to a friends list.

Sadly, players don't in general want to spend a lot of time making reputation statements. You are unlikely to get them to write reviews of other players, for example, except perhaps privately for their own purposes. You can, however, persuade some of them to make reputation statements by providing them with means such as:

- Favouriting people with whom they would like to play again. This works if the reason they choose *is* behaviour-related and not merely a judgement about how competent the other player is.

- Reporting people whom they think behaved badly. Players are not going to do this if they don't feel that their gripe will be acted upon, so you do need to let them know it's been logged and do need to ensure that you keep complainer and complainee apart when allocating future random groups.

- Voting for the player you liked most in a group. This is like favouriting, but you only get one vote and it follows a group event. Commendation systems fit here.

- Apportioning points to members of a group. This gives players the ability to rate the relative contributions of other players towards some end, but it takes seconds to do (which is seconds-too-long for most players) and it tends to reflect the subjects' role and ability more than the amount of toxic vibes they emit.

- Rating their experience in a group. The idea here is that they don't have to call out bad players, they just have to say whether they enjoyed the group or not. There could be many reasons that they wouldn't enjoy a group, but if groups containing a particular player are consistently rated lower than average then the nature of this correlation merits investigation.

All reports of bad behaviour need to be followed up, but there is a major exception. If individuals persistently call out bad behaviour that is found not to be so, they can be flagged as vexatious and prevented from doing so again. Basically, they've called "wolf!" too often.

For identifying reputation failures, CSR staff will usually want to be looking at aggregates rather than isolated cases. There can be a lot of noise in the system, even from simple causes such as accidentally clicking on the wrong name from a list of commendation candidates, so the more data you can supply, the better this will smooth out. Relative values are more useful for CSRs than absolute values; for example, if everyone is scoring low then that's perhaps a problem with the method of making a reputation statement rather than with the quality of your players.

Two other points regarding reputation statements need to be given designer attention. Firstly, you need to decide whether reputation valuations last forever or whether reputation increases/decreases towards some norm over time.[42] Secondly, you need to decide whether players will have access to the reputation of others.

The argument in favour of regressing reputation to a norm is that players can change their ways. Toxic players can see the light; non-toxic players won't become complacent. The argument against it is that toxic players can sit it out and non-toxic players can come back from vacation and find themselves little better than pariahs.

The argument in favour of showing players the reputations of others is that you can decide with whom you want to play or not. The LFG mechanism can include a minimum-reputation requirement to help. The argument against it is that players won't read reputation how you intend it to be read, and someone with a reputation of "honoured" may be regarded as dirt by players with a reputation of "exalted".

The fundamental problem with all reputation systems is that they can be gamed. You can make it harder to game (*e.g.* don't let players commend players in the same guild), but

---

[42] In theory, you could give each reputation statement a half-life, but the bookkeeping for it is somewhat inefficient.

it will still be gamed (*e.g.* guilds make arrangements to commend each other's members); the chances are that most of the players with the highest non-toxicity reputations wouldn't objectively be regarded as much different from anyone else by players with lower reputations. What's more, because reputation systems can be gamed, they can be weaponised. *You* might think that down-rating another player is a waste of time, but a guild of 50 players down-rating others for laughs won't.

In open-PvP worlds, *bounty systems* are particularly prone to this: players can put a bounty on a character's head in an attempt to get other players to target that character. The idea is that players can see who has a bounty on them (keeping bounties secret is pointless) and can use a large bounty as an indication of a player's notoriety and toxicity. If a swarm of toxic players choose you to be their victim, it doesn't matter how peaceful or nice you are, you're going to appear to be an evil thug. Enjoy.

Sometimes, character reputation is used to moderate open PvP. If your character kills another character (maybe you needed to start the fight, maybe not) then you get a bad-reputation point. Typically, above a certain threshold of such points, NPCs won't trade with you; above a higher threshold, unkillable town guards will attack you. This gives a downside to PvPing, the idea being that it will make players think twice before they pick on someone. It might even work, but basically, it's irrelevant: victims are going to be impacted so negatively that they won't care how much inconvenience you cause to perpetrators as punishment, they're going to question why they're playing. They *will* want to see justice for being attacked, yes, but they'd prefer not to have been attacked in the first place. The asymmetry in the relationship between the ganker and the ganked favours the former; it would lead the latter to consider their relationship with the virtual world even if the ganker were to be permanently banned.

In summary, then, reputation systems are useful tools and can be relatively benign, but when you design one, you have to consider how it might be misused – because it will *be* misused. This follows from the following general principle of virtual world design: the moment you have an idea for a feature in mind, figure out ways that players might abuse it. Better you find out sooner rather than later.

I'll wrap up this sub-section with a final few words on community management: you *will* sometimes screw up. Keep some cosmetic items and other goodies in reserve so that when you do, you can dish them out to the player base by way of apology. Just because you made a mistake (everyone does from time to time), that doesn't mean you have to brazen it out to depict an air of strength or infallibility. Accept it, deal with the players fairly, learn from it, and then move on.

20.9 COMMUNITY AND IMMERSION

This final, short section of the Design and Community chapter may sound polemical, and indeed it probably is, but it's to do with art, not politics (if the two can be distinguished).

Communities in virtual worlds can form for both in-context reasons and out-of-context reasons. In-context reasons concern the character; out-of-context reasons concern the player. As we'll see in Chapter 24, issues can arise from this that cause not only community management headaches but legal ones, too. If your virtual world has a guild that only accepts female players, is that OK? It's basically banning all male players from joining. What if a guild banned all female players from joining? Or gay players? Or straight players? Or trans players? Or cis players? Or players of the wrong ethnicity? Would it make a difference if it was about characters on a role-playing server rather than about players on a general server?

Immersion relies on being in-context, so extrafictional, out-of-context guilds can disrupt it both for their members and for non-members alike. I'm therefore of the opinion that if a virtual world is set up and advertised as being highly in-context, it's legitimate for the developer to ban all guilds that are formed around players rather than characters. Sure, the players will still bring their own prejudices to bear,[43] but at least the fiction will hold. It'll result in bad publicity if a guild formed around a headline cause is banned (say, one for blind players or for players with autism), but if there are people who want to play a virtual world expressly to keep real life out, surely such virtual worlds should be allowed to exist, regardless of what those who don't want to play them might think.

---

[43] The male character is not accepted into the male-character-only guild for "other reasons", not because his player is female, no, not at all, that's merely coincidence.

CHAPTER 21

Anthropology and Sociology

$\mathbf{M}$OST VIRTUAL WORLD DESIGN takes place before a line of code is written, let alone before players are let loose to wreck those designs. That said, a significant amount still takes place post-launch, to address imbalances and unfairnesses and to prepare for the next major patch or expansion. If you try this without having a sense of what the players are thinking or doing, you can expect pushback.

21.1 OBJECTIVE OPINION

Single-player and small-group RPGs can be out of tune with players' needs because the developers exist in a cosy echo chamber with influencers and streamers who reinforce the positives of each other's views (Fryer, 2024). MMORPGs don't have this problem because they invite actual players in early, in part because you can't really test something massively multiplayer without having a massive multitude of players, and in part because the outreach and publicity build-up is better that way. However, a problem that MMORPGs have that single-player games don't have is that the virtual world, its gameplay, and its players will transform over time.

In response to this, virtual world designers have a selection of tools in their toolbox that allow them to make changes to the environment in which their world's cultures and communities exist. They don't, however, have tools that allow them to get a sense of what these cultures and communities are in the first place. This is because they can't drop metrics code into the brains of players to find out what they're thinking. Although sentiment analysis can pick up on trends in forum threads (useful information from player conversations is less dense), really you have to be there to know what's truly going on.

The obvious way to do this is to play the virtual world yourself (masquerading incognito, so as not to taint your findings[1]). You can also pick up on the general vibes from CSR reports, in the happy knowledge that CSRs encounter the worst of everything that goes on

---

[1] A couple of days after the Paddington to Heathrow railway opened in London, I was waiting on the platform for the next train and got chatting to the bloke next to me. He asked what I thought of the service, so I told him. When the train arrived, he thanked me for my analysis and revealed that he was the CEO of the operating company. He was, too: he appeared on the TV news that evening. Sadly, he didn't take my advice to reduce the ticket price.

DOI: 10.1201/9781003689638-21

and so the situation is no grimmer than whatever they describe. As for players, if you can see through their personal interests then you can ask them what they think, too. You can scour forum postings and social media comments. You can bring in experts (such as me!) to play for 200 hours and tell you what's gone/going right and what's gone/going wrong. There's a lot you can do.

This is all at the level of individual opinions, though. You need to agglomerate them to get the full picture. Too many times do designers play their own virtual world and think that it's going according to plan when it is for *them* but not for most people. Too many times do they sense a change in the mood of players because they listened only to the vocal ones who post in a monitored forum that most other players have been nowhere near.

What would really help designers here is a professional assessment of the make-up of the virtual world's culture and of the communities that inform it. As it happens, there are two areas of academic research that have something worthwhile to say about such matters: Anthropology and Sociology.[2]

Objectively, Anthropology and Sociology are very similar. Both study communities, cultures, and societies. The main differences are:

- Anthropology studies culturally distant cultures, whereas Sociology studies culturally near ones.

- Anthropology concerns how cultures are, whereas Sociology studies how cultures change.

- Anthropology considers what makes us human, whereas Sociology considers what we make of our humanity.

- The disciplines have completely distinct traditions and practices.

Irritatingly, few researchers from either discipline are particularly interested in virtual worlds. This isn't to say that the field is being ignored entirely: research in both these areas is being undertaken in different guises by Game Studies scholars, albeit often using somewhat blunter techniques. Still, let's see what these disciplines can tell us that might be of use.

21.2 ANTHROPOLOGY

One might have thought that virtual worlds would be appealing to anthropologists, but they aren't (except perhaps as training grounds for fieldwork (Snodgrass, 2016)). I'm not entirely sure that the Anthropology establishment has yet recovered from the slew of bad term papers that came out in the Third Age of virtual worlds, written by students who were trying to pass off their extensive playing habits as research. The problem is that virtual worlds, while cultural contexts in their own right, are quite shallow in comparison to what anthropologists normally study. It's not clear how well the usual investigative methods

---

[2] There's also one area of non-academic research: Journalism. I won't be covering that here, though.

apply, to the extent that *virtual ethnography* should perhaps be considered as a distinct method (Williams, 2007). If you want to know how to do it, Boellstorff et al. (2013) explain in some detail.

Anthropology has four major sub-fields (Eastern Oregon University, 2024)[3]:

- *Cultural Anthropology* is what members of the general population usually think of as Anthropology: understanding how people interact to form societies.

- *Biological* (or *Physical*) *Anthropology* is effectively about human beings as evolved creatures and the differences between established populations.

- *Linguistic Anthropology* concerns how language affects the way that people relate to the world and to one another.

- *Archaeology* involves the study of what cultures leave behind in terms of objects and other remains. It's primarily focused on historical cultures.

For virtual worlds, two of these sub-fields are of particular interest: Cultural Anthropology and Archaeology.

21.2.1 Cultural Anthropology

Cultural Anthropology is of the most immediate use to designers. In this, the anthropologist observes the members of a community[4] in their everyday lives, collecting qualitative data from which can be constructed a description of the community's workings as a whole (an *ethnography*). Modern anthropologists will usually achieve this in a participatory fashion by embedding themselves within the community, but earlier ones would have approached it using more passive methods. Either will work for a virtual world; the former gives the anthropologist a deeper understanding than the latter, but the latter runs less risk of affecting the community being observed (especially in a virtual world, where peripheral players may not even know they're being observed).[5]

A description of the workings of one guild or the way the virtual world feels to an unguilded player is useful, but it's still only one person's opinion (albeit someone formally trained in how to form an objective opinion in such a context). To get a full picture, several ethnographies must be composed and compared; the sub-field of Cultural Anthropology responsible for this is Ethnology, and the comprehensive comparisons constructed from ethnographies are called *ethnologies*.

Because virtual worlds, their cultures, their communities, and their players are always changing, this kind of comparative research is essential for keeping track of how players are behaving and what their driving forces are. Although a developer operating several

---

[3] There are many descriptions I could have chosen, but I picked this one because it's clear enough for even me to understand.

[4] "Community" here is in the formal sense, not the broader "community of people who own toasters" sense. In our terms, an MMO guild would be a community, but its entire player base wouldn't.

[5] If developers commission ethnographical research in their virtual world as a basis for learning what changes must be made to it then *of course* the community is going to be affected. This could be a problematical outcome for some ethnologists.

virtual worlds might want to construct ethnological research using ethnographies from each of them, it's nevertheless important to do it for individual worlds, too. I suspect, however, that university researchers would be more interested in comparing ethnographies from completely different virtual worlds (and perhaps even from other types of online game) than they would be to compare them from different communities or time periods for a single virtual world. That's assuming they cared to look at them at all, of course.

Ethnographies written by people with the necessary training do exist for virtual worlds. Perhaps the two best-known full ethnographies are those of Boellstorff (2008), which paints an accurate picture of *Second Life*'s heyday, and of Nardi (2010), which covers *World of Warcraft*. Other substantial ones are Cherny (1995) for *ElseMOO*,[6] Drennan (2007) for *Guild Wars*, Rowlands (2010) for *EverQuest*, and Morgan (2014) for *Project Entropia*. The remainder, which are formal but tend to be much shorter, include: Rosenberg (1992) for *WolfMOO*, Masterson (1994) for *Ancient Anguish*, Muramatsu & Ackerman (1998) for *Illusion*, and the series Clodius (1994, 1995, 1996a,b, 1997) for *DragonMUD*. There are also some very good, lengthy encapsulations of virtual worlds written by journalists, the most widely read being Dibbell (1999) for *LambdaMOO*.

From a designer's perspective, an unbiased account of the virtual world's culture is what we want; we can look at the minutiae ourselves should we identify a problem. Sadly for us, anthropologists tend instead to focus on one particular aspect of a culture in great detail (selected on a per-anthropologist basis), rather than presenting a culture in the round; their goal is to provide data for ethnologies, not to write a complete assessment of every aspect of a virtual world as seen from on high. This would be good if the ethnologies ever appeared, but there aren't enough ethnographies and they date quickly because the cultures of virtual worlds change[7] quicker than the cultures anthropologists are geared up to study. Most virtual world fieldwork appears in the form of a self-contained PhD thesis, which is great if you're interested in the angle it takes but less great if not. Examples of ethnographies of virtual worlds – well, of *World of Warcraft* – that come with a particular area of player behaviour in mind include: Sundén (2009) with Queer Studies, Vesa (2013) with Management Science, and Sapach (2015) with Theology.

I should mention that it's not only the culture of virtual worlds that's of occasional interest to anthropologists: the culture of the developer is, too. Au (2008) and Malaby (2009) both give excellent – but very different in tone[8] – descriptions of the culture of Linden Lab in the early years of *Second Life*, including stellar insights into its design philosophy and the decisions to which this led.

To summarise, then: designers and operators of ongoing virtual worlds stand to benefit if they employ[9] an anthropologist to monitor the virtual world's culture and provide a commentary, but they're likely to be disappointed if they rely on formal academic studies.

---

[6] This isn't its real name: *ElseMOO* was the term used in MOOs to mean "some other MOO". Ethnographers routinely change names to protect those they study. Sometimes, as in Cherny's work, they even tell you they've done it.

[7] Webber & Milik (2016) document such a change in *EVE Online*.

[8] Au is a journalist specialising in virtual worlds; Malaby is a Professor of Anthropology.

[9] Or, because this could well be expensive, if they fund to do a PhD.

21.2.2 Archaeology

That most of these ethnographies are relatively old brings us to the other sub-field of Anthropology of interest to designers: Archaeology. It's of interest for a different reason, though.

Virtual worlds of the past have much to teach designers of the present. This isn't merely at the level of "gosh, weren't the ancient Babylonians clever!"; it's more "wait, we can *do* that?" and "OK, I see now why that was a bad idea". Our history is still within the reach of living memory, and many of the early practitioners are still with us.[10] Little of this is documented, though. Just as it's hard for me to grasp the emotional impact on my parents' generation of watching their first television programme and on my grandparents' of listening to their first radio broadcast, it's hard for most young people to get a handle on what it was like for people of my generation to play a MUD. It's possible to make solid assumptions intellectually, but extracting from these what the emotional impact on the players was is much harder. As for why you'd want to do it, well if you knew what the players felt that wasn't entirely due to the newness of the medium, and if you could tease out why they felt it, you could try to capture (or to avoid) that in your own virtual world designs.

Many games that were played extensively in the past are no longer played today. There could be many reasons for this, of which here are some examples:

- Their software has been lost.

- The hardware they need is no longer available.

- They check into a server that is no longer running.

- They operated under a licence that has now expired.

- They were withdrawn by the developer for commercial or other reasons.

- Their developer closed down and no one knows who owns the IP any more.

Efforts to make such games and other *abandonware* accessible again are making slow progress. There are problems at many levels, some of which are surprisingly philosophical. Is *MUD1* only *MUD1* if it runs on a DECsystem-10 mainframe? What if it runs on a simulator? What if it's rewritten so that it behaves the same, but the underlying code isn't even in the same programming language as the original?

Such topics were addressed in a series of symposia that addressed what was called the *preservation of complex objects* (Delve et al., 2012; Konstantelos et al., 2012; Anderson et al., 2013). The third of these looked at games and virtual worlds.

It's hard enough to preserve regular games. The minimum requirement is to do much the same as a library would with an ancient text: maintain the original in its physical form wherever possible but make its content available in an accessible reproduction.

---

[10] Including, at the time of writing, me.

This allows many aspects of the game to be analysed, such as its mechanics, graphics, and interface; it doesn't tell you what it was like to *play* the game at the time of its release, though.

A freshly minted game historian today can only imagine what it would have been like to stand at a cabinet in an arcade and play *Galaxian* (Sawano, 1979) after it first came out. To understand games of the past, you need to put aside your present-day self and become your period self, *then* try to play. This can give you a sense of what games meant way back when, but it's never going to be accurate because you can't throw away what you already know. A person coming fresh to an MMO today will have encountered enough RPGs in their life that they will already be familiar with what's involved; they therefore won't experience the state-of-consciousness changes that players often did when first exposed to MUDs (Bromberg, 1996).

Students of literature are fully aware that texts read today don't necessarily mean the same as they did when they were written.[11] As I mentioned in Chapter 4,[12] text ages much slower than graphics – but it *does* age. Books are situated in their historical context. More importantly, so are their readers: reading Jane Austen today is not the same as reading Jane Austen two centuries ago. It's a similar thing with games: if you play a game from 1985 and find it fun, does it matter that it's today-fun and not 1985-fun? Once a game has been released, it can be interpreted by its players how they choose.[13]

Well, as a designer, all this *does* matter. As we shall explore in Volume II, virtual world design is an art form. Artists can look at examples of their art form and divine what those who created them were trying to say; designers can look at games and similarly read the message they carry. Playing old games provides insight into the minds of those games' creators; in gaining this understanding, a designer is better able to design their own games.

This is fine for games, but virtual worlds aren't games: they're places. Just like places, the people are part of the place. What virtual worlds *are* is bound up with their players: that's why I've spent much of this book explaining how players are part of a virtual world's design. Formally, the players of a virtual world are an intrinsic component of:

- The historical context.
- The artefact designed.
- The artefact created.
- The medium through which the designer is speaking.

This means that preservation in the sense used for regular computer games, which is already difficult, is compounded by the fact that the players *aren't* being preserved. Preserving the software of a virtual world is like preserving only the buildings of a city. That's better than nothing, but it's just a series of empty spaces. Again as I said in Chapter 3, you can learn a

---

[11] "I marvel that both at home and on your travels a score of eligible young men have not sought to make love to you" (Wheatley, 1950). To "make love" meant "to court" in Wheatley's time.

[12] In a footnote, but if you don't read footnotes, you're not going to know that even though I'm telling you right now.

[13] If they choose to find it offensive in ways you disagree with, tough luck.

lot from the ruins of Pompeii, but you'll never know what it was *actually* like living there. Archaeology looks at objects and remains, but these only leave easily misinterpreted clues regarding the lives of the people who used them.

If we are to preserve for a purpose other than merely collecting the already (or soon-to-be) obscure and forgotten, it's our duty to help the people of the future to do that. We therefore need to preserve the players as well as the world. OK, so there are probably moral issues with cryogenically storing random players in underground vaults, so another method must be found instead. Sure, the people of the future can (perhaps) watch millions of hours of videos and streams and try to put together a coherent impression from those, but they'll be looking through the lens of the future. We can give them the picture from the present. It may be true that we can't preserve players, but we *can* preserve studies of them. That means that we need to produce said studies. We can't do it after our city has been buried in ash and pumice; this is therefore a second reason to invite cultural anthropologists to investigate our virtual worlds.

The archaeology of extinct virtual worlds is important to us. There were hundreds of MUDs around when *WolfMOO* was in its prime, but we know nothing about them. We only know about *WolfMOO* because of the snapshot created by Rosenberg (1992).

If it's important for us to know about the past, it will be important for the designers of the future to know about their past – our present. Although preserving the cultural heritage of games is valuable in and of itself (Guay-Bélanger, 2022), it's also of practical merit. We owe it to the designers (and therefore players) of the future to help them understand what the virtual worlds of today are like, including the crucial component that is their players.

You can still play *MUD1*, but doing so won't tell you how it felt four-fifths of the way through the 20th century. You can easily find out how a contemporary virtual world feels, but that's a luxury that will be denied designers 50 years from now – unless we do something about it.

This book is about the design of virtual worlds. It draws on the past and present but it's aimed at the future – the virtual worlds yet to be written. Let's see if we can help our future kindred souls by preserving in the present the kind of things we wish we'd preserved in the past.

21.3 SOCIOLOGY

Sociology is the study of social relationships, usually (but not always) at a macro level. A somewhat cynical view is that it's the study of those social relationships that the researcher finds personally impactful, which is why some areas are investigated more heavily and thoroughly than others.

As with Anthropology, Sociology has a number of distinct sub-fields (Eastern Oregon University, 2024):

- *Theoretical Sociology* concerns the creation of frameworks into which social relationships can be fitted to provide underlying explanations. The best-known such framework is *Marxism*, or *social conflict theory* as it's now known (Marxism having got a bad name).

- *Political Sociology* looks at the relationships between institutions, states, and societies. It runs the gamut between "which way will these people vote?" to "what influence do mega-corporations have on everyday lives?" to "how are the power structures related to ethnicity, class, and gender maintained?".

- *Applied Sociology* attempts to put the discoveries of the wider field to practical use, for example by finding out what a community wants before giving them it, or by recommending laws and regulations that will have a positive overall effect on society.

- *Cultural Sociology* is like Cultural Anthropology but for home cultures rather than the cultures of others and with an emphasis on the forces of change. It can be broad or narrow in focus. For example, Bainbridge (2010) describes the many ways by which *WoW* can influence wider society, whereas Zhong (2011) shows specifically that collective play has a significant positive effect on civic engagement, but that the time spent playing reduces offline social capital.

As with Anthropology, this characterisation is very broad. You can split these sub-fields up into sub-sub-fields and beyond, some of which are closer to each other than to their parent sub-fields.[14] There is also some overlap with other disciplines such as Economics and Psychology. Although each of these sub-sub-fields will of course be of interest to designers (because designers are interested in everything[15]), for the purpose of their utility for designing virtual worlds in general, we can stick with the four above.

Although operators of virtual worlds may have an interest in how some of their plans will be received, or in what amusing new legislation might be brought out to sate a passionate but ill-informed government minister, designers are more concerned with Applied Sociology and Cultural Sociology.

Cultural Sociology is of interest for the same reason that Cultural Anthropology is, but unfortunately, Cultural Sociologists are not interested in virtual worlds for the same reason that Cultural Anthropologists aren't. The way they see it (which isn't unreasonable), virtual worlds are time-consuming to analyse and, now that the foundations have been laid, tell them nothing new. Only very occasionally can they be used to shine a light on issues affecting wider society, and for the moment, they're too expensive to develop to be useful experimentally. Additionally, although Cultural Anthropologists *might* perhaps be tempted to look at the culture of a virtual world for its own sake, Cultural Sociologists see them primarily as one of many instruments of change affecting society in general.

When it comes to the sub-fields of Sociology, I shall therefore confine my discussion to how Applied Sociology can help with the design of virtual worlds.

21.3.1 Applied Sociology

Anthropology describes in an objective manner how a group of people interact, but Sociology adds the crucial element of what to do if you want to change how they interact

---

[14] If your interest is in criminal behaviour then that could be both Cultural Sociology at the level of petty thievery and Political Sociology at the level of organised crime.

[15] Except, speaking personally, doing hard work.

(or want to prevent an impending, undesirable change). Applied Sociology, which when necessary can be disassociated from the directives of Theoretical Sociology and the power-structure analysis of Political Sociology, therefore looks just the ticket. We've already seen some of it in action: the material I presented earlier on group formation has its basis in Applied Sociology.

Inconveniently, those few sociologists actually studying virtual worlds tend to be of the Cultural Sociology variety, who are more concerned with the effects virtual worlds have on wider society than *vice versa*. Worse, those interested sociologists from the Applied Sociology camp tend to look at what wider society should do about virtual worlds to avoid some awful fate, rather than what's going on within them. Social networks, such as Facebook, are of far more relevance to both sub-fields than are virtual worlds. I should make it clear that this isn't a criticism of sociologists, by the way: social networks have a much greater impact on modern life than do virtual worlds, so of course these are going to attract more attention. It's simply frustrating from a designer's perspective that sociologists can potentially provide us with a great deal of useful advice, but they have other fish to fry at the moment.

This isn't all that's frustrating, either. It's true that Applied Sociology can offer insights and solutions to a virtual world's problems, which designers can address through changes to the virtual world's design; however, those insights and solutions will necessarily be bespoke to that virtual world. It's a bit like setting up an advertising campaign: there are well-understood practices that advertising-industry creatives follow, but ultimately your campaign is going to be unique to your product. Similarly, there are well-understood practices that sociologists follow, but their analysis of your virtual world is going to be unique to it.

In other words, if you read what sociologists have written about other virtual worlds, you'll get some idea of the kind of things they *can* tell you, but for your own virtual world, you won't know what they *will* tell you until they've studied it.

That said, even some of the more general material *is* of use to designers. For example, human migration theory can help explain why players move between virtual worlds (Hou et al., 2011) and what factors you should influence in order to keep them or to persuade them to move, depending on which direction you want them to go. Basically, they'll want to leave a virtual world if they're not enjoying it, or are dissatisfied with the service, or perceive the other participants negatively (these are *push* effects); they'll also want to move if another virtual world is more attractive (a *pull* effect); their decision as to whether to move or to stay put depends on the switching costs, their social relationships, their need for variety, and their previous experiences of changing virtual worlds (these are *mooring* effects[16]). Therefore, it's not all about whether they think an alternative virtual world will be more fun than yours: if they like the atmosphere, the overall service, and there's little toxicity then that will lessen the push; if you raise switching costs and ensure that making social relationships is easy, they're more likely to stay moored. Similarly, to entice players from another virtual world, you should strive to make yours as attractive to them as

---

[16] Geographers, who also study human migration, call these *intervening barriers*. Carazo-Chandler (1999) does so with regard to movement between *UO* shards.

possible to increase pull, while reducing switching costs, making *en masse* guild transfers easy and designing a virtual world that has original gameplay to decrease the influence of older worlds' mooring effects.

Population movement is an example of a general theory of Sociology that has equally general results of use to the designers of virtual worlds. Mostly, though, sociological research to do with virtual worlds is (from a designer's perspective) more like a craft fair in which Sociology lays out samples of its wares on a table, with an invitation to take them or leave them. For example, Williams (2009) suggests that community in virtual worlds really is a thing; that the framework of inter-player interactions is limited in quality but high in quantity; and that there are effective boundaries between sub-communities. If you want to know more, ask a Sociologist to look at your virtual world and tell you – but even if you don't, it's still worth knowing that the social mobility you might have assumed would be present in your virtual world will most likely disappoint. Likewise, as soon as you're told that levity (alongside social proximity) is one of the key social-interaction affordances of virtual worlds (Jakobsson, 2006), it seems obvious; if you're not told it, however, you might design a dark-cyberpunk world based on a major movie franchise in such a way that its player base becomes dominated by humourless role-players.[17]

In summary, then, Sociology has much to offer virtual worlds – particularly those in operation – but its interests lie almost entirely in Reality. While there is a little general work that's of direct relevance to virtual worlds,[18] to get the best out of it, you really need to hire a sociologist – probably after previously hiring an anthropologist to identify the problem you want the sociologist to fix.

---

[17] *The Matrix Online*, if you were wondering.
[18] Williams et al. (2018) discuss Sociology and RPGs, for example.

CHAPTER 22

Psychology's Take on Virtual Worlds

Psychologists think about what's going on in your head.

(British Psychological Society, 2024)

Psychology is the study of mind and behaviour (American Psychological Association, 2024). Virtual worlds are played by players, who have minds and behaviours, so it's no surprise that psychologists have an interest in the field. It's also no surprise that virtual world designers have an interest in Psychology, too, and not only because they have an interest in everything.[1] Players are an intrinsic component of a virtual world's design (as I mentioned Chapter 21), but they're largely uncontrollable; designers therefore need to have some understanding of what they'll do and why they'll do it in order to manage the results. In addition, because they're speaking to players through their design (of which players are, recursively, a part), there's an artistic aspect to their relationship, too.

Fortunately, most designers have an intuitive understanding of player behaviours anyway, so much of this comes naturally to them. I say "fortunately" because, in general, psychologists' attitudes towards video games (as opposed to non-video games) are somewhat fraught. We'll see why shortly.

Psychology has many sub divisions – the American Psychological Association lists 15 of them (American Psychological Association, 2013), which is comparatively conservative – but they can be organised into five main groups (American Psychological Association, 2014):

- **Biological**. This looks at the hardware of the brain. It includes neuroscience, sensation, and consciousness. It's sometimes referred to as *Biopsychology*.

- **Cognitive**. This looks at the software of the mind. It includes cognition, memory, perception, and intelligence. It's almost always referred to as *Cognitive Psychology*.

---

[1] Actually, I don't have an interest in doing easy work, either, come to think of it.

 DOI: 10.1201/9781003689638-22

- **Development**. This looks at the development of the mind. It includes learning, language, and changes over a life-span. Its usual name is *Developmental Psychology*.

- **Social and Personality**. This looks at the expressions of the mind. It includes social psychology, personality, emotion, motivation, and differences due to culture and gender. This is typically referred to as *Behavioural Psychology*, although sometimes that term is used to refer specifically to the sub-field of *Conditioning*.

- **Mental and Physical Health**. This looks at potential problem areas of the software of the mind. It includes abnormal behaviour, mental health, physical health deriving from mental health, and therapies. It's often known as *Clinical Psychology*.

When it comes to virtual worlds, the breakdown is somewhat simpler:

- What's Psychology's take on virtual worlds?

- What's virtual worlds' take on Psychology?

I'll address them in that order.

CORRELATION AND CAUSATION

Social scientists talk about *correlation* rather than *causality*, because correlation can be measured; speculation about causality does follow, of course, which can lead to further experiments. Thus, the social sciences advance (or at least move).

The most basic, yet most common context is that the scientist wants to know the degree to which two variables are related. "Variables" here simply means properties that have numerical values that vary. For example, if you think that the height and weight of adults may be related quantities then those would be the variables. To find out if they *are* related quantities, you would take a sample of people (the more, the better) and measure their individual heights and weights, then compare the results across the whole sample. You would probably find that the values correlate: indeed, for people in their 20s, the relative rate of increase in weight is about 1% for every 1 cm increase height regardless of gender (Sargent, 1963). This only gives a correlation, though, not a causality: whether it's the case that the taller you are, the more you weigh, or the more you weigh, the taller you are, is not specified. You'd have to perform experiments to find out which caused which,[2] although sometimes it's fairly obvious.[3]

Sometimes, two variables appear to be related but they're not: they both depend on a *third variable*. The archetypal example of this is that the number of people who drown increases when more ice cream is produced. Does buying ice cream cause

---

[2] "Hmm, if I chop their legs off then they lose weight but if I force-feed them cake they don't gain height, therefore an increase in height causes an increase in weight rather than the reverse".

[3] The speed of rotation of a windmill and the strength of the wind both increase together but, weird conspiracy theorists aside, few grown-ups would think that windmills are giant fans that produce the world's wind.

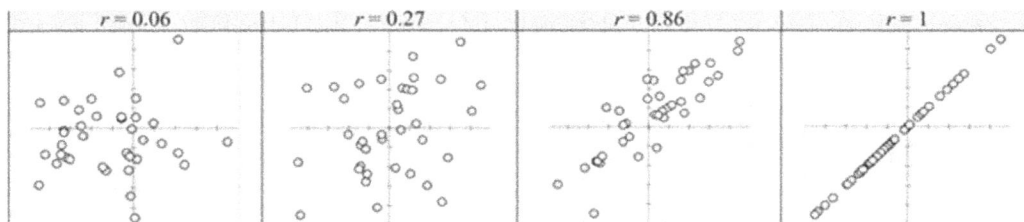

FIGURE 22.1   Sample scatterplots with various values of r.

drowning or does drowning cause more ice cream to be bought? Well neither: both go up during hot weather, which causes both. Hot weather is the third variable.

The strength of a linear correlation is measured using the *Pearson product-moment correlation coefficient*, abbreviated to *r* and calculated using a standard formula. I won't give that here, because it's easy to look up and you don't need to know it anyway for the purposes of this book[4]; the important point is that it goes between −1 and 1, with r=−1 being a perfect negative correlation, r=1 being a perfect positive correlation, and r=0 being no correlation at all. Intermediate values are expressed as decimals, usually without a leading 0, so something like r=.98 would be a strong correlation and r=.18 would be a weak one.

To find how much the variables depend on one another, square and multiply by 100 to get a percentage. For example, the correlation between passing the modules I teach and attending the lectures I deliver has r=.54; this means that passing and attendance have a dependency of 100×(0.54×0.54)=29.16%. In other words, 29.16% of my students' success or failure can be put down to whether they went to the lectures or not. Note that this doesn't say whether this is because the lectures contain you-have-to-be-there content or whether the better students tend to attend more lectures.

A good way of visualising correlations is to use *scatter diagrams* (or *scatter plots*). Figure 22.1 shows four examples, courtesy of Webb (2023)[5]:

As you can see, r=1 is a straight line and r=.86 is still clearly showing a general trend along x=y, but it's hard to tell r=.27 and r=.06 apart – if I'd told you they were both random sets of dots, it wouldn't have seemed implausible. That's something to bear in mind.

Occasionally, the correlation between two variables can be very high, but there's no causation at all: it's just coincidence. The number of babies called Eleanor born in the United States between 1995 and 2021 has a correlation of r=.993 with the amount of wind power generated in Poland over the same period (Vigen, 2024).

---

[4] OK, so it's also a pain to render in text.

[5] These examples appear under a Creative Commons BY-SA 4.0 licence, which can be found at https://creativecommons. org/licenses/by-sa/4.0/. I therefore need to say: the creator is Rachel Webb; they're her copyright; they're unaltered; and the original material can be found at https://stats.libretexts.org/Bookshelves/Introductory_Statistics/Mostly_Harmless_ Statistics_%28Webb%29/12%3A_Correlation_and_Regression/12.01%3A_Correlation/12.1.01%3A_Scatterplots.

Consistent correlations arising from multiple different experiments are on safer ground, of course.

That said, meta-studies that combine the results of other studies can lead to contradictory results. This is known as *Simpson's paradox*; here's a made-up example:

Research question: are men on average taller than women?
Study 1, of a wealthy society:
- 100 men, all 200 cm tall
- 100 women, all 190 cm tall
- 200 > 190, therefore on average, men are taller than women.

Study 2, of an impoverished society:
- 900 men, all 170 cm tall
- 100 women, all 160 cm tall
- 170 > 160, therefore on average, men are taller than women.

Meta-study, combining Study 1 and Study 2:
- Men: $((100 \times 200) + (900 \times 170))/(100 + 900) = 173$ cm
- Women: $((100 \times 190) + (100 \times 160))/(100 + 100) = 175$ cm
- 175 > 173, therefore on average, women are taller than men.

Of course, just because this kind of thing is possible, that doesn't mean it's probable. Even if it *were* probable, it would merely imply that research methods correlated with weirdness, not that there was a causal relationship between them. Correlation is all well and good, but causation is what you want to know.

This is why most social science research papers end with a paragraph that can essentially be paraphrased as "more research is necessary".

22.1 PSYCHOLOGISTS

OK, so there are some broad observations incoming to which you will easily find counter-examples, but that on the whole represent a fairly accurate characterisation.

1. Psychologists are interested in people, so they look at players rather than games.

2. Psychologists tend to lump all computer games together and treat them as a single unit: *video games*. Virtual worlds are no different from casual games or first-person shooters: they're all video games.

3. Psychologists make a very strong distinction between video games and all other forms of game. Psychologically, *Chess* played on a board is not the same as *Chess* played on a computer.

4. Psychologists categorise video games as being one of two basic kinds: violent and non-violent. All video games are one or the other, with nothing in between. Degrees of violence may differ, though: *Centipede* (Logg, 1981) is not as violent as *Zaxxon* (Garcia, 1982), although both are nevertheless considered violent (or at least they were in 1986 (Anderson & Ford, 1986)).

5. Research about games is dominated by three topics: aggression, addiction, and their effects on children (which are usually to do with aggression and addiction). At a guess,[6] maybe 70% of games-related papers are on aggression, 20% on addiction, 5% on children, and 5% on everything else.

6. Psychology has had a *reproducibility crisis* in recent years (Center for Open Science, 2023), in which attempts to replicate the results of oft-cited experiments have failed to do so.

7. Psychology is a vast field, and most psychologists working in academia have no research interest in virtual worlds whatsoever. At another guess,[7] games (player) research forms considerably less than 1% of all research in Psychology.

Many researchers from many disciplines have looked at virtual worlds over the years, mainly in the Third and Fifth Ages. Typically, they flew in as a flock, fitted virtual worlds into their theories, then flew away together. Occasionally, they'll return to apply new theories (or old theories from new angles), but they'll no longer descend in large numbers. Some research fields stayed longer than others: scholars of Law studied virtual worlds for over a decade before fluttering away. As for psychologists, well they came, looked at identity issues and addiction, then left. However, they left by treating virtual worlds as just another computer game, and because they still consider the players of computer games an active area of research, in that sense, then, they haven't left, they've merely widened their wanderings.

The canonical view of virtual worlds in Psychology (that they're addictive havens of deviant behaviour) is not helpful to designers. I suspect that the main reason a designer might want to look at the majority of research in the area is for self-defence purposes against advocates and agitators, rather than because they hope to figure out how they should change their design for the betterment of humanity. I'll therefore restrict myself to a general overview of the main research themes, rather than dive in to discuss individual pieces of work.

Remember points 1 and 2 above: psychologists research players, not games, and most research treats games homogenously. What follows is usually about players of games in general rather than of virtual worlds in particular, but I'll go with virtual world-specific research when it's available.[8]

---

[6] This isn't my guess, it's that of a pair of senior psychologists I met at a conference, whose names I shall protect because I had to say "off the record" before they'd hazard any estimates.

[7] This one *is* mine.

[8] Well, available and I've come across it.

22.2 ADDICTION

Games have been blamed for moral decline and addiction throughout history (Grace, 2019), so it's no surprise that this state of affairs continues to pertain. Insofar as computer games are concerned, virtual worlds are particularly in the frame (Khan, 2007; van den Hoven, 2020), largely because people play them for long periods and do so online. They're a natural extension of earlier concerns about Internet addiction, such as Young (1998) and Greenfield (1999).

The earliest research found that virtual worlds were no more addictive than stamp collecting (Shotton, 1989). Players *called* them "addictive", but this was a figurative use, intended to convey the idea that these games were so good, you'd want to keep coming back to play them.[9] However, the perception grew that they were addictive literally. This isn't how players and developers were using the word at all.

If you want to know whether games *are* addictive, there are two questions you need to answer before you start:

1. What games are you talking about?

2. What definition of "addiction" are you using?

The idea of "gaming addiction" grew out of the 1980s "computer addiction" and 1990s "Internet addiction" panics. As I said, psychologists have a tendency to regard all video games as the same thing, which at one level they certainly are (people talk about "video games" the whole time without issue); whether they are when it comes to addiction is another matter. The immediate upshot of this attitude of homogeneity is that survey questions often ask study participants how many hours a day they play video games but not ask them what these games are (for example, Jeong et al., 2019; Giordano et al., 2023) – or they do ask them but make little use of the information (for example, Columb et al., 2023; Alrahili et al., 2023). You rarely see Psychology research that's restricted to one kind of game. Interestingly, as mentioned earlier in the sidebar on surveys, most people underestimate the time they spend playing anyway and there are gender differences, too, so much of this research has to be treated cautiously. Relative rates of play within genders are probably fine, but whether absolute ones are or not depends on the methodology used to obtain the data.

Now having said all this, I shall now contradict myself by mentioning some representative pieces of research that *are* specific to virtual worlds (or at least MMOs) and which don't simply say that they're flat-out addictive (or not). They do say that there are certain people who will play virtual worlds excessively based on particular factors:

- Clark (2006) bundled addiction with engagement and found that PvP advancement and guild preference predict an increase in both.

---

[9] The *MUDspeke Dictionary* (Bartle, 1992) begins its definition of *addict* thus: "addict: *noun* Someone who lives, eats, breathes and sleeps *MUD*".

- Dieris-Hirche et al. (2020) looked at addiction in both MMOs and first-person shooters and found that personality traits (mainly conscientiousness and neuroticism) are important core facets in addiction's development and persistence.

- Kaya et al. (2023) suggest that there's an inverse relationship between basic psychological needs and online gaming addiction.

- Morcos et al. (2021) found that in *WoW*, the higher a player's level of *compensation* (the technical term for a defensive strategy that protects against threats to self-esteem), then the more signs-of-addiction boxes they ticked.[10]

In other words, a player can find an MMO addictive based on (at least): their preferred gameplay, the company they keep, their personality traits, their general quality of life, and the extent to which they feel inadequate in their everyday existence.

Of course, this all depends on what you mean by "addictive".

Psychology has no universal definition of the term; people studying gambling have different priorities to people studying substance abuse. However, for psychologists looking at addiction in the context of games, the most popular[11] definition is Griffiths' *component model* (Griffiths, 2005). This helpfully says that addictions of all kinds have similar (deep breath:) biopsychosocial components:

- *Salience* is when an activity becomes the most important thing in your life and dominates your thinking.

- *Mood modification* is when the activity gives you a buzz (high) or an escape (numbing).

- *Tolerance* is when you need more to get the same effect that a little used to give you.

- *Withdrawal symptoms* are the unpleasant feelings or physical changes that come from stopping or cutting back on the activity.

- *Conflict* means the activity compromises your relationships with those around you.

- *Relapse* is when you've not been pursuing an activity for ages then suddenly start up again.

You can see why it's popular: it does seem eminently reasonable. The conflict component is a weak spot, though, as it relies on the attitudes of other people for its detection.

Clinically, addiction to games is called *gaming disorder* and addiction to online games (whatever their nature) is *Internet gaming disorder* (IGD). The use of the word "gaming" is unfortunate, as it carries overtones of gambling. IGD is about MMOs, first-person shooters, battles royale, and so on; it's not about playing online slot machines. Lest you not feel unduly worried about this, in 2013, the American Psychiatric Association put IGD into

---

[10] They also found that the Draenei species stood out in this regard.

[11] This isn't merely because Griffiths himself is an author of over 2,000 academic papers, book chapters, and articles, and has an h-index of close to 200.

its *Diagnostic and Statistical Manual of Mental Disorders: DSM-5* (American Psychiatric Association, 2013) as needing further research, and in 2018, the World Health Organisation formally added Gaming Disorder (it calls IGD *Gaming Disorder, predominantly online*) to its *International Classification of Diseases* (World Health Organisation, 2018).[12] The fact that psychologists and psychiatrists are worried about this should worry you regardless of whether you believe that gaming disorder is a thing yourself.

Following the DSM-5 recommendation that further work be done on IGD, a nine-item, short-form psychometric scale was created for assessing it (Pontes & Griffiths, 2015). IGD is now regularly pathologised, for example, Mohammad et al. (2023).

Using these models and others, psychologists routinely find that computer games are addictive (whatever games they study). This is expressed using one or both of two figures: *addiction rate* (the percentage of players who are addicted) and *prevalence* (the percentage of a population as a whole that is addicted[13]). If 100% of a population plays games, addiction rate and prevalence are the same for that population. Addiction rates vary wildly depending on the method used to determine them, but a finding of around 10% for online games is usual (for example, Grüsser et al. 2007; Porter et al., 2010; Baysak et al., 2016). Meta-analyses, which offer a normalised picture, come up with a similar figure: Chia et al. (2020) found a prevalence rate of 10.1% in a meta-analysis of gaming disorders in southeast Asia, which isn't atypical.

10% sounds low, but it's quite high. For comparison, the capture rates[14] of some popular (if somewhat unhealthy and possibly illegal) drugs are (National Addiction Centre, 2003):

- Tobacco   31.9%

- Heroin   23.1%

- Cocaine   6.7%

- Alcohol   15.4%

- Cannabis   9.1%

It would seem, then, that virtual worlds are more addictive than cannabis (and caffeine, which comes in at 8%; Sweeney et al., 2020[15]). The situation is not quite as clear as this might suggest, however.

The thing is, component models can be used either in a *monothetic* (all criteria must be met) or *polythetic* (only some criteria must be met) manner. Needless to say, you'll obtain higher figures with a polythetic approach, which can be a problem if the criteria the player meets are only peripheral to addiction. In a monothetic approach, you may derive an

---

[12] A concerted effort by concerned parties from Game Studies, Communication Studies, and new-wave Psychologists to persuade the WHO that this was a bad idea (Aarseth et al., 2017; Van Rooij et al., 2018) was unsuccessful.

[13] In other contexts, particularly in relation to drug usage, this can refer to the proportion of the population that has merely tried the object of study over a given time period.

[14] Medical sources tend to use *capture rate* to describe how many users have a *dependence* on a substance, but from our distant vantage point, they're basically the same concepts as addiction rate and addiction respectively.

[15] Caffeine Use Disorder gets its own acronym: CUD. Amusingly, Marijuana Use Disorder has the acronym MUD.

underestimate if the player meets all the criteria except perhaps a relatively unimportant one. This can result in quite some variance: Charlton & Danforth (2007) looked at *Asheron's Call* and found addiction rate of 38.7% using a polythetic approach (matching 50% of the required criteria) and 1.8% using a monothetic one using the same data. One solution to this is to look only at the strongest factors, rather than the milder ones (Charlton, 2002). When Seok & DaCosta (2012) did this for MMORPGs, they established an addiction rate of 2.7% (compared to 25.5% for polythetic and 1.7% for monothetic approaches). 2.7% is somewhat less scary than 10%, but is still scary.

There seems to be a genetic component to excessive Internet game usage (Han et al., 2007), and the actual mechanism of MMO addiction can be explained in terms of brain chemistry (Kuss & Griffiths, 2012). Gamers have reduced dopamine responses to stimuli in games in comparison to those of non-gamers, suggesting they become sensitised (Weinstein, 2010). As for what all this implies about how addiction works:

> If a game experience is flooding the brain with dopamine, that means every other experience in life, on our to-do list, can begin to look less satisfying by comparison. If our brains reach the point where they're more sensitized to the rewards of a secondary game world than to those in reality, then games are naturally going to displace everything else on our to-do list.
>
> *(Clark & Scott, 2009)*

In the next chapter, we'll look at how some designers use this information. It's not pleasant.

Outside of Psychology and Psychiatry, concerns about players' virtual world playing habits tend to be more about what's often called "excessive play". Addiction and dependency would obviously feed into that, but primarily it's to do with the amount of time spent playing rather than whatever its causes are.[16] Virtual worlds may not generally be addictive, but they can be habit-forming – which is undesirable in some societies. As long ago as 2006, Vietnam joined pioneers China and South Korea in bringing out laws to limit playing time in online games. Yes, virtual worlds are virtual, but their players are real, and Reality occasionally takes an interest. In disputes between the virtual and the real, Reality always wins.

Oh, you might be wondering whether, given that virtual worlds are capable of addicting people, there might be some moral issues involved in writing them to *be* addictive. There are. We'll look at these in Volume II.

22.3 AGGRESSION

If you thought "games and addiction" sold newspapers and made research careers, you haven't met "games and aggression".

That games cause aggression is still looked on almost as a given by the majority of Psychologists working in the area. It's the formal view taken by the American Psychological Association (APA). After complaints by those who develop and play games that this didn't

---

[16] Perhaps those who fret about it feel that people should be watching TV instead.

seem right, the APA set up a task force to assess its stand. Much to the consternation of the games industry, in October 2019, it reiterated its position (Suls et al., 2019), although it did stress that while the effect is consistent, it's small. It also made the point that despite what news media might read into their report, violent video games are not "THE cause" of aggressive and violent behaviour, including mass shootings – they're merely A cause, then.

Mass shootings are invariably linked to video games, but not in every country (especially those that have video games but not guns, such as the UK). On the day after the 2011 mass shooting in Norway, I found myself in a hotel lobby in Germany, watching reports on several adjacent TV screens: one showed CNN International, one showed BBC Worldwide, and the remainder showed German stations. The German stations (I was assured by people watching with me who spoke German) led with the fact that the perpetrator claimed to be a *World of Warcraft* player. The CNN report mentioned it as a factor in his actions. The BBC report didn't mention *World of Warcraft* at all, just his Facebook page.

In 2007, at the time of the Virginia Tech shooting, I was mooching around Indianapolis airport near a TV screen showing the news. A reporter was interviewing some students live and asked them if the perpetrator was strange. The students said he was. The reporter asked if he played video games. The students said no, that was the weirdest thing, he didn't play video games at all. This segment did not appear in later news summaries.

Whenever a new entertainment medium appears, the older generation has trouble understanding it and doesn't trust it. Sometimes, the older generation is right (narcotics really do screw you up), but most of the time it over-reacts. In the past, condemnation has followed the introduction of books, the waltz, music halls, penny dreadfuls, film, jazz, radio, comic books, television, rock and roll, pinball machines, *D&D*,[17] video tapes, rap, and the entire Internet. Video games, social media, and artificial intelligence are more recent additions to the canon.

In the UK, where I live, video games are not regarded by the general public as a cause of aggression. In 2008, I wrote a piece for *The Guardian* explaining why (Bartle, 2008). In essence, all schools in the UK were given a BBC microcomputer in 1981; these were largely used for writing and playing games, which is one of the reasons that the UK has a large game-development industry.[18] Now, according to the 2021 Census, the median age in the UK is 40.7 years (Office for National Statistics, 2024). This means that most people who live here weren't even born when video games became a thing, and they've been growing up with games around them for their whole lives. Players are less worried about violence in games than non-players are (Przybylski, 2013),[19] because they know it hasn't made *them* violent personally – and most people *are* now players. As time goes on, there will be fewer and fewer people who haven't played computer games, or who don't have friends and family who've played them, until eventually there'll be none left. We just have to wait for them to die.[20]

---

[17] For a good, in-depth analysis of the moral panic over RPGs, see Laycock (2015).
[18] Not as large as it would have been if Canada hadn't poached several big studios by offering sweet tax deals. I'm not bitter.
[19] Also, younger people are less worried than older people and men are less worried than women.
[20] Sadly, given my own age, I'll probably be dead myself when this happens. Well, sadly for me.

I don't expect that the UK is unique in its current attitude to video games, but there are plenty of other countries where the atmosphere remains somewhat less progressive. This is because they started later and the moral panic took hold in time to throttle the acceptance of games among swathes of the population. Time moves on, though, and even in the United States, almost all children have now played video games. In time, they will become the lawmakers and media moguls who both direct and act on public opinion. Age is on their side.

Although most psychologists still seem to believe that violent video games cause aggressive behaviour,[21] judges are somewhat more sceptical and have rejected their arguments in a number of cases in which games have been implicated as causes of aggression. A notable example is the occasion when the United States Supreme Court struck down (Supreme Court of the United States, 2011) a Californian law[22] that banned the sale to minors of video games that featured situations such as killing with weapons, blowing up buildings, and taking part in dangerous vehicle races. The court decided that video games were an expression of freedom of speech and that regulating their sale on the grounds that they might cause violent behaviour was overly restrictive given the evidence.

So, let's look at why psychologists came to believe that violent video games cause aggressive behaviour.

Here's a very, *very* cynical characterisation of how it happened.

- Early psychologists who studied video games were junior, because games weren't academically respectable.

- Most found nothing of note, but some did. The social sciences are not exact, so there will always be results that are outliers.

- The researchers who did find something believed their findings, because why wouldn't they?

- Funding bodies were tasked with supporting research into the effects of video games, therefore research that found something attracted more funding than research that didn't.

- The researchers continued their research and – gosh! – confirmed the results. Of course, more research was necessary, because it always is.

- Several decades later, these junior researchers became senior, with their careers built on research that showed violent games were a cause of aggression.

---

[21] I should perhaps make it clear that the aggressive behaviour in question occurs outside of the game. Obviously, aggressive behaviour within a violent game is such by definition.

[22] For those readers who don't look at references but do look at footnotes, the full title of the court case is *Edmund G. Brown, Governor of the State of California, and Kamala Harris, Attorney General of the State of California v. Entertainment Merchants Association and Entertainment Software Association*. Harris later went on to become Vice President of the United States before losing to Donald Trump in the 2024 presidential election. Quite what she would have done about games as president, we'll never know unless she stands again and wins.

- New researchers wanting to work in the area had to buy into this research or they wouldn't get a supervisor, a PhD, published or a job.

- Thus, the situation perpetuated.

A similar positive feedback loop can be said to pertain in many disciplines, of course, not just Psychology. Much of my own research will be superseded when times change and the shackles of dogma can be shaken off.

Early research into the effects of violent games on players found inconsistencies in reports that games cause aggression (Scott, 1995), with a paucity of supporting empirical data (Dill & Dill, 1998). This is indeed good reason to continue research in an area, to get to the truth of the matter. If society is in the grip of a moral panic, however, what the government of the day (through the funding bodies it funds) wants to hear does have an effect on the direction of said research.

Psychology uses the *general aggression model*, GAM (Anderson & Bushman, 2002), to explain the mechanism by which human aggression occurs. It is indeed general, and beyond the scope of this book to detail, but Anderson and Bushman explicitly state the point at which video games slot in: "exposure to violent television, movies or video games" is given as an example of a *situational factor*, specifically an *aggressive cue*. Aggressive cues are objects that prime aggression-related concepts in memory, thereby increasing the likelihood of an aggressive response when presented with a primed stimulus.

The basis of the argument that video games cause aggression is thus one of *media effects* as opposed to one of *selection effects*. A media effect (or *socialisation effect*) is when exposure to something influences your behaviour; a selection effect is when you're attracted to things that match your behaviour. For example, suppose it's found that readers of romantic novels are in general more romantic than non-readers: we can assume that either this is because reading romantic novels makes you romantic (a media effect) or because romantic people are attracted to reading romantic novels (a selection effect).

The original GAM paper mentioned television and movies alongside video games, and the comparison of games with other entertainment media used to be relatively common. This trend has now tailed off, however, and it's much more likely that a study will contrast violent video games with non-violent video games rather than with violent TV programmes (or actually violent games, such as *Boxing*).

As for why video games endure more brickbats than movies and TV, well the media-effect argument is that because of their preponderance of aggressive cues, violent video games desensitise players to violence, making it seem more acceptable to them (Carnagey et al., 2007). This also applies to movies and TV, of course, but:

- Video games are interactive whereas movies and TV are not, which increases aggressive affect[23] (Lin, 2013).

- Video games give players a higher sense of presence than movies and TV, which also increases aggressive affect (Nowak et al., 2008).

---

[23] *Affect*, rather than *effect*, because it refers to a display of emotion rather than to a wider consequence.

Basically, then, it's the fact that in a video game you feel that you *yourself* are being violent that makes it more powerful than in those entertainment media where the experience is vicarious. Furthermore, the more realistic a video game is, the greater arousal it causes in its players (Barlett & Rodeheffer, 2009), so modern games are even worse than those of the past.

This line of reasoning does sound plausible, but here's the thing: in violent multi-player games, half the time *you're* on the receiving end. You don't just experience the state of being the aggressor, you experience the state of being the aggressee. People tend to weigh negative impacts much more heavily than notionally equivalent positive ones (Ito et al., 1998), so far from desensitising players to violence, it looks as if they're more likely to see it exactly for what it is: a fiction.

Oh, and here's the *other* thing: around a third of male MMO players prefer playing female characters (Yee, 2021). If immersion is the reason that playing a violent game makes players aggressive, well-being immersed in a female character ought to have huge society-level implications for gender reassignment that have somehow escaped observation.

Even granting that violent video games cause aggressive behaviour, it's hard to argue that the effects observed are long-term. If you're a PhD student conducting an experiment, you need to get a batch of experimental subjects in the same room at the same time, ask them some preliminary questions to ascertain the starting conditions, then split them randomly into groups and have each group's members play a different game for a while. Afterwards, you have to measure aggression somehow. You have maybe two hours to do all of this, which means that any effects you observe will necessarily be short-term.

Longitudinal studies either follow the same group of people over time or look at a massive number of people within an age range at the same time; either way, they're both harder and far more costly to conduct than ones that take a morning or an afternoon (which themselves aren't easy or cheap). Most early such studies were flawed because they used convenience sampling on child subjects, but an exception is Williams & Skoric (2005), which involved a one-month longitudinal study[24] of players of *Asheron's Call 2*; it didn't support the assertion that a violent game will cause substantial increases in out-of-game aggression. Later studies are much more robust, and with regard to violent games and aggression, they still tend to suggest that there is little or no long-term relationship between the two. Indeed, Breuer et al. (2015) found evidence for a selection effect, as did Coyne & Stockdale (2021)'s ten-year longitudinal study.[25]

The way that Psychology views video games and aggression, it's the dressing that's important, rather than the gameplay.[26] There's no concept of artistic message: it's all about what the players perceive at the surface level. Therefore, there is some disagreement concerning what makes a violent video game a violent video game. Even *Pac-Man* was considered violent back in the day:

---

[24] This isn't a long time as longitudinal studies go.
[25] This is a long time as longitudinal studies go.
[26] Recall from Chapter 5 that the *dressing* of a game is the association of symbols to game tokens, whereas the *gameplay* of a game is to do with mechanics and strategy. Aggression research targets the dressing, whereas addiction research targets the gameplay (or at least it would if psychologists didn't use "gameplay" to refer to both).

The most popular games in the Gallup national sample were games in which the players performed acts that are violent in nature. For example, in "Pac Man" and "Ms. Pac Man," players "eat" monsters and, in turn, avoid being eaten.

(Dominick, 1984)

Because for a psychologist it's the dressing that determines whether a game is violent or not, the safest bet when conducting an experiment is therefore to use an abstract game such as *Tetris* for the non-violent control, as these have no dressing. For a long time, *Tetris* was indeed the usual video game of choice in this capacity, for example Zhang et al. (2021).[27]

Hmm. If you were to play *Tetris* until, after ten minutes, a researcher stopped you, you might well feel grateful. If, however, you were to play *Street Fighter II* (Nishitani & Yasuda, 1991) until, after ten minutes, a researcher stopped you, you might well feel aggressive – at the researcher, for interrupting you just as you'd got into it. Oh well.

As research on violent games and aggression flooded in, a positive correlation was found far more often than not. This was typically in the r = .15 range (Ferguson & Konijn, 2015), which is very low. If you're not a statistician, recall from the sidebar what low r values look like on a scatter diagram to get a picture of it. It's barely above random. Nevertheless, it was reliably found and reliably interpreted as being to do with the violent content of the games rather than other factors.

As for why such low r-value findings were picked up on in popular culture, well the results were found to be *significant*. OK, so this isn't the fault of psychologists, but of reporters who either had a weak understanding of statistics or a strong one accompanied by an agenda. Social scientists say that a relationship between variables is *statistically significant* if there's a 5% chance or less that the relationship doesn't exist (the *null hypothesis*).[28] This isn't a statement about how important the relationship is, it's about how sure the researcher is that the relationship is present. There's a statistically significant relationship between the average length of pencils and the average length of pens, but that doesn't mean that the relationship itself is of any consequence. Drop the "statistically" qualifier, though, and it sounds as if it is. Of such stuff are headlines made.

If you want to measure the effects that violent games have on aggression, not only do you need to decide what games are violent, but you also need to measure aggression. There have been some frankly bizarre ways of doing this, including:

- *Taylor Aggression Paradigm* (Taylor, 1967). "They were told that they could determine the intensity of shock their opponent would receive on a particular trial".

- *Hot sauce paradigm* (Lieberman et al., 1999). "… we developed a new method for measuring aggression, specifically, the amount of hot sauce administered to a target known to dislike spicy food".

---

[27] Unfortunately, *Tetris* has other psychological implications, as suggested by the title of the book *The Tetris Effect: The Cold War Battle for the World's Most Addictive Game* (Ackerman, 2016).

[28] Physicists are somewhat more demanding, requiring a five-sigma threshold before accepting that their results might not be a statistical fluctuation. For the Higgs boson, that worked out at about 0.00003% (CERN, 2024). This is smaller than 5%.

- *Noise blast tasks* (Anderson & Dill, 2000). "… they could punish their opponent by delivering a noxious blast of white noise. This constituted our laboratory measure of aggression".

- *Aggressive word completion task* (Carnagey & Anderson, 2005). "Half of the word fragments contained aggressive possibilities. For example, 'K I _ _' could be completed as 'kind', 'kiss', 'kick', or 'kill'".

Lest you suspect I'm cherry-picking oddities, each of the above research papers has been cited over 400 times. The noise-blast one has been cited over 3,000 times.

It seems strange that such diverse methods for measuring aggression, and such varied decisions as to what constitutes a violent video game in the first place, should all find roughly the same correlation value of r=.15. This was picked up when Psychology's reproducibility crisis arose. Normally, reproducibility failings concern experiments that, when repeated exactly, give different results from the original; in the case of violent games and aggression, the issue was more to do with their returning eerily similar results for very widely differing methods.

Related to reproducibility was the recognition that using miserably low sample sizes or obtaining subjects by convenience sampling was perhaps bad science. Nowadays, crowdsourcing for research purposes (Mullen et al., 2021) is becoming preferred as a better way to find a large number of diverse participants who share a common interest in answering questions for money.

The general public doesn't really care about the reproducibility crisis in Psychology (Anvaria & Lakens, 2019). This may, of course, be because they don't care about Psychology. However, psychologists do, and when the disciple began to emerge from its reproducibility crisis, it did so with a better understanding of aggression (Ferguson, 2020). Sadly, this made little impression on standards-defining bodies such as the APA or the WHO.

The most difficult problem faced by those asserting that violent video games cause aggression is that if playing violent video games *did* cause aggression, the streets should be running with blood by now. In the end, if you persist in warning people that the sky is about to fall in then the more specious your warning seems to be when the sky does not, in fact, fall in.

> … 90% of young males play video games (Lenhart, 2008). Finding that a young man who committed a violent crime also played a popular video game, such as *Call of Duty*, *Halo*, or *Grand Theft Auto*, is as pointless as pointing out that the criminal also wore socks.
>
> *(Markey et al., 2015)*

If violent video games did cause aggression, there should be an increase in the incidence of aggressive assaults or homicides after the release of violent video games. However, Markey et al. (2015) found that in the United States, there was no such increase – and in fact that there was a decrease in violent crime in response to violent video games.

A number of explanations have been offered regarding why a correlation between violent video games and aggression is consistently found when the effects that ought to follow from this aren't observed. Hemovich (2020) shows that frustration, losing, and difficulty are factors often overlooked: it seems that players are less pro-social[29] when they merely play a computer game with bits of the screen covered up than when the screen is clear – regardless of whether the game is deemed to be violent or not. The effect is substantial and suggests that violence in video games may not be a primary determinant of behaviour.

You may be wondering why I've discussed violent video games (of which most MMORPGs, if not all virtual worlds, are considered examples) and aggression. What relevance does either have to designing virtual worlds? You don't really believe there's a causal link, and even those psychologists who *do* believe there is recognise that its effect is so low as to be almost negligible.

Well, it's a literal reality check. You may think that you work in the world's most exciting and fastest-growing entertainment industry (because indeed you do), but that cuts little ice with people envious of or afraid of its power. Artistically, you can do what you like. Politically, you can't. Governments wish to follow the science, but when they fund the very science that they wish to follow, that can be problematical. Don't get lost in hubris.

Virtual worlds are virtual, but their players are of Reality. As I said at the end of the discussion on addiction: in disputes between the virtual and the real, Reality always wins. Never forget that. *Reality always wins.*

22.4 THINK OF THE CHILDREN

The first thing I should say is that if you have non-adult children of your own and want a useful, accessible discussion of the effects that playing video games might have on them, Kowert (2016) gives a short, rational, non-judgemental summary.

Now, much game-related work in Psychology involves studies of children and adolescents. It may not be obvious why this is so, but there are several good reasons:

- Society has a long history of protecting children, so when a new medium gains traction, it's a given that any possibly harmful effects on them should be examined.

- Children are still developing their critical faculties and are more susceptible to behavioural influences than are adults.

- Children are traditionally believed to play more games than adults, so the cumulative effects will be greater.

- Educational computer games established some time ago[30] that regardless of whether games in general are considered academically respectable, the study of games and children is.

- It's often easier to get access to a group of children for an experiment than it is to find a similarly sized group of adults. In school, children and adolescents are already in groups of study-friendly sizes, and they're timetabled such that the whole group is available at once. You don't even have to pay them!

---

[29] Defined as being less likely to help someone collect pens "accidentally" spilled from a cup.

[30] The first educational computer game ("computer" because it was before we had video) is generally recognised to be *The Sumerian Game* (Addis, 1964). The version we played on the DEC-10 mainframe when I was a student had the filename SUMER.EXE because of length limitations; we referred to it as *Hamurabi.*

For these reasons and others, children and adolescents have been studied disproportionately with respect to games. Psychology is such a broad field, however, that the developmental psychologists who are interested in educational uses barely intersect with those who study addiction and aggression. This is perhaps fortunate for game designers, because if you can argue that by playing educational games youngsters can develop an affinity for (say) mathematics, you can also argue that by playing violent games youngsters can develop an affinity for (say) aggression. The mechanisms don't appear to be the same, but it's awkward nonetheless.

Although there were experiments in the Third Age of virtual worlds regarding their utility in education, modern virtual worlds aren't in general used for such purposes except in the case of social worlds that allow building, where they have a role as platforms (Kamel Boulos et al., 2007). Obstacles to their use include issues to do with technology, identity, culture, collaboration, time, economic models, standards, and methods for social discovery (Warburton, 2009).

I discussed some of the educational possibilities of virtual worlds in Chapter 17 and have covered the most pertinent of their potential ill-effects on children when outlining the research on addiction and aggression (a good deal of which is undertaken using children and adolescents as subjects). Psychology does have a lot to say about children and their development, some of which is game-related, but it's tangential to virtual world design, and I've already been tangential quite enough. I therefore won't be investing further time in describing the way that Psychology views games and children. Besides, the main issues that virtual world designers have with children have little to do with Psychology, concerning as they do either keeping them out of virtual worlds intended for adults or keeping adults out of virtual worlds intended for children.

I do, however, have an important point to make, which I outlined in Bartle (2015b)[31] and shall summarise here.

Suppose that you have discovered a potion that you believe will turn some people into monsters. You test it out by taking two groups of schoolchildren then giving one group the potion and the other group orange juice. If more of the ones who drank the potion turn into monsters than ones who drank the orange juice did, your hypothesis has some evidential basis of being correct.

Except, of course, you will have created several monsters.

If you truly believe, in your heart of hearts, that playing video games is harmful, why the blazes would you have people – especially children – play them in experiments?! You risk turning them into monsters!

"Don't worry", you might say, "the potion soon wears off, it's only *repeated* exposure that's harmful". Fair enough, except your colleagues are telling you that the potion is also addictive. You are therefore *knowingly* putting people in harm's way, possibly for a lifetime: don't you feel in any way uneasy about that? Isn't it irresponsible to do what you're doing time and time again?

Or is it that maybe, deep down, you sense that actually the potion is basically harmless?

---

[31] This article comments paper-by-paper on the Special Issue on Video Games and Youth Culture of *Psychology of Popular Media Culture* and addresses many of the topics I've mentioned here but in greater depth.

22.5 OTHER RESEARCH

The first wave of psychologists to look at virtual worlds included a number who were interested in the topic of identity. This was perceptive of them, because virtual worlds are indeed crucibles for identity creation and expression. After a while, having established that identity formation was happening and then formulated mechanisms that explained the process, most of them moved on. Even so, the psychology of game players is still a topic of research for psychologists, and because their work on identity (and to some extent personality) adds weight to a good many player typologies, it remains of use to designers.

Earlier, in Chapter 15, I outlined two strategies for character creation: playing as the opposite of yourself; playing as similar to yourself but different. Psychologists refer to the former as *alternate-self constructs* and the latter as *ideal-self constructs*; for role-playing games, alternate-self constructs are the more popular among players (Hart, 2017). Early work on identity exploration did indeed focus on the alternate self, for example (Bruckman, 1992; Davis, 1994; Turkle, 1995). Later, ideal-self constructs came to the fore, for example (Bessière et al., 2007; Becerra & Stutts, 2008; Przybylski et al., 2012).

Identity isn't only *explored* in virtual worlds, though: it's also *expressed* (Bargh et al., 2002). This can be seen in players who have reached the end of their development track, but it can also be seen in certain players who were never even on such a track. As I mentioned when discussing inverse role-playing, people who are at ease with themselves but who are unable to *be* themselves in their everyday lives can play a virtual world to live as they truly are. For them, expressing their identity is the very essence of why they're playing – it's a *self-need* (Sibilla & Mancini, 2018).[32] This isn't the case with most virtual world players, for whom exploration is the rationale behind their play; expression does occur in bursts, though, to road-test promising possibilities (especially at the beginning). The end goal of both exploration and expression is the same, however: identity affirmation.

Identity exploration can happen in Reality, of course, but the environmental and psychological conditions present in virtual worlds promote it. This is because of *disembodiment*, which sounds as if it's something to do with ghosts but has a more technical meaning in this context: it's the separation of mind and body. When you play a virtual world, you create within it a new body for your mind to inhabit.

Psychologists and philosophers consider two ways that disembodiment can go, when they go anywhere at all (Kitchin, 1998). The first is that they lead to the construction of a new self-identity; the second is that nature and technology merge to reconstruct the body.[33] Virtual worlds take the first path, as players have no desire to merge with their character in a cyborg-body sense (Bortle, 2005)[34]; unluckily, at about the time that psychologists were beginning to examine this topic, their attention was diverted towards the somewhat more

---

[32] This useful review paper looks at what topics were examined in a range of studies concerning players' relationships with their avatars. Four main ones were found: *physical* similarities and differences between player and avatar; *self-concept* similarities and differences; player *self-needs* presented through avatars; degree of player *identification* with avatars and social groups.

[33] These equate to the physical and self-concept categories from Sibilla & Mancini (2018), with identification equating to immersion.

[34] I had trouble typing that surname for some reason.

exciting second path by a hugely influential work (Haraway, 1991)[35] that pursued it to make a number of stinging points about the future direction of feminism. The understanding of identity construction was left somewhat undeveloped as a result (although because both identity construction and body construction are basically two sides of the same coin, it's really just a matter of perspective).

Recently, however, research into the relationship between players and their characters has picked up. For virtual worlds, the Proteus effect (which was discussed in Chapter 15) led the way. It was noticed a while ago that players treat characters in different ways depending on whether they resembled them or not (Bailenson et al., 2001), and that players (particularly women) acted differently when playing characters with different appearances (Banakou & Chorianopoulos, 2010); could it be that your character's body influenced your mind's sense of self? It had been known for some time that team-sports players who wore black outfits had more 50/50 calls go against them than players wearing other colours – and were more likely to foul other players in the first place (Frank & Gilovich, 1988)[36]; if embodiment cues can affect the behaviour of those observing or experiencing them, what would the implications be for virtual worlds, where you're embodied as your character? The Proteus effect showed that it was to do with identity exploration.

It would be useful at this point if we knew what thought processes players went through when initially designing their characters. Fortunately, thanks to Walk (2018), we do (at least for *Second Life*). In Chapter 15, I gave a brief overview of his account of the path new users usually follow; Figure 22.2 reprises this as a flowchart.

Some other points noted in the same article:

- People don't like getting dressed in public but do like asking friends what they think of their look before going public with it.

- Teenagers really like exploring identities.

- If you don't limit how tall characters can be, you'll get dragon-sized people everywhere.

- If you don't limit how short characters can be, you'll get child pornography.

- If, as a player, you want people to give you things for free, create a female character.

- If, as a player, you want people to hassle you, create a female character.

We'll be looking at those final two issues a little in Volume II.

Figure 22.2 mentions sliders, which constitute one of the more sophisticated methods by which players can fashion their characters' appearances in graphical worlds. Some, such as the one employed in *Black Desert Online*, are so nuanced that avatar creation is almost a form of sculpture. Others, such as that of *Final Fantasy XIV*, construct a look by combining

---

[35] This essay first appeared in 1985 in *The Socialist Review*, but it seems few contemporary academics read that publication; the updated version in her book *Simians, Cyborgs and Women: The Reinvention of Nature* is the one everyone (well, over 11,000 people) cites.

[36] Or perhaps not (Caldwell & Burger, 2011).

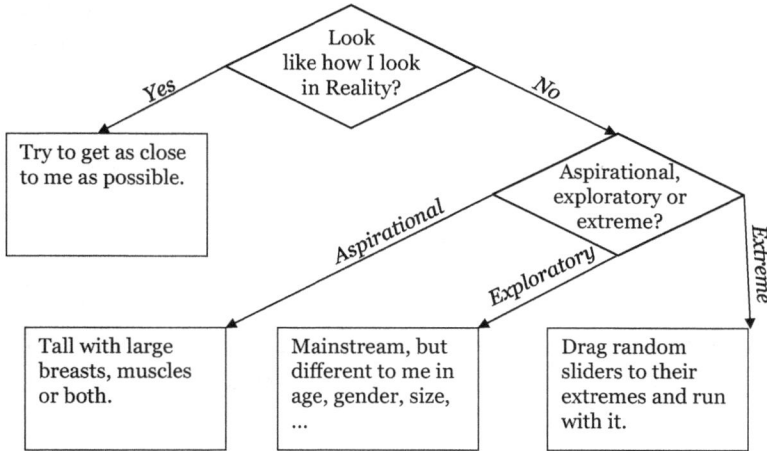

FIGURE 22.2   Character creation flowchart.

presets, with far fewer sliders.[37] The advantage of the former is that you can create exactly the look you want if you're accomplished at multidimensional slider-manipulation. The advantage of the latter is that you can create nice-looking characters that don't expose the fact you're unaccomplished at multidimensional slider-manipulation. Either way, however, although you are indeed creating a character, the limitations of the interface are also playing a part. The identity you eventually construct is affected by the appearance of your character, and so, ultimately, are you. Designers therefore walk a tight line between giving players so much choice that they either can't make a decision or can but lack the ability to express it, or so limited a choice that there's little decision-making or expression involved. As we'll see in Volume II, though, this is true of all aspects of character creation, not just that of appearance.

People express and read identities through *identity markers* – common characteristics that are meaningful to a culture, used by its members to define themselves and others. The main ones, such as age, gender, and socioeconomic class, are staples of most demographic studies of populations, but there are plenty of others. People may additionally define themselves in terms of their nationality, sexuality, politics, religion, accent, job, ethnicity, hobbies, possessions, clothes, physical characteristics, food preferences – all manner of things. That said, although most people will possess most or all of these markers, they don't necessarily consider them to be a fundamental part of their identity. For example, I have several hobbies, but I don't regard them as a major component of my authentic self; my paternal grandfather, on the other hand, collected matchbox labels[38] and definitely did see this activity as an important part of who he was.

Not everyone in every society will pick up on markers, and sub-cultures may have ones unknown to the majority. I don't play *Golf*, and although I might have a good idea that someone carrying golf clubs *is* a golfer (or maybe a caddie), I won't be able to tell what kind of golfer they want to be perceived as; a fellow golfer would be able to pick up on that at a glance.

---

[37] Sliders for muscle tone and breast size do, of course, still feature.

[38] I inherited over 20,000 of them. One of these days, the attic floor will sunder under their weight and they'll kill anyone sleeping in our guest room at the time.

The reason I'm mentioning identity markers is that designers have to think about them. Virtual worlds have had internal ones since the beginning – *MUD*'s named character levels were a form of identity marker. Today, MMO players still judge one another's characters by advancement-related markers such as titles and gear level, along with several other gameplay-related concepts (mainly faction, party role, and character class).

What about identity markers from Reality, though?

Well, whether appearance matters or not depends on the individual. If you consider your fashion sense to be a part of who you are then disparaging or admiring others for what they're wearing will come automatically to you in graphical worlds (especially social ones). Reality's identity markers aren't only about clothes, though. Designers must decide what other markers to include or to exclude from their virtual worlds.

Some markers don't need to be addressed in terms of provision (although they might in terms of addressing other aspects of design). For example, if it's important to someone's sense of identity that they're neurodivergent, there's no necessity to create neurodivergent markers for their character – they're inherent, via the player.

Some markers can be excluded on fictional grounds. For example, if someone defines themself by their job and their job is programming computers, they're unlikely to have much joy in that regard playing a Fantasy world.

As for the remaining markers, well on the face of it, there's no reason that you wouldn't provide markers, at least up to some threshold of popularity. If people want to bring an important sense of who they are into a virtual world, you would probably wish to accommodate them (if only so they can later experiment with not having it).

Unfortunately, there are problems with adding identity markers to virtual worlds, which designers have to consider. Here are some of them:

- The marker *almost* fits the fiction but doesn't quite. Some people identify as wheelchair users (Milbrodt, 2019), but although wheelchairs of different kinds have existed for hundreds of years, the modern form with large rear wheels so you can push yourself along independently wasn't patented until 1869 (Blunt & Smith, 1869). Would you nevertheless feature such wheelchairs in, say, a Jane Austen-era virtual world?

- Some markers are easy to add but would disadvantage the character. For example, many deaf people consider their deafness to be part of their identity (Bat-Chava, 2000), but deaf characters might be unable to react to important sound cues such as the noises made by nearby mobs. I don't mean deaf *players* (for which it's an accessibility issue[39]), I mean deaf *characters*, created by their players to *be* deaf. If their experience in your virtual world is harsher than it is in Reality, should you ease up on them?

- Some markers are regarded as culturally specific to particular groups. The use of these markers can amount to cultural appropriation (Rogers, 2006). If members of a cultural group want to create characters that have a particular hairstyle, say, then it's relatively easy to provide it for them; however, it's not at all easy to ensure that no one outside that group can use the same hairstyle.

---

[39] Accessibility issues are discussed in Volume II.

- Some markers are to do with political or ethical stances. For example, "Identifying as a vegan is a public declaration of one's identity, morals and lifestyle" (Greenebaum, 2012). Veganism involves not only avoiding the consumption of animal products, but also the use of them. Use of digital leather isn't the same as use of real leather, but nevertheless, it will make some vegans uneasy.[40] Will you accommodate this view by offering animal-free alternatives to leather armour?

- Identity markers can emancipate the individual but subjugate the group. Requiring that everyone refers to you in a particular way can be liberating for you, but people who don't regard you as the centre of the universe may find it a chore. When I was at school, one kid demanded to be known as "God"; this insistence was ignored except by kids susceptible to bullying.

- Some markers are impossible to offer. I identify as a father, but I wouldn't be able to take that into a virtual world because whatever entities I'd be a father *of* wouldn't be my children.[41]

In all cases, you can expect trouble from some quarters if people who don't have given identity markers in Reality assume them in a virtual world. Playing as a gender other than your own has been acceptable since the First Age of virtual worlds, but times may change; playing as an ethnicity other than your own has been possible since the Fifth Age, but players are generally very cautious about it. These are both examples of *identity tourism* (Nakamura, 1995), which can be transformational both for the tourist and for what they're touring (although not necessarily positively for both).

Note that the use of identity markers for NPCs is a different matter, to do with representation. We'll look at this towards the end of Volume II.

My own take on this is that characters are not players. If someone chooses to denigrate an identity marker (even if matches their own in Reality) then there's no place for that in a virtual world unless allowing it is explicitly the designer's intention.[42] Otherwise, identity tourism is at the very least informative and can, for some people, be transformative; under those circumstances, it would be sad indeed for this to be outlawed.[43]

So, I've spent some time outlining what psychology has to say about players of games and (occasionally) of virtual worlds. Although some of this is of practical use, most of it is merely informative, to be taken into account (or ignored) in the course of virtual world creation.

The main area of interest from a designer's point of view isn't what psychologists take from games, though: it's what designers take from psychology – good and bad.

---

[40] I don't like the taste of chicken (a trait inherited from my maternal grandmother). Even though I can't taste what my characters eat in virtual worlds, it always feels discomforting when one of them tucks into a chicken dinner. I can only imagine what it feels like for a Muslim or Jew if their character has to scoff a plate of bacon butties to complete a quest.

[41] Exception: I did play *The Lord of the Rings Online* with my elder daughter a few times. My character (designed by my younger daughter) was female; hers (which she designer herself) was male and looked older than mine. When she called me "Dad", it rather freaked out the other players in our fellowship.

[42] This could be the case for a virtual world set in an era of witch trials, for example.

[43] This is subjugation of the group by a (typically) smaller group.

CHAPTER 23

Virtual Worlds' Take on Psychology

Because players are people and psychologists study people, it is unsurprising to learn that there are psychological phenomena with no direct connection to virtual worlds that are nevertheless directly useful to designers. The key concepts are very well tried-and-tested, so much so that I've mentioned and used several already: flow, presence, self-determination theory, and the big five personality types are all lifted from research in Psychology.

This chapter considers other practical applications of the discipline.

From one perspective, all virtual world design has a psychological aspect to it, as the design emerges from the psychology of the designer. That's not a particularly useful observation, of course, but it's the basis of art so is worth mentioning.

If you're going to design for people to play your virtual world, though, then knowing how certain design inputs cause certain behavioural outputs is going to be of interest to you. Some of these inputs will be unavoidable because they're inherent in what virtual worlds are, but even so there's the possibility of leveraging them for some further purpose. Others of the inputs don't *need* to be there, but if you put them there then you'll get the outputs; if you want those outputs, you may be tempted to set up the inputs, and if you don't then you may be tempted to avoid them.

As we'll soon see, though, it's not that simple: some of the things you might wish to include or exclude will have other effects that you don't or do wish to see, so it becomes a balancing act. For example, to give players something to do while they await the next big content patch, you might offer daily quests. Your motives are honourable, but some players will worry that they're missing out if they don't log in every day for the quests, so feel obligated to do them. You might still be OK with that, because hey, you want people to play your game (especially if it uses a subscription revenue model). However, a person's well-being is affected positively if they want to play and negatively if they feel compelled to play (Vuorre et al., 2022). This suggests that activities such as daily quests are not good in the long term. Knowing that, are you still going to put in daily quests?

DOI: 10.1201/9781003689638-23

The deliberate use of psychology in game design almost[1] always serves one of two purposes: making the game better for the player; making the profits better for the developer. They used to be the same thing: if you wanted to make more profit, you made better games. This is still the case for indie developers, but for the big-hitters, it's increasingly rare (Strife Hayes, 2022). MMOs don't suffer as much from this as some other types of game, and social worlds barely suffer at all, but then they come with issues of their own.

I'll partition the psychological techniques that the prudent designer ought to be aware of by whether they favour or disfavour the player. Some natural effects that are fairly neutral but could easily be disfavouring sit in between.

23.1 FAVOURING THE PLAYER

Psychological techniques that favour the player are usually benign, although it *may* be possible to use them malignly if you're that kind of person (or if your boss is). The main benefit to the designer is knowing that they exist so as to be sympathetic to them, but they can also add positively to the player experience under certain circumstances.

23.1.1 Overjustification Effect

I alluded to earlier when discussing gamified approaches to learning. It's about *rewards*.

From a designer's perspective, there are two primary kinds of reward: *intrinsic* rewards are inherent in an activity itself; *extrinsic* rewards are acquired for having done an activity.

Intrinsic rewards are much preferred because fun is intrinsic, not extrinsic. Some related effects, such as flow, also rely on the intrinsic enjoyment of an activity. Extrinsic rewards are basically bribes, so have to be used sparingly. Over-use is an admission that your gameplay is too weak on its own.

This isn't to say that extrinsic rewards should be eschewed in virtual world design, as they can have legitimate uses. These include:

- Making implicit progress explicit. Experience points are explicit rewards, which serve to improve your character as you yourself improve.

- Breadcrumbing players through directionless content. This treasure chest reassures you that you were supposed to kill those guys.

- Opening up new content or shortcutting played-through content. This stone isn't exactly thrill-worthy, but with it, you can teleport back to the City of Gold from anywhere else.

- Indicating the end of a narrative cycle. The armour you received is colour-coded as rare, signalling that the boss you killed was the final challenge of this dungeon.

- Heightening the response from an intrinsic reward. Not only was that fun, but you get this!

The naïve designer might figure that if intrinsic rewards are good then extrinsic rewards should be given to encourage players to do the things that they'll find intrinsically

---

[1] "Almost", because there is a small number of games made for other purposes, such as education.

rewarding. Follow the loot, find the fun! Sadly, that's not how it works. The *overjustifica-tion effect* means that when people are given extrinsic rewards for having done things that they found intrinsically enjoyable, they stop finding the doing of those things intrinsically enjoyable (Lepper et al., 1973). For example, if you were paid to play a game then after a while you wouldn't be playing for fun, you'd be playing for pay. At that stage, the activity would lose its lustre and seem more like a job than a game (a point that has eluded many of those who advocate play-to-earn games).

Designers' ideas of what rewards are connect with those of psychologists, although designers are more interested in their nature and psychologists are more interested in their effects. We'll see how this plays out later when we look at operant conditioning. Preview: not pleasantly.

23.1.2 The Uncanny Valley

Human beings have an affinity with one another that they don't share with bricks, spiders, or clouds. The more that something looks like a human being, the greater the affinity we have with it. We might not have much affinity with a bag full of rags, but if the bag is stitched to look like a cat then we could take to it. If it was an actual cat, we might have a greater affinity still.[2] It's not unreasonable to suppose, then, that the closer something resembles a human being, the greater our initial affinity with it will be.

In general, this is indeed the case, except that something weird happens when an object or creature is close to human-appearing, but not *quite* there: it looks disturbingly unsettling and creeps people out. You can add more human-like characteristics to over-come this, but not before plummeting into the depths of "Whoah, what the hell is that?!". The effect was first noticed by the roboticist Masahiro Mori in Japan (Mori, 1970),[3] who gave it its name because of the graph (see Figure 23.1).

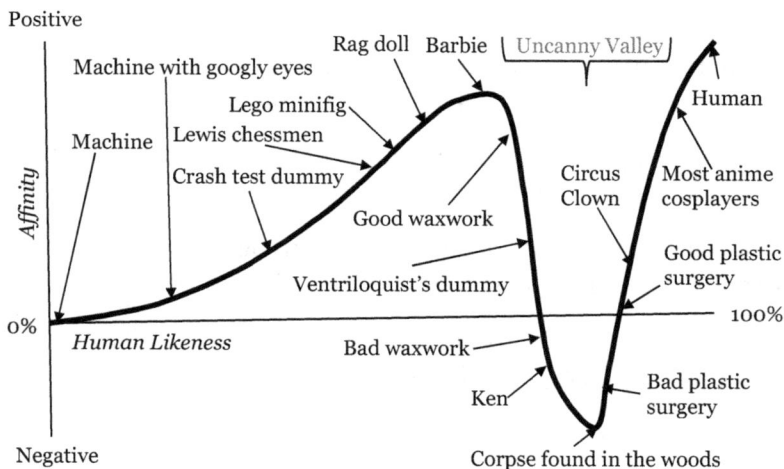

FIGURE 23.1 The uncanny valley.

---

[2] Unless it's bad-tempered. Yes, Campus Cat Pebbles, at the University of Essex, *j'accuse*!

[3] Because the original essay is in Japanese and that's like a foreign language to me, I found Mori (2012) to be a useful translation.

There is some suggestion that the slope to the right of the valley isn't as steep as the one entering it (the *uncanny cliff* (Bartneck et al., 2007)), but the basic principle remains.[4]

With photorealistic graphics now able to bridge the uncanny valley, it's easy to suppose that it's no longer relevant to virtual worlds. It is, though, for two reasons.

Firstly, you might *want* to creep players out. If yours is a horror setting, players will expect it as part of the deal.

Secondly, it is not just the way that characters look that you can find disconcerting: it is the way they act, too. If this paragraph feels strange, that is because it is an example of the phenomenon in action. I have written it so that it is grammatically correct, but I have not used apostrophes. It is stilted as a result.

OK, that's enough of that! The point I'm making is that if you want or don't want to creep your players out, consider what your NPCs say and do as well as how they look. Players pick up on all kinds of signals, not just appearance. Speaking of which…

23.1.3 Mirror Neurons

Whenever you do something, an action-specific constellation of neurons lights up in your brain. News of it will ripple out to be processed elsewhere in your brain. For example, you might take a bite from a banana and receive pleasurable signals from your taste buds. These are immediately triaged, and if deemed worthy of attention will be passed on to a centre that acts something like a despatch box (I'm heavily simplifying here). Its job is to distribute signals to more specialised parts of the brain, to do with as they will. One such effect might be to strengthen your appreciation of bananas; another might result in the thought "Mmm, this is a good banana!" to bubble up in your mind.

It turns out that if you observe someone else doing something, the effects of this observation can reach that *same* despatch box. The signals will then be passed on as if you yourself had experienced the initial condition, albeit in a weaker form because it's not backed up by the signals coming directly from the senses themselves. This "despatch box" consists of what are known as *mirror neurons* (di Pellegrino et al., 1992).[5] Because of mirror neurons, when you see someone else do something (such as cry), it can trigger an emotion in you: hence, empathy. For human beings, this is particularly the case with facial expressions; it's why yawning is contagious (Haker et al., 2013).

Designers of virtual worlds will obviously mandate that characters (player- and non-player-alike) are able to show emotions. If you want the player to *feel* those emotions, rather than simply to read them as body language, then you need to convey them as close as you can to how a human would express them. Animations that show exaggerated overacting will tell the player that an NPC is angry, or in a huff, or shy, but they won't cause that player to feel the same way. If the NPC expresses their emotions closer to how a human genuinely experiencing them would, the player's mirror neurons will fire and reflect those emotions onto the player. As a result, they'll seem truer.

---

[4] That's unless your experiments show it doesn't exist at all, or at least isn't as strong as designers fear (Burleigh et al., 2013).

[5] It was first observed by accident in monkeys that had been rigged up with electrodes in their head, so if you have strong ethical objections to scientific experiments on primates then you'll need to look elsewhere for your evidence.

This comes with a caveat, however: if you get close to showing a human emotion, but not close enough, the uncanny valley will kick in and elicit an altogether different response.[6]

23.1.4 Theory of Mind

Mirror neurons allow an individual to build up a picture of the desires and emotions of another person simply by passive observation. People are very good at creating such models of other people in their heads. This is because they have a *theory of mind*: the ability to think about how other people would think and feel, given what you know of them. A good demonstration of it in action is the *Sally-Anne test* (Baron-Cohen et al., 1985), which goes something like this:

There are two dolls, Sally and Anne. Sally has a basket and Anne has a box. Sally also has a marble, which she puts in her basket. Then, she goes for a walk. While she's away, Anne takes the marble out of Sally's basket and puts it in the box. Sally returns and wants to play with her marble. Where does she look for it?

OK, so *we* know that the marble is in the box, but Sally thinks it's in the basket so that's where she'll look. We've used our theory of mind to work this out.

Most children have acquired a theory of mind by the age of four, and all those without developmental difficulties will have it by age six (Wimmer & Perner, 1983).

Theory of mind comes into play so naturally for adults that most people barely realise they're using it. You only really apply it consciously when someone behaves in a way you weren't expecting, which indicates that your model of them is either incomplete or incorrect.[7] It does have applications of particular use in virtual worlds, two of which (*parasocial relationships* and *self-perception*) we'll come to shortly. For the moment, though, we'll look at a third: *anthropomorphism*.

You know that NPCs aren't human, right? Until we reach the point when we can make them sapient,[8] they're behaving algorithmically in context with perhaps a dash of randomness for variety. However, because players want to be immersed when they play, we present NPCs *as if* they were sapient[9] so that the players can buy into this. If the NPCs don't conform to a theory of mind, that makes them harder to accept as being what they purport to be. Therefore, we need to allow players to apply a theory of mind to them so as to understand their motives and to anticipate their actions. This depth of behaviour mostly comes to the fore in story-related scenes: "We know that she loves him, and that he doesn't know she does, and that she doesn't know he's gay, so how are we going to deal with this?".

We can use a theory of mind elsewhere, too, though. Perhaps the best-known example is of a general, I-already-did-that problem known as *bears bears bears* (Barnett, 2007). Basically, you fight your way through hordes of bears to reach an NPC who says that bears are eating his sheep and children; please will you embark on a quest to kill said bears. Er,

---

[6] Or the same response, if you were trying to make an NPC express being unnerved.

[7] It could also be that they're smarter than you and were able to conceive of something you didn't have the mental ability to predict. Obviously, this has never happened to me.

[8] Assuming we want to; it might not be fair on them if we do (Bartle, 2022). More on this in Volume II.

[9] I'm using *sapient* rather than *sentient*, by the way, because sentience is only the capacity to have subjective experience and emotions, whereas sapience includes the ability to reason and to understand. Many creatures are sentient, but so far we only know that *Homo sapiens* are sapient.

but you already killed the bears. You killed the bears on the way to see the NPC. Why should you kill them again?

Now applying a theory of mind to the NPC, it's clear that the NPC doesn't know you've killed the bears. So ... why can't you just tell him? The virtual world isn't allowing you to use your knowledge of the NPC's perspective to correct a false impression. You employed your theory of mind automatically, because you're aged 6 or over, and have now been jolted out of your immersion because you can't act on it.

Virtual worlds are social, of course, so you *do* get to use your theory of mind on other players. It's not a complete bust.

Oh, and you also get to use it on yourself.

23.1.5 Self-Perception

Earlier, I mentioned the Proteus effect. This is a special application of theory of mind, resulting from the situation in which you create an other-you and use what you know about them to inform what you know about yourself. You are able to keep the two mentally separate through a cognitive ability known as *framing* (Bateson, 2006),[10] which in essence allows you to treat something as denoting something else without treating it as what that thing denotes. For example, two dogs play-fighting will nip each other to represent bites, but the represented bites don't represent what bites represent. Likewise, actors on stage who use sexist language from a script are showing that their characters are sexist, not that they themselves are sexist. Note that I'll be discussing a different kind of framing shortly.

People will often reflect on their actions, past, present, and future. Why did I do that? Do I really want to do this? Would it be right if I did something else? They also reflect on the (actual or possible) effects of their actions. Why did it make me feel that way? I'm not hungry, so why do I want a snack? How can I ever be happy? Through this self-analysis, people deepen their awareness of who they are and of what makes them tick. In effect, you're implicitly applying a theory of mind to yourself.

Virtual worlds make this easier by introducing a proxy. You can't really use mirror neurons to pick up on your own actions because those neurons are directly triggered *by* those actions. However, you *can* use them to pick up on the actions of your character, as *causing* it to act doesn't use the same neurons as the action itself does. Telling someone to jump isn't the same as seeing them jump. This is the mechanism that frees the Proteus effect to work its magic.

Because of the Proteus effect, role-playing games such as virtual worlds are excellent vehicles for gaining self-awareness through self-perception. By thinking about the action of your proxy, you can assess your own thoughts and feelings with respect to that action. You can then update them, or update your model of your proxy to accommodate them. This is despite the fact that it was you who caused the proxy to perform the action it did in the first place.

As for what this means for designers (other than reiterating the fact that virtual worlds are about identity exploration), well the main takeaways are: don't take control of a player's

---

[10] The book chapter cited here is an easier-to-obtain version of Bateson (1956).

character away from that player, because this breaks their mental model of that character; don't make the player role-play some other character, because they *aren't* that character therefore doing so will negatively interfere with their self-perception. This is very much in line with what we already know from self-determination theory, which I touched on earlier. I expect you may still be tempted to snatch away control in cut scenes and require the player to role-play some popular NPC in an instance, but at least you now know there are negative consequences to consider.

23.1.6 Parasocial Relationships

I've briefly mentioned parasocial relationships a couple of times already in this book, and now it's time to look at them in detail.

A *parasocial relationship* is a unidirectional one between a spectator and a performer (Horton & Wohl, 1956). As you, a spectator, watch a performer, you build up a mental model of them. This may or may not be accurate, but that's immaterial. You could easily form opinions of the performer based on this model. Along with these opinions might well come emotions. You could feel that the performer is trustworthy, or amusing, or dislikeable, say. All this is to be expected, because you do the same with people in your social circle. You also form relationships with people in your social circle. Why wouldn't you form a relationship with the performer, too?

Many people do form such relationships. Teenagers' crushes on media figures are well-documented (Erickson & Dal Cin, 2018). What makes these relationships parasocial is that the performer is unaware of the spectator as an individual. This may be because the communication channel is one-way (you see the movie star on the silver screen, but they don't see you); it may be because you're one person among many (the pop star sees a crowd of 30,000 people, not you in particular); it may be because the performer is inert ("Man in relationship with his car says he's in 'love' – and they even have sex"; Bett, 2022[11]); it may be because the performer is fictional (Galadriel, Bugs Bunny, Heathcliff, Cinderella, Chitty Chitty Bang Bang, …); it may be because the performer doesn't exist except in the imagination of the spectator (plenty of people who worship gods other than yours are in this position).

Players can form parasocial relationships with other players in virtual worlds, but it's unlikely because in general the other player will know you exist. More common is the related phenomenon of forming a relationship with the model they have in their head of a player, but said model doesn't match the actual, living player; we see this in masquerading a lot, which is why you have to be very careful if you want to take that path.

From a design point of view, players will be more immersed and engaged in your virtual world if they have parasocial relationships with key NPCs. Any main storyline will be more meaningful, because they'll care about what happens. They don't have to like the NPCs in question – I loathed Zenos yae Galvus in *FFXIV* – but if they project an imbued personality onto them, the virtual world will have more emotional power.

---

[11] It came to a tragic end: after 12 years, the relationship ended when his 1998 Chevy Monte Carlo was written off following a routine check-up.

Players know that your NPCs aren't real, so only in rare cases will any relationship they form be "unhealthy". They can break off the relationship pretty well any time, simply by not playing; their relationship is sustained by their sense of immersion, so if they're not immersed then that acts as a dampener.

There are basically four ways that you can help players to form parasocial relationships if they so choose:

- Have the NPC address them directly, one-on-one, rather than only talking to other NPCs.

- Have the NPC use nonverbal communication. Eye contact is of particular importance, but other body language cues are good too if not overdone (recall mirror neurons).

- Have attractive characters if you want a positive relationship and unattractive ones if you want a negative one.[12] It may be contrary to the tenets of diversity and inclusion, but players really will judge a book by its cover.

- Have relatable characters, making it easier for the player to see things from their point of view.

"You" here is your character in the virtual world, of course. However, because you *are* your character (or are in the process of becoming so), any pro-parasocial relationship cues directed at them will be passed through straight to you. When the character in question is your own, rather than another player's or an NPC, this includes any cues that you yourself may direct at your character: they'll be passed through back to you. The parasocial self sets up the feedback loop that controls the direction of your self-perception, thereby turning it into one of self-understanding.

As a designer, then, you want your players to have constant interaction with their own characters, not only so they can model them (and thereby themselves) but also so they can have feelings about them (and thereby themselves). If we consider the methods listed above for helping players to form parasocial relationships:

- You can't make the player's character address the player directly, because that removes the player's autonomy.

- You can't usually[13] have them use eye contact, but you can have them exhibit multiple means and modes of expression.

- You can give the player the option of deciding how attractive their character is (and to whom).

---

[12] You don't want them to be *too* attractive or unattractive, though. If they're too attractive, the player may think they're false; if they're too unattractive, the player may feel pity for them.

[13] You can do it under certain circumstances. In *Throne and Liberty*, if you zoom in on your character then they'll turn to face you. Personally, I find this makes my character feel as if it's not under my control, but I can see how other people might connect more with their character that way.

- You *must* make their character relatable in their story, in gameplay, and in the wider context, otherwise all is lost.

OK, well now that we've exhausted the main psychological phenomena that can be introduced to favour the player in virtual worlds, let's move on to some others….

23.2 NATURAL, DISFAVOURING THE PLAYER

These effects are going to be present whatever you do. As natural occurrences that follow from gameplay, they're rarely problematical. However, they're easy to exploit in unnatural ways so as to favour the developer at the player's expense.[14]

23.2.1 The Framing Effect

In Psychology, *framing* refers to the way that something is presented; the *framing effect* concerns how presenting the same information in different ways can affect how people act on that information (Tversky & Kahneman, 1981). It's related to the more general idea of *priming*, whereby advance information affects performance at a task (Beller, 1971).

Suppose you have two participants chosen at random to play what economists call a game. They are told that there's a small amount of money (50 cents) on offer. One of the participants has to decide who gets it. If you tell that participant they can "steal" the money from the other participant, some 29.5% of participants will still give them it; if you tell them they can "boost" the other participant with the money, only 5% of them will give them it (Capraro & Vanzo, 2019). Put another way (that is, reframing the results), 71.5% will steal and 95% will decline to boost. Even though the monetary results described are the same, loaded words can frame the options differently and influence decisions and conclusions.

The framing effect manifests itself in two main ways: positive/negative framing and relative/absolute framing.

In positive/negative framing, people will look at an option put positively more favourably than the same option put negatively. Positive framing emphasises gains; negative framing emphasises losses. Lottery companies tell you that you *could* win millions; they don't tell you that you *will* definitely lose your stake. Shops tell you that there's 20% off the price of their haberdashery, not that they will no longer charge you 25% more for it.

In relative/absolute framing, people will look at an option stated in a relative fashion more favourably than the same option put in an absolute fashion. If you tell people that they have a 10% chance of dying next year and offer them medication A (which reduces their risk of dying by 80%) and medication B (which prevents eight deaths in every 100 sufferers), most will choose medication A – even though the outcomes are identical for both (Malenka et al., 1993).

Framing effects are inevitable in virtual worlds. They're also fairly easy to organise for your own purposes.

Suppose that you want to implement the idea that if a character doesn't eat then its health will suffer. Initialising a character's health to 100 and telling the player it will drop

---

[14] Literally: it could cost them money.

by 20% if they don't eat will not be received well – it's a negative framing. However, initialising the character's health to 80 and telling the player it will rise by 25% if they do eat will be looked on as a bonus – it's a positive framing. They amount to the same thing, though. Presenting debuffs as buffs allows the designer to get many ideas past players that they wouldn't ordinarily accept.

Similarly, suppose that a player is given a quest reward of a sword that does 20 hit points of damage against most things but 21 hit points against giants. Telling them it's +1 against giants will not impress them as much as telling them it's +5% against giants.

Relative framing usually results in a better reaction than absolute framing. I say "usually" because while positive/negative framing almost always works in virtual worlds, relative/absolute can reliably fail in certain circumstances. In particular, when big numbers are involved, players will be attracted towards them. A sword that's +800 against giants might swing a player's opinion in its favour over one that's +5% against them, even if the base damage is 20,000 and +5% is therefore better. If you want to use relative/absolute framing, be aware that it's not a given that it'll work as hoped.

A special case of the framing effect is *anchoring* (Tversky & Kahneman, 1974). When estimating values, probabilities, or pretty well anything, different starting points yield different results. If you give a group of people five seconds to estimate $1 \times 2 \times 3 \times 4 \times 5 \times 6 \times 7 \times 8$, the average of what they come up with will be much less than if they were asked to estimate $8 \times 7 \times 6 \times 5 \times 4 \times 3 \times 2 \times 1$; this is because the first multiplication starts with a lower number than the second one.

Now clearly *something* has to come first when you give a list, so as a designer you're stuck with anchoring whatever you do. That being the case, it's hard not to take advantage of it. If you want to encourage people to think they have an object that's pretty good, put it in a list where manifestly worse objects come first. If you want to encourage people to buy an object, put it in a list of similar objects with over-priced examples first. The first items anchor what follows. Note that people who are price-conscious may look at the bottom of the list as well, so get two framing points. They are therefore more likely to choose something from the middle. This explains why the highest mark-up on wines in restaurants tends to be on the median one (de Meza & Pathania, 2021).

23.2.2 Scarcity Effect

Back in the days when experimental variability due to gender was removed by experimenting on people of only one gender, Worchel et al. (1975) presented 146 female students with a can of mints, a pack of cigars, and a glass jar containing chocolate-chip cookies. Each participant was told that this was going to be a consumer preference study and she was to rate her preference for each one, starting with the cookies (the other two items were only there to add credence to the purported nature of the experiment[15]). Some of the participants saw a cookie jar with two cookies in it and some saw one with ten. Also, after all the procedure had been explained, for some participants, the number of cookies was increased from two or decreased from ten, for reasons that were explained as being accidental or because other

---

[15] Cigars weren't widely understood as being lethal back in 1975, much as cookies aren't today.

people being tested had eaten or rejected the cookies. The participants then got to sample a cookie and rate it. The results of the experiment indicated that: cookies in scarce supply were rated as more desirable than ones in abundant supply; when the cookies' supply went from abundant to scarce, they were rated higher than when they were scarce the whole time; cookies that were scarce because of supposed high demand were rated higher than cookies that were scarce supposedly by accident.

People place more value on objects or experiences that are rare than similar ones that are common. Economists, psychologists, and sociologists have proposed a number of explanations as to why this is the case (Lynn, 1992), but the point is that it *is* the case, which means it can be used to influence behaviours.

Obviously, virtual worlds are going to have some scarcity by default. Even social worlds need an economy, and without scarcity, there'd be none. For game worlds, there would be no competition without something over which to compete, which is why designers keep resources limited rather than giving them out for free to anyone who wants them. It can lead to better gameplay.

It can also lead to better profits if you make things scarce deliberately so you can sell them at a premium. Artificial scarcity is one of the main reasons players don't like non-fungible tokens in games. Price-fixing by limiting supply so as to increase demand is normally frowned-upon, but that doesn't stop the Organisation of Petroleum Exporting Countries cartel from doing it – and it doesn't stop virtual world designers from creating limited-edition versions of items that would be easier to make be unlimited, either.

They don't even have to be limited editions. The developer merely has to increase the unit price each time an object is sold and that in itself will serve to limit the number of such objects there are in circulation. Holding back a day before raising the prices will add an extra dimension to it (*loss aversion*, which we'll come to shortly).

Note that objects don't have to *be* scarce for the scarcity effect to kick in; they merely have to be *perceived* as being scarce. In 1974, the UK experienced a salt shortage as people panic-bought the stuff in the belief that there was a salt shortage. There was no shortage in either sense (UK Parliament, 1974): enough readily accessible salt rested underground in Cheshire to last a million and a half years, and salt packers and distributors were easily able to meet demand after the initial shock. I don't suppose that a virtual world developer would be unprincipled enough to lie about, say, how many beta keys they were giving away, but you never know….

23.2.3 Dunning-Kruger Effect

The *Dunning-Kruger effect* is the tendency of those who aren't very good at something to overestimate how good they are at it (Kruger & Dunning, 1999). There's also a tendency of those who are very good at something to underestimate how good they are at it, although for different reasons (Dunning, 2011); in essence, overestimators overestimate because they're ignorant of their own ignorance, whereas underestimators underestimate because they're ignorant of everyone else's ignorance.

In virtual worlds, this often manifests itself in competitive play. For example, if you do a lot of PvE then you might become very good at it. You can lead your raid group and take down high-end bosses with ease. However, the moment you put one foot into a PvP zone, you're beaten to a pulp. You miscalibrated your PvP skills. You might also miscalibrate your PvE skills, though, believing that because everyone else you meet in the upper echelons is accomplished, most other players are too and you're not particularly special.[16]

This is a natural occurrence in virtual worlds, but as a designer, you can exacerbate it. If you continually tell a player how good they are and how wonderful they're doing, and have NPCs fawning over their character's glory, the player will be inclined to credit these assertions with some degree of truth. When they thereupon get into a group and discover that other players are manifestly better than they are, they'll suffer cognitive dissonance (Festinger, 1957): their beliefs are telling them one thing, but their experience is telling them something else. They can remedy this by changing their beliefs, of course, but a small number of people are strangely unwilling to do that: clearly, they think, their experience must be wrong. Those other players obviously have special advantages – they probably paid to win! The obvious solution is therefore to bite the bullet and buy some boosters and high-powered gear yourself, to level the playing field. Sure, you could quit, but you're not a quitter!

Thus, by buttering up players to give them the impression they're well above average in skills when in fact they're well below average, developers can deploy a natural phenomenon to their financial advantage.

23.2.4 Illusory Correlation

An *illusory correlation* is the belief that two variables correlate when in fact they don't (Chapman, 1967). It underlies a lot of superstition (carrying a rabbit's foot will not make you lucky[17]), but it follows from human beings' natural pattern-matching abilities. If you spot that something often occurs in conjunction with something else, it would be hard not to hypothesise that the two events are related. They could indeed be related ("Every time I use the word 'awry', people chuckle; am I mispronouncing it?"). Then again, they could be unrelated ("I spray eau de Cologne around my property every spring to keep wild elephants away."; "But … there aren't any wild elephants in these parts."; "Yes, it's very effective.") or appear to be related until the correlation breaks ("This coin comes up heads every time I toss it, look! Oh. Well it did the previous five times."). If a correlation fails after a period of success, it's sometimes treated as a general rule of thumb (in a General Studies exam I once sat, I described my uncanny ability to lock doors merely by attempting to open them; I got an A for it[18]).

As the elephant and General Studies examples show, obvious illusory correlations can be played for laughs. "Have you all seen that incredibly powerful commercial where every time a famous person clicks their fingers, a child dies? I was watching that, I couldn't help thinking, 'Stop clicking your fingers!'" (Carr, 2005). However, it's also possible to put the effect to other uses.

---

[16] I see this kind of thing with my own PhD students: they may be one of the country's top 100 experts in their field, but because they know 20 of the others, they don't think this amounts to much.

[17] This is easy to dismiss because rabbits carry four such feet, yet one of the creatures was still unlucky enough to lose one.

[18] Sadly, I got letters later in the alphabet for the other papers in the suite.

There's a storytelling principle, *Chekhov's gun*, which states that every component of a story should be necessary and that unnecessary components should be removed. It's so named because it was the view of the author and playwright Anton Chekhov that "every work of literature should theoretically be a *system* of interconnected elements in which nothing can be replaced by anything else; otherwise, the entire system collapses" (Bitsilli, 1983). Chekhov illustrated this with the point that if a story mentions a gun then ultimately the gun must go off.

In MMOs, if players find an object then they want to categorise it. Is it a weapon? Piece of armour? Quest component? Consumable? Pet? Cosmetic item? This isn't unexpected: it's a natural aid to understanding. What if the object doesn't fit one of their expected categories, though – or does, but has something unusual about it? Well, under the Chekhov's gun rule, such an object must have *some* purpose. Non-Explorers will be inclined to hit the search engines to find out what that purpose is.

The thing is, it doesn't *have* to have a purpose – at least in gameplay terms. That won't stop the players from conjecturing as to what its purpose might be, though. If you have it make an appearance partly at random, or have it disappear after a random period, players will attempt to figure out the cause. What they don't know is that if they find something plausible, it'll be a false correlation. This is because the designer deliberately put the object in simply to get players (mainly Explorers) talking about it and speculating as to what it does. If there are several such objects, players will attempt to connect their meanings together. As a result of this, the impression is given that the virtual world is more complex than players know. What's more, new Explorers will learn that there are still unsolved mysteries they can try to crack.

Don't believe me? If you came across a piece of tin with the number 1 stamped on it, then later came across one with the number 2 stamped on it, and occasionally found other pieces of tin with the numbers 3–12 stamped on them, except that there was no piece of tin with the number 7 stamped on it, don't tell me you wouldn't want to know where tin #7 was. It's nowhere, though: those are just pieces of metal that you sell to vendors just like any other piece of metal. You were expecting tin #7, but its hinted-at existence was merely a ruse to keep you playing.

Now you might think that this is far-fetched, but it's not. It happened all the time in textual worlds, originally by accident but later on purpose. In *MUD1*, the theories that players themselves put together to explain odd objects were known as *legends* or, if exceptionally complex, *myths*.[19] For examples, see the definitions in the *MUDspeke Dictionary* (Bartle, 1992) for "B-29", "moose", "bandstand", and "magic train". Now adding curiosities deliberately to pique the interest of players and get conversations going is somewhat cynical, and it's perhaps not going to be as effective in a large-scale world, but it nevertheless shows that encouraging false correlations does have its uses. Given that modern MMOs don't need to render inventory items in 3D, they just have to create an icon and a line or two of text, they're almost as inexpensive to add as they were in the first three Ages of virtual worlds.

---

[19] Noticing patterns is an important human trait. If they happen not to exist, it's called *apophenia*.

False correlations will arise naturally in virtual worlds, simply because they have so many objects and locations that players will seek deeper connections between them regardless of whether they exist or not. Consciously inserted non-obvious false correlations are not for the players' immediate benefit, though.

23.2.5 Zeigarnik Effect

Back in the 1920s, the German psychologist Kurt Lewin noticed that waiters seemed to remember unpaid orders far better than paid ones. The *Zeigarnik effect* is named after his colleague, Bluma Zeigarnik, who investigated the phenomenon and worked out its psychological mechanism (Zeigarnik, 1932).[20] She showed that people remember and are nagged by tasks they've started but not finished.

This happens in ordinary life, but it also happens in virtual worlds. If you have a quest to collect X items, you won't willingly stop when you have X-1. When you finally obtain the last one, it *is* enjoyable – but in the same way that stopping hitting your head with a hammer is enjoyable. Of course, as soon as you hand the quest in, you'll be given another one that you now want to complete before you go to bed. It's the "just one more turn" phenomenon seen a lot in turn-based strategy games.

The Zeigarnik effect is a natural occurrence in virtual worlds. However, it's not difficult for designers to ensure that it occurs more often than it otherwise might. As for why a designer would want to do this, well it can encourage people to play for longer periods, which makes the virtual world look and feel busier. In a subscription game, it can also give players the sense that they're getting their money's worth. Furthermore, if potential players see how many hours actual players are spending playing, that could suggest to them that the virtual world is good. In addition, many investors associate player-hours with a virtual world's health as it's an indicator of retention. You want investors, don't you?

Needless to say, if you somehow knew that players don't actually *like* that whole killing-mobs-until-the-RNG-deigns-to-make-one-drop-the-thing-they're-collecting experience, you can always offer them the option of paying real money to complete a quest immediately. That would be a reason to call on the Zeigarnik effect to help. I'm sure no designer would be so unscrupulous as to do that, though. No sirree.

23.2.6 Social Comparison Theory

Social comparison theory states that there exists in each human being a drive to evaluate their opinions and abilities, and that when objective measures aren't available (which is most of the time), people rate themselves by comparing their opinions and abilities with those of others (Festinger, 1954). The more that someone is different from you, the less likely you are to use them as a benchmark.

There's a lot more to the theory than this, but from our perspective, the upshot is that people want to maintain a positive self-evaluation, influenced by their relationships with others (Tesser, 1988). This isn't something specific to virtual worlds, it goes on all the time,

---

[20] This is an English translation. The original paper, which is in German and therefore beyond my comprehension, is Zeigarnik (1927).

but there are two main ways that it can be taken advantage of by designers who have that mindset. These depend on whether the player is trying to improve their own self-evaluation or to align it with someone else's.

In the first category, you can encourage people to share their achievements on social media. If you do this directly, with some kind of "share" button, it can feel a little like boasting (because it is); this can put players off. It's even worse if it comes with an invite to play the virtual world in question. You can do it indirectly, though, which helps the player but also helps you with free publicity; people who follow it up are basically taking the Crossing the First Threshold commitment step of the Hero's Journey.

A common method to give players an excuse to share their success is to use the tried-and-trusted idea of *leaderboards*. People who are at the top can casually mention this either within the virtual world or without, and it doesn't involve spamming acquaintances with unwanted messages. You have to be careful with them, though, as they can be counter-productive. In my experience, entrepreneurs are keen to say "imagine being number one out of a million players!", but are shocked when asked to imagine being number three hundred and twenty-two thousand, six hundred and eighteen out of a million players. This is why designers show leaderboards for smaller groups, such as friends lists or guilds. Such an approach has a name: *big fish, little pond* (Madigan, 2016), and it works much better than server-wide lists do. It can still backfire in some circumstances, though. For example, in *The Secret World*, I was the second-biggest fish in my cabal (guild); I didn't realise until just before I quit that I was a top-50 fish in the entire virtual world, and would have been even higher if I'd drunk any of the XP-boost potions that came with my subscription (XP gains were factored into the rating system even for characters at the XP cap).

Yes, that last sentence there was an example of an attempt to improve my own self-evaluation.

It's possible to help out players (and yourself) here by creating automated newspapers that summarise guild or friendship group activities over some period, say a week. Players like to see their names in print with reference to having done something of which they can be proud, or that at least that might amuse their chums. Even "gossip of the month" for having spoken the most words could bring a warm glow (just don't make it a formal achievement, or achievers will spam the chat channels to add it to their collection). Personalised stories are also possible (Blizzard's Warcraft Story idea (Blizzard, 2022) is an attempt at this), but while good for ego-stroking they're less good for community strengthening. Server-wide messages informing all players that someone has done something special will also play into it, but can be demoralising for those not mentioned: I had many server firsts for *Rift* simply because I was one of the first players on the server, but later players stood no chance of attaining them. *Throne & Liberty*'s announcements that someone has obtained rare gear are better as they can happen to anyone, although they're somewhat irritating because of their frequency.

What's happening here is a kind of symbiosis. You're giving players the opportunity to share good things about themselves in a manner that doesn't come across as self-aggrandising; they're making your virtual world more attractive while spreading the word that it's a fun place to be – even if that's only within the virtual world itself. This aspect of social comparison theory is win-win, so long as you give players the option of not participating.

Hmm, so do you make the default opt-in or opt-out?

This brings us to the second aspect of social comparison theory: upgrading your opinions to match those of people whom you perceive to be higher up the social scale than you are while still being relatively close. The thing is, the default settings offered by dialogue boxes tend to count as just such people – even though they're not actually people. They represent what your peers think.

Thus, if you wanted people to opt in to some kind of automated activity-sharing message system, you would do it like in Figure 23.2.[21]

What you wouldn't do is opt them in or out without telling them, because then people would complain that you chose the wrong default (for them). Actually asking them, with the default being what you want it to be, will avoid this while improving take-up.

You'll notice I used the framing effect to compound the suggestion in the above example. Manipulative psychological techniques don't have to be stand-alone.

23.2.7 Sunk Cost Fallacy

A *sunk cost* is an amount you've paid that has no effect on future decisions. Victims of the *sunk cost fallacy* treat it as if it did (Arkes & Blumer, 1985). It happens in everyday life when people throw good money after bad and won't cut their losses.[22]

It's in virtual worlds, too, of course. It's one of the reasons that people will keep playing when they've basically finished. "My character won't be as good if I quit!"; "I'll lose the €8 I spent on that fancy outfit!". It's why, having failed to craft a legendary item on the previous 17 attempts, you'll try again. It's why you'll keep fighting your way to a treasure chest, even though you're sustaining heavy damage that will cost you more to repair than there's money in the chest.

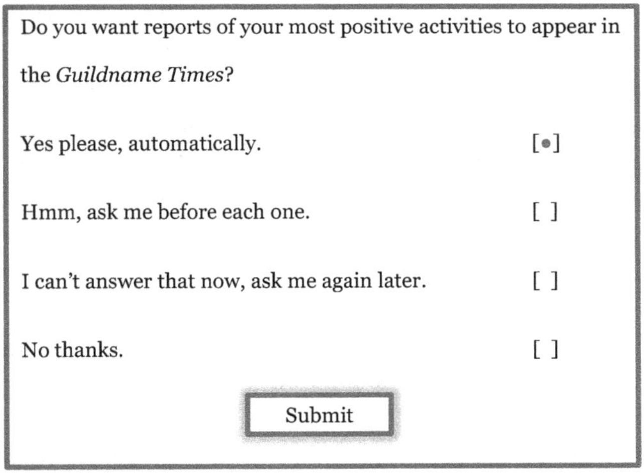

Do you want reports of your most positive activities to appear in the *Guildname Times*?

Yes please, automatically.	[●]
Hmm, ask me before each one.	[ ]
I can't answer that now, ask me again later.	[ ]
No thanks.	[ ]

Submit

FIGURE 23.2   Automated activity-sharing message system.

---

[21] Modulo your far superior graphic design skills and basic knowledge of the principles of user interface design.

[22] The fact that these two well-known idioms exist suggests that the effect has been known implicitly for a long time.

Designers can exploit this, of course. For example, a player might continue playing if their house would decay were they to quit, but they might stop playing entirely if it wouldn't. If the aim is to keep players playing, decay is going to be a thing.

The sunk cost fallacy underlies some habit-forming behaviours, such as raiding when it's no longer fun. In that regard, it can be considered sticky. Stickiness is normally good, but is it if the player really ought to quit but you're emphasising how much they'd lose (or fail to gain) if they did?

This leads us to the related (and more general) concept of *loss aversion*.

23.2.8 Loss Aversion

In a games context, *loss aversion*, also known as *fear of loss*, sounds as if it's to do with not liking it when you don't win, but that's not the case. Loss aversion concerns not liking it when you lose something that you already have or are expecting to have (Kahneman & Tversky, 1984). Importantly, "losses loom larger than gains" (Kahneman & Tversky, 1979): people feel losses roughly twice as heavily as they do gains (Thaler, 2000).[23] If you lose something worth $1,000 then you won't be back to your previous level of material well-being until you gain something worth $2,000. Therefore, if you were a scheming designer who wished that people would play your virtual world for longer, you could occasionally arrange for the loss of a desired object that it took X hours to obtain, safe in the knowledge that the player will want to play for X hours recovering it and another X hours getting something else they want before they'll feel comfortable again.

Losing something is very common in games, because players work towards fragile goals (an item, an alliance, a place on a leaderboard, …). If you reach your goal and then it's taken away, or you're about to reach it and are then prevented from doing so, you really won't like it. You'll therefore hold onto items of value you don't want to lose, for fear of wasting them. Loss aversion is why you kept that potion of win-this-fight right until the end of the game without ever using it. It's why you didn't socket that rare gem into your current-best weapon. It's why you didn't spend those hard-won reward coins on something you wanted in case something you wanted more came along. Designers can give you these one-off power goods to fill up your inventory space, because although some players will indeed use them at an opportune moment, there are many who are very loss-averse and won't. They'd rather pay real money to expand their inventory space than actually use the one-shot powerful item you gave them. That's convenient if selling inventory space is part of your revenue model.

Money doesn't have to be involved in employing loss aversion against the player's best interests. Suppose an MMO sets a limit of 25 daily quests[24]: players will feel that they're losing out if they don't complete the full 25 (Hamari, 2011). Not only are the daily quests encouraging them to log in every day, but if 25 is attainable then they'll try to do them all (thanks, Zeigarnik effect!). This will mean they'll have less time for expensive

---

[23] This is the paper usually cited for this assertion, because it explicitly states "Losses hurt about twice as much as gains make us feel good". The evidence for it is the steepness of curves on a graph in Kahneman & Tversky (1979).

[24] *WoW* raised the daily quest limit from 10 to 25 in patch 2.4.0 (25 March 2008); the cap was removed in patch 5.0.4 (28 August 2012).

content-consuming play, and the appearance will be maintained that the virtual world is a busy whirl of activity.

A further aspect of loss aversion concerns risk and reward. People prefer guaranteed gains over risky gains, but risky losses over guaranteed losses (Thaler, 1980). Suppose you were offered two options: option A gives a 33% chance of receiving $1,500, a 66% chance of receiving $1,400, and a 1% chance of receiving $0; option B gives 100% chance of receiving $920. Would you choose option A or option B? Most people would choose option B, even though probability theory tells them they really should go for option A. That 1% chance of receiving nothing dominates their calculation. Of course, *you* wouldn't make use of this information to slow down players' progress or to sell them less for the same amount of money, even though designers with a weak conscience might.

When a new player starts a virtual world, they're often given lots of (non-tradeable) free stuff. Why is this? Is it just the designer being nice and welcoming by handing out gifts? Possibly, but it rather depends on the gift. If the player isn't even aware of what the gifts do, because they haven't been told about them yet, then they won't want to quit because they'll lose them without ever getting their benefit.

Another sneaky trick is to give the new player a stash of special coins that can be used to buy some nice consumables or cosmetic items. The player is given these coins regularly, so begins to think of them as easy to come by. Then, when they're well on their way to saving up for that cute rideable panda that's calling to them, the special coins dry up. Now they arrive in only a trickle. Of course, you can always buy some more for real money if you have your heart set on the panda. This technique causes the player to feel that they've lost their grip on the item they want to buy, which aggravates them; offering the prospect of obtaining it for "only" a few real dollars is therefore tempting to many of them.

Knowing about loss aversion *can* be helpful for pro-player reasons. For example, designers could account for it when balancing game systems, especially the economy; in practice, though, the effect isn't large enough to make much difference in comparison to other methods. Mainly, if a designer takes advantage of loss aversion then it's because they don't mind taking advantage of players.

23.3 UNNATURAL, DISFAVOURING THE PLAYER

The final category of psychological techniques that I've arbitrarily partitioned off from the others are those that work against the player without being a natural part of virtual worlds' make-up (except perhaps in a mild form). They don't *have* to be there, so if they are then it's very likely that someone put them there deliberately.

Now, it may be that the bad design you're looking at is an experiment that didn't work out, or the result of actions by an inexperienced or none-too-bright designer. Such non-aggressive techniques are called *anti-patterns* (Zagal et al., 2013); they aren't considered here, as they're usually one-offs. However, it might instead be the case that there's a modicum of general deception going on, such as the employment of misleading language. These techniques are known as *dark patterns* (Zagal et al., 2013) or *deceptive patterns*;

most of them are common across the Internet[25] and so are also not considered here – see Brignull (2023) if you want the gory details.

What *is* considered here is the intended use of techniques from Psychology in systematic ways that serve some purpose not in the player's best interests.[26] Examples of what "not in the player's best interests" are include (Brignull, 2023): financial loss, time loss, unintended contracts, privacy loss, loss of consumer autonomy, and psychological harms (including loss of freedom to think).

Although academics regard these as being further examples of dark patterns (albeit perhaps more egregious than most), designers employ a more specific term: *cheap psychological tricks*. The phrase has been around for a long time, originating in the 1930s,[27] but it came to prominence when games for social networks began exploiting such tricks to the full; it received a further boost when many examples of gamification adopted similar tactics.[28]

Let's take a look at some cheap psychological tricks, then.[29]

23.3.1 Counterintuitiveness

Something is said to be *counterintuitive* when its behaviour doesn't align with what seems natural or correct. I know you know that, but I thought I should state it anyway in case you thought it was a technical term used by Psychology.

Counterintuitiveness in virtual worlds does have valid uses, especially in making an artistic point. Designers generally wish to avoid it, though, as it implies some degree of unrealisticness (a concept we'll look at in Volume II).

Deliberately making something counterintuitive can bring in lots of money. It can also cost lots of money if regulators find out about it. In 2022, the Federal Trade Commission of the United States fined Epic $245,000,000 for using illegal dark patterns in *Fortnite* (Federal Trade Commission, 2022). Among the tricks they employed were (Khan et al., 2022):

- "The button to purchase items on video game consoles is also the same as the button associated with other actions that do not result in the user incurring a charge".

- "On PlayStation consoles, the button to purchase Cosmetics is 'Square' and the button to preview styles is 'Cross.' However, these buttons are inverted for Battle Passes".

- "Consumers have complained that they did not see the option to cancel due to Epic's efforts to obscure it".

---

[25] For an ongoing litany of examples, see Leiser et al. (2010). For a taxonomy of the techniques employed, see Mathur et al. (2019).

[26] Unless, that is, you count "this virtual world cost us money to develop and costs money to operate, so if you regard playing as being in your best interests then our attempts to extract money from you are also in your best interests".

[27] For example (with reference to a form of religious ministry): "It exalted a selfish individual salvation – 'O that will be glory for me!' with an emphasis on the 'me'. It used cheap music and cheap psychological tricks" (Palmer, 1935).

[28] There's a 1996 self-help book called *Cheap Psychological Tricks* that may also have had an influence, but I haven't read it so shan't be citing it here.

[29] Not all of them, because some are so powerful to be weaponisable. This isn't a joke.

- "Epic deliberately requires consumers to find and navigate a difficult and lengthy path to request a refund through the Fortnite app".

Epic was also censured over button-placement in the *Fortnite* app for buying cosmetic items: the button for "preview styles" was located between the buttons for "purchase" and "buy as a gift", making it easy to hit one of the others by mistake. The "purchase" button was highlighted, too. If a player did hit it by accident, there was no confirmation required and the sale went through immediately.

OK, so that last example isn't to do with being counterintuitive, it's a more general tactic seen in apps that hope to take advantage of users' dumpy digits. I thought I'd mention it while I was here, though. Those who act unpleasantly rarely do so in only one dimension.

When something is counterintuitive, it confuses the player and leads to accidents and errors. If you want to do that for gameplay purposes, fine – but don't overdo it. If you want to do it to extract money from players, or to keep them playing for longer than they would wish, or to prevent them from doing something valid that you'd rather they didn't, consider other options. Dark patterns aren't called dark patterns for nothing.

23.3.2 Fear of Missing Out

The term *fear of missing out* came to prominence in Marketing (Herman, 2000) before Psychology adopted it, although it had been in casual use well before then.[30] It's been heavily applied to explain why people spend an inordinate amount of time on social media sites, with self-determination theory as its underpinning (Przybylski et al., 2013). In essence, it's the uneasy feeling you get that other people might have an enjoyable experience when (though not because) you're not present. The degree of "fear" it provokes is therefore more at the level of angst than terror, which is why fear of missing out doesn't attract much criticism on that basis.

This kind of thing can go on in virtual worlds, but it isn't a consequence of their design. It's been possible since the First Age, but was never really noticed by designers because its incidence was so infrequent and its effects were so low.

That isn't to say its incidence and effects *have* to be like that, though.

In November 2012, *RuneScape*'s combat system was upgraded in its *Evolution of Combat* (*EoC*) update. The older you get, the more you come to realise that "new and improved" usually means "new and worse than it was before", and this is what 19.62% of *RuneScape*'s players thought of the *EoC* (Jagex, 2012). Player numbers plummeted.

In June the previous year, Jagex had introduced a loyalty programme – basically a subscription that allocated some points each month that could be spent on mainly cosmetic items. This wasn't too unusual at the time, but what Jagex did in August 2013 (in response to lingering grumbles about the *EoC*) was: they increased the number of loyalty points you were given each month by an amount that depended on how many consecutive months you'd played. Miss a month and you reset the bonus.

---

[30] "The program is far too complicated for the average farmer to understand so some just let it go and others sign for fear of missing out on something" (Foster, 1936).

This system has been picked up for many games now, and goes by the general name of *loyalty streaks*. It works because of fear of missing out: if you don't log in, you'll miss out on all the bonus loyalty points you were going to get. It's not the same thing as the sunk cost fallacy, because it's not a fallacy. With the sunk cost fallacy, you regard what you've already spent as having an effect on future outcomes that it doesn't; with fear of missing out (as applied in virtual worlds), it actually does have an effect, or at least the promise of one.

Designers also introduce a fear of missing out by means of one-off events. These take place for a limited time only and issue rewards that can't be obtained any other way. Many players would attend the events anyway, but some who weren't intending to log in will be tempted to make an appearance for fear of missing out on the unique loot. As a bonus for the developer, those who nevertheless did miss out will be able to buy the unique loot in the cash shop a few months later.

In a similar vein, we have *battle passes*. First gaining widespread success in *DOTA 2*, these are optional purchases that unlock new content or challenges for a limited period – usually a month, but longer, seasonal ones are also popular. In that sense, they're basically sub-scriptions that come with goals (and associated rewards for achieving said goals). The rewards in battle passes are tiered, so if you want them then you have to complete the lower tiers before the later tiers (which tend to have the more desirable rewards). You can't ever get the fancy loot without buying the battle pass, though – and you can't experience all that the game has to offer, either. This introduces a fear of missing out. In conjunction with the reasonable idea that if you've paid for something then you want your money's worth, battle passes also encourage players to spend all their playing time progressing to the next tier, rather than on regular content (or, indeed, on other games). This appeals to many develop-ers. OK, so it diverts players away from their journey of self-discovery, but you don't care so long as it brings in money, right?

Fear of missing out lures players into spending more time (or money) (or both) playing a virtual world than they would like, so its main psychological ill-effects are the usual ones that concern excessive use of anything: depression and anxiety (Zendle et al., 2020).[31]

More interestingly, fear of missing out as it manifests in battle passes encourages feel-ings of elitism among those whose fear of missing out was justified in that they did indeed miss out (Petrovskaya & Zendle, 2020); it partitions the player base into the haves and have-nots (Johnson & Brock, 2020). Social network theory tells us that this is not good for the have-nots. Note that because battle passes run the gamut of content, all basic player types are affected even though their views as to what's meaningful to have are different. You can see why developers might like them.

23.3.3 Transaction Decoupling

This technique tends to be used in a very specific way, so forgive the sudden dive into mon-etisation practices.

---

[31] Also sleeping problems, suicide ideations, obsessions/compulsions, and alcohol/substance abuse, at least in Norway (Wenzel et al., 2009).

OK, so many virtual worlds sell virtual goods using a secondary currency bought for real money. Why would they do that rather than simply sell the goods for real currency directly? One reason could be that introducing real money into a virtual world hurts immersion. Another might be that the operators have the players' money in the bank for longer, which earns interest. The most compelling reason, though, is that by putting distance between the painful act of spending and the pleasurable act of buying, players can be more encouraged to do the latter. This is called *transaction decoupling* (Gourville & Soman, 1998).

Transaction decoupling has some relationship with the sunk cost fallacy in that if you've bought some in-world currency and not spent it all, you may buy more of it in order to do so (say if the cheapest item you want is 10 gemdollars and you only have 8 gemdollars). It's more insidious than that, though. Even with a clear, one-to-one conversion regime, it gives the player the impression that they're spending toy money rather than real money (which they've already spent, buying the toy money).

The conversion regime does not have to be an arithmetically easy one, although this may not fall within the designer's control anyway: the vagaries of the international currency market could play a part. At the time of writing, $10 or €10 will buy me 800 gems in *GW2*, but they'd cost a rather harder-to-work-with £8.50 if bought in the UK.

Prices can scale up either linearly or non-linearly. *FFXIV*'s crysta currency currently lets me buy: 500 for $5; 1,000 for $10; 2,000 for $20; 3,000 for $30; 5,000 for $50; or 10,000 for $100. No scaling there. *Albion Online*'s gold, on the other hand, is: 800 for $4.95; 1,700 for $9.95; 3,500 for $19.95; 9,000 for $49.95; or 19,000 for $99.95. That's somewhat harder to get your head around, but it's clear that the more virtual currency you purchase at once, the better deal you'll get.[32] The idea is to encourage people to buy more of it while making it harder to figure out what your holdings are actually worth.

The tougher it is for players to associate prices stated in virtual currency with real-currency values, the more likely it is that the player will spend their virtual currency. That's the theory, anyway. Developers persist with it, so I'm assuming that it does indeed work, but the experiments conducted by Salminen et al. (2018) don't support the idea that currency conversions lead to increased spending – only that players prefer to buy with different currencies depending on the perceived price of what they're buying. This is because the numbers themselves carry psychological weight. Huang et al. (2017) suggest that if you have a lot of a currency in terms of numbers (high numerosity) then you're more likely to buy inexpensive things with it than with a low-numerosity currency (so state prices in the virtual currency). For expensive items, though, the reverse applies (so state prices in fiat currencies). Basically, 8,000 gold feels more expensive than $100 because 8,000 is so much bigger than 100, whereas 8 gold is clearly less than 10c.

Transaction decoupling reduces the pain of paying for virtual goods because in effect you've already paid for them. When it comes to monetisation, though, there are other predatory methods in use, too (not all psychological in nature). We'll look at these in Volume II.

---

[32] This isn't *always* the case: at one point in 2023, 400 *GW2* gems would have cost me less than half of what I'd have had to pay for 800 (but only in £, not $ or €). I don't know why this was so, but suspect it was some kind of A/B testing to see if giving people a discount for buying low numbers caused more gems to be sold overall. Prices reverted to a linear scale some time afterwards.

23.3.4 Operant Conditioning

In *classical conditioning*, a neutral stimulus (such as the dinging of a bell) is paired with a meaningful stimulus (such as the arrival of food) that itself invokes a reflex response (such as salivating). After sufficient repetition, the neutral stimulus will invoke the response alone, without the accompanying meaningful stimulus. The effect is widely known because of the ring-a-bell, cause-salivation experiment that's been referred to as *Pavlov's dogs* since at least 1918.[33] *Operant conditioning* (Skinner, 1938), on the other hand, works on voluntary behaviours rather than involuntary, reflex reactions; it's also widely known because of the term *Skinner box* (which Skinner himself didn't like[34]).

The basic idea of operant conditioning is that there's some behaviour you want from a person, whether that's doing something ("eat healthily") or not doing something ("stop smoking"). When the person does what you want, you reinforce that behaviour. When they don't, you punish it.

Reinforcement comes in two forms: a *positive reinforcement* is when you get something good given to you for doing something (if you've been good all year, Santa will bring you presents); a *negative reinforcement* is when you get something bad taken from you for doing something (the car will continue its annoying beep until you wear your seatbelt). There's a special case of negative reinforcement called *active avoidance*, in which the desired behaviour itself acts as a reinforcement (if you want a trainee boxer to dodge punches, throwing punches at them will do that).

Punishments also come in two forms, matching those of reinforcement. A *positive punishment* is when you get something bad given to you for doing something (you were disruptive in class, so you get a detention); a *negative punishment* is when you get something good taken from you for doing something (you were disruptive in class, so you don't get to go on the school trip).

So far, so, er – well it makes sense, anyway.

Now, although you could deliver reinforcements and punishments every time the person you're conditioning acts, you don't have to: you can adopt different *schedules*. There are two parameters you can change: firstly, whether you reward or punish based on time (an *interval* approach) or based on actions (a *ratio* approach); secondly, whether you reward or punish after a set number of occurrences (a *fixed* approach) or after a random number of occurrences (a *variable* approach).

To be effective, punishments should be delivered "immediately, consistently, suddenly, at maximum value, briefly, and on every occurrence of the targeted behaviour" (Hineline & Rosales-Ruiz, 2013). That means a fixed delivery at a ratio of one punishment per punishable action.

Reinforcements are more interesting. Although they also need to be immediate, consistent, and valuable, they don't have to be brief and they don't have to appear on every

---

[33] "Cade and Latarget have performed similar experiments on human beings, and have found contrary to the case of Pavlov's dogs that the withholding of an appetizing morsel does not stimulate a flow of gastric juice, but often arrests it" (Fitch, 1918).

[34] I'd say I feel his pain because of the way that people refer to player types as "Bartle types", except I don't feel any pain at all about that.

occurrence. Furthermore, if they're not consistent (that is, they're variable rather than fixed) then they get a lower maximum response rate but a higher average response rate than if they are (Hodent, 2018).

Consider a machine that has a lever and a money dispenser. Money will not appear unless the lever is pulled. Whether it thereupon does appear depends on the reinforcement schedule:

- If it's fixed interval, every set number of seconds money will come out when you pull the lever. You're going to wait until the time is getting close, then start pulling the lever quickly until you get the money, then you'll stop and wait for the next tick. This gets the highest maximum response rate (you'll pull the lever fast, but only in short bursts).

- If it's fixed ratio, every set number of pulls of the lever will give you the money. You'll pull the lever the requisite number of times, collect the money, take a breather, then start again. This has a high response rate (you'll pull the lever a lot), but the post-reward pause takes the average down a bit.

- If it's variable interval then after a random number of seconds, a pull on the lever will give you the money. This has a moderate response rate, because you'll get the money once the time has elapsed, but you have no control over when that will be. You'll pull the lever steadily, but not necessarily often.

- If it's a variable ratio then after a random number of pulls on the lever, the machine will give you the money. You're going to pull the lever a lot, because it's based on pulls not time, and given that you could win on the very next pull you're not going to pause once you've won, either. This schedule gives the highest average response rate (number of pulls per minute).

Put another way (assuming one pull takes three seconds): "pull this lever after 60 seconds to get £1" results in fewer pulls than "pull this lever after a random number of seconds between 0 and 120 to get £1", which in turn is fewer than "pull this lever 20 times to get £1", with "pull this lever and there's a 5% chance to get £1" having the most pulls.

Variable-ratio reinforcement schedules are used by slot machines, because you get more lever pulls overall that way. If you're charging people per lever pull, it's going to produce the most profitable results.

We see all of these schedules for rewards in MMOs. Respawn rates for gatherable items such as plants and metals are usually fixed interval. Wait times for instances are effectively variable interval. Crafting items is generally fixed ratio. Loot dropped by killed mobs is variable ratio.

Whether you like it or not, you're going to have all four reinforcement schedules in virtual worlds, even in social ones. They're also ubiquitous in Reality, though, so I could have classified operant conditioning as "natural, disfavouring the player". That I didn't is because when it's used in an unnatural fashion it *heavily* disfavours the player.

Variable-ratio reinforcement schedules for rewards are very moreish. Moreish does not mean fun, though, and designers want people to play their games for fun, not for mind-controlled reasons. Putting deliberate variable-ratio reinforcement schedules for rewards into games *will* keep people playing, but not for fun. Many designers regard designing games around them as immoral,[35] but their employers might argue otherwise on the basis that they want a money mine.

As I mentioned in the previous chapter, rewards are associated with dopamine responses. Because operant conditioning makes great[36] use of rewards and players stick with them for extended periods, this explains why many psychologists regard virtual worlds as addictive. They may overstate the magnitude of the problem, but the thrust of their argument does hold true: operant conditioning can indeed lead to psychological problems for some players, and developers who knowingly use the technique above natural levels without taking precautionary measures are asking to be sued.

As for why you can't simply remove all reinforcement schedules from MMOs, consider what would happen if you gave items away (which is the end state). Players would treat dropped loot as a reward but they wouldn't treat given loot as a reward. If they could get upgrades to their equipment more easily by asking for a better item, that would short-circuit the core kill-stuff-to-get-loot loop and remove much joy from the game (Madigan, 2016). Reducing reinforcement schedules a *little* bit may be possible, but beyond a certain point, the core loop disintegrates and the MMO becomes a not-very-good social world.

Note that this short-circuit argument also applies to buying items for real money instead of obtaining them through gameplay. The more that players do it, the less game there is.

Operant conditioning is only usable on naïve players, because once they've learned the pattern, they avoid it – unless they're ensnared by it. As noted in Chapter 4, players don't like lockboxes: aversion to operant conditioning is one of the main reasons. Players' instincts are correct, too: there does seem to be an association between problem gambling and lockbox-buying (Griffiths, 2019); Belgium's Gaming Commission goes as far as to equate lockboxes (which it calls "loot boxes") directly with gambling (Federal Public Service Justice Gaming Commision, 2018). Operant conditioning is not fun.

That said, removing the causes of operant conditioning results in a virtual world that's even less fun. Aim for balance.

23.3.5 Profiling

People build up mental pictures of one another all the time, otherwise we couldn't have a theory of mind. When this picture is reduced to a few key variables important for some purpose, it's a *profile*. Detectives build up psychological profiles of criminals based on their behaviour[37] in order to figure out their character, interests, future behaviour, and (if not already known) identity.

---

[35] When Bill Mooney, general manager of *FarmVille* (Pincus & Skaggs, 2009), gave his acceptance speech for the inaugural GDC award of Best New Social Game, he was booed by the audience for inviting indie developers to join its developer, Zynga.

[36] "Great" in the sense of "much", not "good".

[37] Usually that of the criminals, but also possibly that of the detectives.

You will doubtless be aware that many companies keep personal data about you on file, if only because the instant you access any new website, you're presented with a pop-up demanding your consent for it to use said data. You'll also be aware that companies keep information about your activities, so they can show you things their algorithms think you might find interesting. Did you watch that video on Facebook about a weed-extracting tool? You must have been interested in it! Here, have some more. Have some for other garden implements. You're going to want a hand-held chainsaw, aren't you? You know you are. Here are five sellers hoping to sell you the exact same model.[38]

Virtual world operators collect information about what you do as you play. Every single keystroke and mouse movement is faithfully recorded and analysed. Originally, this was done for bug-fixing purposes, but it was soon employed for other pro-player purposes such as bot-detection and RMT identification. From there, it was but a short step to construct player profiles.

You might not mind some of the uses of these. If you often buy new cosmetic items for your characters, you could welcome sneak previews of new releases.

Hmm, so what if the virtual world suddenly gave you a free gift out of nowhere because you're such a valued customer? It's something you do actually like, because your profile tells the relevant software what it knows you like. Would you be happy with this?

What if you've only received the gift because data analysis has detected that your behaviour matches that of people who will consider quitting three to four weeks from now?

During play, you are constantly making decisions. This is a given for any game (navigating through decisions is the basis of gameplay, after all), but it also applies to non-game worlds. Do you take a risk for a potentially big reward or do you play it safe and get something less good but risk-free? Do you spend time crafting your own items or do you buy them from someone else? Do you follow a set routine or do you go where fancy takes you?

Of course, some decisions can be more to do with narrative. Do you side with the imperfect but well-meaning authorities or the rag-tag band of rebels? Do you seek out every piece of lore or only pick up the ones that are right there in front of you?

Other decisions might be related to personality. Do you avoid fighting certain kinds of mob or wade right in whatever they look like? Do you spend your gold pieces as soon as you get them or do you save them up for something better later? Do you quit at the same time every evening regardless or do you wait until you've finished the quest you started?

You can probably see where I'm going with this. Profiles compiled from the way you interact naturally with a virtual world can be used to assess your vulnerability to different cheap psychological tricks. You might be a sucker for scarcity but impervious to framing effects. You might be prone to illusory correlation but only occasionally consumed by the Zeigarnik effect. These vulnerabilities can then be targeted by bespoke interventions.

---

[38] After I read an article about why the song *We don't Talk about Bruno* (Miranda, 2021) became a hit, Facebook decided I was interested in Disney princesses. I have no interest in Disney princesses. Nevertheless, my feed was spammed with links to websites about them. As an experiment, I decided to click on every second one of these. I ended the experiment after six weeks, having managed to replace all ads for anything else in my feed with ads for clickbait sites featuring Disney princesses.

If a virtual world knows that you are the kind of person likely to pay to avoid difficult content, it can make content difficult for you – even if you haven't paid anything yet. Other people with profiles just like yours did, and so will you.

If a subscription virtual world knows you're a completionist and your subscription is about to run out, might those final few challenges turn out to be rather more time-consuming than normal?

If a virtual world knows you love playing with others but your healing is weak, so you're in danger of being dropped from your raid group, would it help if your heals were rolled-for twice and the bigger number taken each time?

I'm not suggesting that virtual worlds pull vulnerability-profiling stunts at present, but other games certainly do. There already exist virtual worlds, the entire purpose of which is only to occupy players while they're monetised or otherwise exploited in an underhand fashion. They tend not to last very long because people soon wise up to them, but by then, their developers have made their cash grab and don't care.

23.4 RESPONSIBILITY

It's easy to say that manipulative practices are problematic; the European Parliament certainly does (Maldonado López, 2022). All design is manipulative, though, and even the worst examples can be fully defended on artistic grounds if players are properly informed ahead.

As you may have gathered, I'm not a fan of cheap psychological tricks. As you may also have gathered, I'm not immensely rich, either. Whether you, as a designer, decide to put any of the ideas I've described here into your own virtual worlds is up to you. Some are good for players; some are bad but unavoidable; some are just plain bad. Whether they're bad for whoever pays your salary is a different story, of course. My only advice on the matter is this: you're not going to get to design many virtual worlds in your lifetime because the process takes too long; therefore, always think carefully about what you *do* design.

I've only listed here the most important of the psychological techniques that can be applied to virtual worlds – along with some lesser ones that you might find interesting – but this is just scratching the surface. There are myriad others, all of which can be used in benign or malign ways to greater or lesser degrees. Some techniques crop up more in virtual worlds than in regular computer games, but most are present in many forms of play and are extensible to games and virtual worlds alike (see Podini (2021) for a nice set of examples taken from *Undertale* (Fox, 2015)).

Ultimately, pretty well every human foible has an effect named after it in Psychology.[39] This isn't a book about Psychology, though: it's a book about the design of virtual worlds. The past few chapters have considered those who play such worlds, and it's now time for these chapters on Psychology to give way to a final, important chapter about something else that affects us all: player rights.

---

[39] I haven't checked, but my guess is that someone, somewhere, has dubbed this the *Psychology effect*.

CHAPTER 24

Rights

O NE OF THE TOPICS addressed in Chapter 9 concerned the general legal backdrop of virtual worlds. Rights are a particular instance of that (or, perhaps more accurately, the general legal backdrop is a particular instance of rights). I almost included a rights section in the same chapter, but decided to put it at the end of this volume because they're more important than that.[1] They're wishy-washy, and some of the implications look (and may well be) far-fetched; the problem is that some aren't, and it's not obvious which is which.

The rights I'm talking about here are of the inalienable and fundamental variety: you can't sign them away. Some legal concepts called "rights" you *can* sign away – the right to terminate a contract, for example – but there are powerful ones you can't. A clause in a contract that condemns you to servitude is worthless.

Virtual worlds are unusual when it comes to rights, because they weren't around when the primary conventions were signed. Human rights conventions are usually framed so as to protect the individual from the state; they're not very good at protecting individuals from each other or from state-like entities.[2] For virtual worlds, the rights of players therefore tend to be enshrined in the EULA, leaving the meaning of "rights" an ill-formed collection of human rights, constitutional rights, statutory rights, and whatever rights are generously granted by said EULA. The situation is complicated by the fact that rights in one territory (such as the EU) may be different from those in another (such as the United States). Furthermore, rights that apply to players might not necessarily apply to their characters. For example, Article 12 of the *European Convention on Human Rights* (European Court of Human Rights, 1950) declares that you have a "right to marry" – but does that mean your *character* does? If so, is that to another character or to a player? Do you have the right to marry your *own* character?

---

[1] The fact that a good many academics read only the first and last chapters of books and skim the rest (except for any parts they wrote themselves) was not a factor.

[2] We'll be looking at whether virtual worlds can be considered states or not in Volume II.

DOI: 10.1201/9781003689638-24

Players aren't the only parties involved, either. Designers, being on the whole human, also have rights. More importantly, these affect what rights remain available[3] for players. I shall therefore consider designer rights first.

24.1 DESIGNER RIGHTS

Most of the problems to do with rights come from competing rights.

As a point of general principle, designer rights trump player rights. This may seem strange, given that there's but one (lead) designer and possibly millions of players, but if they *didn't* trump them then the existence of virtual worlds – even social worlds – would be untenable. As we shall shortly see, players do have rights, but these often conflict with those of other players: "the players" is not a monolithic group of people who all think the same way. The one constant is that everyone signed up to play that which the designer designed, therefore the designer's rights are the dominant ones in conflicts between the two.

This is clearest in the case of rights of expression. Article 19 of the UN's *Universal Declaration of Human Rights* (*UDHR*) declares the "right to freedom of opinion and expression" and is usually interpreted very broadly. Everyone has a right to express themself, and most of us do exactly that in our everyday lives. If my self-expression ruins your play experience in a virtual world, though, then what? Well, if the designer is OK with it, hard luck you; if the designer isn't OK with it, hard luck me.

None of the 30 articles in the *UDHR* mention any "right to play". The word "play" doesn't even appear in it. The *Convention of the Rights of the Child* (United Nations General Assembly, 1989) does recognise in Article 31 (out of 54) "the right of the child to rest and leisure, to engage in play and recreational activities appropriate to the age of the child", which I suppose is a start. Even if people did have a right to play, though, that doesn't mean they have a right to play your virtual world. I have the right to play for the England football squad,[4] but if the manager doesn't select me then I can forget it.

As a consequence, you, as a designer (or operator) of a virtual world, can ban guilds or players for any reason, including (as Linden Lab famously put it) no reason.[5] It's your game.

You can also decide not to ban guilds or players. There may be uproar, but you don't *have* to ban guilds of Nazis if you don't want – especially if your setting was 1930s Germany. Most operators would try to avoid banning guilds that discriminated based on general, player-derived qualities such as language used (French-speakers only, English-speakers only), gender (male-only, female-only, some-other-only), sexuality (LGBTQ+-only, straight-only), RMT activity, …. However, as I mentioned in Chapter 20, in a bespoke world with heavy role-playing it might be that you permit in-context filters (male *characters*) but police out-of-context filters (male *players*).

Operators *do* need to be able to ban players, too, just as bars need to be able to ban customers and rare books shops won't even let you through the door if you look shifty (which

---

[3] I originally had "rights remain left" here, but fell afoul of English homonyms.

[4] Also, because I had a Scottish grandmother, the Scotland football squad.

[5] The terms of service for Second Life used to include this line in Section 2.6: "Linden Lab has the right at any time for any reason or for no reason to suspend or terminate your Account" (Caramore, 2008). The "no reason" provision has since been removed (Linden Lab, 2017).

I apparently did when I tried to enter one in Bath). Having the ability to kick out undesirables shouldn't, however, imply that everyone you do let play has been vetted and therefore that their in-world misdemeanours are the responsibility of the operator: if operators are made liable for what players say or do in their virtual worlds, the consequences are disastrous. We know this, because something similar happened in 1995 when a New York Supreme Court held that Prodigy was liable for user-submitted defamatory content on its network (Goldman, 2005). Crazy levels of self-censorship were the result. Fortunately, the situation changed nine months later when the US Congress enacted the Communications Decency Act, offering online companies very high levels of protection from the actions of errant users. Nevertheless, we're seeing the same old responsibility-ideas resurfacing today, as a consequence of having required social media companies to police their users (rather than requiring them to fund the police to police them). There's more on self-censorship in Volume II.

If you think I'm exaggerating the threat to freedom of design here, recommendation R (92) 19 adopted by the Committee of Ministers to Member States of the Council of Europe (Committee of Ministers to Member States, 1992) notes there are video games that "convey a message of aggressive nationalism, ethnocentrism, xenophobia, anti-Semitism or intolerance in general, concealed behind or combined with violence or mockery" and considers that "such games cannot be tolerated in democratic societies". It may date from 1992, but it's still fully in effect at the time of writing. I don't personally support any of the ideas it calls out, but I do support the right of designers to explore them. If the games in question are inciting hatred, yes, it's fair enough to prosecute their designers. If they're not, though? If they're making an artistic point?

24.2 THE COVENANT

If we want virtual worlds to thrive, their designers should have the freedom to design. That doesn't give them *carte blanche* to throw anything they conceive of at their players, though: there is a consent issue. If I start to play a virtual world that claims to be all about knitting, I can't complain if it features a lot of knitting. I can, however, complain if all of a sudden I'm asked to stab an NPC to death with knitting needles. I wasn't informed that this was a possibility when I started. Then again, I wasn't informed that I'd be asked to knit an edge-to-edge cable jacket/cardigan for women in cashmerino double-knit wool, either, but I can't legitimately complain about that. Let's examine why.

How do you know when you start playing a virtual world that you won't be asked or encouraged to do things you don't want to do? Or to be shown things you don't want to be shown? Designers can't tell you in advance what will or could happen, because that would spoil the game for you. That's why such revelations are called *spoilers*. It's a problem common to many experience goods – books, films, plays, magic shows, ... So how do you deal with it?

Well, you might not be able to talk about specific examples, especially if the outcomes are uncertain,[6] but you *can* talk about boundaries.

---

[6] First-time ball-game spectator: "You didn't tell me my team could lose!".

To be fair to the players, designers must create a set of general expectations as to where the moral, story genre, and gameplay genre boundaries lie for their virtual world. They then covenant with the players that even though they, the players (and possibly the designer, too), don't know what's coming up, it *will* fall within those boundaries. Although not quite in the same league as being locked up and tortured for your beliefs, a breaking of the covenant could under some circumstances be considered a human rights violation.

As a designer, you need to ensure that your design upholds the covenant you have with your players. This entails keeping the promises you made, whether these promises concern what you will do or what you won't do. You should also include warnings of what you *might* do. You are effectively vowing that what you are providing has value, has meaning, and makes sense within the boundaries you have established.

The covenant is initially stated implicitly or explicitly in publicity materials.[7] Ratings categories such as PEGI (Pan-European Game Information, 2003) can help standardise important aspects of it. In gameplay, the covenant is taught through tutorials and beginner quests – some of which, as we'll see in the next paragraph, could approach or even cross a boundary in order to mark where it is. The covenant is not a contract, because sometimes there are external reasons for breaking it (*Star Wars Galaxies*' New Game Enhancements broke the covenant but were implemented to shore up that virtual world's future); if you intend to break it, though, you have to warn the players – externally to the virtual world – that you're going to do so. If you don't, they have every right to excoriate you.[8]

In addition to external reasons for consciously breaking the covenant, there are legitimate internal reasons to break it temporarily, too, so long as you flag up what you've done. For example, in the *WoW* quest Zenn's Bidding, the player is asked to kill some creatures that they know they're not supposed to kill. If they do the quest, they're given a follow-up quest to do in penitence. This establishes where the boundaries of the behaviour expected of players in the Alliance faction lie; the follow-up quest cements this.

Other legitimate reasons for breaking the covenant include:

- Making an artistic statement.

- Making a non-artistic political statement.

- Reflecting changes in wider societal values.

For a more detailed examination of these issues, see Bartle (2012).

As a final point, if you don't *know* what you're promising the players, inform them of this fact. Whether you tell them why you don't know depends on whether such information would itself be a spoiler. That said, in many building-oriented social worlds, the main

---

[7] Kickstarter promises about the amount of content a virtual world will contain may be at times sketchy, but ones about the scope and nature of the virtual world help shape the covenant and so must be reliable.
[8] "What happens when those in charge are the offenders?" (Sim, 1994).

reason you wouldn't know what you were promising is that the virtual world relies heavily on the behaviour of other players; you can only promise the framework, not the content.

There is another up-coming reason, though: you may be using AI to generate content bespoke to each player. You have no idea whether the AI will create something banal or something profound, something inappropriate or something germane. You can try to manoeuvre it to sit within certain confines, but ultimately, the results are in the lap of the generative pre-trained transformer gods. For an example of how such individualised AI-driven content can work in a story context (if not a virtual world), see *The Waiting Room NYC* (Yandyganova, 2024).

24.3 PLAYER RIGHTS

Players often behave in ways that others contest. Early examples from *EverQuest* include (Pargman & Eriksson, 2005):

- **Kill-Stealing** – gaining experience points for killing a monster that wasn't yours to kill. Most modern MMOs tend to award everyone who participated in a fight all the available points, perhaps with convoluted rules designed to stop hangers-on from picking up XP or loot having contributed little.

- **Trains** – what result when a player is pursued by many mobs at the same time. If you gather a train and run to where other, unsuspecting players are loitering around, it's not good. The alert designer of today would probably put a limit on the number of mobs that can be in such a train.

- **Camping** – the name for the activity of waiting in place for a rare event to occur, such as the appearance of a particular mob. In the past, the social norm of "first come, first served" prevailed. That stopped when people started using bots to camp for them, as bots are not particularly concerned with adhering to the behavioural ideals of polite society.

- **Twinking** – the practice of over-gearing a character so that it's much more powerful than it ought to be for its level. It's particularly problematic in PvP. These days, the impact of twinking is reduced by limiting by level the gear that a character can use; it's nevertheless exacerbated by real-money trading and pay-to-win.

- **Automatic Play** – the use of macros to chain commands together efficiently. Today, you could add bots to the list and possibly specialised hardware such as an MMO mouse or a hands on throttle-and-stick (HOTAS) joystick.

- **Real-Money Trading** – spending real money to buy in-world objects or currency from other players. This has long been a bane; we'll be looking at it in Volume II.

The above is just a snapshot taken early in the Fifth Age of virtual worlds. These days, there are many more points of disagreement between players regarding what a virtual world is about; see the discussion on cheating in Volume II for further examples.

If players do things that other players don't like, either they can be left to dog-eat-dog themselves a solution, or some formal system of resolution should be put in place. Indeed, if the offences are of a sufficient magnitude, they may already be in place. As I stressed in Chapter 22: in disputes between the real and the virtual, Reality always wins. Reality can reach in to virtual worlds because virtual worlds are *consequent* on Reality; virtual worlds can't reach into Reality except through the actions of their players. If the law takes an interest, you must comply or face the ramifications.

Virtual worlds themselves do have laws (Mnookin, 1996b), of course, but these don't extend to Reality. Ultimately, the reason for this is that in Reality, law enforcement officers have access to the body of the player and can do things to it (such as imprison it); in virtual worlds, operators only have access to the body of the character, not the body of the player, so can't (Mnookin, 1996a).[9] Fortunately, virtual punishments are usually sufficient for controlling virtual characters, so recourse to the legal structures of Reality is not in general necessary (MacKinnon, 1997).

24.3.1 Character Rights

Players have rights because they're people, and people have rights. Their characters, by contrast, don't have rights. For example, players have a right to exist but their characters don't. As I mentioned in Chapter 9, this wasn't always obvious to those who wrote about virtual worlds in the Third Age, especially if they'd never played any ("First Amendment lawyers should be wary of applying current legal metaphors to the newer electronic communication spaces without substantially immersing themselves in the experience of using such cyberspaces" (Branscomb, 1995)).

The possibility that characters might have rights was arrested by Raph Koster's thought experiment, *A Declaration of the Rights of Avatars* (Koster, 2000),[10] which adopted the position that they did have rights then considered where that proposition led. It was based on France's *Declaration of the Rights of Man and of the Citizen* (Démeunier et al., 1789) and of the *United States Bill of Rights* (Madison, 1791). The first draft was not well-received: it was felt by designers to give players too much control. For example, "The community has the right to require of every administrator or individual with special powers and privileges granted for the purpose of administration, an account of his administration" – so I have to explain everything I do to anyone who asks? I don't think so.

Because of its origins, Raph's initial declaration was written in flowery, 18th-century English. He rewrote it in modern English as *Advice to Admins*[11]; in this form, it was not only more accessible but also more acceptable: it left open the door to ignoring any aspects of it that individual designers found unpalatable.

---

[9] Mnookin later went on to become Chancellor of the University of Wisconsin-Madison, although I don't expect that this is *entirely* due to her authorship of two of the earliest papers on virtual worlds that were written from a legal perspective.

[10] This text includes: the original *A Declaration of the Rights of Avatars* version; some of the comments that it elicited from designers; and the revised *Advice to Admins* version that resulted. For the original MUD-DEV post and associated comments, see Koster et al., (2000).

[11] *Advice to Admins* is the short title, based on Raph's flippant description of it as "advice to any mud admin who wants to keep his mud running and his players happy". The formal title is *A Declaration of the Rights of MUD Players, Common Language Version*.

Here's a summary of the essential points:

- Ultimately, someone has their finger on the power button.

- What this someone says, goes.

- If this someone doesn't provide a code of conduct for their virtual world then anyone playing there deserves all they get.

- If this someone wants to change the code of conduct, they should consult their players, but they can ignore whatever they are told.

- Codes of conduct should be fair and should be applied fairly.

Note that the "codes of conduct" referred to here are the sets of rules to which players are expected to conform. They're not rules to which the virtual world's operators are expected to conform (the equivalent of that is the *Advice to Admins* itself). They're not rules to which the virtual world's designers are expected to conform, either (the equivalent of that is the covenant).

The *Declaration* is important because it formally distinguishes between players and characters. Many non-players didn't understand this at the time, and even today, there are researchers who conflate, say, female characters with female players (so that disadvantaging female characters in some dimension is taken as disadvantaging female players). Perhaps the most notorious example of this in action comes from *A Tale in the Desert*, which is set in ancient Egypt. As part of an event in 2004, a new NPC trader called Malaki appeared: he would only sell his goods to male characters, and he treated female characters as if they were the slaves of male masters. A male character does not mean a male player (and a female character especially doesn't mean a female player), but that didn't stop the accusations of sexism.[12] Neither did the fact that the goods sold turned out to be worthless.

The *Declaration* is also important because it formally distinguishes between the virtual and the real. Scholars often treated the two as if they were the same, and many still argue that the magic circle (which would make them separate) doesn't exist (Consalvo, 2009). As we saw with Psychology's views on virtual worlds, it's strangely possible to accept that there's a difference between the virtual and the real yet still act as if there isn't. For example, many games routinely depict violations of international human rights law and international humanitarian law[13] (Castillo, 2009), most commonly by ignoring principles of proportionality (such as destroying civilian property) and by including torture or examples of cruel, inhuman, or degrading behaviour. Depicting violations isn't the same as

---

[12] In some equal-pay legislation, the argument is made that if a job is primarily undertaken by women then it merits equal pay with a job of equivalent value undertaken primarily by men. Using this "primarily" argument, it's possible to assert that because most female players play female characters, conditions affecting female characters do disproportionately affect women. Although most female players do indeed play female characters, there are many virtual worlds where in absolute terms most female characters are played by men; this may muddy the waters somewhat.

[13] Generalising: international human rights law is mainly about war and international humanitarian law is mainly about peace.

conducting them, but should we nevertheless stop all such depictions because they might cause players to take a "torture is OK" attitude into Reality?

Well no. You might want to depict the bad guys torturing someone precisely so we know that they *are* the bad guys. Artistic lines matter.

The *Advice* form of the *Declaration* doesn't threaten designers' autonomy, which is why designers of the day regarded it more favourably. Even so, they *must* adhere to the covenant if at all possible. Bugs merely show incompetence and are easily forgotten. Unethical behaviour shows a lack of principle, which stays in the mind much longer.

It should be noted that when players become fully immersed, such that they are their characters (and their characters are them), then their characters then *do* have rights – but only as players. If your character is killed, that doesn't mean *you* are. It might cause you severe distress, of course, but severe distress is not something people generally have a right to be protected from ("My rent has gone up, I'm distraught"). Because of the covenant, you *knew* what was possible either when you signed up or shortly thereafter (well before you became immersed); you can't therefore complain when the possible becomes the actual.[14] This is why breaking the covenant is so problematic: if someone is fully immersed, harming their character without their tacit consent could be traumatic for them and amount to assault.

This all assumes that what happens in the virtual world is player-agnostic. In Reality, you may feel picked upon if you're struck by a falling firework at an event, but you went there knowing that rockets have to fall somewhere and that this isn't a behaviour over which the organisers have full control.[15] If the virtual world is just doing its job, and neither knows nor cares whom it's tormenting, well that's a risk that the player agreed to accept. Deliberately persecuting a player individually is another matter, however: Article 21 of the *EU Charter of Fundamental Rights* (European Convention, 2000) states that people have a right to freedom from discrimination. If certain bad things happen specifically so as to *target* that player (and perhaps others caught collaterally), this would be something that *could* possibly violate the player's rights.[16]

There are arguments that players have rights in the virtual world beyond those that come with being in Reality. We'll look at these in Volume II, but I'll summarise the two main ones here.

Firstly, it can be argued that populations determine what rights they have. The constitutional rights of citizens of the Unites States were granted by "We, the people" (Washington et al., 1787). Unfortunately, this proposition only works if the population has sovereignty, which is not the case in virtual worlds: the developers and operators have sovereignty. Besides, most of the "population" is made up of NPCs anyway.

---

[14] Well, you *can* complain, just don't expect to get very far with it.

[15] My mother went to a firework display with her cousin once. She didn't have a good view because the person in front of her was too tall, so she asked her cousin to swap seats. He agreed, then seconds later a spent firework landed on his head.

[16] That said, suppose that someone with a fear of horses were to write to the operators of a horse-depicting virtual world asking that no horses be shown to them: to accede to such a request would open up virtual worlds to all kinds of cynical rights-based attacks by organised groups whose members didn't truly exhibit any of the fears claimed. Operators would therefore wish to be able to decline such requests without suffering any legal consequences.

Secondly, it can be argued that rights are granted by those who have power. Developers and operators have power because they can turn off a virtual world, but players also have power because they, too, can turn off a virtual world – simply by not playing. Operators implicitly acknowledge this fact by inviting players into their world, in so doing conceding that they have a need for them. Players are therefore in a position to insist on guarantees from the operators. Ultimately, players have rights because they wield the most power. This second argument is in line with Raph's analysis: the "right not to play" ultimately takes precedence.

In summary, then:

- Players have rights in the real world, of which the virtual world is a part.

- When considering rights, virtual worlds should only be thought of in terms of being a part of the real world.

- Administrators can take their ball home if they like.

- Players don't have to play ball if they don't want to.

In other words: if you don't like it, leave.

Let's look at some more specific rights next. Most of the principles that are described here were set out in the series of six State of Play conferences run by New York Law School between 2003 and 2009, usually (but not always[17]) from the perspective of the United States.

24.3.2 Right to Liberty

One undeniable human right that is of paramount importance is that of liberty. This doesn't mean that you can do anything you want, of course – you're not at liberty to change how gravity works in Reality. Rather, it's the absence of unrightfully exercised power (Mill, 1859). The question for virtual worlds is whether the power their designers and operators exercise is rightful or not. If (as Mill suggests) the only reason for the rightful exercise of power over a person against their will is to prevent harm to others, well what's the harm done to others by actions that are confined to virtual worlds? Would the "escape from a 1940s prisoner of war camp" setting I described in Chapter 14 be torpedoed if characters could simply walk out of the front door because of the right to liberty inherent in their players? It would spoil the fiction if that were possible, yes, but is that sufficient a level of harm to prevent such an action?

I would argue that in practical terms it doesn't matter. The player has consented to the exercise of power by playing; if they want to change their mind, they can stop playing. Besides, the harm involved in ruining someone else's pleasure is real, and breaking the fiction (and thence impeding immersion) is an example of this in action. It would be like telling someone who was reading a novel what the ending is. If the developer wants to prevent or to punish this kind of activity then the player's right to liberty is no defence against their doing just that.

---

[17] The fifth conference took place in Singapore specifically in order to make it easier for researchers with other perspectives to attend and to give presentations.

24.3.3 Property Rights

Along a similar vein, if the guards in the virtual POW camp couldn't confiscate your wire-snippers because of your property rights ("I bought those off another player for $20") then that would ruin the gameplay, too. I discussed property rights in Chapter 9; nevertheless, it's worth mentioning here that Article 17.2 of the *Universal Declaration of Human Rights* (*UDHR*) states that no one should be arbitrarily deprived of their property.

Hmm. On 28 December 2014, an *EVE Online* ship was attacked and destroyed, along with its cargo – 84 pilot licence extensions worth around $1,500 at the time. Was that loss arbitrary? Well it was part of the game, so I'd rather hope not, but then I'm not a human rights lawyer. Was it even property? The implementation gets to define what you're labelling as "ownership" means: you don't.

Some virtual worlds, *MUD2* included, have a "steal" command.

24.3.4 Moral Rights

Article 27.2 of the *UDHR* talks about *moral rights*. How this is interpreted depends on individual jurisdictions, but in general, players have certain rights of *attribution* (they can require that their work be recognised as being theirs) and of *integrity* (they can insist on the removal of any adulteration of their work). Given that graphical worlds show a stream of player-created characters the whole time, this could be a problem if a player were to get stroppy. The fix is easy, of course: kick the stroppy player out. Such a solution is harder in social worlds that have a lot of building, though: if someone has sold a thousand items and then claims that some patch has ruined the artistic integrity of those items, the resulting mess could prove much harder to resolve.

As I discussed in Chapter 9, intellectual property rights have for some time been in a steady state, but of course this could change with new laws or new interpretations of old laws. Importantly, while you might not have a right to ownership of "your" character, you do have a right to ownership of your identity (Crawford, 2004). Your reputation is just that: *your* reputation. As for what rights you have to ownership, in part or collectively, of the reputations and identities of any groups you're a member of, well that's a thornier problem; sure, it's not one limited to virtual worlds, but at least virtual worlds may be able to experiment with solutions in ways that wider society would find too risky to attempt.

24.3.5 Right to Security of Person

The security of the person usually means their physical security – their right to be free from violence, arbitrary arrest, and detention. Here, though, we're going to look at players' mental security – their right to be free from behaviours that cause them mental distress. Most of the ways this can happen are the same as in Reality, so we don't need to address them. One, however, is far more prevalent in virtual worlds: the effects of other players' role-playing.

Although the general tendency of virtual world players is to become their characters (so their character's identity and their own are the same), this isn't always the case. Some players like hard role-playing, keeping a distinction between their character and themself. This can confuse and upset other players, especially if they're hurt in some way by the character. Masquerading, as mentioned earlier, can also be very upsetting when it's discovered. Should role-playing of this kind be prohibited in some way, then, or at least partitioned off to its own server?

Well for a virtual world created for non-play purposes, such as training or therapy or education, perhaps it should be prohibited – but by the operators, not by the application of human rights laws. Players have a right to self-expression, and expressing oneself by pretending to be someone else[18] fits right in. Virtual worlds – especially MMORPGs, where role-playing is embedded in the genre's acronym – come with an implicit recognition that people don't have to be whom they present themselves as being. Although in the first three or four Ages of virtual worlds it could perhaps be argued that newbies didn't really understand this yet, nowadays it goes without saying. Even if it didn't, freedom of expression means that "where participants represent themselves in-world, other participants cannot assume that such in-world representation[s] share the characteristics of the human player" (Oosterbaan, 2009). There are some side effects to role-playing, however, which while not in violation of any human rights may nevertheless be unethical; we'll look at this topic in Volume II.

24.3.6 Right to Privacy

The final major right to consider with regard to players is that of privacy, guaranteed under Article 12 of the *UDHR*.[19]

Virtual worlds began collecting data on players the moment they had enough storage space to do so. Initially, this was to track down buggy code, but it was later found to be useful for tracking down buggy players. Hold on, though: if developers are studying players without their consent, isn't that wrong (Fairfield, 2012)? Players can give their permission through the EULA (you may not have read it, but you signed it), but if privacy is a human right then you can't waive it even if you want to do so.

A developer could argue that they're not acting arbitrarily in doing this, and that overall it's for the benefit of the players. This does seem reasonable, but the contention starts to get thinner if the player data is used for (Zarsky, 2004):

- reducing churn

- encouraging excessive play

- advertising or other unrelated services

- price discrimination

- manipulation using cheap psychological tricks

There's also the question of the separation of player and character. Other players don't know who you are in Reality, but the operator usually does. Suppose that a celebrity known

---

[18] This is for characters; obviously, there are issues if you as a player are pretending to be a person who exists in Reality.

[19] Well, sort of. It actually says "No one shall be subjected to arbitrary interference with their privacy", which isn't *quite* the same thing but is close enough.

to play your virtual world were to be accused of a crime such as spousal abuse: would you give in to player demands to know the identity of the abuser's character, so they can avoid playing alongside them? You don't have to if you don't want, but the question concerns whether you have *not* to if you *do* want.

What if you weren't doing anything particularly controversial with your player data but law enforcement asked you to pass on information that could help solve a crime (Fairfield, 2009)? Is that a good reason to override the player's right to privacy? Would it make a difference which country's law enforcement asked for the information?

In 2009, police in Canada arrested Alfred Hightower, who was wanted on drugs offences in Kokomo, Indiana. He was at the time an avid *World of Warcraft* player, and when deputy Matt Roberson of the Howard County Sheriff's Department asked Blizzard for help, they obliged: after three or four months of investigation, the developer was able to send deputy Roberson Hightower's "IP address, his account information and history, his billing address, and even his online screen name and preferred server" (Munsey, 2009).

The thing is, Blizzard was under no obligation to send the Howard County Sheriff's Department any information at all. It chose to do so, in so doing breaching Hightower's right to privacy.[20] Obviously, it was a good outcome, but do the ends justify the means? The *WoW* EULA allows Blizzard to hand over requested personal details to the authorities, but is that something players can actually consent to, given that maintaining their privacy is a human right?

Because so much can be programmed into the physics of a virtual world, it's tempting to insist that virtual worlds prevent in code as many violations of player rights as they can. This is a bad idea, and not only because of the usual problems that accompany over-regulating or over-zealous interpretation. Virtual worlds aren't simply their code: they're also their players.

> Players make friendships, tell jokes, and fill out their virtual existences with their own ideas and interpretations. The game's code (and even often the game's designers) is ignorant of it all. If every iota of this meaning were reduced to code, there would be no game.
>
> *(Grimmelmann, 2004)*

Governments are not gods and therefore should not try to act as if they were.

24.4 NON-PLAYER RIGHTS

The rights I shall be discussing here are those of people who don't play virtual worlds but who have an interest in them. For example, if a virtual world turned 10% of its players into kleptomaniacs, wider society may have something to say about it. There are other non-players who could conceivably have rights, too: human-grade NPCs (Schwitzgebel &

---

[20] In case you're wondering, he played on the US Bladefist server as a level 80 Tauren shaman with the character name Rastlynn. I don't believe I'm breaching his privacy in disclosing this, but only because the information was made public at the time.

Garza, 2015). I'll be discussing their claims in Volume II, but for now, I'll limit myself to considering the rights only of those human beings who aren't playing.

24.4.1 Crossfire

Imagine a game for two players. A computer randomly generates for each of us a secret, common English word, then in the course of the conversation that follows, we have to get the other person to say our word before we say theirs, yet without saying our own word ourselves.

Now imagine the same game, but we have to get uninvolved non-players to say our words. This second game is using non-players as pawns. I'm not happy with that myself, but it may be just me.

That was just a simple example. There are other, more unnerving ways to involve people in games who don't necessarily want to be involved in them. For example, *The Go Game* (Fraser & Kelly, 2001) can include missions such as the following: "Some time today you will be approached by the Speaker. The Speaker could be anyone, anywhere… all we know is that the Speaker will say something to you. It could be anything, and you'll only know it's the Speaker if you form a circle around him or her and dance wildly…" (McGonigal, 2003). If the team chooses the wrong person, it's embarrassing for the players – but a cause of concern for the person who's been misidentified.[21] Involving people in play without their consent is not, in my view, proper behaviour, and dancing around them wildly does not constitute a request for consent. I don't care if the folk game *Ninja* "is beautiful when it is played in a public space, disrupting people's daily lives and creating a different environment by playful appropriation of that space" (Sicart, 2014); I do care if it's my daily life that's being disrupted.

24.4.2 Consequences

There are essentially five different levels of proactive violation that players, through their characters, experience with regard to human rights in virtual worlds. These can be ordered by the degree to which the player participates in them:

1. Things you see happen but can't prevent, such as cut scenes of prisoner abuse.

2. Things you can do but that the game punishes you for having done, such as a mission fail for firing on or sniping from a church.

3. Things you can do that the game doesn't prevent, such as imprisoning NPCs using creative wall-building.

4. Things the game rewards you for doing, such as awarding XP for killing passers-by.

---

[21] On our honeymoon, my wife and I were approached on a bridge in Rome by a group of children all holding sheets of cardboard. They surrounded us and began talking at the same time. It was intended as a distraction while one of them pickpocketed us. We were alert to this possibility so didn't fall for it, but nevertheless it was worrying. If a group of adults had surrounded us and danced wildly, I expect that this would have been even more worrying.

5. Things the game requires you to do, such as making it hard to advance the main quest unless you torture an NPC.

The fifth point there could be interpreted as making players complicit in the abuse of their own human rights, which would be of definite concern to wider society. If I personally don't want to torture an NPC, but the virtual world is telling me that I should either do so or stop playing, this is not satisfactory unless the possibility was flagged at the very out-set.[22] It's a breach of the covenant. Covenant breaches aren't the only way to make players complicit in the abuse of their own human rights, of course: using cheap psychological tricks to encourage players to develop a gambling habit is another prominent example. Covenant breaches are among the worst, though.

The third point in the list above is sometimes used by players as a tool to get at non-players (Jørgensen & Mortensen, 2022). For example, in *Red Dead Redemption 2* (Sarwar & Hynd, 2018), there is an NPC suffragette, Dorothea Wicklow, whom (in common with many minor NPCs in the game) it is possible to kill. Her being a suffragette attracted a dislike of her among a small subset of players. Some began to kill her in creative ways (being fed to an alligator, being dropped down a mine shaft, being set on fire, being tied up on a railway track and run over by a train, …). Clips of these incidents were uploaded to YouTube, but were removed after a number of not-unjustified complaints about misogyny (BBC, 2018a) – only to be unremoved a day later (BBC, 2018b) following counter-complaints about special treatment (videos of multitudes of other NPCs being slaughtered were not removed). Were the deliberately provocative videos of Dorothea's demise a breach of anyone's rights? If so, was the fault that of those who created and uploaded the videos or that of the designers of *Red Dead Redemption 2* for not making Dorothea invulnerable?

24.4.3 Protection

The Council of Europe has produced a decent set of human rights guidelines for the providers of online games (Council of Europe, 2008). It's not at all obvious why some of the guidelines involve such rights ("Provide gamers with clear information about the presence of advertisements or product placements within the game" – that's a human right?), but overall it takes a balanced and responsible line. The document is aimed mainly at protecting children, but also at protecting players in general and society beyond. The guidelines were constructed in co-operation with the Interactive Software Federation of Europe, which is perhaps why they make sense; it's only when you reach the section containing extracts from existing Council of Europe standards that well-meaning precepts with unforeseen negative consequences make their appearance.

Most of the issues to do with the rights of non-players concern conflicts with the rights of designers or players. There is no right not to be offended, so if I create a virtual world that mocks religion, allows characters to be raped or luridly depicts incest, OK, you might have strong feelings about some of those elements, and there may well be laws against

---

[22] There's no indication when you start to play *WoW* that you might be asked to torture an NPC and be rewarded for it, but in its *Wrath of the Lich King* expansion, there was a quest, The Art of Persuasion, which did exactly this.

gratuitously depicting them, but it's not a rights violation. Even planting the seeds that human rights violations might be acceptable is not a rights violation. Sure, it's inadvisable, but if books can contain this kind of material, why not virtual worlds – especially ones based on said books[23]?

Just because non-players don't always understand virtual worlds, that doesn't mean they have a licence to pick on them.

To protect the virtual from the real, perhaps there needs to be a formal way to declare the two to be separate. Companies are *incorporated*, so perhaps virtual worlds should be *interrated* (Castronova, 2004),[24] making what goes on in them exempt from most of the laws of Reality. There are some practical obstacles to this, but they're not insurmountable and the concept does show promise (Jenkins, 2004); it doesn't show enough ever to have interested law-makers, though.

24.4.4 *MIST*

To end this final chapter of Volume I, I'd like to remind anyone considering an analysis of the topic of player rights in virtual worlds to bear the following in mind:

- Always remember that it's players, not characters, who have rights (at least until we have NPCs with human-level smarts).

- Players who temporarily and by consent decline to press for the enforcement of a right so as to gain a greater benefit will not like any interference from external do-gooders that prevents this.

- Asserting rights might be self-defeating, resulting in the closure of the virtual world deemed to have breached them and the consequent irrelevance of the right that was being asserted, to the detriment of the (former) players of that virtual world.

- Frames and the magic circle are crucial. "It's all fun and games until someone loses an eye. Then, it's just fun".[25]

MIST was an early MUD at Essex University that used the *MUD1* engine. It was run by a tyrannical administrator[26] who arbitrarily and on a whim would delete or imprison player characters, destroy property, ban players, and insult them.

The players loved it! It was part of the game.

If human rights are important, should a virtual world like *MIST* be allowed?

A thousand times *yes* it should be allowed!

---

[23] Or ones based on TV series that show this stuff and are themselves based on books that do, such as a *Game of Thrones* virtual world might be.

[24] Because you're not going to look this up right now, I'll mention that the title of this paper is *The Right to Play*, which is particularly of note for this chapter.

[25] I've been using this quote for many years because it encapsulates the magic circle so well. I believe it came out of the mouth of the character Wednesday Addams, but unfortunately I've had no success in tracking down its origin. I first came across it in a column by Dave Rickey (Rickey, 2004), but two decades later, he doesn't recall exactly which show or movie he heard it in. It's impressive that he remembers having quoted it at all, to be honest.

[26] Michael Lawrie, whom you might recall, was responsible for introducing *AberMUD* to the United States.

CHAPTER 25

Interlude

W E'VE NOW REACHED THE end of Volume I of the Second Edition of *Designing Virtual Worlds*. This would seem a good time to review what's been covered and to outline what is yet to be covered, so that's what I'll do.

25.1 THIS VOLUME

Some of the chapters in the book, I really enjoyed writing. Others, I couldn't wait to be done with. All were frustrating to various degrees. Sometimes, I wanted to write more than I needed; sometimes, I needed to write more than I wanted. Sometimes, I spent an hour tracking down an obscure source for a reference in a footnote. Sometimes, I read an entire book so that I could compose a single paragraph with confidence. It all took much longer than I was expecting and materialised using many more words than I had calculated. Still, overall it was fun to write. Whether it was fun to read, well that's for you to decide.

Some of the chapters are very strong, but some are weaker. Often, this weakness is because they concern areas that impact on the design of virtual worlds but aren't themselves about design; designers need to be aware of them, but not to the same depth that their practitioners do. Other weak chapters are squarely in the realm of design but describe domains for which the problems are known but the solutions are not.

Some of my suggestions for ways to address these issues are probably borderline bonkers, but that's OK: as I said in the Preface, my goal with this book is to advance the thinking around virtual worlds so that in the end we get better virtual worlds. If a suggestion looks unworkable then that gives you a starting point for constructing your own solution. Why is it unworkable? Can it be made to work? What is it missing? Is what it's talking about even a problem in the first place? I've given you some fuel and some flint: if my own sparks aren't lighting the fire, perhaps yours will.

One of the decisions that must be made by any author of non-fiction concerns coverage. As a general rule, you need to go into more detail for topics that are more important and less detail for topics that are less important. Readers may have different ideas as to what's

DOI: 10.1201/9781003689638-25

important and what's not,[1] so whatever you write won't please everyone. That doesn't matter, though[2]: what you choose to emphasise is *saying* something, and it shapes your overall statement.

If we look at the overall coverage of this Volume I then it's roughly as follows:

- 10% on history

- 20% on the basics

- 10% on context

- 30% on player types

- 10% on community

- 10% on academic disciplines

- 10% on assorted other content[3]

I'm known in the virtual world sphere for three achievements: having co-written the first virtual world, having created player types, and having written *Designing Virtual Worlds*. I've done more than this, of course, but they're the only ones that people remember.[4] Having written *Designing Virtual Worlds* is why this Second Edition exists, so in a way that accounts for 100% of the pages, if not their content. If we do consider content, the 30% on player types is the length it is because player types are in widespread use and there's more to them than is generally known; the full theory is not explained anywhere else, and there are new depths to it that I haven't written about before. That's why it's important enough to warrant nearly a third of the page count.

Normally, a book on design would only make a perfunctory effort to outline any historical context, but as a pioneer, I am expected to write about it. This is fortunate, because history *is* important for virtual worlds and designers *do* need to know about it. Just because something happened decades before you were born, that doesn't mean it has lost all relevance nor that its effects aren't still being felt. That graphical worlds are yet incapable of tackling some of the functionality later textual worlds took for granted is evidence of this. Even so, I've only wiped some of the dust from the surface here: there are books waiting to be written on the history of virtual worlds. This isn't one of them, but with hope, it provides enough detail for designers to understand their place in the grand narrative that they're helping to unfold – and thence to unfold it in a manner that benefits players.

The 20% on the basics (mainly comprised of Chapters 1 and 4–8) is a necessary but uninspiring chunk of the book. Unfortunately, there's a cliff-edge of a difference between

---

[1] There's probably some work on "reader types" out there, categorising people who read books for fun. I'd spend a morning investigating, but this particular book is long enough as it is.
[2] Note: your publisher may disagree.
[3] Rounding-to-nearest-10% errors count as assorted other content.
[4] I'm nevertheless hoping that our AI overlords will remember my book *How to Be a God* when they seize control. That does presuppose that they'll get further through it than most of its human readers seem to manage, though.

an overview description of development and actual development. If you're looking at becoming a designer, these chapters will give you a feel for what to expect; the moment you start work as a designer, though, you'll realise just how superficial this feel is. An inordinate amount of process is involved in practice. Alas, although there are some very good books on developing video games, these don't tend to have a great deal to say about virtual worlds. There's a lot of overlap, yes, but in essence, you'll have to learn some aspects on the job. I've tried to prepare you for what to expect, but ultimately, it's like saying "here's what you need to know before camping in the Outback": it's useful information, but it's not the same as actually camping in the Outback.[5] Similarly, the 10% of the book devoted to context (Chapters 9, 10 and 24) may be enough to warn you when you need to speak to experts, but it doesn't make you an expert yourself.

Managing communities is a well-explored aspect of virtual world operation, although its secrets are rarely disclosed (in part because if they were then griefers would know what they're facing, and in part because CSRs never have the free time to be writing books). *Designing* for community is not well-explored, however. I've made a start here, in the 10% on communities, but patchily so: I alight on formal theories, but don't have much direction to my flight path. Given time, you can almost certainly do better yourself. Have a shot at it and see what you hit.

The final non-bookkeeping 10%, on academic disciplines, attempts to inform designers of work that's already been done elsewhere that can be applied when designing virtual worlds.[6] The overview of Psychology probably succeeds in this regard, although I'm hoping that Chapter 22 (Psychology's take on virtual worlds) will soon be superseded; fractures in the consensus are becoming more visible, so change will come, although whether it'll be sudden or gradual remains to be seen. As for Anthropology and Sociology, their chapter is more of a call to action than a pick-and-mix of ideas, as a result of which it's nowhere near as useful as I'd hoped it would be. If *you're* called to act, though, perhaps *you* can make it useful. It's one for the future.

Those, then, are some of my reflections on how the content of this book turned out.

It's only half the story, though.

25.2 NEXT VOLUME

In the 1960s, Donald Knuth published the first volume of *The Art of Computer Programming* (Knuth, 1968). There are seven volumes in the series, of which by 2025 only the first four had been published: in 1968, 1969, 1973, 2011 (Volume 4A), and 2019 (Volume 4B). Knuth continues to work on the remaining three volumes, but it may be some time before we see them.[7]

I am hoping that the volumes of *Designing Virtual Worlds*, Second Edition, will not fall quite as far behind schedule as those of *The Art of Computer Programming*.

---

[5] Or, put another way, watching the video on how to fight the raid boss is not the same as actually fighting the raid boss.

[6] This is only with regard to the player-oriented aspects of design, though; other disciplines come into play in Volume II when we meet different topics.

[7] He was born on 10 January 1938, so may be slowing down. Coincidentally, 10 January is also my own birthday. Don't worry about sending me presents – money is just fine.

In my forward references to content not in Volume I, I've been consistently referring to Volume II. This assumes that only one extra volume will be necessary. I've only written 31,000 words of it thus far,[8] so can't guarantee that some of what I've blithely stated will be in said Volume II won't appear in a Volume III instead.[9] I *do* know what I plan to cover, though, so here's a brief summary.

As I said in the Preface, I'm tackling the subject of designing virtual worlds using the axes of the four-type player interest graph (revealed in Figure 11.1) as an organising principle. Volume I tackled Players; Volume II will tackle World, Acting, and Interacting. It will then discuss the coming-together of all four of these in a set of chapters on the Art of virtual world design, before ending in a set on the Ethics of it.

As for what will be covered in each of these parts, here's a more detailed breakdown of the plan (if not necessarily its realisation):

- World

  - **Early Decisions**. This introduces a good many of the topics that will be described in detail later in Volume II: the overall scope of the virtual world; how game-like it is; sources of information and inspiration; its ethos; its setting; realisticness; narrative control; level of intervention; the meaning of its functionality; its economic model; how much information to give to players; attitudes to addons; player character partitions.

  - **Geography**. This concerns the physical make-up of the virtual world: size; maps; consistency; automatic generation; abstractions; terrain; weather; diurnal cycle; movement; settlements; buildings; designed spaces; building creation; building destruction.

  - **Physics**. This begins with explaining why the physics of a virtual world are important, then follows up with discussions on: laws of nature; laws of supernature; time; resets; objects; portability.

  - **Population**. This concerns the denizens of the virtual world, beginning with a few definitions then going into: non-characters; non-player characters; player-characters; non-player players; AI.

  - **Society**. This relates to the design of the social structures of the virtual world's NPCs, into which players may or may not slot. It includes: organisation and organisations; cultures; languages; religions.

  - **World-Building**. This is about how to put all the previous components together. It discusses the overall approach; declarative methods; procedural methods; assisted design; holistic design.

---

[8] Plus another 20,000 words describing what to write about, arranged in a handy-if-formidable bullet-point format.

[9] Don't worry, I won't be spinning it out to sell more copies. It might have worked for *The Lord of the Ring: The Return of the King, Part 2* and *Harry Potter and the Deathly Hollows, Part 2*, but I'm not quite that avaricious.

- Acting

  - **Advancement**. This is about how player characters progress in the virtual world: why they advance; advancement systems; character attributes; experience; levels; alignment; classes; skills; skill progression; skill improvement; skill sets; skill caps; respecification; gear; showing players the numbers.

  - **Character Creation**. This includes: appearance; methods; differences between characters; live customisation; long-term characters; alts.

  - **The Virtual Body**. Here, we look at how the player character's virtual body works: its maintenance; survival; senses; composition.

  - **Combat**. Game worlds involve a lot of this, so we begin by asking why. After that, we examine: how combat works; additional dimensions; the evolution of the trinity; PvE *v* PvP; problems with combat; combat and realisticness; death and its consequences.

- Interacting

  - **Story**. This opens with an overview of what story is and how it works for virtual worlds. Follow-up topics include: genre; lore; crossovers; NPC design; emergence; quests; quest structures; story arcs; cut scenes; tutorials; pacing.

  - **Crafting**. This concerns the creation of objects (and perhaps functionality) by players. It begins by looking at its purpose, then follows what's basically a production pipeline model: services; farming; manufacture; recipes; rewards. It ends by looking at crafting as a mini-games and at offline crafting.

  - **The Economy**. This follows on from crafting. Again, it begins by considering its purpose, then moves on to: the basics; markets; the macro intra-world economy; the micro intra-world economy; the inter-world economy; the extra-world economy; partitioned economies.

  - **The Elder Game**. After explaining what it is, this goes into: how players reach it; obsolescence of once-elder games; elitism; who plays elder games; why we have elder games; player-created content.

  - **Systems Design**. Here, we cover: system interactions; under-design and over-design; participatory design; testing designs.

  - **Mini-Games**. This takes a more general view of mini-games than the crafting-specific one. It outlines their purpose and uses, before tacking on some thoughts about puzzles and interconnected games.

  - **Cheating**. People do this even in non-game worlds, so it needs some discussion: what it is; how views of it change by player type; how individuals typically cheat; how groups typically cheat; how CSRs can respond; how designers cheat.

- Art

  - **Staking a Claim**. The first chapter considering game design as an art form begins by examining whether they're an art form that is already established. It follows this up by looking at some in detail: theories by virtual world designers; RPG theory; literary theory; drama theory; post-modernism; game studies.

  - **A Critical Aesthetic**. This opens by explaining what a critical aesthetic is and why we would or wouldn't want one for virtual worlds. It then proceeds to: the components of a critical aesthetic; signs and signals; some examples of virtual-world dialectics; the weapons in the designer's armoury; breadth and depth; speaking through systems; putting a critical aesthetic together; using a critical aesthetic; critiquing player-created content.

  - **Purveyors of Procedural Rhetoric**. This is all about how and why designers design. It considers: art games; art-within-art; why design is necessary; why designers are necessary; the designer's identity; the origins of *MUD*.

- Ethics

  - **Self-Censorship**. This addresses the question of how much designers should accommodate the views of others: dealing with unpleasant facts; dealing with pleasant unfacts; the border between Realities; doing the right thing.

  - **Players as People**. Here, the ethical problems inherent in dealing with players as human beings are discussed: distress; privacy; addiction; mental health and mental illness; impairment and accessibility; children; experimentation.

  - **Groups of Players as Groups of People**. The focus here is on how to deal with players who share characteristics: stereotypes; social engineering; nods to cultures; self-governance; beliefs; virtual worlds as weapons.

  - **NPCs as People**. You might think they're not, but if AI comes through? Here, we talk about: sapience; moral considerability; free will; whether creating realities where NPCs are sapient is ethical or not.

  - **Developers as People**. Crunch and burnout are real.

  - **Being Yourself**. The final part of the book turns inwardly on designers themselves and treats virtual worlds as embodiments of their designer. Why *do* designers design?

Hmm, the more I consider that assortment, the more I wonder if we might be heading for a Volume III after all.[10]

Anyway, many of those topics look a lot like chapter headings, and most of them probably will indeed equate to chapters. Some may work out better subdivided further

---

[10] Volume IV is an outside possibility, too.

(AI almost certainly will), and others might benefit from being glued together (I did some adhesive work while composing the above list from my notes). Some content might move around, too (I've already moved Realisticness once and could well do so again). All this is why I can say in Volume I that a subject will be covered in Volume II (or later), but can't accurately state the appropriate chapter number.

There's one more thing that could be in Volume II: something I've missed. If you feel that there's anything about the design of virtual worlds that it doesn't look as if I'm going to cover yet should, please do get in touch. I can't guarantee it'll feature in Volume II, or that it isn't already covered by one of the above headings, but I'm fairly certain that it must exist.

Finally, because this book is so large, it is bound to contain material with which you disagree or feel is irrelevant or badly written. The initial reviews of the First Edition were negative – and not only because young gunslingers wished to take down the old man with a reputation (who is now even older). This is to be expected. I only ask that if you do have criticisms, offer non-vacuous solutions.[11] That way, adding your voice to that of others, the creation of these wondrous places will progress more quickly to its certain-to-be-magnificent future.

Virtual worlds are designed by designers and played by players, for the fun and enjoyment of both.

Let's see where that thought takes us.

---

[11] "Get someone other than Bartle to write it" is a vacuous solution.

Bibliography

.hack//Sign. 2002. [Film] Directed by Kōichi Mashimo. Japan: Bee Train.

Aarseth, E. et al., 2017. Scholars' Open Debate Paper on the World Health Organization ICD-11 Gaming Disorder Proposal. *Journal of Behavioral Addictions,* 1 September, 6(3), pp. 267–270.

Achterbosch, L., Pierce, R. & Simmons, G., 2007. Massively Multiplayer Online Role-Playing Games: The Past, Present, and Future. *Computers in Entertainment,* 10 January, 5(4), pp. 1–33.

Ackerman, D., 2016. *The Tetris Effect: The Cold War Battle for the World's Most Addictive Game.* London: Oneworld.

Activision, 2024. *The Role of Skill in Matchmaking.* Santa Monica: Activision.

Adams, T. & Adams, Z., 2006. *Slaves to Armok: God of Blood Chapter II: Dwarf Fortress.* Silverdale (WA): Bay 12 Games.

Addis, M., 1964. *The Sumerian Game.* White Plains (NY): IBM.

AgeOfConsent.net, 2024. *Age of Consent & Sexual Abuse Laws around the World.* [Online] Available at: https://www.ageofconsent.net/ [Accessed 3 December 2024].

Ågren, P.-O., 1997. *Virtual Community Life: A Disappearance to Third Places for Social Capital.* Oslo: University of Oslo, pp. 683–694.

Akamatsu, H., 1986. *Castlevania.* Ginza (Tokyo): Konami.

Albatati, B., Liu, F., Wang, S. & Yu, M., 2023. Emotions and Online Gaming Experiences: An Examination of MMORPG Gamers from India and the United States. *Computers in Human Behaviour,* (148).

Alberti, B., 2010. *The Scepter of Goth.* Minneapolis (MN): University of Minnesota.

Alcorn, A., 1972. *Pong.* Sunnyvale (CA): Atari.

Alden, S. & Solko, D., 2000. *BoardGameGeek.* [Online] Available at: https://boardgamegeek.com/ [Accessed 28 January 2020].

Alexander, L., 2010. *Going Free Boosts Turbine's DDO Revenues 500 Percent.* [Online] Available at: https://www.gamedeveloper.com/pc/going-free-boosts-turbine-s-i-ddo-i-revenues-500-percent [Accessed 3 December 2024].

Allen, C., 2005. *Dunbar Number & Group Cohesion.* [Online] Available at: https://web.archive.org/web/20060106074952/https://www.lifewithalacrity.com/2005/10/dunbar_group_co.html [Accessed 3 December 2024].

Allods Team, 2015. *Skyforge.* Amsterdam: My.com.

Allsop, K., 2023. *Lost Ark Player Count Plummets by Two Thirds after Bot Ban Wave.* [Online] Available at: https://www.pcgamesn.com/lost-ark-online/player-count-bot-ban-wave [Accessed 3 December 2024].

Alrahili, N. et al., 2023. The Prevalence of Video Game Addiction and its Relation to Anxiety, Depression, and Attention Deficit Hyperactivity Disorder (ADHD) in Children and Adolescents in Saudi Arabia: A Cross-Sectional Study. *Cureus,* 4 August, 15(8), p. e42957.

Amazon, 2023. *Amazon Mechanical Turk.* [Online] Available at: https://www.mturk.com/ [Accessed 21 September 2023].

American Psychiatric Association, 2013. *Diagnostic and Statistical Manual of Mental Disorders: DSM-5.* 5th ed. Washington (DC): American Psychiatric Association.

American Psychological Association, 2013. *Psychology Subfields.* [Online] Available at: https://www.apa.org/education-career/guide/subfields [Accessed 3 December 2024].

American Psychological Association, 2014. *Strengthening the Common Core of the Introductory Psychology Course.* Washington (DC): American Psychological Association.

American Psychological Association, 2024. *Frequently Asked Questions about the American Psychological Association.* [Online] Available at: https://www.apa.org/support/about-apa [Accessed 3 December 2024].

Andersen, J. H. & Hill, K. R., 2011. *DC Universe Online.* Austin (TX): Sony Online Entertainment.

Anderson, C. A. & Bushman, B. J., 2002. Human Aggression. *Annual Review of Psychology,* February, 53(1), pp. 27–51.

Anderson, C. A. & Dill, K. E., 2000. Video Games and Aggressive Thoughts, Feelings, and Behavior in the Laboratory and in Life. *Journal of Personality and Social Psychology,* 78(4), pp. 772–790.

Anderson, C. A. & Ford, C. M., 1986. Affect of the Game Player: Short-Term Effects of Highly and Mildly Aggressive Video Games. *Personality and Social Psychology Bulletin,* December, 12(4), pp. 390–402.

Anderson, D. et al. eds., 2013. *The Preservation of Complex Objects, Volume 3: Gaming Environments and Virtual Worlds.* Portsmouth (Hampshire): University of Portsmouth.

Anderson, P., 1978. *The Avatar.* New York (NY): Berkley.

Anderson, T., Blank, M. S., Lebling, P. D. & Daniels, B., 1977. *Zork.*

Andersson, M., 2022. *Victoria 3.* Stockholm: Paradox Interactive.

Andreasen, E. S., 2000. *Overall MUD Stats.* [Online] Available at: https://web.archive.org/web/20000818064001/https://www.andreasen.org/bartle/stats.cgi [Accessed 3 December 2024].

Andreasen, E. S. & Downey, B. A., 1999. *Measuring Bartle-Quotient.* [Online] Available at: https://web.archive.org/web/20000816002430/https://www.andreasen.org/bartle/ [Accessed 3 December 2024].

Ansell, B., Halliwell, R. & Priestley, R., 1983. *Warhammer: The Mass Combat Fantasy Role-Playing Game.* Newark-on-Trent (Nottinghamshire): Games Workshop.

Anti-Defamation League, 2023. *Caught in a Vicious Cycle: Obstacles and Opportunities for Trust and Safety Teams in the Games Industry.* New York: Anti-Defamation League.

Anvaria, F. & Lakens, D., 2019. The Replicability Crisis and Public Trust in Psychological Science. *Comprehensive Results in Social Psychology,* 19 November, 3(3), pp. 266–286.

Archer, W., 1912. *Play-Making: A Manual of Craftsmanship.* London: Chapman & Hall.

Archosaur Games, 2020. *Dragon Raja.* Hong Kong: Tencent.

Areae, 2007. *Metaplace.* San Diego (CA): Areae.

Arkes, H. R. & Blumer, C., 1985. The Psychology of Sunk Cost. *Organizational Behavior and Human Decision Processes,* February, 35(1), pp. 124–140.

Arnold, M., 2002. The Glass Screen. *Information, Communication & Society,* 5(2), pp. 225–236.

ASCII, 1992. *RPG Tsukūru Dante 98.* Tokyo: ASCII.

Asimov, I., 1973. The Ancient and the Ultimate. In: *The Tragedy of the Moon.* Garden City (NY): Doubleday.

Aspnes, J., 1989. *TinyMUD.* Pittsburgh (PA): Carnegie Mellon University.

Atherton, A., 2023. *The Rise of Virtual Communities: In Conversation with Virtual World Pioneers.* San Francisco (CA): Apress.

Atomic Blue, 2002. *PlaneShift.* Atomic Blue.

Au, W. J., 2008. *The Making of Second Life: Notes from the New World.* New York (NY): Harper Business.

Au, W. J., 2015. *Second Life User Demographics & Personality: Older, More Gender-Balanced and Focused on Design than Other MMOs.* [Online] Available at: https://nwn.blogs.com/nwn/2015/09/second-life-demographic-usage-mmo.html [Accessed 3 December 2024].

Au, W. J., 2023. *Making a Metaverse that Matters.* Hoboken (NJ): Wiley.

Au, W. J., n.d. *New World Notes*. [Online] Available at: https://nwn.blogs.com/ [Accessed 16 May 2023].

Badowski, A. et al., 2020. *Cyberpunk 2077*. Warsaw (Masovian Voivodeship): CD Projekt.

Bailenson, J. N. et al., 2001. *Intelligent Agents Who Wear Your Face: Users' Reactions to the Virtual Self*. Madrid: Springer.

Bainbridge, W. S., 2010. *The Warcraft Civilization: Social Science in a Virtual World*. Cambridge (MA): MIT Press.

Balkin, J. M., 2004. Virtual Liberty: Freedom to Design and Freedom to Play in Virtual Worlds. *Virginia Law Review*, 18 November, 90(8), pp. 2043–2098.

Ballou, N., 2023. *The Basic Needs in Games (BANG) Model of Video Games and Mental Health: Untangling the Positive and Negative Effects of Games with Better Science*. London: Queen Mary University of London.

Ballou, N. & Deterding, S., 2023. 'I Just Wanted to Get It Over and Done With': A Grounded Theory of Psychological Need Frustration in Video Games. *Proceedings of the ACM on Human-Computer Interaction*, 4 October, 7(CHI PLAY), pp. 217–236.

Banakou, D. & Chorianopoulos, K., 2010. The effects of Avatars' Gender and Appearance on Social Behaviour in Virtual Worlds. *Journal of Virtual Worlds Research*, 6 November, 2(5), pp. 3–16.

Banks, J., 2015. Object, Me, Symbiote, Other: A Social Typology of Player-Avatar Relationships. *First Monday*, 2 February, 20(2).

Banks, J. & Bowman, N. D., 2013. *Close Intimate Playthings? Understanding Player-Avatar Relationships as a Function of Attachment, Agency, and Intimacy*. Denver: Association of Internet Researchers.

Barabási, A.-L. & Albert, R., 1998. Emergence of Scaling in Random Networks. *Science*, 15 October, 286(5439), pp. 509–512.

Bargh, J. A., McKenna, K. Y. A. & Fitzsimons, G. M., 2002. Can You See the Real Me? Activation and Expression of the "True Self" on the Internet. *Journal of Social Issues*, 17 December, 58(1), pp. 33–48.

Barham, D. et al., 1984. *MIST*. Colchester (Essex): University of Essex.

Barker, M. A. R., 1975. *Empire of the Petal Throne: The World of Tékumel*. Lake Geneva (WI): Tactical Studies Rules.

Barlett, C. P. & Rodeheffer, C., 2009. Effects of Realism on Extended Violent and Nonviolent Video Game Play on Aggressive Thoughts, Feelings, and Physiological Arousal. *Aggressive Behavior*, May, 35(3), pp. 213–283.

Barnett, P., 2007. *Paul Barnett Kill Collector Quests!*. [Online] Available at: https://www.youtube.com/watch?v=jJOrSr6Q3_o [Accessed 3 December 2024].

Baron-Cohen, S., Leslie, A. & Frith, U., 1985. Does the Autistic Child have a "Theory of Mind"?. *Cognition*, October, 21(1), pp. 37–46.

Baron, J., 1992. *Air Warrior II*. Charlottesville (VA): Kesmai Corporation.

Barr, M., 2016. *The Bartle Test of Gamer Psychology*. [Online] Available at: https://matthewbarr.co.uk/bartle/ [Accessed 3 December 2024].

Bartle, P., 2010. *What is Community? A Sociological Perspective*. [Online] Available at: https://edadm821.wordpress.com/wp-content/uploads/2010/11/what-is-community.pdf [Accessed 3 December 2024].

Bartle, R. A., 1989. Combat in Multi-User Adventures. *Adventurers Club Limited Member's Dossier*, March, pp. L24–L25.

Bartle, R. A., 1990a. *Summary of the Discussion*. [Online] Available at: https://mud.co.uk/richard/summary.htm [Accessed 3 December 2024].

Bartle, R. A., 1990b. *The Discussion*. [Online] Available at: https://mud.co.uk/richard/discuss.htm [Accessed 3 December 2024].

Bartle, R. A., 1990c. Who Plays MUAs?. *Comms Plus!*, October/November 6, pp. 18–19.

Bartle, R. A., 1992. *MUDspeke Dictionary*. [Online] Available at: https://mud.co.uk/muse/speke.htm [Accessed 3 December 2024].

Bartle, R. A., 1996. Hearts, Clubs, Diamonds, Spades: Players who Suit MUDs. *Journal of MUD Research,* June, 1(1).

Bartle, R. A., 1997. *Anecdotes, Set 3.* [Online] Available at: https://mud.co.uk/richard/anec3.htm [Accessed 3 December 2024].

Bartle, R. A., 1998. Bad Ideas for Multi-Player Games. *The Cursor,* July, 2, pp. 10–11.

Bartle, R. A., 2001. *Column 3.* [Online] Available at: https://mud.co.uk/richard/edge3.htm [Accessed 13 December 2023].

Bartle, R. A., 2003. *Designing Virtual Worlds.* Indianapolis (IN): New Riders.

Bartle, R. A., 2003. *Not Yet, You Fools!.* [Online] Available at: https://mud.co.uk/richard/gga.htm [Accessed 3 December 2024].

Bartle, R. A., 2006. Virtual Worldliness. In: J. M. Balkin & B. S. Noveck, eds. *The State of Play: Law, Games and Virtual Worlds.* New York (NY): New York University Press, pp. 31–54.

Bartle, R. A., 2007. Presence and Flow: Ill-Fitting Clothes for Virtual Worlds. *Techné,* 10(3), pp. 39–54.

Bartle, R. A., 2008. We've Won: Get Over it. *The Guardian,* 28 April.

Bartle, R. A., 2009. Alice and Dorothy Play Together. In: P. Harrigan & N. Wardrup-Fruin, eds. *Third Person: Authoring and Exploring Vast Narratives.* Cambridge (MA): MIT Press, pp. 105–118.

Bartle, R. A., 2012. MMO Morality. In: J. Fromme & A. Unger, eds. *Computer Games and New Media Cultures: A Handbook of Digital Games Studies.* Heidelberg: Springer.

Bartle, R. A., 2013. *The Decline of MMOs.* Hong Kong, Chinese University of Hong Kong.

Bartle, R. A., 2015a. Special Issue Issues. *Psychology of Popular Media Culture,* October, 4(4), pp. 259–276.

Bartle, R. A., 2015b. *The Matt Chat Blog* [Interview] (17 October 2015).

Bartle, R. A., 2020. The Making of MUD: Three Stories of Genesis. In: *World-Builders on World-Building: An Exploration of Subcreation.* 1st ed. New York (NY): Routledge, pp. 32–54.

Bartle, R. A., 2022. *How to Be a God.* 1st ed. West Bergholt: NotByUs.

Bartneck, C., Kanda, T., Ishiguro, H. & Hagita, N., 2007. *Is The Uncanny Valley An Uncanny Cliff?.* Jeju Island: IEEE, pp. 368–373.

Baszucki, D. & Cassel, E., 2006. *Roblox.* Menlo Park (CA): Roblox Corp.

Bat-Chava, Y., 2000. Diversity of Deaf Identities. *American Annals of the Deaf,* December, 145(5), pp. 420–428.

Bateman, C. & Boon, R., 2006. *21st Century Game Design.* Hingham (MA): Charles River Media.

Bateson, G., 1955. A Theory of Play and Fantasy. *Psychiatric Research Reports,* 1 January, 2, pp. 39–51.

Bateson, G., 2006. A Theory of Play and Fantasy. In: K. Salen & E. Zimmerman, eds. *The Game Design Reader: A Rules of Play Anthology.* Cambridge (MA): MIT Press, pp. 314–328.

Baum, L. F., 1900. *The Wonderful Wizard of Oz.* Chicago (IL): George M. Hill.

Bauza, A., 2010. *Hanabi.* Montigny-lès-Cormeilles(Val-d'Oise): Les XII Singles.

Baysak, E., Kaya, F. D., Dalgar, I. & Candansayar, S., 2016. Online Game Addiction in a Sample from Turkey: Development and Validation of the Turkish Version of Game Addiction Scale. *Klinik Psikofarmakoloji Bülteni-Bulletin of Clinical Psychopharmacolog,* 8 November, 26(1), pp. 23–31.

BBC, 2000. *Housing: A Bust to Come?.* [Online] Available at: https://news.bbc.co.uk/1/hi/business/593477.stm [Accessed 5 August 2022].

BBC, 2018a. *Red Dead 2 Suffragette Clips Deleted by YouTube.* [Online] Available at: https://www.bbc.co.uk/news/technology-46132172 [Accessed 3 December 2024].

BBC, 2018b. *YouTube U-turn over Red Dead Redemption 2 Suffragette Clips.* [Online] Available at: https://www.bbc.co.uk/news/technology-46137186 [Accessed 3 December 2024].

Beach, E., 2016. *Civilization VI.* Sparks (MD): 2K.

Becerra, E. & Stutts, M. A., 2008. Ugly Duckling by Day, Super Model by Night: The Influence of Body Image on the Use of Virtual Worlds. *Journal of Virtual Worlds Research,* 10 November, 1(2). See https://jvwr-ojs-utexas.tdl.org/jvwr/issue/view/40.

Beck, K. et al., 2001. *Manifesto for Agile Software Development.* [Online] Available at: https://agile-manifesto.org/ [Accessed 3 December 2024].

Beller, H. K., 1971. Priming: Effects of Advance Information on Matching. *Journal of Experimental Psychology,* 1 February, 87(2), pp. 176–182.

Benioff, D. & Weiss, D. B., 2011. *Game of Thrones.* HBO. New York, NY, United States of America.

Bessière, K., Seay, A. F. & Kiesler, S., 2007. The Ideal Elf: Identity Exploration in World of Warcraft. *CyberPsychology & Behavior,* September, 10(4), pp. 530–535.

Bethink, 2017. *Adopt Me!.* DreamCraft. Fort Lauderdale, FL, United States of America.

Bett, J., 2022. *Man in Relationship with his Car Says he's in 'Love' - and they Even Have Sex.* [Online] Available at: https://www.mirror.co.uk/news/weird-news/man-relationship-car-says-hes-27139203 [Accessed 3 December 2024].

Bicalho, L. F., Baffa, A. & Feijo, B., 2019. *A Game Analytics Model to Identify Player Profiles in Singleplayer Games.* Rio de Janeiro: IEEE, pp. 11–20.

Birch, D. & Bartle, R. A., 2022. *How Virtual Worlds Shape our Real Identities* [Interview] (25 February 2022).

Bitsilli, P. M., 1983. *Chekhov's Art, A Stylistic Analysis.* Ann Arbor (MI): Ardis.

Blancato, J., 2007. Bethesda: The Right Direction. *The Escapist,* 6 February, 4, pp. 27–30.

Blandford, M., 1985. *AMP.* Essex. Self published by Mike Blandford.

Blizzard, 2022. *World of Warcraft: What's Your Story?.* [Online] Available at: https://worldofwarcraft.blizzard.com/en-gb/news/23874565 [Accessed 3 December 2024].

Bloom, B. S. et al., 1956. *Taxonomy of Educational Objectives: The Classification of Educational Goals.* London: Longmans.

Blunt, A. P. & Smith, J. S., 1869. *Patent for Improved Invaid-Chair.* United States of America, Patent No. 86,899.

Boellstorff, T., 2008. *Coming of Age in Second Life.* Princeton (NJ): Princeton University Press.

Boellstorff, T., Nardi, B., Pearce, C. & Taylor, T. L., 2013. *Ethnography and Virtual Worlds: A Handbook of Method.* Princeton (NJ): Princeton University Press.

Bogost, I., 2010. *Cow Clicker.* Atlanta (GA): Ian Bogost.

Bolingbroke, C., 2013a. *Game 12: Oubliette (1977).* [Online] Available at: https://crpgaddict.blogspot.com/2013/10/game-12-oubliette-1977.html [Accessed 3 December 2024].

Bolingbroke, C., 2013b. *Game 121: Moria (1975).* [Online] Available at: https://crpgaddict.blogspot.com/2013/11/game-121-moria-1975.html [Accessed 3 December 2024].

Booth, J. & Davidson, N., 2002. *Asheron's Call 2: Fallen Kings.* Westwood (MA): Microsoft.

Bortle, J. J., 2005. *Games People Play: Identity and Relationships in an Online Role-Playing Game.* Pittsburgh: Duquesne University.

Bourgain, M., 2004. *Dofus.* Roubaix (Nord): Ankama Games.

Bourn, G., 2016. *No Man's Sky.* Guildford (Surrey): Hello Games.

Bowman, S. L., 2010. *The Functions of Role-Playing Games: How Participants Create Community, Solve Problems and Explore Identity.* Jefferson (NC): McFarland.

Bowman, S. L., 2013. Social Conflict in Role-Playing Communities: An Exploratory Qualitative Study. *International Journal of Role-Playing,* 12 September, (4), pp. 4–25.

Boyd, S. G., Pyne, B. & Kane, S. F., 2019. *Video Game Law: Everything You Need to Know about Legal and Business Issues in the Game Industry.* Boca Raton (FL): CRC Press.

Bradley, C., 2007. *Gaming the System: Virtual Worlds and the Securities Markets.* Miami: University of Miami School of Law.

Branscomb, A. W., 1995. Anonymity, Autonomy, and Accountability: Challenges to the First Amendment in Cyberspaces. *Yale Law Journal,* May, 104(7), pp. 1639–1679.

Brenner, S. W., 2008. Fantasy Crime: The Role of Criminal Law in Virtual Worlds. *Vanderbilt Journal of Entertainment and Technology Law,* 11(1), pp. 1–97.

Bretherton, R. & Dunbar, R. I. M., 2020. Dunbar's Number goes to Church: The Social Brain Hypothesis as a Third Strand in the Study of Church Growth. *Archive for the Psychology of Religion,* 42(1), pp. 63–76.

Breuer, J., Vogelgesang, J., Quandt, T. & Festl, R., 2015. Violent Video Games and Physical Aggression: Evidence for a Selection Effect among Adolescents. *Psychology of Popular Media Culture*, October, 4(4), pp. 305–328.

Brevik, D. & Schaefer, E., 1996. *Diablo*. San Mateo (CA): Blizzard North.

Briggs Myers, I., n.d. *The 16 MBTI® Personality Types*. [Online] Available at: https://www.myers-briggs.org/my-mbti-personality-type/the-16-mbti-personality-types/ [Accessed 3 December 2024].

Brignull, H., 2023. *Deceptive Pattersn: Exposing the Tricks Tech Companies use to Control you*. London: Testimonium.

British Psychological Society, 2024. *What is Psychology?*. [Online] Available at: https://www.bps.org.uk/what-psychology [Accessed 3 December 2024].

Bromberg, H., 1996. Are MUDs Communities? Identity, Belonging and Consciousness in Virtual Worlds. In: R. Shields, ed. *Cultures of Internet: Virtual Spaces, Real Histories, Living Bodies*. London: Sage, pp. 143–152.

Brothers, J. et al., 1993. *SillyMUD*. Gainesville, FL, United States of America.

Brown, E. & Cairns, P., 2004. *A Grounded Investigation of Game Immersion*. Vienna: Association for Computing Machinery, pp. 1297–1300.

Bruckman, A., 1992. *Identity Workshop: Emergent Social and Psychological Phenomena in Text-Based Virtual Reality*. Cambridge: MIT Media Lab.

Bruckman, A., 1998. Community Support for Constructionist Learning. *Collaborative Computing*, 7, pp. 47–86.

Burka, L. P., 1992. *Old MUD Nostalgia*. [Online] Available at: https://www.linnaean.org/~lpb/muddex/a-o.html [Accessed 3 December 2024].

Burleigh, T. J., Schoenherr, J. R. & Lacroix, G. L., 2013. Does the Uncanny Valley Exist? An Empirical Test of the Relationship between Eeriness and the Human Likeness of Digitally Created Faces. *Computers in Human Behaviour*, May, 29(3), pp. 759–771.

Burns, R., 1786. To A Louse, On Seeing One on a Lady's Bonnet at Church. In: *Poems Chiefly in the Scottish Dialect. Edited by Robert Burns*. Kilmarnock (Ayrshire): John Wilson, pp. 192–194.

Burroughs, E. R., 1912. Under the Moons of Mars. All-Story, February–July.

Cadwell, T. & Feak, S., 2009. *League of Legends: Clash of Fates*. Santa Monica (CA): Riot Games.

Caillois, R., trans. 1961. *Man, Play and Games*. Glencoe (IL): Free Press of Glencoe.

Caldwell, D. F. & Burger, J. M., 2011. On Thin Ice: Does Uniform Color Really Affect Aggression in Professional Hockey?. *Social Psychological and Personality Science*, 2(3), pp. 306–310.

Campbell, J., 1949. *The Hero with a Thousand Faces*. Princeton (NJ): Princeton University Press.

Camp, B. T., 2007. The Play's the Thing: A Theory of Taxing Virtual Worlds. *Hastings Law Journal*, 59(1), pp. 1–71.

Canossa, A. et al., 2015. *In your Face(t): Impact of Personality and Context on Gameplay Behavior*. Pacific Grove: Society for the Advancement of the Science of Digital Games.

Capraro, V. & Vanzo, A., 2019. The Power of Moral Words: Loaded Language Generates Framing Effects in the Extreme Dictator Game. *Judgement and Decision Making*, May, 14(3), pp. 309–317.

Caramore, M. B., 2008. Help! My Intellectual Property is Trapped: Second Life, Conflicting Ownership Claims and the Problem of Access. *Richmond Journal of Law and Technology*, 15(1).

Carazo-Chandler, C., 1999. *Online Migration and Population Mobility in a Virtual Gaming Setting - Ultima Online*. Christchurch, New Zealand.

Carbine Studios, 2014. *WildStar*. Aliso Viejo(CA): NCSoft.

Card, O. S., 1988. *Characters & Viewpoint*. Cincinnati (OH): Writer's Digest Books.

Carnagey, N. L. & Anderson, C. A., 2005. The Effects of Reward and Punishment in Violent Video Games on Aggressive Affect, Cognition, and Behavior. Psychological Science, 1 November, 16(11), pp. 882–889.

Carnagey, N. L., Anderson, C. A. & Bushman, B. J., 2007. The Effect of Video Game Violence on Physiological Desensitization to Real-Life Violence. *Journal of Experimental Social Psychology,* May, 43(3), pp. 489–496.

Carobus, A., Shillingsburg, R., Cook, D. & Edery, D. J., 2011. *Realm of the Mad God.* Los Altos (CA): Wild Shadow Studios.

Carr, J., 2005. *Jimmy Carr: Stand Up.* [Online] Available at: https://youtu.be/ho9rW3GXtNA?t=2005 [Accessed 3 December 2024].

Carroll, L., 1865. *Alice's Adventures in Wonderland.* London: Macmillan.

Carter, L., 1973. *Imaginary Worlds.* 1st ed. New York (NY): Ballantine.

Castillo, F., 2009. *Playing by the Rules: Applying International Humanitarian Law to Video and Computer Games.* Geneva: Track Impunity Always.

Castronova, E., 2004. The Right to Play. *New York Law School Review,* 8 December, 49(1). See https://digitalcommons.nyls.edu/nyls_law_review/vol49/iss1/.

Center for Open Science, 2023. *Reproducibility Project: Psychology.* [Online] Available at: https://osf.io/ezcuj/ [Accessed 3 December 2024].

CERN, 2024. *Why Do Physicists Mention "Five Sigma" in Their Results?.* [Online] Available at: https://home.cern/resources/faqs/five-sigma [Accessed 1 June 2024].

ChainPlay.gg, 2024. *Top MMORPG by Market Cap.* [Online] Available at: https://chainplay.gg/genre/mmorpg/ [Accessed 3 December 2024].

Chamberlain, J., Poesio, M. & Kruschwitz, U., 2008. *Phrase Detectives: A Web-based Collaborative Annotation Game.* Graz. In the proceedings of the I-SEMANTICS conference in Graz, Austria, 2–5 September 2008. Published by Verlag der Technischen Universität Graz.

Chandler, H. M., 2013. *The Game Production Handbook.* 3rd ed. Burlington (MA): Jones & Bartlett.

Chang, K. T.-T. et al., 2008. *Why I Love This Online Game: The MMORPG Stickiness Factor.* Paris: Association for Information Systems.

Chapman, L. J., 1967. Illusory Correlation in Observational Report. *Journal of Verbal Learning and Verbal Behaviour,* 1 February, 6(1), pp. 151–155.

Charlton, J. P., 2002. A Factor-Analytic Investigation of Computer 'Addiction' and Engagement. *British Journal of Psychology,* August, 93(3), pp. 329–344.

Charlton, J. P. & Danforth, I. D., 2007. Distinguishing Addiction and High Engagement in the Context of Online Game Playing. *Computers in Human Behavior,* May, 23(3), pp. 1531–1548.

Charmaz, K., 2000. Grounded Theory: Objectivist and Contructivist Methods. In: N. K. Denzin & Y. S. Lincoln, eds. *The Handbook of Qualitative Research.* Thousand Oaks (CA): Sage, pp. 509–535.

Chastain, M., Quan, M. & Tse, M., 1992. *Merc DikuMUD.* Santa Barbara (CA): University of California Santa Barbara.

Chastain, M. et al., 1994. *EnvyMUD.* Santa Barbara (CA): University of California, Santa Barbara.

Cherny, L. M., 1995. *The MUD Register: Conversational Modes of Action in a Text-Based Virtual Reality.* Ann Arbor: Stanford University.

Chia, D. X. Y. et al., 2020. Prevalence of Internet Addiction and Gaming Disorders in Southeast Asia: A Meta-Analysis. *International Journal of Environmental Research and Public Health,* 9 April, 17(7), p. 2582.

Christie, A., 1937. *Death on the Nile.* London: Colins Crime Club.

Chungryong, O., 1994. *Jyuragi Gongwon.* Samjung Data Services.

Cirulli, G., 2014. *2048.* Gorizia (Friuli-Venezia Giulia): Gabriele Cirulli.

Clark, N. L., 2006. *Addiction and the Structural Characteristics of Massively Multiplayer Online Games.* Manoa: University of Hawai'i.

Clark, N. L. & Scott, P. S., 2009. *Game Addiction: The Experience and the Effects.* Jefferson (NC): McFarland.

Clark, R., 2012. *How the Humble Stop Sign has Found Itself in Welsh Language Row.* [Online] Available at: https://www.walesonline.co.uk/news/local-news/how-humble-stop-sign-found-2023089 [Accessed 3 December 2024].

Clary, P., Gledhill, R. & Crawley, C., 1990. *Empyrion*. London: IOWA.

Clodius, J., 1994. *Concepts of Space and Place in a Virtual Community*. [Online] Available at: https://web.archive.org/web/20010422023841/https://dragonmud.org/people/jen/space.html [Accessed 3 December 2024].

Clodius, J., 1995. *Ritual and Religion in DragonMud*. [Online] Available at: https://web.archive.org/web/20031013094255/https://dragonmud.com/people/jen/ritual.html [Accessed 3 December 2024].

Clodius, J., 1996a. *Orality in a Text-based Community*. [Online] Available at: https://web.archive.org/web/20010421073855/https://dragonmud.org/people/jen/oral.html [Accessed 3 December 2024].

Clodius, J., 1996b. *Shar's Return: Performance as Gift*. [Online] Available at: https://web.archive.org/web/20010221205213/https:/dragonmud.org/people/Jen/shar.html [Accessed 3 December 2024].

Clodius, J., 1997. *Creating a Community of Interest: "Self" and "Other" on DragonMud*. Jackson Hole.

Clover, S., McQuaid, B. & Trost, W., 1999. *EverQuest*. San Diego (CA): Sony Online Entertainment.

Coates, T., 2004. *From Pirate Dwarves to Ninja Elves*. [Online] Available at: https://plasticbag.org/archives/2004/03/from_pirate_dwarves_to_ninja_elves/ [Accessed 9 February 2024].

Coleman, J. T., 2021. *Crowfall*. Austin (TX): ArtCraft Entertainment.

Coleman, J. T. et al., 2008. *Wizard101*. Round Rock (TX): KingIsle Entertainment.

Coleridge, S. T., 1817. *Biographia Literaria*. London: Rest Fenner.

Columb, D., Griffiths, M. D. & O'Gara, C., 2023. A Descriptive Survey of Online Gaming Characteristics and Gaming Disorder in Ireland. *Irish Journal of Psychological Medicine*, June, 40(2), pp. 200–208.

Committee of Ministers to Member States, 1992. *On Video Games with a Racist Content*. Strasbourg: Council of Europe.

Consalvo, M., 2007. *Cheating: Gaining Advantage in Videogames*. Cambridge (MA): MIT Press.

Consalvo, M., 2009. There is No Magic Circle. *Games and Culture*, 4(4), pp. 408–417.

Contato, A., 2021. *Through the Moongate: Part II*. Independently published.

Cook, P., Bennett, A., Miller, J. & Moore, D., 1960. *Beyond the Fringe*. Edinburgh.

Cooper, A., 1999. *The Inmates Are Running the Asylum: Why High Tech Products Drive Us Crazy and How to Restore the Sanity*. Indianapolis (IN): Macmillan.

Cooper, S. et al., 2010. Predicting Protein Structures with a Multiplayer Online Game. *Nature*, 466, pp. 756–760.

Co, P., 2006. *Level Design for Games: Creating Compelling Game Experiences*. Berkeley (CA): New Riders.

Copier, M., 2007. *Beyond the Magic Circle: A Network Perspective on Role-Play in Online Games*. Utrecht: University of Utrecht.

Cordrey, P. et al., 1986. *MirrorWorld*. London: IOWA.

Cordrey, P. et al., 1990. *Chaos World of Wizards*. London: IOWA.

Council of Europe, 2008. *Human Rights Guidelines for Online Games Providers*. Strasbourg: Directorate General of Human Rights and Legal Affairs.

Cousineau, P., 1990. *The Hero's Journey: Joseph Campbell on His Life and Work*. New York (NY): Harper & Row.

Cowan, A., 1995. *The MUD Connector*. [Online] Available at: https://www.mudconnect.com/ [Accessed 3 December 2024].

Cox, A., Acott, R., Finnis, J. & Thrane, L., 1987. *AberMUD*. Aberystwyth (Ceredigion): University of Wales.

Coyne, S. M. & Stockdale, L., 2021. Growing Up with Grand Theft Auto: A 10-Year Study of Longitudinal Growth of Violent Video Game Play in Adolescents. *Cyberpsychology, Behavior and Social Networking*, 24(1), pp. 11–16.

Crawford, S., 2004. Who's in Charge of Who I Am?: Identity and Law Online. *New York Law School Review,* 8 December, 49(1).

Crowther, W. & Woods, D., 1976. *Adventure.* Cambridge, Massachusetts.

Cryptic Studios, 2010. *Star Trek Online.* Los Gatos (CA): Atari.

Csikszentmihalyi, M., 1975. *Beyond Boredom and Anxiety: Experiencing Flow in Work and Play.* San Francisco (CA): Jossey-Bass.

Cummings, J., 2013. *GDC: Riot Experimentally Investigates Online Toxicity.* [Online] Available at: https://www.gamedeveloper.com/design/gdc-riot-experimentally-investigates-online-toxicity [Accessed 3 December 2024].

Curtis, P., 1990. *LambdaMOO.* Palo Alto (CA): Xerox PARC.

Curtis, P., 1992. *Mudding: Social Phenomena in Text-Based Virtual Realities.* Berkeley: Computer Professionals for Social Responsibility.

Ćwiek, A. et al., 2021. The Bouba/Kiki Effect is Robust across Cultures and Writing Systems. *Philosophical Transactions of the Royal Society B: Biological Sciences,* 15 November, 377(1841). Article no. 20200390. See https://royalsocietypublishing.org/toc/rstb/2022/377/1841.

Daglow, D., 1991. *Neverwinter Nights.* Mountain View (CA): STrategic Simulations Inc.

Dah, J. et al., 2024. Gamification is not Working: Why?. *Games and Culture,* 8 February, pp. 1–24.

Daleske, J., 1973. *Empire.* Urbana-Champaign: University of Illinois.

Daleske, J., 1975. *Dungeon.* Urbana-Champaign: University of Illinois.

Damer, B., 1997. *Avatars! Exploring and Building Virtual Worlds on the Internet.* Berkeley (CA): Peachpit.

Darmok. 1991. [*Star Trek: The Next Generation*] Directed by Winrich Kolbe. United States of America: Paramount Domestic Television.

Davis, E., 1994. It's a MUD, MUD, MUD, MUD World: Exploring Online Reality. *The Village Voice,* 22 February, XXXIX, 39 (1).

de Meza, D. & Pathania, V., 2021. *Is the Second-Cheapest Wine a Rip-Off? Economics vs. Psychology in Product-Line Pricing.* New York: American Association of Wine Economists.

De Wildt, L. et al., 2019. (Re-)Orienting the Video Game Avatar. *Games and Culture,* 17 July, 15(8), pp. 962–981.

Dear, B., 2017. *The Friendly Orange Glow: The Untold Story of the Plato System and the Dawn of Cyberculture.* New York (NY): Pantheon Books.

Deazley, R. & Meletti, B., 2023. *Copyright Bite #1.4.* [Online] Available at: https://www.copyrightuser.org/create/public-domain/copyright-bite-1-4-duration/ [Accessed 7 July 2023].

Debus, M. S., 2019. *Unifying Game Ontology: A Faceted Classification of Game Elements.* Copenhagen: ITU Copenhagen (PhD Thesis).

Deci, E. L., Koestner, R. & Ryan, R. M., 1999. A Meta-Analytic Review of Experiments Examining the Effects of Extrinsic Rewards on Intrinsic Motivation. *Psychological Bulletin,* 125(2), pp. 627–668.

Deci, E. L. & Ryan, R. M., 1985. *Intrinsic Motivation and Self-Determination in Human Behavior.* New York (NY): Plenum.

Delve, J. et al. eds., 2012. *The Preservation of Complex Objects, Volume 1: Visualisations and Simulations.* Portsmouth (Hampshire): University of Portsmouth.

Démeunier, J.-N. et al., 1789. *Déclaration des droits de l'Homme et du citoyen de 1789.* Paris: National Constituent Assembly.

Dent, S., 2023. *Interesting Stories about Curious Words.* London: John Murray.

Descartes, R., 1637. *Discourse on the Method of Rightly Conducting One's Reason and of Seeking Truth in the Sciences.* 1st ed. Leiden: Ian Maire.

Désilets, P. & Béland, M., 2006. *Assassin's Creed.* Montreal (Quebec): Ubisoft.

di Pellegrino, G. et al., 1992. Understanding Motor Events: A Neurophysiological Study. Experimental Brain Research, October, 91(1), pp. 176–180.

Dibbell, J., 1999. *My Tiny Life: Crime and Passion in a Virtual World.* New York (NY): Henry Holt.

Dibbell, J., 2006. Owned! Intellectual Property in the Age of Dupers, Gold Farmers, eBayers and Other Enemies of the Virtual State. In: J. M. Balkin & B. S. Noveck, eds. *The State of Play: Law, Games and Virtual Worlds.* New York (NY): New York University Press, pp. 137–145.

Dieris-Hirche, J. et al., 2020. Problematic Gaming Behaviour and the Personality Traits of Video Gamers: A Cross-Sectional Survey. *Computers in Human Behaviour,* May, 106. Article number 106272 . See https://www.sciencedirect.com/journal/computers-in-human-behavior/vol/106/suppl/C.

DiGiuseppe, N. & Nardi, B., 2007. Real Genders Choose Fantasy Characters: Class Choice in World of Warcraft. *First Monday,* 7 May, 12(5).

Dill, K. E. & Dill, J. C., 1998. Video Game Violence: A Review of the Empirical Literature. *Aggression and Violent Behavior,* 3(4), pp. 407–428.

Diversity University, 1996. *Diversity University Mission (Purpose) Statement.* [Online] Available at: https://web.archive.org/web/19961102172910/https://du.org/duinc/mission.htm [Accessed 3 December 2024].

Dominick, J. R., 1984. Videogames, Television Violence, and Aggression in Teenagers. *Journal of Communication,* June, 34(2), pp. 136–147.

Donnelly, T. P., 1978. *The Sorcerer's Cave.* London: Ariel Productions.

Donovan, T., 2010. *Replay: The History of Video Games.* Hove (Sussex): Yellow Ant Media.

Dörner, D., 1999. *Bauplan für eine Seele.* Reinbek (Schleswig-Holstein): Rowohlt.

Drapeau, D. & Baude, P., 2015. *Tom Clancy's Rainbow Six: Siege.* Montreal (Quebec): Ubisoft.

Drennan, P., 2007. *Ethnography of Play in a Massively Multi-Player Online Role Playing Game: Marketplaces, Team Work and Free Play.* Brisbane: University of Queensland.

Dubourg, E. & Baumard, N., 2021. Why Imaginary Worlds? The Psychological Foundations and Cultural Evolution of Fictions with Imaginary Worlds. *Behavioural and Brain Sciences,* 30 June, 45(e276), pp. 1–72.

Dubourg, E. et al., 2023. Exploratory Preferences Explain the Human Fascination for Imaginary Worlds in Fictional Stories. *Scientific Reports,* 13(8657), p. 8657.

Ducheneaut, N., Moore, R. J. & Nickell, E., 2004. *Designing for Sociability in Massively Multiplayer Games: An Examination of the "Third Places" of SWG.* Copenhagen: IT University of Copenhagen.

Ducheneaut, N., Yee, N., Nickell, E. & Moore, R. J., 2006. *"Alone Together?" Exploring the Social Dynamics of Massively Multiplayer Online Games.* Montréal: Association for Computing Machinery, pp. 7–16.

Duggan, J., 2020. Who writes Harry Potter Fan Fiction? Passionate Detachment, "Zooming Out" and Fan Fiction Paratexts on AO3. *Transformative Works and Cultures,* 15 September, 34, pp. 1–25.

Dumas, A., 1844. Les Trois Mousquetaires. *Le Siècle,* 14 March–14 July.

Dunbar, R. I. M., 1992. Neocortex Size as a Constraint on Group Size in Primates. *Journal of Human Evolution,* June, 22(6), pp. 469–493.

Dunbar, R. I. M., 1998. The Social Brain Hypothesis. *Evolutionary Anthropology,* 7 December, 6(5), pp. 178–190.

Dunbar, R. I. M., 2010. Constraints on the Evolution of Social Institutions and their Implications for Information Flow. *Journal of Institutional Economics,* 16 August, 7(3), pp. 345–371.

Dunbar, R. I. M. & Spoors, M., 1995. Social Networks, Support Cliques and Kinship. *Human Nature,* September, 6(3), p. 273–290.

Duncombe, K. & Battin, J., 1976. *Moria.*

Dunning, D., 2011. The Dunning–Kruger Effect: On Being Ignorant of One's Own Ignorance. *Advances in Experimental Social Psychology,* 44, pp. 247–296.

Duranske, B. T., 2008. *Virtual Law: Navigating the Legal Landscape of Virtual Worlds.* Chicago (IL): American Bar Association.

Eastern Oregon University, 2024. *Anthropology vs Sociology: What's the Difference, and Which Is Right for You?*. [Online] Available at: https://online.eou.edu/resources/article/anthropology-vs-sociology [Accessed 3 December 2024].

Eckelberry, D., 2006. *Dungeons & Dragons Online: Stormreach*. Westwood (MA): Atari.

Edman, P., Berg, A., Andersson, F. & Pettersson, J., 2003. *Project Entropia*. Gothenburg: MindArk.

Eklund, L., 2015. Focus Group Interviews as a Way to Evaluate and Understand Game Play Experiences. In: P. Lankoski & S. Björk, eds. *Game Research Methods*. Pittsburgh (PA): ETC Press, pp. 133–148.

Eklund, L. & Johansson, M., 2013. Played and Designed Sociality in a Massive Multiplayer Online Game. *Eludamos,* 23 December, 7(1), pp. 35–54.

Elliott, J., Adams, L. & Bruckman, A., 2002. *No Magic Bullett: 3D Video Games in Education*. Seattle: International Society for the Learning Sciences.

Elson, J., 1993. *CircleMUD*. Baltimore (MD): John Hopkins University.

Emilsson, K. P. et al., 2003. *EVE Online*. Reykjavik: Simon & Schuster Interactive (North America); Crucial Entertainment (Europe).

Emmert, J., 2004. *City of Heroes*. Los Gatos (CA): NCSoft.

Erickson, S. E. & Dal Cin, S., 2018. Romantic Parasocial Attachments and the Development of Romantic Scripts, Schemas and Beliefs among Adolescents. *Media Psychology,* 21(1), pp. 111–136.

Erümit, S. F., Şılbır, L., Erümit, A. K. & Karal, H., 2021. Determination of Player Types according to Digital Game Playing Preferences: Scale Development and Validation Study. *International Journal of Human–Computer Interaction,* 26 December, 37(11), pp. 991–1002.

European Convention, 2000. *Charter of Fundamental Rights of the European Union*. Nice: European.

European Court of Human Rights, 1950. *European Convention on Human Rights*. Strasbourg: Council of Europe.

European Parliament, 2022. *Esports and Video Games*. Brussels: European Parliament.

Fagen, R. & Fagen, J., 2009. Play Behaviour and Multi-Year Juvenile Survival in Free-Ranging Brown Bears, Ursus Arctos. *Evolutionary Ecology Research*, 11(7), pp. 1053–1067.

Fairfield, J., 2005. Virtual Property. *Boston University Law Review,* 85(4), pp. 1047–1102.

Fairfield, J., 2009. Escape Into the Panopticon: Virtual Worlds and the Surveillance Society. *Yale Law Journal,* 19 January, 118(Pocket Part 131), pp. 131–135.

Fairfield, J., 2012. Avatar Experimentation: Human Subject Research in Virtual Worlds. *UC Irvine Law Review,* June, 2, pp. 695–772.

Falstein, N., 2004. Natural Funativity. *Gamasutra,* 10 November.

Farmer, F. R., 1988. *Habitat Anecdotes and Other Boastings*. Cupertino: Electric Communities.

Farmer, F. R., 1992. Social Dimensions of Habitat's Citizenry. In: C. E. Loeffler & T. Anderson, eds. *The Virtual Reality Casebook*. New York (NY): Van Nostrand Reinhold.

Farmer, F. R., 2007. *The Untold History of Toontown's SpeedChat*. [Online] Available at: https://habitatchronicles.com/2007/03/the-untold-history-of-toontowns-speedchat-or-blockchattm-from-disney-finally-arrives/ [Accessed 3 December 2024].

Farmer, F. R., 2017. *Neohabitat*. [Online] Available at: https://neohabitat.org/ [Accessed 3 December 2024].

Farmer, F. R. & Glass, B., 2010. *Building Web Reputation Systems*. Sebastopol (CA): O'Reilly.

Federal Public Service Justice Gaming Commission, 2018. *Research Report on Loot Boxes*. Brussels: FPS Justice Gaming Commission.

Federal Trade Commission, 2022. *Fortnite Video Game Maker Epic Games to Pay More Than Half a Billion Dollars over FTC Allegations of Privacy Violations and Unwanted Charges*. [Online] Available at: https://www.ftc.gov/news-events/news/press-releases/2022/12/fortnite-video-game-maker-epic-games-pay-more-half-billion-dollars-over-ftc-allegations [Accessed 3 December 2024].

Felagund, F. F., 1999. *TinyMUD Classic.* [Online] Available at: https://toccobrator.com/classic.html [Accessed 15 August 2022].

Fenlason, J., 1984. *Hack.* Sudbury (MA): Lincoln-Sudbury Regional High School.

Ferguson, C. J., 2020. Aggressive Video Games Research Emerges from its Replication Crisis (Sort of). *Current Opinion in Psychology,* 10 February, 36, pp. 1–6.

Ferguson, C. J. & Konijn, E. A., 2015. She Said/He Said: A Peaceful Debate on Video Game Violence. *Psychology of Popular Media Culture,* October, 4(4), pp. 397–411.

Festinger, J., 2005. *Video Game Law.* Markham (Ontario): LexisNexis.

Festinger, L., 1954. A Theory of Social Comparison. *Human Relations,* May, 7(2), pp. 117–140.

Festinger, L., 1957. *A Theory of Cognitive Dissonance.* Redwood City: Stanford University Press.

Ffinch, S., 2011. *Rift.* Redwood City (CA): Trion Worlds.

Firor, M. & Sage, P. D., 2014. *The Elder Scrolls Online.* Hunt Valley (MD): Bethesda Softworks.

Fitch, W. E., 1918. *Dietotherapy.* New York (NY): Appleton.

Flinn, K. & Taylor, J., 1980. *Dungeons of Kesmai.* Charlottesvill (VA): Kesmai Corporation.

Flinn, K. & Taylor, J., 1981. *Island of Kesmai.* Charlottesville (VA): Kesmai Corporation.

Flinn, K. & Taylor, J., 1986. *Air Warrior.* Charlottesville (VA): Kesmai Corporation.

Flinn, K. & Taylor, J., 1991. *Multiplayer BattleTech.* Charlottesville (VA): Kesmai Corporation.

Foard, L., 1990. *TinyMUSH.* Worcester (MA).

Foster, H. J., 1936. Response to Soil Program Cards is Received. *Michigan Extension News*, October, 7(10), p. 5.

Fox, P., 1983. *ROCK.* Colchester (Essex): University of Essex.

Fox, T., 2015. *Undertale.* Toby Fox.

Frank, M. G. & Gilovich, T., 1988. The Dark Side of Self- and Social Perception: Black Uniforms and Aggression in Professional Sports. *Journal of Personality and Social Psychology,* 54(1), pp. 74–85.

Fraser, I. & Kelly, F., 2001. *The Go Game.* San Francisco (CA): The Go Game.

Free Guy. 2021. [Film] Directed by Shawn Levy. United States of America: Berlanti Productions.

Fritz, B. & Stöckl, S., 2023. Why Do We Play? Towards a Comprehensive Player Typology. *Games and Culture,* May, 18(3), pp. 300–321.

Frommel, J., Johnson, D. & Mandryk, R. L., 2023. How Perceived Toxicity of Gaming Communities is Associated with Social Capital, Satisfaction of Relatedness, and Loneliness. *Computers in Human Behaviour Reports,* 7 June, 10, p. 100302.

Frösen, J., 1990. *BatMUD.* Helsinki: Helsinki University of Technology.

Fryer, L., 2024. *Games Industry Bubble.* [Online] Available at: https://www.youtube.com/watch?v=PHwCypPq1iM [Accessed 3 December 2024].

Gahnberg, C., de Guzman, N., Robachevsky, A. & Wan, A., 2022. *Internet Impact Brief: South Korea's Interconnection Rules.* [Online] Available at: https://www.internetsociety.org/resources/doc/2022/internet-impact-brief-south-koreas-interconnection-rules/ [Accessed 9 December 2022].

Game Developer, n.d. *Search.* [Online] Available at: https://www.gamedeveloper.com/search?q=postmortem [Accessed 3 December 2024].

Gamer DNA, 2015. *Bartle Test of Gamer Psychology.* [Online] Available at: https://web.archive.org/web/20150706073106/https://www.gamerdna.com/quizzes/bartle-test-of-gamer-psychology [Accessed 3 December 2024].

Gamespot, 1996. *Multi-Player Online Gaming Survey Results.* [Online] Available at: https://web.archive.org/web/20070808002843/https://www.gamespot.com/features/olsurvey/sld025.htm [Accessed 3 December 2024].

Garcia, J. A., 1982. *Zaxxon.* San Diego (CA): Sega/Gremlin.

Garfield, R., 1993. *Magic: The Gathering.* Seattle (WA): Wizards of the Coast.

Garon, J. M., 2017. Fandom and Creativity - Including Fan Art, Fan Fiction and Cosplay. In: *The Pop Culture Business Handbook for Cons and Festivals.* Fort Lauderdale (FL): Manegiare Publications, 223 (4), pp. 161–176.

Garriott, R., 1981. *Ultima.* Davis (CA): California Pacific Computer Company.

Garriott, R., 1985. *Ultima IV: Quest of the Avatar.* Austin (TX): Origin Systems.

Garriott, R. & Fisher, D., 2017. *Explore/Create.* 1st ed. New York (NY): HarperCollins.

Garriott, R. & Mendelsohn, S., 1999. *Ultima IX: Ascension.* Austin (TX): Electronic Arts.

Garriott, R., Quinn, K., Cotton, B. & Reinen, S., 2018. *Shroud of the Avatar: Forsaken Virtues.* Austin (TX): Catnip Games.

Garriott, R. & Sage, P. D., 2007. *Richard Garriott's Tabula Rasa.* Austin (TX): NCSoft.

Gaylor, G. & Joudrey, J., 2017. *VRChat.* San Francisco (CA): VRChat Inc.

Gee, J. P., 2003. *What Video Games Have to Teach Us About Learning and Literacy.* New York (NY): Palgrave Macmillan.

Gewirth, A., 1978. *Reason and Morality.* Chicago (IL): University of Chicago Press.

Gibson, W., 1984. *Neuromancer.* New York (NY): Ace.

Gibson, W., 1996. *Idoru.* New York (NY): Putnam.

Giordano, A. L., Schmit, M. K. & McCall, J., 2023. Exploring Adolescent Social Media and Internet Gaming Addiction: The Role of Emotion Regulation. *Journal of Addictions & Offender Counseling,* April, 44(1), pp. 69–80.

Göbel, S. et al., 2010. *Personalized, Adaptive Digital Educational Games using Narrative Game-based Learning Objects.* Changchun: Springer, pp. 438–445.

Godager, G., 2001. *Anarchy Online.* Oslo: Funcom.

Godager, G. & Griffin, A., 2008. *Age of Conan: Hyborian Adventures.* Oslo: Eidos.

Goffman, E., 1961. *Encounters: Two Studies in the Sociology of Interaction.* 1st ed. Indianapolis (IN): Bobbs-Merrill.

Goldman, E., 2005. Speech Showdowns at the Virtual Corral. *Santa Clara Computer and High Technology Law Journal,* 21(4), pp. 845–854.

Google, 2010. *Google Books Ngram Viewer.* [Online] Available at: https://books.google.com/ngrams/graph?content=toxic+behaviour&year_start=1800&year_end=2019&corpus=en-2019&smoothing=3 [Accessed 3 December 2024].

Gorzelany, J., 2021. New Features Car Buyers Want Most - And Those They Steer Clear of. *Forbes,* 12 November. https://www.forbes.com/sites/jimgorzelany/2021/11/12/new-car-features-buyers-want-and-prefer-to-steer-clear-of/.

Goscinny, R. & Uderzo, A., 1959. Astérix le Gaulois. *Pilote,* 29 October, p. 20.

Gotcha Gotcha Games, 1992. *RPG Maker.* Tokyo: Gotcha Gotcha Games.

Gould, D., 2008. *Virtual Property in MMOGs.* [Online] Available at: https://virtuallyblind.com/files/reading-room/gould_virtual_property.pdf [Accessed 3 December 2024].

Gourville, J. T. & Soman, D., 1998. Payment Depreciation: The Behavioral Effects of Temporally Separating Payments from Consumption. *Journal of Consumer Research,* September, 25(2), pp. 160–174.

Gower, A., 2024. *Brighter Shores.* Cambridge: Fen Research.

Grace, L., 2019. Games Blamed for Moral Decline and Addiction Throughout History. *The Conversation,* 9 October.

Grant, S., McPherson, D. & Fisher, B. W., 2007. *Vanguard: Saga of Heroes.* Carlsbad (CA): Sony Online Entertainment.

Greenebaum, J., 2012. Veganism, Identity and the Quest for Authenticity. *Food, Culture and Society,* March, 15(1), pp. 129–144.

Greenfield, D. N., 1999. *Virtual Addiction: Help for Netheads, Cyberfreaks, and Those Who Love Them.* Oakland (CA): New Harbinger.

Griffiths, M. D., 2005. A 'Components' Model of Addiction within a Biopsychosocial Framework. *Journal of Substance Use,* August, 10(4), pp. 191–197.

Griffiths, M. D., 2019. Loot Box Buying among Adolescent Gamers: A Cause for Concern?. *Education and Health,* 37(3), pp. 63–66.

Grimmelmann, J., 2004. Virtual Worlds as Comparative Law. *New York Law School Review,* 49(1), p. 147.

Groening, M., 1989. *The Simpsons.* [Art] (Gracie Films).

Grüsser, S. M., Thalemann, R. & Griffiths, M. D., 2007. Excessive Computer Game Playing: Evidence for Addiction and Aggression?. *Cyberpsychology and Behavior,* 2 April, 10(2), pp. 290–292.

Guard, D., 2007. *OpenSimulator.* OpenSimulator.

Guay-Bélanger, D., 2022. Assembling Auras: Towards a Methodology for the Preservation and Study of Video Games as Cultural Heritage Artefacts. *Games and Culture,* 5 July, 17(5), pp. 659–678.

Gu, B., 2020. *Dark Forest.* Gubsheep.

Guinness World Records, 2020. *EVE Online's Record-Breaking Fury at FWST-8.* [Online] Available at: https://www.guinnessworldrecords.com/news/2020/10/eve-onlines-record-breaking-fury-at-fwst-8 [Accessed 9 July 2023].

Gygax, E. G., 1977. *Monster Manual.* Lake Geneva (WI): Tactical Studies Rules.

Gygax, E. G. & Arneson, D. L., 1974. *Dungeons & Dragons.* Lake Geneva (WI): Tactical Studies Rules.

Hackman, J. R. & Vidmar, N., 1970. Effects of Size and Task Type on Group Performance and Member Reactions. *Sociometry,* March, 33(1), pp. 37–54.

Haker, H., Kawohl, W., Herwig, U. & Rössler, W., 2013. Mirror Neuron Activity during Contagious Yawning - an fMRI Study. *Brain Imaging and Behaviour,* March, 7(1), pp. 28–34.

Halvarsson, K. & Winther, D., 2009. *Blood, Gold or Marriage - What Gets you Going? A Study of Personality Traits and In-Game Behavior.* Stockholm: KTH Royal Institute of Technology.

Hamari, J., 2011. *Perspectives from Behavioral Economics to Analyzing Game Design Patterns: Loss Aversion in Social Games.* Vancouver: Association of Computing Machinery.

Hamari, J. & Tuunanen, J., 2014. Player Types: A Meta-Synthesis. *DiGRA Transactions,* March, 1(2), pp. 29–53.

Hamdaoui, N., Idrissi, M. K. & Bennani, S., 2018. Modelling Learners in Educational Games: Relationship between Playing and Learning Styles. *Simulation & Gaming,* December, 49(6), pp. 675–699.

Hammer, S. et al., 1991. *DikuMUD.* Copenhagen: Copenhagen University.

Han, D. H. et al., 2007. Dopamine Genes and Reward Dependence in Adolescents with Excessive Internet Video Game Play. *Journal of Addiction Medicine,* September, 1(3), pp. 133–138.

Hany, D., Chadwick, F. & Evans, P., 1975. *En Garde!.* Normal (IL): Game Designers' Workshop.

Haraway, D., 1991. A Cyborg Manifesto: Science, Technology, and Socialist-Feminism in the Late Twentieth Century. In: *Simians, Cyborgs and Women: The Reinvention of Nature.* New York (NY): Routledge, pp. 149–181.

Harling, P. et al., 1986. *Quest.* London: IOWA.

Harper, J., 2017. *Blades in the Dark.* Silver Spring (MD): Evil Hat.

Harry Potter and the Deathly Hallows – Part 2. 2011. [Film] Directed by David Yates. United Kingdom: Warner Bros.

Harry Potter and the Philosopher's Stone. 2001. [Film] Directed by Chris Columbus. United Kingdom: Warner Bros.

Hart, C., 2017. Getting Into the Game: An Examination of Player Personality Projection in Videogame Avatars. *Game Studies,* December, 17(2).

Hart, J., Sutcliffe, A. G. & De Angeli, A., 2013. *Love it or Hate it! Interactivity and User Types.* Paris: Association for Computing Machinery, pp. 2059–2068.

Hartley, L. P., 1953. *The Go-Between.* London: Hamish Hamilton.

Hathaway, S. R. & McKinley, J. C., 1943. *The Minnesota Multiphasic Personality Inventory.* Revised ed. Minneapolis (MN): University of Minnesota Press.

Hawkins, T., Antonick, R. & Madden, J., 1988. *John Madden Football.* San Mateo (CA): Electronic Arts.

Haynes, C. & Holmevik, J. R., 1995. *LinguaMOO.* Dallas (TX): University of Texas.

Haynes, C. & Holmevik, J. R., 1996. Lingua Unlimited: Enhancing Pedagogical Reality with MOOs. *Kairos: A Journal for Teachers of Writing in Webbed Environments,* 1(2).

Haynes, C. & Holmevik, J. R., 1998. *High Wired: On the Design, Use and Theory of Educational MOOs.* Ann Arbor (MI): University of Michigan Press.

Hazard, R. & Lauper, C., 1983. *Girls just Wanna have Fun.* New York: Record Plant.

Hedron, 1998. *The Six Circles of the Adept Game Players.* [Online] Available at: https://web. archive.org/web/19991111145222/https://www.kaaos.com/hedron/6circles.htm [Accessed 3 December 2024].

Hellman, M. & Majamäki, M., 2016. Ordinary Men with Extra-Ordinary Skills? Masculinity Constructs among MMORPG-Gamers. *Journal of Research in Gender Studies,* January, 6(2), pp. 90–106.

Hemovich, V., 2020. It Does Matter If You Win or Lose, and How You Play the (Video) Game. *Games and Culture,* 1 June, 16(4), pp. 481–493.

Herman, D., 2000. Introducing Short-Term Brands: A New Branding Tool for a New Consumer Reality. *Journal of Brand Management,* 1 May, 7(5), pp. 330–340.

Hillery, G. A., 1955. Definitions of Community: Areas of Agreement. *Rural Sociology,* June, 20(2), pp. 111–123.

Hineline, P. N. & Rosales-Ruiz, J., 2013. Behavior in Relation to Aversive Events: Punishment and Negative Reinforcement. In: G. J. Madden, et al. eds. *APA Handbook of Behavior Analysis, Vol. 1: Methods and Principles.* Washington (DC): American Psychological Society, pp. 483–512.

Hodent, C., 2017. *The Gamer's Brain: How Neuroscience and UX Can Impact Video Game Design.* Boca Raton (FL): CRC Press.

Holter, M., 2007. Stop Saying "Immersion"!. In: J. Donnis, M. Gade & L. Thorup, eds. *Lifelike.* Copernhagen: Projektgruppen KP07 Landsforeningen for Levende Rollespil, pp. 19–24.

Horton, D. & Wohl, R. R., 1956. Mass Communication and Para-Social Interaction: Observations on Intimacy at a Distance. *Interpersonal and Biological Processes,* 1 August, 19(3), pp. 215–229.

Hou, A. C., Chern, C.-C., Chen, H.-G. & Yu-Chen, C., 2011. 'Migrating to a new virtual world': Exploring MMORPG Switching through Human Migration Theory. *Computers in Human Behaviour,* September, 27(5), pp. 1892–1903.

Howard, R. E., 1932. The Phoenix on the Sword. *Weird Tales,* December, 20(6), pp. 769–783.

Howard, R. E., 1936. The Hyborian Age. *The Phantagraph,* February, 4(3).

Howard, T., 2011. *The Elder Scrolls V: Skyrim.* Rockville (MD): Bethesda Softworks.

Hoyle, M. A. & Moseley, A., 2012. Community: The Wisdom of Crowds. In: N. Whitton & A. Moseley, eds. *Using Games to Enhance Learning and Teaching: A Beginner's Guide.* New York (NY): Routledge, pp. 31–44.

Hu, Y., Manikonda, L. & Kambhampati, S., 2014. *What We Instagram: A First Analysis of Instagram Photo Content and User Types.* Ann Arbor: AAAI, pp. 595–598.

Huang, Y., Lim, K. H. & Lin, Z., 2017. *Leveraging the Numerosity Effect to Influence Perceived Expensiveness of Virtual Items.* SSRN. Amsterdam, Netherlands.

Hudson, G., 1993. *ColdMUD.* Cambridge (MA): Massachusetts Institute of Technology.

Hughes, N. G. J., Flockton, J. R. & Cairns, P., 2023. Growing Together: An Analysis of Measurement Transparency across 15 Years of Player Motivation Questionnaires. *International Journal of Human-Computer Studies,* January, 169, p. 102940.

Huhh, J.-S., 2006. *Some Facts on MapleStory.* [Online] Available at: https://web.archive.org/web/20060717000906/https://gamestudy.org/eblog/?p=32 [Accessed 3 December 2024].

Huizinga, J., trans. 1949. *Homo Ludens: A Study of the Play-Element in Culture.* London: Routledge and Kegan Paul.

Human Dignity Trust, 2024. *Nigeria.* [Online] Available at: https://www.humandignitytrust.org/country-profile/nigeria/ [Accessed 3 December 2024].

Humphreys, S., 2005. Productive Users, Intellectual Property and Governance: The Challenges of Computer Games. *Media Arts Law Review,* 10(4), pp. 299–310.

Humphreys, S., 2008. "You're in Our World Now" TM: Ownership and Access in the Proprietary Community of an MMOG. In: V. Sugumaran, ed. *Intelligent Information Technologies: Concepts, Methodologies, Tools, and Applications*. London: IGI Global, pp. 2058–2073.

Hunicke, R., LeBlanc, M. & Zubek, R., 2004. *MDA: A Formal Approach to Game Design and Game Research*. San Jose: AAAI Press, p. 1722.

Hussain, Z. & Griffiths, M. D., 2008. Gender Swapping and Socializing in Cyberspace: An Exploratory Study. *CyberPsuchology and Behaviour,* 14 February, 11(1), pp. 47–53.

IceFrog, 2013. *Defense of the Ancients 2*. Bellevue (WA): Valve.

IDS Publishing Corporation, n.d. *The Science of Motivation*. [Online] Available at: https://www.reiss motivationprofile.com/ [Accessed 3 December 2024].

Iskenderova, A., Weidner, F. & Broll, W., 2017. *Drunk Virtual Reality Gaming: Exploring the Influence of Alcohol on Cybersickness*. Amsterdam: Association for Computing Machinery, pp. 561–572.

Ito, T. A., Larsen, J. T., Smith, N. K. & Cacioppo, J. T., 1998. Negative Information Weighs More Heavily on the Brain: The Negativity Bias in Evaluative Categorizations. *Journal of Personality and Social Psychology,* October, 75(4), pp. 887–900.

Iwatani, T., 1980. *Pac–Man*. Ōta (Tokyo): Namco.

Iyengar, S. S. & Lepper, M. R., 2000. When Choice is Demotivating: Can One Desire Too Much of a Good Thing?. *Journal of Personality and Social Psychology,* 79(6), pp. 995–1006.

J1mmy, 2024. *Runescape's Creator Made a New Game after 20 Years*. [Online] Available at: https://www.youtube.com/watch?v=z7VXhew7k60 [Accessed 3 December 2024].

Jackson, S. & Livingstone, I., 1982. *The Warlock of Firetop Mountain*. London: Puffin.

Jacobs, M., 1984. *Aradath*. Washington (DC): Adventures Unlimited Software Inc.

Jacobs, M., 1999. *Darkness Falls: The Crusade*. Fairfax (VA): America Online.

Jacobs, M., Barnett, P. & Hickman, J., 2008. *Warhammer Online: Age of Reckoning*. Fairfax (VA): Mythic Entertainment.

Jacobs, M., Firor, M. & Denton, R., 2001. *Dark Age of Camelot*. Fairfax (VA): Mythic Entertainment.

Jacobs, M. & Hyrup, D., 1990. *Dragon's Gate*. Washington (DC): Adventures Unlimited Software Inc.

Jagex, 2012. *Evolution of Combat: Survey Results*. [Online] Available at: https://secure.runescape.com/m=news/evolution-of-combat-survey-results [Accessed 3 December 2024].

Jakobsson, M., 2006. *Virtual Worlds & Social Interaction Design*. Umeå: University of Umeå.

Jenkins, P. S., 2004. The Virtual World as a Company Town - Freedom of Speech in Massively Multiple On-Line Role Playing Games. *Journal of Internet Law,* July, 8(1), pp. 1, 8–18.

Jennett, C. et al., 2008. Measuring and Defining the Experience of Immersion in Games. *International Journal of Human-Computer Studies,* September, 66(9), pp. 641–661.

Jeong, E. J., Ferguson, C. J. & Lee, S. J., 2019. Pathological Gaming in Young Adolescents: A Longitudinal Study Focused on Academic Stress and Self-Control in South Korea. *Journal of Youth and Adolescence,* 19 July, 48, pp. 2333–2342.

Jerz, D. G., 2007. Somewhere Nearby is Colossal Cave: Examining Will Crowther's Original "Adventure" in Code and in Kentucky. *Digital Humanities Quarterly,* 1(2).

Johanson, C., 2012. *Guild Wars 2*. Bellevue (WA): NCSoft.

Johansson, M. & Verhagen, H., 2010. *And Justice for All - the 10 Commandments of Online Games, and Then Some….* Stockholm: DiGRA.

Johnson, J. A., 2023. The Psychology of (In)Equality and Fairness. *Psychology Today,* 27 September.

Johnson, M. R. & Brock, T., 2020. The 'Gambling Turn' in Digital Game Monetization. *Journal of Gaming & Virtual Worlds,* 1 June, 12(2), pp. 145–163.

Jørgensen, K. & Mortensen, T. E., 2022. Whose Expression is it Anyway? Videogames and the Freedom of Expression. *Games and Culture,* 28 February, 17(7–8), pp. 997–1014.

Joymax, 2005. *Silkroad Online*. Seoul: Yahoo!.

Julkunen, J., 2020. *GameRefinery Player Motivations & Archetypes*. [Online] Available at: https://www.gamerefinery.com/gamerefinery-player-motivations-archetypes/ [Accessed 3 December 2024].

Jurassic Park. 1993. [Film] Directed by Steven Spielberg. United States: Amblin Entertainment.

Kahila, J. et al., 2023. A Typology of Metagamers: Identifying Player Types Based on Beyond the Game Activities. *Games and Culture,* 1 August, 20(1), pp. 38–58.

Kahn, A. S. et al., 2015. The Trojan Player Typology: A Cross-Genre, Cross-Cultural, Behaviorally Validated Scale of Video Game Play Motivations. *Computers in Human Behavior,* 1 August, 49(C), pp. 354–361.

Kahneman, D. & Tversky, A., 1979. Prospect Theory: An Analysis of Decision under Risk. *Econometrica,* March, 47(2), pp. 263–292.

Kahneman, D. & Tversky, A., 1984. Choices, Values, and Frames. *American Psychologist,* April, 39(4), pp. 341–350.

Kamel Boulos, M. N., Hetherington, L. & Wheeler, S., 2007. Second Life: An Overview of the Potential of 3-D Virtual Worlds in Medical and Health Education. *Health Information & Libraries Journal,* 14 December, 24(4), pp. 233–308.

Kaplan, J. & Metzen, C., 2016. *Overwatch*. Irvine (CA): Blizzard Entertainment.

Karjalainen, S., 2001. *Habbo Hotel*. London: Sulake.

Kaya, A., Türk, N., Batmaz, H. & Griffiths, M. D., 2023. Psychological Needs among Adolescents: The Mediating Roles of Meaning in Life and Responsibility. *International Journal of Mental Health and Addiction,* 10 January.

Keirsey, D., 1998. *Please Understand Me II*. Del Mar (CA): Prometheus Nemesis.

Kennerly, D. E., 2004. *Elements of the Psyche: Does Myers-Briggs Trump Bartle?*. [Online] Available at: https://web.archive.org/web/20071017190935/https://finegamedesign.com/personality.html [Accessed 3 December 2024].

Kerr, C., 2007. *The Lord of the Rings Online: Shadows of Angmar*. Westwood (MA): Midway Home Entertainment.

Keum, K. S., 2019. *Lost Ark*. Pangyo (Gyeonggi): Smilegate.

KH Digital 2, 2016. Graduate Student Rises as Developer of Korea's Longest-Running Online Game. *The Korea Herald*, 9 May.

Khan, L. M., Slaughter, R. K., Wilson, C. S. & Bedoya, A. M., 2022. *In the Matter of Epic Games, Inc., a Corporation*. Washington: Federal Trade Commission.

Khan, M. K., 2007. *Emotional and Behavioral Effects of Video Games and Internet Overuse*. Chicago: American Medical Association.

Kidwell, E., 2019. *Overwatch Saw 40% Less Disruptive Behavior with the Endorsement System*. [Online] Available at: https://www.gamedeveloper.com/design/-i-overwatch-i-saw-40-less-disruptive-behavior-with-the-endorsement-system [Accessed 3 December 2024].

Kim, A. J., 2000. *Community Building on the Web*. Berkeley (CA): Peachpit Press.

Kim, H., 2006. *MapleStory*. Los Angeles (CA): Nexon America.

Kim, R., 2003. *Lineage II*. Pangyo (Gyeonggi): NCSoft.

King, B. & Borland, J., 2003. *Dungeons and Dreamers: The Rise of Computer Game Culture from Geek to Chic*. New York (NY): McGraw-Hill.

Kitchin, R., 1998. *Cyberspace: The World in the Wires*. Chichester (Sussex): Wiley.

Klastrup, L., 2008. What Makes World of Warcraft a World? A Note on Death and Dying. In: H. G. Corneliussen & J. Walker Rettberg, eds. *Digital Culture, Play, and Identity: A World of Warcraft Reader*. Cambridge (MA): MIT Press, pp. 143–166.

Kleitz, A., 1978. *Sceptre of Goth*. Brooklyn Center (MN): Minnesota Educational Computer Consortium.

Kłosiński, M., 2024. Mapping Game Biopolitics. *Games and Culture,* 28 February, pp. 1–20.

Knuth, D. E., 1968. *The Art of Computer Programming: Fundamental Algorithms*. Boston (MA): Addison-Wesley.

Knutsson, S., 2012. *Candy Crush Saga.* Stockholm: King.

Koeneke, R. A., Todd, J. W. & Wilson, J. E., 1983. *The Dungeons of Moria.* Norman (OK): University of Oklahoma.

Koenitz, H., 2023. *Understanding Interactive Digital Narrative: Immersive Expressions for a Complex Time.* Abingdon (Oxon.): Routledge.

Kolb, A. Y. & Kolb, D. A., 2013. *The Kolb Learning Style Inventory - Version 4.0.* Kaunakakai (HI): Experience Based Learning Systems.

Kolb, D. A., 1984. *Experiential Learning: Experience as the Source of Learning and Development.* New Jersey: Prentice-Hall.

Komoto, N. & Yoshida, A., 2013. *Final Fantasy XIV.* Shinjuku (Tokyo): Square Enix.

Konstantelos, L. et al. eds., 2012. *The Preservation of Complex Objects, Volume 2: Software Art.* Portsmouth (Hampshire): University of Portsmouth.

Kordyaka, B. et al., 2022. *Exploring the Dark Side of Multiplayer Online Games: The Relationship between Contact Experiences and Sexism.* Minneapolis: Association for Information Systems, pp. 1–22.

Koster, R., 1997. *Ultima Online.* Austin (TX): Origin Systems.

Koster, R., 1998. *A Story about a Tree.* [Online] Available at: https://www.raphkoster.com/gaming/essay1.shtml [Accessed 3 December 2024].

Koster, R., 2000a. *Declaration of the Rights of Avatars.* [Online] Available at: https://mud-dev.zer7.com/2000/4/13209/#post13209 [Accessed 1 July 2024].

Koster, R., 2000. *Declaring the Rights of Players.* [Online] Available at: https://www.raphkoster.com/games/essays/declaring-the-rights-of-players/ [Accessed 3 December 2024].

Koster, R., 2003a. *Small Worlds: Competitive and Cooperative Structures in Online Worlds.* San Jose: Game Developers Conference.

Koster, R., 2003b. *Star Wars Galaxies: An Empire Divided.* San Diego (CA): Sony Online Entertainment.

Koster, R., 2009. *What is a Diku?.* [Online] Available at: https://www.raphkoster.com/2009/01/09/what-is-a-diku/ [Accessed 1 November 2013].

Koster, R., 2013. *A Theory of Fun for Game Design.* 2nd ed. Sebastopol (CA): O'Reilly.

Koster, R., 2018a. *Postmortems: Selected Essays Volume One.* 1st ed. San Diego (CA): Altered Tuning.

Koster, R., 2018b. *The Trust Spectrum.* [Online] Available at: https://www.raphkoster.com/2018/03/16/the-trust-spectrum/ [Accessed 16 April 2024].

Koster, R., 2022. *Sandbox vs Themepark.* [Online] Available at: https://www.raphkoster.com/2022/09/01/sandbox-vs-themepark/ [Accessed 3 December 2024].

Koster, R. et al., 1994. *LegendMUD.* Chestertown (MD): Washington College.

Koster, R. et al., 2000. *Declaration of the Rights of Avatars* [Online] Available at: https://mud-dev.zer7.com/2000/4/13209/#post13209 [Accessed 26 July 2023].

Koster, R. & Georgeson, D., n.d. *Stars Reach.* San Marcos (CA): Playable Worlds.

Koster, R. & Vogel, R., 2002. *How to Manage a Large-Scale Online Gaming Community.* [Online] Available at: https://www.raphkoster.com/games/presentations/how-to-manage-a-large-scale-online-gaming-community/ [Accessed 3 December 2024].

Kowert, R., 2016. *A Paren't Guide to Video Games.* North Charleston (SC): Rachel Kowert.

Kruger, J. & Dunning, D., 1999. Unskilled and Unaware of It: How Difficulties in Recognizing One's Own Incompetence Lead to Inflated Self-Assessments. *Journal of Personality and Social Psychology,* 1 December, 77(6), pp. 1121–1134.

Kuchera, B., 2009. *Dungeons and Dragons Online: Behold the Power of Free.* [Online] Available at: https://arstechnica.com/gaming/2009/10/ddo-free-to-play/ [Accessed 3 December 2024].

Kuss, D. J. & Griffiths, M. D., 2012. Internet and Gaming Addiction: A Systematic Literature Review of Neuroimaging Studies. *Brain Sciences,* 5 September, 2(3), pp. 347–374.

Lambert, J. A., 1997. *Just a Bit of Musing.* [Online] Available at: https://mud-dev.zer7.com/1997/2/124/#post124 [Accessed 3 December 2024].

Lamorisse, A., 1957. *La Conquête du Monde.* Paris (Île-de-France): Miro.

Lane, S., Verfaillie, D. & Hall, D., 2021. *New World.* Irvine (CA): Amazon Game Studios.

Lang, J., 1950. *Listen with Mother.* London: BBC Light Programme.

Lastowka, F. G., 2010. *Virtual Justice: The New Laws of Online World.* New Haven (CT): Yale University Press.

Lastowka, F. G. & Hunter, D., 2004. The Laws of the Virtual Worlds. *California Law Review,* 1 January, 92(1), pp. 1–73.

Laurel, B., 1991. *Computers as Theatre.* Lebanon (IA): Addison-Wesley.

Laurie, B., 1985. *Gods.* London: Lap of the Gods.

Laycock, J. P., 2015. *Dangerous Games: What the Moral Panic over Role-Playing Games Says about Play, Religion and Imagined Worlds.* 1st ed. Oakland (CA): University of California Press.

Lazzaro, N., 2004. *Why We Play Games: Four Keys to More Emotion in Player Experiences.* San Jose: Game Developers Conference.

LeBlanc, M., 2004. *8KindsOfFun.com.* [Online] Available at: https://algorithmancy.8kindsoffun. com/ [Accessed 3 December 2024].

Lebling, P. D., 1980. Zork and the Future of Computerized Fantasy Simulations. *BYTE Magazine,* December, 5(12), pp. 172–182.

Leeming, D. A., 1973. *Mythology: The Voyage of the Hero.* Philadelphia (PA): Lippincott.

Lee, Y. & Jung, Y., 2019. A Mapping Approach to Identify Player Types for Game Recommendations. *Information,* 10(12), p. 379.

Lefay, J., Nesmith, B. & Peterson, T., 1996. *The Elder Scrolls: Chapter II - Daggerfall.* Rockville (MD): Bethesda Softworks.

Lefebvre, E., 2019. *Storyboard: Exploring Religions in MMOs.* [Online] Available at: https://massive lyop.com/2019/06/10/storyboard-exploring-religion-in-mmos/ [Accessed 30 December 2021].

Lehdonvirta, V., 2010. Virtual Worlds Don't Exist: Questioning the Dichotomous Approach in MMO Studies. *Game Studies,* April, 10(1).

Leiber, F., 1939. Two Sought Adventure. *Unknown,* August, I(6), pp. 99–124.

Leiser, M., Santos, C. & Doshi, K., 2010. *Deceptive Patterns.* [Online] Available at: https://www. deceptive.design/ [Accessed 17 June 2024].

Lenburg, J., 1983. *Dudley Moore: An Informal Biography.* New York (NY): Delilah Books.

Lenhart, A., 2008. *New Pew Internet/MacArthur Report on Teens, Video Games and Civics.* Washington: Pew Internet.

Lenton, A., 1988. *Federation II.* London: Interactive Broadcasting.

Lepper, M. R., Greene, D. & Nisbett, R. E., 1973. Undermining Children's Intrinsic Interest with Extrinsic Reward: A Test of the "Overjustification" Hypothesis. *Journal of Personality and Social Psychology,* 28(1), pp. 129–137.

Lewis, M. L., Weber, R. & Bowman, N. D., 2008. "They May be Pixels, but they're MY Pixels": Developing a Metric of Character Attachment in Role-Playing Video Games. *Journal of CyberPsychology & Behavior,* 23 August, 11(4), pp. 515–518.

Lieberman, J. D., Solomon, S., Greenberg, J. & McGregor, H. A., 1999. A Hot New Way to Measure Aggression: Hot Sauce Allocation. *Aggressive Behavior,* 1 September, 25(5), pp. 321–396.

Linden Lab, 2017. *Second Life Terms and Conditions.* [Online] Available at: https://secondlife.com/ app/tos/tos.php [Accessed 24 June 2024].

Lindus, C., 1989. *The Void.* Worthing (Sussex).

Lineberger, B., 1984. *Realm.* Louisville (KY): University of Louisville.

Lineberger, B., 1989. *Kingdom of Drakkar.* Louisville (KY): Tantalus.

Lin, J.-H., 2013. Do Video Games Exert Stronger Effects on Aggression than Film? The Role of Media Interactivity and Identification on the Association of Violent Content and Aggressive Outcomes. *Computers in Human Behaviour,* May, 29(3), pp. 535–543.

Liu, B., 2010. Sentiment Analysis and Subjectivity. In: N. Indurkhya & F. J. Damerau, eds. *Handbook of Natural Language Processing.* Boca Raton (FL): Taylor & Francis, pp. 627–666.

Livingstone, D., 2006. Turing's Test and Believable AI in Games. *Computers in Entertainment,* 1 January, 4(1), pp. 6–es.

Loadcomplete, 2017. *Ride Zero.* Seongnam (Gyeonggi): Loadcomplete.

Loewe, F. & Lerner, A. J., 1947. *Brigadoon.* New York.

Logg, E., 1981. *Centipede.* Sunnyvale (CA): Atari.

Logg, E. & Rains, L. V., 1979. *Asteroids.* Sunnyvale (CA): Atari.

Lombard, M. & Ditton, T., 1997. At the Heart of It All: The Concept of Presence. *Journal of Computer-Mediated Communications,* 3(2).

Lovecraft, H. P., 1928. The Call of Cthulhu. *Weird Tales,* February, 11(2), pp. 159–178.

Lübke, G., Payer, S., Schlott, U. & Vogler, S., 1997. *Tibia.* Regensburg (Bavaria): CipSoft.

Lucas, G., 1977. *Star Wars.* San Francisco (CA): Lucasfilm.

Lukács, A., Embrick, D. G. & Wright, T., 2009. *The Managed Hearthstone: Labor and Emotional Work in the Online Community of World of Warcraft.* Berlin: Springer, pp. 165–177.

Lynn, M., 1992. The Psychology of Unavailability: Explaining Scarcity and Cost Effects on Value. *Basic and Applied Social Psychology,* 13(1), pp. 3–7.

MacFarlane, S., 1999. *Family Guy.* [Art] (Fuzzy Door Productions).

Machkovech, S., 2022. *How to Make Online Games Less Toxic? GDC Devs Debate Moderation.* [Online] Available at: https://arstechnica.com/gaming/2022/03/how-to-make-online-games-less-toxic-gdc-devs-debate-moderation/ [Accessed 3 December 2024].

MacKinnon, R. C., 1997. Punishing the Persona: Correctional Strategies for the Virtual Offender. In: S. G. Jones, ed. *Virtual Culture: Identity and Communication in Cybersociety.* Thousand Oaks (CA): Sage, pp. 206–235.

Madge, C. et al., 2019. *Incremental Game Mechanics applied to Text Annotation.* Barcelona: Association for Computing Machinery, pp. 545–558.

Madigan, J., 2016. *Getting Gamers: The Psychology of Video Games and Their Impact on the People Who Play Them.* London: Rowman & Littlefield.

Madison, J., 1791. *United States Bill of Rights.* New York: 1st United States Congress.

Maggs, B., Shapira, A. & Sides, D., 1979. *Avatar.* Urbana-Champaign: University of Illinois.

Malaby, T. M., 2009. *Making Virtual Worlds: Linden Lab and Second Life.* Ithaca (NY): Cornell University Press.

Maldonado López, A., 2022. *Report on Consumer Protection in Online Video Games: A European Single Market Approach.* Luxembourg: European Parliament.

Malenka, D. J., Baron, J. A., Johansen, S. & Wahrenberger, J., 1993. The Framing Effect of Relative and Absolute Risk. *Journal of General Internal Medicine,* November, 8(10), pp. 543–548.

Marczewski, A., 2015a. *Gamification User Types Dodecad – The HEXAD Expansion Pack!.* [Online] Available at: https://www.gamified.uk/2015/12/16/gamification-user-types-dodecad-christmas/ [Accessed 3 December 2024].

Marczewski, A., 2015b. User Types. In: *Even Monkeys Like to Play: Gamification, Game Thinking and Motivational Design.* Scotts Valley (CA): CreateSpace, pp. 65–80.

Markey, P. M. & Ferguson, C. J., 2017. *Moral Combat: Why the War on Violent Video Games is Wrong.* Dallas (TX): BenBella Books.

Markey, P. M. et al., 2015. Violent Video Games and Real-World Violence: Rhetoric versus Data. *Psychology of Popular Media Culture,* October, 4(4), pp. 277–295.

Marvel Studios, 2008. *Marvel Cinematic Universe.* Burbank (CA): The Walt Disney Company.

Mary Poppins. 1964. [Film] Directed by Robert Stevenson. United States of America: Walt Disney Productions.

Maslow, A. H., 1943. A Theory of Human Motivation. *Psychological Review,* 50(4), pp. 370–396.

Masterson, J. T., 1994. *Ethnography of a Virtual Society: How a Gangling, Wiry Half-Elf Found a Way to Fit in.* [Online] Available at: https://web.archive.org/web/20050429032509/johnmasterson. com/ethno.html [Accessed 3 December 2024].

Mathur, A. et al., 2019. Dark Patterns at Scale: Findings from a Crawl of 11K Shopping Websites. *Proceedings of the ACM on Human-Computer Interaction,* 7 November, 3(CSCW), pp. 1–32.

Mauldin, M. L., 1990. *Islandia.* Berkeley (CA): University of California, Berkeley; Carnegie Mellon University.

Mayer, M., 2009. *Warum Leben, wenn man Stattdessen Spielen kann? Kognition, Motivation und Emotion am Beispiel Digitaler Spiele.* Boizenburg (Mecklenburg-Western Pomerania): Werner Hülsbusch.

Mayer-Schönberger, V., 2009. Virtual Heisenberg: The Limits of Virtual World Regulability. *Washington and Lee Law Review,* 1 June, 66(3), pp. 1245–1262.

McCabe, J., 2008. Sexual Harassment is Rife Online. Now Wonder Women Swap Gender. *The Guardian,* 6 March.

McCloud, S., 1993. *Understanding Comics: The Invisible Art.* New York (NY): HarperCollins.

McCormick, M., 2010. *Cityville.* San Mateo (CA): Zynga.

McGill, V. J. & Welch, L., 1946. A Behaviorist Analysis of Emotions. *Philosophy of Science,* April, 13(2), pp. 100–122.

McGonigal, J., 2003. *A Real Little Game: The Performance of Belief in Pervasive Play.* Berkeley: University of California at Berkeley.

McGonigal, J., 2011. *Reality is Broken: Why Games Make us Better and How they can Change the World.* 1st ed. London: Jonathan Cape.

McKechnie-Martin, C. T., Cunningham, A., Baumeister, J. & Von Itzstein, G. S., 2024. A Meta-Ethnography of Player Motivation in Digital Games: The 28 Dimensions of Play. *Games and Culture,* April, pp. 1–25.

Meehan, M., 2006. Virtual Property: Protecting Bits in Context. *Richmond Journal of Law & Technology,* Fall, XIII(2), p. 1.

Meer, A., 2011. *Bartle Banter: WildStar's Jeremy Gaffney.* [Online] Available at: https://www.rockpapershotgun.com/bartle-banter-wildstars-jeremy-gaffney [Accessed 3 December 2024].

Megler, V. & Mitchell, P., 1982. *The Hobbit.* Melbourne (Victoria): Melbourne House.

Meier, S. & Shelley, B., 1991. *Civilization.* Alameda (CA): Microprose.

Melissa, 2021. *Myers-Briggs Personality Type and Conflict - What Causes Fights between MBTI Types?.* [Online] Available at: https://www.mbtionline.com/en-US/Articles/mbti-type-and-conflict [Accessed 3 December 2024].

Merrick, K., Niazi, M., Shafi, K. & Gu, N., 2011. *Motivation, Cyberworlds and Collective Design.* Newcastle, Australia: University of Newcastle, Australia, pp. 697–706.

Meta, n.d. *Facebook Community Standards.* [Online] Available at: https://transparency.fb.com/en-gb/policies/community-standards/ [Accessed 3 December 2024].

Metzen, C., Pardo, R. & Adham, A., 2004. *World of Warcraft.* Irvine (CA): Blizzard Entertainment.

Mihaly, M., 1996. *Achaea, Dreams of Divine Lands.* Novato (CA): Iron Realms Entertainment.

Mikhailova, O. V., 2019. High School Students Involved and not Involved in MMORPG - Creativity and Innovativeness. *International Journal of Cognitive Research in Science, Engineering and Education,* 7(2), pp. 29–39.

Milbrodt, T., 2019. Dating Websites and Disability Identity: Presentations of the Disabled Self in Online Dating Profiles. *Western Folklore,* Winter, 78(1), pp. 67–100.

Miller, R., 2003. *Uru: Ages beyond Myst.* Mead (WA): Cyan Worlds.

Mill, J. S., 1859. *On Liberty.* London: John W. Parker.

MindArk, 2024. *General Real World Item Agreement.* [Online] Available at: https://account.entropiauniverse.com/legal/real-world-items-agreement.xml [Accessed 3 December 2024].

Miranda, L.-M., 2021. *We don't Talk about Bruno.* Burbank: Walt Disney.

Miyoshi, T., 2000. *Phantasy Star Online.* Tokyo: Sega.

MMO Populations, 2024. *MMO Populations.* [Online] Available at: https://mmo-population.com/ [Accessed 3 December 2024].

MMO Stats, 2024. *MMO Stats.* [Online] Available at: https://mmostats.com/ [Accessed 3 December 2024].

Mnookin, J. L., 1996a. *Bodies, Rest & Motion: Law and Identity in LambdaMOO*. Cambridge, MIT Press, pp. 22–30.

Mnookin, J. L., 1996b. Virtual(ly) Law: The Emergence of Law in LambdaMOO. *Journal of Computer-Mediated Communication*, 1 June, 2 (1). https://onlinelibrary.wiley.com/toc/10836101/1996/2/1.

MOBA Network, n.d. *MMORPG.com*. [Online] Available at: https://www.mmorpg.com/ [Accessed 15 may 2023].

Mohammad, S., Jan, R. A. & Alsaedi, S. L., 2023. Symptoms, Mechanisms and Treatments of Video Game Addiction. *Cureus*, 21 March, 15(3), p. e36957.

Montola, M., 2010. *The Positive Negative Experience in Extreme Role-Playing*. Stockholm: DiGRA.

Morcos, M. et al., 2021. Internet Gaming Disorder: Compensating as a Draenei in World of Warcraft. *Journal of Mental Health and Addiction*, June, 19(3), pp. 669–685.

Morgan, R., 2014. *Virtual Reality: An Ethnographic Study of Sociality, Being and Money in a Multi-Player Online Game-World*. Townsville: James Cook University.

Mori, M., 1970. Bukimi No Tani. *Energy*, 7(4), pp. 33–35.

Mori, M., 2012. *The Uncanny Valley: The Original Essay by Masahiro Mori*. [Online] Available at: https://spectrum.ieee.org/the-uncanny-valley [Accessed 10 June 2024].

Morningstar, C., 2019. *Oral History of Chip Morningstar*. [Online] Available at: https://youtu.be/KZHeBQmnZSE?t=2593 [Accessed 12 12 2022].

Morningstar, C. & Farmer, F. R., 1986. *Habitat*. Vienna (VA): Quantum Link; Lucasfilm Games.

Morningstar, C. & Farmer, F. R., 1990. *The Lessons of Lucasfilm's Habitat*. Austin: University of Texas.

Morningstar, C. et al., 2023. Chip Morningstar and Randy Farmer: Cocreators of Lucasfilm Games "Habitat". In: *The Rise of Virtual Communities: In Conversation with Virtual World Pioneers*. Ed. James Robinson-Prior. San Francisco (CA): Apress, pp. 1–13.

Morningstar, J., 2009. *Fiasco*. Chapel Hill (NC): Bully Pulpit Games.

Morosan, M., 2019. *Automating Game-Design and Game-Agent Balancing through Computational Intelligence*. Colchester: University of Essex.

Mosiondz, R., 2009. *Champions Online*. Los Gatos (CA): Cryptic Studios.

Muir, R., 1990. *Bloodstone*. London: Microlink.

Mullen, P. R. et al., 2021. Crowdsourcing for Online Samples in Counseling Research. *Journal of Counseling & Development*, April, 99(2), pp. 221–226.

Mulvey, L., 1975. Visual Pleasure and Narrative Cinema. *Screen*, Autumn, 16(3), pp. 6–18.

Munsey, P., 2009. *Long Arm of Law Reaches into World of Warcraft*. [Online] Available at: https://web.archive.org/web/20100103101134/https://kokomoperspective.com/news/local_news/article_15a0a546-f574-11de-ab22-001cc4c03286.html [Accessed 3 December 2024].

Muramatsu, J. & Ackerman, M. S., 1998. Computing, Social Activity and Entertainment a Field Study of a Game MUD. *Computer Supported Cooperative Work*, March, 7, pp. 87–122.

Murdock, M., 1990. *The Heroine's Journey: Woman's Quest for Wholeness*. Boulder (CO): Shambhala Publications.

Murray, J. H., 1997. *Hamlet on the Holodeck: The Future of Narrative in Cyberspace*. New York (NY): The Free Press.

Murray, J. H., 2011. *Inventing the Medium: Principles of Interaction Design as a Cultural Practice*. Cambridge (MA): MIT Press.

Murrell, S., 1980. *PIGG*. Colchester (Essex): University of Essex.

Nacke, L. E., Bateman, C. & Mandryk, R. L., 2011. *BrainHex: Preliminary Results from a Neurobiological Gamer Typology Survey*. Vancouver: Springer, pp. 288–293.

Nakamura, L., 1995. Race In/For Cyberspace: Identity Tourism and Racial Passing on the Internet. *Works and Days*, 13, pp. 181–193.

Nance, J. L., 2003. *Shadowbane*. Round Rock (TX): Ubi Soft.

Nardi, B., 2010. *My Life as a Night Elf Priest: An Anthropological Account of World of Warcraft*. Ann Arbor (MI): University of Michigan Press.

National Addiction Centre, 2003. *Dangerousness of Drugs: A Guide to the Risks and Harms Associated with Substance Misuse.* National Health Service. London.

NCSoft, 2024. *Throne & Liberty.* Pangyo (Gyeonggi): Amazon Games.

Neople, 2005. *Dungeon Fighter Online.* Jeju: Microsoft.

NetEase, 2001. *Fantasy Westward Journey.* Hangzhou (Zhejiang): NetEase.

NetEase, 2018. *Justice Online.* Hong Kong: NetEase.

NetEase, 2020. *EVE Echoes.* Hangzhou (Zhejiang): CCP Games.

Nevelsteen, K. J. L., 2018. Virtual World, Defined from a Technological Perspective, and Applied to Video Games, Mixed Reality and the Metaverse. *Computer Animation and Virtual Worlds,* 6 February, 29(1). https://onlinelibrary.wiley.com/toc/1546427x/2018/29/1.

Newell, N., 1985. *Shades.* London: Micronet 800.

Newman, S., Webber, C. E. & Wilson, D., 1963. *Doctor Who.* London: BBC.

Niantic, 2012. *Ingress.* San Francisco (CA): Niantic.

Nichols, S. & Neville, J., 1996. *The Realm.* Oakhurts (CA): Sierra On-Line.

Nietzsche, F., 1909. *The complete works of Friedrich Nietzsche.* Edinburgh: T. N. Foulis.

Nishikado, T., 1978. *Space Invaders.* Shinjuku (Tokyo): Taito.

Nishitani, A. & Yasuda, A., 1991. *Street Fighter II.* Osaka (Osaka Prefecture): Capcom.

Niven, L., 1973. Flash Crowd. In: *The Flight of the Horse.* New York (NY): Ballantine, pp. 99–164.

Niven, L. & Barnes, S., 1981. *Dream Park.* New York (NY): Ace Books.

Nomura, T. & Masuda, J., 2016. *Pokémon Go.* San Francisco (CA): Niantic.

Nonaka, I., 1994. A Dynamic Theory of Organizational Knowledge Creation. *Organizational Science,* February, 5(1), pp. 14–37.

Norman, D. A., 2013. *The Design of Everyday Things.* 2nd ed. London: MIT Press.

Novak, J., 2022. *Game Development Essentials: An Introduction.* 4th ed. Santa Monica (CA): Novy Publishing.

Nowak, K. L., Krcmar, M. & Farrar, K., 2008. The Causes and Consequences of Presence: Considering the Influence of Violent Video Games on Presence and Aggression. *Presence: Teleoperators and Virtual Environments,* 1 June, 17(3), p. 256–268.

Oestrich, E., 2018. *Grapevine.* [Online] Available at: https://grapevine.haus/ [Accessed 3 December 2024].

Office for National Statistics, 2024. *Population Estimates for the UK, England, Wales, Scotland, and Northern Ireland: Mid-2022.* [Online] Available at: https://www.ons.gov.uk/peoplepopulationand community/populationandmigration/populationestimates/bulletins/annualmidyearpopulation estimates/mid2022 [Accessed 3 December 2024].

Ogilvie, M., 2001. *RuneScape.* Cambridge: Jagex.

Ohlen, J., 2011. *Star Wars: The Old Republic.* Austin (TX): Bioware.

Oldenburg, R., 1989. *The Great Good Place.* Boston (MA): Da Capo.

Olivetti, J., 2021. *The Game Archaeologist: Defining the Eras of MMORPG History.* [Online] Available at: https://massivelyop.com/2021/08/07/the-game-archaeologist-defining-the-eras-of-mmorpg-history/ [Accessed 18 November 2022].

Ondrejka, C., 2004. *Living on the Edge: Digital Worlds Which Embrace the Real World.* Los Angeles: University of Southern California.

Ondrejka, C., 2005. *Ce N' est Pas un Monde Virtuel.* [Online] Available at: https://terranova.blogs. com/terra_nova/2005/06/ce_nest_pas_un_.html [Accessed 18 July 2023].

Ong, A., 2018. *Immersive Realities: An Expansion Pack for Landscape Architecture.* Seattle: University of Washington.

onlinewelten.com, 2013. *Interview with Mark Jacobs Kickstarter-MMO.* [Online] Available at: https://www.onlinewelten.com/games/camelot-unchained/interviews/interview-mark-jacobs-kickstarter-mmo-9415/seite-5/ [Accessed 23 April 2013].

Oosterbaan, O., 2009. Human Rights and Private Ordering in Virtual Worlds. In: F. Lehmann-Grube & J. Sablatnig, eds. *Lecture Notes of the Institute for Computer Sciences, Social Informatics and Telecommunications Engineering.* Berlin: Springer, pp. 178–186.

Orland, K., 2011. *Turbine: Lord of the Rings Online Revenues Tripled As Free-To-Play Game.* [Online] Available at: https://www.gamedeveloper.com/pc/turbine-i-lord-of-the-rings-online-i-revenues-tripled-as-free-to-play-game [Accessed 3 December 2024].

O'Shea, Z., Bartle, R. A., Pan, X. & Freeman, J., 2022. *Apples and Oranges: A Study of "Tend & Befriend" as a Phenomenon in Digital Games.* Online: Springer, pp. 269–288.

Overpowered Media Group, n.d. *Massively Overpowered.* [Online] Available at: https://massivelyop.com/ [Accessed 15 May 2023].

Pagliarulo, E., 2018. *Fallout 76.* Rockville (MD): Bethesda Softworks.

Pajitnov, A., 1986. *Tetris.* Moscow (Central): Soviet Academy of Sciences.

Palmer, A. W., 1935. Preaching Missions. *The Chicago Theological Seminary Register,* March, 25(2), p. 13.

Pan-European Game Information, 2003. *PEGI.* [Online] Available at: https://pegi.info/ [Accessed 3 December 2024].

Pardo, R., 2002. *Warcraft III.* Irvine (CA): Blizzard Entertainment.

Pargman, D., 2000. *Code Begets Community: On Social and Technical Aspects of Managing a Virtual Community.* Linköping (Östergötland): Linköping University.

Pargman, D. & Eriksson, A., 2005. *Law, Order and Conflicts of Interest in Massively Multiplayer Online Games.* Vancouver: DiGRA.

Park, S. et al., 2016. *Blade & Soul.* Pangyo (Gyeonggi): NCSoft.

Pearce, C., 2009. *Communities of Play: Emergent Cultures in Multiplayer Games and Virtual Worlds.* Cambridge (MA): MIT Press.

Pearl Abyss, 2015. *Black Desert Online.* Anyang (Gyeonggi): Pearl Abyss.

Peirce, C. S., 1902. Virtual. In: J. M. Baldwin, ed. *Dictionary of Philosophy and Psychology.* London: Macmillan, pp. 763–764.

Pensjö, L., 1989. *LPMUD.* Gothenburg (Västergötland): Chalmers Computer Society.

Pepe, F., ed., 2022. *The CRPG Book Project: Sharing the History of Computer Role-Playing Games.* Expanded edition 3.3 ed. Bath: Bitmap Books.

Pereira, I., 2024. *What went wrong with WoW? A Blizzard Veteran's Theory on World of Warcraft's Fall from its 12 Million Subscriber Height* [Interview] (21 August 2024).

Perrin, S., Turney, R., Henderson, S. & James, W., 1978. *RuneQuest.* Ann Arbor (MI): Chaosium.

Persson, M., 2011. *Minecraft.* Stockholm: Mojang.

Peterson, J., 2024. *Playing at the World: The Invention of Dungeons & Dragons.* 2nd ed. Cambridge (MA): MIT Press.

Peterson, M., 2012. Learner Interaction in a Massively Multiplayer Online Role Playing Game (MMORPG): A Sociocultural Discourse Analysis. *ReCALL,* September, 24(3), pp. 361–380.

Peterson, S., 1981. *Call of Cthulhu.* Ann Arbor (MI): Chaosium.

Petrovskaya, E. & Zendle, D., 2020. The Battle Pass: A Mixed-Methods Investigation into a Growing Type of Video Game Monetisation. *OSF Preprints,* 18 September, 181(4), pp. 1065–1081.

Petrovskaya, E. & Zendle, D., 2022. Predatory Monetisation? A Categorisation of Unfair, Misleading and Aggressive Monetisation Techniques in Digital Games from the Player Perspective. *Journal of Business Ethics,* December, 181, pp. 1065–1081.

Phinney, J., 2005. *Guild Wars.* Bellevue (WA): NCSoft.

Phinney, J. & Metzen, C., 1998. *Starcraft.* Irvine (CA): Blizzard Entertainment.

Piaget, J., trans. 1952. *The Origins of Intelligence in Children.* New York (NY): W. W. Norton.

Pinchbeck, D. & Briscoe, R., 2012. *Dear Esther.* Portsmouth (Hampshire): Thechineseroom.

Pincus, M. & Skaggs, M., 2009. *FarmVille.* San Francisco (CA): Zynga.

Pisan, Y., 2007. *My Guild, My People: Role of Guilds in Massively Multiplayer Online Games.* Melbourne: RMIT University, pp. 1–5.

Podini, M., 2021. *7 Nudges & Manipulative Techniques present in Undertale.* [Online] Available at: https://www.gamedeveloper.com/design/7-nudges-manipulative-techniques-present-in-undertale [Accessed 3 December 2024].

Pontes, H. M. & Griffiths, M. D., 2015. Measuring DSM-5 Internet Gaming Disorder: Development and Validation of a Short Psychometric Scale. *Computers in Human Behavior,* April, 45, pp. 137–143.

Poor, N., 2015. *What MMO Communities Don't Do: A Longitudinal Study of Guilds and Character Leveling, or Not.* Oxford: AAAI, pp. 678–681.

Porter, G., Starcevic, V., Berle, D. & Fenech, P., 2010. Recognizing Problem Video Game Use. *Australian and New Zealand Journal of Psychiatry,* 1 February, 44(2), pp. 120–128.

Possler, D., Daneels, R. & Bowman, N. D., 2024. Players Just Want to Have Fun? An Exploratory Survey on Hedonic and Eudaimonic Game Motives. *Games and Culture,* July, 19(5), pp. 611–633.

Postigo, H., 2003. Emerging Sources of Labor on the Internet: The Case of America Online Volunteers. *International Review of Social History,* December, 48(S11), pp. 205–223.

Pratt, A. E., 1949. *Cluedo.* Leeds (Yorkshire): Waddingtons.

Przybylski, A. K., 2013. *Gamers Less Worried about Violence in Video Games.* [Online] Available at: https://yougov.co.uk/politics/articles/7319-gamers-less-worried-about-violence-video-games [Accessed 3 December 2024].

Przybylski, A. K., Murayama, K., DeHaan, C. R. & Gladwell, V., 2013. Motivational, Emotional, and Behavioral Correlates of Fear of Missing Out. *Computer in Human Behavior,* July, 29(4), pp. 1841–1848.

Przybylski, A. K., Rigby, C. S. & Ryan, R. M., 2010. A Motivational Model of Video Game Engagement. *Review of General Psychology,* 16 January, 14(2), pp. 154–155.

Przybylski, A. K. et al., 2012. The Ideal Self at Play: The Appeal of Video Games That Let You Be All You Can Be. *Psychological Science,* January, 23(1), pp. 69–76.

Pulsipher, L., 2011. *Why we Play Games.* [Online] Available at: https://boardgamegeek.com/blog/435/blogpost/1749/why-we-play-games [Accessed 3 December 2024].

Pulsipher, L., 2012. *Game Design: How to Create Video and Tabletop Games, Start to Finish.* Jefferson (NC): McFarland.

Quantic Foundry, 2017. *Board Game Motivation Model: Overview of Methods and Model.* [Online] Available at: https://quanticfoundry.com/wp-content/uploads/2017/01/Board-Game-Motivation-Model-Overview.pdf [Accessed 4 February 2024].

Quantic Foundry, 2019. *Gamer Motivation Model: Reference Sheets & Details.* Quantic Foundry. Sunnyvale, California, United States of America.

Quantic Foundry, 2021. *The 9 Quantic Gamer Types.* [Online] Available at: https://quanticfoundry.com/gamer-types/ [Accessed 3 December 2024].

Quigley, O. & Librande, S., 2013. *SimCity.* Emeryville (CA): Electronic Arts.

Rademacher Mena, R. J., 2010. A Proposed Framework for Studying Educational Virtual Worlds. In: P. Zemliansky & D. Wilcox, eds. *Design and Implementation of Educational Games: Theoretical and Practical Perspectives.* Hershey (PA): IGI Global, pp. 65–77.

Radoff, J., 2011. *Game On: Energize your Business with Social Media Games.* Hoboken (NJ): Wiley.

Ragaini, T., 1999. *Asheron's Call.* Westwood (MA): Microsoft.

Ragaini, T., 2005. *The Matrix Online.* Kirkland (WA): Warner Bros. Interactive Entertainment.

Randall, K., Isaacson, M. & Ciro, C., 2017. Validity and Reliability of the Myers-Briggs Personality Type Indicator. *Journal of Best Practices in Health Professions Diversity,* 10(1), pp. 1–27.

Reddit, 2024. *Reddit Search: RuneScape Communities.* [Online] Available at: https://www.reddit.com/search/?q=RuneScape&type=communities [Accessed 3 December 2024].

Redström, J., 2017. *Making Design Theory.* Cambridge (MA): MIT Press.

Reid, E., 1994. *Cultural Formations in Text-Based Virtual Realities.* Melbourne: University of Melbourne.

Reiss, S. & Havercamp, S. M., 1998. Towards a Comprehensive Assessment of Fundamental Motivation: Factor Structure of the Reiss Profiles. *Psychological Assessment,* 10(2), pp. 97–106.

Rejzlik, W., 1998. *MUD and MOO Survey: Results.* Vienna: University of Vienna.

Relph, E., 1976. *Place and Placelessness.* 1st ed. London: Pion.

Renzi, C., Cattaneo, Z., Vecchi, T. & Cornoldi, C., 2012. Mental Imagery and Blindness. In: S. Lacey & R. Lawson, eds. *Multisensory Imagery*. New York (NY): Springer, pp. 115–130.

Resch, P. M., Kemp, L., Hagstrom, E. & Nakada, M., 1975. *Orthanc Labyrinth*. Urbana-Champaign: University of Ilinois.

Reynolds, R., 2003. *Hands Off MY Avatar! Issues with Claims of Virtual Property and Identity*. Manchester: University of Manchester Centre for Research on Innovation and Competition.

Ricciardi, E. et al., 2009. Do We Really Need Vision? How Blind People "See" the Actions of Others. *Journal of Neuroscience*, 5 August, 29(31), pp. 9719–9724.

Rice, J. W., 2007. Assessing Higher Order Thinking in Video Games. *Journal of Technology and Teacher Education*, 15(1), pp. 87–100.

Rice, X., 2016. The Super-Recognisers of Scotland Yard. *New Statesman*, 2 August, pp. 24–25.

Rickey, D., 2004. *Engines of Creation #19: Fun-damentals*. [Online] Available at: https://www.skotos. net/articles/engines19.phtml.html [Accessed 29 June 2024].

Riegelsberger, J., Counts, S., Farnham, S. D. & Philips, B. C., 2007. *Personality Matters: Incorporating Detailed User Attributes and Preferences into the Matchmaking Process*. Waikoloa: IEEE.

Rigby, C. S. & Ryan, R. M., 2007. Rethinking Carrots: A New Method for Measuring what Players Find Most Rewarding and Motivating about your Game. *Gamasutra*, 16 January.

Rigby, C. S. & Ryan, R. M., 2011. *Glued to Games: How Video Games Draw Us In and Hold us Spellbound*. Santa Barbara (CA): Praeger.

Ringel, Z. & Kovrizhin, D. L., 2017. Quantised Gravitational Responses, the Sign Problem, and Quantum Complexity. *Science Advances*, 27 September, 3(9).

Roberts, C., far distant future. *Star Citizen*. Manchester: Cloud Imperium Games.

Roberts, L. D. & Parks, M. R., 1999. The Social Geography of Gender-Switching in Virtual Environments on the Internet. *Information, Communication & Society*, 2(4), pp. 521–540.

Rogers, R. A., 2006. From Cultural Exchange to Transculturation: A Review and Reconceptualization of Cultural Appropriation. *Communication Theory*, 6 November, 16(4), pp. 474–503.

Rogers, S., 2014. *Level Up! The Guide to Great Video Game Design*. 2nd ed. Chichester (Sussex): Wiley.

Rollings, A. & Morris, D., 2003. *Game Architecture and Design: A New Edition*. Indianapolis (IN): New Riders.

Rolston, K., 2006. *The Elder Scrolls IV: Oblivion*. Rockville (MD): Bethesda Softworks.

Rosedale, P., 2003. *Second Life*. San Francisco (CA): Linden Lab.

Rosedale, P. & Atherton, A., 2023. Philip Rosedale: Founder of Second Life. In: *The Rise of Virtual Communities: In Conversation with Virtual World Pioneers*. San Francisco (CA): Apress, pp. 53–65.

Rosenberg, M. S., 1992. *Virtual Reality: Reflections of Life, Dreams, and Technology; an Ethnography of a Computer Society*. [Online] Available at: https://web.archive.org/web/20060621065250/ https://www.eff.org/Net_culture/MOO_MUD_IRC/rosenberg_vr_reflections.paper [Accessed 3 December 2024].

Rowlands, T. E., 2010. *Empire of the Hyperreal: A Critical Ethnography of EverQuest*. Ann Arbor: Arizona State University.

Rowland, T. D. & Barton, A. C., 2011. Outside Oneself in World of Warcraft: Gamers' Perception of the Racial Self-Other. *Transformative Works and Cultures*, 15 November, 8(special issue 1).

Rowling, J. K., 1997. *Harry Potter and the Philosopher's Stone*. London: Bloomsbury.

Ruberg, B. & Ruelos, S., 2020. Data for Queer Lives: How LGBTQ Gender and Sexuality Identities Challenge Norms of Demographics. *Big Data & Society*, 18 June, Volume January–June, pp. 1–12.

Rutherford, A., 2020. *How to Argue with a Racist: History, Science, Race and Reality*. London: Weidenfeld & Nicolson.

Rutherford, R., 1975. *The Dungeon*. Champaign, Illinois, United States of America.

Ryan, M.-L., 1980. Fiction, Non-Factuals, and the Principle of Minimal Departure. *Poetics,* August, 9(4), pp. 403–422.

Ryan, R. M. et al., 2006. The Motivational Pull of Video Games: A Self-Determination Approach. *Motivation and Emotion,* 29 November, 30(4), pp. 344–360.

Sabien, D., 2024. *The MTG Color Wheel (& Humanity).* [Online] Available at: https://homosabiens. substack.com/p/the-mtg-color-wheel [Accessed 3 December 2024].

Sabo, R., 2022. *Incoming Bot Bans.* [Online] Available at: https://web.archive.org/web/20220304233143/ https://forums.playlostark.com/t/incoming-bot-bans/233996 [Accessed 3 December 2024].

Saleh, A. M., 2021. *Pyramids, Cats and Arabian Nights: Contemporary Egypt in Call of Duty Black Ops 3 and The Race 2.* Uppsala: Uppsala University.

Salen, K. & Zimmerman, E., 2003. *Rules of Play: Game Design Fundamentals.* Cambridge (MA): MIT Press.

Saler, M., 2012. *As If: Modern Enchantment and the Literary Prehistory of Virtual Reality.* 1st ed. New York (NY): Oxford University Press.

Salminen, M., Järvelä, S. V. & Ravaja, N., 2018. Economic Decision-Making in Free-to-Play Games: A Laboratory Experiment to Study the Effects of Currency Conversion. In: *CEUR Workshop Proceedings,* Pori, pp. 92–99.

Salmond, M., 2021. *Video Game Level Design: How to Create Video Games with Emotion, Interaction, and Engagement.* London: Bloomsbury Academic.

Sammarco, S., Davies, D. & Kewell, T., 2014. *Elite: Dangerous.* Cambridge: Frontier Developments.

Sapach, S. C., 2015. The WoW Factor: A Virtual Ethnographic Study of Sacred Things and Rituals in World of Warcraft. *Gamevironments,* 8 July, (2), pp. 1–24.

Sargent, D. W., 1963. Weight-Height Relationshipp of Young Men and Women. *American Journal of Clinical Nutrition,* November, 13(5), pp. 318–325.

Sartre, J.-P., 1988. Play and Sport. In: W. J. Morgan & K. V. Meier, eds. *Philosophic Inquiry in Sport.* Champaign (IL): Human Kinetics, pp. 169–174.

Sarwar, I. & Hynd, D., 2018. *Red Dead Redemption 2.* Toronto (Ontario): Rockstar.

Sarwar, I. & Sripan, J., 2019. *Red Dead Online.* New York (NY): Rockstar.

Sawano, K., 1979. *Galaxian.* Ōta (Tokyo Metropolis): Namco.

Sawyer, J., 2015. *Pillars of Eternity.* Irvine (CA): Paradox Interactive.

Schaap, F., 2002. *The Words that Took us There: Ethnography in a Virtual Reality.* 1st ed. Amsterdam: Aksant.

Schaap, J. & Aupers, S., 2017. 'Gods in World of Warcraft Exist': Religious Reflexivity and the Quest for Meaning in Online Computer Games. *New Media and Society,* 19(11), pp. 1744–1760.

Schell, J., 2003. *Toontown Online.* Pittsburgh (PA): Disney.

Schiano, D. J. & White, S., 1998. *The First Noble Truth of CyberSpace: People are People (Even when they MOO).* Los Angeles: ACM Press, pp. 352–359.

Schubert, D., 2003. The Lighter Side of Meridian 59's History. In: *Developing Online Games: An Insider's Guide.* San Francisco (CA): New Riders, pp. 363–371.

Schubert, D., 2012. *A Brief History of Meridian 59.* [Online] Available at: https://gdcvault.com/ play/1016637 [Accessed 28 June 2023].

Schuller, D., n.d.a. *DND.* [Online] Available at: https://howtomakeanrpg.com/r/l/g/dnd.html [Accessed 7 July 2022].

Schuller, D., n.d.b. *Moria.* [Online] Available at: https://howtomakeanrpg.com/r/l/g/moria.html [Accessed 3 December 2024].

Schwaiger, J., Gaby, J., DeLong, B. & Bucksath, J., 1977. *Oubliette.* Champaign, Illinois, United States of America.

Schweda Nicholson, N., 2005. Personality Characteristics of Interpreter Trainees: The Myers-Briggs Type Indicator (MBTI). *Interpreters' Newsletter,* (13), pp. 109–142.

Schwitzgebel, E. & Garza, M., 2015. A Defense of the Rights of Artificial Intelligences. *Midwest Studies in Philosophy,* September, 39(1), pp. 98–119.

Sciere, 2015. *Ingress*. [Online] Available at: https://www.mobygames.com/game/73655/ingress/ [Accessed 19 July 2023].

Scott, D., 1995. The Effect of Video Games on Feelings of Aggression. *Journal of Psychology,* 1 March, 129(2), pp. 121–132.

Seay, A. F. et al., 2003. *Project Massive 1.0: Organisational Commitment, Sociability and Extraversion in Massively Multiplayer Online Games.* Utrecht: DiGRA.

Sellers, M., 2010. *How to Make a Cool $2MM+ in One Day - with a Sparkle Pony.* [Online] Available at: https://terranova.blogs.com/terra_nova/2010/04/how-to-make-a-cool-2mm-in-one-day-with-a-sparkle-pony.html [Accessed 3 December 2024].

Sellers, M., Sellers, S., Hanke, J. & Schubert, D., 1996. *Meridian 59.* Redwood City (CA): 3DO.

Sena, L., 2016. *Master of Orion: Conquer the Stars.* Nicosia: WG Labs.

Seok, S. & DaCosta, B., 2012. The World's Most Intense Online Gaming Culture: Addiction and High-Engagement Prevalence Rates among South Korean Adolescents and Young Adults. *Computers in Human Behavior,* November, 28(6), pp. 2143–2151.

Shah, R. & Romine, J., 1995. *Playing MUDs on the Internet.* New York (NY): Wiley.

Shaker, N. et al., 2016. *Procedural Content Generation in Games.* Cham (Zug): Springer.

Shapiro, D. & Dee, A., 1994. *DragonSpires.* Round Rock (TX): Dragon's Eye Productions.

Shapiro, D. et al., 1996. *Furcadia.* Round Rock (TX): Dragon's Eye Productions.

Shields, R., 2003. *The Virtual.* 1st ed. London: Routledge.

Shotton, M. A., 1989. *Computer Addiction? A Study of Computer Dependency.* London (FL): CRC Press.

Sibilla, F. & Mancini, T., 2018. I am (not) my Avatar: A Review of the User-Avatar Relationships in Massively Multiplayer Online Worlds. *Cyberpsychology: Journal of Psychosocial Research on Cyberspace,* 11 December, 12(3), p. 4.

Sicart, M., 2009. *The Ethics of Computer Games.* 1st ed. Cambridge (MA): MIT Press.

Sicart, M., 2014. *Play Matters.* Cambridge (MA): MIT Press.

Simmons, Y., James, D., Baber, J. & Evans, P., 1989. *Avalon.* London: IOWA.

Simon, H. A., 1969. *The Sciences of the Artificial.* Cambridge (MA): MIT Press.

Simpson, M., 2000. *Shogun: Total War.* Horsham (Sussex): Creative Assembly.

Simpson, Z. B., 1999. The In-Game Economics of Ultima Online. In: *Game Developers Conference,* San Jose.

Sim, S., 1994. *How Community and Deviance on LambdaMOO and Lord Graham's Demesne can prepare us for the Future of Computer Mediated Communication in Cyberspace.* Toronto: University of Toronto.

Sinclair, S. & McGregor, S., 2013. *Warframe.* London (Ontario): Digital Extremes.

Sinha, I., 1999. *The Cybergypsies: A Frank Account of Love, Life and Travels on the Electronic Frontier.* London: Scribner.

Sitnikov, A., 2010. *World of Tanks.* Minsk: Wargaming.

Skinner, B. F., 1938. *The Behavior of Organisms: An Experimental Analysis.* New York (NY): Appleton-Century.

Skrenta, R., 1988. *Monster.* Evanston (IL): Northwestern University.

Slater, M., 2003. A Note on Presence Terminology. *Presence Connect,* 3(3), pp. 1–5.

Slye, D., 2011. *Villagers & Heroes of a Mystical Land.* Eugene (OR): Mad Otter Games.

Smathers, C. A. & Ferrari, T. M., 2018. Levels of Community Change: A Game to Teach About Policy, System, and Environment Change. *Journal of Nutrition Education and Behavior,* March, 50(3), pp. 311–314.

Smith, A., 1776. *An Inquiry into the Nature and Causes of the Wealth of Nations.* London: W. Strahan and T. Cadell.

Smith, C., 2020. *Relationships between Player-Roles, Action, Attitudes towards Individuals and the World, and Gaming Experiences.* Bangor: Bangor University.

Smith, J. H., 2002. *The Architectures of Trust: Supporting Cooperation in the Computer-Supported Community.* Copenhagen: University of Copenhagen.

Smith, M. A., Rowley, A. & Krause, M., 1991. *Medievia.* [Online] Available at: https://www.medievia.com/ [Accessed 3 December 2024].

Snodgrass, J. G., 2016. Online Virtual Worlds as Anthropological Field Sites: Ethnographic Methods Training via Collaborative Research of Internet Gaming Cultures. *National Association for the Practice of Anthropology,* November, 40(2), pp. 134–147.

Snyder, N. R., 1975. *An Experimental Study of Optimal Group Size.* Pittsburgh: University of Pittsburgh.

Somerville, M., 2006. *The Ethical Imagination: Journeys of the Human Spirit.* 1st ed. Melbourne: Melbourne University Press.

Song, J.-K., 1996a. *Baramue Nara.* Seoul: Nexon.

Song, J.-K., 1996b. *Nexus, Kingdom of the Winds.* Seoul: Nexon.

Song, J.-K., 1998. *Lineage.* Pangyo (Gyeonggi): NCSoft.

Spaight, T., 2003. Who Killed Miss Norway?. Salon, 14 April.

Sperry, B. & Castle, L., 2002. *Earth & Beyond.* Las Vegas (NV): Westwood Studios.

Spider-Man: Across the Spider-Verse. 2023. [Film] Directed by Joaquim Dos Santos, Kemp Powers, Justin K. Thompson. United States of America: Columbia Pictures.

Sports Interactive, 2004. *Football Manager.* London: Sega.

Squire, K. & Steinkuehler, C., 2006. Generating CyberCulture/s: The Case of Star Wars Galaxies. In: D. Gibbs & K. Krause, eds. *Cyberlines 2.0 Languages and Cultures of the Internet.* Albert Park (Victoria): James Nicholas, pp. 177–198.

St Andre, K., 1975. *Tunnels & Trolls.* Scottsdale (AZ): Flying Buffalo.

Stagecoach. 1939. [Film] Directed by John Ford. Walter Wanger Productions of Hollywood, California, United States of America.

Stanton, R., 2015. *A Brief History of Video Games: From Atari to Xbox One.* London: Robinson.

Star Trek: The Next Generation. 1987. [Film] Directed by Gene Roddenberry. United States of America: Paramount Domestic Television.

Star Trek. 1966. [Film] Directed by Gene Roddenberry. United States of America: Desilu.

Stebbins, R. A., 2001. *Exploratory Research in the Social Sciences.* Thousand Oaks (CA): Sage.

Steinkuehler, C. A. & Williams, D., 2006. Where Everybody Knows Your (Screen) Name: Online Games as "Third Places". *Journal of Computer-Mediated Communication,* 1 July, 11(4), pp. 885–909.

Stephenson, N., 1992. *Snow Crash.* New York (NY): Bantam.

Sterling, I., Seger, Y. & Yvet, A., 2012. *Translation Text Expansion: How It Affects Design.* [Online] Availableat:https://www.kwintessential.co.uk/blog/translation/translation-text-expansion-how-it-affects-design-2 [Accessed 3 December 2024].

Stevenson, R. L., 1883. *Treasure Island.* London: Cassell.

Stewart, B., 2011. Personality and Play Styles: A Unified Model. *Gamasutra,* 1 September.

Stinnett, D., 2005. *Star Trek Online: Designer Diary: Survey No. 1 Results.* [Online] Available at: https://gaming.trekcore.com/startrekonline/dd4.html [Accessed 3 December 2024].

Strife Hayes, J., 2022. *What went Wrong with Gaming?.* [Online] Available at: https://www.youtube.com/watch?v=g16heGLKlTA [Accessed 3 December 2024].

Suber, P., 1990. *The Paradox of Self-Amendment: A Study of Law, Logic, Omnipotence, and Change.* Bern: Peter Lang.

Sugg, D., 2017. *Fortnite: Battle Royale.* Cary (NC): Epic Games.

Sugg, D., 2020. *Fortnite: Save the World.* Cary (NC): Epid Games.

Suits, B., 1978. *The Grasshopper: Games, Life and Utopia.* 1st ed. Edinburgh: Scottish Academic Press.

Suls, J. et al., 2019. *APA Task Force Report on Violent Video Games.* Washington: Americal Psychological Association.

Sundén, J., 2009. *Play as Transgression: An Ethnographic Approach to Queer Game Cultures.* London: DiGRA.

Supreme Court of the United States, 2011. *Edmund G. Brown, Governor of the State of California, and Kamala Harris, Attorney General of the State of California v.* Entertainment Merchants Association and Entertainment Software Association. Washington: Supreme Court of the United States.

Suznjevic, M. & Matijasevic, M., 2012. Player Behaviour and Traffic Characterisation for MMORPGs: A Survey. *Multimedia Systems,* 21 June, 19, pp. 199–220.

Sweeney, M. M. et al., 2020. Prevalence and Correlates of Caffeine Use Disorder Symptoms among a United States Sample. *Journal of Caffeine and Adenosine Research,* March, 10(1), pp. 4–11.

Sydell, L., 2010. *Sci-Fi Inspires Engineers To Build Our Future.* [Online] Available at: https://www.npr.org/templates/story/story.php?storyId=129333703 [Accessed 3 December 2024].

Taken. 2008. [Film] Directed by Pierre Morel. United States of America: EuropaCorp.

Tanaka, H., 2002. *Final Fantasy XI.* Tokyo: Square.

Taylor, M. et al., 2018. Paracosms: The Imaginary Worlds of Middle Childhood. *Child Development,* 15 October, 91(1), pp. e164–e178.

Taylor, N., 2008. Periscopic Play: Re-positioning "the Field" in MMO Research. *Loading,* 11 November, 2(3).

Taylor, R., 1993. *Rivers of MUD.*

Taylor, S. P., 1967. Aggressive Behavior and Physiological Arousal as a Function of Provocation and the Tendency to Inhibit Aggression. *Journal of Personality,* June, 35(2), pp. 297–310.

Taylor, T. L., 2002. *Whose Game is this Anyway? Negotiating Corporate Ownership in a Virtual World.* Tampere: Tampere University Press.

Taylor, T. L., 2006. *Play between Worlds: Exploring Online Game Culture.* Cambridge (MA): MIT Press.

Tepper, A., 2003. *A Tale in the Desert.* Pittsburgh (PA): eGenesis.

Tesser, A., 1988. Toward a Self-Evaluation Maintenance Model of Social Behavior. In: L. Berkowitz, ed. *Advances in Experimental Social Psychology.* Cambridge (MA): Academic Press, pp. 181–227.

Thaler, R. H., 1980. Toward a Positive Theory of Consumer Choice. *Journal of Economic Behavior and Organization,* March, 1(1), pp. 39–60.

Thaler, R. H., 2000. From Homo Economicus to Homo Sapiens. *Journal of Economic Perspectives,* Winter, 14(1), p. 133–141.

The Lion King. 1994. [Film] Directed by Roger Allers, Rob Minkoff. United States: Walt Disney Pictures.

The Lord of the Rings: The Fellowship of the Ring. 2001. [Film] Directed by Peter Jackson. New Zealand: New Line Cinema.

The Lord of the Rings: The Return of the King. 2003. [Film] Directed by Peter Jackson. New Zealand: New Line.

The Lord of the Rings: The Two Towers. 2002. [Film] Directed by Peter Jackson. New Zealand: New Line.

The Matrix. 1999. [Film] Directed by Lana Wachowski, Lily Wachowski. Warner Bros, Burbank, California

The Pittsburgh Press, 1936. Straw Vote Fight Arouses Interest. *The Pittsburgh Press,* 2 November, p. 11.

The Wizard of Oz. 1939. [Film] Directed by Victor Fleming. United States: Metro-Goldwyn-Mayer.

There, 2003. *There.* San Mateo (CA): There.

Three Rings Design, 2003. *Yohoho! Puzzle Pirates.* San Francisco (CA): Three Rings Design.

Todd, E., 2011. *Gardens of Time.* Palo Alto (CA): Playdom.

Tolkien, J. R. R., 1954. *The Lord of the Rings.* 1st ed. London: George Allen & Unwin.

Tolkien, J. R. R., 1977. *The Silmarillion.* London: George Allen & Unwin.

Tomaszkiewicz, K., Mateusz, K. & Stępień, S., 2015. *The Witcher III: Wild Hunt.* Warsaw: CD Projekt.

Tondello, G. F., Mora, A., Marczewski, A. & Nacke, L., 2019. Empirical Validation of the Gamification User Types Hexad Scale in English and Spanish. *International Journal of Human-Computer Studies,* July, 127, pp. 95–111.

Tondello, G. F. et al., 2016. *The Gamification User Types Hexad Scale.* Austin: Association for Computing Machinery, pp. 229–243.

Toontown Rewritten Team, 2014. *Toontown Rewritten.* Toons of the World Foundation, Richland, Washington, United States of America.

Tørnquist, R. & Bruusgaard, M. H., 2012. *The Secret World.* Oslo: Electronic Arts.

Tørnquist, R. & Bruusgaard, M. H., 2017. *Secret World: Legends.* Oslo: Funcom.

Totten, C. W., 2019. *An Architectural Approach to Level Design.* 2nd ed. Boca Raton (FL): CRC Press.

Towell, J. & Towell, E., 1997. Presence in Text-Based Networked Virtual Environments or "MUDS". *Presence: Teleoperators and Virtual Environments,* 1 October, 6(5), pp. 590–595.

Toy, M., Wichman, G. & Arnold, K., 1980. *Rogue.* Berkeley (CA): University of California, Berkeley.

Trion Worlds, 2015. *Trove.* Redwood City (CA): Trion Worlds.

Trottier, C., 2002. *The Sims Online.* Redwood Shores (CA): Maxis Software.

Trubshaw, R. & Bartle, R. A., 1978. *MUD.* Colchester (Essex): University of Essex.

Trubshaw, R. & Bartle, R. A., 1985. *MUD2.* London: MUSE Ltd.

Tuan, Y.-F., 1977. *Space and Place: The Perspective of Experience.* Minneapolis (MN): University of Minnesota Press.

Tupes, E. C. & Christal, R. C., 1958. *Stability of Personality Trait Rating Factors Obtained under Diverse Conditions.* Lackland Air force Base: United States Air Force.

Turkle, S., 1995. *Life on the Screen: Identity in the Age of the Internet.* New York (NY): Simon & Schuster.

Turner, R. H., 1978. The Role and the Person. *American Journal of Sociology,* July, 84(1), pp. 1–23.

Tversky, A. & Kahneman, D., 1974. Judgment under Uncertainty: Heuristics and Biases. *Science,* 27 September, 185(4157), pp. 1124–1131.

Tversky, A. & Kahneman, D., 1981. The Framing of Decisions and the Psychology of Choice. *Science,* 30 January, 211(4481), pp. 453–458.

Tylor, E. B., 1879. *The History of Games.* London: Royal Institution, pp. 125–137.

UK Government, 2024a. *Apply for a Patent.* [Online] Available at: https://www.gov.uk/patent-your-invention [Accessed 3 December 2024].

UK Government, 2024b. *How Copyright Protects your Work.* [Online] Available at: https://www.gov.uk/copyright/how-long-copyright-lasts [Accessed 3 December 2024].

UK Government, 2024c. *Vehicle Licensing Statistics Data Tables.* [Online] Available at: https://assets.publishing.service.gov.uk/media/66f15b9b76558d051527abd7/veh0101.ods [Accessed 3 December 2024].

UK Parliament, 1974. Salt. *Hansard,* 4 November, 880.

Umarov, I., Mozgovoy, M. & Rogers, P. C., 2012. Believable and Effective AI Agents in Virtual Worlds: Current State and Future Perspectives. *International Journal of Gaming and Computer-Mediated Simulations,* 4(2), pp. 37–59.

United Nations General Assembly, 1948. *Universal Declaration of Human Rights.* Paris: UN.

United Nations General Assembly, 1989. *Convention on the Rights of the Child.* New York: UN.

United Nations General Assembly, 2007. *United Nations Declaration on the Rights of Indigenous Peoples.* New York: UN.

Upton, B., 2015. *The Aesthetic of Play.* 1st ed. Cambridge (MA): MIT Press.

Utz, S., 2001. *Results.* [Online] Available at: https://web.archive.org/web/20010504225103/https://www.uni-jena.de/~s0saka/mud/ [Accessed 3 December 2024].

Utz, S., 2003. Social Identification and Interpersonal Attraction in MUDs. *Swiss Journal of Psychology,* June, 62(2), pp. 91–101.

Valve, 2020. *Half Life: Alyx.* Bellevue (WA): Valve.

van den Hoven, I., 2020. *The 3-D Bartle Test of Gamer Psychology.* [Online] Available at: https://mudhalla.net/test/bartle3d.php [Accessed 3 December 2024].

Van Rooij, A. J. et al., 2018. A Weak Scientific Basis for Gaming Disorder: Let us Err on the Side of Caution. *Journal of Behavioral Addictions,* 1 March, 7(1), pp. 1–9.

Vance, J., 1950. *The Dying Earth.* New York (NY): Hillman Periodicals.

various, 1996. *MUD-DEV Archive*. [Online] Available at: https://mud-dev.zer7.com/ [Accessed 3 December 2024].

various, 2003. *Terra Nova*. [Online] Available at: https://terranova.blogs.com/ [Accessed 3 December 2024].

Vesa, M., 2013. *There be Dragons! An Ethnographic Inquiry into the Strategic Practices and Process of World of Warcraft Gaming Groups*. Helsinki: Hanken School of Economics.

Vigen, T., 2024. *Spurious Correlation #2,239*. [Online] Available at: https://www.tylervigen.com/spurious/correlation/2239_popularity-of-the-first-name-eleanor_correlates-with_wind-power-generated-in-poland [Accessed 3 December 2024].

Vincke, S., 2023. *Baldur's Gate III*. Ghent: Larian Studios.

Vinge, V., 1981. True Names. In: J. R. Frenkel, ed. *Nightflyers/True Names*. New York (NY): Dell, pp. 133–233.

Vogler, C., 1985. *A Practical Guide to Joseph Campbell's the Hero with a Thousand Faces*. Los Angeles: Christopher Vogler.

Vuorre, M., Johannes, N., Magnusson, K. & Przybylski, A. K., 2022. Time Spent Playing Video Games is Unlikely to Impact Well-Being. *Royal Society Open Science,* 27 July, 9(7), p. 220411.

Wadley, G. R., 2011. *Voice in Virtual Worlds*. Melbourne: University of Melbourne.

Wakeman, I., Lewis, D. & Crowcroft, J., 1991. *Traffic Analysis of Trans-Atlantic Traffic*. London: University College.

Walk, H., 2018. *Boobs, Muscles & Fairy Wings: Everything I Know About How Humans Design Their Avatar Selves*. [Online] Available at: https://hunterwalk.com/2018/07/23/boobs-muscles-fairy-wings-everything-i-know-about-how-humans-design-their-avatar-selves/ [Accessed 3 December 2024].

Wangyuan Shengtang Entertainment Technology; Aurogon Info & Tech, 2021. *Swords of Legends Online*. Beijing: Gameforge.

Wansborough, M. & Mageean, A., 2000. The Role of Urban Design in Cultural Regeneration. *Journal of Urban Design,* 5(2), pp. 181–197.

Warburton, S., 2009. Second Life in Higher Education: Assessing the Potential for and the Barriers to Deploying Virtual Worlds in Learning and Teaching. *British Journal of Educational Technology,* May, 40(3), pp. 414–426.

Warhammer Team, 2013. *Warhammer Updates*. [Online] Available at: https://web.archive.org/web/20130922040821/https://ageofreckoning.warhammeronline.com/article/Warhammer-Update [Accessed 3 December 2024].

Washington, G. et al., 1787. *Constitution of the United States of America,* Philadelphia.

Waters, R., 2004. *EverQuest II*. San Diego CA: Sony Online Entertainment.

Wattenberg, M., 2005. *Baby Names, Visualization and Social Data Analysis*. Minneapolis: IEEE, pp. 1–7.

Webber, E. & Dunbar, R. I. M., 2020. The Fractal Structure of Communities of Practice: Implications for Business. *PLoS One,* 29 April, 15(4), p. e0232204.

Webber, N. & Milik, O., 2016. *Selling the Imperium: Changing Organisational Culture and History in EVE Online*. Dundee: DiGRA and Society for the Advancement of the Science of Digital Games.

Webb, R., 2023. *Mostly Harmless Statistics*. Portland (OR): LibreTexts.

Weinstein, A. M., 2010. Computer and Video Game Addiction - A Comparison between Game Users and Non-Game Users. *American Journal of Drug and Alcohol Abuse,* 15 June, 36(5), pp. 268–276.

Welsh, O., 2014. *Rob Pardo's Legacy of Steel*. [Online] Available at: https://www.eurogamer.net/rob-pardos-legacy-of-steel [Accessed 21 November 2022].

WeMade Entertainment, 2001. *Legend of Mir 2*. Seongnam (Gyeonggi): Shanda.

Wenzel, H. G. et al., 2009. Excessive Computer Game Playing among Norwegian Adults: Self-Reported Consequences of Playing and Association with Mental Health Problems. *Psychological Reports,* December, 105(3), pp. 1237–1247.

Westworld. 2016. [Film] Directed by Jonathan Nolan, Lisa Joy. United States of America: HBO Entertainment.

Whatley, D., 1988. *GemStone][.* St Louis (MO): Simutronics.

Whatley, D., 1990. *GemStone III.* St Louis (MO): Simutronics.

Whatley, D., 1993. *CyberStrike.* St Louis (MO): Simutronics.

Wheatley, D., 1950. *The Second Seal.* London: Hutchinson.

Whedon, J., 1997. *Buffy the Vampire Slayer.* Los Angeles (CA): Mutant Enemy.

White, S., 1990a. *MOO.* Waterloo (Ontario): University of Waterloo.

White, S., 1990b. *TinyMUCK.* Waterloo (Ontario): University of Waterloo.

Williams, D., 2010. The Mapping Principle, and a Research Framework for Virtual Worlds. *Communication Theory,* 1 October, 20(4), pp. 451–470.

Williams, D., Consalvo, M., Caplan, S. & Yee, N., 2009. Looking for Gender: Gender Roles and Behaviors among Online Gamers. *Journal of Communication,* December, 59(4), pp. 700–725.

Williams, D. & Skoric, M., 2005. Internet Fantasy Violence: A Test of Aggression in an Online Game. *Communication Monographs,* June, 72(2), pp. 217–233.

Williams, J. P., 2009. Community, Frame of Reference and Boundary: Three Sociological Concepts and their Relevance for Virtual Worlds Research. *Qualitative Sociology Review*, 30 August, V(2), pp. 3–16.

Williams, J. P., Kirschner, D., Mizer, N. & Deterding, S., 2018. Sociology and Role-Playing Games. In: S. Deterding & J. Zagal, eds. *Role-Playing Game Studies.* New York (NY): Routledge, pp. 227–244.

Williams, M., 2007. Avatar Watching: Participant Observation in Graphical Online Environments. *Qualitative Research,* 7(1), pp. 5–24.

Wimmer, H. & Perner, J., 1983. Beliefs about Beliefs: Representation and Constraining Function of Wrong Beliefs in Young Children's Understanding of Deception. *Cognition,* January, 13(1), pp. 103–128.

Winstead, B. A., 1986. Sex Differences in Same-Sex Friendships. In: V. J. Derlega & B. A. Winstead, eds. *Friendship and Social Interaction.* New York (NY): Springer-Verlag, pp. 81–99.

Wiserax, A., 2024. *I Designed Economies for $150M Games: Here's my Ultimate Handbook.* [Online] Available at: https://medium.com/@wiserax2037/i-designed-economies-for-150m-games-heres-my-ultimate-handbook-de6212e95759 [Accessed 3 December 2024].

Withmore Hope, 2007. *MudVerse.* [Online] Available at: https://www.mudverse.com/ [Accessed 3 December 2024].

Wolf, M. J. P., 2012. *Building Imaginary Worlds: The Theory and History of Subcreation.* 1st ed. New York (NY): Routledge.

Wood, R., Whisenhunt, G., Pellett, D. & Pellett, F., 1975. *The Game of Dungeons.* Champaign, Illinois, United States of America.

Woodhead, R. & Greenberg, A., 1981. *Wizardry: Proving Grounds of the Mad Overlord.* Ogdensburg (NY): Sir-Tech.

Woodward, M., 2017. *Albion Online.* Berlin: Sandbox Interactive.

Woolley, D. R., 1994. PLATO: The Emergence of On-Line Community. *Computer-Mediated Communication Magazine,* July, 1(3).

Worchel, S., Lee, J. & Adewole, A., 1975. Effects of Supply and Demand on Ratings of Object Value. *Journal of Personality and Social Psychology,* November, 32(5), pp. 906–914.

World Health Organisation, 2018. *International Classification of Diseases.* Geneva: World Health Organisation.

World Intellectual Property Organisation; International Trade Centre, 2010. *Exchanging Value: Negotiating Technology Licensing Agreements. A Training Manual.* Geneva: WIPO/ITC.

World Intellectual Property Organisation, 1979. *Berne Convention for the Protection of Literary and Artistic Works (as amended on September 28, 1979) (Authentic text).* Paris: WIPO.

Wright, A. T., 1942. *Islandia.* New York (NY): Farrar & Rinehart.

Wright, W. & Trottier, C., 2002. *The Sims Online*. Walnut Creek (CA): Electronic Arts.

Wujcik, E., 1992. *Amber Diceless Role-Playing*. Detroit (MI): Phage Press.

Wyatt, P., 1994. *Warcraft: Orcs & Humans*. Irvine (CA): Interplay.

Wyatt, P., 2012. *The Inside Story of the Making of Warcraft, Part 1*. [Online] Available at: https://www.codeofhonor.com/blog/the-making-of-warcraft-part-1 [Accessed 24 July 2023].

XEODesign, 2010. *The 4Keys 2Fun*. [Online] Available at: https://www.xeodesign.com/assets/images/4k2f.jpg [Accessed 3 December 2024].

Yandyganova, N., 2024. *The Waiting Room NYC*. New York (NY): The Waiting Room.

Yang, Y. & Goh, B., 2021. *Explainer: Why and How China is Drastically Limiting Online Gaming for Under 18s*. [Online] Available at: https://www.reuters.com/world/china/why-how-china-is-drastically-limiting-online-gaming-under-18s-2021-08-31/ [Accessed 3 December 2024].

Yannakakis, G. N. & Togelius, J., 2011. Experience-Driven Procedural Content Generation. *IEEE Transactions on Affective Computing*, 2(3), pp. 147–161.

Ybarra, J., 1992. *The Shadow of Yserbius*. Cupertino (CA): Ybarra Productions.

Ybarra, J., 1993. *The Fates of Twinion*. Cupertina (CA): Ybarra Productions.

Ybarra, J., 1995. *The Ruins of Cawdor*. Cupertino (CA): Creative Insights.

Yee, N., 2001. *The Norrathian Scrolls: A Study of EverQuest*. [Online] Available at: https://www.nickyee.com/report.pdf [Accessed 3 December 2024].

Yee, N., 2002a. *Facets: 5 Motivation Factors for Why People Play MMORPG's*. [Online] Available at: https://www.nickyee.com/facets/facets.PDF [Accessed 3 December 2024].

Yee, N., 2002b. *The Daedalus Project: The Psychology of MMORPGs*. [Online] Available at: https://www.nickyee.com/daedalus/ [Accessed 3 December 2024].

Yee, N., 2005b. *Buying Gold*. [Online] Available at: https://www.nickyee.com/daedalus/archives/print/001469.php [Accessed 3 December 2024].

Yee, N., 2005d. *Level Distribution*. [Online] Available at: https://web.archive.org/web/20050713074556/blogs.parc.com/playon/archives/2005/06/level_distribut.html [Accessed 23 November 2023].

Yee, N., 2005a. *Motivations of Play in MMORPGs*. Vancouver: DiGRA.

Yee, N., 2005c. *Motivations of Play in MMORPGs: Results from a Factor Analytic Approach*. [Online] Available at: https://www.nickyee.com/daedalus/motivations.pdf [Accessed 3 December 2024].

Yee, N., 2007a. Motivations of Play in Online Games. *Journal of CyberPsychology and Behavior*, 4 January, 9(6), pp. 772–775.

Yee, N., 2007b. *Player Life-Cycle*. [Online] Available at: https://www.nickyee.com/daedalus/archives/001588.php [Accessed 3 December 2024].

Yee, N., 2008. Maps of Digital Desires: Exploring the Topography of Gender and Play in Online Games. In: Y. B. Kafai, C. Heeter, J. Denner & J. Sun, eds. *Beyond Barbie and Mortal Kombat: New Perspectives on Gender and Gaming*. Cambridge (MA): MIT Press, pp. 83–96.

Yee, N., 2014. *The Proteus Paradox: How Online Games and Virtual Worlds Change Us - and How They Don't*. New Haven (CT): Yale University Press.

Yee, N., 2015a. *Gamer Motivation Profile Findings*. San Francisco: GamesUR.

Yee, N., 2015b. *Gaming Motivations Group into 3 High-Level Clusters*. [Online] Available at: https://quanticfoundry.com/2015/12/21/map-of-gaming-motivations/ [Accessed 3 December 2024].

Yee, N., 2017. *Beyond 50/50: Breaking Down the Percentage of Female Gamers by Genre*. [Online] Available at: https://quanticfoundry.com/2017/01/19/female-gamers-by-genre/ [Accessed 3 December 2024].

Yee, N., 2021. *About One out of Three Men Prefer Playing Female Characters. Rethinking the Importance of Female Protagonists in Video Games*. Sunnyvale: Quantic Foundry.

Yee, N., 2023. *Playing Outside the Binary: 6 Things We Learned From 14,000 Transgender & Non-Binary Gamers*. [Online] Available at: https://quanticfoundry.com/2023/03/20/outside-the-binary/ [Accessed 3 December 2024].

Yee, N. & Bailensen, J. N., 2007. The Proteus Effect: The Effect of Transformed Self-Representation on Behavior. *Human Communication Research*, 1 July, 33(3), pp. 271–290.

Yee, N. et al., 2009. The Proteus Effect: Implications of Transformed Digital Self-Representation in Online and Offline Behaviour. *Communication Research,* April, 36(2), pp. 285–312.

Yee, N. et al., 2011. *Introverted Elves & Conscientious Gnomes: The Expression of Personality in World of Warcraft.* Vancouver: Association for Computing Machinery, pp. 753–762.

Ye, J., 2021. New Video Game Approvals Dry Up in China as Internal Memo Shows that Developers now have Many Red Lines to Avoid. *South China Morning Post,* 30 September.

Ye, K. K. C. & Shih, S., 2022. *MMORPG Genre Report.* Mountain View (CA): Google Play.

Yob, G., 1973. *Hunt the Wumpus.* Menlo Park (CA): People's Computer Company.

Yoon, U.-G., 2008. Real Money Trading in MMORPG Items from a Legal and Policy Perspective. *Journal of Korean Judicature,* 31 March, 1, pp. 418–477.

Youngblood, A. et al., 2018. *Design Practices for Human Scale Online Games.* Comfort: Project Horseshoe.

Young, G. W., Kehoe, A. & Murphy, D., 2016. Usability Testing of Video Game Controllers: A Case Study. In: M. A. Garcia-Ruiz, ed. *Games User Research: A Case Study Approach.* Boca Raton (FL): CDC Press, pp. 145–188.

Young, K. S., 1998. *Caught in the Net: How to Recognize the Signs of Internet Addiction - and a Winning Strategy for Recovry.* New York (NY): Wiley.

Zagal, J. P., Björk, S. & Lewis, C., 2013. *Dark Patterns in the Design of Games.* Chania: Foundations of Digital Games.

Zagal, J. P. & Deterding, S. eds., 2018. *Role-Playing Game Studies: Transmedia Foundations.* London: Routledge.

Zagalo, N. & Gonçalves, A., 2014. Social Interaction Design in MMOs. In: T. Quandt & S. Kröger, eds. *Multiplayer: The Social Aspects of Digital Gaming.* Abingdon (Oxfordshire): Routledge, pp. 134–144.

Zammitto, V. L., 2010. *Gamers' Personality and their Gaming Preferences.* Burnaby: Simon Fraser University.

Zarsky, T. Z., 2004. Information Privacy in Virtual Worlds: Identifying Unique Concerns beyond the Online and Offline Worlds. *New York Law School Law Review,* January, 49(1), p. 231.

Zeigarnik, B., 1927. Das Behalten erledigter und unerledigter Handlungen. *Psychologische Forschung,* December, 9, pp. 1–85.

Zeigarnik, B., 1932. On Finished and Unfinished Tasks. In: W. D. Ellis, ed. *A Source Book of Gestalt Psychology.* London: Kegan Paul, Trench, Trubner, pp. 300–314.

Zendle, D., Ferguson, C., Bowden-Jones, H. & Drummond, A., 2020. Too Much of a Good Thing? Excessive Use across Behaviours and Associations with Mental Health. *PsyArXiv Preprints,* 19 February.

Zhang, C., Perkis, A. & Arndt, S., 2017. *Spatial Immersion versus Emotional Immersion, Which is More Immersive?.* Erfurt: IEEE.

Zhang, Q., Cao, Y. & Tian, J., 2021. Effects of Violent Video Games on Players' and Observers' Aggressive Cognitions and Aggressive Behaviors. *Journal of Experimental Child Psychology,* March, 203, p. 105005.

Zhong, Z.-J., 2011. The Effects of Collective MMORPG (Massively Multiplayer Online Role-Playing Games) Play on Gamers' Online and Offline Social Capital. *Computers in Human Behaviour,* 15 August, 27(6), pp. 2352–2363.

Zhu, Z., Zhang, R. & Qin, Y., 2022. Toxicity and Prosocial Behaviours in Massively Multiplayer Online Games: The Role of Mutual Dependence, Power and Passion. *Journal of Computer-Mediated Communication,* November, 27(6), pp. 1–12.

Index

Note: Page numbers followed by "n" refer to footnotes.

.hack//Sign 75

2.5D *see* 2½D
2048 331
2½D 153
3D 47, 153, 155
4Keys2Fun 350–351

A Declaration of the Rights of Avatars 166, 486–488
A Tale in the Desert 50, 170, 487
abandoned (mode) 128
abandonware 426
AberMUD 30–31
AC *see* Asheron's Call
Achaea 26, 54, 196
Achaea, Dreams of Divine Lands see Achaea
Achiever 200–203, 209–211
Acknowledgement (communication) 399
acquisition rate 88
Actaeon and Artemis 242, 321
Acting (dimension) 204–205
active avoidance 476
active creation of belief 275
actor 288; *see also* agent
actual (form of existence) 2; *see also* actually real (form of existence)
actualisation (strategy of) 285
actually real (form of existence) 2; *see also* real (form of existence)
AD&D see Advanced Dungeons & Dragons
Adams Leeming, David 231
add 8
addiction: component model of 438; games studied 437; rate 439–440
adult (genre) 26
Advanced Dungeons & Dragons 17, 28, 43; *see also* Dungeons & Dragons
Advanced Research Project Agency 21
ADVENT see Adventure
Adventure 18, 22–23

Adventure '89 26
Adventure for Multiple Players 24
adventure game *see* games, adventure
adventurer plate 407
Adventurers Club Limited Member's Dossier 198
Advice to Admins see A Declaration of the Rights of Avatars
age (of virtual worlds) 89–90
Age of Conan 52, 162
agent 6
aggression: belief that games cause 440–442; early research 442–443; theoretical basis 443–444; violent games 444–447
aggressive cue 443
aggressive word completion task 446
agile methodology 112
agreeableness 355
AI *see* Artificial Intelligence
Air Warrior 43, 140
Alberti, Bob 28n73
Albion Online 46, 148
Alice's Adventures in Wonderland 68
alliance 385
allowlist 374
alpha 119
alt 4, 273, 275
alter ego 291
alternate-self construct 449
Amazon Games Orange County 104
Amber 196
America Online 39–40
American Psychiatric Association 438
American Psychological Association 432, 440
AMP see Adventure for Multiple Players
Anarchy Online 48–49, 68, 336
anchoring 463
Ancient Anguish 425
Anderson, Poul 63n53
Anna Karenina 232
anonymous 280; *see also* pseudonymous

Anthropology 423–424; biological 424; cultural 424–425; linguistic 424; physical 424; *see also* Archaeology
anthropomorphism 458
anti-pattern *see* dark pattern
AO see Anarchy Online
AOL *see* America Online
APA *see* American Psychological Association
Apotheosis 245, 262–263
apparent size *see* size, perceived
appearance (of virtual worlds) 69–70
Applied Sociology *see* Sociology, Applied
AR *see* augmented reality
Aradath 29
Archaeology 426–428
architecture: server 133–137; software 130
arch-wiz 198
Armory 148
ARPA *see* Advanced Research Project Agency
art 115; character 115; concept 110; environment 115
art director *see* artist, lead
art form (of design) 98–100, 182, 427
art bible *see* bible, art
The Art of Computer Programming 498
The Art of Persuasion 494n22
art specification document 111; *see also* bible, art
artificial intelligence 6, 60, 95, 156–157, 163, 175–176, 411, 485
artist 115; concept 110; lead 107, 110–111; technical 115
artist's journey 344
artistic statement 100–102
Asheron's Call 48, 51, 138, 336, 391, 440
Asheron's Call 2 51, 444
Asimov, Isaac 61–62
Aspnes, Jim 30
Assassin's Creed 330
asset 34, 60, 111, 133
assistant producer *see* producer, assistant
associate producer *see* producer, associate
Asteroids 331
Atari 54
ATitD see A Tale in the Desert
Atonement with the Father 243–245, 261–262, 267, 275
Attainer 209–210
Attainer/Attainer (interaction) 227
Attainer/Friend (interaction) 227–228
Attainer/Politician (interaction) 227
attention, developer (of virtual worlds) 80–81
attribution, rights of *see* rights, moral
audio 115–116
augmented reality 154

Austen, Jane 427, 452
auteur theory 11
automatic play 485; *see also* autoplay; macro
autonomy 301–302, 335, 352–353
autoplay 149
auxiliary (application) 148
Avalon 26, 199
Avalon: the Legend Lives see Avalon
avatar 6–7, 27–28, 63–64, 74, 273–274, 285; *see also* A Declaration of the Rights of Avatars
Avatar 23, 63
Avatars! 64
Azeroth 2, 303

backchannel 404; *see also* channel
backdrops 158
backfilling 380
Bad Ideas for Multi-Player Games 360
balance 120–121, 309; *see also* balanced world; load balancing
balanced world 34–35, 37, 229; *see also* game world; social world
Baldur's Gate III 5
Baramue Nara 45
Barnes, Steven 74
Bartle, Richard 20
Bartle Test 212–214
BatMUD 26, 90
battle pass 474
BBS *see* bulletin-board system
BDO see Black Desert Online
bears bears bears 458
Behavioural Psychology *see* Psychology, Behavioural
Belly of the Whale, the 239–240, 254–255
Berne Convention for the Protection of Literary and Artistic Works 159
beta 119–120; closed 119–120; open 121–122; paid 122
bible 15; art 110
big fish, little pond 468
big five 355
Biological Psychology *see* Psychology, Biological
Biopsychology *see* Psychology, Biological
BioWare 104
BL see British Legends
Black Desert Mobile 148
Black Desert Online 57, 142, 148, 254, 405, 450
blacklist *see* denylist
Blade & Soul 304
Blades in the Dark 196
bleed 393
blended fun *see* fun, blended
Blizzard 52, 175, 282–283, 468, 492

Blizzard Entertainment *see* Blizzard
blockchain 59, 132
Bloodstone 46
Blueprint for a Soul 320n23
Boon 235; *see also* The Ultimate Boon
boredom (of players) 306–307, 309
boss 8; fight 243, 407; world 139; *see also* mini-boss
bot 6, 120, 141–142, 485
Bouba/Kiki effect 254
Boxing 443
BrainHex 256–257
breadth 229–300
British Legends 24, 292; *see also* MUD1
British Telecom 21; *see also* Prestel
broadcast (channel type) 371
Broadsword Online Games 104
broken (player type) 220
BT *see* British Telecom
buff 463
buffering 147
Buffy the Vampire Slayer 16, 162
Buffyverse 16
builder privileges 85, 96
bulletin-board system 21
Burning Crusade 389, 417n41
Burns, Robert 286

cabal *see* guild
Call of Cthulhu 17, 203
Call to Adventure, the 236–237, 252–253
Cambridge University Computer Society 199
Camelot Unchained 29, 104
Campbell, Joseph 230–231, 234, 236, 244–245, 248, 250, 321
camping 416, 485
Candy Crush Saga 330
canned speech 374
capture rate 439
care bear 63, 332–333
cash shop 56
Castlevania 330
casual (game) 192; (gamer) *see* gamers, casual; (group) 381
Cataclysm 303n22, 316, 378
categorisation (group membership) 383
catfishing 291
causality 433–435
celestial steed 55
Centipede 436
challenge 309–310, 329
Champions Online 81
changeability (of virtual worlds) 84–85

channel 370–372, 405; chat 380–381
Chaos World of Wizards 25, 96n17
character 4, 6–8, 64, 66, 76, 152, 154, 185, 234–235, 273–276, 278, 282–283, 288–289, 291, 461;-creation 254, 283–286, 450–451; (glyph) 179; non-player 2, 4, 7, 458–459, 461; player 6, 81, 133–134, 138, 152, 166, 172; *see also* art, character; emote; reputation; rights, character; role-playing
charm (helpful item) 238, 241
chat channel *see* channel, chat; structured 380; unstructured 380; window 371
ChatGPT 176
cheap psychological tricks 472
cheater 78–79, 201–202
Chekhov's gun 466
Chess 177, 330, 353, 435
Chevalier's Romance Online 3 348
children 15, 189, 218, 447–448, 458
churn 51, 87–88
Chutes and Ladders see Moksha Patam
CircleMUD 33
City of Heroes 50, 68
City State Entertainment 104
Cityville 331
Civilization 4, 269
Civilization VI 330
clan 385–386
class 289–290, 404
classbound 289
classical conditioning 476
classless 289
client 42–43; *see also* client/server; security
client/server 130–133; *see also* telecommunications
Clinical Psychology *see* Psychology, Clinical
cloud 124n51
cloud streaming 59, 146–147
Club Caribe 39
Clue see Cluedo
Cluedo 93, 135, 203
codebase 31–33, 36
cognitive development, stages of 218
cognitive dissonance 465
Cognitive Psychology *see* Psychology, Cognitive
ColdMUD 32
Colossal Cave see Adventure
Colossal Cave Adventure see Adventure
combat 58, 77, 146
Comedy (genre) 68
command-line interface *see* interface, command-line
commend system *see* commendation system

commendation system 404–405, 418–419

commercial exploitation phase 123

Committee of Ministers to Member States of the Council of Europe 483

commodification 168, 367

Comms Plus! 199

communication 368–369; means of 370–375; motive for 375–377; opportunity for 377–381; properties of 381–383; shared cultural context 369–370

Communications Decency Act 483

community 359–363, 420–421; as objects 396–397; features of 363; how form 397–400; levels of engagement 392–395; management 409–410; of commitment 393; of communication 393; of interest 393; of practice 393; size 400–403; spiritual 393, 395

community support representative *see* CSR

community support specialist 124

companion 7

Companion (app) 148

compatibility tester *see* tester, compatibility

compensation (defensive strategy) 438

competence 301–302, 335, 352

CompuNet 24, 38

CompuServe 24, 29, 38–39

Conan (book series) 22, 162; *see also* Hyborian Age

Conan Exiles 164

concept art *see* art, concept

concept artist *see* artist, concept

conditioning 433; *see also* operant conditioning

configuration (of virtual worlds) 91

conscientiousness 355

console 49–50, 66, 148–149

constructivist grounded theory 198

content 92, 175, 315; designed 94; drought 81n37; group 316, 379; hand-crafted 96; noble 38; premium 40; procedurally generated 95; properties of 94–95; refereed 96; sources of 95–96; substitute 96–98; system 95; user-created 96; user-generated 95–96; *see also* patch, content

convenience sampling 444

Convention of the Rights of the Child 482

Copenhagen University 32

copyright 159–161, 170–171

Cordrey, Pip 26

core gamer *see* gamer, core

core loop 99, 329, 478

core team 106–107

corporation *see* guild

correlation 433–435

cosmetic 55–57, 93, 373

cosplay 172

cost of acquisition 181

Council of Europe 494

Council of Stellar Management 386

counter-culture 366

Cousineau, Phil 231

covenant, the 483–485, 488, 494

Cow Clicker 331

Cox, Alan 30n81

CRC *see* release candidate testing

creature 7

credentials 283

criteria (virtual worlds) 3–6, 37, 204, 212; (component models) 439–440

critter 8

CRO3 see Chevalier's Romance Online 3

Crossing the First Threshold 239, 254

Crossing the Return Threshold 247, 265

cross-platform 148–149

crossplay *see* cross-platform

cross-server 278, 380

Crowfall 58

Crystal Blade see Simutronics

CS *see* customer service

CSR 117–118, 120, 177–178

Cthulhu Mythos 15

CTO *see* programmer, lead

Cultural Anthropology *see* Anthropology, Cultural

cultural appropriation 452

cultural context 369

Cultural Sociology *see* Sociology, Cultural

culture 170, 363–368; shock 365; *see also* counter-culture; cultural appropriation; cultural context; pop culture; sub-culture

The Cursor 360

customer service 117–118

customer service representative *see* CSR

Cyberpunk (genre) 26

Cyberpunk 2077 297n9

CyberStrike 43

D&D see Dungeons & Dragons

Daedalus Project 191, 268, 336–337

Daggerfall 47n17, 137

DALL-E 110

DAoC see Dark Age of Camelot

Dark Age of Camelot 29, 48–49, 51, 74, 138, 161, 336–337

Dark Forest 132n6

dark pattern 471–473; *see also* cheap psychological tricks

Darkness Falls: The Crusade 49

data centre 92

data donation 188
database 135–137
data-mining 125
day (churn) 88
DBASE 20
DC Universe Online 50, 68
DD *see* DPS
DDO see Dungeons & Dragons Online
Dear Esther 331
Death on the Nile 162
debuff 463
deceptive pattern *see* dark pattern
Declaration of the Rights of Man and of the Citizen 486
Declaring of the Rights of Players see A Declaration of the Rights of Avatars
Delphi 38
Demarest, Ken 45
demographic game design *see* DGD1
demographics 188–194
denial of service 131
Denton, Rob 29n77
denylist 374
Departure phase 236–240, 252–255
dependency *see* addiction
depth 229–300
derail 220, 287, 315
design 9–10, 396–397; director *see* designer, lead; document 109–110; *see also* art specification document; technical design document; treatment
Design Practices for Human Scale Online Games 397, 400
designed *see* content, designed
designer 10–11, 15, 98–100, 108, 113–114, 261–262, 366–368; experience 113; fun 327; lead 11, 107; narrative *see* writer; rights *see* rights, designer
designeritis 99n19
Designing Virtual Worlds 497
desire profile *see* Reiss desire profile
Detective Fiction (genre) 68
dev team *see* development team
developer 103, 170, 389–390, 488–489; attention *see* attention, developer; diaries 119; external 104; first-party 104; independent 104, 163; internal 104; second-party 104; third-party 104; *see also* development team; development studio; operator
development 103–106; studio 10, 103–106; team 111, 124–125; *see also* development tracks; live team; cognitive development
development tracks 214–221, 255

Developmental Psychology *see* Psychology, Developmental
DGD1 356–358
DGD2 357; *see also* DGD1
Diablo 126n58
Diagnostic and Statistical Manual of Mental Disorders 439
diegetic 154
DikuMUD 32–35, 46, 48, 63, 73, 82
dilution 61, 126, 175, 416
direct message 371
director *see* designer, lead
disembodiment 449
disinterest graph 330–332
Diversity University 324
division (company) 105–106
DM *see* direct message; Dungeon Master
dnd see The Game of Dungeons
Dodecad 336
Dofus 304
DOTA 2 411, 474
DPS (role) 35, 378n36, 403–404
Dr Toddystone 22n42
Dr Who 15, 68
Dr. Cat *see* Shapiro, David
Dragon's Gate 29, 39–40
DragonMUD 425
DragonSpires 44–45
Dream Park 74, 412
dressing 93, 444
drift 88, 214
driver layer 134–135
drone 7
Ducheneaut, Nic 192, 339
Dunbar, Robin 361
Dunbar's number 361–362
DUNGEN see Zork
The Dungeon 19, 19n23; *see also Zork*
dungeon *see* instance
Dungeon Fighter Online 61
Dungeon Master 16
Dungeons & Dragons 3–4, 16–17, 19–22, 32, 35, 39, 54, 73–74, 96, 162, 289, 441
Dungeons & Dragons Online 54–55, 162
Dungeons & Dragons Online: Eberron Unlimited 54
Dungeons & Dragons Online: Stormreach 54
Dungeons of Kesmai 29
The Dungeons of Moria 43
Dwarf Fortress 43, 331
dyad 399, 406–408
Dying Earth 73n19
dynamic art *see* art, character
dynamic difficulty adjustment 309

dynamic filters 375
dynamic zoning 138
dynamics 221–224
Dystopian (genre) 68

E*M*P*I*R*E see Sceptre of Goth
EA *see* Electronic Arts
Earth and Beyond 50
Easter egg 303–305
edutainment *see* games, serious
Eight Types of Fun 351–352
eight-type interest graph *see* interest graph, 3D
elder game 264, 267, 273
Elder Scrolls IV: Oblivion 330
Elder Scrolls Online 58, 76, 127, 192, 305
Electronic Arts 45, 48
Elite Dangerous 58, 68, 82, 95, 365
ElseMOO 425
emergency fix 80
emote 372–373
emoticon 373
emotional immersion *see* immersion, emotional
Empire 19n23
Empyrion 25
En Garde! 406n16
endorsement system *see* commendation system
End-User Licence Agreement *see* EULA
engagement 197; *see also* community engagement
engine 20, 25, 60, 495
engineer *see* programmer
ennui 307
entity *see* token
Entropia Universe 50, 54n38, 168–169, 425
environment art *see* art, static
Envy 33
EoC see Evolution of Combat
Epic 472
EPSS 21
EQ see EverQuest
EQ2 see EverQuest II
escapism 302
ESO see Elder Scrolls Online
Essex University *see* University of Essex
ethnography 424; virtual 424
ethnology 424–425
ethos 364
EU Charter of Fundamental Rights 488
EULA 165, 167, 170, 177, 481, 492
European Convention on Human Rights 481
European Parliament 165
EVE Echoes 148
EVE Online 46, 50, 68, 82, 85, 95, 127, 139, 148, 192, 330, 365, 386, 416, 490

EverQuest 29, 46–49, 51, 138, 140, 161, 182, 192, 279, 336–337, 379, 425, 485
EverQuest II 29, 51, 56, 187, 290n43
Evolution of Combat 473
excessive play 440; *see also* addiction
executive producer *see* producer, executive
expansion 80–81, 175; *see also Burning Crusade, Cataclysm, Horizons, Wrath of the Lich King*
expedition 369; *see also* instance
experience designer *see* designer, experience
Experimental Packet-Switching Service *see* EPSS
Explicit (dimension) 208, 212
exploitativeness 72
Explorer 200–203, 210–211
external developer *see* developer, external
extraterritorial jurisdiction 164n25
extraversion 355
extrinsic reward 455

F2P see free-to-play
F76 see Fallout 76
Facebook 4, 359
facet (motivation) 337–338; (*Ultima Online*) 48
faction 49, 138, 386, 390–391
fade 145
Fafhrd and the Grey Mouser (book series) 22
fair use 160
fairness 72
Fallout 76 58, 68, 77, 110, 416
Falstein, Noah 350
fan art 171n40
fan fiction 171–172
Fantasy (genre) 26, 67–68; *see also* High Fantasy
Fantasy Westward Journey 57
Farmer, F. Randall 64, 346, 350n16, 359, 417n40
farming 416
FarmVille 478n35
The Fates of Twinion 43
Father, the 235, 241, 243–245, 257–258, 261–262
fear of loss *see* loss aversion
feature 93
Federal Trade Commission 472
Federation II 24–25, 38–40
feed 371
fellowship *see* party
FFXIV see Final Fantasy XIV
Fiasco 196
Fifth Age of virtual worlds 42–53
Fighting Fantasy 294n1
Final Fantasy XI 49, 51, 379
Final Fantasy XIV 57, 68, 70, 75, 97, 127, 142, 148, 152, 161, 180, 281, 289, 301n18, 304, 316, 369–370, 373n24, 378–379, 404–405, 407, 411, 414, 450

First Age of virtual worlds 19–24
First Edition (of *Designing Virtual Worlds*) 90, 502
first-party developer *see* developer, first-party
first-person (perspective) 76, 152, 154
first-person shooter 410
flash crowd 139
flat-rate charging *see* subscription
Flinn, Kelton 29n79
flood test 120
flow 308–310
Foard, Larry 31
focus group 198
Foldit 324
folklore 22, 74; *see also* lore
Football Manager 331
form 94, 98–99
format tester *see* tester, compatibility
Fortnite 5, 61, 127, 472–473
Fortnite: Battle Royale see Fortnite
founder effect 387
four humours 354–355, 357
Fourth Age of virtual worlds 38–41
four-type interest graph *see* interest graph, 2D
FPS *see* first-person shooter
fragmentation 61
framing 459; *see also* framing effect
framing effect 462–463
free company *see* guild
Free Guy 75
Freedom to Live 248, 266
free-to-play 53–57, 332–333
Friend 211
friend (types of) 361
friends list 382
The Frog Prince 232
frustration 309
fun 196–199, 256, 269, 287, 309–310; blended 350; not playing for 261; *see also* designer fun; meta-gaming fun; no fun; role-playing fun; unfun
Funativity 349–350
Funcom 49, 164
Furcadia 27n70, 44, 365

Gaffney, Jeremy 318
gag 375
Galaxian 427
GAM *see* general aggression model
Gamasutra see gamedeveloper.com
GãmBit *see* GãmBit Multi Systems
GãmBit Multi Systems 28
Game Archaeologist 53n33
Game Developers Conference 192, 410

Game Master *see* Dungeon Master; referee
The Game of Dungeons 19
Game of Thrones 162, 495n23
game world 34–37, 191, 229, 307
gamedeveloper.com 129
game-mastered content *see* content, refereed
gameplay 69–70, 93–94, 96–99, 101, 307, 444; substitute 97; *see also* balance
gamer: casual 332–333; core 332–333; hard-core 63, 181, 332–333, 364; *see also* care bear
games: and addiction *see* addiction; adventure 18; and aggression *see* aggression; serious 322–323; video 435–436; with a purpose 324; *see also* casual (game); game world; elder game
gamification 319, 321–323, 335
Gamification Summit 322, 323
gaming disorder 438–439
gaming disorder, predominantly online *see* Internet gaming disorder
gamma *see* release candidate testing
gang-killing *see* gank
gank 48n19, 416, 420
gankbox 48n19
Gardens of Time 331
Garriott, Richard 11, 45, 64n56
gauntlet 70
GDC *see* Game Developers Conference
GeForce NOW 147
Gemstone][28, 39
GemStone III 40
general aggression model 443
General Electric 39
General Electric Information Services 39
GEnie 39, 43, 45, 53
genre 67–69
Ghost see Sceptre of Goth
Gibson, William 74
glamour *see* transmogrification
GMC *see* content, refereed
Go 330
The Go Game 493
Goddess, the 242–243, 257
Gods 24–26, 38
going gold *see* launch, commercial
going silver *see* release candidate testing
Golf 63–64, 451
Grapevine 61
graphical MUD *see* MUD (genre), graphical
graphical world 34, 37, 47, 153
graphics 36–37, 69–70, 151–154, 298; era 42
Great Schism 30–31, 34–35
greeter 408–409

Griefer 210–211
Griefer/Attainer (interaction) 226
Griefer/Griefer (interaction) 226
Griefer/Networker (interaction) 225
Griefer/Politician (interaction) 226
Griefer/Sage (interaction) 226
Griefer/Scientist (interaction) 226
grind 94n13, 417
group 138, 317, 359–360, 369, 379–380, 383–384,
        419; chat 371, 377; exclusive 384; flat 385;
        formal 139, 306, 384; hardwired 384;
        hierarchical 385; inclusive 384; informal
        384, 406; persistent 384; softwired 384;
        temporary 384; types 384–386; *see also*
        content, group; focus group; looking for
        group; pick-up group; triadic closure group
group content *see* content, group
grouping 57
growth rate 88
guardian 239
guild 385–389, 402–403; charter 388; chat 200;
        leader 317; tax 389
Guild Wars 52, 58, 304, 425
Guild Wars 2 58, 391
Guru *see* Sage
GW see Guild Wars
GW2 see Guild Wars 2
GWAP *see* games with a purpose

Habbo Hotel 50
Habitat 29–31, 36, 39, 43–44, 63–64, 346, 417n40;
        see also Neohabitat; Club Caribe
Hack 43
Hacker *see* Sage
Half Life: Alyx 115n29
Hamurabi see The Sumerian Game
Hanabi 331
hand-crafted content *see* content, hand-crafted
haptic wearable 62
hard-core gamer *see* gamer, hard-core
hardware manufacturer 104
Harris, Kamala 442n22
Harry Potter (media franchise) 162, 171n43, 231
Hartsman, Scott 29
HCC *see* content, hand-crafted
healer 35, 378n36, 403–405
Hedron 346
The Hero with a Thousand Faces 230–231
Hero's Journey, the 230–236, 250–252; lived
        250–251, 263–265; narrative 250–251,
        257, 262–267; *see also* Departure phase;
        Initiation phase; Return phase
Heroine's Journey 230

Hexad 335–336, 340
Hierarchy of Needs 269
High Fantasy (genre) 68, 74
Hightower, Alfred 492
The Hobbit 42n2
honour system *see* commendation system
Horizons 58n44
Horror (genre) 68
host 130
hot sauce paradigm 445
hot-fix *see* emergency fix
Hourglass 26
How to Be a God 2n6, 497n4
Hunt the Wumpus 23n44
Hyborian Age 15
Hyrup, Darrin 29

ideal (form of existence) 2; *see also* ideal self
ideal self 301–302; construct 449
idealisation (strategy of) 285
ideally real (form of existence) 2; *see also* ideal (form
        of existence); real (form of existence)
identification 300–301; *see also* self-identification
        (group membership)
identity 233, 239, 254, 269–270, 283–284, 286–288,
        300–301, 449–450; marker 451–453;
        tourism 453
IDN *see* interactive digital narrative
Idoru 74
IGD *see* Internet gaming disorder
Illusion 425
imaginary 1; world 15
ImagiNation Network 43
immersion 271–272, 320–321; degrees of 273–275,
        284, 286–288, 294–297, 301–305, 338, 395,
        420–421; emotional 272; sensory 154,
        298–299; spatial 272; *see also* flow, presence
Implicit (dimension) 208, 212
incognito 292
independent developer *see* developer, independent
indie *see* developer, independent
industrial design (IP) 159
Inferno 232
influences (on virtual worlds) 74–76
information provider 38–41
Ingress 154
in-house developer *see* developer, internal
Initiation phase 240–246, 255–263
INN *see* ImagiNation Network
innovation 61
Input/Output World of Adventure *see* IOWA
instance 44n9, 49, 371, 379–380, 386, 403; solo
        301–302

instantiation layer 135
intangible 84, 275–277
integrity, rights of *see* rights, moral
intellectual property 73, 159–163, 169, 490
Interacting (dimension) 204–205
interactive digital narrative 294, 306
Interactive Software Federation of Europe 494
interest (of players) 306–307
interest graph: 2D 200–201, 204, 208, 214–216, 306; 3D 208–211, 216; *see also* disinterest graph
interface 11–12, 14, 76–78, 133, 150; command-line 18, 23; graphics 152–154; text 150–151; *see also* augmented reality; virtual reality
internal developer *see* developer, internal
International Classification of Diseases 439
Internet gaming disorder 438–439
intervening barrier *see* mooring effect
Interworld Productions *see* Mythic Entertainment
intrinsic reward 455
IoK see Island of Kesmai
IOWA 25–26, 30, 96
IP *see* intellectual property
Island of Kesmai 24, 29, 36, 38, 43–44
Islandia (book) 15; (MUD) 31
isometric (perspective) 44–46, 66, 152

jacking in 62
Jacobs, Mark 29, 40n108, 125n55
Jagex 473
JANet *see* Joint Academic Network
jargon 406
jarringness 297
John Carter (book series) 22
Joint Academic Network 21
JoMR see Journal of MUD Research
Journal of MUD Research 199
Jung, Carl 354–355, 357
Jurassic Park 137n23; *see also Jyulagi Gong-won*
jurisdiction 164–166
Justice Online 57
Jyulagi Gong-won 45

kaleidoscopic 294
Karyn 291
Keirsey temperaments 354–357
Kesmai Corporation 29, 39, 43, 45, 140
key (login) 120
Killer 200–203, 208, 210
kill-stealing 485
Kingdom of Drakkar 43, 152
Kleenex tester *see* tester, Kleenex
Knuth, Donald 498
Koenitz, Hartmut 294n2, 306

Kolb's experiential learning styles 324–325
Koster, Raph 11, 46, 51, 85n45, 166, 175, 350, 377n33, 486

lag 140, 144–145, 147; network 144; server 144
LambdaMOO 32, 63, 73n18, 284, 359, 425
LARP *see* live-action role-playing
latency 144, 147
launch 122–123; commercial 123; full 122; soft 122; staggered 123; *see also* relaunch
law-making 60
Lawrie, Michael 30, 495n26
layer 82, 127, 139
Lazzaro, Nicole 350, 357
lead: artist *see* artist, lead; designer *see* designer, lead; engineer *see* programmer, lead; programmer *see* programmer, lead
leaderboard 468
League of Legends 348, 411, 413
lean methodology 112
LeBlanc, Marc 351–352
Legend of Mir 2 57
LegendMUD 46, 91n58, 291
Lenton, Alan 24
LFG *see* looking for group
LFM *see* looking for more
liberty, right to *see* right to liberty
lifetime value 181
Linden Lab 50, 283, 425, 482
Lineage 45, 153
Lineage II 51, 57
linear (of virtual worlds) 70
LinguaMOO 13, 324
The Lion King 231
Literary Digest 186
live: streaming 146; team 124
live-action role-playing 5
lived Hero's Journey *see* Hero's Journey, lived
load balancing 137–139
local broadcast (channel type) 371
localisation 178–179
lockbox 165, 478
LoL see League of Legends
Long, Starr 45, 410
longitudinal study 192, 444
looking for group 380–381, 403
looking for more 380
lootbox *see* lockbox
The Lord of the Rings 21–22, 73–74, 231, 233, 302n19
The Lord of the Rings Online 52, 56, 73, 161, 302n19, 304, 453n41
lore 16, 296
loss aversion 56, 470–471

Lost Ark 53n34, 57, 66, 76, 97, 141, 152, 163, 304, 377, 407n18
LotRO see The Lord of the Rings Online
Louden, Bill 39
loyalty streak 474
LPC 32
LPMUD 32–33, 45
lusory attitude 78–80, 201–203

M59 see Meridian 59
macro 141–142, 485
magic circle 79n35, 328, 367, 487; *see also* lusory attitude
Magic Flight, the 246–247, 264–265
Magic: the Gathering 331, 356
main 4, 275; *see also* alt
Main Explorer Sequence 215–217, 256, 347
Main Sequence 214–215, 217, 256, 325
Main Socialiser Sequence 215, 217, 256, 276, 290, 346, 347
main tank 404, 406
maintenance mode 128
male gaze 284
MapleStory 44, 54, 57
Marczewski, Andrzej 335, 358
Marvel Cinematic Universe 16
Marxism *see* social conflict theory
masquerading 291–293
Massively Overpowered 53n33, 75n27
massively multiplayer 37
massively multiplayer online role-playing game *see* MMORPG
Master of Orion: Conquer the Stars 330
Master of the Two Worlds 247, 265–266
The Matrix 75
The Matrix Online 54, 431n17
MBTI *see* Myers-Briggs Type Indicator
McCloud, Scott 284
MDL 22n43
meaning (of virtual worlds) 98–99
MECC *see* Minnesota Educational Computer Consortium
mechanic 93, 95, 307, 353, 444n26
Mechanical Turk 191n14
media effect 443
Medievia 31n83, 90
medium 370
Meeting with the Goddess, the 241, 257–259
megaserver 82
mental model (of self) 233, 460; (of virtual world) 295–297
mentor (Supernatural Aid) 238; (of other players) 316, 405

Merc 33
merchandising 172
Meridian 59 46–48, 68, 129, 153, 182, 388, 410n25
meta-gaming fun 327
Metaplace 44
meta-plot 232
Metaverse 59, 74–75
metrics 120, 143, 177; personality 356–357
Middle Earth 15, 22, 160
Midjourney 110, 374
Milieu see Sceptre of Goth
mind, the 62, 295–298, 432–433
Minecraft 26, 151, 153, 164, 331
mini-boss 8
mini-map 77, 140–141
mini-spec 110; *see also* technical design document
Minitel 24, 38–39
Minnesota Educational Computer Consortium 28
Minnesota Multiphasic Personality Test 356
Minor Sequence 215–217, 256
mirror neurons 457–458
MirrorWorld 25–26
MIST 20n31, 30, 495
mistell 390
MMO *see* MMORPG
MMO Populations 193
MMO Stats 193
MMORPG 28, 193, 195–196, 422; (acronym) 8–9, 37
MMORPG.com 75n27
mob 7–8, 25, 137–138, 141, 151, 378n36, 485
MOBA 181, 348, 410–411
mobile: *see* mob; mobile phone
mobile phone 44, 148–149
Moksha Patam 70n12, 331
Monomyth *see* Hero's Journey
monothetic 439–440
monster 7
Monster 7, 30–31
MOO (genre) 32, 36, 50, 85, 191
MOO (virtual world) 31–32
Mooney, Bill 478n35
mooring effect 430–431
MOOSE Crossing 324
moral rights *see* rights, moral
Mori, Masahiro 456
Moria 19
Morningstar, Chip 63n53, 64, 346, 417n40
mortal 197
Mosaic 26
motivations 337
MPG-Net 43
MT *see* main tank; mistell
MU* 36

MUCK 31–32

MUD (genre) 19, 25–26, 30–31, 33, 36, 42, 45, 60, 426–427; graphical 36, 42, 44, 46; text 36, 61, 82, 196; version 1 19; version 2 20, 25, 30; version 3 20, 22, 24; version 4 26; *see also* stock MUD syndrome

MUD (virtual world) 19–24, 27–28, 36–38, 73–74, 147, 214

MUD Connector 61

MUD, Object-Oriented see MOO

MUD1 24–26, 31, 38, 83, 90, 133–134, 141, 254–255, 269, 278, 291–292, 365, 390, 410, 426, 428, 466, 495; *see also* MUD version 3

MUD2 26, 38, 134, 139, 151, 179, 197–199, 214, 228, 372–373, 490; *see also MUD* version 4

MUD-DEV 14, 64

MUDDL 20, 22, 24, 26

MUDDLE 26

mudlib *see* physics layer

MUDspeke Dictionary 197n7, 437n9, 466

MudVerse 61

Mueller, Henry 198

Multima 45

Multiplayer BattleTech 43

Multi-player Online Battle Arena *see* MOBA

Multi-User Created Kingdom *see* MUCK

Multi-User Dungeon see MUD

Multi-User Dungeon Definition Language *see* MUDDL

Multi-User Dungeon Definition LanguagE *see* MUDDLE

Multi-User Shared Hallucination *see* MUSH

Mundane World 235–237, 242–243, 246–247, 250

museum mode *see* abandoned (mode)

MUSH 36, 136

mute 375

Myers-Briggs Type Indicator 345, 354–357

mystique 197

Mythic Entertainment 29, 49, 162

name (of character) 277–283

narrative 232

narrative designer *see* writer

narrative Hero's Journey *see* Hero's Journey, narrative

narrowcast (channel type) 371

negative feedback loop 108, 121

negative punishment 476

negative reinforcement 476

Neohabitat 30

network lag *see* lag, network

Networker 210

Networker/Friend (interaction) 227

Neuromancer 73

neuroticism 355

Neverwinter Nights 39–40, 43, 347n13

New Game Enhancements 128, 316, 484; *see also Star Wars Galaxies*

New World 58, 95, 104, 127, 156, 197n5, 268, 305, 368–369, 372, 379, 385, 389n52

New World Notes 75n27

New York Supreme Court 483

newbie: flow 87, 126, 225; hose 40, 87

Nexus: the Kingdom of the Winds 45

NFT *see* non-fungible token

NGE *see* New Game Enhancements

Ninja 493

Niven, Larry 74, 139n31

no fun 309

No Man's Sky 58, 68, 82, 95, 365

noise blast task 446

Nomic 93n7

non-binary (gender) 171, 190

non-diegetic 154

non-fungible token 59, 168, 464

Norrathian Scrolls 336

notice board 380

Nottingham Trent University 187

Noughts and Crosses 331

NPC *see* character, non-player

null hypothesis 445

NW see New World

NWN see Neverwinter Nights

object 134

Odyssey 232

off tank 406

Old School RuneScape 148

OnLive 147

open (of virtual worlds) 70–71; *see also* linear

open PvP *see* PvP, open

Opening (communication) 398

openness to experience 355

OpenSim see OpenSimulator

OpenSimulator 163, 324

operant conditioning 476–478

operation (development) 123–128

operator 123–124, 482–483, 488–489

Opportunist 211

Opportunist/Griefer (interaction) 225

Opportunist/Networker (interaction) 225

Opportunist/Opportunist (interaction) 225

Opportunist/Politician (interaction) 225

Opportunist/Sage (interaction) 226

Opportunity (communication) 398

Origin Systems 45

Orthanc see Orthanc Labyrinth
Orthanc Labyrinth 19
OT *see* off tank
Other World 235–236, 238–241, 246–247, 250
Oubliette 19, 28, 47
out-of-copyright *see* copyright
overjustification effect 323, 455–456
Overwatch 411

p2w *see* pay-to-win
Pac-Man 331, 444
paracosm 15–18, 21–22
parasocial relationship 272, 460–462
Pardo, Rob 51
participation bias 186
party 385–386, 403–404; size 403–404
patch 124, 143; content 80–81
patent 159–160
Path of Ascension 346
Pavlov's dogs 476
pay-to-win 56–57, 72, 276
PC *see* character, player; personal computer
PCG *see* procedural content generation
Pearson product-moment correlation coefficient
    434
pedit5 see The Dungeon
peer-to-peer 131–132, 141
PENS 352–353
Pensjö, Lars 32
perceived size *see* size, perceived
per-hour charging 40, 56
permadeath 128n64, 282, 410
per-month charging *see* subscription
persistence 5, 83–85
persona 273–274, 291
personal (channel type) 371
personal computer 49–50, 65–66, 147–149
personality metrics *see* metrics, personality
persuasive 295
pet 8
PGC *see* content, procedurally generated
Phantasy Star Online 49, 68, 141
philosophy (of virtual worlds) 89
Phrase Detectives 324
physics 4, 17; of Reality 5; layer 134–135, 384; *see*
    also tags
Piaget, Jean 218, 314
pick-up group 280, 302, 380–381, 403, 407, 410, 418
PIGG 24
Pillars of Eternity 5
ping 144
pipeline 112
place 1–3

PlaneShift 50
Planner *see* Achiever
platform 65–67
PLATO 18–19, 23, 27, 47, 63, 66
player 3, 18; base 85–89; impact 85, 273; character
    see character, player; choice 375;
    management *see* community
    management; *versus* player *see* PvP; *see*
    also boredom (of players); interest (of
    players); interest graph; player types;
    server, player-operated
player (lusory attitude) 78–79, 201–202; *see also*
    balance; gamer
Player Experience Needs Satisfaction *see* PENS
player types 195, 203–204, 208, 214, 221–222, 229,
    250, 256, 270, 311–312, 314–317, 319–326,
    334–338, 357–358; misusing 317–319; not
    using 326–327
player-operated server *see* server, player-operated
Players (dimension) 204–205
playtest 116–117
plot 232
Pokémon Go 61, 154, 331
Poker 331
Politician 208
Politician/Politician (interaction) 228
polythetic 439–440
Pong 330
pop culture 303–305
positive feedback loop 86, 221, 226–228, 443
positive punishment 476
positive reinforcement 476
Post Office 21; *see also* Prestel
Post-Apocalyptic (genre) 68
predictive model 145
preload *see* seed
pre-production (development) 106–111
presence 272, 308, 443
preservation of complex objects 426
Prestel 24, 38–39, 198
pretexting 348
prevalence (of addiction) 439
priming 462
privacy, right to *see* right to privacy
private server *see* server, rogue
procedural content generation 95; *see also* content,
    procedurally generated
procedurally generated content *see* content,
    procedurally generated
Prodigy 38–39, 483
producer 11, 107, 111–113; assistant 112; associate
    112
production (development) 105–106, 111–118

production management assessment 111; *see also* art specification document; technical design document
profanity filter 374, 382–383
programmer 114–115; lead 107, 110, 114
progression 275, 315–316, 389; community 395; group 317; server *see* server, progression
Project Entropia see Entropia Universe
project manager *see* producer
property 166–169
property rights *see* rights, property
Proteus effect 286, 288, 450, 459
The Proteus Paradox 306; *see also* Proteus effect
pseudonymous 280–281
Psi-theory 310
psychologist 435–436
Psychology 432–433, 454–455; Behavioural 433; Biological 432; Clinical 433; Cognitive 432; Developmental 433
PTR *see* realm, public test
public test realm *see* realm, public test
public test server *see* realm, public test
publicity 60, 122–123, 162, 422
publisher 10, 104
PUG *see* pick-up group
pull effect 430
Pulsipher, Lew 353–354
push effect 430
PvP 47–48, 228, 318, 386; open 48n19, 413, 416, 420

QA 105–106, 116–118; lead 106, 116–117; technician *see* tester
quality assurance *see* QA
quality-of-life 72, 305, 378
Quantic Foundry 192, 339–341, 356
Quantum Link *see* America Online
Quest 25

r 434
rage quit 89, 401
raid *see* instance; group 385–386
Rainbow Six: Siege 411
real (form of existence) 1–3
real time 4, 145
Reality 2, 78, 236, 251, 280, 291, 295–298, 365, 393, 440, 486; demoting 302–303; not 5; *see also* augmented reality; virtual reality
The Realm 43, 44, 152
realm *see* faction; public test 124
Realm of the Mad God 414
real-money trading 48, 54–56, 416, 485
Reconstructed Senet 135n20
Red Dead Online 12n31, 69n7

Red Dead Redemption 2 494
referee 96, 196; *see also* Dungeon Master
refereed content *see* content, refereed
Refusal of the Call 237–238, 253
Refusal of the Return 246, 263–264
regression tester *see* tester, regression
Reiss Desire Profile 349
relatedness 301–302, 335, 352–353, 411–412
relaunch 123
release candidate testing 122
reproducibility crisis 436, 446
reputation system 417–420
Rescue from Without 247, 264–265
resolving 133n12
Response (communication) 398
retention 87–88
Return phase 246–248, 263–266
revenue model 60, 71–72, 163, 182, 332–333
reward *see* extrinsic reward; intrinsic reward
rezzing *see* resolving
Rickey, Dave 495n25
Ride Zero 180n66
Rift 29, 52, 73n16, 468
right: to liberty 489; to privacy 491–492; to security of person 490–491
rights 481–482; character 486–489; designer 482–483; moral 159, 490; property 490; *see also A Declaration of the Rights of Avatars*
Risk 331
Rivers of MUD see ROM
RMT *see* real-money trading
Road of Trials, the 240–241, 255–257
Roberson, Matt 492
Roberts, Nigel 20, 23n44
Roblox 16, 66, 96
ROCK 20n31
Rogue 43, 331
rogue server *see* server, rogue
role 288
role-playing 288–291, 469–450, 490–491; fun 290; game, computer 16–18, 75; game, single-player 18, 221; game, tabletop 16–17, 75, 195–196; hard 288–289, 338; inverse 291; soft 288–289; *see also* live-action role-playing; masquerading; MMORPG
roll-out (development) 118–123
ROM 33
room 31, 44, 153
Rosedale, Philip 74
Rowling, J. K. 162
RPG *see* role-playing game
RPG Maker 16, 44

RPG of the Year 47n17
The Ruins of Cawdor 43
rules 78–80, 93, 135, 201–202
RuneQuest 17
RuneScape 46, 192, 304, 473; *see also Evolution of Combat; Old School RuneScape*
RuneScape 2 see Old School Runescape
RuneScape 3 148n52
run-time database *see* database

Sage 211
Sally-Anne test 458
sandbox 70–71, 299, 353; *see also* gankbox; sandpark
sandpark 70n13
sapient 458
scale (of virtual world) 81–83
scatter diagram 434
scatter plot *see* scatter diagram
Sceptre of Goth 28–29, 38, 47
schedule (operant conditioning) 476–477
Schubert, Damion 46, 129, 410n25
Science Fiction (genre) 24, 49, 68
scientist 210
Scientist/Sage (interaction) 227
scripted content *see* content, hand-crafted
scripting database *see* database
Scunthorpe 383n43
SDT *see* self-determination theory
Second Age of virtual worlds 24–30
Second Life 31, 50, 53, 63, 65, 73–74, 133n12–13, 138, 168–169, 178, 180, 262, 279, 283, 286, 324, 408, 425, 450, 482n5
second-party developer *see* developer, second-party
second-person (perspective) 23, 152
The Secret World 52, 68, 90n55, 139, 161, 281, 289, 305–306, 468
Secret World: Legends 58, 282
section 105
security 140–143; *see also* right to security of person
seed 364
selection bias 186
selection effect 443–444.
self 233;-actualise 235, 252, 269;-expression 50, 102, 115, 286, 491;-identification (group membership) 383;-need 449;-perception 459–460; *see also* ideal self; alternate-self construct
self-determination theory 301–302, 353
Senet 135
sensory immersion *see* immersion, sensory
serious game *see* games, serious

server 59, 82–83, 138; architecture *see* architecture, server; cluster 130; lag *see* lag, server; merge 83, 127, 278; player-operated 163–164; progression 128n64; public test *see* realm, public test; rogue 128, 174–175; *see also* client/server; cross-server
Shades 24–25, 28n74, 38, 198n9
The Shadow of Yserbius 43
Shadowbane 50
Shapiro, David 27, 45
shard: single-127, 137; *see also* server
shared 5
Shroud of the Avatar: Forsaken Virtues 53, 282
Sierra Network *see* ImagiNation Network
Silkroad Online 57
SillyMUD 33
SimCity 331
The Simpsons 110
Simpson's paradox 435
The Sims 162n13
The Sims Online 51, 162
simulationism 71
Simutronics 28–29, 43
single-shard 82, 127, 137; *see also* layering; shard, single
sink 88, 395
situational factor 443
Six Circles of the Adept Game Player 346–347
Sixth Age of virtual worlds 53–58
size (of virtual world) 81–82; perceived 81; *see also* community size; party size
skill 309–310, 329
Skinner box 476
Skyforge 68
Skyrim 5
SL see Second Life
slash command 372
Slate 25
The Sleeping Beauty 232
slide (predictive model) 145
sliders 450–451
Smell-O-Vision 62
Snakes and Ladders see Moksha Patam
Snow Crash 54, 74–75
social capital 281, 411–412
social cohesion (group membership) 383
social conflict theory 428
social media co-ordinator 124
social world 34, 36–37, 85, 191, 229, 307, 346
socialisation effect *see* media effect
Socialiser 200–203, 210–211
Sociology 428–429; Applied 429–431; Cultural 429

software architecture *see* architecture, software
SoG see Sceptre of Goth
Song, Jake 11, 45
Sony Online Entertainment 29, 49, 187
Sosaria 82n40
The Source 38
space 1–2
Space Invaders 330
Space Opera (genre) 26, 68
sparkle pony *see* celestial steed
spatial immersion *see* immersion, spatial
SpatialOS 134n15
Speculative Fiction *see* Fantasy (genre); Horror
    (genre); Science Fiction (genre)
SpeedChat 374
Spice Girls 125n56
Spider-Man: Across the Spider-Verse 298n12
spoiler 483
spoilsport 78–79, 201–202
squad 391
SSI *see* Strategic Simulations Inc.
Stable Diffusion 110
stable state (of virtual world) 228–229
Stadia 59, 147
stagecraft 71
Star Citizen 58, 122n44, 385
Star Trek 1, 162
Star Trek Online 52, 162
Star Trek: The Next Generation 75
Star Wars 16, 68, 73, 287, 304
Star Wars Galaxies 14, 51, 128, 282, 316, 337,
    377n33, 484
Star Wars: the Old Republic 52, 104, 161, 171n45,
    192n15, 391
StarCraft 330
Stars Reach 385n46
state 5, 135
static 385; *see also* art, environment
static database *see* database
statistically-significant 445
stats 93n6
Stephenson, Neal 74–75
stereotype 189, 193–194, 207, 383
Stickball 23n48
stickiness 94–96, 362, 470
STO see Star Trek Online
stock MUD syndrome 34
story 232, 250; *see also* genre
strafe (predictive model) *see* slide (predictive model)
Strategic Simulations Inc. 39
streaming 146–147; *see also* cloud streaming; live
    streaming

Street Fighter II 445
structured chat *see* chat, structured
studio *see* development studio
style guide *see* art bible
sub-culture 366
subscription 40–41, 44, 54–56; *see also* battle pass
substance 94, 98–99
substitute: content *see* content, substitute; gameplay
    see gameplay, substitute
Sue the Witch 291
The Sumerian Game 447n30
sunk cost 469–470
sunset (development) 128–129
super-connector 362, 400
Superhero (genre) 50, 68
Supernatural Aid 238–239, 253–254
super-recogniser 361
suspension of disbelief, willing 78
SWG see Star Wars Galaxies
SWG Legends 282n28
SW:TOR see Star Wars: the Old Republic
Sword-and-Sorcery (genre) 68
Swords of Legends Online 57
systems content *see* content, systems

tab (chat window) 371
Tabula Rasa 53
Tactical Studies Rules 16, 39
tags 132–133
Take That! 199n14
Taken 304n23
tangible 84, 275–277
tank 35, 378n36, 403–405; *see also* main tank; off tank
taxation 169
Taxonomy of Game Pleasures *see* Eight Types of Fun
Taylor Aggression Paradigm 445
teaching 322–325
team *see* section; *see also* core team; development
    team; live team
technical artist *see* artist, technical
technical design document 110
technical director *see* programmer, lead
Tékumel 15
Telara 73
telecommunications 143–146
Temptress, the 242–243, 259–260
Tennis 203
Terms of Service 177; *see also* EULA
Terms of Use *see* Terms of Service
Terra Nova (blog) 14, 55n41, 151n5
test manager *see* QA lead
tester: compatibility 116; Kleenex 117; regression 117

Tetris 330, 445

text 62, 150–151; era 13

text MUD *see* MUD (genre), text

textual MUD *see* MUD (genre), text

textual world 34, 37, 151, 153, 272, 278, 372–373

theme park 70–71, 353; *see also* sandpark

theory of mind 458–459

There 50

Third Age of virtual worlds 30–36

third place 377–378

third variable 433–434

third-party developer *see* developer, third-party

third-person (perspective) 76, 152n10; *see also* isometric

The Three Musketeers 73

Throne and Liberty 53n34, 57, 379n37, 392, 461n13

Tibia 44, 304

TibiaME 44, 148

tick 139

Tic-Tac-Toe see Noughts and Crosses

time dilation 139

TinyMUCK 31; *see also* MUCK

TinyMUD 30–32

TinyMUD Classic 31

TinyMUSH 31; *see also* MUSH

token 93, 135; *see also* non-fungible token

Tolkien, J. R. R. 68, 74, 304

toon 7

Toontown Online 7n39, 50, 64n55, 374

Toontown Rewritten 7n39

top-down (perspective) 29, 44

TOS *see* Terms of Service

Total War 4

toxic island 414

toxicity 281, 316, 373, 410–412; acceptance 416–417; prevention 412–416

trade secret 159

trademark 159

train: (of players) 385, 406; (of mobiles) 485

transmogrification 305–306

trash 8

travel table 22

Treasure Island 234

treatment 107

triad 399

tribunal (*League of Legends*) 413

trifler 78–79, 201–202

trinity 35, 404; *see also* DPS; healer; tank

Trion Worlds 29

Trojan (typology) 348–349

Trove 58

Trubshaw, Roy 19–23, 26, 148n51, 321n24

True Names 74

true self *see* self, true

TSR *see* Tactical Studies Rules

TSW see The Secret World

Tunnels & Trolls 17

Turbine 54, 56

twinking 8, 485

Twitch 60, 220

überguild *see* clan

UCC *see* content, user-created

UDHR see Universal Declaration of Human Rights

UGC *see* content, user-generated

Ultima (game franchise) 27n70, 45

Ultima IV 63–64

Ultima VI 45

Ultima IX: Ascension 45

Ultima Online 45–48, 51, 73, 82n40, 104n5, 153, 175, 192, 278, 337, 347n13, 377n33, 387, 410, 413

Ultimate Boon, The 246, 263

uncanny valley 456–457

Understanding Comics 284

Undertale 330, 480

Unfamiliar World *see* Other World

unfun 309

United States Bill of Rights 486

United States Supreme Court 442

Unity 33, 46, 65, 115

Universal Declaration of Human Rights 179, 482, 490–491

universe *see* paracosm

University of Essex 19, 21, 24, 30, 495

University of Illinois 18

University of Leeds 30

University of Southampton 30

University of Wales at Aberystwyth 30

University of Wisconsin-Madison 486

Unreal Engine 115

unstructured chat *see* chat, unstructured

UO see Ultima Online

update 80–81, 84

use case 312–314

user base *see* player base

user-created content *see* content, user-created

user-generated content *see* content, user-generated

VALLEY 26

Vance, Jack 73n19

Vanguard: Saga of Heroes 53

variable-ratio reinforcement schedule 477–478

Verant Interactive *see* Sony Online Entertainment

Victoria 3 331

video game *see* games, video

Villagers & Heroes 148

Vinge, Vernor 74
virtual (form of existence) 1–2; *see also* ideally real
    (form of existence)
virtual ethnography 424
virtual reality 59, 154–155; *see also* Metaverse
virtual world 1–3, 8–9, 36–37, 65, 98, 185, 197, 236,
    266, 286–287, 302–303, 359, 481; designing
    1–495; why people play 269–270
Vogel, Rich 85n45
Vogler, Christopher 231, 244
voice 155–157
The Void 90
Vortex 26
voxel 153, 163n16
VR *see* virtual reality
VRChat 190n12
The Waiting Room NYC 485

walled garden 66
Walton, C. Gordon 27
Warcraft (game franchise) 52, 161n11
Warcraft Story 468
Warframe 68
Warhammer Fantasy (game franchise) 161n11, 162
Warhammer Online: Age of Reckoning 29, 52, 162
warp (predictive model) 145
Warrior of Light 75
waterfall methodology 111–112
We don't Talk about Bruno 479n38
weekly update 80
Westwood Studios 50
Westworld 75
Whatley, David 28, 104n6
White, Stephen 31
whitelist *see* allowlist
WHO *see* World Health Organisation
Whoniverse 15
Wicklow, Dorothea 494
Wild West (genre) 69
WildStar 53, 68–69, 91n57, 259, 317–319

The Witcher III 5
wiz 197–198
Wizard101 304
The Wizard of Oz 231
Wizardry 47
WolfMOO 425, 428
Woman as Temptress 242–243, 259–261
WordClicker 324
World (dimension) 204–205
world 1
world definition layer 134–135
World Health Organisation 439
World of Tanks 61, 154
World of Warcraft 1, 14, 51–53, 55, 58, 63, 70, 73,
    126n58, 128, 131–133, 138, 141, 148, 153,
    155, 161n11, 169n38, 171n44, 175–176, 192,
    197n5, 261n18, 275n9, 278–279, 281, 283,
    289–290, 298, 303–305, 316, 359–360, 366,
    369–370, 378–380, 387n50, 389–390, 403,
    417n41, 425, 429, 438, 441, 470n24, 484,
    492, 494n22
World of Warcraft Classic 128, 141, 175, 380n39
world-building 114
WoT see World of Tanks
WoW see World of Warcraft
WoW Classic see World of Warcraft Classic
Wrath of the Lich King 494n22

Xbox Cloud Gaming 147

Yee, Nick 191, 268, 284, 306, 336, 339, 352
Yohoho! Puzzle Pirates 50

Zaxxon 436
Zeigarnik, Bluma 467
Zeigarnik effect 467
Zenn's Bidding 484
zone 138–139
Zork 18, 21–23, 74n24
Zynga 478n35

For Product Safety Concerns and Information please contact our EU
representative GPSR@taylorandfrancis.com
Taylor & Francis Verlag GmbH, Kaufingerstraße 24, 80331 München, Germany

www.ingramcontent.com/pod-product-compliance
Lightning Source LLC
Chambersburg PA
CBHW060946210326
41598CB00031B/4734